Evolutionary Biology and Human Social Behavior

Evolutionary Biology and Human Social Behavior

An Anthropological Perspective

Edited by

Napoleon A. Chagnon
The Pennsylvania State University

William Irons
Northwestern University

Duxbury Press
North Scituate, Massachusetts

Evolutionary Biology and Human Social Behavior: An Anthropological Perspective was edited and prepared for composition by *Mary Ann Harrell*. Interior design was provided by *Trisha Hanlon*. The cover was designed by *Trisha Hanlon*.

Duxbury Press
A Division of Wadsworth, Inc.

Library of Congress Cataloging in Publication Data

Main entry under title:

Evolutionary biology and human social behavior.

Based on papers presented at two symposia organized for the
American Anthropological Association's 1976 annual meeting.
Bibliography:
Includes index.
1. Sociobiology—Congresses. 2. Social structure
—Congresses. I. Chagnon, Napoleon A., 1938– II. Irons,
William. III. American Anthropological Association.
GN365.9.E96   301.2   78–14564
ISBN 0–87872–193–2
Printed in the United States of America
1 2 3 4 5 6 7 8 9 — 83 82 81 80 79

Contributors

Richard D. Alexander
Division of Biology and Museum of Zoology
University of Michigan, Ann Arbor

David P. Barash
Departments of Psychology and Zoology
University of Washington, Seattle

Daniel G. Bates
Department of Anthropology
Hunter College, CUNY

William P. Bernds
Departments of Psychology and Zoology
University of Washington, Seattle

Paul E. Bugos, Jr.
Department of Anthropology
The Pennsylvania State University

Napoleon A. Chagnon
Department of Anthropology
The Pennsylvania State University

Mildred Dickemann
Department of Anthropology
California State College, Sonoma
Sonoma State University

William H. Durham
Department of Anthropology and
Program in Human Biology
Stanford University

Mark V. Flinn
Department of Anthropology
The Pennsylvania State University

Robin Fox
Department of Anthropology
Rutgers University and
The Harry Frank Guggenheim
Foundation

Raymond B. Hames
Department of Anthropology
University of California, Santa Barbara

John L. Hoogland
James Ford Bell Museum
University of Minnesota, Minneapolis

Richard D. Howard
Department of Biology
Bowling Green University, Ohio

William Irons
Department of Anthropology
Northwestern University

Jeffrey A. Kurland
Department of Anthropology
The Pennsylvania State University

Susan H. Lees
Department of Anthropology
Hunter College, CUNY

Bobbi S. Low
School of Natural Resources
University of Michigan, Ann Arbor

Thomas F. Melancon
Department of Anthropology
The Pennsylvania State University

Katharine M. Noonan
Division of Biology
University of Michigan, Ann Arbor

Paul W. Sherman
Department of Psychology
University of California, Berkeley

James N. Spuhler
Department of Anthropology
University of New Mexico,
Albuquerque

Lionel Tiger
Department of Anthropology
Rutgers University and
The Harry Frank Guggenheim
Foundation

Edward O. Wilson
Frank B. Baird Jr. Professor of Science
and Museum of Comparative Zoology
Harvard University

Contents

Preface

This volume is an outgrowth of two symposia entitled "Sociobiology and Human Social Organization, I and II" which were organized by the editors for the American Anthropological Association's 1976 Annual Meeting. The papers have been expanded and revised, and several papers have been added in the hope of presenting readers with a clearer picture of the implications of sociobiology for anthropology. These symposia were organized in conjunction with two other symposia entitled "Sociobiology and Anthropology: The Implications for Theory I and II," which were initiated by Irven DeVore. DeVore has edited a volume presenting the papers from those symposia, as well as additional papers, which will appear with the title *Sociobiology and the Social Sciences* (I. DeVore, personal communication, 1978).

The primary focus of the four symposia was the implications of recent refinements of Darwinian theory for social and cultural anthropology. Biologists now generally agree, after much debate, that the evolved traits of organisms do not exist because they have contributed to the survival of species, breeding populations, or social groups but because they have contributed to the survival of some alleles over their alternatives (Williams 1966). In other words, evolved traits can be expected to be adaptive for individual organisms, or smaller units such as individual genes, but not for larger units such as breeding populations. Acceptance of this principle within biology necessitated rethinking many aspects of basic theory. The most prominent question in need of rethinking was the evolution of sociality, which often appears to involve individual sacrifices for the benefit of social groups. Such behaviors have been explained in the past as adaptations for the survival of species or breeding populations. The challenge of explaining sociality in terms of selection at the individual level, or lower levels, has led to the development of the ideas of kin selection (Hamilton 1964) and reciprocal altruism (Trivers 1971). These ideas have proven powerful as principles explaining social behavior among a wide range of species, and have given rise to a growing interest among some evolutionary biologists in the possibility of explaining human behavior in similar terms (Alexander 1971, 1974, 1975a, 1977a; Hamilton 1975; Trivers 1971; Wilson 1975:547ff, 1978). The discipline within biology which is concerned with explaining sociality in terms of natural selection has come to be labeled sociobiology. Sociobiology is viewed by its advocates as nothing other than the application of evolutionary biology to the study of certain characteristics of organisms, specifically, their social behavior.

Sociobiology when applied to human sociality converges in important ways with the theoretical views of those social and cultural anthropologists who have advocated the value of a biological perspective for their discipline (see for example Alland 1972; Alland and McCay 1973; Fox 1975b; Freeman 1966; Tiger 1969; Tiger and Fox 1966, 1971; Tiger and Shepher 1975). To the extent that it entails the view that behaviors are adaptations to specific environments it also shares important elements with ecological anthropology (see for example Bennett 1969, 1976; Damas 1969; Goldschmidt 1966; Netting 1968, 1971; Rappaport 1968; Richerson 1977; Spooner 1972; Vayda and McCay 1975; Vayda and Rappaport 1968). It differs, however, from these theoretical perspectives which have developed in anthropology by rigorously defining adaptation in terms of maximization of genetic representation in future generations, or, in the technical language of sociobiology, maximization of inclusive fitness (Hamilton 1964).

Human sociobiology also differs from most current theoretical points of view in anthropology and the other social sciences in claiming that biology is of central importance to an understanding of human behavior.

Sociobiology, or as it is sometimes labeled behavioral biology, is theory, not proven fact. As such, however, it is for some anthropologists and other social scientists very exciting theory since it holds out the possibility of providing the social sciences with a theory which is both more basic and more general than any of its predecessors (Alexander 1971, 1975a; Blurton Jones 1976; Wilson 1975:4, 547–575, 1977, chapter 21, 1978). Whether this possibility will be realized or not depends on the outcome of research directed at refining and testing the theory. This volume is intended as a contribution to such research efforts.

Work of the sort undertaken in this volume is best done by anthropologists and biologists in collaboration. The editors of this volume, both social anthropologists, have relied heavily on the assistance of a biologist, Richard D. Alexander. We would like to acknowledge his extensive contribution to the editing of this volume. In particular, Irons would like to acknowledge Alexander's generosity in providing detailed criticisms and suggestions for revisions of chapter 1 and the five brief essays that introduce sections of the book.

We would also like to acknowledge the patient assistance of Jeremiah Lyons, Managing Editor of Duxbury Press, in the preparation of this volume. We also wish to thank our reviewers: Barbara Ayers, Leo Despres, and Dale M. Madison. The final responsibility for editorship, for better or for worse, lies with ourselves.

We owe an apology to many of the contributors of this volume for our seemingly endless delay in completing editorial responsibilities and thereby missing our original publication date by a very wide margin. The melding of biological and anthropological insights is proceeding at such a rapid pace that we might have inadvertently deprived a number of the contributors of the privilege of getting important ideas into print before others have done so, and should this be true, we are sincerely sorry. The contributors most likely to be affected delivered their papers at the 1976 meetings of the American Anthropological Association and the abstracts were published in that year. We hope that readers will keep in mind that most of the papers presented here were available for limited distribution from that time on, although the versions presented here have in most cases undergone some revision.

We intended this to be a volume of original papers and, therefore, expected that the contributors would not publish their papers elsewhere prior to their appearance here. Because of delays in publication, however, William Durham submitted his paper to another volume (C. A. Caplan, ed., 1978. *The Sociobiology Debate.* New York, Harper & Row.) where it appeared as our volume was being sent to the printers. While Durham expected that our volume would be published before Caplan's, we were unaware that he had submitted his paper to that volume. This may have caused a further injustice to other contributors to this volume who also might have wished to publish their contributions sooner than they appear here. For this we apologize.

Two of our graduate assistants, Carolyn McCommon and John Hadidian, deserve very special thanks for the herculean tasks they so admirably executed in correcting the original bibliography; we and others, in our collective preoccupation with prose, often paid insufficient attention to the less exciting, but important, tasks of referencing other works. The burden of rectifying and correcting this oversight fell largely to these two people. Finally, we owe an immeasurable debt to Mary Ann Harrell, who so efficiently and insightfully edited the manuscript and who, because of her intellectual breadth and familiarity with a remarkable amount of technical literature, saved the editors from numerous academic, not to mention grammatical, indelicacies. But despite the numerous improvements her labors made to the volume, the final responsibility rests with us.

Further, we would like to acknowledge the generous support of the editors' research by the Harry Frank Guggenheim Foundation, the Ford and Rockefeller Foundations' Program for Population Policy Research, the National Science Foundation, and the National Institutes of Health. Without such support, we would never have conducted the research reported in our individual papers in this collection, and we would never have developed the interests which led us to organize the 1976 symposia and to edit this volume.

Our individual contributions to the joint task of editing this volume have been equal, as best as we can measure them, and therefore, the order of our names as editors is alphabetical.

N. A. Chagnon
W. Irons

February 1979

Prologue

Philosophy, throughout its history, has consisted of two parts inharmoniously blended: on the one hand a theory as to the nature of the world, on the other an ethical or political doctrine as to the best way of living. The failure to separate these two with sufficient clarity has been a source of much confused thinking. Philosophers, from Plato to William James, have allowed their opinion as to the constitution of the universe to be influenced by the desire for edification: knowing as they supposed, what beliefs would make men virtuous, they have invented arguments, often very sophistical, to prove that these beliefs are true. . . . [T]he true philosopher is prepared to examine all preconceptions. When any limits are placed, consciously or unconsciously, upon the pursuit of truth, philosophy becomes paralyzed by fear, and the ground is prepared for a government censorship punishing those who utter "dangerous thoughts"—in fact, the philosopher has already placed such a censorship over his own investigations.

Bertrand Russell,
A History of Western Philosophy
1945:834–835.

Much of the criticism that has been leveled at the application of sociobiology to human beings is based on the argument that biological analyses of human sociality invariably encourage reactionary politics (see for example Sociobiology Study Group of Science for the People 1976, 1977; Sahlins 1976a:101). To the degree that such criticism reflects the experience of the living present as well as decades and centuries past—the experience of repression and slavery and exploitation—it not only claims attention, it commands respect. The concerns of ethics in private life and of politics for the public good are beyond question legitimate issues.

Yet to say this leaves Russell's point unshaken. As no idea is beyond abuse and debasement, no search for truth can shirk its proper quest.

Our search concerns theory as to the nature of the living world. We seek to separate this as best we may from any received ethical or political doctrine—not to encourage reaction, but to think clearly. We would hope that clear thinking would arm us against any baseness if need be.

We believe this ideal valid for any scientific theory and for any empirical study.

In our research, we have tried as best we can to reach conclusions consistent with logic and with the data available to us. We do not think that our conclusions, or those of others presented in this volume, support any partisan view in ethics or politics. For one thing, we need more and better data. For another, our conclusions are as yet provisional. Our work is just beginning—and distortions of it, if they arise, must be met as they appear.

Let us confront one difficulty squarely. A theory that human behavior is purely "genetically determined" would imply that attempts to change behavior by changing the social environment are futile and that political programs designed to change the nature of social relations are bound to fail. But the theories explored in this volume maintain that behavior is the product of both genetic and environmental influences, which interact in complex ways throughout the life history of an individual. Such a view implies that one can change behavior by changing the social environment, and, at the same time, suggests that attempts to change behavior will be most successful if based on a real understanding of human beings as biological organisms (Alexander 1977b, 1977c; Fox 1973; Tiger 1970; Rossi 1976). Be that as it may, the objective of the editors in editing this book is only to understand and explain human behavior.

N.A.C.
W.I.

I. Some Statements of Theory

The central issue addressed by this volume is the nature of the relationship between biological evolution and human social behavior. This initial group of papers addresses this issue in terms that are both general and theoretical.

In the first chapter, an introduction to human sociobiology, I take up four points. First, I argue that viewing human behaviors as adaptations shaped by natural selection does not imply that these behaviors have inherited fixed forms. Rather, it is perfectly compatible with the view that human behavior is highly flexible in its response to environmental influences. Second, I argue that the complexity and consistency of the anatomical structures and ontogenetic processes which create the "capacity for culture" imply that not only this general capacity but also specific forms of culture must have been adaptive during most of human evolution. Third, I discuss what types of behavior are in fact adaptive. This discussion consists of a review of basic principles of, and issues in, sociobiology and should be useful for readers not familiar with this discipline. Fourth, I discuss the extent to which human sociobiology is compatible with the basic theoretical views which have developed in anthropology.

The following chapters by Durham and Alexander delve further into the relationship between culture and biological evolution. In chapter 2, Durham advocates a somewhat different theoretical perspective than I advocate in chapter 1 and Alexander in chapter 3. He argues that human behaviors are shaped by two complementary processes: natural selection and cultural selection. Cultural selection is an aspect of the learning that maintains cultural traditions. Durham hypothesizes that in this process individuals selectively retain—from both traditional and innovative traits—those traits which most promote survival and reproduction and hence the contribution of genes to future generations. This selective retention is influenced by certain biases (chapter 2:44–46) in the process of socialization, most of which are independent of any genetic influence. These biases cause the retention of traits encouraging the maximization of genetic representation in future generations even though the selective process is largely independent of genetic influence and hence largely independent of natural selection.

Recently a number of authors have presented theoretical views that depict the development of culture not only as independent of natural selection but also as causing human behavior to diverge significantly from forms which are adaptive (Cloak 1975; Dawkins 1976; Richerson and Boyd, 1978). In an important sense, Durham's view is intermediate between those of Alexander and myself (presented here) and those of Cloak, Dawkins, and Richerson and Boyd (presented elsewhere).

Alexander, in chapter 3, looks at some of the objections to Darwin's central thesis that all of the characteristics of life forms are the cumulative products of natural selection. He argues that these criticisms are misplaced and gives his reasons for seeing natural selection as the only satisfactory explanation of the evolution of all features of life forms, including attributes such as behavior and culture, which change in response to environmental change without genetic change. He addresses at length the relationship between culture and natural selection, defending the theory that culture has been shaped by the cumulative inclusive-fitness-maximizing behavior of the aggregate of all human beings who have lived. Since human beings have conflicting reproductive interests, this cumulative product cannot be viewed satisfactorily as something optimally serving the reproductive interests of particular individuals, or something completely (or even largely) under the control of any particular individual. Rather, he says, it is more realistically viewed as the environment to which an individual must adapt as best he or she can. This unresponsiveness of culture to the wishes of individuals, Alexander believes, is what has given rise to the view that culture is beyond the control of individual human choice. Alexander is convinced (and I agree) that this impression is largely correct—in most situations, individuals are unable to change culture. He clarifies the matter by stressing that the ultimate forces shaping culture are the *conflicting* reproductive strivings of all individuals. Starting from this premise, he discusses such issues as the conditions under which culture can be expected to change, and reasons for the arbitrary nature of many aspects of culture.

It is not surprising that the application of natural selection theory to sociality has led to efforts to develop functional theories of human social behavior and culture, based ultimately on the proposition that during human history individuals have tended to behave so as to maximize their inclusive fitness. Whether such a theory succeeds, and if so, in what form it will ultimately emerge, will depend on the results of future research. Their differences—with one another and with the alternate views mentioned above—hinge on the essentially untested question of the degree to which the processes shaping culture are independent of individual efforts to survive and reproduce. To the extent that this question is sensible, fruitful lines for future research are suggested by the arguments posed here. Some of the later essays in this volume begin the pursuit of these lines of research.

W. I.

1. Natural Selection, Adaptation, and Human Social Behavior[1]

William Irons

> I should like to see professional anthropologists trespassing on the fields of the other sciences, and particularly, perhaps, on the study of animal behavior.
>
> J. B. S. Haldane
> "The Argument from Animals to Man: An Examination of its Validity for Anthropology"
> 1956

Human beings, like other organisms, are products of natural selection. This simple and widely accepted proposition has led a number of scientists to believe that human behavior can best be understood if studied from the perspective of evolutionary biology. This volume is an attempt by a number of anthropologists and biologists to contribute to the research objective implied by this belief. The basic issue it confronts is whether human behavior is adaptive (in the biological sense) and what specific forms it would assume in response to various environments if it is adaptive. This issue is addressed in this volume both theoretically and empirically. The purpose of this introductory chapter is to summarize briefly the relevant principles of evolutionary biology and to explain why they can be expected to apply to human behavior.

The principles of biological theory which are relevant to the study of behavior are all extensions of the modern synthetic theory of biological evolution which combines Darwin's concept of natural selection with Mendel's discovery of the nature of inheritance. This theory holds that the evolution of all life forms is the outcome of five processes: inheritance,

[1] In writing this chapter, I profited greatly from extensive commentary and criticism by Richard D. Alexander. Napoleon A. Chagnon, Mildred Dickemann, Mark Flinn, Jeffrey A. Kurland, Thomas Melancon, and Marjorie Rogasner also read early drafts and made helpful comments. Carolyn McCommon did service above and beyond the call of duty in typing and retyping the several drafts of this paper. Work on this paper was also assisted by support of my research by the Harry Frank Guggenheim Foundation and the National Science Foundation.

mutation, drift, gene flow (including isolation), and natural selection. It is the central proposition of modern evolutionary biology that, of these five processes, natural selection is pervasive in determining the traits of organisms (Mayr 1963). Most anthropologists and other social scientists are familiar with these basic tenets of evolutionary biology. However, a useful examination of behavior from the point of view of evolutionary biology requires familiarity with additional theoretical principles and issues which are generally less familiar to anthropologists and other social scientists. These additional areas of theory deal with adaptive phenotypic plasticity and with sociality. Theory relating to these topics is summarized below and discussed in relation to topics of traditional anthropological concern.

Phenotypic Plasticity and Genetic Inheritance

The hypothesis that human behavioral propensities are adaptations shaped by natural selection does not imply that human behavior is not plastic or that differences in behavior among human populations are the result of genetic differences. The most reasonable hypothesis is that the behavioral differences exhibited by different populations are environmentally induced variations in the expression of basically similar genotypes (cf. Haldane 1956), and that the ability and propensity to vary behavior in response to environmental differences is itself an adaptation.

Natural selection sometimes favors genes which canalize developmental processes in such a way as to produce the same phenotype under all of the various environmental conditions commonly encountered by members of the particular breeding population in which these genes occur. Blood types in human populations are familiar examples of this sort of trait. If an individual has a genotype for type A blood, it is very unlikely that any environmental influence will modify the expression of the genotype in such a way as to cause the individual to have type O, or type B, blood. Traits of this sort are referred to as obligate traits.

In other cases, natural selection favors genes which produce different phenotypes in different environments (Schmalhausen 1949; Seger 1976; Maynard Smith 1975: 19–26). Skin color in chameleons is a familiar example. Part of the genetic material of chameleons causes them to develop anatomical structures and physiological processes which lead to a continual change in skin color which causes their color at any time to match the predominant color of the animal's immediate environment. The resulting coloration is an adaptation against detection by predators. Adaptively flexible traits of this sort are sometimes referred to as facultative traits in contrast to obligate traits. Other familiar examples of adaptive flexibility are the tanning responses and the development of calluses in response to pressure or friction.

Not all examples of phenotypic variation in response to environmental conditions are instances of adaptive flexibility. Rickets and scurvy are examples of environmentally induced changes in the phenotypic expression of particular genes, but these changes are not adaptive—that is, they do not make survival on an inadequate diet more probable. Rather, these changes represent failures to cope with particular environmental conditions. Whether or not a particular example of change in the phenotypic expression of particular genes is an example of adaptive flexibility is in many cases difficult to determine. However, there are certain features which support the hypothesis that a particular instance of variable phenotypic expression is adaptive (cf. Williams 1966: 10, 81–83). Such an initial hypothesis is appropriate if the variation results from a complex structure or process which is controlled by many genes and is relatively constant throughout a population. If change in any one of the many genes would radically change the phenotype, then its actual constancy can best be explained by natural selection. The hypothesis of adaptiveness is also strengthened if the structure appears well designed to produce a particular change, and the change can be shown to favor survival under the conditions inducing it.

An initial hypothesis to the effect that a particular form of phenotypic variability is adaptive is also strengthened if the anatomical structures and physiological processes causing the variability impose a high cost on the organism in terms of energy, nutriments, or the assumption of risks. In such a case the maintenance of these structures and processes by natural selection is plausible only if the organism is receiving some benefit in return for the cost (cf. Humphrey 1976:303).

It is also important to note that when adaptive flexibility of phenotype does occur it is only adaptive to a limited range of environmental conditions. This is so partly because natural selection can only produce adaptation to the conditions actually encountered by a population of organisms. There is no reason to expect an organism to produce an adaptive response, especially one based on the interaction of many genes, to a set of environmental conditions never encountered by its ancestors. Also, if a particular condition has only rarely been encountered by a population and a structure capable of producing an optimal response to that condition is expensive in

I. Some Statements of Theory

terms of energy or nutritive material, then natural selection may favor organisms that do not have this structure: its cost is not, in the majority of cases, repaid sufficiently in terms of survival and reproduction. The most reasonable expectation is that a phenotype which varies in response to environmental change will be adaptive only within the range of conditions frequently encountered by the population in which the particular flexible phenotype evolved.

Considerations of this sort are essential to an understanding of behavior, because behavior is one aspect of an organism which is especially likely to incorporate an element of adaptive flexibility. Stated differently, behavior is likely to be facultative rather than obligate in character. It is in fact difficult to think of behaviors, even in simple organisms, which do not vary in some way in response to some environmental cue. Anthropologists are most concerned with learned behaviors, and more especially with behaviors which are learned as a result of living in a particular society, i.e., culturally transmitted behaviors. In my opinion, it is a reasonable hypothesis that the different forms of culturally transmitted behavior found among human societies represent the adaptively flexible expression of genetic material which is basically the same from one human population to another.

Human behavioral flexibility is based on a number of complex structures and processes which suggest that this flexibility is an adaptive character produced by natural selection: (a) these structures and processes are basically constant throughout the species and appear to be controlled by many genes; (b) they impose a heavy cost in terms of energy and other limited resources and in terms of risks; and (c) they appear to be designed to encourage the learning of culturally transmitted behaviors, i.e., to produce a particular form of phenotypic flexibility in response to a specific type of environmental variation. Most salient among these traits are the long period of maturation and dependence on the care of older individuals, the large brain, and the complex neural and vocal apparatus which expresses itself in the learning of language. It is more difficult to identify the specific physiological and anatomical underpinnings of aspects of human culture other than language. Still, it seems a reasonable hypothesis that the neural and endocrine systems responsible for the human propensity to form intricate long-term social relations and to absorb the values and belief systems of specific societies also impose a cost on organisms, and hence can be maintained by natural selection only if there is some benefit as well (cf. Fox 1971). Such a benefit would be present if the behavioral end products of socialization were in the majority of cases successful adaptations to the specific environments in which the individuals exhibiting the behavior find themselves.

Much is already known about how learning in various species works as a mechanism for tracking specific environmental parameters and molding behavior to what is optimal given the organism's particular environment. The research of ethologists on learning has shed light on this topic (Hinde 1970:425–654, 1974; Hinde and Stevenson-Hinde 1973; Tinbergen 1965). Different species, which have been subject to different selective processes, react to the same environmental stimuli very differently. Whether a particular stimulus provides positive or negative reinforcement (or no form of reinforcement), whether its effects on future behaviors are strong or weak, are all things that vary from one species to another. Some behaviors can even be established without reinforcement (Tinbergen 1965). The exploratory behaviors which are elicited by a novel environmental element and which can then be either positively or negatively reinforced also vary from one species to another. The end result of these species-specific learning processes is that members of each species tend in their usual environments to learn behaviors which are adaptive, given the species' way of coping with and exploiting its environment—its niche.

Learning in human beings is facilitated by culture, i.e., learning as a result of interaction with other members of an individual's species. This process is not unique to human beings (Kawai 1965; Kummer 1971: 117–130), but human beings carry the process much further than any other species. Culture change is both rapid and Lamarckian (cf. Wilson 1977 and chapter 21, this volume). The rapidity of cultural evolution is a result of the fact that the transmission of behavioral phenotypes from one individual to another can be independent of reproduction and genetic inheritance. Acquired traits can be passed quickly not only between related but also between unrelated individuals. The speed of cultural evolution is further enhanced by the fact that, to some degree, individuals retain the ability to substitute new behaviors for old ones throughout their life histories. All of this makes possible the rapid spread, in a population, of successful behaviors that could only be learned slowly and by serendipity if individuals were unable to draw on the experience of others.

The capacity of human beings to use problem-solving abilities to innovate also plays an important role in giving culture its Lamarckian qualities. When faced with novel environmental elements, human beings increase the rate of behavioral innovation. The innovations produced are not random, but rather cluster around adaptive responses to the novel ele-

I. Some Statements of Theory

ments (cf. Boehm 1978). It is as if an organism in a novel environment could increase its mutation rate, and somehow induce mutations that produce phenotypes approximating the optimal form given the novel element. As a result of its rapid, Lamarckian character, culture greatly increases the power of individuals to track their environment and adjust behavior effectively to specific sets of environmental conditions.[2]

These observations about culture, however, do not, in my opinion, alter the argument stated above supporting the hypothesis that the end products of socialization should, in most cases, be adaptive behaviors. Both the argument in terms of complexity and constancy, and that in terms of cost, apply as much to culturally transmitted behaviors as to other forms of phenotypic flexibility.

The proposition that culture can change without genetic change and the proposition that culturally transmitted behaviors approximate what is optimal in terms of natural selection appear superficially to be contradictory. How can changes in phenotype which are independent of genetic change be optimal in terms of natural selection, which can be defined as the differential reproduction of genotypes? The answer lies in a selective element built into the process of socialization or enculturation. The capacity for culture could be favored by natural selection only if accompanied by a propensity to behave as if the individual were weighing both innovative and established modes of behavior in terms of their effect on his or her inclusive fitness and adopting only those behaviors which increase inclusive fitness the most. It is clear that people do consciously weigh the probable consequences of alternative behaviors, and choose those which they evaluate as probably producing the most desirable consequences. The view expressed here assumes that what is consciously evaluated as desirable would equate with the biologically optimal in the environments in which human beings evolved. It is also important to be aware that the reproductive interests of different individuals are to some degree in conflict. Thus, while individuals try to choose behaviors which are optimal for their inclusive fitness, the overall group pattern of behavior is unlikely to be ideal for any one individual. Rather, it can be expected to represent the outcome of conflict and compromise among individuals with differing interests.

It should be noted that this hypothesis concerning adaptiveness of culturally transmitted behavior is not compatible with those views which

[2] The discussion of culture in this essay is phrased in terms of behavior, rather than of ideas, beliefs, and sentiments, because it is actual behavior which influences reproductive success directly. Ideas, beliefs, and sentiments, from the point of view of behavioral biology, are important to the extent that they influence behavior.

accord human beings a largely passive role in relation to the cultural traditions to which they are exposed (for examples of this view see White 1949: 330–359; Sahlins 1976a: 1–16). Rather, it is compatible with a view which assumes that each individual plays an active role in his own socialization. This means that in learning behavior from others, an individual does not imitate behaviors slavishly. Instead, individuals are seen as evaluating what they are offered, accepting some things, modifying others, rejecting still others, and occasionally inventing new behaviors of their own. Out of this process the culturally acquired behavior of individuals can be seen as constantly changing (whether slowly or rapidly) and in the process molding behavior to what is adaptive in a continually changing environment (cf. Barth 1966, 1967; Bailey 1969; Britan and Denich 1976; Burnham 1973; Kapferer 1976; Murdock 1949). This issue of the relationship between the individual and culture is taken up again in the last section of this essay.

The above hypothesis about the adaptiveness of culturally acquired behavior is an empirically testable one. The most straightforward way of testing it is to attempt to determine whether actual behavior in the majority of human societies does approximate forms which are optimal in terms of natural selection. This brings the discussion to the question of what kinds of behavior natural selection can be expected to favor. A number of evolutionary biologists have concerned themselves with this question and the results of their work are summarized below under the headings of group versus individual selection, kin selection, return benefit theory, sexual selection and parental investment, and sex ratio theory.

Group Versus Individual Selection

Natural selection in the form of the differential reproductive success of individuals proceeds much more rapidly than does natural selection in the form of the extinction of whole breeding populations or species, and the expansion of competing populations or species. Therefore, traits which cause organisms to increase their genetic representation in future generations outcompete traits which favor the survival of breeding populations or species at the expense of maximizing individual genetic representation in descending generations.

The question of the level at which selection operates has been a theoretical issue with far-reaching implications in biological theory. It became an issue largely in response to the publication of Wynne-Edwards' theory of social regulation of population density, which was predicated on

I. Some Statements of Theory

the assumption that populations adapt as a result of selection at the population level (Wynne-Edwards 1962). Wynne-Edwards hypothesized that natural selection, in the form of the extinction of some entire breeding populations and the expansion of others, favored certain characteristics of entire populations. The most salient of these, according to Wynne-Edwards, was a social regulation of population density which prevented overexploitation of food resources (cf. Divale and Harris 1976; Harris 1977a). He reasoned that populations which failed to evolve social behaviors which limited population density, before starvation or malnutrition arose, would lose out to those which did. The former populations, once food shortages arose, would begin to exploit their food resources more heavily. This heavier cropping would set up a vicious cycle whereby heavier cropping would lead to population growth, which would lead to still heavier cropping, until the species serving as food resources were driven to extinction. Once extinction of food species occurred within a breeding population's territory, the latter population itself would go extinct. Then the food species would recolonize the area, leaving open the possibility that "cropping" populations related to the extinct ones, but able to control their numbers, could move into the area vacated by extinction.

The expectation derived from this model is that animal populations should socially regulate fertility so as to maintain a population below that at which overcropping of food resources might begin. Since food resources vary in abundance over time, population density would have to be low enough so as to not initiate the vicious cycle described above at a time when food resources were at their minimal abundance. This would, of necessity, mean holding a population stationary at a density below the maximum which could be supported by the food resources when they were above their minimal level of abundance. Empirical evidence does indicate that many populations do stabilize at such low densities, although alternate explanations are available in terms of a number of factors which cause density-dependent increases in mortality such as disease, parasites, predators, and intraspecific aggression motivated by individual-level selection (McLaren 1971; Williams 1966:234–246; Williams 1971). On the other hand, direct evidence of whole breeding population extinctions of the sort hypothesized by Wynne-Edwards is rarely reported in the literature (Wilson 1975:116).

The real difficulty for group selection and group-level adaptation, however, came from theoretical considerations. The Wynne-Edwards hypothesis maintained that group selection would produce populations of individuals predisposed to hold their reproductive success below the level that physiology and resources will permit. If individuals predisposed to produce the maximum numbers of viable offspring should enter the population through gene flow or mutation, these high reproducers would produce a disproportionately large portion of each succeeding generation. In other words, individual level selection would favor organisms adapted to behave contrary to the pattern favored by group selection. This means that, within any population consisting of individuals genetically predisposed to limit fertility for the long-term benefit of the group, genes predisposing a maximization of an individual's genetic representation in descending generations would spread rapidly and would destroy the group level adaptation. Once such genes entered a population adapted at the group level, they could be eliminated only by extinction of the entire population. Before this happened, unless interpopulation migrations were very rare, the genes for selfish reproductive strategies would be very likely to spread to neighboring populations. The greater the frequency of migration, the more neighboring populations they would spread to. Thus it seems probable that several populations would have to be eliminated in order for the selfish genes to be removed by natural selection. In short, a very high rate of whole population extinction and a low rate of interpopulation gene flow would be necessary for group selection to favor social regulation of fertility for the benefit of the group against the countervailing effect of individual selection (Boorman and Levitt 1972, 1973; Levins 1970; Williams 1966, 1971). Empirical evidence indicates that these conditions are rarely met, and that most forms of social behavior can be explained adequately by models assuming that selection is effective only in producing adaptations at the individual level (Alexander 1975a; Alexander and Borgia, in press; McLaren 1971; Williams 1966, 1971). As a result very few theoretical biologists presently support the proposition that group selection can be expected, under any but very rare circumstances, to overcome the effects of individual selection and produce group level adaptations.

This has meant that all explanations of traits in terms of benefits to the species or breeding populations have had to be replaced by new explanations based on the assumption that evolution is guided by individual level selection, or lower-level selection such as genic selection. Forms of social behavior are aspects of animal life which, before the resolution of the group selection issue, were very frequently explained by appeals to group benefits (as they still frequently are among anthropologists), and as a result sociality has been extensively reexamined by biologists in recent years. This rethinking of sociality in terms of individual level selection has given rise to the theoretical ideas and literature which are variously labeled behavioral biology/selfish gene theory/sociobiology/natural selection theory (Alexander 1975a; Dawkins 1976; Wilson 1975).

Many of these ideas are phrased in the idioms of altruism and selfishness. Altruism as defined by behavioral biologists means behavior by which an organism decreases its own reproductive success and increases that of another organism or other organisms. Selfishness is defined as behavior by which an organism increases its own reproductive success and decreases that of another organism or other organisms. Reproductive success/Darwinian fitness/classical fitness in this context is a measure of the number of offspring an organism produces which survive to become part of the breeding pool of the next generation. It should be clear how these technical concepts are relevant to the preceding discussion of group and individual selection. These special uses of the words "altruism" and "selfishness" are similar to, but not identical with, everyday usage. Confusion can arise if these special meanings are not kept in mind. As will be seen in the following discussion, the "altruistic" behaviors favored by natural selection turn out to be genetically selfish (cf. Trivers 1971:35). For this reason, some behavioral biologists have used the term "apparently altruistic" behavior rather than "altruistic behavior" (e.g. Sherman 1977). Terms such as "solidarity," "cooperation," "assistance," and "generosity" are frequently used in social anthropology to refer to behaviors which in the technical vocabulary of behavioral biology are "altruistic."

Kin Selection

Behavior by an individual organism which reduces its own Darwinian fitness can be favored by natural selection if the behavior also has the effect of increasing the Darwinian fitness of genetically related individuals in sufficient degree to cause the individual's genetic material to increase in descending generations (Hamilton 1964). This aspect of natural selection has been labeled kin selection (Maynard Smith 1964), and the behavioral strategies favored by this aspect of selection have been labeled nepotism (Alexander 1974). It is most effectively measured in terms of inclusive fitness, an individual organism's genetic representation in descending generations as a result of its own reproduction AND that of genetically related individuals (Hamilton 1964). Kin selection appears to be important in shaping many forms of sociality, including kinship among human beings.

The above conclusions imply that natural selection can only favor forms of behavior which are genetically selfish, that is, which maximize the genetic representation in future generations of the organism exhibiting the behavior. In fact, this is the basic premise of the new refinements of Darwinian theory which have come to be known as sociobiology (Alexander 1975a; Dawkins 1976; Wilson 1975). The various theoretical issues and hypotheses that fall under this label are in fact attempts to predict the form of behavior from the basic premise that behavior is genetically selfish.

On the surface, the conclusion that natural selection is potent to produce adaptations only at the individual or lower levels would seem to imply that the evolved behavioral propensities of organisms should be directed toward maximizing their own Darwinian fitness and diminishing that of competitors. However, there are special circumstances in which an organism can increase its genetic representation in future generations by behaving in ways which diminish its own reproductive success and increase that of competitors, that is, by behaving altruistically. Specifying these circumstances has been the central theoretical concern of sociobiology (Wilson 1975:3).

The first rigorous definition of a set of conditions under which altruism will be favored was supplied by W. D. Hamilton (1964). The conditions he dealt with can arise only among genetically related organisms. Hamilton defined these conditions in terms of Darwinian fitness, and in terms of the portion of genes shared by related organisms. Hamilton's theory of kinship maintains that altruistic behavior will be favored by natural selection when the cost to the altruist is less than the benefit to the relative devalued by the portion of the altruist's genes present in the relative. These conditions can be expressed by a simple inequality

$$C < r B$$

in which C is the cost in Darwinian fitness of a particular altruistic act to the altruist, B is the benefit to the beneficiary, and r is the coefficient of relationship between the two individuals, that is, the fraction of genes shared by the two organisms. Hamilton (1964) originally put this inequality in the form $k > 1/\bar{r}$ in which k represents the ratio of gain in fitness to loss in fitness (i.e., B/C) and $\bar{r}$ represents the average coefficient of relatedness for the total group of relatives who are beneficiaries of an altruist's assistance.

The variable in this inequality represented by r is Sewall Wright's coefficient of relationship. In sexually reproducing diploid organisms, sex cells contain half the genetic information of each parent. When two sex cells are joined to form a new individual, the new organism has gained half its genetic material from each parent. Therefore, parent and child each have half of their genes in common; that is, for this pair $r = \frac{1}{2}$.[3] Full siblings are individuals who share both parents; that is, their genetic material was assembled from different sex cells, drawn from the same set of parents. Because of crossing over in the formation of sex cells, an individual's total genetic material is in effect randomly divided in half, and that random sample of one half the individual's total genetic material forms the hereditary material in each sex cell. Therefore, two sex cells from the same individual will *on the average* have half their genetic material the same and half different. This, however, is the most probable outcome. Actual pairs of sex cells will vary in the portion of genetic material they have in common, some having more and some having less. Thus, on the average for full siblings, $\frac{1}{2}$ of the genetic material from *each* parent will be the same and $\frac{1}{2}$ different; for a total of $\frac{1}{2}$ of their genes the same, $r = \frac{1}{2}$. However, in the case of siblings, the value of r is a mean for a large sample of full siblings. Actual pairs of siblings will vary in their genetic relatedness around this mean owing to random variations in the assortment of genes during meiosis. In contrast, for parent and child r is always exactly $\frac{1}{2}$. Half siblings have only one parent in common. They, as a result, will have half of the genes from that parent in common, but none in common from the other parents (assuming the other parents are unrelated). Since the common parent provided half of their entire genome, they have $\frac{1}{2} \times \frac{1}{2} = \frac{1}{4}$ of their genes in common. An individual is related by $\frac{1}{4}$ to a full sibling's child, because that sibling in reproducing passes on half of the genes they have in common. Each meiotic link in a pedigree reduces relatedness by a half. By this logic grandparent and grandchild are related by $\frac{1}{4}$, and full first cousins by $\frac{1}{8}$.

The logic of the conditions for adaptive altruism toward kin discovered by Hamilton, can be demonstrated by considering the hypothetical case of an organism which "chooses" not to reproduce at all in order to assist a full sibling to reproduce. Whether natural selection will favor such a "choice," depends on C and B in the above inequality. For the sake of illustration, let us assume the individual in question would have had two

[3] In this chapter and in chapters 6 and 7, it is assumed that individuals are related through only one known link. Thus r always appears in these chapters as a common fraction—$\frac{1}{2}$ for full siblings, $\frac{1}{4}$ for half siblings, $\frac{1}{8}$ for full first cousins, etc. This is a heuristic simplification useful in clarifying theoretical models. In real life, however, human beings may be aware of multiple genealogical ties and may act in terms of the degree of relatedness implied by all of these known ties. Thus, in the empirical discussions of the Yąnomamö (chapters 4 and 8), r usually appears as a decimal fraction carried to several places as a result of adding the degree of relatedness contained in several genealogical links. Keep in mind that r refers to genes identical by descent, not homozygosity.

offspring had it made the choice of reproducing itself and so would its sibling. If it helps the sibling as stated above, however, it has none and—let us assume—its sibling has eight offspring. In this case the cost, C, to the altruist is two offspring, and the benefit, B, to the related organism is six offspring. The coefficient of relationship, r, is $\frac{1}{2}$, so that the benefit devalued by r is 3. Thus, the inequality is satisfied and the behavior is adaptive. Translating the same consideration into a more direct measure of genetic representation in the first descending generation, the cost of two offspring represents one copy of the altruist's genes (each offspring carrying $\frac{1}{2}$ the altruist's genes) and the benefit of six additional sibling's offspring would represent $1\frac{1}{2}$ replicas of the altruist's genes (each sibling's offspring carrying $\frac{1}{4}$ of the altruist's genes).

The word "choice" was placed in quotation marks because the processes by which organisms come to exhibit altruistic behaviors of various sorts are not all "choices" in the usual sense of the word. Among many hymenopteran species the "choice" of being sterile and assisting a sister to reproduce is made for an individual by her caretakers while she is a larva. Those larvae fed one diet develop into sterile workers, those fed another become fertile queens. This is an example of phenotypic flexibility built into the developmental process, and to the extent that a "choice" is made it is not made by the individual herself. Another example of altruism toward siblings is that of bitter-tasting caterpillars (Fisher 1958 [1930]:177–181). A caterpillar cannot prevent itself from being eaten by tasting bitter. By the time the predator is aware that its prey is unpalatable it is too late to do the prey any good. However, similar caterpillars in the immediate vicinity will benefit, including a large number of siblings. Here the word "choice" is purely metaphoric, since protective bitter taste in caterpillars is presumably an obligate trait.

On the other hand, one could cite a number of mammalian cases of altruism based on kinship, or nepotism, in the form of the protection of off-spring from predators by their mothers. In cases such as these, the psychological processes leading to specific protective acts may, in fact, closely parallel in nature the process we subjectively know as making choices. The important point to be drawn is that Hamilton's formulation of kin selection does not make any assumption about the flexibility of the processes leading from genotype to phenotype. The conditions favoring altruism toward kin may in some cases produce obligate traits—bitter taste in caterpillars—and in other cases may involve psychological processes which we might label learning or decision making.

Whether selection favors nepotism and whether it favors pheno-

　　　　　　　　　　　　　　　　I. Some Statements of Theory

typic plasticity are separate issues. There is good reason, as pointed out in the preceding section of this essay, to believe that highly flexible traits will reflect strategies of nepotism as much as do obligate traits. The same can be said as well of the other aspects of selection discussed below under the headings of return benefit theory, sexual selection and parental investment, and sex-ratio theory. Frequently models appearing in the biological literature explicitly make the assumption that the alternate behaviors they are dealing with are obligate traits controlled by alleles at a single genetic locus (see for example Trivers 1971:36–37). The use of such an assumption in constructing a simple logical or mathematical model is not meant to imply that all examples of the forms of sociality under discussion are either based on alleles at a single locus or are obligate as opposed to facultative traits (cf. Trivers 1971:53–54). The mistaken notion that human behavioral biology implies strict limits to plasticity seems to arise from a failure to appreciate this fact.

The hypothetical example of an individual choosing to forego reproduction and assist a sibling discussed above illustrates some of the other heuristic simplification common in behavioral biological models. The effect of the environment is represented in a simple form in the B's and C's, which have fixed values implying that the same behavior in a particular population will always have the same effect on reproductive success. Actual situations are likely to be more complex in that the values of B and C are likely to vary over time in ways that are only partly predictable. Modeling this sort of situation mathematically is more complex than the above inequality with fixed values of C and B (e.g., Kurland, chapter 6; Irons, chapter 7). Nevertheless, if the conditions of the above inequality are satisfied most of the time, selection should operate as the simpler model predicts. The important thing to note is that a biologist's use of a simple model does not imply that he believes reality is as simple as his model. He need only believe the model will be in some way a useful predictor of observable variables, such as the presence or absence of altruistic assistance of siblings. Models of this sort appear frequently in the literature in behavioral biology. They are also common in other disciplines that use logical or mathematical predictive models. Their value should be judged by their intended use: predictions that can be tested empirically.

In order to express the effect of altruism among kin on genetic representation in future generations, Hamilton (1964) defined a quantity which he labeled inclusive fitness. Inclusive fitness is a measure of an individual's genetic representation in descending generations. It takes into account both an individual's own reproduction *and* that of relatives who share some of the individual's genes. The absolute number of replicas of an individual's genome in the first descending generation consists of half the number of that individual's offspring (half because each offspring contains half the parent's genes), one-quarter the number of full sibling's offspring, one-eighth the number of half sibling's offspring, one-sixteenth of the number of full first cousin's offspring, and so on. Inclusive fitness may seem impossible to calculate since potentially an organism's distant kin extend *ad infinitum*. However, behavioral biologists are not interested in inclusive fitness by itself, but rather in the effect of behavior on inclusive fitness. (Past a certain degree of relatedness, the effects of behavior on inclusive fitness usually become trivial.) In practice, a given pattern of behavior usually has a significant effect on the reproductive success of only a limited range of related organisms. Thus, determining the effect of that behavior on inclusive fitness can be done by examining its effect on a limited number of organisms affected.

The variables which Hamilton drew attention to in his 1964 paper can be used to predict selfish as well as altruistic behavior. In a later publication (1971) Hamilton in fact extended his attention to selfish behavior. The variables relevant to the condition under which selfish behavior will be adaptive are the same as those relevant to altruism. If for a particular selfish behavior the benefit to the actor, B_a, and the cost to a relative, C_k (a for actor; k for kin), are such that

$$B_a > r\, C_k$$

then organisms which behave selfishly toward kin will be favored by selection. It is important to emphasize that kin selection theory does not predict that individuals will always be altruistic to close relatives. Rather, it predicts that they will be altruistic in some circumstances and selfish in others depending on the cost and benefits involved.

For example, in studying the relationship of parent to offspring, behavioral biologists are concerned with selfish as well as altruistic behaviors. Assuming that all of a parent's offspring are subject to equal probabilities of survival and reproductive success, a parent would be favored by selection if it invested equally in each offspring.[4] Its genetic representa-

---

[4] All of the following discussions of parent-offspring conflict are based for simplicity on this assumption. In some empirical cases, different offspring may have different chances of achieving a high reproductive success. In such cases, parents would be expected to scale their expenditure of limited resources in caring for different offspring, expending somewhat more in nurturing those with higher chances of reproductive success. However, in such

I. Some Statements of Theory

tion in each offspring is the same, and the chances are roughly the same for each offspring that a given unit of energy or some other limited resource expended in care will pay off in a given number of grandoffspring. It is also reasonable to assume that past a certain point further expenditures of limited resources in a particular offspring will have decreasing benefits in terms of improving that offspring's chances of survival and eventual reproduction. In short, investment in each offspring eventually reaches a point of diminishing returns. The initial units of effort expended in feeding and protecting a given offspring vastly increase that offspring's chances of survival, but once its basic nutritional needs are met and it has been shielded from the major hazards of its environment, the expenditure of further effort in caring for that offspring will have smaller incremental effects on its life expectancy and probable reproductive performance. Given these constraints, a parent's advantage lies in cutting off its care to an offspring once the point of diminishing returns is met, and directing further care to other offspring which have not yet reached that point. Assuming that a parent has the ability to invest care in all of its offspring up to the point of diminishing returns, one would expect it to do so. Further, if past the point of diminishing returns each additional unit of care invested in a particular offspring will yield less benefit than the previous unit of care, one would expect a parent, after it has brought all of its offspring to the point of diminishing returns, to divide any remaining resources equally among its offspring.

In the parent's eyes—given the above conditions—each offspring is of equal value: each, in effect, represents an equally effective vehicle for projecting genes into future generations. From the offspring's point of view, however, the situation is quite different. It is related to itself by $r = 1$, but to each of its siblings by $r = \frac{1}{2}$. Thus, from its point of view, it is twice as valuable as a vehicle for projecting its own genes into future generations as is each of its siblings.[5] For it, the ideal distribution of parental care would consist of twice as much care for itself as for each of its siblings. Thus, one would expect disagreement between parent and offspring over the amount of care the parent should give the offspring. These considerations underlie

cases the conflict of interest discussed below still arises for the same reason, i.e., the genetic distinctness of parent and offspring in sexually reproducing species. The parent's preferred division of resources among offspring and the offspring's preferred division, as a result, will still not be congruent.

[5] This value is based on the assumption that the next offspring will be a full sibling. If it is a half sibling, Ego would be four times more valuable.

the theoretical discussions which come under the heading of parent-offspring conflict (Trivers 1974).

A number of empirical expectations concerning behavior between parent and offspring can be derived from Trivers' model. Among mammals for example, one would expect parent and offspring to disagree concerning the ideal time for weaning (Trivers 1974). A relevant mammalian family for anthropologists to consider is that of primates. Most higher primates produce a single offspring at a time, and following birth, the mother's parenting activities are directed for a period of time primarily toward the new offspring. Part of this care consists of suckling the infant. Lactation imposes a nutritional burden on the mother which fits the definition of cost used above. To some degree it weakens the mother's survival chances. If a mother were to be pregnant at the same time, this would impose an additional cost, further lessening the mother's survival chances. There is evidence that among many primates, there is an adaptive mechanism which prevents females from assuming the dual burden of lactation and pregnancy. The process of lactation itself suppresses the estrous cycle so that lactating females cannot become pregnant. This in a sense represents a trade-off between survival and fertility. A female that could become pregnant while lactating could produce—if she survived—more offspring than a competing female which could not become pregnant while lactating. However, such a gain in fertility would impose a heavier cost on the mother lessening her chances of survival. Further, she would be able to invest less nutritionally in each offspring during the period of gestation and lactation. Other forms of care of offspring would also of necessity diminish as the number of offspring produced increased. The effect of these costs would be a lower life expectancy for the mother and offspring. Thus, increasing fertility usually imposes a cost in lowered survivorship. Conversely, reducing mortality often imposes cost in the form of lowered fertility. Modern Darwinian theory would state that natural selection would favor the combination of mortality and fertility rates which leads to the highest genetic representation in descending generations. In primates this has taken the form of fertility lower than that characteristic of many mammals. Producing one offspring at a time, and suppressing estrus for a long period of lactation after each offspring, are part of this optimal pattern for primates of low fertility and high survivorship. The optimal pattern from a primate mother's point of view entails at some point ceasing to suckle an offspring. This point occurs when the parent's reproductive success is best served by producing an additional offspring rather than continuing to suckle the last. This lowers the survival chances of the weanling, but if the right time is

20

chosen, this consequent diminution of expected genetic representation in the next generation of breeding individuals is less for the mother than that gained by producing an additional offspring. However, as a result of the considerations discussed above, the point that is ideal for a mother primate to wean and become pregnant again is calculated on the assumption that each offspring is of equal value. From the point of view of the offspring, the ideal time for being weaned is calculated on the assumption that it is worth twice as much as the next offspring to be born. That is, its potential contribution to future generations of descendants has twice the value of that of a sibling. Thus, one would expect a primate mother to want to wean her offspring sooner than the offspring would like. This sort of conflict over weaning has been observed among a number of mammalian species including some primates (Kurland 1977:117–120; Wilson 1975:341–343). A young primate that attempts to persuade its mother to extend the suckling period is behaving selfishly. If successful, it will increase its own inclusive fitness and diminish that of its mother. If the inequality (on page 18) is satisfied natural selection will favor individuals that behave selfishly in this situation. The mother can be expected to behave in her own reproductive interest, contrary to that of her offspring, and to resist attempts by offspring to extend suckling beyond the point that is optimal for her.

This evolutionary perspective on selfishness can be used to analyze not only weaning conflicts but a number of problems such as infanticide, or armed conflict in any of a number of forms (cf. Chagnon and Bugos, chapter 8; Chagnon, Flinn, and Melancon, chapter 12; Dickemann, chapter 13). It can be noted by considering the inequalities above, that as r diminishes, the likelihood that altruistic behavior will be adaptive also diminishes, and at the same time the likelihood that selfish behavior will be adaptive increases—assuming B and C for a particular altruistic or selfish act maintain the same value as r diminishes. Evidence that this is true for some areas of human behavior is available (Alexander 1975a; Chagnon 1975 and chapter 4; Chagnon and Bugos, chapter 8; Hames, chapter 9).[6] It is important to note that in many cases B and C will not remain constant as r diminishes, but that this is a good assumption for the ethnographic situations dealt with by Hames (chapter 9) and by Chagnon and Bugos (chapter 8).

[6] Sahlins (1976a:17–67) presents some evidence to the contrary. His discussion rests on the assumption that if one cannot predict co-residence and co-membership in descent groups from r, then it follows that one cannot predict altruism and selfishness from r, B, and C. This does not follow logically, and unless one favors the abuse of logic, one can ignore his argument (cf. Alexander 1977c:919; Etter 1978:163. Alexander discusses this point in terms of k, Hamilton's original variable which is equivalent to B/C).

Return Benefit Theory

Altruistic behavior can be favored by natural selection if there is a high probability that the organism assisted by this behavior will eventually reciprocate with altruistic behavior toward the original altruist (Trivers 1971; Darwin 1871:92; Williams 1966:93–99). By definition, such behavior is favored by natural selection only if the final effect for the altruist is an increase in its own genetic material in descending generations. Exchanges of altruistic assistance of this sort are labeled reciprocal altruism (Trivers 1971) or reciprocity (Alexander 1974). Conditions under which this behavioral strategy will be favored by natural selection are limited by the fact that reciprocal altruists can easily be exploited by individuals who accept the benefits of another's altruism but do not reciprocate (Trivers 1971).

One possible concrete example of this sort of behavior is that of warning calls given by birds after observing a predator (Trivers 1971:43–45). Such a warning call carries with it a cost, since the bird giving the call is more likely to be located by the predator. The benefit, to other birds in the vicinity, is a greater chance of escape. An example of a set of conditions under which natural selection might favor such behavior could be the following: (a) issuing a warning call only increases by a small amount an individual's chances of being caught; (b) the warning to other birds greatly increases their chances to escape; (c) each bird inclined to give such warning calls lives in a flock consisting of other birds similarly inclined, so that it more frequently receives the benefits of warning calls than it pays the cost of giving them.

The last condition, however, is one that is unlikely to be consistently met over an evolutionary time scale. This is because in such a population any bird which is inclined not to give warning calls will enjoy a selective advantage over the other birds. Such a non-altruist would enjoy the benefits of warning calls given by other birds, but would never pay the cost of issuing such calls. Thus, whenever mutation or gene flow introduces a non-altruist of this sort into a population of altruists fitting the above description, natural selection will favor the spread of the propensity to refrain from warning calls at the expense of the propensity to give them.

In a population of warning-givers, a bird that refrains from giving warnings enjoys a selective advantage. The result is that genes predisposing birds to refrain from giving warning calls will spread. As the proportion of altruists diminishes, the number of warning calls given goes down, and considering the population as a whole the advantage of selfish birds declines. In contrast, the disadvantage of altruists increases; they continue to give warnings and to pay the cost, but the number of warnings they receive declines. The end result in a finite population is that the genes predisposing birds toward altruism will be eliminated once genes are introduced which predispose individuals not to issue warnings. For similar reasons, altruistic genes cannot be introduced into a population consisting of selfish birds.

Reciprocity, thus, can be established as an adaptive strategy in a population only if some additional set of conditions are met which give altruists an advantage over selfish strategists. A number of such conditions have been suggested.

One condition suggested with reference to warning calls as an anti-predator adaptation is the following. Successfully capturing a prey of a particular species in a particular locality, may help the predator to learn better how to capture that type of prey in that specific setting and also may habituate the predator to hunting that species in that particular location (Trivers 1971:44). Thus a warning call could have an additional direct benefit to the giver of the call, in that it would decrease the chance of a specific predator's returning to that location. This could compensate for the failure of some individuals to reciprocate warning calls and shift the relative costs and benefits of giving versus not giving calls in favor of the former.

Another set of conditions under which reciprocal altruism might be sustained is this: the benefits given are directed exclusively to specific recipients, the altruists monitor each individual they assist, and the altruists stop helping a particular individual if it fails to reciprocate (Trivers 1971:36, 46–53). A hypothetical case might consist of an animal coming to the assistance of another animal in intraspecific fights, and then waiting to see whether the beneficiary reciprocates in kind. Such a behavior will entail an unrepaid cost if not every individual reciprocates. However, if enough reciprocate, and the success of individuals in fights is greatly increased by an ally, the benefits could outweigh the cost. Whether such a strategy can win out over a strategy of no assistance depends on the composition of the population. A single team fighter, in a population of solitary fighters, will pay a cost and derive no benefit. Thus, team fighters cannot establish themselves in a population of non-assisters unless they initially enter in large numbers with established alliances and spend little effort in the new population attempting to form new alliances. An animal that assists any unfamiliar individual it encounters which is caught up in a fight, and then waits to see if similar assistance is reciprocated, would not do as well as an animal that is more cautious. One can envision a more cautious strategy of observing unfamiliar individuals for some time to determine their propensity to reciprocate before coming to their rescue. A careful sizing up of strange individuals before attempting to initiate reciprocal exchange of benefits is something that is possible only in an animal that collects large amounts of information about conspecifics it comes in contact with and weighs this information in a sophisticated way. Human beings are one species which would seem capable of accomplishing this (Trivers 1971:46–53).

Another way of avoiding the cost of non-reciprocation would be to punish non-reciprocators when they are discovered (Trivers 1971:49–50). Again, this is a strategy which one can imagine among human beings more easily than among any other species. The possibility of a strategy of this sort as a buttress to reciprocal altruism has led to the suggestion that moral outrage, the bearing of grudges, and even the satisfying quality of vengeance are all adaptive responses to the reciprocal altruist's problem of dealing with non-reciprocators (Trivers 1971:49–50).

One of the functions of language, accurate memory, and high intelligence among human beings may be that they enable people both to agree on complex exchanges of benefits and to monitor one another's behavior closely. Through the vehicle of language human beings learn a lot about the behavior of other individuals. One human being often reacts to another largely in terms of his or her reputation, that is, in terms of information gathered from third parties, rather than through direct experience with the individual in question (cf. Trivers 1971:52). In fact, concern about reputation, and the evaluation of individuals through information gathered via third parties, is probably an important universal of human social life.[7] A combination of language and long memory can in fact make a single failure to reciprocate very expensive, especially in small communities where one only interacts with individuals who know one another's life histories well. Thus, human beings are in many ways the most likely of all social animals to have refined strategies of reciprocal altruism, and any attempt to understand human sociality should be based on careful attention to reciprocity. Anthropologists have long been aware of the importance of reciprocity.

Reciprocity is especially likely to develop when the costs are low and the benefits high (West Eberhard 1975:11–14). Reciprocity is also possible among related individuals, in which case an altruist is rewarded in

[7] This also gives rise to such things as gossip as a possible sanction and possible aggressive strategy, and at the same time some skepticism about gossip.

I. Some Statements of Theory

two ways: (a) an increase in inclusive fitness resulting from benefits enjoyed by kin, and (b) an increase in Darwinian fitness resulting from the return benefits (Trivers 1971:46). Reciprocal altruism is favored between related individuals whenever

$$(B_s - C_s) + r (B_k - C_k) > 0$$

where B_s and C_s are the benefits and costs to self, B_k and C_k are the benefits and costs to the related individual, and r is the coefficient of relatedness between the two related individuals (West Eberhard 1975:19–21). The first term of this equation represents the gain in Darwinian fitness, and the second the gain in inclusive fitness by means of increasing a relative's reproductive success.[8] As individuals become progressively less related, i.e., as r becomes smaller, the second term becomes progressively less significant until eventually only the first is of any real importance. Once this point is reached the inequality closely approximates that which would apply to reciprocal altruism among unrelated individuals. However, when r is relatively large the second term on the left side of this inequality may be important.

This inequality is especially important for human societies since there are few kinship relations among human beings in which the expectation of reciprocity is not an important element in the relationship. Among many animals, altruism is limited primarily to care for immature offspring, and once offspring are mature the parent's altruism or parental investment ceases. In such a case altruism is favored by natural selection almost exclusively as a result of kinship. In human societies, such altruism justified only by kinship is hard to find. In most societies, adult and adolescent children are expected to reciprocate some benefits to their parents. The benefits returned may frequently be less than those received, but this should not obscure the fact that reciprocation is expected and usually occurs. Relations among kin of the same generation are even more strongly characterized by exchanges rather than a one-way flow of benefits.

The precise nature of the social relationship between specific pairs of kin in human societies usually reflects the history of exchange between the individuals involved and not just the degree of relatedness or the culturally shaped expectations of the society. Some pairs of brothers are close, reflecting mutual satisfaction with their history of reciprocal ex-

---

[8] The use of Darwinian and inclusive fitness here is not meant to imply that they are mutually exclusive measures. Darwinian fitness is a component of inclusive fitness, the more encompassing measure.

changes, and others are distant, reflecting a lesser satisfaction with their history of exchanges. Other factors can, of course, be cited to explain differences in relations between pairs of kin which are socially defined as equivalent—such as the extent to which similarity of age has made them competitors for the same limited pool of parental benefits or for the same limited number of potential mates. The point to be emphasized here, however, is that human kinship relations are importantly based on reciprocity and only when viewed in this way can they really be understood. One would expect that relationships based on reciprocal altruism (even if only in part) would be monitored closely by the individuals involved to determine whether the benefits and costs involved are fairly distributed. One would further expect that the willingness of each individual to incur further costs for the benefit of the other would depend on each participant's evaluation of the history of exchanges. Human kinship relationships certainly do have this characteristic. From the perspective of behavioral biology, however, one would expect that an individual is willing to behave altruistically to some degree toward close kin with whom the history of exchange has been unsatisfactory. Close here, in my estimation, would mean $r \geqq \frac{1}{8}$.

Another possibility that should be noted in reference to reciprocal altruism is the possibility of indirect reciprocity. An altruistic act need not be rewarded by the beneficiary in order to be adaptive. It is only necessary that as a consequence of the act some gain in inclusive fitness will flow to the altruist. Since a gain in inclusive fitness can be accomplished by a benefit accruing to a relative of the altruist, an altruistic act to individual B by individual A may be adaptive if the probable consequence is that B will in the future act altruistically to C, a relative of B (cf. Trivers 1971:52). In such a case the benefit to C would have to be devalued by the coefficient of relatedness between A and C, and by the probability that the benefit will actually flow to C. If in this devalued measure it is greater than the cost to A, the altruistic act is adaptive. One can also easily imagine other forms of indirect reciprocity, as for example when individual A assists B, B assists C, and C assists A. Many human institutions entail such indirect exchanges. Human societies are characterized by many complex patterns of indirect exchanges of benefits, and questions as to whether a particular form of behavior is adaptive or maladaptive, should be approached with cognizance of this fact (West Eberhard 1975:20–22).

Before turning to another topic, it should also be noted briefly that the issues raised by return benefit theory in many ways converge with the long-established interest in the social significance of reciprocity among social anthropologists (Lévi-Strauss 1949; Malinowski 1926; Mauss 1954; Sahlins 1965).

Parental Investment and Sexual Selection

Trivers (1972: 139) defined parental investment as anything a parent does to nurture and protect an offspring which increases the offspring's chances of reproductive success at the cost of limiting the parent's ability to nurture and protect other offspring. An organism's total expenditure of time, energy, and other resources and its total assumption of risk toward the end of producing and nurturing offspring are referred to as its parental effort. In most species members of one sex invest more than members of the other in the care of each offspring and as a result are capable of producing fewer offspring than members of the opposite sex. Given this, members of the sex investing less can increase their reproductive success by acquiring multiple mates. This, in turn, leads to two processes, both of which were defined by Darwin (1871) as sexual selection: competition for mates among members of the sex investing less, and differential choice, as mates, of members of the sex investing less by members of the sex investing more. This sort of selection leads to sexual dimorphism in morphology, physiology, and behavior. When the investment of each sex per offspring is approximately equal such dimorphism is minimized. Mate choice and competition for mates are referred to as mating effort. Both mating effort and parental effort are subdivisions of a broader category of striving referred to as reproductive effort (cf. Low 1978). The concept of parental investment if broadened to include care and assistance of relatives other than offspring can be referred to as altruism investment (Dawkins 1976).

In the majority of species males (defined as the sex producing smaller gametes) are the ones that invest less per offspring and females are the sex that invests more. This appears to be the primitive condition among mammals. Females under these conditions invested considerable energy, time, and risk in gestation, lactation, and other forms of nurturance. Males in contrast devoted little or nothing to the care of offspring. The energy investment of males in the production of a single gamete is trivial in comparison to the female investment needed to bring a newly conceived zygote to the end of the period of parental care. The result is that males can potentially produce far more offspring than females, and females become a limiting resource for males. Females are in effect in shorter supply than potential male demand, and each female is virtually assured of a mate. Females are, therefore, selected to choose mates which will produce the fittest offspring. They are ordinarily approached by a number of courting males, but do not consent to mate until some male has demonstrated his suitability in various ways. Discrimination in choosing mates is for males with better genes (and for males with greater willingness to supply their share of parental investment if males do ordinarily supply some investment). The result of female choice, given low male investment, is that males who can demonstrate their superior suitability as mates are chosen over and over again as mates, and inferior males are not chosen at all. Thus female choice not only tends to cause a greater variance in male reproductive success than occurs among females, it also causes selection for males who have the particular qualities that cause them to be chosen as mates. These traits include various kinds of showiness and a behavioral propensity to court females vigorously. They also include traits such as strength and agility which demonstrate health and indicate the male in question has good genes. Males, under these conditions, also tend to compete directly with one another using aggression to exclude other males from opportunities to mate. This causes selection for greater size and fighting ability. The results of these selective pressures are sexual dimorphism in both morphology and in behavior.

In some species, these conditions are reversed with males investing more per offspring than females. In these cases females become the larger, showier, more aggressive sex and males exercise careful discrimination among the many female suitors who approach them. Matings tend to be polyandrous, and females have a higher variance in reproductive success. Pipefish, seahorses, and phalaropes, a type of polyandrous bird, are examples. Some species are also characterized by relatively equal investment, monogamy, and limited sexual dimorphism. The majority of species of birds fit this pattern.

The secondary development of male parental investment has occurred in many mammalian species including most notably the human species. The secondary evolution of male parental investment introduces a number of elements into male and female strategies. Males to be successful must devise strategies for assuring accurate identification of their own offspring. These strategies take such forms as long courtship before mating and preventing other males from access to one's mates by means of territoriality. The greater the male investment, the greater the importance of paternity knowledge. The presence of male investment and potential difficulty in identifying paternity, also make cuckoldry an alternate male strategy (cf. Trivers 1972: 146). These strategies are then countered in some

I. Some Statements of Theory

areas by greater male efforts to exclude mates from contact with other males. Males' strategy may in some cases consist of jealously guarding their own mates while simultaneously trying to cuckold other males. On the other hand, so long as male investment is less than female investment, male desertion of mates and subsequent mating with additional females is likely to remain a successful strategy (cf. Trivers 1972: 146–150). Thus, for females counterstrategies to prevent desertion and assure male investment in their offspring become important (cf. Alexander and Noonan, this volume). The evolution of male parental investment in the human line is also associated with a limited sexual dimorphism and a limited degree of polygyny (cf. Alexander et al., this volume). Thus human males are somewhat larger, and apparently more aggressive, than females and they are facultatively polygynous. They also appear to be somewhat inclined toward cuckoldry as a reproductive strategy. Male choice in selecting mates is important among human beings, but females appear to remain the more discriminating sex.

Sex Ratio Theory

Natural selection consistently favors only one strategy over several generations in regard to the sex ratio of offspring: equal parental investment in offspring of each sex (Fisher 1958; MacArthur 1965; Hamilton 1967; Leigh 1970). Under certain circumstances, selection can favor the ability to make facultative variations from a 50/50 ratio in response to the temporary condition or environmental circumstance of particular parents.

    R. A. Fisher, in his classic work of 1930, was the first to shed light on the question of why sex ratio so frequently approximated 50/50. He observed that if a population had a surplus of females, any individuals genetically predisposed to produce more males would leave more offspring in the second descending generation. Their male progeny would find it easy to acquire mates simply because there would be more females than males in the population. However, once such selection caused male-producing genes to spread sufficiently, the sex ratio would approach 50/50 and the advantage of a genetic predisposition toward producing more male offspring would vanish. If the initial situation were one of an excess of males, the reverse process would occur. In either case the population would stabilize at 50/50. This means that there is no lasting advantage to a tendency to produce offspring predominantly of one sex. Producing offspring of each sex in roughly equal proportions is the only strategy which is consistently favored over a number of generations. Later authors have refined "Fisher's principle" by demonstrating that selection favors not equal numbers of offspring but rather equal parental investment in offspring of each sex (MacArthur 1965; Hamilton 1967; Leigh 1970). Thus, if for example it costs a parent twice as much to bring a male to the end of the period of parental investment as it does a female, one would expect, other things being equal, that parents would produce twice as many females as males. Half of the genes in each generation come from males of the preceding generation, and half from females. If parental investment, on average, is equal for young of each sex, then both the cost and benefit of rearing each sex will be equal. If more is invested in one sex than the other, as a population average, the benefit will remain equal (half the ancestry of each generation must come from each sex), but the total investment in one sex will be greater than in the other. This causes selection favoring those who invest more in the sex which in the population as a whole receives less investment. As in Fisher's reasoning above this selection tends to bring the ratio back to 50/50, and the only consistently favored strategy is one of equal investment in each sex as a population average.

Differential mortality as well as differential cost can affect the numbers of each sex born. Consider for example a situation in which the average male born dies at a point at which half of the parental investment needed to bring a male to maturity has been expended, but the average female dies at a point at which nine-tenths of the investment needed to bring a female to maturity has been expended. If males and females each require equal investment and if equal numbers of each are produced, more investment will be expended on females than on males, and the effect will be selection favoring individuals who produce more than 50 percent males at birth.[9] Such individuals will in effect be investing more in the sex which is underrepresented in terms of investment. Again the only strategy consistently favored over several generations is one which adjusts numbers at birth so as to equalize investment in each sex. In the case above this would be a ratio of 9 males for every 5 females.

Trivers and Willard (1973) have provided another insight into sex ratio. They observed that if it is predictable from a female's condition or circumstances (her health or the abundance of resources available to her) that her offspring will be either at the high or low end of the variance in reproductive success, then selection should favor in females the ability to

[9] Actually all investment from conception on could logically be considered, but assuming equal investment per offspring and equal mortality before birth provides a reasonable approximation to real cases, and is suitable for explaining the general principles.

I. Some Statements of Theory

vary the sex ratio of their offspring in response to these conditions. Selection would favor females who respond to conditions indicative of highly successful offspring by producing more male offspring, since the most successful males have a higher reproductive success than the most successful females. By the same logic, selection would favor females who respond to conditions indicative of offspring near the low end of the variance by producing more females. Crucial elements in the sets of conditions favoring this kind of selection are (a) the predictability of offspring's place in the variance in reproductive success from the mother's conditions or circumstances, and (b) a polygynous breeding system in which variance in male reproductive success is higher than variance in female reproductive success. If either of these elements is missing, selection for this sort of variation in sex ratio cannot be expected. It is important to note that when this sort of flexibility in the sex ratio of offspring does evolve, the overall population averages do not deviate from the refinement of "Fisher's principle" which predicts equal investment on average for each sex.

The above predictions about sex ratio may seem esoteric to many social and cultural anthropologists, but they are relevant to hypotheses about human infanticide discussed by Bates and Lees, Chagnon et al., and Dickemann in this volume. It is also relevant to the subject of spontaneous abortion discussed later in this volume by Bernds and Barash. The fact that the same theoretical principle can shed light both on events of a physiological nature and on forms of behavior such as infanticide suggests that our traditional division of phenomena into distinct biological and cultural categories is for some purposes artificial.

Behavioral Biology and Anthropology

The theoretical principles from evolutionary biology which are summarized in the preceding pages are compatible with most but not all of the theoretical views widely accepted among anthropologists. The central and most widely agreed upon theoretical ideas in anthropology are the following: (a) human behavior varies widely between societies and is largely shaped by culture, i.e., things individuals learn as a result of growing up in and living in a particular society; (b) cultures are integrated wholes, or at least institutions in the same culture are frequently functionally interrelated; (c) all value judgments are relative to the culture in which they are made; and (d) culture develops as a result of its own internal dynamics, not

*as a result of human input. Of these views, only the last is incompatible
with behavioral biology.*

Up to this point, I have presented a biological view of human
behavior and sociality. The crucial questions at this juncture are: (1) how
does this view contrast with the views of human behavior which are at
present commonly accepted among cultural and social anthropologists?
and (2) can this view fruitfully be combined with anthropological views
of human behavior which are at present commonly accepted among cultural and social anthropologists?

Most anthropologists would agree that the following quotation
from Ruth Benedict's *Patterns of Culture* summarizes the central finding
of anthropological research.

> *The life history of the individual is first and foremost an
> accommodation to the patterns and standards traditionally handed
> down in his community. From the moment of his birth the customs
> into which he is born shape his experience and behavior. By the
> time he can talk, he is a little creature of his culture, and by the
> time he is grown and able to take part in its activities, its habits
> are his habits, its beliefs his beliefs, its impossibilities his im-
> possibilities. Every child that is born into his group will share
> them with him, and no child born into one on the opposite side
> of the globe can ever achieve the thousandth part. [1934:2–3]*

The basic objective of much of anthropology up to the present
has been documentation of the tremendous influence of culture on human
experience and behavior. This has been the task of anthropology more
than of any other discipline. Culture can be described, as Ruth Benedict
describes it above, as the shaping of an individual's behavior by the experience of growing up and living in a particular human community.
Whether one admires or abhors polygyny, sets as one's goal getting
through medical school or becoming a shaman, and a host of other aspects
of each individual's experience, one is shaped by the fact of growing up
and living in one community rather than another.

A number of other ideas have been combined with this basic notion
that human experience is strongly influenced by culture. One is the idea
that a culture—the ways of behaving, speaking, and thinking learned in a
particular society—is an integrated whole. As such the parts cannot be
understood without relating them to the whole (Benedict 1959:52–61;
E. Wolf 1964:92–93). For example, polygyny in a particular locality cannot

be understood without reference to household form, the economic role of female labor, and so forth. A common but less rigid version of this view maintains that while all aspects of a culture may not be tightly integrated into an overall pattern, at least many aspects of a culture can be expected to be functionally interrelated (E. Wolf 1964:92–93).

A third idea commonly considered important by anthropologists is the notion of cultural relativism. This view states that, since particular views as to the rightness or wrongness, appropriateness or inappropriateness, etc., of particular ideas, behaviors, or social relationships are different from one community to another, there is no absolute standard by which one can judge such things as goodness, correctness, etc.

A fourth idea which is widely accepted as basic is the idea of the superorganic nature of culture. This view, in essence, states that culture is an independent variable and human behavior and ideas are dependent variables. Culture changes over time as a result of its own internal dynamics, and human behavior and thought are carried along to new forms in response to this change. According to this view, human thought and action do not shape culture. Only the reverse occurs. Our impression that we can change culture is an illusion, since our act in changing some pattern of acting or thinking is itself the product of previous cultural patterns (Kroeber 1917, 1944; Sahlins 1976a:3–67; White 1949:330–359).

Not all anthropologists have accepted all of these views, but these ideas have been more widely accepted as the basic principles of social and cultural anthropology than have any others. The words chosen to express these ideas often vary more than the ideas themselves. Thus, the view that behavior is largely a response to social structure is not fundamentally very different from the view that behavior is largely shaped by culture (cf. Radcliffe-Brown 1965:188–204). The Durkheimian notion of the independence of collective representations as constraining forces on human behavior is not basically very different from the view that culture is superorganic (Durkheim 1958: 1–13).

Of these four basic principles, only the fourth stands in definite disagreement with evolutionary biology. If culture evolves in its own terms without responding to human attempts to shape it, and at the same time determines the form of human behavior, then it is hard to see how evolved behavioral tendencies could cause behavior to assume the form that maximizes inclusive fitness. In view of this fact it is interesting that the notion that culture has a dynamic of its own has received a serious challenge within social anthropology from people who have no apparent interest in introducing biological principles into social anthropology.

A number of anthropologists have suggested that social systems can only be understood if the conscious actors in the system are studied in terms of the factors shaping their choices as to how to behave (Barth 1966, 1967; Bailey 1969; Dyson-Hudson 1970; Goldschmidt 1966; Kapferer 1976).[10] Similar theoretical views have also been developed by sociologists (Blau 1964; Homans 1961). The theoretical work of these anthropologists and sociologists has been strongly influenced by game theory (von Neumann and Morgenstern 1964). Their approach to analyzing human behavior begins with the observation that people make choices among alternative forms of behavior. Explaining behavior is then seen as the task of determining what influences their choices. What choices are possible is determined by the technological knowledge available in the community in which an individual finds himself, and also by the other individuals in the community and their probable ways of behaving. These can be labeled cultural constraints on behavior. There are also ecological constraints. The natural setting in which a community is located also limits what forms of behavior are possible. The same cultural and ecological constraints also determine what consequences will flow from a particular form of behavior. People place different values on these consequences: some are more desirable than others. These evaluations influence the likelihood that these behaviors will be repeated.

Occasionally people innovate, try some new form of behavior. If the consequences of this new behavior are more desirable than those of earlier alternative behavior, the innovator is likely to repeat the novel behavior, and other members of his or her community are likely to imitate it. If the consequences are less desirable than those of earlier forms of behavior, the behavior is not likely to be repeated. Thus, change is determined not only by innovation but by a process of evaluation in which people choose in some cases to imitate innovative behavior, and in some others not (Barth 1967:668). The actual consequence of the behavior and whether it is seen as desirable or undesirable are the determinants of whether a behavior becomes frequent, i.e., institutionalized in a community.

Seen in this way, behavior is not a dependent variable shaped by culture as an independent variable. Rather, culture—the things individuals learn as a result of growing up in and living in a particular community— is the outcome of a continuous process of choices as to how to behave and evaluation of the consequences of behavior. Human beings play an active

[10] Raymond Firth (1964:30–87) in many ways anticipated the views of these theoreticians. It is interesting that Sahlins, who claims the autonomy of culture makes sociobiological reasoning invalid (1976a:3–67), ignores these dissenting views completely.

I. Some Statements of Theory

role in this process, and current behavior is in effect the product of past behavior rather than of an entity called culture which is somehow apart from human beings, influencing their behavior but not influenced by it.

Social behavior in terms of this point of view is seen as transactions between individuals in which each attempts to gain more from the exchange than he gives (Barth 1966:1–11). This need not imply cheating, only that each party to an exchange must value what he or she gets above what he gives. Thus if an individual has crops to harvest but insufficient labor to harvest them and another has time he cannot profitably spend, each can gain more than he gives if they exchange labor for part of the crop. One exchanges otherwise idle time for produce, and the other exchanges produce he could not harvest himself for the labor needed to harvest his full crop. In fact most institutionalized, i.e., frequently repeated, transactions are of this sort in which each gives something that has more value to the other party than to himself. Attempts at cheating do occur, but cheated individuals are rarely willing to repeat the bargain unless coerced, and others rarely are willing to imitate the transactions in which they see the probable outcome as unfair to themselves. Coercion, where it is possible, changes this picture, but it can nevertheless be seen, in terms of the same model of choice, as a form of behavior aimed at producing desirable consequences. Those who apply coercion do so in order to produce results they desire. Those coerced choose the best of possible courses of action given the coercion.

This view also does not assume that all of the individuals in a community will behave in the same way. Rather the behavior of different individuals in the same community will be the same only to the extent that they face the same constraints and opportunities and have the same knowledge and experience. Members of the same community will often behave in very similar ways because the things influencing their choices will be the same, but complete conformity to one stereotyped pattern of behavior by all the members of a community is not to be expected. The anthropologist's habit of saying, for example, that Nayar live in matrilateral extended families, and Turkmen in patrilateral extended families, is a descriptive shorthand. In fact, there is variation within a society as well as between societies and the reasons for it are the same: variation in the factors influencing choices among alternative behaviors.[11]

The above discussion amounts to a suggestion that the view of

[11] This view need not imply that people are conscious of, or accurately verbalize about, the factors influencing their choices. It is only necessary that these factors be identifiable by outside observers and that their effect be somewhat predictable.

culture as an independent variable and behavior as a dependent variable be replaced by a view which more explicitly emphasizes the process out of which both culture and behavior are generated. This view maintains that there is a constant process of feedback between behavior and culture, i.e., the things people learn by interacting with other people. Current behavior is shaped by things learned in the past, and at the same time influences what will be learned in the future. Sorting out one of these two things as an independent variable and the other as a dependent variable is nonsense. Present behavior and culture are dependent variables in response to past behavior and culture. Past behavior and culture are translated into present behavior and culture by sentient, intelligent creatures who evaluate past events in order to choose how to try to influence future ones.

A theoretical view of this sort is much more compatible with behavioral biology than the superorganic view of culture. It should, of course, be carefully noted that those who have presented theoretical views of this sort have no apparent interest in incorporating biological notions into social anthropology. For all I know, they may be chagrined at my suggestion that their views are especially compatible with behavioral biology. In order to integrate these game-theory approaches which have emerged in social anthropology into behavioral biology, all one has to do is add the hypothesis that the evaluations of consequences flowing from different behaviors are ultimately determined by preferences which are universal traits of human beings.[12] Whether they are so or not should be an empirical question.[13] If behavior can be shown to maximize inclusive fitness as a general result, this would constitute empirical support for this assumption.

A theoretical model of human behavior as adaptation at the individual level combined with a game-theory approach of the sort discussed above is quite compatible with the other commonly accepted basic principles of anthropology noted above. The most basic principle, that behavior varies widely among human societies, is logically expectable in terms of biological considerations. As noted earlier, natural selection can favor phenotypic variation in response to environmental variation. Human beings invest a large portion of their nutrient resources in constructing organs like the brain and vocal apparatus which are specialized for acquiring and processing information from their environment. They also

---

[12] This represents an alteration of the theoretical models at least as presented by F. Barth, who sees these evaluations as being cultural (1966:12–21).

[13] It is curious that proponents of the superorganic view, which is in many ways counterintuitive, never attempted to devise empirical tests of this view.

I. Some Statements of Theory

invest a large portion of a typical life history in learning, while prolonging the process of maturation and deferring reproduction. Given this heavy investment in things enabling them to vary their behavior in response to different environmental conditions, one would expect actual behavior to vary extensively from one environment to another.

Since culture is a process in which individuals maturing in a particular society learn by drawing on the information gathered by other individuals, one would expect that the things learned would vary greatly. The kind of information that is useful varies from one environment to another and so the kinds of information people bother to gather, retain, and pass on to others vary from one environmental setting to another. The information at hand in a particular society at a particular point in time limits possibilities for change in response to environmental change. For example, modern industrial society adjusts to food shortages in a different way than can a group of hunters and gatherers simply because the information and accumulated capital equipment it has available is very different. This means that different societies respond differently to similar or even identical environmental change. The specific events of history become determinants of human behavior, which are as important as current environmental circumstances.

Other factors also contribute to the importance of the specific history of a society in determining the current behavior of its members. A large part of the environment to which individuals adapt consists of other individuals and their expected behavior. Thus, learned social behavior can stabilize in a particular form because given existing behavior patterns the most adaptive response is to repeat the existing patterns. However, a different society in the same natural environment might arrive at a different set of stable social behaviors (cf. von Neumann and Morgenstern 1944 [1964]:31–45; Maynard Smith 1975). Given a horticultural economy in a tropical environment, a system of patrilineages may become a stable system but so may a system of matrilineages. This element of historical particularism is not only compatible with the game-theoretic thinking of behavioral biology, but is also expectable for a culture-bearing animal.

This same sort of game-theoretic thinking also leads to the expectation that different aspects of behavior will be to some extent integrated. It does not lead to an expectation that each form of behavior will necessarily have as its function maintaining the overall social system, although many behaviors may have this effect (cf. Radcliffe-Brown 1965:5–7, 12–14). However, it does lead to an expectation that individuals choosing strategies in one area of behavior will be influenced by the strategies they have chosen in other areas. Thus, it is not surprising, for example, that residence choice and household organization in many societies should be influenced by the prevailing sexual division of labor.

A biological perspective of the sort discussed above also does not alter the principle that value judgments are relative to the social context in which they are made. The criterion of adaptiveness is introduced by such a perspective, but the adaptiveness of a particular behavior is determined by the environment in which it occurs. Thus, the idea of relativity is not lost. Also, the statement that a particular form of behavior is adaptive in a particular environment does not alter other value judgments about that behavior. It might, for example, be possible to show that a particular form of behavior in a particular society is maladaptive, but nevertheless evaluated, in that society, as morally good. In such a case the fact of maladaptiveness does not change the moral judgment applied by members of the society in question. It also does not imply that the behavior is morally incorrect by any universal standard that I am aware of. The statement that a particular form of behavior is adaptive to a particular environment is a statement about its effect on survival and reproduction and nothing more. Whether that behavior is also good—morally, esthetically, or otherwise—is a separate issue.

The notion of cultural relativism carried to its logical extreme can be a source of embarrassment, as for example when it makes it difficult to find a reason for condemning cannibalism if it occurs in a society in which it is socially approved (cf. Jarvie 1975:263). I see no way in which the introduction of behavioral biology into social anthropology alters this embarrassment. If behavioral biology should eventually be generally accepted as a source of basic theory in social anthropology, it seems to me cultural relativism will remain as much a source of embarrassment as it is a source of pride.

Thus, there is a simple answer to the question of how behavioral biology contrasts with the views of human behavior commonly accepted by social and cultural anthropologists. It differs in two ways: (1) in adding the expectation that most forms of behavior will either be biologically adaptive, or will be expressions of evolved tendencies that were adaptive in the past, and (2) in challenging the notion of the superorganic. Beyond this there is reason to believe that most of the existing anthropological literature can be fruitfully combined with behavioral biology in order to provide a broader approach to the study of the social and cultural variation found among human societies (cf. E. O. Wilson, this volume). Also, the methodologies that have been developed by anthropologists, such as participant observation and cross-cultural comparison, would in no way be rendered less valuable by the introduction of behavioral biology into anthropology. They would remain as research tools which can be used to answer the questions posed by behavioral biology as readily as they were used to answer other questions in the past.

Whether or not such an approach is useful depends, as noted earlier in this essay, on whether or not the concepts of natural selection and adaptation can provide valid predictions about culture and behavior. Logically deriving such predictions and testing them empirically will determine the usefulness of behavioral biology to anthropology.

---

2. Toward a Coevolutionary Theory of Human Biology and Culture[1]

William H. Durham

Introduction

At the heart of the controversy over sociobiology and human social behavior lies a distinction between two separate kinds of mechanisms by which human attributes may come to exist at high frequency in a population. One of the mechanisms, the one most familiar to biologists and to sociobiologists in particular, is a *genetic* mechanism. An attribute, introduced to a human population's gene pool by mutation, migration, or recombination, may spread via gene propagation *if* it confers a reproductive advantage to its carriers *and if* that reproductive advantage results from genetic differences between carriers of the trait and non-carrier conspecifics. In this case, a trait is said to spread by "natural selection": the differential reproduction of individuals because of genetic differences between them.

The other mechanism, the one most familiar to social and cultural

[1] I thank Robert Boyd, Kathleen Durham, David Gordon, Brian Hazlett, Sarah Blaffer Hrdy, Frank Livingstone, Marlene Palmer, Elizabeth Perry, Roy Rappaport, Peter Richerson, Eric Smith, Victoria Sork, Joel Samoff, Alfred Sussman, John Vandermeer, and Jim Wood for thoughtful discussion and criticism of this work. Copyright © 1978 by William H. Durham.

anthropologists, is a *cultural* mechanism. An attribute may increase in frequency in a human population when it is spread by learning and maintained by tradition. Here the transmission of the attribute may be completely distinct from the biological processes of inheritance. Instead of differential reproduction, theories of cultural evolution propose that human attributes result from the differential replication by learning and imitation of variants introduced into a "cultural pool" by innovation and diffusion. By contrast, this process might be called "cultural selection" (see Durham 1976a).

Because these models of inheritance may be readily distinguished on the basis of mechanism (essentially genes versus brains), both biologists and anthropologists have assumed that human biology and culture must therefore be studied in mutually exclusive fashions. Scholars in both fields habitually ignore that other inheritance mechanism which is not conventionally a part of their own discipline, or at most assign to it some small, "modifying" influence. Most biologists and anthropologists have unfortunately overlooked a possible coevolutionary relationship between human biology and culture and continue to attempt the separation of their interwoven effects.

Sociobiology, although widely touted as the "new synthesis," has not yet proven to be an exception to this rule. Instead the field has been defined as "the application of evolutionary biology to the social behavior of animals, including *Homo sapiens*" (Barash 1977:2). Sociobiologists have repeatedly analyzed particular human social behaviors in terms of natural selection theory which, by definition, assumes the genetic-inheritance mechanism for the behavior under study (see, for example, Wilson 1975; Barash 1977). Without explicit incorporation of the alternative cultural mechanism, sociobiological explanations of human social behavior have automatically implied that observed behaviors are the end products of cumulative genetic change.

While it has long been argued that human behavioral *plasticity* is a product of our biological evolution, it is quite another matter to suggest that particular behaviors themselves evolved by natural selection. First, correlations between theories from evolutionary biology and observed human behaviors in no way constitute evidence of causation. As I have argued elsewhere (Durham 1976a) and continue to argue below, these correlations may equally result from the *cultural* inheritance mechanism and a complementary process of *cultural* evolution. Second, by singling out the genetic-inheritance model, sociobiologists have overlooked the fact that culture is, as Simpson (1972) recently put it, "the more powerful

I. Some Statements of Theory

means of human adaptation." The cultural mechanism provides a way to modify phenotypes that is (a) more rapid than changes resulting from natural selection, (b) better able to track environmental change or stability, and (c) sometimes even more responsive to perceived human need as described below. Given that human beings do have two principal inheritance mechanisms, and that the cultural mechanism is surely no less influential than the biological one, a preoccupation with natural selection and genetic models is likely both to distort our understanding of human social behavior and to prolong the unnecessary debate of biology versus culture. More progress is likely to be made by a theoretical perspective that includes *both* mechanisms of inheritance and makes no a priori assumptions about their relative importance in the evolutionary development of a given form of social behavior. In the pages that follow, I would like to discuss some of the conceptual features that such a coevolutionary theory might have.

This paper, then, has three objectives. First, I shall continue an argument made earlier (Durham 1976a, 1977) that where the natural selection theories of sociobiology have been right in their predictions or explanations of human behavior, it has often been for the wrong reasons. The apparent consistencies between biological theory and human behavior suggest *not* that there is necessarily an underlying biological basis that guides, steers, controls, programs, predisposes, or inclines every human activity, but rather that the traditions and customs produced by cultural processes are often adaptive in the "biological sense." I propose that these consistencies are best explained by the joint evolution of human biology and culture.

Second, my arguments here will imply that the whole "adaptive functionalism" approach to understanding human attributes has a theoretically circumscribed value, even when expanded to include cultural processes. For a number of reasons, the adaptive consequences of these attributes are not their sole significance. A perfectly valid endeavor for anthropologists and human ecologists is to seek an understanding of the meaning that cultural traits have for their bearers. In the eyes of the natives, this meaning may or may not be related to adaptation.

Third, this paper will elaborate on some earlier attempts to formulate a theory of cultural evolution which is adequate for explaining how adaptive cultural attributes evolve when they do (Durham 1976a, 1976b). I speak of "cultural selection" and "phenotype" not with any deliberate intention of "biologizing" culture and thereby alienating anthropologists. Rather, my motivation is to work for a real synthesis of presently antithetical doctrines espoused by biologists and anthropologists. I see the key to that synthesis to lie in the notion of *coevolution of the cultural and biological influences* on human phenotypic traits including behavior. For this, the need arises for a model of cultural evolution that is, at once, an outgrowth of earlier theories from cultural and ecological anthropology, and an explicitly complementary or coevolutionary theory with the theory of organic evolution by natural selection (see also Blurton Jones 1976).

Biological and Cultural Evolution

According to neo-Darwinian evolutionary theory in biology, the genetic traits of a given population of plants or animals track, over generations of time, one or more optimal character states that are specific to the organism and its environment. Changes in phenotype are thought to result most commonly from individual-level natural selection (together with some forms of kin and group selection) which acts to preserve those genotypes that direct the formation of phenotypes best suited to the prevailing conditions. This theory has now proven to be very successful in explaining the genetically coded traits of most organisms.

Particularly in human beings, however, there is an important non-genetic or cultural component of phenotypes as mentioned above. What was apparently selected for during the organic evolution of human beings was an *unusual capability for modifying and extending phenotypes on the basis of learning and experience.* Within limits, culture enables us to alter and build onto aspects of morphology, physiology, and behavior without any corresponding change in genotype. This means, of course, that natural selection by itself is neither adequate nor appropriate for explaining the culturally acquired phenotypic traits of human beings.

Anthropologists realized long ago that nonbiological process or processes were behind the cultural component of human phenotypes, and they have led the search for alternative models or theories for the evolution of this important cultural aspect. Widely varied theories are explicit and implicit in the anthropological literature (see, e.g., Kaplan and Manners 1972) and a number of them have been successful at explaining some within- and between-group variations in human cultural attributes. Curiously, a large number of these models represent a process of selective retention analogous in some sense to natural selection (Campbell 1965, 1975; Durham 1976a), although the phenotypes retained in time would be those which best suited a given cultural criterion. Unfortunately, there has been little agreement to date regarding the effective criterion or criteria behind any such cultural selection. The list of candidate criteria now includes free energy, satisfaction, profit, population regulation, homeostasis, and even ease of replication of a cultural instruction. Again, each has proven useful for the analysis of cultural characteristics in certain societies, but none has proven adequate for a general theory.

Part of the problem has been that, in the search for theories to explain cultural phenomena, one key factor has been continually overlooked, and that factor has much to do with the relationship between human biology and culture. Many scholars have failed to appreciate that the organic evolution of the *capacity* for culture had, at least at one time, important implications for the actual *process* of cultural evolution. Presumably what was genetically selected for in our ancestors was an increasing ability to modify phenotypes through learning and experience, true enough, but only because those ancestors persistently used that ability to enhance their survival and reproduction. The capacity for culture, one could say, continued to evolve not merely because it *enabled* superior adaptations, but also because it was used to *produce* superior adaptations. Our hominid ancestors must therefore have had ways of keeping culture "on track" of the adaptive optima as those optima varied from place to place and changed from time to time. The conclusion is important: as the capacity for culture evolved, *the developing culture characterizing a group of people must have been adaptive for them in the survival and reproduction sense whatever else it may have been.*

It is important to note that this conclusion does *not* require that the cultural meaning of things was consciously or unconsciously related to their consequences for survival and reproduction. It means only that, however culture changed and evolved, and whatever meaning was given by people to their cultural attributes, the net effect of those attributes was to enhance human survival and reproduction. There is an important deduction from this argument. Although a coevolutionary theory has potential for contributing to an understanding of the adaptive significance of cultural attributes, it is not necessarily the key to understanding the meaning and symbolic significance people may give to those attributes (see also Sahlins 1976b).

Obviously things have changed since the days when the capacity for culture was evolving because it was used by proto-hominids to produce superior adaptations. It is then appropriate to ask, is culture still used by human beings as a way to enhance their survival and reproduction, or have we lost the ability to keep culture "on track"? Has cultural evolution by some other principle of optimization, for example, more recently run counter to individual survival and reproduction, and has culture therefore lost its original adaptive significance for human existence?

It is, of course, impossible to give a definitive answer at this time, but for a number of reasons I am inclined to think that there is still an important adaptive dimension to human cultural attributes. These reasons can be divided into two parts: those related to the action of cultural selection within groups as discussed in the next section, and those related to cultural selection between groups as described later.

Cultural selection within groups

For convenience in the description of levels of cultural selection, I shall define *social group* to be any subset of a deme or breeding population containing individuals whose survival and reproduction are directly and substantially interdependent because of interactions among them. It can be thought of as a collection of individuals whose behavior creates at least a given arbitrary amount of interdependence so that the collection is bounded by frontiers of far less interdependence. Of course there are a whole variety of ways to be interdependent in this fashion, including ties arising from goods and services exchanged between members, but for most of the arguments that follow, the exact nature of interdependence is not important. It may be helpful here to think of a deme as some entire ethno-linguistic population or "culture" and to think of social groups as smaller, more interdependent camps, bands, or villages within that population.

Basic to any theory of cultural change and adaptation, of course, is the way in which distinct human social groups acquire their cultural attributes. In this section, I propose the hypotheses (a) that the cultural characteristics of human social groups result to a large extent from internal, individual-level selective retention, and more importantly, (b) that this process generally "selects for" cultural attributes that enhance the ability of their carriers to survive and reproduce.

My reasons are these. First, I believe that there is ample evidence that some process of selective retention continues to operate on the accumulation and modification of cultural attributes within human societies. People remain somehow selective in their receptivity to cultural innovation, for we know that many more innovations are introduced by invention and diffusion than are retained at length within any given society (see, e.g., Barnett 1953). Second, I believe that this ongoing selective retention is, and always has been, influenced by a number of human biases described in the literature which, I propose, tend to keep people from selectively retaining cultural attributes that counter their individual survival and reproduction, provided they have a choice. Of these, perhaps the most important are learned biases. Robert LeVine (1973) has argued that the process of socialization teaches children from an early age not only adherence to social norms and traditional patterns of behavior, but also selectivity in the adoption of new forms, on the basis of what is held to be adaptive and "for their own good." Two properties of this bias make it particularly important. First, the development of this selectivity is at least partly in the combined interest of the parents, the child, and even the social group as a whole (this is not to deny some amount of conflict among these interests). To some extent, all participants in the process have their own survival and reproduction at stake. Second, it is urgent. Because of the special vulnerability of children, the ability or inability to discriminate between positively and negatively adaptive practices in childhood can have direct and immediate consequences in addition to long-term effects.

A second sort of bias might be called the bias of "satisfaction" (see Ruyle 1973, 1977). Presumably throughout the organic evolution of hominids there was a persistent, genetic selective advantage for a neurophysiology that rewarded with sensory reinforcements and a feeling of "satisfaction" those acts likely to enhance survival and reproduction and those which produced unpleasant, distressing, or painful feedback in response to potentially dangerous behaviors. When the capacity for culture began evolving, there was already some built-in bias of this kind, biologically programmed in the design of the pre-human nervous system. Eugene Ruyle, among others, has argued that the selective retention of cultural traits has continued to be influenced by the general sense of "satisfaction" that they do or do not bring to their bearer. While we disagree over the definition and relative utility of the concept of satisfaction, I concur with Ruyle that cultural evolution has probably not ignored nor completely overridden the feedback from the neurophysiology that we are born with (cf. Durham 1977). I agree that "Square wheels, crooked spears, and sickly children are unlikely to provide much satisfaction" (Ruyle 1977:54), but I feel that this is because they are unlikely to do much for survival and reproduction.

There is potentially a third source of bias to be found in the learning structures and functions of the human brain, although I hasten to add that this possibility remains poorly documented at present. A knowledge of the structures and functions of the human brain is certainly crucial to understanding the relationship between biology and culture, but I have not been persuaded by hard-core genetic structuralists (e.g., Laughlin and d'Aquili 1974) that there is a determinism rather than a bias to be found therein. To my knowledge, the best evidence of any learning "canalization" that might affect culture comes from studies by Seligman (1971) and others, showing that some common human phobias are learned with an exposure and rapidity which suggest that these may represent a form of "prepared learning." Other examples of prepared learning have been documented for nonhuman animal species where they are thought to result from built-in neurophysiological mechanisms of the brain. To the extent that there is a bias on culture imposed by the biochemistry and physiology of the human brain, the organic evolution of that organ would mean a bias in favor of the selective retention of more-versus-less adaptive cultural traits.

A fourth kind of bias, which might be called "circumstantial bias," has been suggested recently by Cloak (1977:50) and by Alexander (1977b). This kind of bias may occur when the customary organization of child-rearing practices and enculturation in a social group ensures some regularity of learning and reinforcement for culture carriers. Consider the simple example where parents customarily rear and enculturate their own children. "Wherever that is true, a cultural instruction whose behavior helps its human carrier-enactor (or his/her relatives) to acquire more children thereby has more little heads to get copied into." As a result, cultural instructions that enhance survival and reproduction will differentially propagate through social groups as generations go by, "until most extant cultural instructions have that effect" (Cloak 1977:50).

These four biases (and probably others unrecognized and undiscovered) taken together represent a reasonably strong probabilistic "force" tending to keep culture on track of the adaptive optima. This "force" would operate at the level of individual human beings and bias them as culture carriers. As a result, individuals would tend to select and retain from competing variants those cultural practices whose net phenotypic effect best enhances their individual ability to survive and reproduce (Durham 1976a, 1976b). Hypothetically, this process of cultural selection would result in the spread and maintenance of cultural attributes that are adaptive in the general biological sense of contributing to their bearer's reproductive success. To be more explicit, I therefore hypothesize that *cultural features of human phenotypes are commonly designed to promote the success of an individual human being in his or her natural and sociocultural environment* and, to be consistent with the biological meaning of adaptation, I suggest that *success is best measured by the extent to which the attribute permits individuals to survive and reproduce and thereby contribute genes to later*

I. Some Statements of Theory

generations of the population of which they are members (adapted from Williams 1966:97).

Several implications of this hypothesis deserve elaboration. First, it suggests that successful adaptation be measured by the long-term representation of an individual's genes in a population, a quantity which ecologists and evolutionary biologists often call "individual inclusive fitness" (see, for example, Williams 1966; Alexander 1974; West Eberhard 1975), even though the phenotypic trait in question here need have no special genetic basis whatsoever. This suggestion often leaves both biologists and anthropologists a bit uncomfortable—anthropologists because even cultural ecologists are not accustomed to think in explicit terms of "reproductive success" and "genetic representation," and biologists because they are used to thinking primarily in terms of differentials in reproductive success that stem from genotypic differences. Indeed, for rigorous population genetics, fitness is conventionally defined between genotypes in a given environment. With culture, however, inter-individual differences in the long-term representation of genes can result from acquired phenotypes that have no special underlying genotype. Put differently, the representation of a wide variety of genotypes may actually benefit (they may or may not benefit equally) from a given cultural phenotypic change. To minimize confusion on this matter I therefore suggest that *individual inclusive fitness* be used to refer to the long-term representation of an individual's genes in a population, and *genotypic inclusive fitness* be used to refer to the differential representation of particular genotypes. Where differences in phenotypes result from genetic differences between organisms, individual inclusive fitness contributes to the genotypic fitness of particular genotypes and there is no problem. However, for humans in whom phenotypes may be culturally altered, extended, and transmitted, individual inclusive fitness differentials can result from phenotypes with no special genotypic basis. The analysis of the adaptive significance of cultural attributes thus requires a focus on individuals, their phenotypes, and associated differences in reproductive success. With these qualifications in mind, I suggest that relative, individual inclusive fitness (as approximated by the long-term differential reproductive success of an individual and appropriately weighted kin) remains the best measure by which to assess the adaptiveness of a given biological and/or cultural trait.

Second, an important distinction must be made between "the extent and effectiveness of design for survival" and the actual reproduction record of a given individual or sample (cf. Williams 1966). There may always be chance effects that render a trait in a given case maladaptive or suboptimal. Furthermore, the extent and effectiveness must be judged relative to the particular environment in which the adaptation arose. Third, the analysis of the adaptiveness of a characteristic must always be made in consideration of the alternative phenotypes historically or presently available in a given social context. At any given time, the nature of culture change and the rate of this change will be affected by the availability of alternative forms and the degree of relative advantage and disadvantage among them. Adaptiveness must then be seen as a statement of relative, not absolute, advantage among phenotypes.

To summarize, I hypothesize (1) that human beings are not just passively receptive to cultural innovation but (2) that we have and develop a number of selective biases which result in (3) a tendency to acquire those aspects of phenotype which past experience and some degree of prediction suggest to be most advantageous for personal inclusive fitness. Although the resulting process of cultural selection would normally result in adaptive phenotypic attributes, I should point out that it is actually easier to conceive of cultural influences getting "off track" in the evolution of a phenotype than it is for biological influences. Maladaptive cultural practices *can* be maintained at substantial frequency in a population, particularly when the biases previously mentioned are overridden or prevented from functioning by force, threat, misinformation, or restrictions on alternatives. Maladaptive behaviors can also recur through the conscious or deliberate choice of individuals to behave counter to their reproductive interests for whatever reason, but I am suggesting that this behavior is not likely to become a long-lasting cultural tradition. I am reminded of the "rather extreme example" mentioned in Ruyle (1973:206) of "a religious sect in nineteenth century Russia whose cultural pool contained a total ban on sexual intercourse. Lacking an adequate alternative method of recruitment, the sect disappeared. . . ."

Where circumstances do permit the preceding biases to operate, however, culture would hypothetically evolve to an important extent by the selective retention of nongenetic traits that enhance the ability of human beings to survive and reproduce in their particular habitats (Durham 1976a, 1976b). In principle, this cultural selection may proceed consciously or unconsciously; and, ironically, it may proceed according to any number of other "proximate" or "cognized" criteria (like free energy yield, homeostasis, etc.) that are closely correlated with the reproductive success of human beings in the given environment. In fact, the process may proceed through selective retention not related in any obvious way to reproduction or survival as long as the net effect enhances (or at least does

I. Some Statements of Theory

not reduce) the relative fitness of the culture carrier. In this way, cultural characteristics may take on a meaning and value which themselves are not explained by individual inclusive fitness although their adaptive consequences may then be so explained.

Michael Harner implied a way to summarize this hypothesis for cultural selection within groups when he wrote recently (Harner 1973b:152) that "Culture is learned and transmitted through human effort; therefore it seems unlikely that cultural institutions and traits can be successfully passed on through centuries and millennia without having some regular reinforcement for their maintenance." For the sake of simplicity, let us say that the individual effort involved in culture increases monotonically over the range of a quantitative phenotypic trait that is culturally variable. Further, let us assume that these "phenotypic costs" to an individual from the effort and/or risk associated with the cultural trait are proportional over the range to any "fitness costs" however slight of maintaining and perpetuating the practice (see figure 2–1, cost curve). What I am suggesting here is that individual-level cultural selection would act in time to increase the frequency of any available phenotype whose resulting net fitness benefits (total benefits minus costs) conferred a differential reproductive advantage relative to other phenotypes. In other words, I am suggesting that the reinforcement proposed by Harner is largely to be found in the inclusive fitness benefits of culture. Cultural selection as used here could then be "directional," "stabilizing," or "disruptive" analogous to the modes of natural selection, depending on the shape of the cost and benefit curves. Figure 2–1 shows a hypothetical case for stabilizing cultural selection. In an environ-

Figure 2–1   Model of Stabilizing Cultural Selection

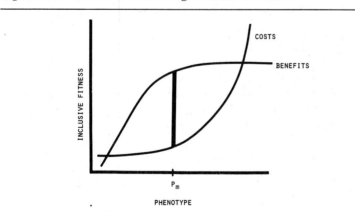

ment where the costs and benefits shown as a function of phenotype persist for some time, the hypothesized process of cultural selection would result in convergence on the intermediate phenotype P_m which effectively optimizes human survival and reproduction in that environment. It should be emphasized that such a trait would spread by individual-level selective retention to all individuals in the given social group for whom these costs and benefits apply. The trait could also spread by diffusion to other groups in the same deme or even other demes. If it continued there to confer individual fitness benefits, this phenotype could spread still further by individual-level selective retention.

One final qualification must be included in this argument. A large number, perhaps even a majority, of the identifiable cultural aspects of human phenotypes involve extremely low fitness costs and/or benefits for their carriers. Cultural traits in some cases may be virtually inconsequential to inclusive fitness and there may be essentially no relative fitness advantage among existing alternative forms. With little basis for fitness discrimination, the hypothesized process of cultural selection would not be effective for these traits. The spread and perpetuation of recognizably low-cost attributes are then likely to be better explained in other ways (like momentary phenotypic reward, or arbitrary symbolic value). As I have argued elsewhere (Durham 1976a), the importance of inclusive fitness to our understanding of human cultural attributes is therefore expected to be conditionally dependent upon the degree to which an attribute taxes the highly variable time, energy, and resource budgets of individuals. My hypothesis is that there are few, if any, cultural practices that are maintained in the absence of force or threat and persist even though individual parents would achieve substantially higher fitness without them or by available alternative practices.

This argument suggests that where cultural evolution proceeds through a process of selective retention within groups, resulting attributes are not likely to require what may be called "fitness altruism" by any individual. Cultural selection, like natural selection, would incessantly oppose any phenotype whose net effect was to assist reproductive competitors in the same population (Alexander [1974] makes this point for genetic selection). This does not mean that cultural selection somehow precludes mutual assistance. On the contrary, cooperative phenotypes would have a cultural selective advantage in any circumstance where joint effort results in mutually enhanced fitness. Nor does this imply that cultural selection within groups necessarily opposes all forms of self-sacrifice. There are now a number of theories showing ways in which genetically based social altru-

I. Some Statements of Theory

ism may actually increase fitness and thereby evolve by natural selection: through reciprocity (Trivers 1971), mate selection (see, e.g., Blaney 1976), social rewards (Ghiselin 1974), and kin selection (Hamilton 1964) to name a few. To the extent that cultural evolution is complementary to organic evolution, as I propose, analogous processes may favor cultural forms of social altruism that actually require no net fitness altruism.

Cultural selection between groups

Where the spread of some cultural trait within a group or population can be traced to an individual-level process, the preceding arguments may appear rather plausible. Problems arise, however, when a trait spreads through a deme or between demes because of some group-level process. Where the selective retention of cultural evolution results from group selection, it is not altogether obvious that individual-level fitness costs and benefits are particularly relevant to understanding changes in the distribution of phenotypes.

As with organic evolution where an individual- versus group-selection debate has been argued for over a decade, the important question concerns not the possibility of cultural selection at group and higher levels, but rather the relative effectiveness and direction of selection at those levels. When the two processes work in the same direction, either for or against a given cultural variant, there is no problem. They are likely to have complementary and reinforcing effects. Questions arise, however, when individual- and group-level processes run in opposition, namely: (1) can group-level cultural selection retain cultural traits advantageous to group reproduction (making it less likely that the group will go extinct or more likely that the group will propagate and colonize) although they decrease individual inclusive fitness and are therefore altruistic? and, conversely, (2) can individual-level cultural selection maintain traits advantageous to individuals while simultaneously being detrimental to the group?

Again, a definitive answer is difficult at present owing both to our general ignorance of the processes behind cultural change and to the paramount importance of situation-specific variables (like rates of innovation, diffusion, group extinction, etc.) to the outcome. However, if we assume that individual-level selection operates continuously and rapidly when choice is available, it is reasonable to hypothesize that the answer to (1) is negative, in general, judging from parallel arguments in organic evolutionary theory (reviewed in Maynard Smith 1976). The *origin* of an altruistic phenotype by cultural processes would require that groups be small for there to be, through "cultural drift" or some "founder effect," no alternative phenotype more individually beneficial within the groups to be selected. In addition, the *maintenance* of the altruistic trait would then depend on there being low rates of introduction of alternative "selfish" variants to groups of altruists (as through diffusion, migration, and invention) at the same time as rapid extinction of groups where any selfish variant is found. These conditions may well obtain in special circumstances and there groups of altruists could prevail. In general, though, group selection is not likely to be the mechanism maintaining the frequency of altruistic cultural traits. Where fitness altruism exists, it is more likely a result of incomplete or impeded individual-level selection, and therefore only a characteristic of certain individuals within a group.

When individual selection is not permitted to function as described above, it is hypothetically possible for group selection to aid in the perpetuation of altruistic cultural attributes. Consider a social system in which force or misinformation may be used by some members of a social group to create a degree of altruism in others that is not likely to result from the operation of individual selection under noncoercive conditions. If that altruism is then put to use to lower the probability of group extinction or raise the probability of group reproduction, group selection could favor that social system, which in turn would perpetuate the coercive practices creating real altruism. A few altruists could be especially effective in group selection by intergroup aggression (see below).

My hypothesis would be that possibility (2) is also not likely to be a major factor behind cultural evolution. In most cases, the long-term reproductive success of an individual human being is dependent upon a stable, functioning social group for any number of group benefits (e.g., increased security or efficiency of resource harvest, defense of resources and progeny). Where these benefits are real and apparent, individual-level cultural selection would act to constrain selfishness to a group-preserving form. This argument implies that cultural selection cannot be seen as leading to some sort of universal adaptive optimization, but rather to relatively beneficial compromises required by group living. In order to obtain the benefits of sociality for self and descendants, an individual must behave in ways that at least do not eliminate some net benefit of sociality for others. Where social benefits are real and apparent, the result of cultural selection would likely be norms, rules, and cultural controls on excessively selfish individual behaviors in the interest of preserving group integrity.

That individual- and group-level cultural selection are unlikely to be successful in opposing one another in the long run does not mean that

I. Some Statements of Theory

group selection is without important consequences for understanding cultural evolution. As a number of authors have now argued, the *acceleration* of changes made possible by group-level extinction and replacement may be the key to understanding the rapid pace of *Homo sapiens* evolution (see discussion in Durham 1976a). Once a trait like P_m in the example above gets established by individual-level cultural selection within a social group, that trait may then give its bearers an advantage *as a group* in competition with other groups. Group selection may then result, reinforcing the spread of the cultural trait within the population. This form of group selection has the interesting property of conserving or even enhancing the original relative fitness value of the trait for the individual culture carriers.

A Coevolutionary Synthesis

In the preceding sections, I have proposed that processes of cultural selection operating within and between human social groups generally result in the selective retention of cultural traits, including behaviors, that past experience and some degree of prediction suggest to be most advantageous to the inclusive fitnesses of individual members. To the extent that this proposition is valid, cultural selection would remain functionally complementary to natural selection although there need be no genetic basis to the selected aspects of phenotype. Operationally, the process would also be independent of organic evolution rendering it thus more rapid, better able to track environmental change or stability, and at times even responsive to perceived human need. At the same time, cultural attributes which evolved in this way can have the interesting property of reducing or eliminating organic selection pressures. Similar phenotypic traits acquired by different genotypes may make the genotypes equally or almost equally "fit" (Durham 1976a). As Dobzhansky (1951) once put it, "The transmission of culture short-circuits biological heredity." On the other hand, cultural change has the opposite potential—that of creating new and different organic selection pressures (cf. Washburn 1959, 1960; Geertz 1973).

The combination of these features gives reason to believe that cultural selection may account for the origin and maintenance of more forms of human social behavior than do mutation and transgenerational changes in the frequency of presumed behavior genes. It will be seen that this theory of cultural evolution shifts the burden of proof for any explicitly *biological* basis for particular adaptive human behaviors over to the sociobiologists. Until we have direct and compelling evidence that a given human behavior has a discrete genetic basis, the demonstration that such behavior has adaptive functions does *not by any means* prove it to be the product of natural selection. Chances are good that it is partly, largely, or even *entirely* a product of cultural selection. Biologists interested in human adaptations would therefore do well to make explicit allowance for the cultural mechanism for the transmission of traits in a population.

While distinguishable on the basis of their means of transmission, biological and cultural inheritance by the arguments above would be functionally complementary. Indeed, the biological influences molded by natural selection and the cultural influences molded by cultural selection could easily be confounded in human phenotypes. Consequently, I suggest that models for the evolution of human social behaviors should explicitly integrate both the genetic and the cultural-inheritance mechanisms.

Simply stated, my hypothesis is that the selective retention in biological *and* cultural evolution generally favors those attributes which increase, or at least do not decrease, the ability of individual human beings to survive and reproduce in their natural and social environments. This perspective has the advantage of explaining both how human biology and culture can often be adaptive in the same sense (cf. Durham 1976a), and how they may interact in the evolution of human attributes. In addition, a coevolutionary view can explain the adaptive significance of human social behaviors without forcing them into natural selection models— indeed without forcing *any* separation of the confounded influences of genes and culture.

For the analysis of adaptive patterns in human social behavior I therefore suggest that "Selection" (capital S) be used to refer to the selective retention of differentially advantageous phenotypic traits by the fitness criterion regardless of whether the predominant process is a variety of cultural or of natural selection.

A coevolutionary perspective implies that for both biological and cultural reasons the interdependence of individual fitnesses among members of a social group can be viewed as the "social glue" that holds human (and non-human) groups together. It further suggests that the *kinds* of fitness interdependence among individuals (e.g., interdependence based on kinship, control of resources, or exchange of goods and services) and the *relative degree* of the interdependencies that exist can be used to define "social structure" in a population. Social structure from this point of view reflects the fact that not all individuals in a social group are interdependent in the same way or by the same amount. Indeed, structural asymmetries in dependence relations can give rise to a degree of manipu-

I. Some Statements of Theory

lative control by some over the behavior of others (Durham, ms.). In extreme cases, these structural constraints on the adaptations of individuals within society can result in behaviors which appear to require altruistic reproductive sacrifice. I should point out, however, that to those in control, manipulated behaviors may yield handsome survival and reproduction benefits. For those being manipulated, on the other hand, such behavior can actually be seen as another adaptive compromise required by powerful structural constraints. For this reason, social structure defined by fitness relations deserves to be considered an integral part of an individual's environment. Structural influences on the adaptations of individuals may have major effects upon the joint biocultural evolution of social behaviors within a group.

Human intergroup aggression constitutes a particularly suitable form of social behavior for testing the coevolutionary approach and many of the preceding arguments about biology, culture, and levels of selection. Not only is intergroup warfare commonly held to be dysfunctional for the individual participants, but it is also one of the more obvious mechanisms for high frequency group selection in human organic and cultural evolution. Coevolutionary theory suggests the following hypothesis:

Human social behaviors including intergroup aggression are generally adaptive (i.e., individual fitness enhancing) for all participants. Where there are exceptions so that net reproductive sacrifice is demanded of some or all participants, this is either because of some unusual degree of group selection or because of coercive manipulation within a social system.

From this, the need arises to analyze how human intergroup aggression is organized and conducted, paying special attention to the distribution of costs and benefits among the participants.

Elsewhere, I have begun an attempt at such an analysis by comparing aspects of intergroup warfare as waged by members of some "primitive" human societies with models for the coevolution of adaptive intergroup aggression in social groups faced with resource competition (Durham 1976b and ms.). The models suggest that "individually sacrificial participation in organized group aggression" may have non-obvious fitness benefits in two ways. First, where human groups compete for limited resources, participants in successful group aggression may themselves directly benefit from the fitness value of resources defended or acquired. The requirements for this to be adaptive are only that (1) the spoils must not be shared throughout the deme but must be shared within the group or subgroup of aggressors, so that (2) the fitness value of resources gained by each participant must exceed his or her accumulated costs. Second, intergroup aggression may have circuitous benefits so that when the participants do not each derive direct resource benefits from the conflict, their fitness costs are more than compensated by other benefits from within the group. For this to be adaptive, (1) at least one important figure in the group must secure resource benefits from the war, and (2) the benefactors must provide other goods and/or services upon which the other participants' fitnesses depend. What appears to be the self-sacrificing participation of warriors in this case may actually be an imperative for them to continue receiving other benefits from within the group.

These two models for group aggression suggest that knowledge of group structure (i.e., fitness interdependencies among individuals within the group), of factors or resources constraining the reproductive success of some or all individuals, and of fitness costs likely to be incurred when rival groups clash, allow the prediction or explanation of group-level human behavior. In both cases, this information gives direct means for predicting the characteristics of groups from the behavior of individuals.

The reinterpretation of ethnographic descriptions of primitive warfare in terms of these models reveals that at least some cases of human intergroup aggression can be seen as biocultural adaptations to conditions of competition for limiting resources. The evidence suggests that to an important extent, processes of both organic and cultural evolution result in the selective retention of phenotypic traits that enhance the ability of individual human beings to survive and reproduce in a given environment. This finding calls into question the continued practice of analyzing human social behaviors in terms of natural selection models alone, for such analyses consider only one aspect of what may be truly coevolutionary influences on human social behavior.

Summary and Conclusion

Because the capacity for culture allows human beings to modify aspects of phenotype without any concomitant genotypic change, I have argued that it makes no sense to view the evolution of human attributes, including social behavior, solely in terms of the natural selection models of sociobiology. Instead, I have suggested that a process of "cultural selection" functionally complements natural selection by retaining over time those cultural variants whose net effect best enhances the inclusive fitnesses of individuals. Where cultural selection operates in this way, human phenotypes would then evolve *subject to both biological and cultural influences* in the direction of character states that maximize inclusive fitness under prevailing environmental conditions (for additional discussion, see Durham 1976a, 1976b).

As I have argued, this coevolutionary perspective has the advantage of explaining both how human biology and culture are often adaptive in the same sense, and how they may interact in the evolution of human attributes. This theory, moreover, contains an important irony. *If* cultural differences between human societies are largely the result of individual-level cultural selection for more-versus-less adaptive traits (possibly reinforced by a process of group selection) as proposed, then our capacity for culture has meant a capacity to reduce or even eliminate many of the organic selection pressures that would have favored the refinements of genetic control required by theories which rely solely on the mechanism of natural selection. Put differently, the operation of cultural selection—what some would call only a "proximate" mechanism—may at times replace and preclude the operation of natural selection, which is scarcely then the "ultimate" mechanism. In short, this theory can explain the biocultural evolution of human attributes without presuming a genetic basis or predisposition for any specific adaptive form. To the extent that humans do behave in ways that maximize their individual inclusive fitnesses, this would suggest that it is generally for both cultural and biological reasons.

This coevolutionary view of human biology and culture may be of help to human ecologists and cultural ecologists who have studied human adaptation but have often failed to identify exactly who benefits from a given practice and how in fact they do benefit. It suggests, for example, a renewed emphasis on individuals and their problems of survival and reproduction in society. This may lead to new interpretations of ethnographic studies which have commonly focused on group-level behaviors. It also suggests new directions for future research. Measures of reproductive success may prove useful both as analytic tools for understanding specific social behaviors and as modeling devices for formulating new research questions. This kind of approach should be most helpful when the "costs" of a given practice can be factored out in terms of time, energy, and resources and where it is possible to detect associated differentials in reproductive benefit. Thus I suggest that coevolutionary analysis is most appropriate in studies of medical anthropology, nutrition and food taboos, human intergroup aggression, population regulation and demography, migration, trade and exchange, and other "high cost" practices. I believe that the theory is also adequate for predicting its own limitations. Considering the abundance of day-to-day cultural practices which involve little time, energy, or resource cost, I re-emphasize that this argument does not say that everything we do is best explained in terms of reproductive success.

The approach suggested here bears some resemblance to recent works by Ruyle (1973), Cloak (1975), Campbell (1975), Richerson and Boyd (1978), and Dawkins (1976: chapter 11). These authors hypothesize, as I do, that the mechanism of cultural evolution can operate independently of the mechanism of natural selection. But they go further than I go to suggest that the differential replication of cultural attributes is independent of the individual fitness criterion as well. Dawkins, for example, proposes the term "meme" to refer to the basic conceptual unit of cultural transmission and he argues in a fashion similar to the other authors that competition among memes results in a selection process (analogous to natural selection) favoring "memes which exploit their cultural environment to *their own advantage*" (p. 213, emphasis added). Like Dawkins, I believe that it is important to ask what gives memes stability and penetrance in their cultural environment, but unlike Dawkins and the others, I argue that the fate of a meme in its pool usually depends upon the meme's fitness costs and benefits to *carriers*. A coevolutionary perspective does not postulate the gradual and cumulative organic evolution of an organ (the brain) that meanwhile often functions antagonistically to natural selection. It seems to me that these other perspectives do.

In conclusion, without prolonging once again the debate of biology versus culture, nature versus nurture, and instinct versus learning, I believe real gains in understanding human social behavior can now be made in several ways. First, we must concentrate our efforts on theories which integrate human biology and culture in the study of human adaptation (see also Durham 1976b; Wilson, this volume). Again, I suggest that "Selection" (capital S) be used to refer to the selective retention of differentially advantageous phenotypic traits by the fitness criterion regardless of whether the predominant process is a variety of cultural or natural selection. Second, we need to examine the specific processes of selective retention in operation so that more is learned about the mechanisms of cultural selection within and between groups. This endeavor has the interesting prospect of adding a *historical* dimension to theories of adaptation, allowing practices observed in the "ethnographic present" to be studied in light of their specific paths of coevolution.

Third, we need to develop theories of transition between organizational levels, so that knowledge of behavior on one level can be used to predict behavior on another level. Paradoxically, in all of this, there is a new danger of overemphasizing individuals as independent entities. Gains will be made when individual-level theorists remember that the adaptations of individuals are not independent nor are they dependent solely because of shared genes. The effort to understand the characteristics of groups and social systems beginning with a focus on individuals will need a better theory of "interest group" activities, where interest groups are defined by any form of fitness interdependence including control of access to strategic resources. Related to this is a need for incorporating social structure into coevolutionary models for human social behavior.

Finally, in addition to any understanding of the present gained from a coevolutionary view of the past, the insights from these endeavors should prove useful as tools for contemporary social change.

3. Evolution and Culture[1]

Richard D. Alexander

The basic argument developed by Darwin, and destined to become the central principle upon which all of biology rests, was two-part in nature. The first part was that all of life is continually and relentlessly subjected to a process of differential reproduction of variants, which Darwin termed natural selection or "survival of the fittest." The second was that all of the attributes of life are owing, directly or indirectly, to the cumulative effects of this process. No significant doubt has ever been cast on the first part of this argument, and the only alternatives to the second, advocated since 1859, have been divine creation and culture.

[1] I thank Laura Betzig for allowing me to read an essay of hers which prompted me to begin immediately to develop and write down some of the ideas in this paper.

Debates over the Scope of Selection

Concerning divinity

The effects of accepting both parts of Darwin's argument are that (1) the traits of modern organisms are, in terms of the environments of history at least, assumed to be means of maximizing genetic reproduction and (2) the patterns of long-term change observable from paleontological data are assumed also to be owing to natural selection. Creationists believe that unfilled gaps in the paleontological record imply creation, hence did not involve change by natural selection; and most thoughtful people would agree that some extensive changes during human history, evidenced in the archaeological record, are likely to have been unaccompanied by genetic change, hence also did not involve change by natural selection.

A degree of importance for natural selection has been granted by both creationists and the most radical adherents to the idea that culture and biology have been independent throughout human history. Thus, the organized supporters of creation as an alternative to evolution, such as members of the Creation Research Society (see the *Creation Research Society Quarterly*), have found it necessary to accept the process of natural selection, which they refer to as "microevolution" (e.g., Moore and Slusher 1970). They have established their line of defense chiefly against "macroevolution," which is their name for natural processes, supposed by others to account for the formation of "major organs" and for the origin of large changes or differences among organisms, such as exist between species or "major groups." The creationists argue that because the formation of major groups or major organs cannot be observed directly or studied by experiment, its analysis is outside science; and they argue that this process is best explained as creation. Understandably, they have remained indefinite about the precise nature of major groups and major organs, or the levels at which divine creation is unavoidable.

Many lines of evidence indicate that creationists are wrong in their efforts to distinguish long-term and short-term changes in evolution. Darwin offered a devastating critique of this view, and anticipated the small, cumulative effects of gene mutations as well, when he noted that major organs are the products of large numbers of small changes of the observable kind attributed by creationists to "microevolution." This fact is easily demonstrated by crossing organisms with variant forms of a given major organ or attribute. Darwin went so far as to offer the challenge that "If it could be demonstrated that any complex organ existed, which

I. Some Statements of Theory

could not possibly have been formed by numerous, successive, slight modifications, my theory would absolutely break down" (1967[1859]:189). A related class of evidence derives from laboratory or forced hybridization of different species or genera, a procedure which clearly shows that differences between such forms are also accumulations of small mutational changes of the directly observable kind (see also Alexander, 1978b).

Concerning humanity

Creationists thus deny that the second part of Darwin's thesis applies to humans by denying that the *earliest* of human attributes—i.e., those actually responsible for the designation "human"—originated through natural selection. Students of culture, on the other hand, tend to deny that the most *recent* of human attributes can be understood by reference to natural selection—i.e., the details of cultural patterns and differences—because they feel that the advent of traditionally transmitted learning signaled the end of any necessary relationship between behavior and the differential reproduction of alternative genetic elements.

Some recent authors have developed arguments, often explicitly about human behavior and culture, as alternative to natural selection in ways that may seem to cast doubt upon even the first part of Darwin's argument. Three such arguments seem most prominent.

Is Selection Tautological?   The first argument is that the basic thesis of natural selection is tautological. Supporters of this view (e.g., Peters 1976) contend that we are unable to identify the "fittest" organisms or traits except retrospectively, and that, accordingly, we can only identify them as those which *have survived*. This argument ignores an enormous body of evidence confirming its falsity. Biologists, as well as plant and animal breeders, are continually able to identify as unfit individual organisms whose phenotypic attributes reveal ahead of time that their chances of reproducing are either nonexistent or relatively small (see also Ferguson 1976; Stebbins 1977). Success in such predictions is possible, as with the maintenance of adaptation, only to the extent that environments are predictable. But all environments of life have some predictable aspects. We can prove this directly, and the countless fashions in which organisms are marvelously and intricately tuned to their environments show that we are correct in assuming that the empirical evidence of environmental consistency is relevant to the process of evolution. Modern evolutionary biology depends upon an ability to generalize about adaptiveness, both across genetic lines and across generations, and remarkable success is being re-alized from such generalizations, especially with attributes common to most or all organisms, like sex ratios, senescence, and parental investment, and others for which the social environment is crucial, like group-living, nepo-tism, and sexual competition (see references in Alexander 1977a, 1977b, and Alexander et al., this volume, chapter 15). In the first case more effective comparisons are possible; in the second, the winning strategies are more stable and more easily identifiable.

Criticisms that statements about natural selection are tautological only concern their predictive value, but some detractors have supposed that they also cast into doubt the existence or universality of the entire process. Even retrospective judgments, however, are entirely sufficient to demon-strate the inevitability of differential reproduction, whether or not humans are aware of its workings or capable of assessing its consequences.

The argument that natural selection is tautological is often linked with statements by prominent evolutionists, such as Mayr (1963) or Simp-son (1964), that evolution is not a particularly predictive or predictable phenomenon, to suggest that evolution does not even qualify as a scientific theory. The misapprehension involved is failure to see that Simpson and Mayr were talking about our inability to predict or give the adaptive reasons for ancient or long-term phylogenetic changes because we are necessarily ignorant of the environments of selection during geological time. We are not so ignorant of the current and recent environments of selection, and our understanding of them grows constantly.

Organic evolution leads to patterns of change in morphology, physiology, and styles of life. Some of these patterns are reflected by fossil remains and some by the array of organisms present at any given time. Evolution also involves speciation, which results in irreversible divergences of different patterns of life. Pattern changes and speciation together lead to phylogenies or family trees that presumably, if the record were complete, could be reconstructed to illustrate the whole history of life. But phylo-genetic patterns, although they are outcomes of evolution, are not the essence of the process. The essence of the process is differential reproduction, or, as Williams (1966) put it, the maintenance of adaptation. Phylogenies are reconstructed with little understanding of the selective forces that produced their patterns because the environments of long-term history cannot be reconstructed with the precision necessary to reconstruct the generation-by-generation effects of natural selection. Efforts to "predict" phylogenies, or the nature of species (i.e., to presage what will be dis-covered about either the past or the future when more complete information is available) fail to the extent that we are ignorant about environments and the array of living organisms present at each time and place in history. They do not fail, as Peters (1976) suggested, because of the demonstrable independence between the causes of mutations and the causes of selection. Our inability to make long-term evolutionary predictions thus does not mean that the nature of the process yielding evolutionary patterns is itself to be doubted, or that evolutionary propositions are so tautological as to fail as scientific theory. Predictions about adaptiveness are most accurate when they concern short-term changes in the present, and there is every reason to believe that they fail increasingly with longer time spans, or when other eras are considered, simply because our information about environments is more incomplete in such cases.

Arguments about the relationship of long-term pattern changes during evolution to the process of natural selection, which is widely accepted as responsible for short-term changes, have relevance here because of the common failure to realize that long-term pattern-tracing (paleontology, archaeology) can be carried on without direct attention to or concern for the process responsible. In biologists' terms, the process of change is guided largely by natural selection. For anthropologists, it is probably fair to say that there is no universally accepted *guiding force* to account for the changes commonly called cultural evolution or for modern variations in culture. The question we must ultimately address is: what is the nature of this guiding force and to what extent has it been the differential reproduction of genes, realized through reproductive striving of individuals? In this question there is no implication that reproductive striving is consciously so directed.

Is Selection Often Impotent Because of Lack of Genetic Variation? The second argument seeming to cast doubt on the universality of natural selection is that genetic variations relevant to selective forces are not always present, rendering selection ineffective. But this argument only specifies rare and temporary situations. As any plant or animal breeder knows, even in genetic lines on which directional selection has been practiced for a very long time, genetic variants and combinations now and then appear which are relevant to a desired direction of change. Because of their unpredictability, the only way to take advantage of such variants is to maintain selection. This realization causes humans to practice artificial selection in a way that parallels the differential reproduction of organisms induced by natural environments, which is also inexorable whether or not the variations involved are heritable (and also ineffective when they are not).

For this reason we may assume that in natural populations most novel variants which increase reproduction spread and become characteristic of the population, and that this is the usual process of evolutionary change.

The reasons why natural selection is regarded as the guiding force of evolution are not commonly discussed, but they are obviously crucial (see Alexander 1977a, for a fuller discussion). The most apparent ones are the following: (1) altering directions of selection alters directions of change in organisms (probably always, even if there is sometimes delay owing to specialization as a result of previous selection), (2) the causes of mutation (chiefly radiation) and the causes of selection (Darwin's "hostile forces" of food shortages, climate, weather, predators, parasites, and diseases) are independent, (3) only the causes of selection remain consistently directional for relatively long periods (thus, could explain directional changes), and (4) predictions based on the assumption that adaptiveness depends solely on selection are met (e.g., consider the history of sex-ratio selection: Fisher 1958[1930]; Hamilton 1967; Trivers and Willard 1973; Trivers and Hare 1976; Alexander and Sherman 1977; Alexander et al., Chagnon et al., this volume).

The greatest constraints on selection occur then, paradoxically, in two opposite situations: when the change of selective direction is very great and when unidirectionality persists for a very long time. In the first case, specializations as a result of previous selection reduce the likelihood of adaptive changes in certain directions; thus, moles are almost certainly less likely than squirrels to evolve wings. In the second case, alleles causing change in the favored direction are apt to be fixed by selection faster than mutants arise; thus, after generations of selection for increased milk production, dairy farmers know that "management" (i.e., environment) is crucial but, obviously, they will continue to favor breeding stock from their best producers in the expectation that once in a while the differences will be heritable. Unlike many aspects of phenotypes, cultural variations of humans, which lack correlation with genetic variations, may nevertheless be heritable because of traditional transmission of learned behaviors. Thus, as is well understood, culture has the unusual property of being able to evolve cumulatively in the absence of genetic change. Rates of cultural change within historical times are clear evidence that massive cultural change does indeed occur without genetic change, or in its virtual absence. However, for cultural change to be independent of natural selection, the following hypotheses would also have to be true: (1) because directions and rates of cultural change are potentially independent of many or most human genetic changes, they are independent of the history of natural selection upon humans; and (2) genetic change through natural selection is not induced by cultural changes. Until very recently, both of these hypotheses have remained largely untested; should they eventually be rejected, as I believe likely, then even for human culture the second part of Darwin's argument will stand as stated above.

Does Evolutionary Theory Suggest Genetic Determinism? The third argument about the relationship of biology and culture is exemplified by the newspaper announcement of the British Broadcasting Corporation film "The Human Animal," which identified sociobiology as "The field of study built on the theory that behavioral patterns in humans are inherited through genes." This definition is, perhaps innocently, a version of the argument that efforts to invoke biological explanations of human behavior are efforts to defend the notion that behavior is "genetically determined." It cannot be denied that some statements by biologists also suggest this kind of naïveté. But there is equal naïveté in supposing that merely to consider genes as influences upon behavior (or any other aspects of phenotypes) means that one is automatically excluding the environment or underplaying its role. To argue that behavior is a product of a history of natural selection, however, is in no way an argument that behavior is determined by the genes. It is almost the opposite—a declaration instead that the behavior of each organism is determined, not by the genes, but by the genes and the developmental and experiential environment together. That the mere introduction of genes as influences on behavior is construed as an unsupportable kind of genetic determinism is indicated by the tendency to contrast explanations which include genes with explanations invoking learning. For so many years we asked: "Is this behavior learned or genetic?" Finally, we are coming to realize that the answer is always "Both." The consequence of this realization is not the exclusion of biology from considerations about human behavior but its appropriate reintroduction into them. (For fuller discussions see Alexander 1978a, 1977b, 1977c.)

Traits, Learning, and Genetic Variation To explain this paradox it is fruitful to consider still another question recently made prominent by self-professed critics of evolutionary approaches to the analysis of human behavior. What is a "trait"? This question seemingly has two aspects. First is the problem of how much or what part of the phenotype can be viewed as a unit in terms of function. In other words, upon what parts and amounts of the phenotype is selection acting in a given circumstance or environment? How much of the phenotype does a given kind or aspect of selection affect?

The second part of the question involves how the genes work together during ontogeny to create the phenotype—in other words, how do the genes in the genotype relate to the identifiable components of the phenotype? A history of natural selection suggests that in some sense these two problems resolve into a single one: How do the units within genotypes (genes, supergenes, chromosomes, etc.) interact (through epistasis, pleiotrophy, linkage, etc.) to produce the functional units (appendages, sensory devices, reproductive organs, etc.) of the phenotype?

This question relates to the genes/learning dichotomy because of a common confusion between (1) whether or not a particular behavioral variant characterizes a particular genotypic variant and (2) whether or not a particular *set* of behaviors characterizes a particular genotypic variant. If a particular behavioral act was learned, then its individual presence as a variant is clearly not a result of genetic variation. But genes are necessarily causal (together with their environment) in the production of all behavior; the only problem is to understand how. To reach this understanding we must consider entire sets of learned behaviors in the set of different individuals possessing the same set of genes influencing that behavior in the collection of environments in which the set of individuals developed. Ideally, such entire sets of learned behaviors would be compared with other sets of learned behaviors in other sets of organisms which do differ genetically. In a species with a great deal of immediate-contingency learning in the behavioral repertoires of individuals, then, the effects of genes on learned behavior can only be understood by analyzing the behaviors expressed by *numerous* individuals who *collectively* have experienced the array of environments in which the behavior in question has evolved, or the environments in which it has usually been expressed. Traits can only be identified by examining the variations in learned activities in the normal range of environments of learning. Genetic change could shift the ease of learning in such a group of organisms one way or another along one or more axes, or reduce or abolish certain possibilities. The adaptive or evolved aspect of learning traits so identified will be the nature or range of expression correlated with the usual environments of history, with nonadaptive, maladaptive, or evolutionarily incidental aspects represented by those appearing in novel or rare environments. Obviously, such "incidental" or non-evolved aspects of learning are crucial in understanding human behavior because of the extraordinarily rapid changes induced by culture and technology. What would be left is a set of learning abilities, the range and relative ease of which have been tuned by natural selection acting on the genetic makeup of the population. It is difficult for me to conceive of *any other relationship* between learned behaviors and the process of natural selection.

Indeed, what I have just described is the general relationship between natural selection and all kinds of expressions of the phenotype, whether behavioral, physiological, or morphological. This is the reason why—even though learning, or variation resulting from environmental variation, is an explanation for observed behavioral variations which is alternative to an explanation based on genetic variation—cultural evolution is not an *alternative* to natural selection as a general explanation for the nature of human activities. Cultural patterns are, like all expressions of the phenotype, outcomes of different developmental environments acting on sets of genetic materials accumulated and maintained by natural selection. Culture differs from other aspects of phenotypes in the degree to which it can change without genetic change; but behavior in general differs from morphology and physiology in the same regard. This is the raison d'être of behavior. It is a way of responding to a greater proportion of the information available to the organism from immediate contingencies in its environments. Culture is a particular and elaborate system of behavior for doing the same. The questions we are led to ask about culture, after considering it in a biological context, are the same that would be asked from any other analytical approach: What forces influence its patterns? What do its expressions mean? The only distinctive aspect of a biological approach is that we are apt to ask these questions in relation to biological functions, or reproduction. This attitude may seem alien to social scientists, but the correct answers to questions about the significance of culture will be the same regardless of the manner in which they are approached.

Concerning culture: natural selection and culture theory

Probably because anthropologists and others tended to identify the possession of culture and the capacity for culture as peculiarly human traits, the concept of culture has acquired and retained a certain singularity: hence, perhaps, efforts to seek general or singular theories of culture; and perhaps also the assertion by investigators reluctant to see culture in this way that "Culture is dead"—that is, that it does not possess the singularity attributed to it and that truly general theories of culture are therefore unlikely. Others, still convinced about the generality of the concept of culture, have come to the notion that, in the absence of acceptable functional explanations, culture can only be explained in terms of itself, or as a set of arbitrarily assigned meanings or symbolizations (White 1949; Sahlins 1976b), and specifically cannot be explained in terms of utilitarianism of any sort or at any level. White, for example, writes skeptically of man's "vaunted control of civilization" and of the fond belief that it "lies within man's power . . . to chart his course as he pleases, to mold civilization to his desires and needs."

Culture, such authors seem to be arguing, is something greater than humans collectively and almost independent of humans individually: It continues on courses perhaps unpredictable, and certainly swayed but slightly by the wishes of individuals, who are merely its "passive" transmitters. Sahlins comes very close to describing culture as an aspect of the environment of humans about which they can do little but accept it in just those terms, thereby almost paralleling the biologists' concept of the genotype and the phenotype as parts of the environment of selection of the individual genes.

But, if human evolution, like that of other organisms, has significantly involved selection effective at genic levels, realized through the reproductive strivings of individuals, neither humans as individuals nor the human species as a whole have had "a" course to chart in the development of culture but rather a very large number of slightly different and potentially conflicting courses. In such event it would indeed be difficult to locate "a function for," or even "the functions of," culture; instead, culture would chiefly be, as Sahlins' view may be slightly modified to mean, the central aspect of the environment into which every person is born and must succeed or fail, developed gradually by the collections of humans that have preceded us in history, and with an inertia refractory to the wishes of individuals, and even of small and large groups. Culture would represent the cumulative effects of inclusive-fitness-maximizing behavior (i.e., reproductive maximization via all socially available descendant and non-descendant relatives) of the entire collective of all humans who have lived. I here advance this as a theory to explain the existence and nature of culture, and the rates and directions of its change.

If this theory is appropriate, then aspects of culture would be expected to be adversary to some of the wishes of each of us; few aspects of it would be viewed with equal good humor by all of us; and in just this circumstance we would not expect grand utilitarian views of culture, general theories of culture, or efforts at purposeful guidance of culture to succeed easily. These are exactly the kinds of failures that have always plagued culture theorists. Yet, by this theory, the inertia of culture would exist *because* individuals and groups did influence its directions and shape, molding it—even if imperceptibly across short time periods—to suit

I. Some Statements of Theory

their needs, thereby incidentally increasing the likelihood that subsequent individuals and groups (a) could find ways to use it to their own advantages as well and (b) could not alter it so greatly or rapidly.

It would also be a source of confusion, in attempts to relate directions and rates of cultural change to utilitarian theories, that the reproductive efforts of individuals would not actually be directed at *changing* culture, as such; nor would such efforts lead to any particular directions of change in culture as a whole. The striving of individuals would be to *use* culture, not necessarily by changing it, to further their own reproduction. No necessary correlation would exist between success in the reproductive striving of an individual and the magnitude of the individual's effect on cultural change, or between the collective success of the individuals making up a group or society and the rate of cultural change. It would not matter if one were a legislator *making* laws, a judge *interpreting* them, a policeman *enforcing* them, a lawyer *using* them, a citizen *obeying* them, or a criminal *circumventing* them: Each of these behaviors can be seen as a particular strategy within societies governed by law, and each has some possibility of success.

Again, it would tend to be contrary to the interests of the members of society that cultural changes of any magnitude could easily be effected by any individuals except for inventions seen as having a high likelihood of benefiting nearly everyone. The reasons are that (1) changes, effected by individuals or subgroups in their own interests, would likely be contrary to the interests of others; and (2) once individuals have adopted and initiated a particular set of responses to the existing culture around their own interests, changes of almost any sort have some likelihood of being deleterious to them. These arguments not only suggest how anthropological interpretations of culture may be entirely compatible with the notion of reproductive striving principally effective at the individual (or genic) level, but also may explain the genesis of views that culture is somehow independent of individuals and groups and their wishes, and not easily explainable in utilitarian terms.

The Evolution of Culture

It is a fundamental characteristic of culture that, despite its essentially conservative nature, it does change over time and from place to place. Herein it differs strikingly from the social behavior of animals other than man. Among ants, for example, colonies of the same species differ little in behavior from one another and even, so far as we can judge from specimens imbedded in amber, from their ancestors of fifty million years ago. In less than one million years man, by contrast, has advanced from the rawest savagery to civilization and has proliferated at least three thousand distinctive cultures [George Peter Murdock, 1960b:247].

If long-term changes in human phenomena, as evidenced for example in the archaeological record, are cultural, and were not induced by natural selection or accompanied by genetic changes relating to cultural behavior, then we should be interested in answering two questions: First, what has guided cultural evolution? What forces can account for its rates and directions of change? Second, what degrees and kinds of correspondence exist today between the patterns of culture and the maximization of genetic reproduction of the individuals using, transmitting, and modifying culture? Are the degrees and kinds of correspondence, and of failure to correspond, consistent with the forces presumed to underlie rates and directions of cultural change?

At one end of a spectrum lies the possibility that all of the cultural changes during human history have been utterly independent of genetic change, neither causing such nor caused by it. At the other end is the possibility that changes in human behavior have correlated with genetic change to approximately the same degree as changes in the behavior of other species, such as non-human primates. Observations within recorded history are sufficient to show that neither of these extreme possibilities is likely. As examples, cultural changes, such as eyeglasses and treatments for diabetes, obviously influence genetic change; and cultural changes clearly have accelerated tremendously in recent decades without any evidence of parallel acceleration in genetic change. At least, then, cultural changes do influence genetic change although there is apparently no clear evidence that genetic changes are causing cultural changes, or that there is any close correlation between cultural changes and genetic changes that specifically influence behavior in relation to culture. Now, it is easy to understand, on theoretical grounds, how culture can change cumulatively without accompanying genetic changes that relate to the behaviors involved—and easy to argue that numerous such changes have occurred within recorded history when strikingly different cultures merged. Therefore the significance of the

I. Some Statements of Theory

above two questions about the forces which change culture and the relationships of culture to maximization of reproduction by individuals is brought into an even sharper focus. We expect that the answers to these two questions will be complementary, and that the efforts to answer them should be conducted simultaneously and jointly.

Some changes in culture, such as those influenced by climatic shifts, natural disasters, and diseases, predators, and parasites (of humans and the plants and animals on which they depend), are beyond human control; others are explicitly under such control, although such control may be very direct (invention and conscious planning) or not so direct (resource depletion and pollution). The difficult question, in understanding the relationship between culture and our inevitable history of natural selection, is not in discovering the reasons behind cultural changes, as such, which are actually fairly obvious. Instead, it is in understanding exactly *how* such changes influence culture: What is done with them? What *direction* of change do they induce, and why? Those changes in culture which are consequences of human action appear to represent products of the striving of individuals and groups of individuals. Such changes, as with extrinsically caused changes, are also *responded to by changes* in the striving of individuals and groups of individuals. Inventions are seized upon. Pollution and resource depletion are lamented, and cause geographic shifts in population or efforts at inventions or practices which will either offset their effects on the lives of those showing the effort or allow them to take advantage of such effects. Attempts are made to predict and offset natural disasters and climatic shifts. All of these responses are easily interpretable as part of efforts by individuals, acting alone or in groups, to use culture to their own advantage in the fashion already suggested. But culture is not easily explainable as the outcome of striving to better the future for *everyone equally:* If that were the case, then surely conscious planning would quickly become the principal basis for cultural change, and it would be carried out with a minimum of disagreement and bickering (perhaps we shall actually be able to make our interests coincide to a greater degree by realizing that we have a background of competition in genetic reproduction, which may be less interesting to us once exposed to our conscious reflection).

It is possible to examine the problem of cultural change in a fashion parallel to that used for evolutionary change (e.g., Alexander 1977a). We can ask about the same five phenomena which characterize the process of genetic change (the most closely parallel argument is probably that of Murdock [1960b]).

1 *Inheritance:* Just as the morphological, physiological, and behavioral traits of organisms are heritable, given consistency in the developmental environment, the traits of culture are heritable through learning. They may be imitated, plagiarized, or taught.

2 *Mutation:* Like the genetic materials, culture is mutable, through mistakes, discoveries, inventions, or deliberate planning (Murdock's "variations," "inventions," and "tentations").

3 *Selection:* As with the phenotypic traits of organisms, some traits of culture reinforce their own persistence and spread; others do not, and eventually disappear for that reason (Murdock's "social acceptance," "selective elimination," and "integration"). (See also Campbell 1965, 1975.)

4 *Drift:* As with genetic units, traits of culture can also be lost by accident or "sampling error."

5 *Isolation:* As with populations of other kinds of organisms, different human societies become separated by extrinsic and intrinsic barriers; they diverge, and they may come into contact and remerge or continue to drift apart; items and aspects of culture may spread by diffusion (Murdock's "cultural diffusion" and "cultural borrowing").

Immediately, differences are apparent between the processes of change during genetic and cultural evolution. Unlike genetic evolution, the causes of mutation and selection in cultural evolution are not independent: Instead, there is a feedback between need and novelty. Most of the sources of cultural "mutation" are at least potentially related to the reasons for their survival or failure.

Some culture theorists have tended to deny utilitarian connections between the sources or causes of cultural change and the reasons for their survival or failure. I suggest that the reason for these denials is that such theorists have never sought function both in terms of reproduction and at the individual level, as biologists now realize must be the case in organic evolution. Some, such as Franz Boas and Ruth Benedict, have emphasized the individual; others, such as Bronislaw Malinowski and A. R. Radcliffe-Brown, have emphasized function as survival value—even, sometimes, to the individual. None, however, has seen function as reproductive value. Instead, most functionalists have either sought group-level utilitarian effects or have regarded survival, not reproduction, of the individual as crucial (for reviews of such views, see Hatch 1973; Harris 1968).

Some recent investigators, such as Cloak (1976), Dawkins (1976),

I. Some Statements of Theory

Durham (1976a), and Richerson and Boyd (1978), have concentrated on heritability of cultural traits (or cultural novelties or "instructions") and argued that their separate mode of inheritance thwarts the operation of natural selection of genetic alternatives. I regard this approach to the history of culture as similar to a view of the natural history of organisms that sees phenotypes in general (as opposed to no phenotypes) as essentially thwarters of natural selection. In one sense they are, since they necessarily render the action of selection on the genes less direct: Selection must now act through the phenotype. But this change had to have occurred because those genes that reproduced via phenotypes outsurvived their alternatives in the environments of history. So must it be with the capacity for culture, as the above authors for the most part acknowledge. Even if culture out-races organic evolution, creating blinding confusion through environmental novelties, to view the significance of its changes and its traits as independent of, or as mere thwarters of, natural selection of genetic alternatives, would be parallel to supposing that the function of an appetite is obesity.

The important question in cultural evolution is: Who or what decides which novelties will be perpetuated, and how is this decided? On what basis are cultural changes spread or lost? In other words, we are led to analyze exactly the same part of the process of cultural change as for genetic change. In cultural change the answer to this question of who decides, and how, actually determines the heritability of culture, since heritability of cultural items at least theoretically can vary from zero to 100 percent from one generation to the next, or even within generations. Any cultural trait, unlike a gene, theoretically can be suddenly cancelled and just as suddenly reinstated, in the population as a whole. Again, in theory at least, this can be done as a result of conscious decision based on what the involved parties see as their own best interests at the time. This reinforcing relationship among selection, heritability, and mutation in culture means that, unlike organic evolution, heritability of culture traits will not be steadily increased; nor will mutability be depressed because the majority of mutations are deleterious in the individuals in which they arise owing to the lack of feedback between mutational directions and adaptive value. Some cultural mutations appear (that is, are implemented, or translated from thought to action) because they are perceived to have value. Unlike evolutionary change, then, cultural change will acquire inertia to the extent that the interests of individuals and subgroups *conflict* (and have a history of conflicting), and whenever the distribution of power is such as to result in stalemates. In part this means that cultural change may be expected to continue accelerating, and this acceleration, I believe, will not only make it increasingly difficult to interpret human behavior in terms of history, but will also increasingly become apparent as the source of novel ethical problems, bound to increase in numbers and severity as cultural change accelerates, because ethical problems derive from conflicts of interest and these are bound to become more complex (Alexander, in press a).

Most recent and current efforts to relate genetic change and cultural change, then, seem really to be efforts to divorce them—to explain why and how culture and genes came "uncoupled" during human history. These arguments generally assume that the uncoupling is essentially synonymous with the appearance of culture—that culture is, by definition, an uncoupling of human behavior from gene effects.

I think these are the reasons why virtually all efforts to understand culture in biological terms have failed. We can easily assume that the capacity for culture *allowed* (as an incidental effect) various degrees of uncoupling of human behavior from reproductive maximization. In modern urban society, for example, such uncoupling is rampant. But to assume that uncoupling is the (historical, biological, evolutionary) function of culture, or its basic significance or attribute, is, as already suggested, like assuming that the function of an appetite is obesity.

There is enough evidence, even in everyday life, to indicate that in general human social behavior is remarkably closely correlated to survival, well-being, and reproductive success. If one accepts this assumption then it is easy to agree that the real question is: What forces could cause the continued coupling between culture and genes? In effect, we must discover, for cultural as well as genetic evolution, the nature of the "hostile forces" (paralleling Darwin's "Hostile Forces" or predators, parasites, diseases, food shortages, climate, and weather [see Alexander 1977a] responsible for natural selection's effects on gene frequencies) by which variations in human social behavior and capacity are selected, by the adjustment of strategies or styles of life, consciously and otherwise, by individuals and groups.

Few people would doubt that positive and negative reinforcement (learning) schedules relate, respectively, to environmental phenomena reinforcing (1) survival and well-being and (2) avoidance of situations deleterious to survival and well-being. With ordinary physical and biotic stimuli this relationship is easy to understand: We withdraw from hot stoves, avoid poisonous snakes, seek out tasty foods, appreciate warmth in winter, dislike getting wet in cold rains, etc.

What about social stimuli? Should it not be the same? Should we

I. Some Statements of Theory

not seek social situations that reward us and avoid those that punish us? Should not the actual definitions of reward and punishment in social behavior, as with responses to physical stimuli, identify for any organism those situations that, respectively, improve or insult its likelihood of social survival and well-being, with appropriate connotations for reproductive success? Is it possible that Sheldon (1961) was right in suggesting that ". . . the reason why many pleasures are wicked is that they frustrate other pleasures"? That evil consists ". . . in frustrations, as the Thomist says, in privation of one good by another"? Is what is pleasurable, hence, "good" and "right," that which, at least in environments past, tended to maximize genetic reproduction?

Arbitrariness in culture

The symbolic or seemingly arbitrary nature of many aspects and variants of culture is commonly regarded as contrary to any functional theory, and especially to the notion that culture can somehow be explained by a history of differential reproduction by individuals. Of course, *seeming* arbitrariness may represent observer error based on failure to understand the significance of environmental variations. Arbitrariness may also be a consequence of the inertia to cultural change in the face of environmental shifts; of mistakes about what kind of behavior will best serve one's interests—especially in the face of the constant and accelerating introduction of novelty, primarily through technology. But, even if the assessment of arbitrariness is actually correct, it need not be contrary to a theory based on inclusive-fitness-maximizing, particularly if culture is explained as a product of the different, as well as the common, goals of the individuals and subgroups of individuals who have comprised human society during its history. Thus, however symbolism and language arose—say, because they were superior methods of communication—their existence, as the major sources of arbitrariness, also allowed the adjustment of messages away from reality in the interests of the transmitting individual or group. In other words, as abilities and tendencies to employ arbitrary or symbolic meanings increased the complexity and detail of messages, and the possibility of accurate transmission under difficult circumstances (e.g., more information per unit of time or information about objects or events removed in time or space), they also increased opportunities for deception and misinformation. It would be a consequence that arbitrariness could typify some of the different directions taken by cultural changes which were nevertheless crucial to their initiators and perpetuators.

Consider the relationship between status and the appreciation of fashion, art, literature, or music. What is important to the would-be critic or status-seeker is not alliance with a particular form but with whatever form will ultimately be regarded as most prestigious. If one is in a position to influence the decision he can, to one degree or another, cause it to become arbitrary. Fashion designers, the great artists, and the wealthy are continually using their status to cause such adjustments. In no way, however, does such arbitrariness mean that the outcomes are trivial or unrelated to reproductive striving. Precisely the opposite is suggested— that arbitrariness may often be forced, in regard to important circumstances, because the different circumstances involved represent important alternatives and because forcing arbitrariness is the only or best way for certain parties to prevail.

These various suggestions may simultaneously explain the genesis of "great man" theories of culture and their failure as general explanations. Great men do appear, and their striving, almost by definition, is likely now and then to have special influences; but, for reasons given above, not necessarily great influences and not influences leading to particular, predictable, overall changes in culture.

The old saw that "one hen-pecked husband in a village does not create a matriarchy" also emphasizes not only that individuality of striving occurs within culture but that it does not necessarily lead to trends. Similarly the argument about status and arbitrariness is a variant of the adage that "when the king lisps everyone lisps," and it bears on the notion of a "trickle-down" effect in stratified or hierarchical social systems. But it indicates that the "trickle-down" effect, rather than being a societal "mechanism for maintaining the motivation to strive for success, and hence for maintaining efficiency of performance in occupational roles in a system in which differential success is possible for only a few . . ." (Fallers 1973) is a *manifestation* of such striving, and a *manifestation of degrees of success*.

As already noted elsewhere in this volume, several recent studies have suggested that many aspects of culture, involving such items as patterns of marriage, inheritance, and kinship behavior, and varying in expression among societies, are neither arbitrary nor independent of predictions from a theory dependent upon inclusive-fitness-maximizing by individuals (Alexander 1977a).

Like learning theory and other theories that stop with proximate mechanisms, Malinowski's "functional" theory of culture, which was couched in terms of satisfying immediate physiological needs, did not account for the existence of those needs (Alexander 1977b). Thus, Sahlins

I. Some Statements of Theory

(1976a) was led to say that for Malinowski culture represented a "gigantic metaphorical extension of the digestive system." But Malinowski's theory would have made sense in the terms suggested here if it could only have been interpreted as seeing culture as a gigantic metaphorical extension of the *reproductive* system.

The ideas I have just suggested are alternative to recent efforts to explain the relationship of culture and genetic evolution—or, more particularly, their apparent lack of relationship—by suggesting that "cultural instructions" (Cloak 1975) or "memes" (Dawkins 1976) are selected in the same fashion as, and often in opposition to, genes or genetic instructions; or that two kinds of selection, often in opposition, are necessarily involved (Richerson and Boyd 1978). Arbitrariness, then, in fashion or any other aspect of culture, may not be contrary to the genetic reproductive success of those initiating and maintaining it, only to that of some of those upon whom it is forced, in particular those who are least able to turn it to their own advantage. To understand the reproductive significance of arbitrariness as a part of status-seeking, one need only understand the reproductive significance of status. One might suggest that there are *genetic instructions* which somehow result in our engaging in arbitrariness in symbolic behavior in whatever *environments* it is genetically *reproductive* to do so.

I suggest, then, that the rates and directions of mutability and heritability in culture are determined by the collectives and compromises of interest of the individuals striving at any particular time or place, together with the form and degree of inertia in the cultural environment as a result of its history; that the "hostile forces" that result in cultural change have tended increasingly to be the conflicts of interest among human individuals and subgroups in securing relief from Darwin's "Hostile Forces of Nature" (see above); and that, among these "Hostile Forces of Nature," increasingly prominent and eventually paramount have been what amounted to predators, in the form of other humans acting in groups or in isolation, with at least temporary commonality of interests (Alexander 1971, 1974, 1975a, 1977a).

By these arguments four outcomes are predicted: (1) a reasonably close correspondence between the structure of culture and its usefulness to individuals in inclusive-fitness-maximizing, (2) an even closer correlation between the overall structure of culture and those traits which benefit everyone about equally, or benefit the great majority, (3) extremely effective capabilities of individuals to mold themselves to fit their cultural milieu, and (4) tendencies for culture to be so constructed as to resist significant alteration by individuals and subgroups in their own interests and contrary to those of others. If these predictions are regarded as important we shall be led to analyze the variations in culture potentially as the outcomes of different strategies of inclusive-fitness-maximizing under different circumstances, and the proximate or immediate physiological and social mechanisms whereby inclusive fitness is maximized as potential explanations of degrees and directions by which cultural patterns diverge from actual inclusive-fitness-maximizing behaviors when technological change and other events create novel environments outside the limits of those in which earlier behaviors functioned.

Concluding remarks

I think we may regard as settled the universality and inevitability of natural selection and the rarity of effective selection above the individual level, and as relatively trivial for social scientists the problem of the relative effectiveness of selection at the individual level as against some lower level. I also suppose that culture can evolve without genetic change, and that it does so frequently without diminution of inclusive-fitness-maximizing effects. It would appear that the immediate future in other areas of investigation will see concentration on two questions: (1) to what extent are cultural patterns actually independent of predictions from natural selection, and why, and (2) how could patterns of cultural behavior be consistent with natural selection in ways that do not do violence to our knowledge of the extent and nature of learning? The papers in this volume suggest this trend and indicate that in most cases the data, if they are to lead to convincing answers, will have to be gathered with these questions actually in mind.

The complexity of the picture developed by these arguments and conclusions indicates both the difficulty involved in extensive and thorough testing of an inclusive-fitness-maximizing theory of human sociality and the potential generality of such a theory. Such testing is the major challenge that lies ahead on the border between the social and biological sciences, together with the problem of dealing with the moral and ethical questions that arise along with any increase in understanding of human behavior and how to modify it. The tasks so identified are not likely to be easy or simple. But, then, no one who ever thought about human behavior in analytical terms is likely to have supposed that they would be.

II. Kinship

Kinship has long been an important topic in anthropology, and yet anthropological research has left unanswered the basic question of why kinship is important in every human society. Hamilton's theory of kin selection (1964) suggests a possible answer to this question. In combination with Trivers' theory of reciprocal altruism (1971), Hamilton's theory provides a new way of looking at human kinship. A number of anthropologists and biologists believe that kinship is an important area of convergent interest between anthropology and the evolutionary biology of social behavior. The six chapters in this section attempt in various ways to combine anthropological and biological approaches to the study of kinship.

The suggestion that human kinship might profitably be studied in terms of sociobiology has, in my opinion, given rise to a number of misunderstandings. Before turning to the essays dealing with this topic, I would like to comment on some of these views which I see as misconceptions.

The first such view is the notion that sociobiology implies that altruism is predictable from the coefficient of relatedness alone (Sahlins 1976a: 24–54). This is untrue for two reasons. First, Hamilton's theory of kinship (1964) predicts altruism in terms of three variables: the coefficient of relatedness, the cost of altruism to the altruist in Darwinian fitness, and the benefit of the altruism to a related beneficiary in terms of Darwinian fitness. The extent of altruism displayed toward different kin would be predictable from the coefficient of relatedness alone only if the cost and benefits of altruism were the same for every category of kin. This may be true in some social contexts (see Chagnon, chapter 4, and Chagnon and Bugos, chapter 8, in this section for example), but is unlikely to be true in all contexts (see for example Irons, chapter 7). The second reason why altruism is not predictable from the coefficient of relatedness alone is that interaction among human kin is often adaptive in terms of reciprocal altruism, a strategy which need not occur among genetically related individuals to be successful (Alexander 1974, 1975a, 1977a; Trivers 1971; West Eberhard 1975).

Another possible source of confusion is a tendency to equate all social interaction with altruism. Human kinship may be influenced in important ways by strategies of mate competition and strategies relating to optimal degrees of inbreeding and outbreeding (cf. Alexander 1977a; Chagnon, chapter 4; and Fox, chapter 5). These strategies are not likely to be altruistic, but they are social and the total pattern of interaction among human kin in a particular society may not be comprehensible without reference to these strategies as well as those entailing altruism.

Another misconception is that kin selection through nepotism—or the maximization of inclusive fitness by helping relatives—can only take place through some kind of unlikely "genetic" recognition of relatives, and could not be realized through social interactions acquired by learning, in a fashion consistent with psychological views of the ontogeny of human social behaviors. In his original paper on inclusive fitness, Hamilton (1964) explained why it is extremely unlikely that genes leading in some direct fashion to recognition of relatives could explain patterns of nepotism appropriate to maximizing inclusive fitness. He pointed out that any such gene would have to, first, have an effect on the phenotype; second, cause its bearers to be able to recognize the effect in others; and, third, also cause its bearers to take the appropriate social action. These requirements of gene action are unreasonably complex. Also, such a mutant would act on the basis of its own presence in the genome of related individuals, independent of the probability that other genes in its genome would, or would not, be in these same relatives. Thus, it would necessarily act against the interests of all the other genes in its own genome, and the extraordinary organization of the genome could not be sustained if such genes became prevalent. Any gene mutating so as to suppress such an "outlaw" effect would thereby help itself, and in any large genome the mutational probabilities of suppression, as opposed to the probability of sustaining "outlawry," would be enormously high (Alexander and Borgia 1978).

Hamilton (1964) did not propose any proximate mechanisms of kin recognition which he thought might actually occur. Alexander (1977b), however, has suggested that inclusive fitness becomes a meaningful concept in evolution only to the extent that social interactions permit accurate assessment of genetic relationships. This means that parents must learn who their offspring are, and all individuals must learn who their various other relatives are, as a result of particular kinds, numbers, timings, or rates of social interactions with them. That this is so is suggested, for example, by the fact that human mothers are unable to identify their own babies if they are anesthetized during labor, depending for identification upon others such as hospital personnel and upon identification marks or bracelets placed upon the baby, also by others. Thus, even the intimate and crucial mother-offspring interaction is established through social not genetic circumstances. That the same is true of other kinds of interactions between relatives seems a foregone conclusion, and some of the relevant contingencies are already obvious: in many cases we are instructed by our relatives about our relationships to others; relationships among family members develop out of the long-term associations that occur within the household; etc. I am convinced that readers will be better able to evaluate the papers presented in this section if the misconceptions discussed above are avoided.

The chapter by Chagnon points out that the patterns of alliance formation, intervillage warfare, and village fissioning which he described in earlier publications on the Yąnomamö (1968a, 1974, 1975) appear to be the outcome of mate competition among males. Lineages appear to be coalitions of related males seeking to assist one another in such competition; and the pairs of intermarrying lineages, which form the cores of most villages, appear to be united because of reciprocal obligations to supply each other with mates. This paper also provides basic information on the Yąnomamö research which will be useful to readers in evaluating the later papers in this volume on the Yąnomamö.

The hypothesis that Yąnomamö politics and warfare follow predictably from mate competition among males has important implications for anthropological theory. The Yąnomamö have a classical form of reciprocal marriage exchange and one of the most common forms of kinship terminology found among preliterate societies, Iroquois terminology. The two culture elements are very much bound up with the Yąnomamö pattern of warfare and alliance formation. Since most other groups with these traits were studied after pacification, it is possible that systematic reciprocal marriage exchange and Iroquois kin terms were similarly related to warfare and alliance formation and in a parallel way were expressions of mate competition in many preliterate societies before absorption into modern industrial states—even though ethnographers did not detect such functions.

The most elaborately argued previous explanation of Yąnomamö warfare maintains that it is a group-level adaptation preventing population growth that would lead to protein shortage (Divale and Harris 1976; Harris 1974, 1977a). As such this interpretation runs into the same theoretical difficulties as the Wynne-Edwards hypothesis. In chapter 11, Bates and Lees review those theoretical difficulties in detail. Much of the evidence supporting the Divale and Harris interpretation is sex-ratio data. Alternate explanations of sex ratios deviating from 50/50 are examined at length by Chagnon, Flinn, and Melancon in chapter 12 and by Dickemann in chapter 13. It has also been argued that warfare among groups like the Yąnomamö is individual-level competition for protein (Durham 1976b). This has been definitively refuted by Chagnon and Hames (1979) for the Yąnomamö.

Fox's chapter looks at the universal practice of classifying kin as a form of biological adaptation. What he says here is an extension of earlier work in which he showed that the culture-nature dichotomy is misleading since culture is itself a part of nature. He begins by observing that human beings classify kin in every society, but that the actual set of categories into which kin are placed varies from one society to another. He argues that kinship categories are ways of regulating both nepotism and the extent of outbreeding in human populations, although regulating outbreeding appears to be the more important function. As such they do not define specific behavior—such as specifying precisely who shall marry whom—but rather set limits on behavior—such as dividing relatives into marriageable and unmarriageable categories. Fox takes issue with those sociobiologists who denigrate the importance of what people say (such as how they classify and label kin) and claim that only what they do is worthy of attention. He emphasizes that such cultural things as kin classification are worthy of study in their own right and that they can be explained as products of natural selection: that is, they exist because they make it easier for individuals (or perhaps groups) to project their genes into future generations. Since human beings everywhere invest differentially in different types of relatives, this pattern often makes sense as a search for an optimal balance of inbreeding and outbreeding, it is expectable that they would everywhere classify kin—as they do. Since human beings occupy highly varied niches, it is expectable that the optimal pattern of differential investment, and of inbreeding versus outbreeding, would vary. Thus, one would expect kin classification to be highly facultative—as it is. Fox shows in some detail how simple shifts in the rules defining kin categories can produce highly varied breeding patterns. Thus, human beings are able to adjust the extent of outbreeding to what is optimal in a wide range of very different niches.

In this paper Fox takes issue with a theoretical position accepted by most of the other contributors to this volume. He argues for a form of group selection. The argument, which is not extensively elaborated, is that kinship systems create sufficient interdependence among members of a group to make group and individual interests indistinguishable. Others have argued that human beings are a species for which the generally improbable conditions for group selection may in fact be met (Alexander 1974:376–377; Wilson 1975:572–574). Thus, although most of the contributors to this volume are convinced that in general individual- and lower-level selection alone are potent in producing adaptations, some reservations and room for further debate remain in the case of the human species.

Fox also comments briefly on chapter 8, by Chagnon and Bugos, and chapter 9, by Hames, who have a very different, but not necessarily contradictory, approach. These chapters are concerned with the effect of precisely remembered genealogical information on behavior (as opposed to ideology) and are able to demonstrate an effect that is not predictable from kinship categories. It seems reasonable to conclude, as Fox does, that actual behavior is influenced both by relatedness and by cultural categories, as well as by other information, and that which factor is more important depends on the circumstances. For example, relatedness appears to be more important in shaping differential assistance, whereas kin categories seem more important in shaping mate choice.

In chapter 6, Kurland explores the relationship between low paternity probability and a number of aspects of social organization. He shows that the level of paternity probability appears to be connected in important ways with such aspects of kinship behavior as paternal investment, the avunculate, inheritance, residence rules, and marital stability, as well as with such elements of culture as theories of the male role in reproduction. In so doing he is building on Alexander's observation (1974: 373; 1977a:319) that the avunculate might be explained as a form of nepotism in a social environment in which men are on average more related to sisters' children than to their wives' children, as a result of widespread promiscuity and inaccurate ascertainment of paternity.

Parental care can be a successful reproductive strategy only when parents can identify their own offspring with some degree of accuracy (Alexander and Borgia, 1978). A male mammal can identify a mate's offspring as his own only by excluding other males from copulating with her over a fairly long period of time. This can be accomplished by various behaviors such as guarding a mate continuously against contact with other males or excluding other males from a defined territory. These behaviors, however, entail a cost which is worth paying only if there is sufficient benefit to be gained by directing effort toward paternal care rather than toward some other end, such as additional matings with fertile females (Alexander and Borgia, 1978). The time period over which a female must be monitored to assure paternity confidence is longer for mammals than for members of most other phyla. This means that paternity confidence for mammals is not only costly, but also highly variable. As a result of this variability, paternal care in mammals should be highly facultative: that is, it should be easily turned on or off as subtle changes in the environment shift levels of paternity probability.

Human males appear to be far more committed to nurturing members of the next generation than most mammalian males (cf. Alexander and Noonan, chapter 16), but nevertheless there is an important facultative element present. In some human societies, males appear not to pay the cost of paternity confidence, and instead direct their nurturance toward sisters' children. In other societies, they appear to pay only part of the cost, assuring that wives' children are on average more related than sisters' children but tolerating some infidelity. In these societies, although men may invest heavily in wives' children, relatedness is generally higher through uterine links, so that a man's assistance to relatives other than his wife's children may be directed more extensively toward uterine kin. Other recent papers dealing with this issue are Greene (1978) and Alexander (1977a:310, 319–324).

In terms of the two variables relevant to kin selection—r and k— Kurland's chapter deals primarily with one: namely, r. The following chapter by Irons is intended to complement this discussion by looking at variations in the other; k, or B/C as it was described in chapter 1 (14–16). Broadly speaking, organisms do two things in order to be represented genetically in future generations: they gather resources and they use these resources for reproduction. I would include such processes as ontogeny in the category of gathering resources, but in the human case the category certainly includes such things as acquiring wealth, securing political power, or building up the obligation of others to assist oneself in various ways. Reproduction includes not only such obvious matters as acquiring mates, but also altruistically assisting kin. The resources individuals are able to gather are very different from one human society to another. Usually they also vary among members of the same society with the age and sex of the person in question. Likewise the value of any specific resources for relatives of a particular age and sex category also varies vastly from one human society to another. These differences can be conceived of as differences in the values of B and C associated with altruism toward different categories of kin (brother, sister, son, or daughter for example) and can make optimal a biasing of altruism investment toward some kin categories at the expense of others. Such a skewing of altruism investment may underlie such social institutions as patriliny, matriliny, virilocality, uxorilocality, the avunculate, or any other institution which is an expression of greater interaction with, or assistance to, one category of kin at the expense of another equally related category.

The paper by Chagnon and Bugos tests a specific set of predictions about aggressive behavior against data on a fight in a Yąnomamö village. The data used are especially relevant to the testing of sociobiological hypotheses and are a type unfortunately rare in the ethnographic record. Much of the data was drawn from a film of the fight itself, later edited to produce the film "The Ax Fight." Readers may gain additional understanding of this particular paper by viewing this film. This chapter makes a very important contribution by supplying data supporting the hypothesis that kin selection underlies much of human sociality and by showing that, contrary to what many anthropologists think, genetic relatedness is an important determinant of human kinship behavior.

The paper by Hames provides data from another society relevant to the issue of kin selection in human populations. It allows further inference in favor of the hypothesis that nepotistic strategies are an important element in human sociality by bearing out the prediction that human beings will more frequently cooperate with more closely related individuals, other things being equal. Hames' data also show that, for the Ye'kwana, actual cooperative behaviors (which are probable loci of altruism) fit this prediction more closely than do patterns of household co-residence. This suggests that the more refined types of behavioral data which Hames, and Chagnon and Bugos, have presented are necessary for truly sophisticated tests of the applicability of kin selection theory to human sociality.

W. I.

4. Mate Competition, Favoring Close Kin, and Village Fissioning Among the Yąnomamö Indians[1]

Napoleon A. Chagnon

Introduction

For the vast portion of human history we have lived in small, kinship-dominated groups. Basic requirements for survival in such groups—defense against predators and conspecific outsiders, nutrition, and reproduction—were met within a matrix of kinship ties and were subject to the qualities of those ties. It was important to have kinsmen, for they defended you and helped you find food and mates.

Anthropologists have known for a very long time that kinship was important in tribally organized societies and that kinship, marriage practices, and notions of descent from common ancestors constituted the fundamental social building blocks of most tribal societies. With the development of the notion of inclusive fitness and the theory of kin selection (Hamilton 1964; West Eberhard 1975) we must now seriously consider the possibility that there is an explanation for human kinship behavior in terms of natural selection, and that favoring of close kinsmen is a human behavioral tendency with profound implications for reproductive success and survival (Alexander 1974, 1977b).

The first reaction of most social anthropologists, myself included, was to dismiss the arguments about the biological quality of kinship out of hand. My own training had constrained me to think of human kinship taxonomies in terms of abstract models that classified and included both kin and non-kin, or that kinship reckoning depended fundamentally on

[1] The research on which this paper was based was provided by the Harry Frank Guggenheim Foundation, the National Institutes of Health (NIMH Grant No. MH26008) and the National Science Foundation (Grant No. SOC75–14262). I would like to thank the following people for criticisms of earlier drafts of this paper, and for many helpful suggestions from them that improved the style, content and theoretical dimensions of the final draft: Richard D. Alexander, Mark Flinn, Mary Ann Harrell, William Irons, and Thomas Melancon. The deficiencies and shortcomings that yet remain are entirely my responsibility.

language, of which humans were the exclusive possessors. The recent rapid growth of long-term, detailed primate studies, however, began to challenge some of my own convictions, and the mounting evidence indicated that recognition of relatives occurred in societies of nonhuman primates, and that the social behavior of these primates could be understood more fully when the patterns of kinship recognition were considered (e.g., Kurland 1977).

Moreover, my own work among the Yąnomamö Indians of Venezuela (Chagnon 1968a, 1968b, 1974) had focused on kinship, genealogy, and marriage practices and I was always struck with the degree to which actual genealogical relatedness, as distinct from "fictive" kinship, seemed to be important to the Yąnomamö. They discriminated in many subtle and not-so-subtle ways against non-kin, no matter how they "classified" them. I concluded, after a detailed analysis of their kinship relatedness, that closeness of kinship, measured genealogically, was an important variable in predicting village fissioning and that village size and cohesion had something to do with the amount of genealogical relatedness within the group (Chagnon 1975).

But one of the most compelling aspects of Yąnomamö social behavior, the feature of their society that puzzled and intrigued me most, was the constant fighting over women and sex (Chagnon 1966, 1968a, 1968b, 1974). That behavior, more than any other, made a great deal of sense when considered in terms of Hamilton's theory of inclusive fitness. Clearly this concern was related to reproduction and "fitness." In investigating scores and even hundreds of different fights and village fissions or relocations, I would ask the Yąnomamö: "Why did you fission there?" or "What caused that fight?". Patiently, and slowly, my informants would sigh and say: "Women!". If the informant was new and had never worked with me before, the answer would be somewhat more animated, and the informant astonished: "What? Don't ask such a stupid question! It is women! Women! We fight over women!" [2] After having spent some forty months among the Yąnomamö, witnessing their fights and arguments, I would not attempt to defend the proposition that Yąnomamö behavior makes sense as a strategy to *minimize* reproductive success or inclusive fitness. There is, in brief, enough evidence to warrant an examination of their kinship and marriage behavior from the perspective that individuals are attempting to maximize

[2] Once a war begins between two villages and people are killed, much of the fighting that follows is explained, by the Yąnomamö, as attempts to get revenge. Still, the wars almost invariably begin in disputes over women.

their inclusive fitness and that part of doing this entails favoring of close kin. As a social anthropologist, therefore, I must conclude that my earlier skepticism about the value of biological models for interpretations of human social behavior must be reconsidered.

But the Yąnomamö, like all humans, behave reproductively in the context of defined social groups. Competition for mates involves coalitions between individuals who are members of different kin groups, particularly lineal descent groups. This feature of mate competition among the Yąnomamö, and presumably in all human societies characterized by lineal descent and formal marriage-alliance patterns, complicates an otherwise simple picture of individuals devising reproductive strategies that are set into play within an undifferentiated mate pool. One implication of exogamic lineal descent organization is that the reproductive potential of an individual is not exclusively a function of his or her own behavior: it is very much dependent on the support of kin in one's own group *and* the willingness of individuals in other, similar groups to give marriageable partners. The strategies that emerge reflect this, and they entail soliciting aid from kin, manipulating kinship terminology, promising to repay women at some later time, giving of daughters in the expectation that others will repay later, favoring individuals of particular kin groups as potential marriage exchangers and investing in them, defending brothers-in-law against brothers, etc. The direct application of theory from evolutionary biology to human marriage behavior and mating strategies is, in my estimation, not possible until the theory is modified to take into consideration the interdependency of individuals in human mating systems and how their interdependency—coalitions and alliances—structures human mating behavior. In brief, recent developments in evolutionary biology suggest that social anthropologists can learn a great deal about human marriage systems, but it is clear that biologists must learn a great deal more than they presently know about human marriage systems before they can render them intelligible in terms of evolutionary biology (see Wilson, this volume, for a discussion of mutual transformations that are likely to occur in biology and social anthropology).

The first wave of excitement and controversy over the applicability of evolutionary biology to human social behavior is now over. The work of testing hypotheses must now begin. Unfortunately, the field research required to generate the kind of data needed to make rigorous tests has only just begun in human societies. Existing data even remotely related to the major hypotheses of evolutionary biology are not abundant, but some data can be re-examined to determine the extent to which human behavior in particular societies appears to conform to predictions from the emerging new body of theory. Such a re-examination of existing data will at least permit us to arrive at conclusions regarding the *possible* applicability of biological theory to human social behavior and help us decide whether or not future research should include the collection of specific kinds of data that are germane to the rigorous testing of sociobiological hypotheses.

This paper is, then, a re-examination of already existing data on Yąnomamö social behavior in an attempt to explore the possibility that Yąnomamö marriage practices, kinship behavior, and village fissioning make sense in a sociobiological context. I hope to show that competition for mates among males involves strategies in which "coalitions" among some males are developed in order to secure marriageable females for themselves, their brothers, and their sons. These coalitions are usually made between males who are related to each other genealogically, a consequence of previous marriage alliances (coalitions) in ancestral generations. The intensity of mate competition and the strategies that emerge vary from village to village and are largely a function of the composition of the village in terms of the size and number of patrilineages—individuals who are related to each other through the male line. The more complex the composition, the greater the competition and, therefore, the more compelling are the advantages for individual members of specific lineages to "pair" with each other in reciprocal exchange agreements. Village fissioning reduces the size of the village and tends to redistribute patrilineages in such a way that competition for mates is greatly reduced: the new villages tend to have a less complex patrilineal structure, and, in some cases, have a markedly "dual" structure. Marriage exchanges in the less complex villages are less fraught with complications that arise when members of other lineages attempt to penetrate the exchange network of the two matrimonially bound patrilineages.

The above arguments will be made in the context of several other objectives this paper has. In the order that they will appear below, these involve the following:

(1) *Ethnographic Context.* This is the first of four papers that deal with aspects of Yąnomamö social behavior in this volume. Accordingly, I summarize here selected aspects of Yąnomamö culture relevant to all four, drawing on my previously published accounts. At times my descriptions may seem assertive and not sufficiently documented in the somewhat spartan narrative I provide. They are essentially summaries of ethnographic accounts I have published elsewhere, and the interested reader might wish to con-

sult the more fully documented arguments and claims: Chagnon 1966, 1967, 1968a, 1968b, 1968c, 1968d, 1972, 1974, 1975, 1976a, 1976b.

(2) *Models*. Traditional models of kinship and marriage systems used in anthropological publications are inadequate to represent the dynamics of individual behavior. I introduce a number of slightly more complex models to reveal more clearly how coalitions between adult males emerge and how they take form and persist over several generations. These models should make clear how competition emerges and how kinship relatedness builds up as males ally themselves with other related males from different lineages, locking themselves and their descendants in matrimonial exchanges that endure over time.

(3) *Egocentric Kinship*. Relatedness between any pair of individuals can be expressed in precise terms using a variation of Sewall Wright's (1922) Inbreeding Coefficient. I present a discussion of the methods used in analyzing genealogical data with this statistic to show how measurements of kinship closeness have been established.

(4) *Data*. In support of the arguments I present, I provide summaries of large amounts of data on Yąnomamö kinship and relatedness collected between 1964 and 1975 during the course of nine field trips. One deficiency in the anthropological literature is the paucity of information on the quantitative aspects of human kinship: how many people in a tribal village are actually related to one another? How closely are people related to one other? How many "strangers" are there in the village? Where, in fact, do a person's closest kin live?

(5) *Future Research*. A number of specific research topics are suggested that would lead to the development of bodies of quantitative data to be used in testing specific hypotheses on human kinship behavior. It is suggested that closeness of kinship relatedness, measured with the techniques described in this chapter, would be a better predictor of human behavior than a knowledge of the kinship terminology and the supposed obligations that characterize specific dyadic relationships.

Yąnomamö Villages and Population

Nobody knows for certain, exactly how large the Yąnomamö population is or precisely how many villages there are, for there are still regions of the tribe that have not been visited by outsiders. These regions are known to contain Yąnomamö villages. I have visited approximately fifty or sixty villages over a wide area of the tribe, both in Venezuela and Brazil. During these trips I made complete censuses of the villages I visited and attempted to make estimates of the sizes of other, nearby villages with information given to me by Yąnomamö informants and, on occasion, by local missionaries. In addition, I have consulted the published accounts of other experienced field researchers and have spoken to many of them. The information thus collected suggests that the Yąnomamö population is of the order of magnitude of 15,000 people, the vast majority living in Venezuela (see figure 4–1). They live, widely scattered, in approximately 150 villages. Villages range in size from 25 to 30 people at one extreme, to upward of 300 at the other extreme. Warfare is endemic among the Yanomamö, but it is more intense in some regions of the tribe than in others. But even where it is chronic, there are long periods of relative peace.

A census and village distribution map made this year would be out of date next year, since some of the 150-odd villages will have fissioned during the year. The resulting factions split away from each other to begin their careers as autonomous political entities. Fissions are not just simple events, however. They are processes. Tensions build up as the village gets

Figure 4–1   Location of the Yanomamö Indians in South America

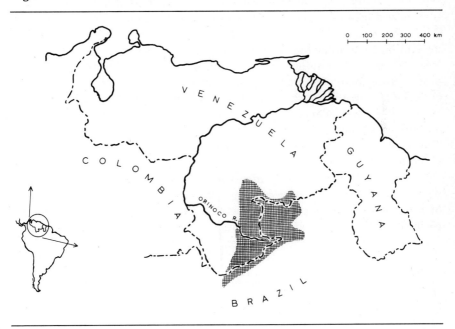

large and fighting becomes chronic within the group. As club-fights increase in frequency and become more violent, groups of people decide to move off and start a garden elsewhere. It may take a year to get the new garden established and a new *shabono,* the village structure and clearing, built. At that point one faction can move away and its members begin life as a new political entity—a new village. Still, families periodically return to the original village for long visits, or families from the original village go to live with the new group, and for a period of several years there will be some migration between the two interrelated groups. In time the two groups might migrate far apart from each other—a week to ten days' walk—and then visiting between them all but ceases.

Each of the 150-odd villages is an autonomous political entity whose members cherish their independence and strive to maintain it. While they look forward to and enjoy the periodic intervillage feasting and visiting that characterize most of the tribal area, they are suspicious of their neighbors—even those to whom they are related historically and genealogically—and are ever wary of the designs that neighbors have regarding the acquisition of women. The pattern and intensity of intervillage warfare in most regions of the tribe is such that members of all villages have to rely on friendly ties with neighbors, cemented in part through intervillage trading and feasting (Chagnon 1967, 1968a, 1968c; Asch and Chagnon 1975). Through these friendly ties—political alliances [3]—neighboring groups can depend on each other for aid in raiding common enemies, or turn to each other for temporary refuge when the chronic raids of enemies drive whole groups from their permanent gardens. This is not to say that the conflicts entail sieges with attacking raiders storming their enemy's village to slaughter the defenders. Rather, the raids are clandestine, unpredictable, and more like ambushes, leading only to one or two casualties if successful. The cumulative effects of worrying about the unpredictable appearance of raiders often leads the members of villages, particularly small villages, to abandon their village and garden temporarily and visit a distant, friendly neighbor for several weeks or even months, subsisting largely on the produce of the ally's garden during that period. Eventually they return to their garden and village; if raiding continues at a high frequency, they usually begin clearing a new garden at a great distance away from their enemies—

[3] I shall speak in this paper of *two* kinds of marriage alliance. One is the kind of alliance that binds discrete villages to each other through the giving of a girl in marriage. The other is in the exchange of women *within* a village between two lineages. Yąnomamö marriages are of the latter kind, i.e., village endogamous.

II. Kinship

two or three days' walk in many cases. When the new garden begins producing, the group permanently abandons its old site and moves to the new one (Chagnon 1968a).

During the periods of time that members of one village take refuge with their allies, they expose themselves to the possibility of losing women to their hosts. The refugees' wives and daughters are attractive to the local men and are more or less continuously harassed by them for sexual favors, and the visiting men are pressured into ceding marriageable girls to their hosts as marriage partners. The longer a group must rely on such refuge, the more difficult it is for them to resist the requests for women or tolerate attempts at seduction or actual seduction. Very often allies part on strained terms, invariably because of arguments over women, preferring to return to the uncertainty of life in their own chronically raided village than to tolerate the machinations of their erstwhile hosts. In short, allies often need each other, but do not always like and seldom trust each other.

Intervillage alliance is far more significant for members of smaller villages who are more vulnerable targets of raids from larger villages and less capable of mounting an effective, long-term pattern of retaliatory raiding. In addition, the geographical position of a village has a great deal to do with the extent to which its members must depend on and enter into alliances with unpredictable neighbors. Thus, villages on the periphery of the tribe have an additional option when local political stresses—raiding and threats from neighbors—grow intolerable: they can migrate outward, away from the source of threat, and simply evade their neighbors (Chagnon 1968a, 1972). This is especially true on the west, south, and eastern periphery of the tribe where unoccupied vast expanses of tropical forest surround the Yąnomamö. On the northern frontier, the expansion of the Yąnomamö is hampered by the presence of an unrelated tribe: the Ye'kwana (for descriptions of Ye'kwana, see Hames 1978; Arvelo-Jiménez 1971).

Expansion and relocation of villages at the center of the tribal distribution is not characterized by the same degree of freedom, for each village is more or less surrounded by other villages and the members of any particular village appear to be most reluctant to "leap-frog" past a neighbor and resettle beyond that neighbor. Each village is therefore limited in its freedom to move by the mere existence of neighbors: it is "socially circumscribed" (Chagnon 1968c). In most parts of the tribal distribution the villages are sufficiently far apart that considerable freedom in choosing a new site does in fact exist—closest neighbors may be three or four days' walk away. Elsewhere, particularly in the Parima Mountains, villages are geographically closer together, but the shorter distance separating them consists of rugged terrain that is difficult to cross. Still, the population density of the Yąnomamö is extremely low—less than one person per square mile, a density that puts them closer to the normal range of hunter-gatherers than to the general range of horticultural people like themselves (Chagnon 1974:127).

The population is growing, perhaps as much as 2 to 3 percent per year in some regions of the tribe.[4] Genealogical data, demographic information, and political histories—all obtained from informants—indicate that the recent history of most Yąnomamö groups has been characterized by population growth, followed by village fissioning and dispersal. While the rate of growth may differ from one region to another (Chagnon 1974), the pattern of village fissioning is generally the same over the entire tribal distribution. Figure 4–2 gives the schematic pattern of village fissioning

Figure 4–2   Schematic Diagram of Village Fissions in Two Yanomamö Populations, Showing Historical Connections of Existing Villages

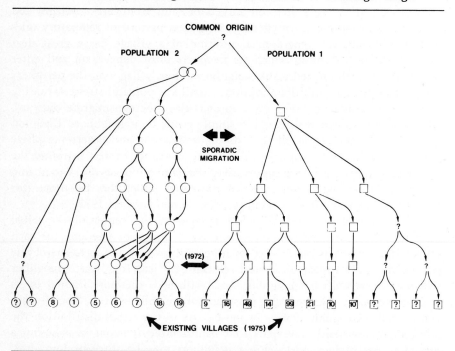

---

[4] Recently introduced diseases have modified the growth rate substantially, and the prospects for continuing population growth appear dim (Chagnon 1977).

II. Kinship

for two "population blocs" of Yąnomamö that have been the focus of my more intensive field research since 1964. The data presented in the remainder of this paper are drawn from these two population blocs, the Shamatari (Population 1) and the Namoweiteri (Population 2).

As figure 4–2 indicates, each village (bottom row) is merely an element in a larger cluster of related villages. The more recent the fission, the more closely related the members of the two independent villages and, by extension, the more remote the fission, the more remote the genealogical relatedness between individuals from the two distantly related villages. I shall return to this point momentarily. Geographical distance between villages also correlates with the closeness or remoteness in time of the fissions that separated the villages. That is, recently fissioned villages tend to be found closer to each other than to members of villages that separated earlier in time.

The dynamics of fissioning hinge on the internal structuring of the village and how this affects the gradual deterioration of "amicability" or "solidarity" as a village grows in size and complexity. Internal order and cohesion derive primarily from (1) the number and size of lineage groups within the village, (2) how often members of these lineages have intermarried among themselves over several generations, and the resulting *patterns* of relatedness, (3) how closely individuals are related to other individuals within the village, i.e., the kind and *amount* of relatedness, (4) the effectiveness of leaders—headmen—in settling internal disputes, (5) whether or not there are several headmen who are members of the same lineal descent group and who, therefore, are competitors for the available marriageable women, and (6) the relative level of intervillage fighting, which increases internal cooperation and inhibits fissioning of groups into two less defensible, separate villages (see also Chagnon 1975). I shall explore the statistical nature of these several factors later in this paper and in other papers in this volume, but for the moment let me describe the general properties of village fission in macroscopic, qualitative terms.

As a village grows in size, tensions within the group mount, internal friction and fighting increase, and bitter arguments are chronic. The major source of the conflict is sex and seduction: younger men frequently attempt to seduce the wives of other men, and seize every opportunity to approach the women when their husbands are not around. Men who go on several-day hunting trips, for example, keep their ears close to the ground when they return to pick up any telltale gossip that suggests infidelity on the part of their wives, and often beat them soundly if there appears to be substance to the rumors. The wronged husband usually challenges the suspected lover to a club-fight as well. Such fights rapidly explode and involve large numbers of the village men, who take sides with close kin (see Chagnon and Bugos, this volume, chapter 8). In smaller villages, the incest taboos and kinship obligations are such that sexual trysting is greatly reduced, and a relatively high level of trust among male co-residents prevails.

Let me illustrate with an example. Small villages are of the order of magnitude of thirty to fifty individuals. As the village grows, the passing of each generation leads to the emergence of villages whose residents are, on the average, progressively more remotely related to each other (see below for statistics). In a small village, for example, an older man with four or five adult sons and several daughters might be bound, through marriage ties, with another man and *his* adult children, each having given his sons and daughters reciprocally to the other's children as marriage partners. Figure 4–3a shows this situation: a "dual" composition. There is considerable harmony and amity within the sibships, based largely on age differences between brothers and the respect and trust that full brothers of discrepant ages have for one another (Chagnon 1966). The brothers as a unit also look out for the welfare of their sisters, interfering on their behalf should their husbands be excessively harsh. The sets of brothers who have married each other's sisters are especially amicable with each other, and the brother-in-law tie is one of the most amicable relationships in Yąnomamö culture. In a biological sense, the inclusive fitness interest of brothers-in-law (who are *also* cognatic kin) overlaps strongly, and the warmth of the ties between them is consistent with expectations derived from kin selection theory. They support each other in fights, share food and goods, hunt together, and, as they have children of their own, may arrange the marriages of these children to each other: the children of brothers-in-law are marriageable partners.

Thus, the coalition formed between men who have married each other's sisters has long-term fitness consequences for all parties united by the marriage. A man gives his sister to another man, and continues to monitor her welfare and well-being long after the marriage begins. He has a special and warm relationship to her children—the classic mother's brother/sister's child relationship—and is expected to invest both materially and socially in these children (see Kurland, chapter 6, this volume, for an analysis of the mother's brother/sister's son tie). His sister turns to him when her husband beats her and he exercises a mollifying influence over the husband, encouraging him to be less harsh. Since he is married to that man's sister, the relationships are reciprocal from the latter's point of view.

As their children reach marriageable age, each man and his sister

Figure 4–3 **Models of Yanomamö Society Based on Reciprocal Marriage Exchange, Lineage Exogamy, and Bilateral Cross-Cousin Marriage**
Figure 4–3a′ is the most parsimonious model encompassing the relevant marriage, descent, and exchange rules and the type of model most frequently given to characterize the interrelationships of these rules. Figures 4–3a and 4–3b are somewhat more complex, but have the virtue of encompassing all the rules as well as revealing the demographic and kinship bases for male/male competition for mates.

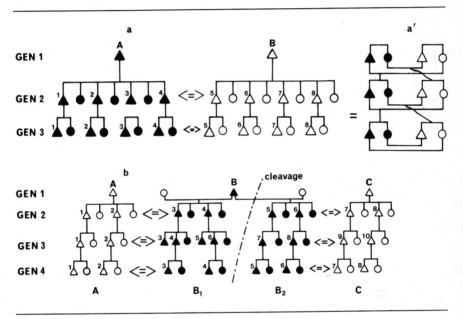

gain potential increases in inclusive fitness by arranging for their children to marry each other, thus reducing the competition for mates for their sons. I might add that *all* women get married, are married young, and married during their entire reproductive period, but not all men are successful in finding wives, and many only do so later in their reproductive life spans (see Chagnon, Flinn, and Melancon, this volume, chapter 12). Moreover, given some paternity uncertainty, reciprocal marriage exchanges of this type are ideally suited to reducing the probability that a man is investing in unrelated offspring: he invests in his spouse's children, whose genetic relationship to himself might be questionable (if they are not cognates), and he also invests in his sister's children, whose genetic relationship to him is more certain [5] (see Alexander 1974, 1977b; Greene 1978; Kurland, chapter 6, this volume). By arranging the marriage of own-children with sister's-children, he can be sure that some of his grandchildren, in whom he also invests, are in fact his descendants. If he is the genitor of his own children, then his grandchildren are that much more closely related to him and among themselves.[6]

Marriage coalitions of this sort—bilateral cross-cousin marriages linking the same groups of relatives—appear to make considerable sense when viewed as social strategies to maximize inclusive fitness and secure mating opportunities in highly competitive situations. I have elsewhere (1974) shown that Yąnomamö groups that practice first cross-cousin marriage more regularly than others are characterized by: (1) a faster rate of growth than others, (2) larger village size and therefore greater advantage in a milieu of chronic warfare, (3) younger age at first marriage for men, (4) greater variation in reproductive success among males, and (5) higher degrees of within-group relatedness, which appear to have an influence on internal village amity and cohesion (Chagnon 1975).

Models Let us return to our village fissioning example as specified in the model given in figure 4–3a. If the village were comprised of just these two sets of relatives (two patrilineages "A" and "B" bound to each other in marriage-exchange obligations), internal harmony would probably be high and conflicts within the group rare. The headman, probably one of the two older lineage heads (or perhaps both as co-headmen), would have very little difficulty or even opportunity to stop arguments and fights: all the adult males are (1) his sons, (2) his brothers-in-law, or (3) his daughters' husbands, who are obligated to heed his advice and defer to him.

I have provided, to the right of figure 4–3a, a much more simplified representation of the processes, rules, events, and prescriptions entailed in figure 4–3a. The simplified model (figure 4–3a′) is the kind of "structural" model commonly used by anthropologists to "represent" a society, like the Yąnomamö, that is characterized by (1) patrilineal descent; (2) bilateral cross-cousin marriage—every male is marrying a female who is simultane-

[5] Even if a man is not the genitor of his wife's children, the children may in fact share some of his genes: Yąnomamö men are frequently related to their wives.
[6] Paternity probability appears to be very high among the Yąnomamö, based on paternity exclusion tests conducted by my medical colleagues at the Department of Human Genetics, University of Michigan Medical School. Using several different antigen systems we tested blood samples from parent/offspring triads and, allowing for possible errors due to mislabeling specimens, estimated that the nonpaternity level is about ten percent.

ously his Father's Sister's Daughter (FZD) and Mother's Brother's Daughter (MBD); and (3) reciprocal exchange between two lineal descent groups (A and B). Furthermore, Yąnomamö kinship equations (Iroquois/Dravidian) (Chagnon 1974: Appendix C; Lizot 1971) are consistent with the model, and in fact men call all female cross-cousins (FZD and MBD) by the term used for "wife." While such a model (figure 4–3a′) parsimoniously represents all the crucial variables needed to describe the "structure" of Yąnomamö society, it in fact misrepresents it by glossing over important conditions and aspects of social behavior, only a few of which are shown in the models given in figures 4–3a and 4–3b. Thus, in the parsimonious model (3a′), all men of Lineage A in any generation are "represented" by a single individual and therefore it is difficult for nonspecialists to appreciate the fact that men of any particular generation in the same lineage might be competitors for the same potential mates. Even the specialists are prone to misunderstand the degree to which such models oversimplify the nature of reality. While figure 4–3a is only slightly more complex than the parsimonious model (3a′), it at least permits us to contemplate more variables—demographic imbalances, the fact that not all "brothers" are equally related, etc.—when we attempt to explain and understand kinship and marriage systems of this sort. I shall come back to this point at the end of the paper.

But few Yąnomamö villages approach "dual" composition this closely, even though there is a strong tendency for such a pattern to emerge in some villages (infra). More commonly, there are three or more sets of brothers (patrilineages), and this automatically leads to a situation in which options for marriage are numerous. Figure 4–3b illustrates how the more complex village composition sets into motion possible conflicts over marriage partners and how such competition expresses itself in fighting and village fissioning. In this situation (figure 4–3b), we have a village in which three older men and their children must arrange marriages among themselves, and how the marriage interests of some of the individuals will be in direct conflict with those of other individuals. In the first case, i.e., dual composition (figure 4–3a), the rule of lineage exogamy alone requires that members of Lineage A must seek their mates outside of their descent group to avoid incest violations (marriage within the lineage is, by Yąnomamö definition, incest). There is only one category of people who are not own-lineage members: the people in descent group "B." Thus members of A and B *must* exchange their children in marriage. But in the second situation, described in figure 4–3b, members of A can obtain mates from Lineage B *or* C, and members of B can get mates from A or C, etc. Let us assume that the village is just being founded and the initial population consists of just the three heads of the lineages (A, B, and C) along with their wives and children. Founder B (Generation 1) in this hypothetical example gives two daughters to Founder A for his sons and gets Founder A's two daughters back for his own sons. Founder B then gives his other two daughters to Founder C in exchange for C's daughters for his remaining two sons. If the village is relatively small, harmony is likely to prevail within the group, but the possibility exists that B's sons numbered "3" and "4" in Generation 2 would be tempted to seduce the wives of their brothers (individuals "5" and "6" of Generation 2). This would be even more likely if B's sons "3" and "4" had a different mother than sons "5" and "6," as shown in the diagram; full brothers would tend to have greater respect for each other's marital and domestic well-being than half-brothers. A cleavage within B's lineage already exists by virtue of the fact that B had two sets of children by two different, unrelated wives. This cleavage is made more apparent by the way in which B arranged the marriages of both sets of children, setting each set of children off on a matrimonial and political career that binds them to totally different sets of kin (A on the one hand, and C on the other). In the next generation (Generation 3), B's grandsons are members of B's lineage and are "brothers" according to Yąnomamö kinship classification (Chagnon 1968c, 1974), but from *their* vantage, there are some fundamental differences. Individuals "3" and "4" of Generation 3 are full brothers and more likely to cooperate strongly among themselves than with their other "brothers" of that generation. If they are to stick up for any of their other "brothers," it is very likely to be individuals "5" and "6" rather than "7" and "8."

Note that a demographic problem now exists in Generation 3: there are six adult males of Lineage B, all of whom are seeking a wife. They have only four sisters among them to give in exchange. Individuals "3," "4," "5," and "6" can count on having an important say in how *their* full sisters are to be deployed in marriage negotiations, but to make things balance and ensure that all four men get wives, they must come up with two more "sisters." Thus, they must try to persuade "7" and "8" to give up their full sisters, an event that is not to the best interests of "7" and "8." However, the cleavage in Lineage B aligns "3," "4," "5," and "6" with each other and they outnumber their "brothers" in the other half of the lineage. If "7" and "8" are young or show little tendency to resist, they may have little say in how their own sisters are given in marriage.[7] If they are mature

[7] The fathers of these men (individuals "5" and "6" of Generation 2) would, of course, be the more likely competitive manipulators of the marriage-arranging tactics, but the interests of the two sets of elders would differ as I describe them for the sons.

II. Kinship

adults and aggressive, it is to their best interests to give their sisters to individuals "9" and "10" of Lineage C in exchange for their sisters. Note, however, that the sisters of "9" and "10" of Lineage C would be legitimate mates for individuals "3," "4," "5," and "6" of Lineage B, since *all* members of Lineage B can marry into Lineage C (as well as into A).

But our example considers competition for *marriage* partners alone; competition for sexual partners—clandestine liaisons—is also part of the social fabric and complicates the internal social dynamics of villages. Both the competition for wives and the possibilities that sexual affairs will disrupt village life increase in the situation represented in figure 4–3b when the individuals of Generation 4 are entering adulthood, especially if demographic imbalances occur in such a way that men of more powerful groups have few sisters to exchange.

It should be clear from the discussion thus far that (1) in order to obtain women in marriage one must give some women in exchange; (2) as the composition of a village becomes more complex by adding more lineages, the types and frequencies of competitive encounters can increase markedly and the reproductive interests of individual males are less easily constrained by rules of exogamy and kinship obligations; (3) as villages grow over time, members of the same lineage grow progressively less related to one another in each generation and become one another's competitors for wives.

If we now add to this situation the fact that there is an overall scarcity of marriageable women in the Yąnomamö population, it should be clear that competition among males for mates can become a severely disruptive force in the internal ordering of large, heterogeneously composed villages. One expression that this takes is a tendency for men to represent themselves as aggressively as possible, indicating to potential competitors that affronts, insults, and cuckoldry will be immediately challenged and met with physical force. In addition, displays of masculinity, such as fighting prowess and *"waiter"* (ferocity) are admired by Yąnomamö women, and particularly aggressive men have an advantage both in soliciting the sexual favors of larger numbers of women as well as depressing the temptation of other men to seduce their wives. For example, it would be hazardous for a young braggart to try to seduce the wife of one of the village "fierce ones," for it is certain that the young man would be severely beaten in a club-fight by the older, fiercer men—and perhaps even killed. On the other hand, many of the older, fiercer men will openly flirt with and try to seduce the wives of younger men, and in some cases, they even do so to the wives of their younger "brothers."

Mate competition among Yąnomamö males must be seen in a broader context, i.e., against the general pattern of mating strategies by sex in the greater organic world. The first and most obvious feature of sexual reproduction bearing on the issue of competition is the fact that males "invest" much less in gametogenesis than females, producing millions of sperm daily. Females, by contrast, produce only a few ova monthly. (See Katchadourian and Lunde 1975:112–113 for estimates of sperm count per ejaculation, and Trivers 1972 for discussion of the investment differentials implied by the biological asymmetry of gametogenesis between males and females.) Thus, males are theoretically capable of producing many more offspring during their lifetimes than females. Given that any community contains more than one mature male and that all males are maximizing their reproductive success, there will be competition among them irrespective of the number of females in that population. Thus, the relative or absolute shortage of females in Yąnomamö villages should not be taken as a "peculiar" or "special" source of competition among males: competition would exist in any event, depending mainly on the degree to which males are involved in investing in the offspring they sire. Ultimately, the source of competition lies in the asymmetry between males and females in both gametogenesis and investment patterns.

Investment by parents inevitably entails resource accrual and disposition, and among humans there is always a flow of necessary resources to the expectant mother from other members of the group. The most common pattern, of course, is for the consort of the expectant female to invest in her and in her offspring. Among humans, the efficacy of the division of labor by sex and the pair bond make the family an efficient unit for assembling and distributing resources and for reproducing offspring. Thus, theoretically, any degree of parental investment by males—husbands—limits the degree to which males can be expected to compete for mates. If the resources required by males to successfully rear their mate's offspring to maturity are abundant and easy to acquire, then males can be expected to compete for multiple mates to the degree that they are capable of rearing their offspring to maturity. Where resources are not abundant and where it is costly to obtain (and defend) them, they may be insufficient to permit males to rear many offspring to maturity, and we should expect males to expend more effort at accruing resources and less effort competing for multiple mates.[8]

[8] However, if males can cuckold and have other males "invest" in the resulting offspring, that, too, is consistent with reproductive maximization strategy and is commonly found in the realm of biology.

II. Kinship

In human societies, however, cooperation and sharing of resources are such that *individual efforts* at economic production are not the limiting factor insofar as acquiring resources is concerned. Among the Yąnomamö, for example, sons-in-law, younger brothers, brothers-in-law, and other relatives contribute food, support, and aid to the mature males. The headman, for example, has a continuous flow of material and other resources—game, cultivated foods, wild foods, labor, services—to his family's hearth and probably subsists better than most individuals in the village. In brief, insofar as resources are concerned, he is in a good position to be able to invest in his mates' children and ipso facto in a good position to acquire multiple spouses. Reciprocally, he helps his younger male kinsmen to secure mates, takes enormous and frequently mortal risks on behalf of his kin during periods of active raiding, and keeps order and relative peace within the village. His ability to acquire resources is predicated on the size and extent of his following, and this resource base likewise permits him to compete effectively for additional mates. As will be demonstrated in chapter 12, headmen *are* more successful in obtaining multiple spouses and siring more offspring than other men of comparable age. (See also Chagnon, chapter 14, this volume, for further discussion of paternal investment, status differences, and reproductive success.)

One of the implications of this argument is that anthropologists will have to take a much more sophisticated view of the relationships between resources available to local populations, competition within and between groups, and reproductive variations within populations. What makes polygyny a possible mating strategy for some males cannot be read directly from an undifferentiated per capita consumption statistic that gives an "average" level of consumption for the group. *How* the resources are distributed and utilized within the group by particular individuals is a far more important factor, even in egalitarian societies characterized by the "domestic mode of production." Wherever polygyny occurs, one should expect differential utilization of resources; and the important question at this point is how individual strategies of production and reproduction are organized, and how this organization relates to inclusive fitness interests of individuals of both sexes and at different points in their life cycle (see also Goody 1976).

Should the above general relationship between resource availability, paternal investment patterns, competition for mates, and polygyny be essentially correct, it would appear that among the Yąnomamö resources are sufficiently abundant to permit a relatively high amount of competition for multiple spouses (see Chagnon and Hames, 1979). In short, it is reasonable to interpret mate competition in terms of relative numbers of males and females in existing Yąnomamö villages as *proximate* determinants of immediate behavior, but, in evolutionary terms, mate competition ultimately derives from the asymmetry in gametogenesis and the costs of investment by males and females. One should expect mate competition to obtain in a wide range of demographic (sex-ratio) situations, provided that resources required by males in their investment obligations remain relatively abundant and/or are differentially utilized by males. In the discussion that follows, therefore, I focus on the proximate terms; a later chapter (chapter 12) dealing with sex-ratio variations will consider the longer-range dimensions of mate competition.

The absolute shortage of females in the Yąnomamö population is a reality that is quite simple to document by taking a census of a large number of villages (see chapter 12 for age/sex distribution). How that shortage actually comes into being is difficult to document in a scientifically satisfying way, but the major logical possibilities are few in number: (1) physiological processes that result in the conception and/or birth of fewer female children, (2) preferential female infanticide at birth such that fewer females are permitted to survive, and (3) differential treatment of female children shortly after birth such that female infant mortality is higher than male infant mortality. Yąnomamö sex-ratio variations are dealt with in a different paper in this volume (Chagnon, Flinn, and Melancon, chapter 12); here it will suffice to say that there is an overall shortage of females in the Yąnomamö population, a shortage that is more pronounced in the younger age categories (see table 4–1, p. 113).

In the competition among males to find mates, there are, first of all, not enough females to go around even if each male acquired only one wife. This problem is dampened in part by the differences in ages of males and females at first marriage: girls are promised in marriage as early as late infancy and, in a few cases, even before they are born. Thus a larger fraction of the female population is marriageable. Cohabitation begins later in a girl's life, usually shortly after her first menses, but copulation is relatively common even before first menses. Males marry between the ages of sixteen and twenty, and thus are from five to eight years senior to their wives in first marriages. Young men from particularly prominent lineages have an advantage, for their elder brothers and men of their fathers' generation are usually more successful at finding them spouses earlier than would be the case for young men from smaller lineages.

Complicating the competition for marriageable girls is the tendency for males from the politically prominent, larger lineages to have multiple spouses: headmen in particular are especially successful in acquiring multiple wives, and very often the younger brothers of headmen are likewise successful in obtaining two or more wives (see Chagnon et al., chapter 12). It is common, in addition, for headmen to obtain additional wives and later pass them on to their younger brothers. Finally, there are taboos against coitus during pregnancy and for more than two years after the birth of a woman's child while the woman is nursing her infant. A polygynous headman, for example, might have as many as four or five wives, but it can happen that all four are either pregnant or nursing a newborn—and the husband may not have sexual relationships with any of them. He must therefore satisfy his sexual desires by seducing the wives of other men. The situation is even more restricting, sexually, for men that have only one wife—or no wife at all. It would be fair to say that most adult male Yąnomamö have healthy sexual appetites and are usually alert for opportunities to engage in sexual affairs with any woman who is not otherwise prohibited as a sexual partner because of incest proscriptions.

Indeed, even in the latter situation, the particularly "fierce" men do not seem to be especially concerned about engaging in incestuous sexual affairs with kinswomen, and the tendency to engage in incestuous sexual liaisons is strongly identified in Yąnomamö beliefs with male aggressiveness and "waiteri" qualities.[9] Moreover, some men, often headmen, break the incest prohibitions and formally marry "sisters" (i.e., parallel cousins who, in their kinship classification, are called by "sister" terms and are prohibited as marriage and sexual partners), setting into motion a redefinition of whole categories of people and opening up new marriage possibilities for the brothers of the initial violator (see Chagnon 1968a, for an example of this). Thus, some headmen might flout the rules and marry women to whom they are related as "brother," an act that takes considerable boldness. Their brothers, who might have been unwilling to be the first to break the incest prohibition, then manipulate the situation to their own advantage: since the headman, their brother, calls his mate "wife" instead of "sister," *they* in turn use this as a precedent. They begin calling *her* sisters by "wife" terms rather than by the correct "sister" terms, thereby making themselves eligible to marry the sisters of the headman's wife!

The redefinition of these women as "legitimate" mates for the headmen's brothers sets into motion jealousies and resentment among the men

[9] The association with "waiteri" qualities was aptly put by one of my informants, who was bragging about his son's potential qualities: "My son is going to be really fierce when he grows up! He'll probably commit incest all the time!"

in other lineages who had, through the incest proscriptions, a prior privileged claim to these women. They now must compete with the political power of the village for opportunities to marry the very women that their traditional rules specified as legitimate mates for them and illegitimate for members of the headman's lineage.[10]

Security and the ability to attract and keep wives in such a milieu are difficult, but can be optimized or maximized by entering into long-term reciprocal marriage ties with individuals in other, similar-sized lineages and agreeing to exchange women back and forth over time. Even when there are demographic imbalances, such as a situation where a man has two sons and four daughters, it would be to the benefit of his lineal descendants (sons especially) for him to give all four daughters in marriage and accept just two in return for his two sons. He might, for example, give all four daughters to the single son of his brother-in-law in exchange for his brother-in-law's two daughters. This binds the two groups intimately together and "obligates" them to continue in the next generation, even though there is a temporary imbalance. A man with four wives is certain to have many children, and the female children are subsequently "returned" as marriage partners to the sons of the polygynous man's brother-in-law.

Investing marriageable females in this fashion can also be considered as a prudent move in a system of mate competition where there are "cheaters." A significant number of Yąnomamö arguments and fights occur when wife-givers renege on a promise. In some cases, the wife-receivers will appropriate the woman by force, dragging her away from her family. In terms of a bookkeeping analogy, the wife-givers have overexpended by promising the same girl to several men; they cannot deliver her to more than one, yet they have taken advantage of bride-service from one or more males or have enjoyed the security, if the marriage promise involved two villages, of an alliance with neighbors. Given the possibility of reneging on marriage promises, it would be to the advantage of a father with several daughters to give them *all* to men in those descent groups that are linked by several generations of reciprocal exchange even though at that time he might receive fewer in return for his sons. A nubile female is a kind of resource that cannot be stored and hoarded until a more propitious "investment situation" emerges. If the father must cede her in marriage, then it is to his advantage to give her to those people who would seem more likely to reciprocate in the future and less likely to cheat. Because of demographic

[10] Chagnon 1968c, 1972; Chagnon and Fredlund, in preparation.

II. Kinship

fluctuations, most families with marriageable sons and daughters eventually find themselves in a temporary situation when they have more sons than daughters. The probability of later getting a reciprocal return would appear to be highest when the parties to the exchange are linked by several generations of similar exchanges and are, for that reason, cognatic relatives as well as wife-givers/wife-receivers to each other. An examination of the reciprocal aspects of exchange, statistically, reveals that there are always imbalances between matrimonially-paired descent groups at any specific point of time. However, the history of those same groups shows that over several generations the imbalances even out—despite the fact that the Yąnomamö have a very limited verbal, numerical system, "one," "two," and "more-than-two" (Chagnon 1968a, 1968b)—and each group receives about as many women as it has given to the other. This tends to be true only provided that the two exchanging groups are of approximately the same size. Otherwise, a numerically-dominant group attempts to coerce smaller groups into ceding more women than they themselves are willing to give. A specific example of balanced reciprocal exchange will be given below.

Mate competition among the Yąnomamö is, therefore, not simply a matter of individuals striving to attract any and all members of the opposite sex. Success depends on aid from close male kin in the patrilineal line on the one hand, and expectations of reciprocity from individuals in other patrilines. It also happens that the members of the other patriline are kinsmen as well, a direct consequence of the fact that earlier marriage exchanges in ascending generations have bound the two groups not only by alliance, but also by blood ties. (See Chagnon and Bugos, this volume, chapter 8, for "alliance" and "descent" aspects of Yąnomamö marriage.)

It is customary for anthropologists to distinguish sharply between cross- and parallel cousins and to emphasize the "solidarity" of the lineage group. These traditional distinctions and emphases must be reconsidered in examining Yąnomamö marriage practices, especially to understand how kinship—cognatic kinship ties—function to keep groups or coalitions bound to each other when a village fissions. Viewed as a biosocial process, village fissioning separates clusters of individuals who are more closely related among themselves than they are to those from whom they fission (see Chagnon 1975 for data). One could argue that it is the reproductive interests of such clusters of closely related individuals that keep them together, for they continue to optimize or maximize their reproductive success by removing themselves from a competitive situation in which other competitors are invading their resources, i.e., appropriating their potential mates. Setting off on a new political career as a separate, smaller village reestablishes a mating system that is usually much more to the advantage of the matrimonially bound kin groups and their respective members.

When a fission occurs, however, it is not always true that the members of each newly established village "gain" to the same degree in the reduction of competition for mates (Chagnon ms.). It is generally true that the putative solidarity of the lineage group disappears, for distantly related members of the same lineage separate from each other and remain with the lineage segments to which they are bound by blood and marriage (Chagnon 1968a, 1968b, 1968c). This can be seen diagrammatically in figure 4–3b: when the village fissions, the line of cleavage running vertically through the middle of Lineage B will define membership in the two new villages. Those to the left of the cleavage ("B1" segment) will remain with the members of Lineage A and start their own village. Those to the right of the cleaving line will remain with members of Lineage C, constituting a separate village. Thus, Lineage B will be redistributed in two new villages and constitute roughly half the membership of those two villages, returning the composition more to a "dual" pattern of the kind shown in figure 4–3a, where competition for mates is less severe and more readily constrained by exogamic rules.

The process of village growth, followed by fissioning, occurs at such a rate that in most areas of the tribe the adults in all villages have, during their lifetimes, fissioned away from others and have relatively large numbers of kinsmen in nearby villages. Nevertheless, the closest relatives of any individual remain in the same village and the process of village fissioning leads to the separation of more remote kinsmen from each other (see Chagnon 1975 for data on coefficients of relatedness before and after village fissions and Chagnon, ms. a, for further analysis of the consanguineal aspects of village fissioning).

Egocentric Relatedness and Kinship

The resolution of mate competition by forming marriage alliances with other kin groups and reciprocally exchanging marriageable partners over several generations leads, as would be expected, to the build-up of relatively close degrees of consanguineal kinship between individuals in the village. The more often that matrimonially bound groups of kin exchange mates and the longer, generationally, they have done it, the closer the degree of relatedness between any particular individual and any other to whom he or she is compared within that kinship group. Periodic exchanges between *all* lineal descent groups occur, contributing to the build-up of relatedness among all co-residents of the village (see Chagnon, chapter 14, table 14-1, and table 4-1, below, for statistics).

Competition for women and the corresponding tendency for men to maximize their chances of obtaining mates through forming and continuing exchange coalitions lead, as I have suggested, to the "bonding" of kin groups—patrilineal descent groups—to each other. However, not all patrilineages are as intimately "integrated" into the village through such bonding patterns as some. For example, a small faction from one village leaves its natal group and joins another village, beginning a coalition based on marriage with some particular kin group in the new village. The offspring in the first generation are not likely to have many relatives in the village, but as they continue and build on the coalition by marrying into the appropriately bound kin groups, *their* offspring become increasingly "integrated" through kinship to the rest of the village members. This can be related to the notion of group "cohesiveness" and "solidarity." We can view the process of village fissioning as, essentially, a failure of the "integrating mechanisms," a diminution of "solidarity." Anthropologists have long argued that solidarity is a critical feature in tribal societies (Durkheim 1958; Lévi-Strauss 1949). Moreover, anthropologists have also argued that integration or solidarity in tribal societies is very much a function of kinship, descent, and marriage alliances. It is not, therefore, such a difficult stretch of the imagination to view social solidarity in populations like the Yąnomamö as deriving largely from kinship ties, and to conclude that measurements of the latter in some sense reflect the "amount" or "quality" of solidarity (Chagnon 1975).

It is clear that as villages grow in size, the amount of overall relatedness between individuals diminishes, in part because competition for mates often leads to marrying more remotely related spouses (second cousins instead of first cousins, for example). Larger villages tend to attract hangers-on who migrate into them to seek mates and who are either unrelated to the village members or only remotely related. Women abducted from distant villages also contribute, through their reproductive efforts, to the diminution of relatedness (Chagnon 1975). Thus, over time, the larger a village becomes, the more likely it is that the average degree of relatedness among its members will decline. At a certain point the village fissions: i.e., "solidarity" is reduced to such a tenuous level that kinship amity can no longer integrate the village members into a cooperative, amicable whole, and clusters of more-related individuals separate from the group. In brief,

I suggest that the amount of relatedness in a village is a measure of the village's "solidarity" and that the more closely related individuals there are in a village, the larger the village can grow before a critical threshold is reached and fission occurs (Chagnon 1975). And it seems clear that the greatest threat to internal harmony is the chronic competition between men for sexual access to women: fissioning reduces this competition.

Method of measuring kinship closeness

It is possible to discuss closeness and remoteness of kinship and to quantify kinship relatedness in a precise mathematical way. I have been using a variant of Sewall Wright's Inbreeding Coefficient to discuss quantitative aspects of Yąnomamö relatedness (Chagnon 1974, 1975), despite the fact that Wright's statistic ("F") was developed to express the probability that alleles at a particular locus on a chromosome are identical by descent from a common ancestor. Wright's formula is

$$F = \Sigma[(\tfrac{1}{2})^{n_1 + n_2 + 1} + (1 + F_A)]$$

where n_1 is the number of generational links back to the common ancestor through one parent and n_2 the number of links back to the same ancestor through the other parent. The total value of F results from summing the coefficients over all separate inbreeding loops, i.e., when there are two or more common ancestors. The expression $(1 + F_A)$ is the inbreeding coefficient of the common ancestor. I have eliminated this expression from my calculations, mainly because it is not possible to collect genealogies that are sufficiently deep (six, seven, eight generations) to determine the inbreeding coefficient of remote ancestors.[11]

Doubling the inbreeding coefficient of an individual gives the coefficient of relatedness between the parents of that individual. Since the inbreeding coefficient and the coefficient of relatedness are both a function of genealogical "steps" or "loops," it is possible to express the relatedness

---

[11] Eliminating the expression $(1 + F_A)$ is probably justified in a behavioral sense as well. Extremely remote events of past generations are of relatively little moment when one is concerned with the immediate tactics and strategies of individuals who are arranging marriages, lining themselves up in factions and supporting others in conflicts. In small villages characterized by a long history of previous consanguineal marriage, for example, all related individuals are related in many different ways—some of them very remote ways. It is the closest relationships that appear to count most, and to establish what these are, only a few generations' genealogical depth is required and "inbreeding" of remote ancestors is superfluous.

between *any* pair of related individuals as a statistic. I have labeled my modification of Wright's F-statistic "F_g," the Coefficient of *Genealogical* Relatedness. F_g is an estimate of r (see chapter 1:14–15) using all known geneologies and assuming paternal links in these geneologies are correct.

The Data Base

While I have visited some fifty or more Yąnomamö villages that are distributed over most of the tribal area, my major field research effort has been devoted to an intensive study of the demographic, genealogical, and social attributes of just a fraction of these. The sample, in fact, consists of two clusters of villages—the two clusters shown in figure 4–2 (above, p. 94) as the "Shamatari" and the "Namoweiteri." The population for these villages consists of 3,270 individuals, of whom 1,541 were alive in 1975, the date of my last census.[12] Of the seventeen variables I have coded for most of the 3,270 individuals, only a few are relevant to the following discussion of kinship relatedness (see Chagnon 1974 for a discussion of some of the variables).

In calculating relationships between individuals for comparative purposes, only four variables are of interest: (1) population identity ("1" for Shamatari, "2" for Namoweiteri), (2) living or dead ("0" and "1" respectively), (3) village identity (each village is designated by a number, such as 01, 04, 05, 19, 49, etc. up to 99), and (4) genealogical data. The genealogical information is, of course, more complete for younger people than for old people or people long dead, since it is collected by interviewing informants whose knowledge about the present is more precise. For the youngest people, the depth of the genealogies is usually five or six generations, occasionally seven; for the oldest people, it may be no more than two or three generations. The individuals—"Egos"—are all assigned a discrete, four-digit identification number. The parents of each Ego are listed by their respective identification numbers and also occur as Egos. *They* have parents, who in turn are listed as Egos, and so on, until the apex of the pedigree is reached and the genealogical information is exhausted. A computer program, especially developed to analyze these data, searches the Ego array and generates a complete, exhaustive pedigree for as many generations as there are data. In comparing *two* Egos, an ancestor

---

[12] Of these 1,541, only 1,326 are considered here—the residents of just the thirteen villages listed in table 4–1.

tree is generated for each one and the common ancestors in each tree are identified. The exact genealogical path from each Ego to that particular common ancestor is specified, the Coefficient of Genealogical Relatedness calculated, etc.

An example might be instructive and simplify the illustration. Village 14 (see table 4–1) of Population 1 contains 119 individuals. The first individual in the list of residents for that village is a woman, born in 1950, whose name is Amahimi and whose identification number is 0055. The next Ego in that village is a girl named Amima whose identification number is 0063. Comparing them as described above to establish how they are related to each other (if at all), we learn that in fact they are related as follows:

0055 and 0063 are related as:
FMF DD, $F_g = 0.0312$, Common Ancestor $= 1221$
MMFFSDD, $F_g = 0.0078$, Common Ancestor $= 1222$
Cumulative $F_g = 0.0390$

where F = Father, M = Mother, S = Son, and D = Daughter.

Since they are related in two discrete ways via two common ancestors, two 'loops' are defined, each associated with a value of F_g. The total relationship between them is the sum of the F_g values. Many compared individuals are related to each other as many as ten or fifteen ways—a reflection of the degree to which their ancestors intermarried. Thus the number of 'loops' reflects, in an important sense, the quality of the bond between both individuals and their respective lineages.

Table 4–1 summarizes a staggering amount of genealogical/kinship data of this kind. Each individual in every village was compared to *every other individual* in the same village and a summary of their relatedness was made. Continuing our example to illustrate the procedure, Ego 0055 was compared to all 118 other residents of Village 14. She was related to 102 of them by at least one common ancestor, but in most cases she was related by many loops. In fact, the average number of loops between Ego 0055 and all 102 other (related) co-residents was 5.176 (not shown in table 4–1); i.e., *each* of the 102 known relatives she has living in the village with her is related to her, on the average, more than five different ways. Her average coefficient of relatedness to these 102 people is $F_g = 0.0985$, a value only slightly below that associated with the relatedness between full first cousins. If we average in the unrelated individuals (i.e., divide the total coefficient of relatedness by 118 instead of 102), Ego 0055 is, on the average,

Table 4–1   Aspects of Relatedness within Yanomamö Villages   Six villages of Population 1 (top half) and seven villages of Population 2 (bottom half) were examined and the following variables compared (columns): Village = numerical identification of village (see figure 4–2 for historical relationships); Size = population of village in 1975; 0–13 Sex Ratio = number of males 13 years old or younger divided by the number of females 13 years old or younger, the quotient in turn divided by 100; Average Prop. Rels. = the average proportion of co-residents that any individual in the village is related to genealogically; S. D. = standard deviation of Average Prop. Rels.; Average Mean Relatedness All = the average mean relatedness of any individual in the village to all other co-residents, whether or not a genealogical connection exists to all (see text); S. D. = standard deviation; Average Mean Relatedness, Cons. = the average mean relatedness of any individual in the village to just those genealogically demonstrable consanguines (see text); S. D. = standard deviation. The bottom rows summarize the variables for the pooled villages of both populations.

Village Comparisons

Village	Size	0–13 Sex Ratio	Average Prop. Rels.	S.D.	Average Mean Relatedness All	S.D.	Average Mean Relatedness, Cons.	S.D.
Population 1								
9	97	1.17	.923	.165	.111	.018	.124	.019
14	119	1.50	.889	.153	.106	.018	.117	.017
16	116	1.47	.881	.195	.092	.014	.112	.029
21	95	0.83	.955	.139	.167	.024	.172	.023
49	77	2.13	.804	.188	.098	.019	.127	.025
99	37	1.43	.880	.188	.167	.034	.186	.034
Population 2								
1	100	1.59	.584	.281	.067	.018	.137	.052
5	127	1.07	.737	.238	.063	.013	.102	.043
6	94	1.64	.578	.227	.060	.011	.106	.021
7	116	1.42	.716	.214	.071	.015	.101	.021
8	122	1.68	.638	.281	.060	.015	.127	.054
18	147	1.43	.851	.205	.071	.011	.087	.022
19	78	1.19	.862	.197	.090	.013	.106	.025

Population Comparisons

Population 1: N = 542			.892	.172	.118	.025	.133	.027
Population 2: N = 784			.714	.259	.068	.014	.108	.038

related to *everyone* in the village by a value of $F_g = 0.0845$. The next Ego, 0063, was related to 93 of the 118 other co-residents, with an average value of $F_g = 0.0578$ to actual consanguineal co-residents and $F_g = 0.0452$ to all residents, the unrelateds averaged in. These calculations were continued until all 119 residents were individually compared to all others. The *averages* of these calculations are the values given in table 4–1. Thus, in Village 14, each individual is related, on the average, to 88.9 percent of all the residents of the village. The average coefficient of relatedness between any individual chosen at random and any of his consanguineal relatives is 0.117, slightly below the value of full first cousins. The average coefficient of relatedness between any individual and *any* other, whether or not they are demonstrably related, is $F_g = 0.106$. The latter statistic is useful to gain an appreciation of the overall consanguineal structure of a village, since it will be a low value if a village is comprised of just a few closely related individuals and a large number of unrelated people. It will be relatively high if the village contains many related individuals but only a few hangers-on or unrelated individuals.

Discussion of table 4–1

A number of striking features regarding Yąnomamö kinship and mate competition emerge from the data in table 4–1. First, as the sex ratios for the 0–13-year-old category indicate, all villages (except Village 21) have a severe shortage of young girls. In one village there are over twice as many young boys as there are young girls (Village 49). The conditions under which mate competition occurs will, therefore, characterize the population for some time to come and will be particularly severe in specific villages.

Second, it is clear that there are high amounts of internal relatedness in the population as a whole as shown by the average proportion of relatives, but there is wide variation between villages in this regard. In Village 21, for example, every individual is, on the average, related to over 95 percent of the rest of the members of the village, but in Village 01 that value is only 58.4 percent. These figures, however, gloss over some very important facts: there are individuals within both villages who have very few relatives and there are individuals who are related to nearly every other co-resident. Moreover, individuals are related more closely to some of their relatives and less closely to others, and these pieces of information about individuals might be critical to understanding both how they are treated within their villages and how they, in turn, treat other individuals.

These variations can be seen, in part, in the diagrams below (figure 4–5), which break the relatedness data down into comparisons of the proportion of people in a village who have varying proportions of relatives in the village. These data will be discussed below. For the time being, it should be noted that the Shamatari villages (Population 1) are more "consanguineal" than the Namoweiteri villages (Population 2). The "Population Comparisons" portion of table 4–1 brings this out most clearly. All differences in means are significant at the 0.05 level (t-test).

Third, both the values of F_g among relatives and among all residents are considerably higher in the Shamatari population than in the Namoweiteri population. This is relatable in large measure to the high proportion of marriages with close consanguineal relatives over several generations on the one hand, and the peculiarities of differential reproductive success of Shamatari males on the other (Chagnon 1974; Chagnon, this volume, chapter 14; Chagnon, Flinn, and Melancon, chapter 12). Among the Shamatari, it appears that extremes of reproductive success are associated with the practice of particular lineages to "bind" to each other more closely than is the case in the Namoweiteri population. Put into other terms, the males of one Shamatari lineage in particular (Lineage 1222, so named for the identification number of its most remote identifiable male ancestor) have been extremely successful in obtaining women for their sons, with the consequence that many polygynous marriages in that population are associated with dramatic levels of reproductive success. If the 30 most fertile males in the entire data set are identified and placed on a genealogy, a very high fraction of them are males who belong to Lineage 1222 (see Chagnon, this volume, chapter 14, for this genealogy and data). One man in particular had 43 children; one of his sons had 33 children, illustrating that success in mate competition by the father has a pronounced influence on the success in mate competition of the sons and daughters . . . and, for that matter, grandchildren.

In short, table 4–1 reveals that very large fractions of people in all Yąnomamö villages studied are (a) related among themselves, (b) closely related in many cases, and (c) that there is variation among villages in overall relatedness. In addition, whole *subpopulations* differ from each other in the levels of relatedness despite the fact that the "ideal" marriage rules and kinship equations are identical for all members of these populations. The differences stem from the consequences of individual strategies and the degree to which marriage alliances and coalitions successfully resolve the problem of finding mates.

Village fissioning, lineage composition, and kinship

The coalitions and marriage alliances are essentially agreements made between individuals (older men) representing their close male and female relatives. They attempt to obtain young women for marriage partners for their sons or younger brothers, and promise to give their daughters and sisters in return. These clusters of marriage-arrangers are essentially the members of shallow patrilineages—men who are related among themselves through the male line, as described in figure 4–3a and 4–3b above.

In the competition for marriage partners, it is important to have large numbers of patrilineal relatives to aid you in finding a mate, if you are a male, or to protect you from harsh treatment at the hands of a fierce husband if you are a female. The fissioning scheme discussed above in figure 4–3a and 4–3b implied that lineages segment and become redistributed among several villages. The evidence given in table 4–2 shows how this happens and that, within particular populations, some lineages are represented in all or nearly all the villages that have a common origin.

If we examine the kinship relatedness data in all villages and arranged them in terms of lineages, the relationship between strategies of mate competition through alliances, village fissioning, and kinship ties will become clear. Table 4–3 summarizes the relevant information. Part A provides the variables for villages in Population 1 (Shamatari) and part B for Population 2 (Namoweiteri).

The villages are broken down into lineages, giving (a) the size of the lineage, (b) the average number of relatives in the village each member of that lineage has, (c) the number of relationship loops on the average each person in that lineage has to all related co-residents, (d) the average coefficient of relatedness of each lineage member to all relatives (lineal and non-lineal) in the village, and (e) the average relatedness of each lineage member to all co-residents, whether or not they are related to them (see above for a discussion of the value of this statistic).

For example, in Village 14 of Population 1, the largest lineage in the village is 2936, composed of 35 men, women, and children who are related to each other through male (patrilineal) links. Each of these 35 individuals is, on the average, related to 112.6 of the 119 co-residents an average of 5.12 different ways, etc. The adult males of this lineage arrange the marriages of their sisters and daughters and, politically, are the single most important group in the village. The headman of the village, as is the case in all known Yąnomamö villages, comes from the largest lineage and, in fact, the headman of this village is the man who led the fission separat-

Table 4-2 **Distribution of Major Lineages by Village** The male "founders" of each major lineage are listed across the top by identification number (1222, 2967, etc.) and the total number of agnatic (through males) descendants each has in the core villages (09, 14, 16, etc.) is given beneath the founder's identification number. Note that particular individuals (founders) have most of their lineal descendants concentrated in the villages of one population bloc (Population 1 or 2). The individuals who do not belong to these major lineages are not enumerated in table 4–2; the exact number of these can be determined by summing all the numbers for each village and subtracting this value from the village size (given in table 4–1).

		1222	2967	2936	0081	0200	1443	2700	2954	2886	1598	2856	0916	3445	1829	3466	2250
Population 1	09	48	11	7	0	1	6	14	0	0	0	0	0	0	0	0	0
	14	20	27	35	0	25	1	1	0	5	0	0	1	0	0	0	0
	16	56	5	2	2	1	32	13	0	0	0	0	0	0	0	0	0
	21	4	74	7	1	5	0	1	0	0	0	0	0	0	0	0	0
	49	23	26	20	0	0	4	0	0	0	0	0	0	0	0	0	0
	99	5	1	5	0	17	1	1	0	0	0	0	0	0	0	0	0
Population 2	01	0	0	5	0	0	0	0	9	0	41	3	0	5	0	1	5
	05	3	3	1	1	0	7	0	44	27	6	4	10	0	0	0	0
	06	4	9	6	0	0	0	0	19	24	0	5	19	0	0	0	0
	07	8	1	2	1	3	0	1	41	22	6	0	4	0	23	0	0
	08	0	0	1	0	0	0	0	6	7	38	1	1	10	0	16	9
	18	0	2	0	2	0	1	1	42	53	2	35	0	5	0	0	0
	19	0	4	0	0	0	0	0	30	31	5	3	0	0	0	0	0

Villages

Table 4–3 **Egocentric Relatedness by Lineages** The six villages of Population 1 (part A of table 4–3) and the seven villages of Population 2 (part B of table 4–3) have been analyzed to show the correlation of high degrees of interpersonal relatedness with membership in the larger lineages. Thus, in Village 09 of Population 1, there are 48 individuals belonging to Lineage 1222; these 48 individuals have, on the average, 92.4 consanguineal relatives in the village, are related to each of these relatives an average of 4.06 different ways by an average coefficient of genealogical relationship of 0.137. The members of this lineage in Village 09 are, on the average, related to *all* members of the village (non-consanguines averaged in) by a coefficient of relatedness of 0.132. Note that the individuals (Others) who do not belong to the large lineages of the village(s) have generally much lower values of these measures of relatedness.

A. Population 1 Shamatari

Lineage	No.	Average No. Cons. Relatives	Loop Avg.	Average Relatedness to Relatives	Average Relatedness to Everyone
Village 09					
1222	48	92.4	4.06	0.137	0.132
2700	14	91.1	3.15	0.130	0.123
2967	11	88.5	3.38	0.095	0.089
Others	24	79.7	2.62	0.106	0.073
Village 14					
2967	27	106.9	4.52	0.105	0.094
0200	25	105.1	4.39	0.125	0.110
1222	20	108.7	4.52	0.098	0.091
2936	35	112.6	5.12	0.144	0.136
Others	12	82.0	3.00	0.090	0.064
Village 16					
1222	56	107.4	4.44	0.097	0.091
1443	32	104.4	3.58	0.128	0.114
2700	13	100.1	4.09	0.104	0.089
Others	15	73.4	2.86	0.136	0.052
Village 21					
2967	74	91.8	6.60	0.190	0.186
2936	7	92.0	6.42	0.132	0.130
0200	5	91.8	6.97	0.113	0.110
1222	4	89.8	5.91	0.145	0.138
Others	5	53.2	3.47	0.077	0.067

Table 4–3 *(cont.)*

Lineage	No.	Average No. Cons. Relatives	Loop Avg.	Average Relatedness to Relatives	Average Relatedness to Everyone
Village 49					
2967	26	66.5	3.74	0.142	0.123
1222	23	61.1	3.06	0.096	0.079
2936	20	63.9	4.37	0.126	0.104
Others	8	36.6	2.39	0.173	0.062
Village 99					
0200	17	34.2	4.25	0.221	0.209
1414	6	30.3	4.63	0.245	0.205
1222	5	28.4	3.40	0.113	0.094
2936	5	32.4	4.27	0.136	0.125
Others	4	26.3	2.63	0.101	0.072
B. Population 2 Namoweiteri					
Village 01					
1598	41	73.5	5.27	0.120	0.089
2954	9	71.0	5.20	0.143	0.103
1805	8	74.5	4.40	0.114	0.081
3445	5	37.4	2.95	0.113	0.028
2936	5	44.8	2.33	0.218	0.047
Others	32	35.1	2.54	0.155	0.034
Village 05					
2954	44	106.0	3.81	0.088	0.074
2886	27	104.9	5.09	0.098	0.082
0916	10	88.0	2.97	0.101	0.058
1443	7	100.6	2.48	0.056	0.045
1598	6	95.8	3.58	0.069	0.053
2814	7	109.9	4.51	0.081	0.071
Others	26	52.7	2.31	0.158	0.033
Village 06					
2886	24	65.7	5.07	0.103	0.072
0916	19	59.2	2.99	0.121	0.070
2954	19	61.1	5.16	0.102	0.067
2967	9	39.8	3.42	0.073	0.031
Others	23	36.3	3.20	0.114	0.046
Village 07					
2954	41	94.6	4.92	0.101	0.081
1829	23	93.5	5.99	0.111	0.091
2886	22	91.8	5.87	0.089	0.072
1222	8	51.0	3.19	0.100	0.043
Others	22	49.8	3.17	0.104	0.039

Table 4-3 *(cont.)*

Lineage	No.	Average No. Cons. Relatives	Loop Avg.	Average Relatedness to Relatives	Average Relatedness to Everyone
Village 08					
1598	38	94.9	5.16	0.098	0.077
3466	16	95.4	6.24	0.115	0.090
3445	10	88.9	5.72	0.098	0.068
2250	9	38.1	2.17	0.155	0.035
Others	49	62.3	3.16	0.155	0.039
Village 18					
2954	42	133.3	5.61	0.087	0.080
2856	35	126.9	4.81	0.079	0.068
2886	53	131.2	5.06	0.083	0.074
3445	5	135.4	4.26	0.064	0.059
Others	12	50.3	2.85	0.138	0.035
Village 19					
2954	30	70.3	5.86	0.101	0.093
2886	31	70.6	7.05	0.112	0.103
1598	5	65.6	3.37	0.074	0.064
2967	4	59.8	4.21	0.085	0.062
Others	8	39.5	4.48	0.128	0.057

ing Village 14 from Village 21 some twenty-five or thirty years ago. Note the composition of both Village 21 and Village 14 and how the major lineages in both groups are the same.

The composition of Village 14 is "complex" and can be likened to the hypothetical situation described in figure 4-3b above: several equal-sized lineages with men competing among themselves for one another's sisters and daughters. Lineage exogamy requires only that the men of, for example, Lineage 2936 find their mates in some other lineage; no rules specify *which* lineage. If exogamy were the exclusive prescription guiding marriage, we might expect these men competing to find their mates in relatively equal numbers from all the other major lineages of the village. In fact, this is not the case, since reciprocity between the members of Lineage 2936 and just a *few* other lineages has prevailed. There are ten adult males in Village 14 who belong to Lineage 2936. Among them, they have had twenty-one marriages to date. In twelve of these, their wives came from Lineage 2967—the males of Lineage 2967 have 'invested' their daughters in the males of the strongest, politically speaking, lineage of the village. The men of 2967 gave many of their daughters in return. This pattern of reciprocal exchange has led to a concentration of relatedness: note that the individuals in Lineage 2936 are, on the average, related to 95 percent (113/119) of all village residents by an average $F_g = 0.136$—more than the value associated with full first cousins.

Let us compare another village to this pattern and relate it to our earlier discussion of figures 4–3a and 4–3b. Village 19 of Population 2 fissioned away from Village 18 in 1973–74, building a new site just yards away from the original village—a decision based on their desire to separate from their competitors on the one hand, and, on the other, to remain living close to them because of the intensity of raids from common enemies. The result was that the original, relatively heterogenous village (in terms of number and size of lineages) fissioned to produce at least one group whose composition approached duality: Village 19's membership is heavily dominated by the members of Lineages 2954 and 2886 (78 percent of the village members belong to these two lineages). Not surprisingly, the men of Lineage 2954 are bound, through marriage, to the people in Lineage 2886: the five adult males of Lineage 2954 have had nine marriages—eight of them to women in Lineage 2886. Conversely, the six adult men of Lineage 2886 have had eight marriages, six of them with women from Lineage 2954. We shall explore the genealogical and kinship implications of this below.

The point I make here is that internal harmony in Village 19 is likely to be higher than that in Village 14, since the major fraction of the adult males of the village is bifurcated into wife-givers and wife-takers whose interrelationships have been set by previous marriage exchanges and for whom it is relatively simple to continue harmony by continuing the reciprocal exchange of their daughters.

The most important general feature of the data shown in tables 4–3a and 3b is the fact that villages are composed of different lineages—interest groups—whose members are competing to find mates. A village with a "dual" pattern is likely to have fewer explosive encounters between competitors. A village with a heterogenous composition—one with several lineage groups of approximately equal size—is more likely to be fraught with internal strife, particularly if it is a large village. A village heavily dominated by just a single lineage (Village 21, for example) might also have fewer internal problems, since the adult males of the dominant lineage can keep order through the exercise of their political superiority—provided the men of that lineage are relatively closely related and not actively competing among themselves for the women of the several smaller lineages.

Finally, there are always some people in all villages (Others) who belong to no large political faction or lineage; they are fair game, insofar as the women are concerned, for the sexual advances of members of all the larger lineages. The men in the "other" category are the source of sexual controversy in most cases. Being less closely related to others in the village (see data in tables 4–3a and b), they are usually less constrained by incest prohibitions and more able to establish sexual liaisons with a larger fraction of the village women. However, they are discriminated against for the most part, and sexual infractions by them are generally more severely punished. This applies as well to "other" women. In Village 14, for example, there is one individual who has no relatives whatsoever; she is a captive from a distant village. Attractive to a larger number of males than most women in the village (she has no kin, and therefore all men may copulate with her), she is more often exposed to attempts to seduce her. Her husband is a jealous man. The mere suspicion that she has been unfaithful enrages him: on one occasion, he shot her with an arrow in the stomach, and she nearly died.[13] His violent actions are largely unrestrained, since she has no brothers to protect her. Villages that are allied, moreover, send young men to each other to look for mates. These men are always suspect, since they try to seduce the young girls in the village and, when caught, they flee for home. If the alliance is a particularly critical one for either or both villages, the culprit might be able to return after a cooling-off period and resume his bride-service for a promised wife. If the alliance is not critical, relationships between the two villages deteriorate.

In some cases, the people in the "Others" category are in fact related to many of the people in the village. This comes about in two ways. First, women who have been abducted from previous enemies reproduce in their captors' village and often have large numbers of descendants. If the villages later make peace, migrants who come to the captors' villages and marry into it are very often related to people there through the offspring of the original captive women. The composition of Villages 5, 6, and 7 for example (table 4–3b) reflects this phenomenon. Second, if two otherwise unrelated villages enter into a long-term alliance that involves the exchange of several marriageable people, then both will contain numbers of "outsiders" who are closely related among themselves—sets of brothers and sisters.

---

[13] Members of the New Tribes Mission heard of her injury and had her brought to their mission and flown to the Territorial Capital for surgery, without which she would have died.

Both tables 4–1 and 4–2 indicate that the various villages of Population 1 are more "consanguineal" than villages in Population 2. An analysis of village size and relatedness based on census data up to 1972 revealed that villages of Population 1 were able to grow larger before fissioning than those in Population 2. There was a clear correlation between the numerical size of a village and the amount and structure of relatedness as measured by F_g (Chagnon 1975). Since 1972, however, the health pattern has changed markedly and it is no longer possible to demonstrate the correlation with recent (post-1972) census data. In 1973–74, several of the Shamatari villages were struck by an exotic respiratory infection that was communicated to them through the contacts with outsiders they initiated in 1973. In one case, 43 percent of the members of one village died (mostly young children and old people). Again, the possibility of gaining access to exotic, manufactured goods (machetes, axes, aluminum cooking pots, fishhooks) by fissioning and migrating toward missions constituted a new force in the dynamics of Shamatari population structure: at least two villages (Villages 16 and 14) fissioned because portions of the original group wanted to move toward the missions where such goods were abundant, despite the fact that former Yąnomamö enemies lived at the missions. In brief, the influences of the outside world are now affecting the aboriginal demographic and social patterns. Still, it is clear that the Shamatari villages were, and still are, characterized by higher degrees of interpersonal relatedness, practice closer degrees of cousin marriage, and have traditionally grown to larger sizes than Namoweiteri villages. In terms of the solidarity implications of kinship relatedness, the Shamatari (Population 1) villages appear to have been able to do this because of the building-up of high levels of relatedness and, therefore, kinship amity—the amity in turn a consequence of their tendency to resolve mate competition by establishing long-term and enduring marriage alliances with closely related (cognatic) kin in other lineages.

It appears, in short, that favoring close kin in marriage alliances is a strategy that has enabled the Shamatari to resolve competition over mates while at the same time giving them a numerical advantage, through the larger size of their villages, in military competition with their neighbors.

The pattern continues, even with the effects of introduced diseases and modifications of the settlement pattern due to desires to obtain manufactured goods: village fissions after the 1973 epidemic deaths continue to result in the formation of new villages whose members are more closely related among themselves than they were in the pre-fission village. Such is the case in the recent fission of Village 14 into Villages 14 and 99, and the fission of Village 16 into Villages 16 and 49 (groups affected by the recent epidemic). The same is true in Population 2, where recent (post-1972) fissions in Village 8 (producing Villages 1 and 8) and Village 18 (producing 18 and 19) have led to smaller, but more highly intrarelated new villages (Chagnon, ms.).

Reciprocity and the structure of marriages

In discussing the composition of Village 19 above, I drew attention to the fact that the adult males of one of the two largest lineages obtained all but one of their wives from the other largest lineage and, conversely, the adult males of the second lineage obtained a large fraction of their wives from the first. The duality of the village structure in terms of lineage composition is maintained by reciprocal exchanges between members of the two lineages. These marriages and the kinship bonds that result from the birth of offspring add cohesion to the village, and create new obligations to continue to exchange marriage partners over time. These new marriages reinforce the accumulating bonds of amity between all members of the two lineages (see Chagnon and Bugos, chapter 8).

The strategy of resolving mate shortage by investing daughters reciprocally results in the development of consistent genealogical patterns— marriage "structures." These can be identified several different ways. One

Table 4–4   Patterns of Reciprocal Marriage Exchange in a Ya̧nomamö Village

Male Egos of Lineage 2954 [1]	Lineage of Spouses [2]	Type of Pattern [3]
2274	2886	8
	2886	8
	2886	8
1113	2886	7
0223	2886	5
	2886	5
1006	0000	0
0569	2886	0
	2886	0

[1] Identification number of the male.
[2] Lineage identity of the spouses, all males coming from Lineage 2954.
[3] Pattern type of each marriage (see text for definitions of types).

II. Kinship

way is to examine the exact genealogical links between spouses and represent the structure in graphic terms in such a way that the statistically most common patterns are acknowledged. Another way, one that more adequately reflects the degree of long-term bonding between specific lineages, is to search for correlations in the lineage identity of certain ancestors of both the husband and the wife. Table 4–4 shows the results of such an inquiry, summarizing the marriages of the adult males of Lineage 2954 in Village 19 to the eight women of Lineage 2886. The "Types" identifying each marriage reflect patterns of exchange between the members of these two lineages over several generations, showing that reciprocal exchanges in this case are not recent and novel. Moreover, the number of genealogical loops likewise reflects the intensity of reciprocal exchange between the lineages of husband and wife.

The types shown are correlations between lineage identities as follows:

Type 8: Spouse Lineage = Father's Mother's Lineage
= Mother's Lineage
Type 7: Spouse Lineage = Mother's Mother's Lineage
Type 5: Spouse Lineage = Mother's Lineage

The structures specified by these types are given in figure 4–4 and are consistent with the demonstrable genealogical and kinship facts. Note that in Type 8, both Ego and his father have taken wives from the same lineage, and in both cases they are marrying cross-cousins (mother's brother's daughters). Type 7 represents one way in which children of cross-cousins become legitimate marriage partners.

Finally, Type 5 is a simple case of Mother's Brother's Daughter marriage, like Type 8 above, but not entailing the same pattern for the father of the Ego shown here. Of all Yąnomamö marriages thus far examined, Type 5 predominates as the most frequent "choice" of mate, at least insofar as "types" based on lineage correlations are concerned.

Summary

The traditional models used by social anthropologists are inadequate to represent the reality of social behavior in general and marriage behavior in particular. The standard representation of the type of social structure

Figure 4–4 **Genealogical Specifications for Selected Marriage Patterns** Darkened circles and triangles in each type indicate membership of those individuals in the same lineage.

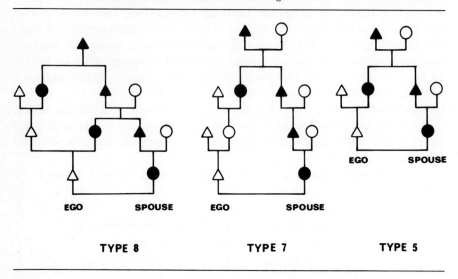

TYPE 8   TYPE 7   TYPE 5

found in the Yąnomamö would be given by the oversimplified diagram shown in figure 4–3a′ (above), where only one male and female are shown to represent their lineage in each generation and where everyone marries according to the rules. Such models also imply a demographic paradise, where there are enough mates for everyone, and where the system of rules and regulations are rigorously followed by thoughtless Egos who are non-participants in the social arena—except as positions on a hypothetical diagram. The diagrams in customary use simply gloss over the dynamics of social behavior and, in so doing, grossly misrepresent social reality.[14]

The real world is much more complex and, accordingly, some attempt must be made to represent it with more realistic models. We know a great deal about the ideal structure of primitive societies, about kinship classifications and equations, ideal marriage rules, and beliefs about descent and filiation. It should be clear from the above data that the outcome of actual behavior varies markedly from one village to the next. Yet all the Yąnomamö groups considered operate according to the same

---

[14] The simple models are appropriate if taken to be ultimately simple expressions and *not* as representing behavior or explaining it. I wish to explicitly distinguish my analysis from structuralism, the latter being an equally legitimate analytic approach, but useless for statistical models.

     II. Kinship

"ideal" rules. The deviations away from the ideal models are the important things to understand, and to achieve this, we must examine actual behavior and document it statistically.

Viewing Yąnomamö society as a system in which there is intense competition among males for reproductive opportunities brings out more clearly the significance of the dynamics of social life on the one hand, and on the other illustrates how demographic reality, kinship behavior, village fissioning and individual strategies all operate together and constitute a meaningful system. Moreover, the predictions we can make using this approach are more likely to be testable with real data. This is not to say that our understanding of principles of structure or kinship terminologies is irrelevant, for it is clear from the above demonstration that the outcome of mate competition can in fact be represented in terms of the general kinds of models used by structurally oriented analysts. But the models that we should turn to now are more complex than the ones customarily found in the anthropological literature, and they are more consistent with the statistical dimensions of actual behavior, the outcome of real people struggling to marry someone and entering into enduring alliances and coalitions to achieve that end. Not everyone is successful in the competition to the same degree, nor are the strategies followed always the same (see Chagnon, this volume, chapter 14, for discussion). Some people violate the rules— commit incest. Others take advantage of the first violation and manipulate kinship terminology to their benefit, expanding their pool of eligible mates, annoying and aggravating the would-be potential mates of the women in the now-redefined category. Despite all the variations, the general pattern and quality of actual behavior appear to be the same: individuals form coalitions with close relatives and attempt to ensure that their children will have mates by reciprocal giving and receiving of women. This builds up a large amount of within-group relatedness and simultaneously pits men of allied lineages against others. Beyond a certain point, internal village struggles, fights, and animosity over and about sex or women become too intense for kinship, descent, and the charisma of leaders to satisfactorily resolve; and then the village simply bifurcates: it fissions. The new groups are internally more consanguineal, and generally, because of the structure of the lineage group, better able to control the competition and constrain it.

Suggestions for future field research

The dynamics of Yąnomamö social behavior in the context of mating and village fissioning seem to be consistent with the prediction, from evolutionary biology, that people behave in such a way that they consistently favor close kin, people with whom they have overlapping genetic interests. They may not consciously reflect on this, any more than a rock can reflect on its mass or velocity as it falls according to predictions from the Law of Gravity. But the fact that rocks have no conception of fractions is an inadmissible "proof" that gravity does not exist. The fact that "fractions are of very rare occurrence in the world's languages" (Sahlins 1976a:45) and calculations of relatedness within the ken of few does not, for the same reason, render kin selection mystical or demonstrate that the process does not occur among humans or animals. The scientific issue is whether or not the behavior of organisms or the fall of a sparrow conforms to predictions based on theories of selection or gravity.

The data presented in this paper immediately suggest a number of hypotheses that could be tested in the field, in villages whose composition is known in detail and where the structure of kinship relatedness has been worked out through prior field investigations and computer analyses.[15] The distribution of relatives in the villages under discussion (figure 4–5), for example, shows that in most villages a large fraction of the people are related to 75 percent or more of the rest of the village residents (the largest quartile, shown on the extreme right of each of the diagrams). There are also varying numbers of people in all villages who are related to 25 percent or fewer of the village residents. Since all Yąnomamö in all villages apply and extend kinship terms to everyone, even those individuals with few kin have "kinship relationships" with *all* village residents and call them all by specific kin terms. A simple test of the predictive value of kinship terminology in the context of social behavior could be made and compared to predictions of behavior in which genealogical relatedness, marriage ties, and coefficients of relatedness are used as the basis of prediction. For example, one could take a specific kinship category—"brother" for example—and determine, for a number of individuals, whom they address as brother. Detailed observations of the behavior of pairs of "brothers" should then be made and coded, using ethological field techniques, covering such things as sharing, touching, threatening, grooming, supporting in fights, etc., and then compare these data to the degrees of relatedness between the pairs (see Hames, this volume, chapter 9, for one example of this kind of study). A prediction from evolutionary biology would be

15 Actually, it could be accomplished through a sampling procedure before the genealogies are known or collected. The fieldworker would have to make a sample of individuals within the selected kinship category and document the behavior, checking it later against the genealogical relationships he also discovers.

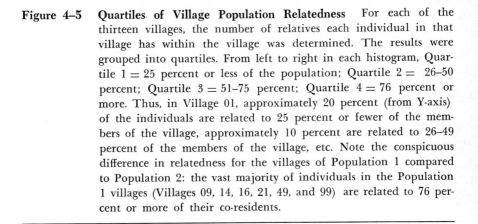

Figure 4–5 Quartiles of Village Population Relatedness   For each of the thirteen villages, the number of relatives each individual in that village has within the village was determined. The results were grouped into quartiles. From left to right in each histogram, Quartile 1 = 25 percent or less of the population; Quartile 2 = 26–50 percent; Quartile 3 = 51–75 percent; Quartile 4 = 76 percent or more. Thus, in Village 01, approximately 20 percent (from Y-axis) of the individuals are related to 25 percent or fewer of the members of the village, approximately 10 percent are related to 26–49 percent of the members of the village, etc. Note the conspicuous difference in relatedness for the villages of Population 1 compared to Population 2: the vast majority of individuals in the Population 1 villages (Villages 09, 14, 16, 21, 49, and 99) are related to 76 percent or more of their co-residents.

Population 1

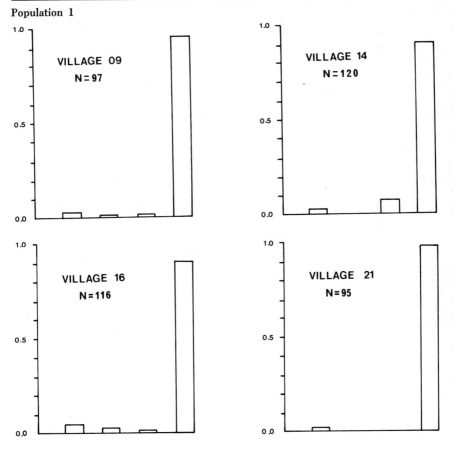

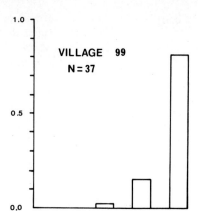

VILLAGE 49
N = 77

VILLAGE 99
N = 37

Population 2

VILLAGE 01
N = 100

VILLAGE 05
N = 127

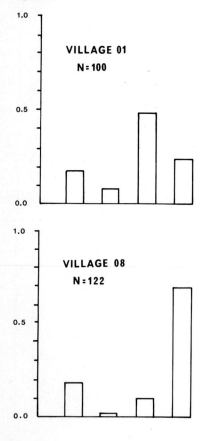

VILLAGE 08
N = 122

VILLAGE 18
N = 147

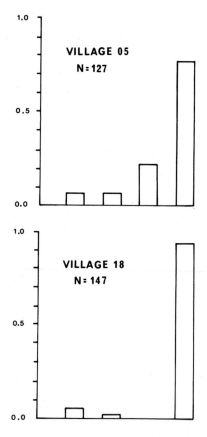

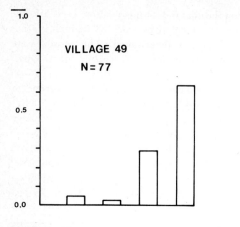

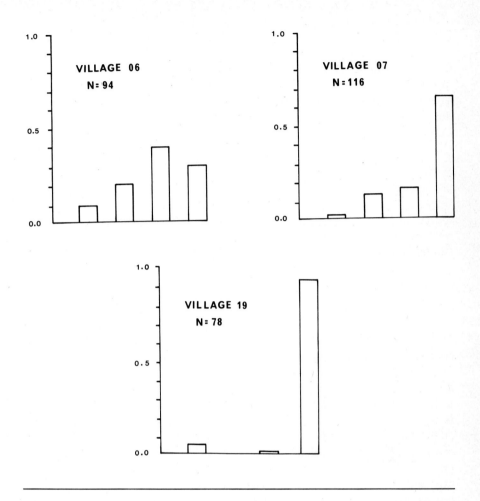

that "brothers" who are more closely related are more amiable with each other and supportive, while those who are less related treat each other less amiably. The prediction from general anthropological theory, in contrast, might be that all men who are "brothers" behave toward each other in precisely the same way. Most anthropologists would wince at the suggestion on the basis of their own experience in field situations, knowing full well that not all brothers in a terminological sense treat each other the same way.

The major question, then, is Why? Is there a pattern? If so, does it have anything to do with kinship relatedness and reproductive interests?

These are questions that students of evolutionary biology are trying to answer—especially the "Why" question. It is my personal conviction that anthropologists should play a prominent and decisive role in this multidisciplinary inquiry. We cannot know on first principles that the question is trivial on the argument that we already have the answer. We do not.

5. Kinship Categories as Natural Categories[1]
Robin Fox

Our starting point must be the accepted universality of kinship classification. This is as universal as language itself, and more universal than, for example, a nuclear-family incest taboo. There exists no known society which does not have classification of kin: it must therefore be accepted as a universal human attribute in the same way as language, of which, of course, it is a part. It is also a function of another attribute which Lévi-Strauss (1962) has claimed to be universal, namely the tendency to classify for its own sake. Although both classification itself, and its subset kin classification, are dependent on language, they do not follow logically from it. One can imagine a species that evolved language, but that neither classified nor named categories of kin. Especially with the latter, there has to be some reason—or perhaps we should say some function, some survival value—for so doing, independently of the capacities to speak and classify themselves. It is not simply *that* we classify, but *what* we classify that matters; and universally we classify kin.

It is commonly stated in anthropology that this very fact makes us totally different from the rest of animal nature, and hence it is not amenable to the same form of analysis that might be applied, say, to a universal

[1] The preparation of this paper has been facilitated by the Harry Frank Guggenheim Foundation.

feature of the behavior of some animal species. This is because we act *in terms of* these classifications, not in terms of genes or whatever is assumed to motivate animals. We imbue nature with cultural meanings and act in terms of these meanings rather than of nature itself. Kinship categories are, in this sense, "cultural" categories and hence outside the realm of "natural" explanation.

I have already argued (1971) that this general position is based on an untenable distinction between nature and culture, and here I wish to pursue this argument into the heartland of the culturalist position: meanings and categories, and in particular kinship classifications. To accept the position of those who, like Lévi-Strauss (1949) (at least in his earlier version [2]), wish to make the nature-culture division the pivot of analysis, is to end up with some odd logical difficulties. Let us take his argument on the incest taboo: it is universal, therefore biological (a natural feature of the species), yet at the same time a rule and very variable, therefore cultural. This he describes as a situation that is theoretically scandalous, and one he seeks to resolve by making the taboo the fulcrum which tips the balance between nature and culture, "partaking" of both.

The same argument can be applied to kinship classification: it is universal therefore biological, but involves rules which are variable and hence is cultural, etc., etc. Of the incest taboo, I have argued (1975a) that what is cultural is only the rule, not the avoiding of incest—which is common to most sexually reproducing species and certainly all mammals (cf. also Bischof 1975). To say the rule is cultural, then, and hence unique, is not to say much, because we are, by definition, the only animal that makes rules since we are the only animal that has language in which to couch them. Thus our uniqueness lies in the use of language, not in any incest-related behavior.

Similarly with kinship classification: our uniqueness lies not in having, recognizing, and behaving differentially to different kin (this happens throughout nature), it lies in giving this process names and rules of naming; in the classification not the kinship.

Incest avoidance does not make us unique: the rule does. Kinship grouping and kin-derived behavior do not make us unique: the naming of kin does. In each case a universal, hence biological, feature is associated with a "cultural" practice.

[2] But see his modified position in the introduction to the English translation: *The Elementary Structures of Kinship*, trans. J. H. Bell and J. R. von Sturmer, ed. and trans. R. Needham (Boston: Beacon Press, 1969).

But by the same logic, the cultural practice—ruling and naming, i.e., classification—if universal, must also be biological.

Hence one set of biological features—the propensity to classify and regulate—comes into conjunction with two others: the propensities to outbreed and to behave differentially toward kin. All this is possible through the mediation of language.

The latter, however, being universal, is also biological, and hence the unifying feature of the other two biological features is itself biological.

Ergo, there is no nature-culture distinction, everything is natural-biological. Hence the argument that we cannot use analyses developed for nature to interpret culture fails since by its own logic the supposedly unique cultural features turn out to be natural.

This tedious demonstration fortunately leads us easily, and without having to bother with most culturalist arguments, to ask some simple questions of evolutionary biology about language, rules and naming systems, whatever these apply to.

The argument with the incest taboo is simple: the propensity to avoid incest exists; what the taboo does, literally, is to give voice to this propensity via rules couched in language.

The argument then with kin classification is the same: the propensity to discriminate among kin exists, and what the kin-term systems do is to give voice to this via systems of linguistic classification which operate according to certain rules.

This is not a cultural "intrusion" (Lévi-Strauss) into nature in either case, but a set of naturally occurring phenomena for this species.

The outbreeding propensity requires different degrees of flexibility under different circumstances in nature. There is no absolute requirement. It is all relative to group size, rates of mutation, adaptational requirements, etc. Degrees of outbreeding and inbreeding, in other words, differ according to adaptational circumstances. Both different species, and populations within species, exhibit different patterns.

For the species *Homo sapiens,* the consequence of this trajectory of evolution that included the origination of language, classification and rule-obedience, was the rapid migration of populations into numerous very varied niches. Therefore, adaptational circumstances changing as rapidly as they did in space and time, *H. sapiens* required a mechanism for regulating degrees of outbreeding more flexible, say, than mere recognition of individuals.

The feedback between these processes—linguistic and mental advance making more rapid adaptive movement possible and in turn requiring greater linguistic and mental advance . . . and so on—selected for creatures that could define and re-define outbreeding/inbreeding boundaries to suit the differing circumstances. That is, it selected for speaking, classifying, and rule-making creatures *who could apply these talents directly to the breeding system.*

Differing human systems of incest prohibition, exogamy, and endogamy are therefore to be understood as products of natural selection.

By extension, the same reasoning applies to the concomitant evolution of the classification of kin and its development into systems of kin categories. The kin-discriminating tendency requires flexibility in its handling in non-humans; in the rapidly evolving hominids, this requirement was many times compounded. Therefore selection was in favor of creatures who could define and re-define degrees and kinds of kin-relationships according to changing circumstances.

Again, the processes that enabled this greater complexity to evolve—language, categories and rules—in turn were re-demanded by the more complex creatures they helped to provoke. Once more the feedback process selected for creatures that could utilize these procedures better in the business of kin definition.

The flexible use of categories of kin, then, by *Homo sapiens,* is to be considered a natural product of natural selection.

The current complexity and variability of systems of kinship classification cannot be used as an argument for not treating human kinship systems as natural phenomena amenable to sociobiological explanation—in the widest sense. Language, as we have seen, must be considered a naturally evolved propensity itself. The complexity of natural languages does not argue against this. In the light of the work of transformational grammarians, we see that a few basic components, and the rules for their transformation, can account for endless complexity. The whole issue of "variability" is in fact a red herring. That universal features do not, under varying conditions, produce uniform responses, is a well-enough established fact for all natural phenomena. Variables—which is what we are concerned with—vary: by definition.

With systems of kinship classification, whatever method of componential analysis (widely understood) one chooses, one finds a system of few elements with rigorous rules for the generation of any set of terms. The number of elements and rules is small and well within human mental capacity. The generation of complex systems requires nothing more complicated than the following of half a dozen rules of logical application. The results can be quite complex; the procedures are basically simple.

Tax (1955), for example, following the example of Kroeber and Lowie, lists a "set of rules that seem to be fairly universally followed." They number twelve, and some are not necessary to an understanding of terms per se: they apply to customary behaviors and even then are suspect. The true list is probably nearer six items (like Kroeber's). Needham (1971) comes up with six "elementary modes" of descent, and, I think, two basic dimensions of terminology (linear/non-linear; symmetric/asymmetric). Murdock (1949) finds four types of parental-generation terms and six types of cousin terminology. Complexity is easy to achieve in this latter case since by combination, ninety-four types are possible. Surprisingly few actually occur. One could go on citing examples, but the moral is the same: few elements, many combinations. (The minimum "elements" seem to be: generation, sex, affinity, collaterality, bifurcation, and polarity.)

Given a small set of elements and combinatorial principles, *Homo sapiens* was able, via naming and simple logical processes, to produce flexible and adjustable systems of classification. The nature of the classification would depend on the types of discrimination demanded by different circumstances. These would determine who should be (a) classed as kin versus non-kin, (b) classed as marriageable or unmarriageable, (c) classed as close or distant, etc., etc. What is remarkable is that there are in fact, as Morgan (1870, 1877) realized, so *few* types that emerge when such a finite but huge variety is possible. There is after all no logical reason why each society should not be totally different.

Having established that the classification of kin is a specific, naturally evolved propensity (like language itself), requiring names and rules of application to make discriminations, we should try to establish in a preliminary way the basic principles for a naturalistic analysis of these systems. How are they to be understood in terms of evolutionary biology?

We shall be concerned with classification. As far as behavior is concerned, the analysis is easier and is in any case proceeding (see especially Chagnon and Bugos, chapter 8; Hames, chapter 9). With institutions, customs, etc., we can go forward immediately. I have chosen here to attack "meanings" directly, since it is these that are, as we have seen, offered as the bulwark of human cultural uniqueness.

We must start again with the very universality of kinship classification. This reflects the universal, hence biological, fact of kin selection,[3]

---

[3] The literature on kin selection (and inclusive fitness generally) is by now very large. See the works cited in this volume, and in the bibliographies of E. O. Wilson (1975) and Robin Fox and Usher Fleising (1976).

rooted in the evolutionary processes characteristic of all sexually reproducing species. With animals, as far as kin discrimination is concerned, certain rules of thumb seem to apply: "those animals around you—that you grew up with, that are close to your mother, etc.—are likely to be kin." (Nature only needs probabilities, not certainties, to operate kin selection adequately. The same is true of incest avoidance.) With *H. sapiens,* once exogamy is invented, more specificity is required.

Exogamy requires not just random outbreeding but specified and bounded exchanges. Therefore, to arrange the breeding systems of human populations, specifications of marriageable and unmarriageable are required. This is ultimately the basic classification: the alliance theorists are correct. In whom should one invest—parentally—becomes an issue for more than just individuals. *Categories* of "invest in" and "not invest in" become necessary, and are invented.

Thus kin classifications and outbreeding principles are "run together" in human kinship systems. To repeat the crucial point: the biological propensity to (a) classify and (b) regulate, embraces, through the biological feature of (c) language, the two biological tendencies to (d) outbreed via exchanges (exogamy) and to (e) behave differentially toward kin.

Kinship systems then, can be seen as assortative mating systems (in one of their aspects), and kin classification as a flexible means of adjusting the categories of marriageable and unmarriageable kin. At its most extreme it can define simply "kin" versus "non-kin" and specify "marry non-kin." Mostly, however, it either (a) specifies "degrees of kinship" from Ego and varies the restricted degrees, or (b) it specifies the kind and composition of descent groups and varies the details of their exogamic relationships, or (c) it categorizes kin and specifies categories of marriageable and unmarriageable.

On the surface these might appear very different; in practice they can have similar effects. The first is best known in the so-called Eskimo and Hawaiian systems where various forms of reckoning—by degrees, stocks, etc.—decide where the circle of "non-marriageable" ends: first cousins, fourth degree, etc., etc. The second can vary from a simple injunction not to marry into one's own clan, for example, to an injunction not to marry into some or all related clans, through a positive injunction to marry into certain clans other than one's own. The third method includes all those systems of preferential (or prescriptive) marriage where types of categories of kin like mother's brother's daughter (MBD) or mother's mother's brother's daughter's daughter (MMBDD) or father's father's sister's daughter's daughter (FFZDD), etc., are specified as marriage partners. (This can encompass some of the second category, but one must allow for the cases where such specifications are made but where unilateral descent groups do not exist.)

The similar effects, in small populations, can be seen by comparing three possible examples of the above three variations. In (1) we could have a prohibition on marriage with kin up to first cousins—second cousins and beyond can be married. In (2) we could have a ban on marriage into one's own clan (assume this to be matrilineal) and one's father's clan (mother's mother's and father's mother's clans), but a positive injunction to marry into mother's father's and/or father's father's clans. This is common in many "Crow" systems (e.g., Cherokee). In (3) we could have a positive rule to marry MFZDD or FFZDD, or, more commonly, MMBDD (irrespective of the existence or type of unilineal groupings). All of these are quite common and standard examples in kinship analysis.

In effect, in each case, in a relatively small community (500–1000)—our typical human breeding pool for evolutionary purposes—the effect for the individual investor might look much the same. In each case, for example, the children of brother and sister could not marry (first cousins), but some of their grandchildren could, and in a small community, even without positive injunctions, they would likely have to. This possibility increases further as the "degrees" are pushed out (to second and third cousins, for example), or the categories made more stringent.

This can be viewed schematically from the point of view of the descendants of a brother and sister:

Figure 5–1   Descendants of a Brother and Sister

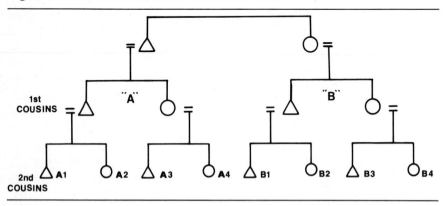

Taking the simple case of a "first-cousin" marriage rule (common in western Europe), we can see that any of the "second cousins" from group A can marry any of those from group B. But in a small breeding pool, if this is pushed to a "second-cousin rule," it is going to be hard to find anyone to marry who is *not* a third cousin anyway. This has a similar effect, then, to a "positive" third-cousin rule de facto. But note that, if this were a matrilineal system with our previously noted injunction to avoid mother's mother's and father's mother's clans, but to marry into mother's father's or father's father's, then A3 would have to marry B4, and similarly A1 would have to marry B4's sister. If this were variation 3, then in the case of a MMBDD rule, B3 would marry A4, and with a FFZDD rule, A1 would marry B4. (All the combinations cannot be shown since for simplicity we have not shown the offspring of the siblings of the spouses of the original brother and sister.)

These various systems of classifying kin (by degrees, by descent group, by category) can then be seen as various ways of combining an out-breeding tendency with a closely endogamous tendency: to avoid sibling, and often first-cousin marriages, but to encourage, or render inevitable, second- and other cousin marriage. The "range of marriageability" can be narrowed or widened by simple devices such as extending prohibited degrees (as the Church did in the Middle Ages to profit from the sale of dispensations), changing the specification of marriageable and unmarriageable clans (see next paragraph), or changing the specification of category from MBD to MMBDD and so on as happens, for example, in the geometric progressions from "two-class" up to "eight-class" systems in Australia; or by combining two or more of these principles for somewhat more hair-raising effects. Marriageable and unmarriageable groups can also be differently aligned by creating asymmetric rules, for example, and banning one set of cousins while prescribing another, thus potentially widening the range while controlling the "flow" and containing it. The examples are familiar, as is the demographic argument that suggests an inbuilt tendency to asymmetric flows (Fox 1965).

This possibility of easily redefining the categories of marriageable versus unmarriageable, can be seen in the variations of "Crow" systems. It is for this reason that I have argued (in press), following Lévi-Strauss, that such systems as "Crow" or "Omaha" should be regarded as descriptive of tendencies, not as static types. These matrilineal systems with "lineal" classifications can work in three basic ways. (1) There can be a simple rule against marriage into one's own matriclan (mother's clan); (2) there can be a rule banning not only one's own clan but that of one's father (i.e., father's mother's clan), and one's mother's father (the two clans, incidentally, to which Ego's clan has "given" women matrilineally related to him); (3) a rule banning two clans (mother's mother's and father's mother's) but enjoining marriage (or at least preferring it) with father's and mother's father's clans. This easily can be seen schematically in figure 5–2.

Figure 5–2

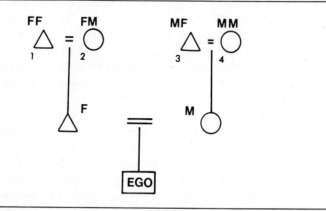

Under rule (1) Ego is simply banned from clan 4, his own. Under rule (2) he is banned from 2, 3, and 4. Under (3) he is banned from 4 and 2, but should marry into 1 and/or 3. Thus in the first case Ego can technically marry into any other clan in the tribe (although, interestingly, all parallel cousins are usually banned); in the second he is banned from "wife-taking" clans, and must look beyond this linked series, his nearest possibility being his father's father's clan (this all has a decidedly "asymmetrical" appearance); in the last case he is banned from the two "closest" but enjoined to marry the *next* two closest (they are all, of course, genetically as close—but thereby hangs a tale). In effect, in the third type, he is well into the classic "second-cousin marriage" pattern typical of his counterparts in a "four-section" system.

I have not been able to go into all the complexities here, but the essential point is that the system of "lineal classification" makes such switches from simple exogamy, through asymmetric flow, to second-cousin direct exchange, very simple—however complicated it may seem in analysis. The reasons why such switches and changes might have been made are not our immediate concern (nor are they all known) and neither is the question of their possible developmental sequence (which is still conjectural).

All we are establishing is that they have an inbuilt flexibility that allows for simple but dramatically effective changes in the specification of marriageable and unmarriageable; changes that can alter significantly the range and type of spouses "at risk of marriage" to any person in the breeding pool. The next step in analysis should be the examination of the various payoffs of the various systems under different circumstances.

The classification systems, then, give human breeding groups the degree of specificity and flexibility they obviously need to combine kin selection, outbreeding, and boundary maintenance. They put the assortative mating system under the possibility of simple conscious control. This may not always seem to be exercised, and indeed changes may often occur without conscious intervention (just by the gradual dropping of a rule, etc.); but as Lévi-Strauss points out, someone has to initiate the changes even though once established they are regarded as having existed from time immemorial. Whether the switches are conscious or not, however, they are easily made and readily available in the logic of the classificatory systems.

The evolutionary function, then, in this interpretation, of something as simple as "lineal terminology," is that it allows (like "classification by degrees," etc.) for an easy manipulation of breeding units to meet changing circumstances. Other functions can of course accrue. As we have seen, in small groups (our evolutionary context after all) different devices may have similar "breeding effects," despite apparently large "cultural" differences in style. But a small change—for example in population size from 1000 to 5000 or more—can have far-reaching effects, and give an adaptational advantage to certain systems over others. Again the point is that whatever the specifics of such changes, the potential for making them is latent in the system of classification.

Thus we can see that the objection that "social" rather than "genetic" classifications are used by man and hence render his kinship systems outside the realm of sociobiological analysis is wrong if it merely means that persons genetically equivalent are classed differently. If the classification is seen as a breeding classification, then its biological significance may be even more far-reaching than would a simple one-to-one "genetic" classification. The latter might be, for assortative mating purposes, largely irrelevant anyway. Most of the argument within anthropology on this point has therefore been equally irrelevant up to now.[4] But the socio-

---

[4] See D. Schneider (1964:180–189) and the references therein to the debate between Gellner, Needham, Barnes, and Beattie.

biologists are in danger, paradoxically, of making exactly the same mistake.

Thus, it appears from the growing amount of work in this area (largely unpublished) that sociobiologists of the "kin-selection" persuasion often wish to oppose "what people do" (i.e., maximize their inclusive fitness) to "what the system says they should do" (i.e., act in terms of social categories). What they "really" do, the implication is, is the former, whatever the rules might be about categories: they will act nepotistically or altruistically toward close relatives genetically and symmetrically defined whatever the categories say. Similarly, their opponents, when they find that there are cases when human beings do not so act, reckon to have disproved the "kin-selection hypothesis."

There is a double confusion here. For a start, according to kin-selection theory, the formula for action is $k > 1/r$. To assume, either pro or con kin-selection hypotheses, that all behavior, or all institutions, can be predicted from "r" alone is erroneous: this is to ignore "k" (see Kurland, chapter 6; Irons, chapter 7). Some behavior can be predicted from "r" undoubtedly, when people know their exact genealogical relationships. But a lot cannot. There are undoubtedly cases (Chagnon and Bugos, chapter 8; Hames, chapter 9) where "r" will predict behavior. But there are plenty of cases where it will not, while "cultural r" will. This is clearest in the case of marriage proscriptions and prescriptions. Here marriage choice is governed by category, that is, by "cultural r." (People of course break the rules: no one is suggesting they act like machines.) My point is, however, that in acting exogamically according to "culturally redefined r," people are *not* doing the opposite of acting according to "real r." This is the nub of the argument: the propensity to redefine "r" for purposes of assortative mating is as entrenched in the selection process as the propensity to act according to real r. In a very profound sense it is just as real, and part of the same process.

The second confusion is this: while both proponents and critics of kin-selection theory are concerned with the prediction of actual behavior, that is not the issue here. The nearest we can get to a prediction is that "people are likely to choose mates from the approved categories and not from the disapproved "—not much of a prediction about specific behavior, although not a trivial statement about the species. And this is the point: We are concerned here with the evolutionary (teleonomic) functions of kin categories, not with the prediction of fitness-maximizing behavior, connected as the two may be. We are asking, in other words, why certain institutional arrangements exist at all. Any "prediction" then—and I would not go further than suggesting some covariation—would be at the institutional level.

We should be careful, therefore, to distinguish the level or explanation that is involved. As far as social (kinship) categories are concerned, in this view, they are largely to do with the definition of exogamy. Other functions—definition of inheritance, succession, etc.—are accruals. Most of the things sociobiologists wish to "predict" have to do with actual interaction—who favors whom, and the like. At best, here, we can only say that categories provide a reservoir of potential recipients of discriminatory behavior, in the same way that categories of "potential spouse" provide a reservoir of actual mates. Which actual relatives will be nepotistically or altruistically favored is another matter.

There is nothing really very strange in the human propensity to act, for some purposes, in terms of categories. Even animals do not act symmetrically toward genetically related other animals, since all these relatives may not, physically, be available. Animals act according to the rules of thumb we have already noted—largely in terms of proximity. Human systems of kinship classification are the equivalent of the differential behavior of animals, only they are more precise. With animals, some physical mechanism puts one "category" literally closer than another. Kinship classification does the same thing definitionally, conceptually, as is the human way. But the end result is similar, differing in the degree of precision with which categories can be defined. We can do two things more precisely: we can trace and remember actual genealogical connections, thus allowing us to override category in favor of genealogy; we can classify together genetically disparate relatives, thus allowing category to override genealogy. But these are two sides of the same coin and it would be a terrible pity if sociobiologists should through misunderstanding of the true evolutionary significance of categorization re-erect the false dichotomy that their opponents favor.

The above was written before the advent of Sahlins' (1976a) critique, but my response to him will be obvious without further comment since his basic misunderstandings are answered by the whole argument of this paper—as are those of the people he is criticising. I am also, on the basis of this argument, forced to support a modified notion of "group selection" against the "individual selection" attacks. Thus it is possible that gene frequencies change within a population as a result of individual selection, itself a result of maximization of inclusive fitness. But the individuals do this—particularly in the human case—within the framework of a system that itself has adaptive properties. (This is another reason we cannot separate out "individual" from "system.") Thus an individual's "success" in such maximization may result from his pursuit of a strategy that in fact maximizes the benefits that the system itself—as a successful adaptive device—makes possible for him. There is, in other words, selection at the system (i.e., group) level, as well as at the individual. The two need not, but could, be incompatible. This is an empirical matter.

It will be obvious that, from the point of view of the "natural" analysis of systems of kin classification (as products, that is, of natural selection), we should favor the "categorical" approach rather than the "extensionist." The latter is too close to our own ethnocentric notion of "real" relationship. Also, an "alliance" approach is preferable to its rivals overall, since it concentrates on kin units as breeding units—although its proponents might not see it quite that way. It also, by the central position it gives reciprocity, opens the way for an analysis of human kinship systems as systems of reciprocal altruism—where calculations of real relatedness are not needed. Thus we have come the full circle to Lévi-Strauss, classification, exchange, and alliance, but fully within the neo-Darwinian mandate and without the obfuscations of the nature-culture distinction. The aim has been simply to demonstrate that a fact like the classification of "father's sister's daughter" with "father's sister" in some systems, with "sister" in others, and with "grandmother" in yet others, is a fact of the same order and open to the same analysis in principle, as the sterility of certain relatives of the queen bee, the regurgitation of food by canid predators, or the gamble with death of the Cleaner Fish. Now the task begins.

6. Paternity, Mother's Brother, and Human Sociality[1]

Jeffrey A. Kurland

Petruchio:	...I pray you, tell Signior Lucentio that his father is come from Pisa and is here at the door to speak with him.
Pedant:	Thou liest: his father is come from Padua and is here looking out at the window.
Vincentio:	Art thou his father?
Pedant:	Aye sir; so his mother says, if I may believe her.

Act V, scene 1
The Taming of the Shrew
Wm. Shakespeare

Genetic relatedness is a major determinant of social behavior among living nonhuman primates (Koyama 1967; Kurland 1977; Massey 1977; Sade 1972b). In many primate species, for example, among macaques and baboons, social groups consist of genetically related adult females with their immature offspring. The tenure of adult males in the social group is variable. This social organization can be described as "matrifocal" in that males who sire offspring are not permanently associated with the group and as "matrilocal" in that the core members of the local group are females related through maternal links. Males born in the group quite predictably leave as they approach sexual maturity (Kurland 1977; Packer 1975). Not all primates live in such a permanent association of uterine kin, but it is this type

[1] This paper is dedicated to Irven DeVore, friend and teacher, who first made me aware of the relationship between paternity and the avunculate. I wish to thank Paul Bugos, Napoleon Chagnon, Martin Daly, Irven DeVore, Martin Etter, Mark Flinn, Meyer Fortes, Robin Fox, Eric Fredlund, Penelope Greene, Carolyn McCommon, Tom Melancon, Warren Morrill, Ralph Smallberg, Alice Schlegel, and Lionel Tiger for contributions to earlier versions of this paper. I am especially grateful to William Irons for tutorials in social anthropology; Robert Trivers for invaluable discussion and encouragement, Steven Gaulin for criticism beyond the call of duty, and Mary Ann Harrell for comments and queries that greatly helped me to articulate in ordinary and hopefully comprehensible English the arguments developed in this paper. These generous critics are, of course, in no way responsible for the inevitable errors that remain. Finally, I am indebted to the Harry Frank Guggenheim Foundation for support throughout the development and writing of this paper.

of primate social organization that is of some interest to anthropologists who seek the evolutionary basis for human kinship systems (Fox 1975a).

It is tempting to characterize the stable association of nonhuman primate uterine kin, or what will be referred here as the "sisterhood," as a form of "matrilineal" social organization. Female members of a macaque group, for example, cooperatively maintain a traditional home range that is passed on to female descendants. Reproductive males are recruited from outside the social group. Indeed, some macaque groups have been observed to do quite well without any resident adult males (Kawamura 1965; Neville 1968). However, there is an obvious structural and functional difference between the primate sisterhood and the human matrilineal society: the role of adult males. In human societies, men often maintain key roles of authority and control over the social and economic affairs of the matrilineal group. Throughout his life, a man interacts with his uterine kin as well as with his wife and her kin. Adult male behavior within the human matrilineal society differs radically from adult male behavior within the primate sisterhood. In particular, a special pattern of interaction between mother's brother and sister's children is a prominent feature of human sociality. This relationship is referred to as the "avunculate." The avunculate rests on a particular sibling relationship, namely, that between brother and sister.

The model presented here serves to focus on those biological variables that make the brother-sister relationship particularly important in some human societies. It is not the purpose of this paper to trace the phylogeny of the avunculate from some reconstructed ancestral nonhuman primate society. There are psychological, structural, and economic explanations of the avunculate (Homans and Schneider 1955; Lévi-Strauss 1969; Needham 1962; Radcliffe-Brown 1924; Schneider 1961a). However, in this paper, I attempt to explicate this aspect of human kinship and social organization in terms of basic evolutionary biological principles. Such a functional explanation of the avunculate can indicate only why such behavior is biologically adaptive, that is, specify its *ultimate* causes in the process of natural selection (Wilson 1975:23). Functional explanations of behavior rest on such evolutionary arguments. This does not imply that the many previous explanations about the *proximate* psychological or economic causes of human kinship behavior are incorrect or irrelevant. A "norm of reaction" model for gene effects portrays the individual's genotype as a mechanism that developmentally maps specific environments onto specific behavior, physiology, or morphology (Schmalhausen 1949). The proximate cause of any behavior is therefore necessarily environmental. Evolution by natural selection can be conceived of metaphorically as a trial-and-error learning process that creates a memory/survival machine which retains, to varying degrees, the correct responses to the environments in which it has been tested. Evolutionary biologists who study the evolution of sociality are concerned with the prediction or explanation of how behavior maps onto the environment, *not* how genes map into behavior. For an evolutionary biologist who investigates social behavior, the particularly salient environmental stimuli relevant to explanations of an actor's behavior are those very stimuli generated by the ongoing behavior of other actors in the population. Hence, the subdiscipline of evolutionary biology now known as "sociobiology" (Wilson 1975). Postulating the existence of a gene that obligately codes for "altruism" is only a simplifying and heuristic procedure useful in modeling the adaptiveness of the behavior. It is simply part of the paradigm characteristic of evolutionary biology. Such modeling procedures in no way commit one to strict determinism or reactionary politics.

Relatedness, Investment, and Paternity

Parental care is perhaps one of the more obvious examples of biological *altruism*—that is, reproductively self-sacrificing behavior. This can be made more explicit if the parent-offspring relationship is analyzed in terms of what Trivers (1972, 1974) refers to as *parental investment*—that is, anything done by the parent for the offspring that increases the offspring's reproductive success and decreases the parent's future reproductive success. Dawkins (1976) generalizes Trivers' parental investment into what he calls *altruism investment*. An individual (altruistically) invests in another whenever such behavior increases the recipient's reproductive success at a cost to the actor of investment in other individuals, including himself; all costs being weighted by the relevant degrees of genetic *relatedness*. The concept of parental investment is thus meant to emphasize the particularly potent selective effects of altruistic investment between parent and offspring (see also Irons, chapter 1, for a review of these and other sociobiological concepts).

The different adult male roles within a primate sisterhood and a human matrilineal society result primarily from different levels of male investment. In a primate sisterhood, indeed in any species exhibiting this kind of social organization, adult males invest much less in offspring than do females. Although while resident, males may protect group members, including their own offspring, from predators or conspecific competitors, by far the greatest investment in offspring comes from the mother. Consequently, male reproductive strategies within such systems will be characterized by behaviors that increase the probability of inseminating females (Trivers 1972). This can sometimes lead to extreme forms of male-male competition resulting in group takeovers and infanticide (Sugiyama 1967; Blaffer Hrdy 1974).

Human males are capable of considerable investment in offspring. In addition to the energy and time required for basic parental care, investment may consist of economic and status contributions to the offspring during the parent's life, or perhaps the inheritance of wealth and status after death. Moreover, in the process of socialization, subtle behavioral interactions between the parent and the offspring may further affect the realized reproductive success of the offspring. For those species in which the male's relative parental investment approaches that of the female, a male will be selected to guard against "cuckoldry"—that is, against the possibility that he might invest in offspring which are not his (Trivers 1972). Thus, a high *probability of paternity*, or *paternity probability*, is a necessary condition for increased male parental investment. The sequestering of a female for an extended period during courtship, as in some birds, or the territorial exclusion of other males, as in monogamous primates, may be examples of some of the behavioral mechanisms by which males establish the paternity of their mate's offspring (Trivers 1972).

The ethnographic data suggest that human males sometimes invest in wife's children or sister's children or both. The avunculate is more conspicuous within matrilineal societies, but also exists within non-matrilineal societies (Radcliffe-Brown 1950). The anthropological issue of why the avunculate is such a critical relationship can be translated into a biological question: under what conditions would a male increase his *inclusive fitness* (Hamilton 1964) by investing in his sister's children rather than his wife's children?

Alexander (1974:373) provides a clear answer by pointing out that since a man is always related to his sister's children by at least 1/8, whereas he may be totally unrelated to his wife's children (ignoring inbreeding effects), a man's sister's children may have more and more of a positive effect on his inclusive fitness as it becomes more and more likely that another man (or men) has begotten his wife's (or wives') children. A man's confidence in or certainty about paternity may very well affect his altruistic investment in his wife's children. However, depending on the probability of paternity, investment in wife's or sister's children will be evolutionarily adaptive, regardless of the man's knowledge of or emotions about paternity (Hartung 1976, footnote 7). On the other hand if the probability of paternity has been low and variable throughout human history, then natural selection is expected to have favored the evolution of proximate mechanisms that allow investing males to better ascertain paternity. Thus, there may well be some correlation between a man's probability of paternity and his confidence of paternity. Alexander suggests that the ability of males to assess their phenotypic similarity to putative offspring will be favored whenever the probability of paternity has been persistently low. Of course, women, their offspring, and other kin may attempt to manipulate to their own advantage male perception of father-offspring similarities (see below, "Paternity Ignorance"). Inbreeding levels, genetic "outlawry," and deception all make the use of particular phenotypic attributes in the dispensation of altruistic benefits toward offspring and other kin exceedingly unlikely (Alexander 1974, 1977a; Kurland, in press). More importantly, a man will never be completely certain of paternity given the reproductive biology of the human species: as in most mammals, there is a highly invariant proximate and genetic correlation between mother and offspring, and a rather low and highly variable genetic correlation between a male and his mate's offspring. This element of uncertainty about paternity is expected to favor the evolution of a variety of anti-cuckoldry tactics by human males when they do invest in a mate's children.

In this paper, I translate Alexander's model into a mathematical form in order to make its assumptions more explicit, to facilitate derivations from the model's axioms, and thus to provide additional predictions about how paternity probability is expected to affect human social behavior. In addition, some ethnographic data are used to test these predictions. Since Alexander's original formulation of the relationship between paternity and the avunculate, we have developed some similar extensions of the model (Alexander 1977a; Kurland 1976; Greene 1978). Dawkins (1976: 114–115) also calls attention to the potential effects of paternity probability on male altruistic investment toward spouse's and sister's children: "perhaps social anthropologists might have interesting things to say."

The Paternity Threshold and the Avunculate

By definition, if there is a low probability of paternity, a man may be unrelated to a wife's child. But clearly the level of paternity probability will also affect sibling relatedness, because an individual and his brother or sister may or may not have the same father, making them either full or half siblings. Paternity probability thus affects both sibling and father-offspring relatedness. Therefore it is necessary to analyze the inclusive fitness effects of altruistic investment in Ego's (or Ego's mate's) offspring as compared to Ego's sibling's offspring. Such an analysis will define alternate "strategies" with characteristic inclusive fitness "payoffs" determined by relatedness, investment, and paternity.[2] To simplify the analysis, it is assumed that a hypothetical individual can invest in either his offspring or his sibling's offspring, and that only these individuals are relevant to his inclusive fitness (see appendix, page 177).

Female Ego and Sister Under what hypothetical conditions should a woman put investment into her children or into her sister's children, given $k =$ the actor's benefit-to-cost ratio due to this behavior? The payoff to her inclusive fitness for investment in her own offspring is $r_o(k)$, whereas it is $r_o(\bar{r}_s)(k)$ if she invests in her sister's children; where $r_o =$ relatedness between a woman and her offspring and $\bar{r}_s =$ expected relatedness between siblings as a function of paternity probability. It follows that investment in a woman's own children as compared to comparable investment in her sister's children is adaptive whenever:

$$r_o(k) > r_o(\bar{r}_s)(k). \tag{1}$$

Unless these siblings are identical twins, (1) can be shown to be always true, Thus, (1) can be reduced to

$$1 > \bar{r}_s. \tag{2}$$

If $r_f =$ relatedness between full siblings, if $r_h =$ relatedness between half siblings, and if $p =$ paternity probability,[3] then it follows that $\bar{r}_s = r_f(p^2)$

---

[2] In this paper, the use of game theory ("strategies," "payoffs," etc.) in the analysis of sociality is based on Hamilton (1967) and especially on Maynard Smith (1972). See also Dawkins (1976) for an excellent explication of game theoretic modeling in evolutionary biology.

[3] Kurland (1976) originally defined p as "the probability that a wife's offspring are the husband's, which is also the probability that siblings share the same father." This gives $\bar{r}_s = r_f(p) + r_h(1-p)$. But Greene (1978) correctly points out that this represents an inconsistent use of the variable p, which must refer only to the probability that a man is the father of his mate's offspring. Sibling relatedness is then derived, in part, from this p. Given this proper definition of p, it follows that the probability that any two siblings have the same father is the product of the independent probabilities that a given man is the father of each sibling through their mother: that is, $p(p)$ or p^2. Although some of the quantitative results of Kurland (1976) and Greene (1978) differ by a small amount, be-

II. Kinship

$+ r_h (1-p^2)$. It therefore follows that

$$1 > r_f (p^2) + r_h (1 - p^2). \tag{3}$$

If the effects of inbreeding are ignored, then $r_f = 2 (r_h)$, and thus

$$\left[\frac{1 - r_h}{r_h}\right]^{\frac{1}{2}} > p. \tag{4}$$

Under an assumption of complete outbreeding, $r_h = \frac{1}{4}$, and (4) reduces to $\sqrt{3} > p$ which can never be false, since p only varies between 0 and 1. Therefore it is always adaptive for this hypothetical woman to direct all investment to her own children.

Female Ego and Brother In the case of a woman and her brother, there is a potential inclusive fitness of $r_o(k)$ due to her investment in her own children. But her brother has a probability p that his wife's children (Ego's sister-in-law's children) are in fact sired by him. This woman obtains a potential inclusive fitness of r_o ($\bar{r}_s$) (k) (p) from comparable investment in her brother's children. Consequently, investment in her children in comparison to her brother's children is adaptive whenever

$$r_o \ (k) > r_o \ (\bar{r}_s) \ (k) \ (p). \tag{5}$$

Given $\bar{r}_s = r_f(p^2) + r_h(1-p^2)$, $r_f = 2(r_h)$, and $r_h = \frac{1}{4}$ as above, this reduces to $4 > p(p^2 + 1)$ which is true over all values of p. Again the hypothetical woman increases her inclusive fitness by investment in her children as opposed to investment in her brother's putative children.

Male Ego and Brother For a male Ego considering investment in his wife's children or his brother's children, it is necessary to evaluate:

$$r_o(k) \ (p) > r_o \ (\bar{r}_s) \ (k) \ (p). \tag{6}$$

This, like inequality (1), reduces to $\sqrt{3} > p$, which is always true. Therefore a given man increases his inclusive fitness more by investing in his

cause of the different values of $\bar{r}_s$, the previous behavioral analysis and ethnographic corroboration used by Kurland (1976) is not at all affected by Greene's (1978) mathematical correction.

wife's children than by investing in his brother's children. However, this is true only when $p > 0$. If $p = 0$, then a male's reproductive success and inclusive fitness due to his investment behavior are both zero! Clearly, male promiscuity with no investment beyond the sperm cells ("k" refers to behavior) can result in gains to a male's Darwinian and inclusive fitness.

Male Ego and Sister   For a male Ego considering investment in either his wife's or his sister's children, there is a *paternity threshold*, p_t. Above this he increases his inclusive fitness more by switching investment from his sister's children to his wife's children. The payoff inequality for the brother-sister dyad has the form

$$r_o \, (k) \, (p) > r_o \, (\mathring{r}_s) \, (k) \tag{7}$$

which immediately reduces to

$$p > \mathring{r}_s. \tag{8}$$

But since $\mathring{r}_s = r_f(p^2) + r_h(1-p^2)$, $r_f = 2(r_h)$, and $r_h = \frac{1}{4}$, it follows that

$$o > p^2 - 4p + 1. \tag{9}$$

There are, of course, two positive real roots of $p^2 - 4p + 1$, but only one, namely p_t, falls within the zero-to-one range of p. The unique solution of (9) that conforms to the assumptions of the present model is $p = p_t = 0.268$ (see also Greene 1978). Thus, only if $p > p_t$ does a man increase his inclusive fitness more by investment in his wife's children than by investment in his sister's children; otherwise, his sister's children do make a potentially greater contribution to his inclusive fitness. The entire model can be represented graphically by plotting parent-offspring, sibling, and sibling-sibling's offspring relatedness against paternity probability (figure 6–1). A man's expected relatedness to his sister's offspring (r_{zo}) intersects his expected relatedness to his wife's offspring at p_t, the paternity threshold.

Considering all possible strategies for a hypothetical human population, it is apparent that there are two pure sex-specific "evolutionarily stable strategies" (Maynard Smith 1972), given alternate investment behavior:

> 1 A female will invest in her children instead of her sibling's children.

Figure 6–1   Relatedness and Paternity Probability   This figure shows genetic degrees of relatedness, r, between a parent and offspring (r_o and r_{mo}), between siblings ($\bar{r}_s$), and between an individual and a sibling's offspring (r_{zo} and r_{bo}) as a function of the paternity probability, (p). In particular, r_o = relatedness between a woman and her children; r_{mo} = relatedness between a male and his mate's offspring; r_{zo} = relatedness between an individual and sisters' offspring; r_{bo} = relatedness between an individual and brother's offspring; and $\bar{r}_s$ = relatedness between siblings.

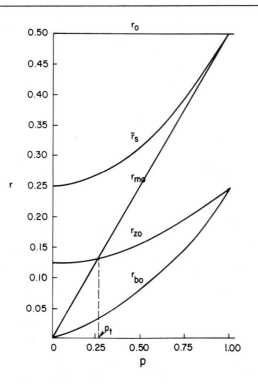

2   A male will invest in his wife's children beyond the paternity threshold, or he will invest in sister's children; he will always ignore brother's children.[4]

[4] Men, of course, do sometimes invest in brother's children. The rather artificial result that males are always to ignore brother's offspring follows from the heuristic assumption that "k" is constant and nonpartible. In reality, of course, the benefits and costs of

The asymmetry between the male and the female strategy rests on the fact, implicit in the model, that although a female always has a high probability of maternity, a male does not always have a high probability of paternity.

According to the model presented here, male altruistic investment is adaptively applied to a wife's child if the probability is approximately greater than a fourth, or the odds better than one-to-three, that he is the father of the child. Male paternity certainty may not ever be perfect; but so long as the probability of paternity is above the rather low paternity threshold, a man can increase his inclusive fitness by investing in his wife's children. If men correctly ascertain their paternity more than a fourth of the time (no matter what proximate mechanisms they use), then natural selection is expected to favor male investment in these children rather than in some sister's children. However, investment may not be able to be directed preferentially toward particular children of a wife. That is, investment may be nonpartible. Often, for example, when a man builds a shelter, or works in a crop field, the fruits of his labor will go to himself, to his wife, and to *all* of his wife's children. In this case, more than a fourth of the wife's children who reside with the husband, and who presumably benefit from his parental behavior, must have been sired by the husband for his altruistic investment to increase his inclusive fitness. If this does not hold, then his altruistic investment is "diluted" by the benefits conferred on unrelated children (see below: "At the Paternity Threshold").

There are two aspects of the human social environment that can contribute to low probabilities of paternity: namely, promiscuity and marital instability. Whenever premarital and extramarital sexual behavior are prevalent, males may have low paternity certainty correlated with low paternity probability. In such an extremely promiscuous environment, a man may suspect that few of a given wife's or lover's children are his. Such extremes of low confidence in and probability of paternity may be characteristic of the few human societies where seasonal or annual male migration leads to long absences from the household, or where visits by members of a revolving set of husband-lovers lead to institutionalized promiscuity. On the other hand, if marriage is short-lived, and in this sense unstable, because males have a shorter life expectancy than females or because divorce is easy and frequent, then remarriage may create a situation in which men find themselves living with and attending to a woman (or women) and

---

altruism will vary from situation to situation in such ways that investment in more distant kin may actually sometimes be adaptive (see below, "Tracking Paternity: Mixed Strategies").

children *known* to have been sired by other men. Marriage, divorce (or a spouse's death), and remarriage generate a system of serial monogamy or serial polygamy. Within such a marriage-mating system, male paternity certainty may be quite high—that is, a man may very well know which of his wife's children are his—but his effective probability of paternity may still be low whenever his nonpartible investment is applied to his wife's children, and where fewer than a fourth of these children were sired by him. If the probability of paternity approaches or falls below the paternity threshold due to promiscuity or marital instability, then natural selection will favor males who can direct investment toward sister's children rather than toward wife's children.

In this hypothetical human population, relatedness and paternity covary. Given maternity certainty, and the covariance between relatedness and paternity probability, there is a fundamental asymmetry in relatedness such that Ego's uterine kin will on average be more closely related than Ego's agnatic kin. Indeed, each male link between Ego and a given relative potentially reduces their relatedness by adding an element of uncertainty. Thus, with a low paternity probability, there is an inherent matrilineal bias to kin relationships and concomitant investment patterns. This may be significant for the formation of matrilineages as opposed to patrilineages.

The range of a man's relatedness to his sister's children is smaller than the range of relatedness to his wife's children—or in other words, the slope of sister's children relatedness is much lower than the slope of wife's children relatedness over the paternity probability (figure 6–1). The brother-sister relationship, which is the basis of the avunculate, will thus be a significant aspect of human social behavior, because, beyond the parent-offspring relationship, and given the right environment, it is this sibling relationship that can contribute most to a male's inclusive fitness. This might explain the prominence of the avunculate in some non-matrilineal societies (e.g., Radcliffe-Brown 1924).

If the paternity probability is less than 100 percent, there is a matrilateral bias in kin relatedness and potentially in behavior. Siblings, siblings' offspring, and other collateral kin are not necessarily genetically equivalent (cf. Sahlins 1976: 35). Indeed, when $p < 1$, parallel and cross-cousins are not equally related (cf. Alexander 1977a:324 ff.). Under the outbreeding assumption of the present paternity threshold model, $r_f = 2(r_h)$ and $r_h = \frac{1}{4}$. It follows from this that M, the genetic degree of relatedness between matrilateral parallel first cousins, is $(\frac{1}{2})$ $(\frac{1}{2})$ $(\bar{r}_s)$ or simply $(p^2 + 1)/16$. Similarly, the degree of relatedness between cross-cousins (X) is $p(p^2 + 1)/16$; and between patrilateral parallel cousins (P), it is $p^2(p^2 + 1)/16$. Only matrilateral parallel cousins are genetically related when p = 0. Even when p is greater than p_t, the paternity threshold, matrilateral parallel cousins are more closely related than cross-cousins, who in turn are more closely related than patrilateral parallel cousins (figure 6–2). If $p = \frac{1}{2}$, matrilateral parallel cousins are four times as related as patrilateral parallel cousins and twice as related as cross-cousins. Not only are matrilateral parallel cousins more closely related, but the degree of relatedness between Ego and his or her matrilateral parallel cousin varies less with paternity probability, making this kin class potentially a more important feature of Ego's kin network and inclusive fitness. This relatedness asymmetry can be generalized to more distant kin—matrilateral relatives will be more closely related to Ego than patrilateral relatives. Anthropologists seem to have some difficulty accounting for the prevalence of the "husband-father status" within the vast majority of matrilineal societies (e.g., Schneider 1961a:14–15, and footnote 8). However, if $p = \frac{1}{2}$, men may be selected to invest in a wife's rather than a sister's children and yet also to favor altruism and cooperation toward

Figure 6–2   Relatedness and Paternity Probability for First Cousins   This figure shows genetic relatedness, r, between first cousins as a function of the paternity probability (p); where $M = (p^2 + 1)/16 =$ relatedness between matrilateral parallel cousins, $X = p(p^2 + 1)/16$ = relatedness between cross-cousins, and $P = p^2(p^2 + 1)$ = relatedness between patrilateral parallel cousins.

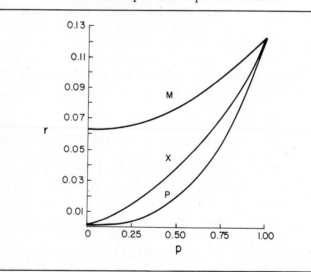

matrilateral rather than patrilateral relatives. In other words, all things being equal, the sociobiology of such a human population facilitates the emergence of a matrilineal society in which the father-child dyad is particularly well developed. Cooperation or altruism between individuals in populations with low or variable paternity probability may favor the creation of households composed of matrilateral relatives. In particular, sisters and sister's children are expected to be the core of some kinds of cooperative and altruistic group activities—for example, household chores, adoption, or child care. Thus, there may be an underlying implicit "sisterhood" within human social groups.

The analysis of sibling relationships demonstrates that the brother-sister relationship, which generates the avunculate, is of singular importance to human social behavior. This kin relationship will be of particular salience for a male whenever circumstances lead to a reduction in the probability of paternity. Thus, where promiscuity is more prevalent, more tolerated, or more easily achieved, where long-term marriage is nonexistent or highly unstable—that is, where divorce and serial monogamy or serial polygamy predominate—there will be lower levels of paternity certainty. There will be a concomitant emphasis on the avunculate and other matrilateral relationships as evidenced by investment patterns, residence, and other forms of social behavior. To the extent that a man can or will invest beyond his own children, he is expected to invest in his sister's certain children in preference to his brother's putative children. A woman may similarly bias any additional investment toward her sister's children. Thus, the higher relatedness between matrilateral kin (e.g., matrilateral parallel cousins), and the subsequent lowered threshold for cooperation and altruism between such kin, will bias social interactions by creating conditions conducive to the emergence of the avunculate, matrilineal inheritance of property and status, matrilocality, and matrilineages.

The Limitations of Ethnographic Examples

Testing this model by means of the ethnographic literature is difficult. The major concern of anthropologists has been with terminological, cognitive, ideological, or economic systems at the level of the group. Structure, function, and adaptation are all conceived of as properties of a group. Examples are too numerous to cite, but a group-level analysis is the rule in social anthropology (see, for example, Keesing 1975, a recent review). Evolutionary biology takes the gene as the proper level for a functional analysis of behavior (Dawkins 1976).

The data pertinent to the present model are observations of what people actually do. Instead, much of the ethnographic literature contains reports by anthropologists on what the native informant says the natives say about what they do, or ought to do. It is often difficult to separate, in ethnographic reports, statements about ideology from descriptions of behavior. The preoccupation with native models of cognition and social rules creates a static picture of human social behavior in which the actors exhibit modal forms of invariant behavior. Obviously the variables described in the ethnographic literature are only partly isomorphic to the relevant biological parameters. Evolutionary biological models of human social behavior are not definitely tested by direct appeals to the typological concepts and qualitative or anecdotal data often found within anthropology.

Unfortunately, corroboration of the model must at present rely on interpretations of ethnographic information. The relevant data on relatedness, paternity, investment, and individual behavior patterns rarely exist. The ethnographic examples used here are in no way meant to be a synoptic survey of matrilineal societies, let alone of the entire range of human cultural and societal organization. But the emphasis must be clearly placed on what human actors are doing, not on the articulated beliefs about what they or others say they are doing. This is not to deny the importance, or the singularly perplexing nature, of human thoughts and utterances. Instead, for the time being, it is human social behavior that is to be analyzed. What an individual says about his own beliefs and behavior is often irrelevant as an explanation of his behavior. It might be that the actor is the last to know or understand explicitly why he does what he does, or thinks what he thinks—a view not inconsistent with other theories of human behavior, such as those of Freud (repression) or Marx (false consciousness). Indeed, Alexander (1975a), and Trivers (1975) have already begun to develop a theory of human consciousness from an evolutionary biological perspective. Given some understanding of the adaptive nature of human social behavior, it should be possible to analyze the relationship between behavior and ideology, instead of assuming the primacy of the latter.

Below the Paternity Threshold

In some matrilineal societies, it appears that social conditions lead to probabilities of paternity that are below the paternity threshold. Among the

Central Kerala Nayar (reviewed in Gough 1961a), a man did not live with his wife; instead, he remained in his natal household within the context of the *taravad* matrilineal descent group. The most important relationships for a man were with his mother, his sisters, and their children. After the *tali* ritual group marriage, a woman might have from three to twelve visiting "husbands" at one time, and more, serially. Patrilateral kin had no particular rights or obligations, perhaps due to difficulty of ascertaining paternity. Thus, although the physiological role of males in procreation was known, it was also claimed that "no Nayar knows his father" (Gough 1961a:364). Services obtained from lower castes, political and military rewards, or the education of sister's son, were directed towards the matrilocal household. Thus, sister's children and other close matrilateral kin were the focus of male investment. Sisters, although sometimes characterized as rivals, were often highly supportive of and nurturant toward each other and their children. Motherless children were reared by their mother's sisters. In marked contrast, brothers maintained a somewhat formal and indirect relationship among themselves based only on links to their mother and sisters in the *taravad* (Gough 1961a:354). The low probability of paternity and the high level of male investment in the matrilocal household are consistent with predictions from the model presented above.

The Minangkabau, living under somewhat different economic and residence circumstances, approach the Nayar investment-paternity pattern (reviewed in Gough 1961d). A Minangkabau man could present only small gifts to his wife, and required permission from his lineage to give self-acquired property to his wife or children. Otherwise a man directed his economic activity to his natal matrilocal-matrilineal household. There may be other societies with inordinately low probabilities of paternity; however, the Nayar are particularly well documented, in contrast to the Minangkabau.

At the Paternity Threshold

In comparison to the Nayar or Minangkabau, other matrilineal societies apparently do not exhibit such inordinately low probabilities of paternity for all males. But the paternity probability may be low enough that the avunculate remains a critically important relationship for male investment and inclusive fitness. The ethnographic information is rich enough in some studies for at least a preliminary test of the proposed model.

Although adultery is exceedingly difficult to quantify, for obvious reasons, ethnographies of matrilineal groups report that the practice is common, frequent, or as it is often coyly put, not infrequent. There is typically, therefore, a great concern with marital fidelity, and jealousy may run high. For example,

> *In Dobu adultery is considered pretty, and a very fine achievement. Virtue in marriage is the dullness of a fool. . . . It is because of this custom of casual bush encounters that a husband in Dobu tends to fall into the habit of mentally timing his wife when she goes off in performance of the natural functions [Fortune 1963: 242 and 247].*

Among the Ashanti, two-thirds of all wives do not live with their husbands, and although households are near each other, separate residences would only seem to encourage the possibilities for extramarital sex (Fortes 1950). After sea voyages of a year or more, a Trobriander man may return home to find his wife has one or two new children—"cheerfully" accepted as proof that coitus has nothing to do with conception (Malinowski 1929:193).

Many patrilineal societies present a marked contrast—for example, the Nuer (Evans-Pritchard 1940, 1956), the Dinka (Deng 1972), the Tikopia (Firth 1936), the Yąnomamö (Chagnon 1968a, 1974), and the Akwẽ-Shavante (Maybury-Lewis 1967). In these, adultery appears to be not only much less tolerated and more severely punished, but also less frequent—insofar as illegitimacy due to extramarital sex is less often reported by the ethnographer. However, since sanctions against extramarital sex are so strong, it is to be expected that adultery would be much more difficult to detect. On the other hand, Chagnon (chapter 4) estimates that the level of mistaken paternity is about 10 percent in some Yąnomamö groups. In other words, $p = 0.9$ for these particular human social groups. Within matrilineal societies, where women have more control over their reproductive activity and less need of investment from husbands (as opposed to male kinsmen), the paternity probability may be much less than 0.9.

In addition to extramarital sex, premarital promiscuity and trial marriage may also alter the paternity probability. Indeed, at least one cross-cultural study suggests that in matrilineal-matrilocal societies sanctions against premarital sex, when they exist, are quite mild, whereas such sanctions are severe in patrilineal-patrilocal societies (Goethals 1971). Although premarital sex is especially tolerated in matrilineal societies (e.g., Malinowski 1929), unwed mothers and illegitimacy leading to lower probabilities of paternity are not tolerated. In one Dobu community, Fortune (1963:239), estimated one illegitimate child out of twelve. However, the Dobuan sanction against unmarried mothers is so strong that pregnant

II. Kinship

women get married (or have abortions), though it is not clear whether they attempt to marry the suspected biological father. There is then the real possibility of mistaken paternity (cuckoldry)—whether intentional or unintentional. On the Trobriand Islands, premarital promiscuity, illegitimacy, and subsequent adoption mediated by a rather flexible classificatory kin terminology, create an environment in which about one percent of the children are publically recognized not to be the offspring of the wife's husband (Malinowski 1929: 196). As in Dobu, marriage upon the first signs of pregnancy might be practiced by Trobriand women since children born out of wedlock are not accepted by a male. However, it is important to note that, unknown to both ethnographer and native, more children than are publically recognized may in fact be begotten by males who are not the spouses of these mothers. Both extramarital and premarital promiscuity may generate enough uncertainty that the average paternity confidence is lowered in the population.

In most matrilineal societies divorce is reported to be quite frequent, and can be initiated by either party without social stigma. Moreover, the remarriage rate seems to keep pace with the divorce rate. Fortune (1963: 9) reports that "an overwhelming majority of" Dobuan had several successive wives, most having from three to eight. Thus, along with considerable promiscuity, the mating system for most individuals is characteristically one of serial monogamy, though often headmen or chiefs are serially polygynous. The majority of a woman's children may therefore have different fathers.

Under some ecological conditions, male investment may be nonpartible—that is, investment such as agricultural labor will necessarily be directed toward an entire household, and hence toward all of a wife's children. A man then has little control over who gets how much of his investment. Consequently, to the extent that a man's labor, valuables or goods are part of his wife's household, or to the extent that his investment is put into the ensemble of a wife's children, such investment will necessarily be directed toward some children that are not his. Now his investment is "diluted," because children from previous marriages, resident in the household, are among the recipients of it. Moreover, a wife may be able to control some means of male investment (e.g., wealth obtained from cash crops) and she may eventually use them for children from later marriages (e.g., in the Nayar, Ashanti, or Plateau Tonga). The complex dynamics of the local group's marriage, residence, and economic patterns can have far-reaching effects on paternity probability.

Clearly, the kind of investment and the degree of male/female control will determine how much male investment is dissipated. For example, a Yao or Bemba or Ashanti man who contributes to a woman's household with four children, when he is the father of only one child, is in effect investing in wife's children when $p = \frac{1}{4}$—below the paternity threshold. In this situation, male investment in spouse's offspring is not adaptive—that is, a man would increase his inclusive fitness more by investing in his sister's children. Consequently, as the husband and his kin resist such investment behavior (see below), additional investment required by the wife for her children will be more easily obtained from her brother (who may be in the same predicament with *his* wife) than from the husband. As the duration of the monogamous relationship increases, so that more than a fourth of a wife's children are really her husband's, husband's and wife's investment interests will come to overlap more and more; and brother's and sister's investment interests, less and less.

Reports on several other societies suggest that a strong avunculate relationship and a matrilateral kinship bias correlate with high levels of premarital and extramarital promiscuity, and serial marriages. Among the Navaho (Aberle 1961), virginity is not at all valued, and in many instances fatherhood is a question hotly disputed. Adultery is most often cited as the grounds for divorce, and divorce most frequently ends the characteristically short-term Navaho marriages—although desertion and death also play their part. Indeed, only a third of the women and a fourth of the men remain married to the same spouse into old age. The Navaho brother controls inheritance for his sister's children, and often their marriage arrangements as well. He takes on the paternal role of strict disciplinarian, and he is the paradigm of the woman's brother who replaces her husband in this. A somewhat similar ethnographic description for the Siuai of the Solomon Islands (Oliver 1955), the Kaguru (Beidelman 1971), and the fascinatingly complex Tiwi of Melville and Bathurst Islands (Hart and Pilling 1961; Goodale 1971) also lend some support to the paternity threshold model.

Above the Paternity Threshold

A man may be able to obtain a high probability of and confidence in paternity by means of large bride payments, or high status, and thus invest in his children. For example, it appears that some aristocratic Nayar men were assured of paternity by their wives (Gough 1961a: 364 and 379). These men provided their sons with military or political offices. Such a response, predicated on a male's knowledge of paternity, may result primarily from

II. Kinship

his wife's behavior. Paternity certainty is something that a woman can give a man. In the hypergamous marriage system of the Nayar, a woman might increase her reproductive success by guaranteeing paternity to a high-status man who would therefore be willing to, and capable of, investing in the child. In theory a woman can always increase her reproductive success by additional investment in her offspring from a man. She will prefer it from a potential mate only if his investment is more certain or greater than that from some other male, such as her brother. This preference can be realized by exercising *female choice* (see Trivers 1972) in mating and by conferring paternity upon her mate. The man, of course, must somehow increase the correlation between paternity certainty and the probability of paternity. He might achieve this by isolating his wife from other males, guarding her (or having others guard her), severely punishing the slightest extramarital transgression (real or suspected), or by making coitus unpleasant and difficult (e.g., by means of chastity belts).

It may be that a low-status or young man must rely more on investment in sister's children, or other matrilateral relatives, to increase his inclusive fitness, until such time as he can establish or gain the paternity of wife's children and then invest in them cf. Irons, chapter 7). Paternity certainty becomes a source of male-male competition in that males may strive for those economic and political attributes that will more often guarantee paternity of a woman's offspring. For her part, a woman and her kin will give such paternity, and the knowledge of it only when she herself gains from this marital arrangement—that is, when it increases her own reproductive success. For instance, she may do this by accepting virilocality. But she is under no particular pressure to do so. If her brother, or other male matrilateral relative, is also of high status or wealthy, and willing to invest in her offspring for whatever reasons, she might prefer to remain near him and her other kin rather than move into an affinal village or house. But, of course, the brother as a result of these high-status attributes may be obtaining paternity certainty from his own wife or wives. If so, he may well prefer to invest in his spouse's children rather than in his sister's children.

There are other ethnographic examples that suggest that men of high status or wealth, such as chiefs or headmen, have an assurance of paternity that allows them to invest in their children, particularly sons, while minimizing matrilineal control of their behavior. For example, among the Yao, the headman immediately takes his wife to his own village where he maintains authority over her and her children (Richards 1950). A large bride payment by a rich Mayombe man guarantees the right to his children and complete authority over his wife (Richards 1950). Presumably, a woman and her offspring in these situations benefit from the husband's investment. Among the Trobrianders, all men practice *urigubu* in which each is obliged to contribute food to his brother-in-law, in effect investing in his sister and her children (Malinowski 1929). This practice works to the advantage of a chief who, in contrast to other men, is polygynous (which presumably increases his reproductive success), and therefore collects *urigubu* from many brothers-in-law. Other aspects of the Trobriand social system work to the advantage of men of high status. Chiefs and village headmen are usually able to keep their adult sons in their village, while insisting that their sisters' adult sons leave their parents and reside with them. Thus, a chief may have higher paternity certainty and, given his wealth and power, invest heavily in his children as well as his sister's children.

Tracking Paternity: Mixed Strategies

The major artificiality of the proposed model of the avunculate results from the idealized actors' lack of behavioral flexibility. These hypothetical human beings can only invest in one set of children or another, not both (but see appendix). Indeed, the model generates population parameters such as p, the paternity probability, with an idealized value and no variance. Real human beings are not so invariant in their behavior. In reality, males are expected to monitor and track paternity. A man might invest in a sister's child, or keep some minimal investment in sisters and other matrilateral kin, and then attempt to invest in a wife's child when he knows or has reason to believe that he sired the child.

Within some matrilineal societies, men clearly do invest in at least some of a wife's offspring—presumably those known or suspected to be sired by the husband himself. Although jural norms and moral sanctions may dictate inheritance from a man to his sister's son, he may still maintain a particularly warm and close relationship with a wife's child and even favor it with substantial gifts. Among the Bemba, Ashanti, and Trobrianders, for example, there are rather strong elements of "patrifiliation" indicative of significant father-offspring relationships that can be overlooked by emphasizing "matriliny" or "mother's right."

No doubt there are circumstances in which the paternity probability increases such that a woman's offspring become critically important to the inclusive fitness of her husband and his patrilateral kin. Robinson (1962) argues that with respect to the *urigubu* practice, marriage negotiations, and inheritance, a Trobriand man can be of considerable importance in the economic and political affairs of his offspring. By means of such activities he can invest in them. If there is some variance in the paternity probability, even when the average paternity probability is above the paternity threshold, then males may utilize a mixed strategy of investment in sisters' children and wives' children. Patrilateral kin will therefore become more prominent within the social system. Thus some men will exhibit a closer relationship to wives' children or particular offspring, some a closer relationship to sister's children. Indeed, within societies where the probability of paternity is low as a result of high divorce and remarriage rates and/or high levels of extramarital and premarital sex, a man may prefer partible forms of investment that can be given to those certain offspring, nephews, and nieces most relevant to his own inclusive fitness (see also Irons, chapter 7). For her part, a woman will prefer a nonpartible investment that her husband must provide for the entire household, and hence for all her children. Her kinsmen, of course, will concur in this (see below).

A mixed investment strategy by males might even occur with a high probability of paternity within non-matrilineal societies. Investment activity and its associated benefit-to-cost ratio may not be fixed, but rather may vary depending on particular characteristics of the recipient. Such differences in the "efficiency" with which recipients utilize investment may outweigh or counterbalance considerations of paternity probability. That is, as West Eberhard (1975) suggests, the probability of altruism is increased if the recipient is a "super-beneficiary" and/or the altruist a "super-donor." For example, age, sex, or status differences between wife's offspring and sibling's offspring might lead to a bias of investment in the sibling's children. Because in most "primitive" societies a woman begins her reproductive life at an age significantly younger than a man's, he may have more nephews and nieces through sisters than through brothers (Irons, chapter 7). Local demographic conditions will determine how many and how often matrilaterally or sororally connected relatives exist in comparison to patrilaterally or fraternally generated relatives (Hajnal 1963, Rose 1960, Goodman et al. 1974). Thus the demography of "primitive" human social groups may bias siblings' interactions toward the brother-sister relationship.

Where male reproductive success varies more than female reproductive success, as it does in some societies (Chagnon, chapter 14), a man may increase his inclusive fitness more by investing in his sister's son than in his own daughter, despite a marginal relatedness difference that favors the daughter. If the nephew, perhaps because of polygyny, can be expected to have a realized reproductive success greater than the average male reproductive success, altruistic investment in that nephew may yield a larger return to a male's inclusive fitness than the same investment in a daughter.

Age differences between potential recipients of investment can also have considerable effects on inclusive fitness. Given survival and fertility schedules for a population, it can be shown that individuals of different ages have different expected genetic contributions to make to the next generation. This component of fitness, referred to by Fisher (1958) as the *reproductive value,* is the individual's age-specific expectation of future offspring. When a man has both an immature son (low reproductive value) and a sister's mature son (higher reproductive value), his inclusive fitness may increase more by investment in the nephew. On the other hand, if the nephew and son have equal Fisherian reproductive value, but the nephew is a member of a high-status local matrilineal group and the son a member of a low-status group, and if status and reproductive success positively correlate, then the best strategy is to invest in the nephew.

Even the type of investment can, in part, determine optimal recipients. If the investment consists of "perishable" items that can only be utilized immediately (e.g. agricultural produce or, bizarre as it may seem, potential mates—see Chagnon, chapter 4), then even if the status differential favors the immature son, the investment might be better conferred upon the sister's son who can use it now. On the other hand, "nonperishable" goods (e.g., wealth or land) can be saved and passed on to a son or daughter when they can best utilize these limiting resources. This, of course, assumes that wealth and reproductive success are positively correlated. This does appear to be the case within at least one human society (Irons, chapter 10). Thus a man's best strategy for inclusive-fitness maximization requires that he weigh long-term provisions for wealth against current benefits for those near him. He need not think in terms of inclusive fitness, to be sure, to assess economic matters. To invest in a nephew now by giving him land may greatly decrease the land available for a son in the future, whereas this year's gifts of yams in no way necessarily diminishes next year's yam gifts to wife's children and sister's children.

Paternity probability therefore can account only for some of the variance in male and female investment behavior. Obviously, age (reproductive value), sex (fitness variance), kinship (relatedness), alliance (status), and recipient-donor efficiency (benefit-to-cost ratios) all combine to determine the natural selection of behavioral strategies. Finally, the male role should not be overemphasized. The optimal female investment strategies may sometimes be at odds with male strategies. And indeed, a woman and her matrilateral relatives may attempt to coerce her husband into acting in ways that increase her inclusive fitness at a cost to his. Disagreements between kin and affine over a male's investment behavior may lead to conflict over, among other things, inheritance or residence.

Kin Versus Affine

There are basic asymmetries in relatedness within the nuclear family that can lead to conflict between parents and offspring or between siblings (Trivers 1974). A parent, equally related to two offspring, will be selected to support altruism between them whenever $B > C$, where $B =$ the benefit to one offspring and $C =$ the cost to the other offspring. An offspring as well as a parent can be thought of as an actor who attempts to maximize his own inclusive fitness. Thus, an offspring, twice as related to itself as to its sibling, will be selected to act altruistically toward the sib only when $B > 2C$. One can expect conflict between parent and offspring, involving not only parental investment but divergent tendencies to altruism and selfishness in the offspring. Trivers (1974) develops the parent-offspring conflict model into a general biological theory of the family that has broad implications for human psychology. Extending Trivers' analysis to more distant relatives, it is apparent that the model has special import for social anthropology (Trivers 1974:261).

It follows from the paternity-threshold and parent-offspring conflict models that low paternity probability will automatically produce a parental bias in favor of daughters whenever interactions between offspring affect the reproductive success of grandoffspring. A parent of either sex will support a son's altruistic investment in a daughter's children whenever $B > qC$; where $B =$ benefits to grandchildren through the daughter, $C =$ costs to grandchildren through the son's wife, and $q = 1/n =$ the probability that a son's wife's children are indeed the son's parent's grandchildren. That is, "q" represents the proportion of male altruistic investment "squandered" on his wife's children (his parent's putative grandchildren) that he did not sire. So long as the chance of paternity is less than 100 percent (q is less than 1), the son's wife's children can incur n times the cost and still increase parental inclusive fitness by means of his altruism toward the daughter's progeny. One son's altruism toward another son's offspring will be adaptive for the parent whenever $qB > qC$ (or simply $B > C$); in the case of two daughters, such altruism increases parental inclusive fitness whenever $B > C$. The B's and C's refer to the benefits and costs to each set of grandchildren. But altruism by a daughter toward a son's spouse's children will only be adaptive for the parent if $qB > C$, where $B =$ benefits to the son's spouse's children, and $C =$ costs to the daughter's children. In this case, the benefits to son's spouse's children must be n times higher than would be the case were the son's probability of paternity perfect. Thus, even at or above the paternity threshold ($n = 4$), the parent will more often favor a given act of altruism by sons toward grandoffspring through daughters. Note that the father and mother will have congruent inclusive fitness interests with respect to offspring and grandoffspring so long as the father has an equal chance of having sired both offspring. Disagreement between the parents themselves can arise if, for example, the husband is the father of the son and not of the daughter.

If Ego, and the relevant inclusive fitness calculation, is shifted from the parental to the filial generation, and thus offspring altruism is transformed into sibling altruism, then there is a potential parent-son conflict not present when paternity is certain. Male Ego's sibling altruism toward a sister and her children is simply the biological avunculate relationship modeled above. Given a choice of investing in his wife's or sister's children, a male is selected to invest in his sister's children whenever $p < p_t$. But his parents may still prefer his altruistic investment in sister and her offspring at $q = p > p_t$ when, above this paternity threshold, investment from his point of view is best put into a wife and her children. Indeed, a man becomes a focus for cooperation, conflict, and manipulation between kin and affine whose interests are defined by the basic brother-sister, parent-offspring and husband-wife relationships.

Given variability in the paternity probability, there may be conflict over male investment. A man who has good evidence that his wife's offspring are his own will prefer to invest in those children. His matrilateral kin will be more closely related on average to his sister's children than to his children, because of the "weakening" effects of any low paternity probability. All things being equal (which they rarely are), his matrilateral relatives prefer that his investment go to his sister rather than to his wife. At the same time, and by the same logic, his wife's kin prefer for the man to invest in her children instead of his sister's children who may be only distantly related to them. A married man is thus caught in a bind. Alternate adaptive investment strategies involve kin bolstering the man's brother-sister relationship and affines emphasizing his husband-wife relationship. Richards makes a similar point about such conflicts of interest:

*In matrilineal societies the man's control over his wife and her chil-
dren can never be complete, except in the case of a union with a
slave woman, but he can gain considerable power over his wife's
labour, her property, and her child-bearing powers, as well as rights
over his children's work and their marriage, by virtue of the service
or payments he makes to his father- or brother-in-law. Moreover,
the ways in which domestic authority is divided between a man and
the head of his wife's kinship group are surprisingly varied. In some
cases there is a formal allocation of rights and privileges between
father and mother's brother in return for service and payments. In
other cases, the balance is less well defined, and every marriage produces what can only be described as a constant pull-father-pull-
mother's brother, in which personality, wealth, and social status of
the two individuals or their respective kinsmen give the advantage
to one side or the other, and a number of alternate solutions are
reached within the same tribe [1950:208].*

Indeed, Fortune's (1963) classic monograph on Dobuan psychology
and religion described in detail this conflict between Ego and spouse's
matrilateral kin, exacerbated by the couple's annual residence relocation.
Richards (1950) describes in some detail the various attempts to resolve this
conflict between patrikin and matrikin, husband-wife and brother-sister, or
exogamy and matriliny that represent the various facets of the "matrilineal
puzzle."

Among the Ashanti (Fortes 1950; Basehart 1961), there is sometimes
conflict between a man's wife and his sister because each wants him to do
what he can for her children. That is, each wants him to invest in her
children. This sometimes leads to divorce, which frees the man from obligations to his wife and children and thus increases his chances of investing in
his matrilineal relatives. Part of the ambivalence and conflict between an
Ashanti man and his nephew may result from attempts on his part to give
wealth to his own children (as noted above) or to deplete the nephew's inheritance in other ways. The Trobrianders also consider it bad for a father
to give gifts to his children, though this certainly occurs (Fathauer 1961;
Malinowski 1929). Among the Plateau Tonga, a man's matrilateral relatives
see his wealth as part of their estate, not as part of his wife's or children's
(Colson 1961). Thus the wife will attempt to divert as much wealth as possible to her children, and often encourages the children to break away so
that their labor does not go to her husband and his kin. It is therefore not

surprising that the Plateau Tonga find the brother-sister conflict to be the most serious sibling rivalry, since it threatens matrilineal inheritance of a man's wealth. Among the Yao, there is some evidence of hostility between a woman's children and her sister's children over the male investment, when a senior man establishes virilocality of a sororal family (Richards 1950).

However, all things being equal, sororal polygyny should generate on average less selfishness (in the sociobiological sense) between members of a household, than nonsororal polygyny, given the closer degree of relatedness between the wives in the former case. This does seem to be the case among the Akwẽ-Shavante (Maybury-Lewis 1967: 87) and the Tiwi (Hart and Pilling 1960; Goodale 1971). With virilocal residence in the Mayombe, this conflict between husband's and wife's family over his potential investment is kept in balance by the return of the children to the mother's brother at puberty, and by the right of the wife to give any earnings to her brother for her children's inheritance (Richards 1950). Among the Navaho (Aberle 1961), the husband provides the labor necessary for economic support of his wife and her children, but her children take care of the husband in his old age. Indeed, some of the complex interactions characteristic of the mother's brother-sister's child, father-child, and husband-wife network may be based on *reciprocal altruism* (Trivers 1971) in which benefits deferred to later life will offset costs incurred earlier. If a man shows signs of shifting investment from his sister's son to his wife's son, tension or conflict between him and the nephew will arise (as noted above). Indeed, within any system of reciprocity, the possibility of cheating would seem to lead inevitably to tense relationships between the actors (Trivers 1971).

The existence of highly variable residence arrangements essentially vitiates such static typological concepts as "matrilocality," or "virilocality." Moreover, as Richards emphasizes, it is exceedingly artificial to characterize a human social group as "matrilineal," when there are always some "patrilineal" elements present (see also Robinson 1962). A typology is best replaced by a set of variables for functional explanations. Variable residence patterns occur not only between and within matrilineal societies (Richards 1950:210), but also during the life of the individual. This variable residence cycle results in part from the conflict between patrikin and matrikin about the right of the husband to determine and control the household, wife, and children. Without a statistical inventory of actual observed household composition and formation for a given group, it is impossible to determine to what extent paternity certainty, relatedness, and investment are the adaptive basis of such residence cycles (but see Gough 1961c, Schneider 1961b). However, the available data lend some support to an interpretation that conflict between husband's and wife's kin and the concomitant residence cycles are determined in part by variable paternity and investment interests. Individuals will differ with respect to how much investment is directed toward which relatives as a result of the degree of paternity certainty established. Variability in behavior and residence is therefore expected. Modal residence patterns of "matrilocality" mask such variability, as Richards (1950) was keenly aware.

Parent-Offspring Ideology

Given variable paternity probabilities, a male life-history may involve investment in sister and her children prior to marriage, but then a shift of investment away from the sister to a wife and his known children (Irons, chapter 7). Of course, male Ego as a grandparent may, depending upon paternity probability and confidence, attempt to divert investment from his son's putative to his daughter's certain children just as his own parents did. Moreover, he may himself still be embroiled in conflict with his sister, matrilateral kin, or even parents (if they are still alive) over investment in his wife and her children. While the behavior of the actors changes over the life cycle in, perhaps, highly predictable ways as a function of changing reproductive status, various aspects of the matrilineal ideology (for example, paternity ignorance, female ancestral spirits, naming customs, or classificatory kin terms) will remain adaptively constant. Until a young man or woman is an independent actor, the dominant belief system is clearly congruent with the parents' and older kinsmen's own biological interest. By the time these young actors can actually affect real control of their own lives, the ideology will be advantageous in interactions with their own offspring, kin, or affines.

The articulated and dominant ideology, expressed in language, religion, or politics, can be thought of as essentially a parental system that serves to create an environment in which the offspring generation, handicapped because of inexperience, will be more easily molded into individuals whose behavior is ideal from a parental viewpoint. Offspring, of course, will resist as best they can and may at times have their way. However, the socializing environment may in fact often work to produce the parent's ideal offspring, particularly in the offspring's early stages of life. But as offspring mature, the "system" becomes an excellent deceptive shield behind which the actor attempts to do what is in his or her interest while literally mouthing parental views. By adulthood, the parental line *is* the offspring's line!

Society, and its members, in the most subtle and complex ways may take part in a fabric of deception and self-deception (Alexander 1975a). This perspective on human social life, though repulsive to some, is quite consistent with the ideas of Freud, Marx, Lévi-Strauss, and others who postulate the workings of an "unconscious," and cannot be dismissed as (or because it is) a "descent into the kingdom of tabu" (Sahlins 1976:106). Instead, part of the function of human behavior, speech, and even cognition, must be sought in the ultimate causes defined by evolutionary biology. Human actors, like other organisms, are also subject to natural selection. While we certainly should not "abandon all understanding of the human world as meaningfully constituted" (Sahlins 1967:107), to deny the relevance of biology to our behavior and its meaning will without doubt make self-knowledge forever incomplete and illusory.

Paternity Ignorance

In some matrilineal societies, individuals explicitly deny the role of sexual intercourse in conception and reproduction (Schneider 1961a). If this "ignorance of paternity" belief is challenged by the ethnographer, as Malinowski (1929) did, the native may argue that coitus and procreation are in no way necessarily connected. Trobrianders maintain that the unborn child journeys from the matrilineal spirit world (*Tuma*) and enters the woman's womb through the unobstructed vagina. Although a "virgin cannot conceive" (Malinowski 1929:180), intercourse is not necessary for conception—any mechanical deflowering is apparently sufficient. The neighboring, matrilineal Dobuans "say bluntly that the Trobrianders lie" (Fortune 1963:239). Obviously, ideology is not simply determined by biology. A number of idealized belief systems may be possible within particular biological boundary conditions.

The Trobrianders also point to the often obvious physical resemblance between father and offspring. Indeed, it is offensive to suggest, as Malinowski did out of ignorance of local custom, that a mother and child, or siblings, or, in fact, any matrilateral relatives, resemble each other. But to "resemble one's father . . . is the natural, right, proper thing for a man or woman to do" (Malinowski 1929:204). When paternity is less than certain, both males and females will be sensitive to any proximate cues that provide paternity information, family physical resemblances being an obvious candidate. The invariant mother-offspring biological connection creates none of these problems.

These two facets of Trobriand ideology appear to represent Richards' conflict in yet another form. The institutionalized inheritance of property and wealth from mother's brother to sister's son, a diagnostic feature of matrilineal society, keeps these aspects of male investment for matrilineal and matrilateral relatives. By emphasizing the lack of any "natural" connection between a man and his children, a man's matrilateral relatives keep the various forms of male investment within the matriline. On the other hand, his wife's (matrilateral) kin, by emphasizing father-offspring resemblance, create a situation where some male investment might be more easily directed to his putative (and thus the wife's) children. Paternity ignorance emphasizes the female role in providing the *substance* of the child, whereas paternity resemblance points to the male's creative role in giving *form* to the child. Within the ideology both sexes are necessary for the creation of a new being. Behaviorally, promiscuity belies the articulated ignorance. Thus, paternity ignorance serves the interest of male Ego's matrilateral kin, whereas paternity resemblance potentially benefits male Ego's spouse's matrilateral kin. Ideology becomes a means for manipulating others by denying particular behavioral or physical states of affairs. Such "deception" will be adaptive whenever it increases the actor's inclusive fitness. Some biologists have suggested that since selection will also favor individuals who can spot the deception, convincing deception might necessarily entail self-deception about the actor's own deceptive behavior (Alexander 1975a; Dawkins 1976; Trivers 1976b). Thus, while he engages in extensive extramarital sexual activity, a Trobriand man may vehemently deny the outsider's (ethnographer's) claim that there is a substantive male role in conception. Indeed, Malinowski himself points to this conflict between behavior and belief. He describes a case in which some Trobrianders denied that a rather ugly woman ever had intercourse, but agreed that nonetheless she bore children, vindicating the Trobrianders' denial of paternity.

> *This was one more of several cases in which I found how strongly convention (ideals of behaviour) obsesses the mind of the natives, but only on the surface and controlling their statements rather than their behaviour. Things about which he would not like even to speak, much less admit to having done, a native simply denies with consistency and vigour, although he is perfectly aware that they do happen, perhaps even under his own roof.* Tout comme chez nous! [*1929:294–295*]

Similarly, among two Australian groups, women and suspected adultery are reported to be the cause of the overwhelming majority of legal disputes, fights, and homicides, despite an ideology of paternity ignorance (Hart and Pilling 1960; Hiatt 1965).

Although one might expect that a woman would not be so deceptively naive about the relationship between intercourse, conception, and her own reproduction, an articulated ignorance of paternity can be to her advantage also. In general, if some male attributes that potentially increase parental investment (e.g., wealth or status) are often obtained fortuitously, perhaps because of some social inheritance custom or historic accident, then male investment ability and genotypic fitness may not always be correlated positively. Consequently, females should be selected to be able somehow to evaluate both the investment and the genetic contribution males can make to their reproductive success. Given her ability simply to assert who is the "father" of her children, and given a man's inability to know with certainty who is the "father," a woman may be in a position more easily to determine who will be the genetic father (genitor) and who the social father (pater) of her children. A man will, of course, not always be so naive about such pronouncements of paternity, but a woman may sometimes succeed in eliciting investment for her children from the pater by convincing him that he is indeed the genitor. These two aspects of male reproduction (genes and investment) may be more easily separated and thus manipulated to the advantage of a woman and her children when there is an institutionalized ignorance of paternity. That is, a woman may have more latitude for choosing separate paters and genitors of her children. It may therefore be quite adaptive for a woman not to articulate what must be to her the more obvious facts of life.

Of course, for males, paternity ignorance represents a rather impressive "smokescreen" for increased promiscuity. Thus, one male response to the low paternity probability induced by paternity ignorance is simply to increase the number of matings, thereby increasing the number of offspring reared by others. A simple positive feedback between promiscuity and paternity will lower the paternity probability even more. Paternity ignorance creates a social environment that is, in part, defined by a complex of male and female reproductive strategies and counter-strategies.

Paternity and the Sex Ratio

According to the paternity threshold model, low and/or variable paternity certainty will often make male investment in a sister's progeny adaptive. With reference to the parent's own inclusive fitness, altruism between sons and daughters can be shown to have an effect on the optimal sex ratio of offspring produced by parents. That is, paternity certainty itself may be a determinant of sex ratios.

Evolutionary biologists have recently suggested that in addition to parental investment, or what Fisher (1958:158) calls "parental expenditure," cooperation and competition between relatives can determine sex ratios (Alexander 1974; Hamilton 1967 and 1972; Trivers 1974; Trivers and Hare 1976; Trivers and Willard 1973). That is, the sex ratio may vary as a function of social behavior. Sex ratios within a population, within a subgroup of the population, or over the lifetime of individuals can be used to test predictions from evolutionary models of social behavior. For example, Trivers and Willard (1973: footnote 21) point out that if one sex acts altruistically toward kin of the opposite sex more than toward those of the same sex, parents will be selected to direct more than 50 percent of the available investment to the more altruistic sex. The altruistic sex "pays back" the parent by freeing some investment for production of others of its sex.

If within a human social group the cost of rearing a typical son or daughter is about the same, and *if* sons are more altruistic toward the offspring of female kin, particularly daughters (i.e., there is a rather prominent avunculate), during the parental investment period, then there should be a male-biased sex ratio by the end of the period. Indeed, assuming that corrections can be made for other sex ratio determinants, the degree of male bias in this tertiary sex ratio will measure the extent to which males invest in female kin, especially in sisters and their offspring, or in their own offspring.

Paternity: Cause and Effect

The paternity threshold model predicts how idealized human actors ought to respond to given levels of paternity certainty. However, this model may give the impression that low paternity probability "causes," for example, the avunculate. Not only is this an absurd use of mechanical causation, but it is equally reasonable to conclude that the avunculate "causes" low paternity probability. These aspects of human sociality and biology do seem to correlate, but clearly this association must be mediated by a host of biological, demographic, economic, and psychological variables that are at present rather imperfectly understood. Simplicity and comprehensibility, virtues of a scientific model, are also sometimes its major weakness when realism is lacking (Levins 1966). The tradeoffs between generality, realism, and robustness of prediction from a model are often difficult to evaluate, especially in the early stages of scientific investigation. The present model of human sociality is thus only a crude first attempt.

The ecology of some human populations may result in economic and political processes that are conducive to male movement and female sedentariness, and thus lowered probabilities of paternity. It is apparent that if one sex is to be relatively more mobile, for whatever reasons, it will be men. A human child is so dependent upon its mother's care that only the father can be easily separated from spouse and children. Rossi (1978:75) points out that although human family patterns reveal extreme diversity in the roles for father (from absence to nurturance), "there is little or no variation in the cultural rule for the relationship of mother and children: A close bond between them is the universal demand." Indeed, there are no human societies in which the household is built around a man and his children, while the mother resides elsewhere. This suggests that human sociality is, perhaps, less variable and arbitrary than most social anthropologists traditionally assert. However, exactly how a social environment arises that generates lowered paternity probabilities is a difficult and complex issue (but see Irons, chapter 7).

The present model lends some support to Murdock's (1949) contention that matrilocal-matrilineal societies easily revert to patrilocal-patrilineal societies. The paternity threshold ($p_t = 0.268$) is low, and thus may be easily realized. This low paternity threshold easily leads to the emergence of patrilineal, patrilateral, or patrilocal patterns that are, in fact, found in many matrilineal groups (Richards 1950). Once the paternity threshold has been passed, only a radical alteration in residence, male mobility, promiscuity, or female choice will bring the average paternity probability again below a fourth. Thus, it is not too surprising that only 15 percent of societies in Murdock's (1957) sample are matrilineal.

Sexism as expressed in kinship, alliance, descent, or other institutions and behavior, can be seen as an obviously self-serving male ideology that creates a social environment in which most males are more able to ascertain and maintain paternity. Human males may attempt to control female reproductive behavior by marriage arrangements. If this fails, they may resort to clitoridectomy, foot-binding, infibulation, chastity belts, wife-battering, and other violent forms of domination, in order to establish paternity. Indeed, these practices may represent frustrated male responses to the paternity uncertainty built into human reproductive biology.

If this is so, it demonstrates that we cannot explain everything by invoking reproductive biology, precisely because one need not be female to find such practices degrading and morally repugnant. In this regard as in others, to increase self-knowledge may increase self-mastery; and we should not forget that culture itself is our response to the uncertainties as well as the biological inevitabilities of life.

A biological perspective on human social behavior assumes that males and females are actors who differ with respect to the particular strategies used to attain reproductive success. Issues of sexual equality, inferiority, or superiority are simply meaningless within biology. The theory of sexual selection implies only that conflict and cooperation between and within the sexes are expected (Trivers 1972). A comprehensive understanding of how paternity and relatedness affect optimal investment patterns and therefore human social organization, and presumably ideology, requires much more information about female behavior and physiology. Indeed, the proposed model implies that in some social contexts women will have reproductive strategies in which paternity for and investment from a husband are of no particular importance. Moreover, it remains to be demonstrated— although most anthropologists take it as axiomatic—that men typically maintain effective control of human social groups, in general, and female reproduction, in particular. More importantly, a sociobiological perspective provides a way of describing human kinship and reproductive behavior in terms of dynamic, frequency-dependent interactions, rather than in terms of static, dualistic, and pejorative concepts (e.g., dominance/subordinance, equality/inequality, autonomy, power, etc.) that are regularly used in the charged arena of sexual politics. Since sexuality itself necessarily entails the contributions of both sexes, there is simply no meaningful way to establish or assert the superiority of one sex over the other.

Although the ethnographic literature cited above lends some support to the model developed in this paper, a more rigorous test is obviously required. It will be no easy task, for it requires rather detailed field research that can provide data on the relevant behavioral interactions, investment patterns, residence cycles, relatedness measures, and paternity probabilities within a human social group. But it is only with such data that such biological models of anthropological phenomena can be scientifically tested.

Appendix: Partible Investment

The paternity threshold model presented above assumes that an actor can invest an equal amount in either a set of potential offspring or a set of potential nephews and nieces, but not both. What would be the optimal (inclusive) investment strategy if investment were partitioned between, and differentially utilized by, offspring and sibling's offspring?

1. For a woman and her sister, it is necessary to re-evaluate equation (1) (p. 150) such that

$$r_o (k_i) > r_o (\bar{r}_s) (k_j), \tag{a}$$

where k_i = benefit-to-cost ratio of investment in offspring, k_j = benefit-to-cost ratio investment in sibling's children $k_i \neq k_j$, and $k_i + k_j = k$ = total return-on-investment to the actor. Thus, "k" represents the benefit-to-cost ratio of the actor's altruism investment. Given $\bar{r}_s = r_f(p^2) + r_h(1-p^2)$; with $r_f = 2r_h$, and $r_h = \frac{1}{4}$, it follows that

$$1 > \frac{k_j}{4k_i} (p^2 + 1). \tag{b}$$

Now if $k_i > k_j$, that is, if female Ego's investment is more efficiently used by her children, then (b) is always true. But suppose that the investment yields a higher return when applied to her sister's children, then $k_j > k_i$. Indeed, assume that $k_j = k_i + e(k_i)$, where e is any positive real number, then

$$1 > \frac{k_i + e(k_i)}{4k_i} (p^2 + 1). \tag{c}$$

Solving for e, it follows that

$$\frac{3 - p^2}{p^2 + 1} > e. \tag{d}$$

If $p = 1$, then the investment in sister's children is adaptive only when $e > 1$. But $e > 1$, when $p = 1$, simply means that $k_j > 2k_i$. In other words, investment in a *full* sister's children must be more than twice as beneficial as investment in a woman's own children, if there is to be a net gain to her inclusive fitness. But this is essentially the Hamiltonian condition for adaptive altruistic behavior between individuals whose degree of relatedness is $\frac{1}{2}$, namely, $B > 2C$, where B = the benefit to sister's children, and C = the cost to female Ego's offspring due to her altruistic investment.

As p decreases, e will increase, until the limit where $p = 0$ and $e > 3$, that is, where $k_j > 4k_i$. This is the condition for adaptive altruistic investment between *half* siblings: namely, $B > 4C$.

2. Exactly the same result is obtained for a male Ego and his brother, with the stricture that $p \neq 0$. As noted above, when $p = 0$, a male's Darwinian and inclusive fitness as a result of his investment behavior are zero. Thus, even if $k_i \neq k_j$, the paternity threshold model demonstrates that altruistic investment between parent and offspring will be more frequent than between siblings of the same sex, since two to four times more investment must be put into an Ego's sibling's progeny.

3. In the case of a woman and her brother, it is necessary to analyze equation (5) (p. 151) such that

$$r_o (k_i) > r_o (\bar{r}_s) (k_j) (p), \tag{e}$$

where all variables are as defined above. This reduces to

$$1 > \frac{k_j}{4k_i} (p^3 + p). \tag{f}$$

If $k_i > k_j$, then (f) is always true, and a female Ego can invest more in her children than in her brother's children. However, if $k_j > k_i$, in particular, if $k_j = k_i + e(k_i)$, as above, then it follows that

$$\frac{4 - p - p^3}{p^3 + p} > e. \tag{g}$$

If $p = 1$, then again e must be greater than 1 for a sister's investment in her brother's children to yield a net increase to her inclusive fitness, that is, $B > 2C$. But as p approaches zero, e becomes infinitely large, and investment in brother's offspring becomes increasingly maladaptive. It is expected that a female will rarely invest more in her brother's spouse's putative offspring than in her own known offspring.

4. To understand the brother-sister dyad, it is necessary to re-evaluate equation (7) (p. 152) such that

$$r_o(p) (k_i) > r_o (\bar{r}_s) (k_j), \tag{h}$$

where all variables are as previously defined. If investment is more efficiently used by a wife's (or wives') children than by sister's (or sisters') children, for whatever reasons, then $k_i > k_j$, or simply, $k_i = k_j + e(k_j)$. Substituting this in (h) above leads to

$$p > 2(1 + e) - (4e^2 + 8e + 3)^{\frac{1}{2}}. \tag{i}$$

In this case, e and p are proportional to each other, and thus, with a paternity probability ($p = 1$), e must be greater than 1. That is, a man's sister's children must benefit more than twice as much as his wife's children. With a decreasing paternity probability, more and more investment can be put into sister's progeny, and taken away from wife's offspring, despite the better utilization of the investment by his mate's offspring, and still increase a male's inclusive fitness.

  If investment in sister's children benefits them more per investment unit than investment in wife's children, then, by definition, $k_j > k_i$, or simply, $k_j = k_i + e(k_i)$, and (h) simplifies to

$$p > \frac{2}{1 + e} - \left[\frac{4}{(1 + e)^2} - 1 \right]^{\frac{1}{2}} \tag{j}$$

Since p and e vary inversely, the paternity threshold will be lower than 0.268, only if $e > 0$. That is, whenever wife's children, contrary to the assumption that $k_j > k_i$, actually do benefit more than sister's children. This implies that additional male investment in a wife's offspring, as compared to sister's offspring, can be *reduced* as the paternity probability increases, and yet still increase a man's own inclusive fitness.

  These machinations should suffice to demonstrate that even under the extreme artificialities of the earlier paternity threshold model, the qualitative results of that model still hold. Variable and divisible investment among an Ego's immediate relatives does not alter the basic argument presented in this paper.

  This appendix is dedicated to my friend Martin Daly, Department of Psychology, McMaster University, who unfortunately asked what would happen if investment were partible.

7. Investment and Primary Social Dyads[1]
William Irons

Anthropologists have long been fascinated with the question of why systems of kinship and marriage differ from one human society to another. This chapter suggests reasons for certain aspects of this variation based on the assumption that human kinship behavior is directed toward maximizing inclusive fitness (Hamilton 1964).

The discussion begins with the observation that altruistically assisting kin appears to be an important means of increasing inclusive fitness in all human societies (Alexander 1977a). Opportunities for employing this strategy are ordinarily greatest in interaction with one's closest relatives—parents, siblings, and offspring—and in cooperating with mates for the care of offspring. For convenience, in the discussion below, these categories of related individuals (parents, siblings, offspring, and mates) are referred to as primary social allies, and the relationships one has with these individuals are referred to as primary social dyads/relationships/ties. One cannot ordinarily interact extensively, during one's adult years, with all categories of primary social allies. Rather, the usual pattern is to interact, in adulthood, more extensively with certain types of primary allies than with others. These patterns of social interaction are the outcome of what can be described as investment choices. In this paper, investment is broadly defined as anything which an individual does to increase his or her inclusive fitness which also limits his or her ability to do other things that would serve the same end in a different way. Investment defined in this way is similar to, yet somewhat broader than, Trivers' concept of parental investment (1972) and Dawkins' concept of altruism investment (1976:133). It involves, for example, any expenditure of limited resources—energy, nutriment, or time—toward a particular end, such as mate acquisition or assisting a particular relative, which limits possibilities of expending such resources toward other ends. It also involves assuming risk in pursuit of

[1] Richard D. Alexander, Napoleon A. Chagnon, Mildred Dickemann, Mark Flinn, Jeffrey A. Kurland, Carolyn McCommon and Marjorie Rogasner read earlier drafts of this paper and made helpful comments. The importance of female networks among the Tiwi was first suggested to me by Carolyn McCommon. Work on this paper was supported by the Harry Frank Guggenheim Foundation and the National Science Foundation.

181

such ends, since the number of risks an individual can afford to assume is limited.

The things that organisms do in order to project their genes into future generations can be thought of as several different kinds of effort. The broadest categories are those of somatic effort, which includes ontogeny and activities aimed at preserving the mature soma, and reproductive effort, which includes all activities aimed at the production and nurturance of other individuals that will serve to carry the organism's genes into descending generations (Williams 1966, Hamilton 1967, Hirschfeld and Tinkle 1975). Reproductive effort can be divided into mating effort, which includes all activities directed toward acquiring a mate and toward the actual process of mating (such as gamete formation), and parental effort, which includes all forms of nurturance of progeny (Trivers 1972, Low 1978). For many species, nurturance of siblings or other relatives which are not offspring is also important. This is certainly true of human beings and it might, therefore, be useful in human sociobiology to refer to kin effort, one subcategory of which is parental effort. It might also be useful in human sociobiology to refer to resource-gathering effort as a broad category which includes somatic effort but also includes such things as acquiring wealth, political power, or various kinds of knowledge. (These various concepts are reviewed and refined in Alexander and Borgia, 1978; Low 1978; Kurland and Gaulin, in preparation.) The most basic investment choices an individual makes are to direct time, energy, or resource toward one of these broad categories of effort rather than another. Investment choice, however, also can be narrower, such as aiding one particular sibling at the expense of another.

A simple example of an investment choice is the choice a woman can make in many societies between residing in the same household as her sisters or in the same household as her husband. Among Ashanti (Fortes 1950), for example, this is often a real choice and different women choose differently. Usually a woman can assist, and be assisted by, the individuals she lives with more than those who live elsewhere. Assuming that it is impossible to live with both her husband and her sisters (which is true in some societies but not all), the expected choice would be the one which would lead to a higher inclusive fitness.

It should be noted that choices of this sort are made in terms of probable, rather than certain, outcomes of alternative courses of action. It should further be noted that such choices are not consciously made in terms of inclusive fitness. Exactly what sort of thought processes do lead to actual decisions is a complex issue not dealt with in this paper. Here it is merely assumed that whatever these thought processes are they tend to produce the same result that a conscious weighing of choices would have in terms of their effects on inclusive fitness. Phrased in these terms, a woman can be expected to choose *as if* she had weighed the probable effect on her children and her sisters' children of (a) staying with a closely cooperating group of sisters, and perhaps some of her brothers, who share in caring for all of the various sisters' children, and, at the same time, forgoing a measure of assistance from her husband, or (b) moving to her husband's household and obtaining greater assistance from him in rearing her children, but less altruistic assistance from the women of her husband's household than from her own sisters. The assumption that unrelated females will be less altruistic in this situation follows from kin selection theory.

Which choice is more desirable depends on such variables as (a) the value, in terms of the reproductive success of her children, of a co-resident husband's versus a non-co-resident husband's investment in her children, (b) the value, in the same terms, of the assistance of co-resident sisters over that of less related co-resident females, and (c) the value, in terms of her inclusive fitness, of the assistance she can give her sisters in rearing their children. These variables are in turn potentially determined by a large number of other variables which have been shaped by the population's peculiar history, its mode of dealing with its natural environment, and its way of relating to other human populations. A few of the more salient of these variables are (a) the division of labor among the sexes, which is in turn strongly influenced by the mode of economic production, and (b) the nature and extent of assistance men can give their children in the social environment in question. Specific examples of such determinants of investment choices are discussed below.

It is assumed in the discussion below that interaction among primary allies is adaptive both in terms of kin selection (Hamilton 1964) and in terms of reciprocal altruism (Trivers 1971). The gain in inclusive fitness resulting from interaction with any particular primary ally can be expressed as

$$\Delta I = (B_s\text{-}C_s) + r(B_k\text{-}C_k)$$

where C_s and B_s are the costs and benefits to the individual in question in terms of Darwinian fitness, C_k and B_k are the costs and benefits to the primary ally in terms of Darwinian fitness, and r is the coefficient of relatedness for the allies in question. In choosing one overall pattern of interaction rather than another, as in the Ashanti example above, an individual should choose, of the various possible patterns, the one which yields the highest $\Sigma\Delta I$. In making such choices, the possible patterns to choose from are limited by what other actors in the system are willing to do. Only those patterns of interaction which yield a high ΔI for the other party are likely to be real possibilities to choose from.

Operationalizing all of the variables involved in the above expression for a particular empirical setting is likely to be difficult. It may, however, be possible in some cases to make testable predictions based on the assumption that, in a particular society, the dyads in which individuals invest heavily entail high benefits or low costs, or both, and those which they neglect entail low benefits, or high costs, or both. Examples of this sort of prediction are discussed below. It is suggested that empirical hypothesis testing based on such predictions will shed light on such topics as the formation of domestic, residence, and descent groups, patterns of inheritance of property, succession to office, and exchanges associated with marriage such as bridewealth, dowry, and brideservice.

Apparent Differences: Four Societies

Below, four specific societies—the Nayar, Tiwi, Yąnomamö, and Turkmen—are discussed in terms of this hypothesis.

The objective is to demonstrate how one can derive specific testable hypotheses from the general proposition that interaction among primary social allies is governed by investment choices aimed at maximizing inclusive fitness. An attempt is made to show how such choices can be made differently in response to variation in environmental characteristics. Environment in this context, it should be noted, includes everything external to an individual which affects his or her inclusive fitness. Other individuals and their expected modes of behavior are often the most salient feature of the environment when it is defined in this way.

The Nayar: M-S, M-D, Z-Z, B-Z

The Nayar before the beginning of the eighteenth century were an example of a society in which institutionalized cooperation between spouses in rearing their offspring was nonexistent. Individuals throughout their lives remained members of their natal household, which consisted of a group of brothers and sisters (by the same mother but not necessarily the same father) and usually by old age included two generations of their descendants in the female line. Both the male and female members of such households formed over a lifetime a number of mating relationships which entailed no obligations beyond the granting of sexual favors by the female party to the male party. These relationships were not exclusive: individuals of either sex were free to enter into as many such relationships at one time as they wished. These could be broken easily and new ones entered into at any time. Women reared their own children with the aid of other members of their household, and males, to the extent that they invested in any children, were supposed to invest in their sister's children rather than their own. Despite some instances of male investment in their own children, the rule that males should aid only in the rearing of their sister's children appears to have been followed by a large portion of Nayar males. Fuller ethnographic details are given below before turning to the question of what environmental circumstances could cause individuals to prefer an investment pattern of this sort.

The Nayar were a group of castes in the region of southern India known as Central Kerala. The descriptive material below is drawn from K. Gough (1961a). The households mentioned above were the primary property-holding and residential units of Nayar society. The oldest male of each unit acted as its head, managing the group's property and income for the benefit of all its members. Several households related genealogically in the female line formed an exogamous matrilineage. Among the lower Nayar castes, several such matrilineages which entered into formal marriage arrangements with each other, and which interdined, formed a single caste. Higher-ranking Nayar castes often, however, consisted of a single lineage which interdined with no other lineage and married only hypergamously (or more precisely hypergynously).

All Nayar women went through a Hindu marriage ceremony before puberty, but this ceremony did not create a set of legal, economic, or social obligations between a woman and her husband. The relationship created between husband and wife by this ceremony was purely ritual in character. Passing through this religious marriage ceremony, however, legitimized, for the woman, entry into relationships of another type known as *sambandham* relationships. *Sambandham* relationships were basically those of lovers. A *sambandham* relationship was initiated and maintained by the man's giving of certain gifts to the woman. The gifts were trivial in value, and the relationship created no obligation on the woman's part other than that of granting sexual favors to the man. The relationship could be terminated at will by either party, and both men and women were free to enter into a number of such relationships at the same time. It was a matter of indifference whether a woman ever entered such a *sambandham* relationship with the man to whom she was married in the formal religious ceremony before puberty.

When a woman became pregnant one of the men who had a *sambandham* relationship with her at the time of conception had to acknowledge paternity. This acknowledgment, however, created no institutionalized relationship between father and child. Children belonged to the mother's household, and their only institutionalized relationship with men of their mother's generation was with their mother's brothers. A child's mother's brothers, and mother's mother's brothers if living, were its disciplinarians and the ones responsible for the child's care and education. Male children would in turn as adults assume the same role toward their sisters' children.

At first glance this form of social organization might seem to be far from optimal for Nayar men. Other things being equal, a man should prefer to invest his time, energy, and other resources in the rearing of his own rather than his sister's children. He is related to his own children by $\frac{1}{2}$, to those of a full sister by $\frac{1}{4}$, and those of a half sister by $\frac{1}{8}$. Given the loose nature of *sambandham* relationships most of his sisters were probably half sisters. Thus, if a Nayar man conformed to the rules of his society, it would appear, he could only invest extensively in members of the first descending generation to whom he was related by $\frac{1}{8}$. In contrast, if he could successfully break the rules of his society and establish an exclusive sexual relationship with a woman, he would be able to identify with reasonable certainty members of the first descending generation to whom he could be related by an r of $\frac{1}{2}$. Assuming he could, further, break the rules of his society and invest his resources in these children rather than his sister's children, he would be better serving his inclusive fitness. This pattern in fact did become the norm after the British established their colonial rule in Kerala, and the pattern described above was replaced by monogamy both as the usual form of marriage and as the normatively expected one. The question raised by considerations of kin selection is why the system described above ever became established.

A possible answer can be found by looking at the role of the Nayar castes in Central Kerala society at the time when this system was functioning. These were warrior castes who had vassal-like relationships with the occupants of various political offices. Kerala was divided into a number of petty kingdoms each headed by a sovereign who was drawn from a small caste of rulers ranked as Kshattriyas, the second highest of the four categories by which all Indian castes are ranked. These small royal castes are generally considered to have been originally Nayars who had improved in ritual rank after establishing themselves as rulers. (Nayar castes were considered to fall in the third highest category of castes and, therefore, were distinctly lower in ritual rank). Below the royal castes were chiefly Nayar castes from which the rulers selected vassal chiefs. Below these were headman and retainer Nayar castes from whom vassals of progressively lower status were drawn.

Marriages (i.e., *sambandham* relationships) among the higher Nayar castes, those of rulers and chiefs, were always hypergynous. Women of royal castes married only wealthy Nambudiri Brahmins who stood at the top of the Hindu hierarchy of ritually ranked castes. Nambudiri Brahmins were themselves patrilineal. Ordinarily only the eldest son of each Nambudiri family was allowed to marry one or several Nambudiri women and produce Nambudiri heirs. Younger Nambudiri brothers entered *sambandham* relationships with Nayar women, and many Nambudiri females were forced to remain celibate (cf. Dickemann, chapter 13). Nayar women of chiefly caste married only royal Nayars (i.e., Kshattriyas) and Nambudiri, with marriage with royal Nayars following the lines of lord-vassal relationships. Nayar women of headman castes married higher-caste men as well as within their own caste. Retainer Nayars married predominantly within their own caste but also occasionally married men of higher caste.

Warfare among the petty kingdoms was continual, and military forces consisting of Nayars were recruited along lines of vassalage. Nayars held rights to manage and enjoy the income of certain lands on condition that they provided satisfactory military service to their lords, whether headmen, chiefs, or royalty. Military training and actual fighting were the only occupations of Nayar men. Agricultural labor on the land they held was done by persons of lower caste who are described as serfs. Men who were very successful in their military careers were rewarded by additional grants of land to their households and sometimes by elevation to offices of headman or chief which they did not previously hold. Once acquired, these offices were hereditary so long as they were satisfactorily executed. Thus there were opportunities for upward mobility. Downward mobility was also possible. Collateral branches of chiefly and headman lineages eventually assumed the status of retainer castes. Also, either cowardice in battle, or defeat and permanent acquisition of one's land by another ruler, could lead to downward mobility.

The literature on the Nayar suggests that the loose marriage system was ideally suited to men whose military careers necessitated frequent absence from their home villages for campaigns (Gough 1961a: 372). From the point of view of rulers, it is stated that the Nayar were more effective as military men because they were free of attachments to wives and family. From the point of view of Nayar men, the family system described above would make sense if viewed as a choice to invest more in resource-gathering effort at the expense of limiting kin effort to assistance of less related individuals than offspring. Being effective as a military man and thereby pleasing one's headman, chief, or ruler, led to a gain in the ability to invest, at the cost of having to invest in less related individuals. The cost took the form of conferring one's benefits on individuals related by $\frac{1}{8}$ as opposed to the opportunity to invest in individuals related by $\frac{1}{2}$, i.e., one's own children. This would mean that any gain in reproductive success (ΔF) resulting from his investment in a member of the first descending generation would increase his inclusive fitness by $\Delta F/8$. If he were able to invest in a child of his own, the same investment would result in an increase in inclusive fitness of $\Delta F/2$. However, following a military career, which was for a Nayar incompatible with exclusive sexual access to wives, meant the value of ΔF itself would be larger than if he attempted to follow a non-military career. If we represent the fitness value of his investment given a military career as ΔF_m and the value of his investment given a nonmilitary career and marriage entailing exclusive access as ΔF_a ("a" for alternate), we can say that following the conventional Nayar pattern would be predicted from kin selection theory if ΔF_m were more than four times as great as ΔF_a. (This is based on the assumption that an alternative mating pattern yielding perfect paternity knowledge was open to men who followed nonmilitary careers.) This indicates stringent conditions, but ones that are certainly possible given what we know of the Nayar. For a Nayar to refuse to follow a military career would have had drastic effects on his ability to invest in any kin. The consequence, according to available information, would have been reduction to the status of slave or execution (Gough 1961a: 331–332, 339–340). Coercion on the part of superiors in a sharply stratified society is an important element in choice for Nayar of retainers, headmen, and chiefly caste. However, I see this fact as entailing no special theoretical difficulty. It seems to me reasonable to assume that individuals make the best of coercive situations which they are unable to alter. It is equally reasonable to assume that as long as a man had to follow the Nayar type of military career, attempts to establish an exclusive sexual relationship with any women were futile.

It may be possible to investigate the probable validity of the above inequality ($\Delta F_m > 4\Delta F_a$) using the methods of historians and ethnohistorians. The Nayar were part of a literate civilization, and records of some of their activities are available. I doubt that exact operationalizing of the values of ΔF_m and ΔF_a would be possible. It might, however, be possible to document for a number of cases what did happen to Nayar men who refused to serve as military men, and to men who served in a way that displeased their leaders. It might be possible, using historic records, to test the proposition that lack of success as a military man meant a great decrease in a Nayar man's resources for nurturing the next generation, and diminished chances to mate. The downward mobility of militarily unsuccessful Nayar, and the lower reproductive success of individuals of lower status (slaves or members of polluting castes) might be things one could demonstrate—or, alternately, cast doubt on—using documentary sources. It might also be possible to document the attempts by Nayar men to maintain exclusive sexual relationships with a particular woman and to invest in her children.

It should also be noted there are many ways of reacting to rules backed up by coercion which eliminate what would otherwise be good strategies for maximizing inclusive fitness or any other goal. One is circumvention of the rule without openly challenging it. There is evidence that despite the loose nature of the mating practices of the Nayar castes, men often did feel they could identify particular individuals as their children. We are told that both moral censure and sorcery were used to discourage men from transferring gifts and cash to favorite wives and their children (Gough 1961a:361). Attempts to block such transfers probably indicate that men were occasionally trying to invest in their own children. From the point of view of sisters, such transfers would be detrimental to their interests. Moreover, as long as knowledge of paternity was less than perfect, a man's brothers and mother's brothers would also prefer that he invest in his sister's rather than his own children (Kurland, chapter 6:167–169). As long as paternity certainty is less than perfect, a man is more closely related on average to his sister's children than to his brother's children (chapter 6:151–153). For the Nayar the comparison would in most cases be between children of half sisters and children of half brothers, i.e., between an r of $\frac{1}{8}$ and an r somewhat less than $\frac{1}{8}$. Kurland (chapter 6) discusses how low paternity probability diminishes average relatedness through all male links, and thus shifts the optimal recipients of kin effort.

The effect of paternity probability is especially relevant to the issue of Nayar men investing in sister's children rather than wife's (i.e., *sambandham* partner's) children. Greene (1978) has shown that men will be on average more related to sister's children than to wives' children if paternity probability falls below a value of $2-3^{1/2}$, or approximately .268. In very simple terms, this means that if paternity is accurately identified for slightly more than one in four children, a man is more closely related to his wives' than his sister's children. Given the Nayar pattern of mating, paternity knowledge may well have been below this threshold. A crucial question, however, is this: could a Nayar man hope, by circumventing the rules of his society and monopolizing the sexual activities of a particular woman, to raise his certainty that her children were his children above that threshold, and if so at what cost to his resource-gathering effort? Again the question would be difficult to answer, but documents of record might yield some indication of whether such a strategy was likely to be successful. If a man were successful in raising paternity certainty above the .268 threshold, but not raising it to a value of one, all the other members of his household—sisters, brothers, mother, and more distant kin—would still be more closely related to his sister's children than his *sambandham* partner's children (Kurland, chapter 6:151–153). For them, conformity to ideology would still be preferable, and this may explain the persistence of the ideology at least as long as only a minority of men seriously tried to circumvent the rules (Kurland, chapter 6:171–173).[2] The assumption is made that if the majority of men wished very strongly to change the system, it is at least possible that they might overcome both ideology and coercion from above.

One can also suggest that for the higher Nayar castes, who were less subject to coercion from above, there would be more attempts to monopolize the sexual favors of particular women so that a man could identify his children, and invest in them (cf. Gough 1961a:360, 379). The literature does say that men of royal lineage consistently did this even though in theory they were subject to the same rules as their Nayar vassals (Gough 1961a:378–379). Marriages among these groups were all hypergynous with men drawing wives from among their vassals. Because these

---

[2] Returning to the situation discussed on p. 188 of a man who refused a military career in order to monopolize the sexual activities of a woman and identified her children as his, one could consider what a paternity probability of less than one would imply. The inequality on p. 188 would then have to be modified. Assuming a limiting case in which a man was dealing with wives versus a known half-sister's children, the inequality justifying abandoning a military career would become $\Delta F_m < 4 \Delta F_a \, p$ where p, having a value of less than one, would represent the degree of paternity probability. This would probably be hard to test from historic records given the difficulty of estimating p from such records. One could, however, test as a limiting case the situation obtaining with a half sister and $p = 1$: $\Delta F_m < 4 \Delta F_a$. If this condition could not be met, then the strategy of not following a military career would not work. Adding a p of less than one, would only diminish the chances that this inequality will be satisfied.

men monopolized the sexual favors of particular women, they were able to identify their own sons, who were also their vassals, and made a practice of conferring military and political offices on them (Gough 1961a:379). One could also suggest as a reasonable hypothesis that these vassal sons were behaving in the interest of their own inclusive fitness when they pursued the interests of their lords/fathers with great vigor. It is interesting that the filial bond to chiefs and rulers was what in Nayar ideology justified dying in battle for one's lord, and also justified denying oneself rights over one's own children (Gough 1961a:323). (I suspect, however, the lower-ranking retainer Nayars for whom the ideology was less realistic were more frequently the ones who, in response to coercion, carried the ideology into practice.)

The pattern of strict hypergyny among the highest castes, it should also be noted, allowed Nambudiri and royal Nayars opportunities for high male fertility of the sort ordinarily associated with polygyny. Since marriages had to be hypergynous and Nambudiri and royal Nayars together were less numerous than the lower castes from whom they drew wives (Gough 1961a:298, 306–312), the number of available mates per male would be high. From a biological point of view, the social organization of Kerala was very adaptive for the uppermost castes.

Although the above requirement—a fourfold greater success in resource-gathering effort as a result of a military career which makes paternity knowledge impractical—is stringent, there are two facts which suggest it is not unrealistic. One fact providing limited support for the above interpretation is the speed with which the Nayar shifted to a pattern of monogamy, once Central Kerala was pacified by the British and the value of Nayar as soldiers to local rulers was eliminated. Thirty years after the British disbanded the armies of the petty kingdoms of Central Kerala, monogamy had become common and fathers had assumed a definite role in rearing their children (Gough 1961a:372). It is a reasonable interpretation that after pacification, rulers and chiefs no longer were interested in punishing Nayar who sought nonmilitary careers or rewarding those who did follow such careers. This would shift the relative value of each type of career as a form of resource-gathering effort, diminishing the greater value of a military career over a nonmilitary one. Once the difference in the expected value for resource gathering of a military over a nonmilitary career slipped below the fourfold threshold, one would expect Nayar men to shift their strategies and begin to abandon military careers and simultaneously to try to raise paternity confidence. This means that after the cessation of warfare among the petty kingdoms of Kerala, one would expect the mating system to shift toward one which would yield greater paternity confidence. This, in fact, did occur.[3] Whether or not the precise sequence of changes in environmental constraint and strategy suggested here actually occurred should be testable using historic records.

A second fact which suggests that the conditions underlying the Nayar kinship system were unusual is the fact that systems entailing so little father-child investment are extremely rare. They may have existed among some groups neighboring the Nayar at earlier periods in history for the same reasons (Gough 1961a:370–371). Otherwise a system approaching this extreme of low institutionalization of paternity is only reported for the poorly described Minangkabau of Sumatra, a group whose men reportedly traveled widely for purposes of trade (Gough 1961:588–590).

The Tiwi: Z-Z, H-W

The Tiwi, an aboriginal group on Melville and Bathurst Islands in North Australia, are another population which has attracted much attention because their social organization represents an extreme form. The data reviewed below are drawn from Hart and Pilling (1960) and Goodale (1971). In this case the pattern carried to an extreme is what might be described as gerontocratic polygyny. This is a marriage pattern in which the older males through polygynous marriages monopolize the females of reproductive age and thereby exclude younger males from marriage. While this tendency is present in milder form in many societies, the Tiwi carried it to an extreme by having all females, regardless of age, married all the time, and excluding most males from legitimate opportunities to reproduce before their late thirties (Hart and Pilling 1960:14–16).

Females were in fact betrothed as a rule before they were born. When a girl had her first menses, she was put through a puberty ceremony. The final stage of this consisted of a betrothal in which the girl's father (defined by the Tiwi as her mother's current husband) would betroth all of her as-yet-unborn daughters to a particular man or boy (Goodale 1971:51–54). He thus would be marrying off his as-yet-unborn granddaughters. The mean age for men married in this way was a little over thirty, with a

[3] C. J. Fuller (1976) argues that the loss of military careers for Nayar men did not *cause* the change in mating pattern, but rather weakened the traditional system so that other forces—such as the desire of lovers to strengthen the social ties between themselves—were no longer held in check. These other forces then caused the change. His argument does not detract from the interpretation I have developed here, and, in fact, the data he presents, in my opinion, support the model discussed here.

range from fourteen to about sixty-five (Goodale, 1971:53, 65–66). Betrothal in this form established a relationship of mother-in-law to son-in-law between a pubescent female and a male who was usually a number of years older than she was. A son-in-law was obligated to, as the natives said, "feed" his mother-in-law. This meant not only supplying her with food from his hunting activities but also providing other kinds of goods and services. In order to fulfill these obligations he normally had to live in the same camp group as his mother-in-law or at least visit it frequently. The mother-in-law had the right to abrogate the marriage of her unborn daughters to her son-in-law if he did not perform his duties satisfactorily. Should this happen, her father, i.e., her mother's current husband, had the right again to assign her a new son-in-law. If, as was more likely, a son-in-law fulfilled his duties satisfactorily, any daughters born to his young mother-in-law would become his wives. These wives lived with their parents until a point at which as young pre-pubescent girls they were taken by their fathers to their husband's camp fire and told that from this point on they must sleep by their husband's fire. It was required that at this point the husband be co-resident with his parents-in-law in the same camp which would assemble each evening at the same place to share the food from that day's hunting and gathering activities and to spend the night. This meant that although she was now under the supervision of her husband and, if there were any, his older wives, her parents were in a position to observe how she was treated in her new role. If she was treated improperly they could reclaim her. Usually a wife finished growing up and learning the economic and domestic duties of a wife while a member of her first husband's household. On reaching puberty she would acquire a son-in-law to serve her while she continued to serve her husband.

Because women were ordinarily much younger than their first husbands, most became widows while still relatively young. Some, in fact, were widows before moving to their husbands' camp fires. A series of rules defined the process by which widows would be assigned new husbands. One rule stated that if a bride had gone through her puberty ceremony, her husband's brothers, by virtue of participating in this ceremony, had residual claims on her as wife (Goodale 1971:54–56). If this condition was met, one of these men simply assumed the obligations of a son-in-law to her mother, and thus laid claim to her as a wife. However, if she had not gone through her puberty ceremony, or her deceased husband had no brothers, her father (i.e., mother's current husband) would betroth her again.

Eventually a woman's mother died; and, since father was defined as mother's current husband, she now had no father. The right to betroth her then passed to her brothers. If the day should come when she had no living brothers, the right to betroth her would pass to her sons. Thus rights of betrothal passed, at least potentially, from mother's father, to father, to brother, to son. The literature on the Tiwi states that although these were the explicitly recognized rules, in fact as women grew older they exerted considerable influence themselves over the choice of their husbands.

Older males who had acquired many wives had many daughters for whom they could assign husbands or sons-in-law. These men bestowed their female descendants in marriage upon other old men like themselves with the expectation of reciprocity, or upon likely young men in return for the promise of economic and political support to the old man and his household. Most of Tiwi politics was concerned with the various transactions by which men strove to acquire first wives, or to increase the number of wives.

An important aspect of this system was that ordinarily all the daughters of one mother stayed together as co-wives to the same husband throughout their lives. Often also they would have as co-wives other groups of sisters to whom they were closely related in the female line, such as the mother's sister's daughters (Goodale 1971:76). The brothers of such a cohesive group of sisters would frequently reside elsewhere as their marital duties demanded, but contact with and support of their sisters was maintained.

Thus, the pattern of interaction among primary allies that emerges among the Tiwi is one in which the bond among sisters is given the greatest emphasis. This is especially clear if one thinks in terms of a lifelong pattern of interaction. The husband-wife bond is also an important locus of interaction and includes the unusual feature of a husband's assumption of primary responsibility for rearing immature girls who are later to be his mates and are already socially defined as his wives. The emphasis on these bonds limits opportunities for interaction among other primary allies, although none are as attenuated as the husband-wife and father-child bonds among the Nayar. Parents were, for example, still actively engaged in overseeing the welfare of a daughter after she moved to her husband's campfire, but less so than the girl's husband himself. Brothers attempted to stay together, but there was less emphasis on brother-brother co-residence and mutual assistance than on sister-sister co-residence and cooperation.

Keeping together groups of closely related women, especially sisters, was possible only with a marriage system emphasizing sororal polygyny. Maintaining such co-resident groups of closely related women as well as such a high degree of polygyny was significant in the light of Hart and

Pilling's hypothesis that households with larger numbers of women were better off economically than those with smaller numbers of women (1960:33–36).

Vegetable materials were the only dependable daily source of food for the Tiwi, and gathering food of this sort was the work of women. Men hunted and supplied meat which may have been nutritionally very valuable. Products of the hunt, however, were sporadic and could not be relied on for daily caloric needs. Vegetable food could be relied on, but only if a large enough group of cooperating women under the experienced leadership of an older woman were involved in the task of gathering such food (Hart and Pilling 1960:33–35).

Households of older men who had many wives had work forces of this sort and residents of such households could expect to eat well day by day. Households of younger men with few wives were, in contrast, unable to depend on a steady daily food supply. For hunters and gatherers with no effective means of food storage, this was a serious problem. Small households usually wandered in the vicinity of large households, so that on days when they were unable to feed themselves they could approach a large household with the expectation of being fed. Hart and Pilling state as a hypothesis that the Tiwi pattern of polygyny was, in effect, an adaptation to the need to maintain a steady food supply.

Assuming for the sake of hypothesis formation that this is correct, one can construct the following model of investment choices underlying Tiwi social organization. Female work forces were more effective if large and if they included experienced older females to supervise the work. From Hamilton's kinship theory, one would expect women to prefer joining a work force consisting of close kin, over one consisting of distant kin or non-kin: to the extent that others in her work group would benefit from her efforts, she would prefer that these benefits be shared by close relatives. Also, other things being equal, one could expect more effective cooperation and less internal conflict in a work force consisting of closely related individuals. The crucial constraint which this situation placed on investment choice was the fact that, from a woman's point of view, the most useful form of investment in her children, other than her own, was the assistance of other females rather than of males. This situation stands in contrast to one in which male investment in children is valuable and a woman is willing to leave parents and siblings to co-reside with a husband as a condition of his investing in her children. Among the Tiwi, women found the assistance of sisters in rearing their children more valuable than the assistance of husbands. Given this situation, sharing a husband with many other women and changing husbands several times during one's life was an acceptable cost to pay for the benefit of co-residing permanently with one's sisters, and perhaps close female cousins as well, on a lifetime basis. Gerontocratic polygyny, in this case, can be interpreted as the outcome of female strategies aimed at holding together groups of closely related women.

Given this female preference and the low value of male investment in children, the most effective male strategy was to maximize the number of one's wives—that is, to invest more in mating effort and less in parental effort. As in many societies lacking important forms of exchangeable wealth such as livestock, shell-money, or whatever, the only way to obtain wives was to give kinswomen in exchange for them. Thus, men with many daughters could exchange them for wives who would bear them more daughters. The fact that male investment in children was not important meant there was no difficulty—from either a male or a female point of view—in a man's having an extremely large number of wives. In fact, all parties to the arrangement benefitted if Hart and Pilling's hypothesis is correct.

Holding a large number of males together—because of the lesser importance of male economic activities—would offer no comparable advantage. This meant that a highly polygynous man with many daughters to bestow would gain little if he exchanged these daughters for wives for his brothers or sons on condition that they reside with him. It was preferable to obtain wives for himself even if this meant the male work force of his ménage would be smaller, less closely related to him, and less solidary. Thus males emphasized competition with other males for the opportunity to enjoy high fertility at the expense of forgoing extensive cooperation with related males. Men invested some resources in assisting brothers, but these were small compared to their investment of resources toward acquiring wives for themselves (Goodale 1971:71–97). The father-son bond, once a man approached puberty, is described as a hostile one entailing virtually no cooperation (Hart and Pilling 1960:34). We are told that the best thing a son could do for his father on reaching puberty was to go away and make way for sons-in-law.

The interpretation offered here of Tiwi social organization cannot be rigorously tested given the existing data. Alternate interpretations which are also supported by the available data (largely qualitative in character) could be suggested. It is important to note, however, that the interpretation suggested above is, in principle, testable. A large enough body of data on the fertility and mortality experience of Tiwi, associated with different life-history experiences in terms of kinship interaction, would allow direct tests of the hypotheses suggested above. Such a test would require a comparison of the reproductive success of women who differ in terms of the size of the female work forces they participated in at comparable points in their life history, and in terms of the number of close kin among the members of their work force. The above hypothesis would be defensible only if the reproductive success of females were positively associated with the size of their work force, and with the number of close kin in their work force. Further predictions which can be derived from the above interpretation for purposes of empirical testing are the following: for males, reproductive success should correlate positively with the number of their wives, and with the size of the female work force on which they depend, but show no correlation—or at least a clearly weaker correlation—with the number of males attached to their household and with the number of closely related males with whom they cooperate on a daily basis.

The Yąnomamö: F-S, B-B, H-W, B-Z

The Yąnomamö are of great theoretical importance in anthropology because they exhibit a classical form of dual organization and because the available data on them demonstrate the connection between this dual organization and the condition which Sahlins labels warre (1968:5–13). Warre is the condition under which there is no central authority which monopolizes the use of violence within a society, which takes upon itself the resolution of internal disputes by adjudication, and which protects the rights of person and property of those under its authority with its own means of violence. Given warre each man has the recognized right and real opportunity to use violence against others for whatever purpose suits him. An individual's protection against arbitrary victimization in such societies lies in the willingness of a kin coalition to meet violence with violence. The Tiwi also were subject to warre before the establishment of Australian administration in their territory. However, in their case violent male-male competition was less prominent. The description of the Yąnomamö below is drawn primarily from Chagnon (1968a, 1974). Chapters 4, 8, 12, and 14 in this volume contain further material on the Yąnomamö, and, therefore, the discussion of their kinship system here is brief.

In the case of the Yąnomamö, men invest much of their time and other resources in the formation and maintenance of alliances with other males which are directed toward two objectives: protecting themselves and their close kin from violence, and using violence against others for acquisition of wives (see Chagnon, chapter 4). The most solidary ties among males are those between father and son, brother and brother, and brothers-in-law. The brother-brother tie tends to be strongest in the case of full brothers, and in the case of brothers who differ widely in age. Those who are closer in age are more clearly competitors for the same mates, and this weakens solidarity. As men grow older they tend to ally more closely with brothers-in-law and to weaken their ties with brothers.

Wives are expected to co-reside with their husbands and husband's close kin and thus by residence are drawn away from close cooperation in adulthood with their siblings and parents. Although husbands and wives are expected to cooperate in many ways, the relationship is frequently characterized by antagonism. Wife beating is common, and women in general are expected to work hard for their husbands for relatively little return benefit other than protection for themselves and their children from the coercion of other men. Brothers are solicitous of their sisters' welfare and attempt to curb potential abuse of their sisters by sisters' husbands. Women who have many powerful brothers living in their village are treated better by their husbands than are those with few brothers, brothers without power, or brothers who live in different villages.

The close tie between brothers-in-law is based in part on the potential for future exchange of daughters as son's wives, but also has much to do with attempts by brothers to protect the interests of their sisters. Thus, the strength of the tie between brothers-in-law is to some extent an aspect of a strong supportive relationship between brother and sister.

The Yąnomamö come closer to a pattern of equal interaction and equal investment among primary allies than do the Tiwi or Nayar. Nevertheless, choices to invest more in certain allies than in others are evident. Women must live with their husbands (after a period of bride-service by the husband) and work the gardens cleared by their husbands. If they are fortunate enough to have parents and siblings in the same village, mutual assistance is possible between a woman and these kin, but it is secondary to her cooperation with her husband and her direct care of her own children. Thus the husband-wife bond takes precedence over the ties of a woman to all her other primary allies other than immature children and adult sons. This combines conveniently with preservation of ties of men to their brothers and parents in adulthood. The ties of a woman to her brother and father, however, do remain significant. Although they reside either in different parts of a village or in different villages, and cooperate little in economic or domestic activities, there is an important political bond between them in terms of protection afforded by brothers to their sisters, and fathers to their daughters. The benefit to men in this relationship is of two types:

altruism to close kin, and also the potential return benefit of a sister's daughter as a son's wife, or an ideal marriage arranged for a daughter to a sister's son. Thus the exchange of benefits between brothers and sisters is not only less than that between husband and wife, but also differs very significantly in the form of the benefits exchanged.

The interesting and well-described pattern of village fissioning among the Yąnomamö (Chagnon 1968a, 1974, 1975) reflects this relatively even division of investment among different categories of primary allies. Yąnomamö villages tend statistically to consist of two intermarrying local patrilineal descent groups of several generations' depth. When they fission owing to internal conflict each of the descent groups tends to split along the line of greatest genealogical distance, and each segment of these severed lineages tends to form a new village with its close relatives in the other lineage. Thus brothers stay with brothers, brothers with sisters and sister's husbands, while cousins and distant affines go off to form a different and frequently hostile village.

Violent male-male competition among Yąnomamö places a high value on brother-brother and father-son alliance. Unlike the Tiwi, sister-sister cooperation offers no great advantage. The obvious solution is for women to leave their natal groups at marriage, for sisters to scatter (unless a group of sisters are able to marry a group of brothers or polygynously marry the same man), and for men to stay together with their closest male kin. However, two features of Yąnomamö society prevent the bias in favor of agnatic bonds from being carried as far as they are in many societies. One is the fact that brothers can, as in many societies, contribute to their sisters' well-being, and hence reproductive success, by protecting them against their husbands when necessary. The second is the fact that there is heavy competition among men for mates and that mates are obtained primarily by exchanging women, or by exchanging women for promises of women in the future. The exchanges are usually arranged by men who trade daughters in order to obtain wives for their sons. Such exchanges, especially of women for promises of women in the future, are most reliable if several exchanges are made with the same man or group of brothers. Therefore, a man can gain by investing a significant portion of his potential pool of benefits in sisters and brothers-in-law with the hope he may obtain mates for his sons or brothers' sons in return.

There are a number of ways in which the above model can be tested empirically. The most basic testable prediction is that the reproductive success of Yąnomamö men should correlate with the number of closely related males who have been co-resident with them (see Chagnon, chapter

4, chapter 14). Male reproductive success should also correlate with the stability of their marital alliances with lineages from which they can draw mates. It should further be possible to test the above model by looking for a correlation between high reproductive success and cross-cousin marriages of the preferred category (see Chagnon, chapter 4, chapter 14). For women reproductive success should be higher if they are co-resident with large numbers of brothers, and also if their marriages are of the preferred form.

The Yomut Turkmen: F-S, B-B, H-W

The Yomut Turkmen offer an instructive contrast to the three groups above in that they represent a pattern of strong emphasis on the father-son and brother-brother bonds. Women are cut off from extensive interaction with parents and siblings in order to be firmly integrated into households and larger cooperative groups built up along the lines of father-son and brother-brother ties. The data below are drawn from my own field research. Much of the descriptive material is available in Irons (1975).

The most significant contrast with the Yąnomamö lies in the fact that usually wives are not obtained by exchanging women for women, but rather by exchanging livestock for women. The required payments are basically the same in amount for all brides and do not vary significantly with the wealth of the two families transacting the marriage. The payments of livestock are exorbitant; they represent the equivalent of several years' income for families in the middle ranges of wealth. Poor families frequently find it necessary to impoverish themselves further by giving away most of their capital in exchange for a bride for one of their sons.

These substantial bridal payments are associated with a pattern of interaction among primary allies which goes further than most in weakening a woman's ties to her parents and siblings in order to strengthen her ties to her husband. This can most clearly be seen by examining the role of women in the organization of domestic units.

The Yomut are divided into households which are property- (livestock and agricultural land) owning units, which act as autonomous groups in organizing and carrying out economic production, and which are responsible for the economic needs of their members. Ordinarily these households go through a developmental cycle beginning with a nuclear family of a man, his wife, and maturing children freshly separated from the husband's father's household. As the sons of the head are married and have children, these new households grow into extended families consisting of a head, his wife or wives, and his sons and their wives and children.

The cycle is then repeated as the sons separate from their parental unit and a portion of the parental household's capital in land and livestock is given to the son as the basis for a new economically independent unit. This usually occurs at about the time a son has children of his own approaching marriageable age.

Marriages are arranged between the heads of households and are thought of by the Yomut themselves as the exchange of livestock for a girl. Livestock is given by the bridegroom's domestic unit to the bride's, and the bride ceases to be a member of her natal unit and becomes a member of her husband's group. She is required to reside with her husband, she must carry out all of her economic and other activities as a member of that household, and any income from her labor (as from carpet-weaving, for example) is the property of the head of the unit. A bride occupies a very subordinate position within her new household. She is expected to obey without question orders from her parents-in-law, her husband, her husband's older brothers, and wives of her husband's older brothers. She is expected to demonstrate her subordination to these individuals by not speaking to them, by covering her face with her head-cloth in their presence, and by not eating with them. New brides are kept busy at one form of work or another, as are most Yomut women throughout their lifetime. It should perhaps be noted that women do all of their work in, or near, the family's living quarters, and heavy work such as plowing or hauling water long distances is regularly done by men. Agriculture and the care of herds, the primary sources of income, are men's work.

As a married woman grows older and becomes the mother of a number of children, her status within her marital household improves, but she always remains subordinate to her parents-in-law as long as she remains a part of their household. Once her husband becomes a household head, her status improves, and she may succeed in exerting considerable influence even though she is supposed to remain subordinate to her husband.

Once married and resident in her husband's household, a woman plays no regular role in her natal household. If her natal household is nearby she may visit frequently so long as it does not interfere with her work. Although her brothers and parents are interested in her welfare, the norms of acceptable behavior discourage them from overseeing her role in her new household. Her parents and brothers may visit her new household and frequently do if distance permits. She is expected, however, to stay out of sight of her own parents and brothers during the visits, and she is a taboo topic of conversation between her parents and parents-in-law, or brothers and husband. Staying out of sight is preferably accomplished by being absent from the tent, or house, in which her parents or brothers are present, but can also be accomplished by covering her face with her head-cloth and saying nothing.

Divorce among the Yomut is extremely difficult to arrange and is statistically very infrequent. Yomut themselves if asked about divorce by outsiders usually respond by saying that it does not exist among them.

Paralleling this limited interaction and opportunities for cooperation or altruistic assistance between an adult woman and her parents and siblings is a pattern of extensive cooperation and assistance between father and adult son, and among brothers. A Yomut man normally remains a member of his father's household and works under the supervision of his father and older brothers until he is somewhere between the ages of thirty and forty. Following his establishment as an independent household head, he usually continues for some time to reside near his father and brothers, and continues many forms of cooperation with them. A man who is an independent household head is normally willing to contribute, when called upon, several days of labor to his father's household, or to an independent brother's household, and expects similar assistance when he has a special need. Such assistance is granted without overt discussion of, or apparent concern for, any specified reciprocal favors. Often, although not always, an independent household head who becomes impoverished, for example as a result of severe livestock losses, will be given aid from a brother, father, or independent son in the form of an outright grant of capital, or in the form of a merging of the impoverished household with a more prosperous one.

Later in life when a man has several independent sons he will as a rule interact somewhat less with his brothers, and instead cooperate more frequently with his sons. His sons will carry the process further in later years as they interact more among themselves than with their father's brother's sons. Thus the sphere of closely cooperating males is not extended indefinitely, but kept to smaller circles of more closely related individuals.

The investment choices underlying this pattern can be summarized as follows. From a male point of view, investments in parents, brothers, and wives are extensive, and are accomplished at the cost of sacrificing any substantial or dependable opportunity to invest in sisters. From a female point of view, opportunities to cooperate with, or exchange benefits with parents or siblings, are sacrificed so that a wife can cooperate closely with her husband and concentrate all of her altruism on her own children.

A pattern of investment of this sort makes sense if the following is true. The size and efficiency of the groups of cooperating males in a household strongly affect the reproductive success of household members, but the size and efficiency of the group of cooperating females in a household have no comparable effect. There is some evidence to suggest that this is the case (Irons 1975:156–158; chapter 10), and analyses to validate this proposition more rigorously are currently in progress. Wealth is an important intervening variable, as is discussed elsewhere in this volume. Households with a large number of able-bodied males who can work together with a minimum of conflict do better at accumulating wealth. Increasing wealth improves the survivorship of both sexes and the fertility of males (without affecting female fertility positively or negatively). The number of females in a household and their ability to cooperate without conflict have no favorable effect on vital rates.

Given these constraints, men can do much to improve their inclusive fitness by cooperating with their closest male relatives. Cooperating with close female relatives offers no similar benefits and is sacrificed to allow concentration on the more adaptive pattern of cooperation among male kin.

From a woman's point of view, her own children are best served by being under the care of an effective cooperating group of males, and her behavior is directed toward facilitating this. For a woman to attenuate her commitment to her husband (by demanding rights of divorce, or the possibility of residing with her natal group) would limit the benefits flowing from her father-in-law and brothers-in-law to her children, and bring no compensating gain. For a woman to form a cooperative network with her sisters would bring no gain, and her brothers would be disinclined to invest in her children rather than their own.

This interpretation can be tested by showing that a woman's reproductive success correlates with the size and effectiveness of the male cooperative group with which her husband is associated, but not with any measurable characteristic of the female cooperative group with which she is associated. The situation is in a real sense the reverse of the Tiwi situation, where the size and effectiveness of female work groups correlate positively with reproductive success and where male cooperative groups are of secondary importance. Among the Yomut, women best serve their own reproductive interests by trying to see to it that their children enjoy the investment that can flow from an effective male cooperative group. Tiwi men accommodate to their situation both by trying to place their children under the care of an effective female work force, and also by competing with other males for large numbers of wives and hence opportunities for very high fertility.

Underlying Regularities

The four societies discussed above clearly indicate the great extent to which investment of kin effort among primary allies can vary from one human society to another. Nevertheless, it is possible to hypothesize certain underlying regularities. The regularities exhibited by these four societies, I suggest, are either universal or nearly so among pre-industrial humans. Industrial societies with their low fertility and high investment per child introduce some new variation which is not discussed here.

In all four of these societies, women concentrate on resource-gathering effort and parental effort, and invest little in other kin effort or mating effort. The assistance that is given to close kin other than their own children is justified as much by reciprocity as it is by nepotism. Hence, it is ultimately parental effort. In all four of these societies, women's interacting with other kin is aimed at getting the other kin to invest in their children in one way or another. Nayar women call on the assistance of the brothers and mother's brothers to maintain, and, if possible, increase the landed property from which they and their children derive economic support. Tiwi women call on their sisters, and to a lesser extent more distantly related females, to form a cooperative group of economic producers that is more effective in providing for children than would be a woman alone, or a husband-and-wife pair. Yąnomamö women and their children need protection from violence, as well as some male labor in garden construction, which they get first from their husbands but also in significant measure from their fathers and brothers. Yomut women are heavily dependent on their husbands and husband's close male kin for economic support for their children. Thus, the thing that is most variable for women is where they turn for additional investment for their children beyond what they can supply themselves. To the extent that they invest in primary allies other than their own children, it is primarily with an eye to return benefits conferred on their children. In each of the four societies, women seek additional investment in their children by turning to those primary allies whose assistance has the highest probability of increasing the survivorship and eventual reproduction of their children. This probability is determined both by the relative ability of various categories of primary allies to confer benefits on a woman's children and their willingness to do so. The ability of various types of primary allies to confer benefits is determined, in turn, by the society's mode of economic production (Tiwi and Yomut) and by the politics of their society (Nayar and Yąnomamö). The willingness of these allies is largely determined by the availability of alternative recipients of particular benefits (lacking in the Nayar case) and the value of what a woman can give in exchange for another individual's investment in her children (e.g., her own children as potential mates for brother's children among the Yąnomamö).

In contrast to female behavior, male behavior is more variable from one society to another. This reflects a greater variation for males than for females in the optimal pattern of investment among mating effort, parental effort, and other kin effort. Underlying this greater variation in some social environments are possibilities of gaining greatly in fertility by emphasizing mating effort at the expense of kin effort, and the fact that because of low paternity probability, parental effort for males is often less adaptive than for females. In many pre-industrial societies, such as the Tiwi, males emphasize mating effort at the expense of kin effort. In other pre-industrial societies, males invest more in kin effort (Yąnomamö and Yomut), but still far less than females.[4] In the Nayar case, reflecting low paternity probability, males devote nothing to parental effort, but much to other forms of kin effort. At the same time, Nayar mating effort contains none of the familiar institutions of bridewealth, brideservice, or elaborate patterns of alliance and exchange which absorb so much male effort in most other pre-industrial societies.

It is interesting to note in passing that in industrial societies male and female investment patterns have come to resemble each other. Both sexes are characterized by low fertility, high parental investment in a few offspring, and little kin effort other than parental effort. If the sexes in fact have basically the same reproductive strategies, one would expect all other areas of behavior to lose gender distinctiveness as well. This indeed seems to occur.

It should further be noted that while such categories as mating effort and kin effort are useful in distinguishing the strategies underlying certain patterns of interaction with primary social allies, some activities are examples of more than one of these categories at the same time. For example, Yąnomamö brother-brother alliances are used for mate acquisition and investment in kin at the same time; and the underlying strategies would be justified both in terms of nepotism and of gaining, for oneself, opportunities to reproduce.

[4] In pre-industrial societies, females may in some cases exercise mate choice. The time and resources devoted to this activity are a form of mating effort. However, expenditure of time and resources under this heading is always much smaller than for males.

As noted earlier, the difference between male and female investment patterns is in part a result of the different possible routes to high reproductive success open to the two sexes. (See the earlier discussion of parental investment and sexual selection: chapter 1, pp. 27–29.). Female investment in reproduction is of necessity high. Carrying a child to term, giving birth to it, and then suckling it are, in pre-industrial societies, inescapable investments that a woman must make in each child. This by itself, as a theoretical minimum investment, is high and the number of children a woman can produce in a lifetime is limited. Also female-female competition for mates, in pre-industrial societies, is very limited. Most women are assured a mate throughout their reproductive years without heavy investment in acquiring mates. Given this, the best strategies, for a woman in most pre-industrial societies, are to seek a high quality mate (in terms of both his ability to invest and his apparent genetic qualities), to invest heavily in her own children, and to seek to direct the investment of other individuals (husband, brothers, sisters, parents) toward her children. If a woman is successful, her limited number of children have good chances of survival and good chances of being successful in terms of mate acquisition, alliance formation, property acquisition, or whatever is necessary for reproductive success in the society in question. Thus, for women, high reproductive success is usually achieved by low fertility (in comparison to what is possible for males) and high parental investment.

For males, high fertility and low parental investment per child is often an optimal strategy (Tiwi).[5] Also, males often are characterized by a higher variance in success at resource gathering. Thus, in some societies the most successful males have unusually high resources available to them and follow strategies of high fertility and high investment per offspring (Yomut).

In societies where some males pursue strategies of high fertility, there is always a shortage of women. That is, there are always more males seeking mates, than there are unmarried females available as mates. This

---

[5] Also among the Yąnomamö and the Yomut, the more successful males are often polygynous—although they have fewer wives than the most successful Tiwi. Whether more successful Nayar males of the retainer castes enjoyed higher fertility is hard to say, although the literature does suggest this as at least a possibility. High caste Nayar, however, probably did, since they drew their wives from lower castes which were more numerous than their own caste (Gough 1961a:319–329). Ruler, chiefs, and some of their high-status relatives appear to have in effect married polygynously, i.e., maintained exclusive sexual access to several wives, and also to have invested in their children (Gough 1961a:378–379).

II. Kinship

may be an artifact of the longer period of potential male fertility (roughly 15–60 in contrast to the female fecund years, 15–45) if higher male mortality does not compensate sufficiently by removing more males than females from the adult population. In the case of the Yąnomamö and the Yomut, this situation is exaggerated by a high sex ratio (Chagnon 1974:157–159; Irons 1975:144). However, even without such a sex ratio, a population in which a substantial number of successful males monopolize the reproductive potential of several women will always be a population in which the demand for female mates exceeds the supply.

This situation, in effect, means that nearly all females are married by their early reproductive years if not sooner, and remain married throughout most of their fecund years. Widowhood and divorce may remove a few fecund women from active reproduction for a time, but this is a limited phenomenon. In these societies, women for the most part are guaranteed opportunities to reproduce and they do not expend effort or resources acquiring mates. Efforts to choose the best possible suitor may be a relevant strategy in each of these societies, but this does not absorb much time, energy, or other resources. Mate choices for females are initially made for them by their older kin, and do not involve careful investment choices by the women themselves. Later choices—those of second or later husbands— often do involve women in the choice of their own mates, but even here, while the choices may be carefully weighed, investment of large measures of time, energy, or other resource is not involved.

For males the situation is often very different. Males usually acquire their first wives long after becoming fecund, and through most of their lives they have fewer opportunities to reproduce than they desire, given the possibilities for polygyny. Thus males, in many—perhaps most— pre-industrial societies, face a problem that females do not. This is the need to invest heavily in mating effort. Whatever form this investment of resources may take—gathering property for bridewealth, serving other men politically, etc.—the underlying situation is one of competition among males for opportunities to reproduce. The patterns of interaction which males establish with their primary allies usually reflect this competition for mates in addition to strategies of investment in children. They must attempt to establish a pattern of interaction which is optimal in terms of mate acquisition as well as in terms of passing benefits to offspring and other close kin.

Another reason—as noted earlier—for the greater variability in male strategies is the problem of identifying paternity. This was discussed at length by Kurland in chapter 6.

Summary of basic model

The most fundamental variable influencing the pattern of interaction among primary allies is the variation in the specific activities which individuals are able to carry out in a particular environment to increase their own and their allies' reproductive success, and the magnitude of the effect of these activities on reproductive success. Environmental constraints and opportunities define an optimal pattern of investment and this, in turn, defines an optimal pattern of residence, rules for inheritance of property, the nature of marriage contracts, and other social patterns governing relationships among primary allies. It should, of course, be noted that these statements apply to actual residential arrangements, actual dispositions of the property of deceased individuals, and in general refer to actual behavior as opposed to stated rules of behavior. It is a well-documented fact that overt rules are not reliable guides to actual behavior. The above model is intended as a source of predictions about behavior rather than ideas or rules. Rules themselves are best understood as means by which certain individuals try to influence the behavior of other individuals.

Pinpointing what people are able to do in order to influence inclusive fitness, or predicting anything about the distribution of investment among allies, requires a large amount of information about the particular social environment in which the choices occur. What particular problems and opportunities individuals face in a specific society and how these affect survival and reproduction (i.e., how alternate courses of action affect vital rates) would have to be known in some detail before one could test predictions of the sort discussed above. Although it is possible as in the case of the Nayar and Tiwi above to combine good ethnographic data with a theoretical model and produce testable predictions, further research is necessary before the predictions can actually be tested. In the case of the Tiwi, the course of social change has probably eliminated opportunities to test rigorously predictions about earlier social behavior. Predictions about the social behavior of nineteenth-century Nayar could probably be tested to some extent from written records. The existing data on the Yąnomamö and the Yomut are in the process of being analyzed to test predictions of the sort discussed in this paper, and some results of these analyses are reported in this volume. The point to be underscored is that theoretical models of human kinship behavior derived from sociobiology, like any other new theoretical perspective, cannot be adequately tested with existing data. New theories demand new types of data and data analyses.

Investment and kinship institutions: further implications in reference to the avunculate and matriliny

This paper has explored reasons for variation in kinship institutions on the assumption that such institutions are generated by the interaction of related individuals pursuing mixed strategies of nepotism and reciprocity. The relevant variables are the fitness costs and benefits to various related individuals of particular patterns of behavior, and the extent of relatedness by descent between various pairs of individuals. In chapter 6, Kurland explores variation in kinship behavior associated with variation in relatedness as it is affected by paternity probability. This chapter has explored variations in kinship behavior associated primarily with variation in costs and benefits. A broader approach can be achieved by looking at both relatedness and costs and benefits at the same time, and by seeking possible interrelationships between relatedness on the one hand and costs and benefits on the other hand. This final section of chapter 7 examines the question of the avunculate and matriliny from such a broader perspective.

Specifically, it asks what environmental conditions would make the avunculate and matriliny good strategies for individuals seeking to maximize their inclusive fitness, and seeks answers in terms both of relatedness mediated by paternity probability and of the fitness costs and benefits of various patterns of investment. It is useful initially to consider marriage, in many societies, as a transaction in which a woman gives a man paternity confidence in return for his investing in her children. The granting of paternity confidence imposes a cost on the woman which is presumably justified by the benefit of her husband's investment in her children. The transaction also imposes a cost on a man in that he too must expend some time and effort in maintaining paternity confidence, and in that the time and resources invested in his wife's children cannot be invested toward other ends, such as the pursuit of additional mates. When men find the transaction satisfactory it is presumably because the benefit of accurately identifying their own children and directing investment toward them outweighs these costs. Virilocality and uxorilocality can similarly be viewed in terms of costs that must be justified by some return benefit. Presumably the individual moving is paying a cost which must somehow be justified by sufficient return benefit.

Low paternity probability and confidence occur when the costs of this transaction are not justified by the benefits. The conditions which can cause the costs to be greater than the benefits are likely to be different for males and females. Societies in which the costs are not justified for either men or women should be societies in which paternity confidence is low and institutions such as the avunculate and other matrilateral biases in kinship behavior are well established. Those in which the benefits justify the costs for both sexes should be characterized by stable marriage and high paternity confidence. In societies in which the costs are justified for one sex but not the other, there should be considerable tension over the issue of who are the proper recipients of male investment (cf. Kurland, chapter 6:168–174; see also Alexander 1974 and Greene 1978 for further discussion).

A number of conditions of the social environment can be identified which would encourage males to forgo paternity confidence. One is an environment in which the resource, time, and effort that might be invested in wives' children will yield higher inclusive fitness payoffs if invested in further mating effort. This can be so either because male investment has relatively little effect on the success of children, or because opportunities for very high fertility will yield unusually high payoffs for mating effort. These conditions appear to hold for the Tiwi.

Another condition which can encourage males to forgo paternity confidence is one in which men can accumulate resources only by being highly mobile and women and children can use these resources only by being sedentary (Kurland, chapter 6:154, 176). This is the condition faced by the Nayar, in which men can acquire wealth only by military careers entailing high mobility, but wealth in the form of land can only be exploited by a sedentary household of women, children, and older retired males. The difficulty in trying to combine high mobility with paternity confidence through such aberrations as chastity belts is presumably too great to make them a satisfactory society-wide strategy.

It might seem at first glance that women would always be interested in securing male investment for their children and that a husband who is convinced he is related to her children by $\frac{1}{2}$ would always be a more reliable investor than a brother who can be related by no more than $\frac{1}{4}$. However, this would not be the case if a cooperative group of related females is more effective at rearing children than a husband-and-wife pair or a polygynous group consisting of one husband and several unrelated females. This is apparently the situation faced by Tiwi women. Given this condition, women may not be willing to do anything for a husband which disrupts the effectiveness of a cooperative group of related females. This could easily mean a woman would be unwilling to move at marriage or to tolerate a husband who interferes in the relations between herself and her co-resident female kin. This condition may underlie uxorilocality and frequent divorce in many societies. If the value for child rearing of a related group of females is very high and the value of male assistance in child rearing very low, women may be reluctant to move at marriage, disinclined to value a marriage once conflict emerges between husband and wife, and setting little store in fidelity as a means of giving a man paternity confidence.

Such a situation will, of course, encourage males to channel more time and resources into mating effort through polygyny, promiscuity, or both. Another expectable male reaction to this situation would be to favor types of investment that a man can pass on to some of a woman's children, but not to others, and can limit to children who are actually his children, or who he believes are actually his children (cf. Kurland, chapter 6:165). The ethnographic literature on matrilaterally biased societies commonly states that men are interested in their own children and often pass on substantial gifts to them, sometimes much to the chagrin of their matrilateral kin. Such gifts have the advantage of being voluntary rather than prescribed and, therefore, can be restricted to children a man believes are his own. Also, they are passed directly to a single child rather than to a wife who distributes them among all her children.

It should further be noted that some social environments may encourage a less extreme reaction in which there is some effort by women to give their husband paternity confidence and some male interest in identifying and investing in their own children, but at the same time only limited restraint on promiscuous behavior by either sex. Such conditions are likely to create a paternity probability above the threshold of .268, but significantly below 1.0. Men are likely to react to this situation by investing primarily in wives' children but preferring to form larger solidary groups along matrilateral lines (Kurland, chapter 6:156–157). This appears to fit the characteristics of many matrilineal societies.

There is another environmental condition which may encourage the avunculate without necessarily entailing a low paternity probability. This is the condition of a great difference in the average or modal age at marriage for males and females. In many polygynous societies the majority of males marry and have children (at least, socially recognized children) considerably later in life. The Tiwi are an example. Given a situation of this sort a man in his early adult years may not have children, but may have sister's children. To the extent that such a man has resources to invest in something other than male-male competition for mates, his sister's children might be the ideal recipients of his investment. Older unsuccessful males in such societies may face a similar situation. Females would naturally be expected to exploit a situation of this sort by encouraging their brothers to invest in their children. Ideologies denying the male role in paternity might have their origin in such female strategies (Kurland, chapter 6:172–174).

Other institutions common in societies emphasizing solidarity along matrilateral lines could have a similar function. In many such societies the bridewealth paid when a girl marries goes to her mother's brother rather than her father. A practice of this sort could serve as a means by which a woman persuades a brother to invest, at an earlier time, in her children. Avunculocal residence could have a similar function. In one case wealth, in the other a claim on labor, is, in effect, given by a sister to her brother as her children mature. A reciprocal exchange of benefits of this sort could fit nicely into the typical life history of males and females in many societies. If a male marries and has children late, in his younger years he would have sister's children who because they are young can benefit greatly from his assistance; and later when he has children of his own, his sister's children, or at least some of them, will be reaching maturity and in a position to return benefits to him in the form of bridewealth or labor. Not all men would have sisters of the right age, nor all women brothers of the right age to make this pattern work, but this does not prevent those who can from establishing such an exchange. Actually, it is equally näive to assume that the ideal always works out when it is a simple pattern of a man living with his wife and investing primarily in his own children. Given the mortality schedules of pre-industrial societies, this ideal, like the one above, could only be realized for a portion of the population. However, if for many individuals it is a real possibility, normative rules and ideology encouraging and justifying such a pattern could develop.

The fact that a man waits some years for the return benefit—in bridewealth or labor—from a sister's children creates a situation of risk and conflict. A sister's child may actually be better able to serve his inclusive fitness by shirking his obligation to move at adolescence to his mother's brother's household and make his labor available to his uncle. The fact that the mother's brother-sister's son relationship in matrilineal societies is frequently characterized by tension may reflect this fact. The inheritance of a mother's brother's status and property may also be both an important sanction by which mother's brother controls a sister's son who might otherwise be tempted to evade his heavy obligations to his uncle and, at the same time, another example of a delayed return justifying still greater assistance from sister's son to mother's brother.

Although a great difference in modal age at marriage for males and females could give rise to the avunculate in the manner described here even in the presence of high paternity confidence, this condition could also exist in conjunction with some of the conditions discussed above which encourage low paternity confidence. Thus, the avunculate may in some cases be a response to more than one environmental condition. Determining exactly which environmental constraints are responsible for the avunculate or some other matrilateral bias in kinship interaction in a particular society may often be difficult with the existing data. However, the above models of conditions giving rise to the avunculate and matriliny are in principle testable by the technique of deriving distinct predictions from the alternate models and conducting fieldwork to check them. Indeed, new field research designed to test models of the sort discussed in this chapter, and of the sort discussed by Kurland in chapter 6, cannot help but expand our understanding of human sociality.

---

8. Kin Selection and Conflict: An Analysis of a Yąnomamö Ax Fight

Napoleon A. Chagnon and Paul E. Bugos, Jr.

> The social behavior of a species evolves in such a way that in each distinct behavior-evoking situation the individual will seem to value his neighbors' fitness against his own according to the coefficients of relationship appropriate to that situation.
>> W. D. Hamilton, 1964
>> "The Genetical Evolution of Social Behavior: II"

> The span of social distance between those who exchange conditions the mode of exchange. Kinship distance, as has already been suggested, is especially relevant to the form of reciprocity. Reciprocity is inclined toward the generalized pole by close kinship, toward the negative extreme in proportion to kinship distance . . . close kin tend to share, to enter

into generalized exchanges, and distant and non-kin
to deal in equivalents or in guile.

Marshall D. Sahlins, 1968
"On the Sociology of Primitive Exchange"

From the days of Lewis Henry Morgan on, students of primitive culture
have generally come to the same kind of conclusion so eloquently summarized in Sahlins' characterization of the nature of primitive exchange:
closeness of kinship is an important mediator of interpersonal relationships
of many kinds in human societies.[1]

The implications of Hamilton's arguments about inclusive fitness
(1964) and the nature of behavior involving related individuals raise the
possibility that we can develop a general scientific explanation for kinship
behavior in terms of natural selection. This is a powerful and, to some,
uncomfortable possibility, for anthropologists have long considered kinship
their special domain and an invasion from biological theory is, to some of
us, inappropriate and perhaps even threatening.

The "nature" of kinship in human societies, particularly those
kinds of societies traditionally studied by field working anthropologists, is a
question for which many different kinds of answers exist. It is, to many,
mostly symbolic in content; to others, the vehicle through which other
kinds of relationships are expressed—economic, political, jural, domestic,
etc. With few exceptions, the general and widely held anthropological views
on human kinship seem to play down—or even deny—that the facts of
relatedness have much to do with human "kinship." In many societies,
especially those whose members have been decimated by exotic epidemics,
there may be a relatively poor relationship between kinship classifications
and putative biological relationship; in some, there may be so few survivors that kinship systems are known primarily through one or just a
handful of individuals. In others, where it might be possible to elucidate
the relationship between genealogical relationship and kinship classifications, the investigations seem not to have been conducted at all—and what
we know about the "kinship systems" has been gotten by the observer
from just a few informants. Or, if the investigations have been conducted,
they tend not to be made available in the literature. There are, in fact,

[1] We wish to express our gratitude to the officers of the Harry Frank Guggenheim
Foundation who generously supported the senior author's research efforts during 1974–7.
We are also indebted to the National Science Foundation (Grant No. SOC75–14262) and
the National Institute of Mental Health (Grant No. MH26008) for additional support
during the same period of time.

II. Kinship

relatively few ethnographic descriptions that tell us how the observer collected his or her information about the "kinship system" found in any particular society, and for that reason it would be difficult to make a general summary of what it is anthropologists really do know about human kinship systems, especially the associated "kinship" behavior.

All of this is not to say that kinship in human societies is nonsymbolic or does not serve as a vehicle for other kinds of relationships. An analysis of kinship behavior from the perspective of inclusive fitness theory does not obviate other, more traditional concerns and approaches to the same subject; it supplements them and increases our understanding of kinship. More important, we believe that such an approach can answer the larger question of *why* kinship is such an important category of human concern and why, as Robin Fox argues (chapter 5, this volume), it is one of the kinds of preoccupations with which humans seem to universally concern themselves . . . a preoccupation they apparently learn very easily.

Hamilton specifically phrased his argument in terms of "valuing" or "comparing" fitness according to closeness or remoteness of relationships *in particular situations*. Those of us who have spent considerable periods of time studying kinship behavior in the field will appreciate the significance of context in interpersonal kinship behavior. People manipulate relatives, exaggerating closeness at times, denying it at others. In some cases, one can even get the impression that kinship is almost irrelevant to the humdrum workaday activities in which individuals engage, while at other times questions of relationship and associated privilege, dues, or prerogative dominate what otherwise seems like a trivial matter to the uninformed outsider.

There is one context or situation in which, we believe, some of the most essential and rock-bottom characteristics of kinship come to the fore and reveal themselves clearly: conflict or crisis situations. Here, in Fortesian terms, the axiomatic qualities of human kinship as prescriptive altruism take on form and substance (Fortes 1969). Ambiguity and metaphorical aspects of kinship, it would seem, should be minimized as the actors elect to follow particular courses of action exercising choices that have obvious costs and benefits. If we are interested in examining individual human behavior with an eye toward understanding the extent to which that behavior is "tracking" biologically relevant dimensions of kinship relationships, it seems that crisis or conflict situations involving potential hazard to the actors are a reasonable place to begin looking.

This paper analyzes one such crisis event, an ax fight, that occurred in a Yąnomamö village in southern Venezuela in 1971. The Yąnomamö are characterized by a wide range of formalized and unformalized fights, ranging in seriousness from chest-pounding at the lowest end to outright raiding with intent to kill at the upper extreme (Chagnon 1966, 1967, 1968a, 1968b). Ax fights fall somewhat closer to the more violent end of the spectrum, since injuries during such fights can be very serious—and even fatal. The ax, of course, is an exotic item of material culture and such fights must therefore be of relatively recent origin in their culture.[2] Ax fights are, however, similar to the more traditional club-fights and probably are just refinements and improvements on them as a result of the introduction of new technology. Indeed, during the particular fight in question, the initial skirmish began with clubs—and clubs continued to be used when the fight escalated to more serious dimensions after a few men took up axes.

We have chosen to analyze this particular fight primarily because the event was filmed with 16mm motion-picture, synchronous-sound equipment and it has become the subject of a motion picture publication. The published film, however, deals with social organization, particularly marriage and alliance practices, and how the anthropologist, through his analytical techniques, renders apparently chaotic events intelligible.[3]

In addition to that filming, the senior author of the present paper photographed the fight with 35mm still equipment from a slightly different and somewhat closer angle. This combination of photographic coverage of the event, which makes it possible to identify all the participants, and genealogical and demographic data collected by the senior author during the several years prior to and after the fight, make it possible to do a very detailed analysis of the event from the perspective of kin selection theory. While the senior author has witnessed many such fights during his twelve-year study of the Yąnomamö, none have been so meticulously documented by photography and none have been described in such a way that all participants are identifiable. Such fights erupt with explosiveness and usually last such a brief time that without some kind of photographic documenting techniques, detailed analysis of the kind presented here would be very difficult except for just the smallest of fights. An important point to make, however, is that this fight is in no way unique or even unusual. It may

[2] It may be that axes have replaced a particular kind of hard, palm-wood dueling weapon called *himo,* a type of double-edged, heavy, sword-like instrument. Himo clubs can still be seen in many villages, although the senior author had never seen a fight in which they were used.

[3] The film, *The Ax Fight* (Asch and Chagnon 1975), can be rented or purchased through: (1) Documentary Educational Resources, 24 Dane Street, Somerville, Massachusetts 02143, or (2) Psychological Cinema Register, 17 Willard Building, The Pennsylvania State University, University Park, Pennsylvania 16802.

II. Kinship

be taken as a specific example of a much larger universe of similar kinds of Yąnomamö conflicts characterizing the geographical area of the senior author's major field of research effort (see Chagnon 1974).

Another point is in order. The data required to make the following analysis were collected long before "sociobiology" entered the theoretical repertoire of social anthropologists and, therefore, could not have been systematically gathered with kin selection or reciprocal altruism arguments in mind. Two consequences of this fact should be obvious. First, it is not likely that the information systematically favors or disfavors the outcome of tests of kin selection theory. Second, had the data been collected with tests of kin selection in mind, it is likely that the definitiveness of our conclusions would be enhanced, for no one is more painfully aware of the kinds of supplementary detail necessary to make convincing statements about the applicability of kin selection theory to human kinship behavior than we. One consequence of our attempts in this paper is the strengthening of our conviction that extremely meticulous, quantitative studies of kinship behavior are absolutely essential if broad generalizations about the "nature" of human kinship behavior are to be developed.

The Fight

The fight, in its broad features and significance, was largely the extension of earlier disputes and of antagonisms that plague all Yąnomamö villages as they grow in size and begin to fall apart. The mechanisms of kinship, marriage exchange obligations, and the authority of the village leaders become increasingly ineffective in organizing the villagers into a cohesive, cooperative whole (Chagnon 1974, 1975). The village in question, Mishi-mishimaböwei-teri, had fissioned several years earlier when its numbers had reached approximately 400 individuals, a size that is staggeringly large by Yąnomamö standards. After the fission, one group, still calling itself Mishimishimaböwei-teri, vacillated in size from about 230 to about 275 people, depending on the numbers of families that temporarily rejoined it, the main group, from the splinter village. This pattern—families leaving and rejoining—characterizes most Yąnomamö village fissions in this area of the tribe, since the "core" of the splinter group often consists of a few authoritative men and their families who have more antagonisms against the core leadership in the original village than do particular heads of households in either group. Thus, individual families often return to the original village in an attempt to patch up grievances and continue their social and economic pursuits in somewhat less strained circumstances. Purely in terms of energy, it is simply more efficient to return to an already-producing garden in the original village than to begin clearing a new garden at a great distance away (Chagnon 1968a, 1968c, 1974).

As the splinter group formed by a fission takes on its own political identity and characteristics, subsequent visits to the original village become, in themselves, political events. The relationships between visitors and hosts during such visits are no longer exclusively dominated by the kinship and marriage ties between them, but are increasingly subject to residential realities and political principles. Thus, visitors are received with considerable formality and tendered particular forms of hospitality and generosity that are assumed to be short-term perquisites. Proper decorum in such cases requires that the visitors depart for home after a politely long visit, their departure usually being met with some relief by the hosts who, if they had fulfilled their obligations as proper hosts, can return to the workaday tasks of gardening and other domestic duties.

The fight that we are about to analyze erupted between a group of recently fissioned ex-residents of the village and a few of the members of the original village. The fission that separated them had occurred too recently in the past to permit the splinter group to assume its own political identity, yet they had returned as visiting dignitaries, expecting to be fed and feted. Moreover, they were deliberately finessing their kinship ties to the local group, expecting to be received not only as a delegation from an independent village but as kinsmen as well—they were trying to have it two ways. In addition, marriage exchanges over a number of generations linked one particular group of the hosts to some of the politically prominent men among the visitors in very complex and intimate ways. Indeed, the host men thus tied by kinship and marriage to the visitors supported them in the fight, and were sincerely interested in bringing these visitors back into the village as permanent residents. One of the more prominent local men had gone so far to demonstrate his sincerity that he cleared a moderately large garden, planted it, and offered to present it to the headman of the visiting faction—his brother-in-law. There was, however, much less enthusiasm among the rest of the members of the village (mostly the leaders from Lineage 1222) for having this group return as permanent residents, so the longer they stayed as visitors the more thinly veiled the local antagonisms became. The overall situation, in terms of the politics of fissioning, was extremely ambiguous. Many of the local people were growing weary of entertaining and feeding the visitors, who appeared to them to be taking advantage of a good thing: they stayed far too long for proper decorum, ate ravenously, complained about not being treated as was their just due as both visitors and kin, and loafed around all day while the hosts worked to support them.

Matters came to a head when one of the men from among the visitors (Mohesiwä 1246) ran into a party of women in the garden and demanded that one of the women (Sinabimi 1744) give him a share of the plantains she was carrying back to the village for her own family. She refused to give him plantains, punctuating her refusal with an insult. Mohesiwä was incensed, and beat Sinabimi with a piece of wood. She fled, screaming and crying, into the village, revealing her story to the others. This angered her kinsman Uuwä (1897) in particular. Some of the relevant social dimensions of the reaction by Uuwä are:

1 Uuwä was a member of the most prominent descent group (Lineage 1222) in the village, the group from which the undisputed local headman came. Thus Uuwä was a brother to the local headman, and in a sense, represented local authority.
2 Uuwä was also a half-brother to the beaten woman, and as is frequent in Yąnomamö domestic group organization, brothers stand up for and defend sisters against cruelty inflicted on them by other men.
3 The affront—beating of a woman—was inflicted by a visitor during a situation of mounting tensions, tensions that were the result of visitors wearing out their welcome in the host village. In an important sense, overstaying the visit was a kind of political coercion, reflecting the capacity of the visitors to compel the hosts to treat them with deference beyond a socially appropriate point.

Uuwä took up a large club and rushed to the center of the village hurling insults at Mohesiwä, who met the challenge by coming forth with an unstrung palmwood bowstave. The two men flailed wildly at each other with their weapons, but since Uuwä's club was longer than Mohesiwä's bowstave, he managed to deliver a painful blow to the latter's forearm. By this time, supporters of both men were quickly arming themselves with long clubs, but Mohesiwä's supporters were clearly more committed to supporting him than were Uuwä's supporters, probably being more concerned about their own disadvantage as visitors and overall numerical inferiority. As soon as Mohesiwä's younger brother came to his aid with a long club and held Uuwä at bay, the conflict stabilized and the male contestants—just a handful of men—glared menacingly at each other. Their female supporters, especially Mohesiwä's sister and mother, hurled vicious insults at Uuwä. Still, the fight appeared to be over at this point and the main antagonists turned, stalked haughtily away, and returned to their respective hammocks.

Meanwhile, the husband of the beaten woman—Yoinakuwä (2248), and his brother, Keböwä (0910), were scurrying about in their own houses looking for more dangerous weapons. No sooner had the club-fighters reached their hammocks than these two men emerged from their houses brandishing a machete and an ax, respectively. They were coming to the aid of their brother-in-law, Uuwä, and simultaneously protecting a "wife." They ran across the village clearing toward Mohesiwä's house, weapons raised conspicuously. They plunged into the house to attack Mohesiwä, but were met with a sea of arms and bodies and were partially immobilized and unable to strike Mohesiwä with their weapons. A struggle ensued within the house, and Keböwä wrested his ax from the resisters. He then grabbed Mohesiwä by the arm and began beating him on the legs and back with the blunt side of his ax, managing to deliver several crunching blows.

The fight had clearly escalated, and large numbers of men began arming themselves with clubs and other weapons. Mohesiwä's younger brother, Tourawä (1837), again came to his rescue, discarding his club, taking up first a machete and then an ax. He attacked Keböwä from the blind side and managed to deliver a series of equally crunching blows to Keböwä's legs, arms, and back with the blunt side of his ax. Stunned and distracted—and in pain from the blows—Keböwä stopped beating Mohesiwä and turned to identify his new adversary. Tourawä backed away a few steps and menacingly turned his ax head up, as if to strike Keböwä on the head with the sharp edge. As he stood there, poised to strike, someone reached up and grabbed his ax-handle from behind him, twisted it so as to turn the sharp edge back down, and dragged him out of the fight. The youth turned to struggle for control of his ax, but as soon as his back was turned, Keböwä rushed him from behind and delivered a powerful over-head blow with his ax, blunt side exposed, striking him squarely in the middle of the back between his shoulder blades, just missing his spine. The sound of Keböwä's ax thudding into Tourawä's back was sickening, and the youth collapsed instantly.[4] At this point, several older men stepped into the

---

[4] The senior author of the paper was standing a few feet from Tourawä when Keböwä hit him with an ax. The filmmaker, Timothy Asch, was some thirty yards away filming the fight with a 16mm motion picture camera, unable to move closer with the bulky equipment without missing significant portions of the fight.

II. Kinship

fight, enraged. A rapid series of blows were exchanged with clubs and the two groups alternately charged and withdrew.

With the entry of the most prominent men, the fight again stabilized. It gradually de-escalated to a series of insults, hostile stares, and ended. Tourawä, the youth felled by Keböwä's ax, painfully regained consciousness and was led off to his hammock. At this point, all the partisans of both sides returned to their homes and tempers cooled down, save for a period of time when the women of both groups screamed insults at each other before withdrawing. The next day some of the visitors packed their possessions and left for home.

The Analysis

Hamilton's formulation of the inclusive fitness hypothesis (1964) accounts for the preservation of altruistic tendencies in a population through natural selection operating at the level of individuals (cf. Williams 1966). Individuals, in maximizing their inclusive fitness, should be expected to favor other individuals who are genetically related to them, i.e., who are ultimately in a position to contribute the altruist's genes to succeeding generations. If the potential costs (in fitness units) to the altruist are the same should he/she favor (1) a close relative, (2) a distant relative, or (3) a non-relative, then one should expect the altruist to "invest" in that individual who, by receiving the benefit, is most likely to yield an equivalent or greater fitness benefit to the original altruist.

An analogy with banking and interest rates might be useful to illustrate the principle. Assume that you have three friends who each own a bank, and all "need" investors, or they will collapse. Your $100,000 would benefit all of them equally. But Bank A will give you 5 percent interest, Bank B 6 percent interest, and Bank C 10 percent. The cost to you in each case will be risking your $100,000, but the potential return is greater if you place your investment in Bank C. One would predict that you would invest in Bank C, on the assumptions that you would attempt to maximize your return and that the chances of each bank's folding are equal.

General predictions

Kin selection theory predicts that if you sustain the same "costs" to your potential fitness in helping a (1) close relative, (2) a distant relative, or (3) a non-relative, your inclusive fitness would be better served by aiding the relative that is genetically most related to you. In addition, the theory also predicts that as the costs to your own potential fitness increase, you would increasingly favor more closely related kin over more distantly related or unrelated individuals, providing that the benefits to the recipients of your aid remain approximately the same. Conversely, if the risks to your own fitness are very small, the theory would predict that individuals would help close relatives in a high proportion of cases, more distantly related relatives in a lesser proportion of cases, the proportion ultimately being predicted by the coefficient of relatedness of the distantly related kinsman to the altruist. If the risks are very small indeed, then it would be expected that an individual would aid even a non-relative on the expectation that such a person would ultimately, at some future date, reciprocate the aid in a similar circumstance (Trivers 1971; Alexander 1974).

There are, of course, intervening variables in the many sociocultural circumstances in which humans normally operate. One might expect, for example, an individual to aid a relative with high reproductive potential over an equally closely related individual with lower reproductive potential, i.e., a child over a parent. Since the child has a greater probability of further enhancing the altruist's inclusive fitness than the parents of the altruist, the altruist would potentially gain a higher inclusive fitness by aiding the younger relative (Alexander 1977b). In other circumstances, overlapping fitness interests of pairs of individuals must be considered. Thus, it might be more beneficial to take risks to aid an affine, say a brother-in-law, than to aid a lineage mate who might be more closely related. This is especially true in human societies characterized by systematic marriage exchanges involving cross-cousins. Since a brother-in-law (say, a second cross-cousin) ultimately provides you with your spouse, and your lineage mate (say, a first parallel cousin) of the same sex is your competitor for that spouse, your inclusive fitness interests might be better served by taking a higher risk for a less closely related individual (brother-in-law) whose inclination to favor you in return by continuing to provide you with mates might be a function of your willingness to help him. Other examples of asymmetry in costs and benefits for specific kinship and other social dyads are discussed elsewhere in this volume (see Irons, chapter 7).

For the example under discussion here, the ax fight, the major variable appears to be closeness of genetic relatedness: individuals seemed primarily to "decide" to aid others on the basis of the degree of relatedness obtaining between themselves and other participants in the fight. That is to say, the "risks" to the potential fitness of each individual seemed to be high and the potential fitness benefits each would derive from joining the fight would therefore appear to depend on closeness of relatedness.

One point of clarification is in order. It is not necessary, in testing kin selection hypotheses, to assume that the individual actors in any social situation are cognizant of "fitness" or are capable of "calculating" coefficients of genealogical relatedness. Natural selection favors organisms that behave adaptively, whether or not they are aware of the evolutionary consequences of their behavior. This aspect of the general theory of evolutionary biology constitutes a major stumbling block to social scientists in general and to social anthropologists in particular, many of whom conceive of "kinship" behavior in explicitly or implicitly mentalistic or ideological terms. For example, one prominent anthropological critic of kin selection theory, Marshall D. Sahlins, misunderstands this central aspect of natural selection when he claims that the "failure" of "sociobiologists" to address the problem of an organism's lack of cognitive appreciation of the evolutionary effects of its behavior ". . . introduces a considerable mysticism in their theory" (Sahlins 1976a:44–45). One could argue, with the same logic, that physicists are behaving "mysteriously" when they suggest that planetary orbits conform to Newtonian models, since it is "mysterious" to suggest that the planets describing these orbits are aware of Newtonian principles.

Specific predictions and relevant data

In the analysis of the ax fight that follows, then, we shall look for evidence that individuals help closer relatives over more distant ones: we expect that if someone comes to the aid of another person in the fight, the helper will be more closely related to the individual he or she is helping than he is to the village at large or to the opponent in the fight. One would predict, from kin selection theory, that the supporters of Mohesiwä will be more closely related to him and to each other than to Mohesiwä's opponent, Uuwä, and his supporters. Conversely, we also expect that Uuwä's supporters would be more closely related to him and among themselves than they are to Mohesiwä or his supporters.

By relatedness, of course, we mean actual genealogical relatedness, not merely terminological salutations. This is not to say that all men who are called "brother" by, for example, Mohesiwä actually participated in the fight as his supporters or that we are so naive as to assume that all kinship terms invariably reflect the minimal English biological equivalent when translated. We are, in short, examining the genealogical dimensions of kinship in this section of the paper. The extent to which these genea-logies are accurate reflections of biological relationships can be judged by examining an earlier work of the senior author, where a detailed discussion of the field methods used in collecting the data is given (Chagnon 1974). We do not assert, however, that the genealogies are absolutely accurate and that they are entirely free of any errors; we only argue that a scru-pulous attempt was made during the twelve-year period of the study to collect genealogical data that was as close to biological accuracy as possible, and that paternity-exclusion tests performed on blood samples suggest that there is good reason to believe that the genealogies are reasonable approxi-mations to biological reality (Chagnon, chapter 4:98). We know of no reason to assume that the errors in the data are large or that they contain any bias that could make the statistics cited below specious.

The method we use to express kinship relatedness is essentially Wright's Inbreeding Coefficient (as described in chapter 4, this volume p. 110). See also Chagnon 1974, 1975), converted, by doubling the value, to the coefficient of relatedness, i.e., the statistic used by Hamilton in his formulation of the kin selection theory. We call this statistic the "coeffi-cient of genealogical relatedness," F_g, to remind the reader that it is based on informants' statements about their genealogical relatedness.

A word of caution should be added here: we, as observers, might have more genealogical information at our disposal than the Yąnomamö individuals might be utilizing as they "track" their social environment and make decisions about aiding various relatives. When we express the closeness of relationship between any pair of individuals as a coefficient of relationship, we are utilizing nearly *all* of the genealogical information available to us.[5] A major theoretical and methodological question is: do the Yąnomamö appear to utilize the same amount of information?

An example is in order to clarify the problem. Because of the sys-tematic exchange of marriage partners over many generations, individuals are, in many cases, related to each other in multiple ways. Some of these relationship "loops" are close, some are distant; i.e., an individual might be related to another as a first cousin by one genealogical loop but also as third cousin by a different loop. The coefficient of relationship would sum the values of all loops and express the relatedness between both indi-viduals as a simple statistic, whether or not the more "remote" loops are even known to the actors. On the other hand, the multiplicity of related-

---

[5] We have not calculated the coefficients of relationship beyond common ancestors of the fourth ascending generation. Thus, increments of relatedness through more remote ancestors are not included in the F_g values.

ness loops does reflect the degree to which systematic marriage exchanges in previous generations have "bound" kinship groups to each other and obligated them to continue exchanges in the current or future generations. In general, the closest genealogical loops account for the major fraction of the value of the coefficient of relatedness; i.e., a multiplicity of relationship loops does not necessarily change the coefficient of relationship by a large increment, for in most cases the additional multiple loops reflect remote degrees of relationship. At this stage in the application of kin selection theory to predictions about Yąnomamö behavior, we are utilizing all of the genealogical information in arriving at coefficients of relationships.

In a future publication, we shall refine the methodology in an attempt to determine the utility of segregating complex patterns of relationship into components that might enable us to predict social behavior more accurately. The issue to be addressed there has to do with the possibility that the closest genealogical connections are properly considered from the perspective of kin selection whereas the more remote connections might be taken to express marriage obligations, i.e., reciprocity expectations.

Table 8–1 gives the matrix summarizing the degree to which each member of Mohesiwä's group (the visitors) is related to all other members.[6] The individuals are listed in the table according to their identification numbers, and occur in the table because they participated in the fight in some active way. Their participation is known from (1) notes taken in the field when the fight occurred, (2) their appearance in the 16mm motion-picture film and (3) their appearance in the 35mm still photographs taken during the fight.

Table 8–2 gives the matrix summarizing the degree to which each member of Uuwä's group (the hosts) is related to all other members of that group that supported him in the fight.

Table 8–3 summarizes the coefficients of relationship between members of the visiting group to the host group, and vice versa.

It is clear from the three tables that the members of each team are more closely related among themselves than they are to their opponents, i.e., that mutual supporters are more closely related genetically among themselves than they are to the individuals they are opposing. It is also clear that the visitors are, as a group, much more highly related among themselves than are the members of the fighting group that opposed them

---

[6] We are using the terms "visitors" and "hosts" to distinguish the two groups of fighters from each other in a simple way. It must be remembered, however, that some local people sided with and supported the visitors. See table 8–4 for identities by village.

Table 8–1 **Genealogical Relatedness of the Supporters of Mohesiwä among Themselves** Each individual who supported Mohesiwä in the ax fight was compared to all other individuals in that group to establish, through computer analysis of their genealogies, whether or not they were related. The coefficient of genealogical relatedness was calculated for each related pair and displayed in the matrix. The last column gives the average coefficient of relationship between each individual and all other individuals in that group. The value 0.2124 at the bottom of the last column is the average of the averages within that group.

	0029	0067	0259	0336	0517	0714	0723	1246	1278
0029	.	.2656	.2656	.2656	.1718	.1250	.1250	.2656	.2656
0067	.2656	.	.5156	.2656	.1718	.1250	.1250	.5156	.5156
0259	.2656	.5156	.	.0312	.0468	.2500	.2500	.5156	.5156
0336	.2656	.2656	.0312	.	.3126	—	—	.2656	.2656
0517	.1718	.1718	.0468	.3126	.	—	—	.1718	.1718
0714	.1250	.1250	.2500	—	—	.	.2500	.1250	.1250
0723	.1250	.1250	.2500	—	—	.2500	.	.1250	.1250
1246	.2656	.5156	.5156	.2656	.1718	.1250	.1250	.	.5156
1278	.2656	.5156	.5156	.2656	.1718	.1250	.1250	.5156	.
1312	.2656	.5156	.5156	.2656	.1718	.1250	.1250	.5156	.5156
1335	.2656	.2656	.5000	.0312	.0468	.2500	.2500	.2656	.2656
1568	.3204	.1954	.1406	.2500	.1562	.1250	.1250	.1954	.1954
1837	.2656	.5156	.5156	.2656	.1718	.1250	.1250	.5156	.5156
1929	.2656	.5156	.0312	.5000	.3126	—	—	.5156	.5156
2194	.2656	.2656	.0312	.5000	.3126	—	—	.2656	.2656
2505	.0390	.0390	.0626	.0156	.0156	.0312	.0312	.0390	.0390
2513	.1094	.1094	.1562	.0626	.0626	.1406	.2032	.1094	.1094

in the fight. Part of this is due to the fact that the host fighters came primarily from one of the *smaller* descent groups in the village (Yoinakuwä and his brother, Keböwä, are the chief spokesmen for that group), one that has not yet become intimately integrated into the genealogical structure of the village through multi-generational marriage ties. An examination of table 8–4, however, reveals that the members of the fighting team from the host group are more closely related among themselves than they are to the rest of the members of their own village. That is, the members of the host fighting group are somewhat more related among themselves than we would expect to occur by chance alone (they are approximately 8 percent more related among themselves than they are to the village at large),

1312	1335	1568	1837	1929	2194	2505	2513	$\overline{X}$
.2656	.2656	.3204	.2656	.2656	.2656	.0390	.1094	.2217
.5156	.2656	.1954	.5156	.5156	.2656	.0390	.1094	.3076
.5156	.5000	.1406	.5156	.0312	.0312	.0626	.1562	.2715
.2656	.0312	.2500	.2656	.5000	.5000	.0156	.0626	.2061
.1718	.0468	.1562	.1718	.3126	.3126	.0156	.0626	.1435
.1250	.2500	.1250	.1250	—	—	.0312	.1406	.1123
.1250	.2500	.1250	.1250	—	—	.0312	.2032	.1162
.5156	.2656	.1954	.5156	.5156	.2656	.0390	.1094	.3076
.5156	.2656	.1954	.5156	.5156	.2656	.0390	.1094	.3076
.	.2656	.1954	.5156	.5156	.2656	.0390	.1094	.3076
.2656	.	.1406	.2656	.0312	.0312	.0312	.0626	.1933
.1954	.1406	.	.1954	.2500	.2500	.0234	.1016	.1787
.5156	.2656	.1954	.	.5156	.2656	.0390	.1094	.3076
.5156	.0312	.2500	.5156	.	.5000	.0156	.0626	.2842
.2656	.0312	.2500	.2656	.5000	.	.0156	.0626	.2061
.0390	.0626	.0234	.0390	.0156	.0156	.	.0312	.0337
.1094	.1562	.1016	.1094	.0626	.0626	.0312	.	.1060
								.2124

but, although the difference in relatedness is in the right "direction," it is not statistically significant. The fighters from the visiting group and their local supporters, on the other hand, are related among themselves 234 percent more than they are to the village as a whole and 335 percent more among themselves than they are to their opponents.

Table 8–4 also summarizes how the supporters of the major principals in the fight—Mohesiwä (1246) and Keböwä (0910)—are related to their respective champions and to the opponent of their champion. Thus, Mohesiwä's supporters are related to him 780 percent more closely than they are to his opponent, and Keböwä's supporters are related to him 210 percent more closely than they are to his opponent.

Table 8–2 Genealogical Relatedness of the Supporters of Uuwä and Yoinakuwä among Themselves *

	0390	0777	0789	0910	0950	1062	1109
0390	.	—	.0468	.0626	.0312	.0938	.0704
0777	—	.	.2500	—	.5000	—	—
0789	.0468	.2500	.	.0468	.2656	.0782	.0860
0910	.0626	—	.0468	.	.0312	.1250	.0626
0950	.0312	.5000	.2656	.0312	.	.0312	.0782
1062	.0938	—	.0782	.1250	.0312	.	.0938
1109	.0704	—	.0860	.0626	.0782	.0938	.
1744	.0626	—	.1406	.0626	.0312	.0626	.0626
1827	.5000	—	.0468	.0626	.0312	.0938	.0704
1897	.0938	—	.1718	.0626	.0312	.3126	.0938
2134	—	—	—	—	—	—	—
2209	.0626	—	.0468	.5000	.0312	.1250	.0626
2248	.0626	—	.0468	5000	.0312	.1250	.0626

* The same analyses described for table 8–1 were used to generate this matrix.

Finally, Figure 8–1 gives the distribution of average relationship coefficients for every individual in the village, including the visitors, for comparison. The mean value for egocentric relationship, using the F_g statistic, is 0.0790. That is, if any individual were taken at random from the village and systematically compared to all 267 other members of the village, we would predict that the average relationship would be $F_g = 0.0790$. Clearly the members of the fighting teams do not represent a random selection of the village; indeed, the average relationship among Mohesiwä's group falls entirely outside the range of the village distribution of average F_g values with its value of 0.2123.

Number of relationship loops: alliance versus descent

The number of different ways any pair of individuals are related—relationship loops—can be taken as a crude measure of the extent to which their immediate ancestors engaged in reciprocal marriage exchanges over several generations. This statistic, however, cannot be used by itself to express "closeness" of kinship, for many of the remoter relationships are associated with very low values of the F_g statistic. That is to say, individuals with two grandparents in common will be more closely related than individuals with

1744	1827	1897	2134	2209	2248	$\overline{X}$
.0626	.5000	.0938	—	.0626	.0626	.0905
—	—	—	—	—	—	.0625
.1406	.0468	.1718	—	.0468	.0468	.1022
.0626	.0626	.0626	—	.5000	.5000	.1263
.0312	.0312	.0312	—	.0312	.0312	.0911
.0626	.0938	.3126	—	.1250	.1250	.0951
.0626	.0704	.0938	—	.0626	.0626	.0619
.	.0626	.2500	—	.0626	.0626	.0717
.0626	.	.0938	—	.0626	.0626	.0905
.2500	.0938	.	—	.0626	.0626	.1029
—	—	—	.	—	—	.0000
.0626	.0626	.0626	—	.	.5000	.1263
.0626	.0626	.0626	—	.5000	.	.1263
						.0883

two great-great grandparents in common, even though in both cases the number of "loops" may be just two.

Table 8–4 (p. 232) summarizes the number of ways (or "loops") members of each fighting group are related to both their champion and their opponent, i.e., how many ways they are related to the person they are supporting versus the person they are opposing in the fight. Thus the supporters of Mohesiwä are related to him, on the average, 4.75 ways, suggesting that they are in part obligated to support him because of previous marriage exchanges that tie their families to his. Note, however, that the magnitude of the value of F_g does not correspond perfectly with the number of relationship loops in all cases: individual 2505 is related to Mohesiwä (1246) four different ways, but the value of F_g derived by summing the four separate fractions of that value comes to only 0.0390. That is, the four different relationship loops involve remote ancestors. By comparison, individuals 0714 and 0723 are only related to him (Mohesiwä) by one relationship loop each, but the associated value of the F_g statistic in both cases is 0.1250, i.e., the common ancestor is a "close" ancestor (Mohesiwä is their sister's son).

Mohesiwä's supporters are much less related to Keböwä in terms of loops: they are, on the average, related to him only 1.00 ways each. In one case, however, the relationship is relatively close: individual 2505 is

Table 8-3 **Genealogical Relatedness between Members of the Two Fighting Groups** Each individual from each group was compared to each individual from the opposing group to establish any genealogical connections that might exist between them. The matrix displays Mohesiwä's supporters along the left (first column) and the supporters of Uuwä and Yoinakuwä along the top (first row). The coefficients of relationship for each compared pair comprise the cells of the matrix. The last column and the bottom row give the average relatedness of each individual to the members of the opposing faction.

	0390	0777	0789	0910	0950	1062	1109
0029	.0390	—	.1094	.0312	.0156	.0860	.0938
0067	.0390	—	.1094	.0312	.0156	.0860	.0938
0259	.0782	—	.1562	.0626	.0312	.1094	.1562
0336	—	—	.0626	—	—	.0626	.0312
0517	.0156	—	.0626	—	—	.1250	.0312
0714	.0626	—	.1406	.0626	.0312	.0626	.0626
0723	.0626	—	.2032	.0626	.1562	.0626	.0626
1246	.0390	—	.1094	.0312	.0156	.0860	.0938
1278	.0390	—	.1094	.0312	.0156	.0860	.0938
1312	.0390	—	.1094	.0312	.0156	.0860	.0938
1335	.0782	—	.1562	.0626	.0312	.1094	.1562
1568	.0312	—	.1016	.0312	.0156	.0626	.0468
1837	.0390	—	.1094	.0312	.0156	.0860	.0938
1929	—	—	.0626	—	—	.0626	.0312
2194	—	—	.0626	—	—	.0626	.0312
2505	.0626	—	.0312	.1562	.0156	.0390	.1094
2513	.0468	.2500	.3594	.0468	.2032	.0782	.0860
X̄	.0395	.0147	.1209	.0395	.0340	.0796	.0804

related to Keböwä two different ways with a summed F_g value of 0.1562 and, interestingly enough, 2505 is related to Mohesiwä four ways—but more remote ways ($F_g = 0.0390$).

Turning to the patterns of relationship Keböwä's supporters have to him, we find that while the F_g average values show they are more closely related to him than they are to his opponent, the number of relationship loops between themselves and his opponent is actually much larger: 4.09 compared to 1.50 for number of loops to Keböwä and, as in the case of Mohesiwä's supporters mentioned above, some of the supporters of Keböwä are more closely related to his opponent than they are to their own champion. However, it is clear that despite the relatively large numbers of loops connecting Keböwä's supporters to his opponent, they are in fact

1744	1827	1897	2134	2209	2248	X̄
.1250	.0390	.1796	—	.0312	.0312	.0601
.1250	.0390	.1796	—	.0312	.0312	.0601
.2500	.0782	.2968	—	.0626	.0626	.1034
—	—	.0626	—	—	—	.0168
—	.0156	.1250	—	—	—	.0288
.2500	.0626	.2500	—	.0626	.0626	.0854
.2500	.0626	.2500	—	.0626	.0626	.0998
.1250	.0390	.1796	—	.0312	.0312	.0601
.1250	.0390	.1796	—	.0312	.0312	.0601
.1250	.0390	.1796	—	.0312	.0312	.0601
.2500	.0782	.2968	—	.0626	.0626	.1034
.1250	.0312	.1562	—	.0312	.0312	.0511
.1250	.0390	.1796	—	.0312	.0312	.0601
—	—	.0626	—	.0626	.0626	.0265
—	—	.0626	—	—	—	.0168
.0312	.0626	.0390	—	.1562	.1562	.0661
.1406	.0468	.1718	—	.0468	.0468	.1172
.1204	.0395	.1677	—	.0432	.0432	.0633

more closely related to their champion—even though the number of relationship loops is small. In brief, the larger number of relationship loops, because of their remoteness, does not necessarily result in closer relationships as measured by the F_g statistic.

The factors behind the composition of the team of supporters that formed around and defended Keböwä and his brother, Yoinakuwä, appear to be largely affinal in overall quality. Figure 8–2 shows the descent and marriage patterns that are relevant. Three of Keböwä's thirteen supporters are men who have married his brother's daughters, men who would, by the extension of Yąnomamö kinship logic, be his "sons-in-law" as well (Egos 1109, 0789, and 2134). Three other men (Egos 1062, 0390, and 1827) are his brothers-in-law, having either married his sister or having given a sister

Table 8–4 **Relatedness to Main Fighters** Part A compares the supporters of Mohesiwä to members of own faction, other faction (team), to the members of the entire village, and to the main fighters. The Village column identifies the village of residence of the fighters: I = Ironasiteri (Visitors), M = Mishimishimaböwei-teri. Part B compares the supporters of Yoinakuwä and Uuwä to members of own faction (team), other faction (team), to members of the entire village, and to the main fighters.

A.

	Ego I.D.	Name	Sex	Age	Village
1.	0029	Ahsökawä	M	15	I
2.	0067	Amomiawä	M	16	M
3.	0259	Borowama	F	39	M
4.	0336	Daramasiwä	M	41	M
5.	0517	Hemoshabuma	M	26	M
6.	0714	Husiheami	F	21	M
7.	0723	Iyäböwä	M	27	I
8.	1246	Mohesiwä	M	24	I
9.	1278	Morokaböwä	M	14	M
10.	1312	Nakahedami	F	23	M
11.	1335	Nanokawä	M	33	I
12.	1568	Ruwämowä	M	27	M
13.	1837	Tourawä	M	19	M
14.	1929	Wadoshewä	M	46	M
15.	2194	Yoroshianawä	M	27	M
16.	2505	Hererewä	M	16	M
17.	2513	Huuhuumi	F	17	I

to him in marriage. This point was made in the more sociological analysis in the 16mm film—that alliance ties figured prominently in the structure and organization of the fight.

Viewing the affinal ties in a temporal and developmental perspective, it seems reasonable to argue that the incorporation of small lineage segments such as that represented by Keböwä and his siblings is initiated predominantly through marriage ties. The "solidarity" that characterizes the relationships of the small group to the larger co-residential group, in this view, rests primarily on affinal obligations and the expectations that

	F_g Value						
To Own Team	To Other Team	To Village	Mohe-siwä Loops	1246 F_g		Keböwä Loops	0910 F_g
.2217	.0601	.0949	8	.2656		1	.0312
.3076	.0601	.0986	6	.5156		1	.0312
.2715	.1034	.1166	3	.5156		1	.0626
.2016	.0168	.0698	4	.2656		0	—
.1435	.0288	.0653	8	.1718		0	—
.1123	.0854	.0779	1	.1250		1	.0626
.1162	.0998	.1162	1	.1250		1	.0626
.3076	.0601	.0996				1	.0312
.3076	.0601	.0986	6	.5156		1	.0312
.3076	.0601	.1005	6	.5156		1	.0312
.1933	.1034	.1138	4	.2656		1	.0626
.1787	.0511	.0814	5	.1954		1	.0312
.3076	.0601	.0986	6	.5156		1	.0312
.2842	.0265	.0778	3	.5156		0	—
.2061	.0168	.0688	4	.2656		0	—
.0337	.0661	.0537	4	.0390		2	.1562
.1060	.1172	.1075	7	.1094		3	.0468
$\overline{X}$ .2124	.0633	.0906	4.75	.3076		1	.0395

future marriage exchanges will occur, cementing the inter-group ties more effectively. As these exchanges develop over several generations, filiative ties ramify, adding a new and perhaps even more enduring nexus, transforming the relationships into those of kinship or, to borrow Fortes' felicitous term, into relationships of "prescriptive altruism."

One might argue, further, that affinal relationships are essentially the initiators of social cohesion and yield only transient amity, and that they must be bolstered and supported by filiative links realized through additional marriage exchanges involving already related individuals. In

Table 8-4 (*cont.*)

B.

	Ego I.D.	Name	Sex	Age	Village
1.	0390	Häämä	M	14	M
2.	0777	Ishiweiwä	M	70	M
3.	0789	Kaaböwä	M	19	M
4.	0910	Keböwä	M	32	M
5.	0950	Kodedeari	M	22	M
6.	1062	Kumishiwä	M	32	M
7.	1109	Maiyahariwä	M	30	M
8.	1744	Sinabimi	F	34	M
9.	1827	Tomömamowä	M	20	M
10.	1897	Uuwä	M	27	M
11.	2134	Yakahawä	M	32	M
12.	2209	Yaukuima	F	40	I
13.	2248	Yoinakuwä	M	42	M

terms of the important debate between Fortes and Leach (see Fortes 1959, 1969), alliance *initiates* the relationships of solidarity that bind lineal descent groups to each other. Descent and filiation add, over time, the more enduring and more binding cohesion, a cohesion that can be continually reinforced and renewed through subsequent marriages of consanguineally related individuals, but a cohesion that can likewise wane if such marriages do not occur. The relatively large number of consanguineal loops that relate Keböwä's supporters to his rival in this fight can be viewed as representing a set of earlier affinal exchanges that have been allowed to lapse because they were not consolidated through additional and more recent marriage exchanges. Conversely, both the number of relationship loops and the high values of F_g tying Mohesiwä's supporters closely to him represent a historical development of affinal exchanges that were continuously bolstered and reinforced through additional marriage exchanges in each generation, marriages that involved already-related individuals.

Interestingly enough, both affinal ties and consanguineal relationships are clearly involved as bases of recruitment—Keböwä/Yoinakuwä supporters seeming to rely on the former mode and Mohesiwä's supporters on the latter. One logical conclusion from this set of facts is that alliance

234

| | F_g Value | | | | | | |
	To Own Team	To Other Team	To Village	Mohe-siwä Loops	1246 F_g	Keböwä Loops	0910 F_g
	.0905	.0395	.0703	2	.0390	1	.0626
	.0625	.0147	.0983	0	—	0	—
	.1022	.1209	.1067	7	.1094	3	.0468
	.1263	.0395	.0863	1	.0312		
	.0911	.0340	.0909	2	.0156	2	.0312
	.0951	.0796	.0854	6	.0860	2	.1250
	.0619	.0804	.0750	10	.0938	3	.0626
	.0717	.1204	.0876	3	.1250	1	.0626
	.0905	.0395	.0703	4	.0390	1	.0626
	.1029	.1677	.1038	8	.1796	1	.0626
	.0000	.0000	.0113	0	—	0	—
	.1263	.0432	.0872	3	.0312	2	.5000
	.1263	.0432	.0924	3	.0312	2	.5000
$\bar{X}$	.0883	.0633	.0820	4.08	.0601	1.50	.1263

and descent are not opposite or mutually exclusive alternatives to the development of social cohesion, but complementary and, in a temporal sense, additive. It might very well be that some societies exploit and utilize one or the other of these mechanisms in ordering the calculus of social life (Barnes 1962), but it seems apparent that the Yąnomamö take advantage of both, and do so within the same village.

One feature of the fight that puzzled the senior author at the time the fight occurred was the intensity with which Keböwä reacted to the beating of Sinabimi—a woman who was married to his brother. To be sure, kin selection predicts that brothers would aid each other in this situation, but Keböwä, in effect, took the initiative to escalate the fight to axes. A "benefit" that ultimately accrued to Keböwä, unpredictable at the time of the fight, was the untimely death, two years later, of Yoinakuwä, the brother that he aided: Keböwä married Yoinakuwä's widow, Sinabimi, and assumed the responsibilities of rearing their family. That family consisted of six children, three of whom were nubile young girls whose future marriage and reproductive careers are now largely under Keböwä's control. Since marrying Sinabimi, Keböwä has sired one child, a son born in 1973, as of the last census update made by the senior author in 1974–75.

Figure 8–1 **Distribution of the Average Coefficients of Relationship for Every Individual in the Village Compared to All 267 Other Co-Residents** If the members of the fighting groups were selected at random, with respect to genealogical relatedness, from the village at large, one would expect the factions to be characterized by an average interindividual relatedness of $F_g = 0.079$—the village average. As tables 8–1, 8–2, 8–3, and 8–4 show, the factions appear to be recruited according to closeness of genealogical relatedness.

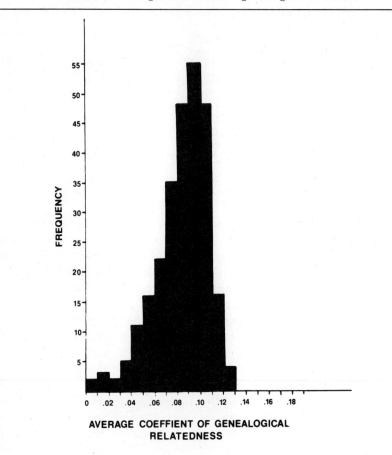

AVERAGE COEFFIENT OF GENEALOGICAL
RELATEDNESS

Conclusion

It is clear that closeness of relationship measured genealogically serves as a mediator of interpersonal behavior in the conflict situation under discussion. Members of the group that supported Mohesiwä in the fight are not a random set of individuals from the village and, to the extent that the genealogical data are an accurate reflection of biological relatedness among them, their participation in the fight can legitimately be seen as having considerable relevance to kin selection theory. Contrary to the extravagant claim made by Marshall Sahlins ". . . no system of human kinship relations is organized in accord with the genetic coefficients of relationship as known to sociobiologists" (1976a:57), there is good reason to believe that additional research will reveal similar patterns in other human societies. We believe that the evidence—and the theory—are of sufficient import at this point that new research projects should be developed to document the extent to which human kinship behavior is consistent with predictions based on inclusive fitness theory. The primitive world is, after all, on the wane and unless the research is done now, only questions will remain.

It is also clear that relatedness alone cannot account for all the bonds of attraction or tactics of recruitment in events such as the one analyzed here, and that affinity or alliance likewise operates to build coalitions. Apart from all considerations of theory in evolutionary biology, the collection of data of the kind described in this paper would, we believe, likewise contribute to a fuller understanding of systems of human marriage and mating, and by extension, to systems of social organization that can be appreciated in both quantitative as well as qualitative terms. We can make the invidious distinctions about the relative attractiveness of different styles of social science research later, but the empirical work must be done now.

Figure 8–2   **Genealogical Connections between Individuals Who Participated in the Ax Fight, Showing Marriage and Kinship Relationships**

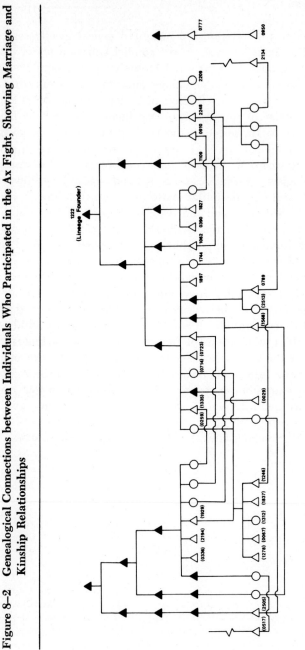

9. Relatedness and Interaction among the Ye'kwana: A Preliminary Analysis[1]

Raymond B. Hames

Introduction

Recent theoretical developments in the field of evolutionary biology and their application to traditional ethnographic problems have caused a great deal of controversy among anthropologists. The relevance of one of these theories, kin selection (Hamilton 1964), as a possible explanation of human systems of reciprocity (Alexander 1974, 1975a, in press b), and as a general tool for the comprehension of human social organization (Wilson 1975) and reciprocal altruism (Trivers 1971) has prompted Sahlins to vigorously condemn kin selection because "The cultural organization of reproductive success, exactly as it is based on kinship properly so called, has nothing to do with an inclusive fitness calculated on biological connections" (1976a:30).

Sahlins argues that since most people do not consciously calculate kinship distances in terms of genealogical (or biological) principles of descent but rather by idiosyncratic cultural principles that vary from culture to culture, kin selection is useless as a broad generalizing theory. Sahlins' critique is off the mark largely because he confounds two levels of analysis. Kin selection does not pretend to account for how humans conceive of, or mentally order, relatedness. The theory simply states that ceteris paribus, behavioral patterns of interaction (such as nepotism and reciprocity) vary according to the amount of relatedness shared by the individuals interacting. Therefore, if kin selection in humans is to be discon-

[1] I would like to thank Napoleon A. Chagnon for providing financial support from his National Institute of Mental Health project for computer programming and time. Don Symons, Mark Flinn, and N. A. Chagnon read the manuscript and provided many useful comments which were incorporated in the present text. Special thanks go to Robert Hemman of the Pennsylvania State University for writing several original computer programs that were used in this work and for spending many long nocturnal hours with me cleaning up the data. Finally, I would like to thank Thomas Foor and Robert Whitacre for statistical advice and my wife, Ilene, for typing and editing several versions of this paper. Financial support for research and writing was provided by the National Institute of Mental Health, Grant #NIMH 5 ROI MH 26008-SSR.

239

firmed, one must do so with behavioral data and not with data on ideological systems. And, although the relationship between mentalistic classifications and attitudes, and behavior, is an interesting problem, it is peripheral to a study of social interaction and relatedness.

Ironically, one of Sahlins' major works, on the theory of primitive exchange (1968), has been used by evolutionary biologists, especially Alexander (1974, 1975a), as evidence that kin selection operates in human societies. Alexander's reinterpretation of Sahlins' work under the rubric of kin selection is both logical and compelling, but it is not totally convincing because of a lack of quantitative data. This lack of precise data is not the fault of those evolutionary biologists who would like to apply their deductive models to human behavior, but rather a problem in most ethnographic data-collection techniques.

Ethnologically based studies on humans and nonhuman primates have shown age and sex to be important factors determining rates of interaction between individuals. Perhaps the best work on this subject has been done by primatologists such as Altmann (1968), Sade (1972a), and Dunbar and Dunbar (1975). Studies on interaction in humans have been conducted mainly in experimental and semi-natural situations and have focused almost exclusively on children (cf. Blurton Jones, ed., 1973). However, studies on children in natural environments are beginning to emerge; thus far, such work has dealt with the !Kung Bushmen of Botswana, yielding invaluable comparative data (Blurton Jones 1973; Draper 1975, 1977). Still, we have no comprehensive work that describes the rates of interaction for other age and sex groups in tribal communities in natural settings.

Recently genealogical relatedness has been conclusively demonstrated to be an important determinant of interaction between individuals in primate societies. Massey's studies on pigtail macaques (1975) and Kurland's on Japanese monkeys (1977) are the first to demonstrate empirically that the amount of relatedness between individuals, along with age and sex, is a strong determinant of interaction for a variety of behaviors. Anthropologists have long realized that kinship is the most important organizational feature of egalitarian societies. Regardless of which particular theory of kinship one subscribes to, I feel it is safe to say that most anthropologists, if not all, regard age, sex, and relatedness (as modified by conceptions of descent) as basic to kinship organization. Ethnographic works attempt to describe how the above factors structure behavior in a variety of circumstances. Unfortunately, most accounts tend to be qualitative or normative. The only studies which have taken a rigorously quantitative approach to the problem of how relatedness varies with behavior (aside from Chagnon and Bugos, chapter 8, this volume) are Chagnon's study of Yąnomamö village fissioning (1975) and Weisner's Ph.D. thesis (1977) on !Kung reciprocity. Chagnon shows that as relatedness declines in a village population the probability of fissioning increases, and residents of the resulting villages are more highly related among themselves than they were as a single village. Weisner demonstrates that meat exchange is a function of relatedness in that those individuals who are closely related exchange meat more often than those who are more distantly related.

My aim here is to report the results of some preliminary computer analyses of data collected on the Ye'kwana Indians of southern Venezuela which convincingly show that Wright's coefficient of relatedness (1922) is a useful predictor of interaction between individuals. My discussion is tentative and broadly sketches the outlines of this relationship. Although at present I am concerned with any kind of interaction, subsequent work will involve breaking interaction into its social and economic components, as well as examining a similar set of data collected on the Yąnomamö Indians, neighbors of the Ye'kwana.

Population and Context

At present there are approximately 2,000 Ye'kwana inhabiting the Upper Orinoco basin of Venezuela. These Carib speakers are principally found on the banks of the Ventuari, Caura, Cunucunuma, and Padamo Rivers, all major affluents of the Orinoco. They have had intermittent contact with civilization and its emissaries for the past 200 years, but the degree of acculturation experienced by each village population varies. Generally, villages at the headwaters are less disrupted than those downriver. Nevertheless, even in the most acculturated villages, the native tongue is invariably used between village members and most of the fundamental aspects of traditional social organization still function. Major factors of change have been the introduction of a cash economy and the evangelical activities of Catholic and Protestant missionaries.

Ye'kwana social organization is characterized by cognatic descent, a mixture of Hawaiian and Iroquois kin terminology (referred to as quasi-unilineal by Murdock 1960a), joint families, and an uxorilocal post-marital residence rule. Villages range in size from 20 to 160 people, with an average of 40 to 50. (The highest figures occur in heavily acculturated villages.) Detailed information on Ye'kwana social organization can be obtained from the following sources: Wilbert (1958), Fuchs (1962), and Arvelo-Jiménez (1971).

The focus of this study is the village of Toki, located on the middle course of the Padamo River. The gently rolling countryside surrounding Toki is covered with primary tropical rainforest, flourishing in equatorial heat and humidity and more than 110 inches of rain per year. The subsistence economy is based on hunting, fishing, gathering, and most importantly, gardening. Some cash cropping is done, but only enough to purchase steel goods, gasoline for outboard motors, and clothing. The village is relatively isolated, receiving non-Indian visitors such as missionaries and malaria inspectors only several times per year. The most common visitors to Toki are members of seven Yąnomamö villages located on the Padamo. The area around Toki is a frontier separating the westernmost extent of the Yąnomamö population and the easternmost Ye'kwana. Until the 1930s the two peoples engaged in chronic warfare. After the Ye'kwana defeated several large Padamo Yąnomamö villages in the 1930s, all fighting ceased, with the Ye'kwana dominating politically. However, the Yąnomamö still carry on active warfare among themselves.

The village of Toki consists of eleven nuclear families living in eight separate dwellings. Six of the nuclear families belong to three joint family units, with all members of each joint family sharing the same house. Although they have separate houses, three of the remaining nuclear families retain strong social and economic links with the senior joint family of the village. In Ye'kwana culture the uxorilocal joint family is the basis of social, economic, and ritual life. The domestic cycle begins with a founding nuclear family. As its children come of marriageable age, males leave the household in order to live uxorilocally with their spouses. Thus a joint family is formed, consisting of a senior founding family and one or more junior families. Junior families usually separate from the joint family soon after their daughters marry and bring sons-in-law into the home. But the founding family's youngest daughter and her spouse remain in the household until the founding couple die. While the senior couple live, they exert some social and economic managerial authority over all of their junior families remaining in the village, even if the latter live in separate houses and have formed joint families of their own. However, the degree of authority exercised by the founding family is stronger towards those families still living with them. Joint family members usually have a common garden from which everyone harvests, and they perform a great many activities cooperatively.

Data Collection and Analysis

Instantaneous scan sampling (see Altmann 1974, for a discussion of this method and other behavioral sampling methods) was chosen as a method for sampling behavior because of the nature of the problem and population studied. The primary aim of my study was to collect time budgets of economic activities for all members of the village, in order to show how the division of labor was structured according to age-sex groups, and how individual variations in time budgets within each age-sex group are related to the demographic composition of each minimal economic unit (i.e., the nuclear family). Also, social activities were sampled as they occurred, forming an integral part of my economic study. The results of this work are contained in my Ph.D. dissertation and elsewhere (Hames and Hames 1976; Hames 1978; Chagnon and Hames 1979).

In the present analysis the population used consists of eighty-eight full-time members of the Ye'kwana village of Toki.[2] I sampled behavior in the following way. Once or twice daily I made a round through the village, observing and recording the behavior of each individual encountered. I recorded his or her name, activity, location, time and date of the scan, and each individual, if any, with whom he or she was interacting (on a hand-held tape recorder). If an individual was absent from the village I inquired as to his or her activity, location, and companions.[3] After each circuit was completed I returned to my mud house, I listened to the tape, and recorded the data directly on FORTRAN coding sheets. Daily sampling hours and starting points were chosen by consulting a table of random numbers so my appearance would not be predictable by the Ye'kwana. Sampling began in September, 1975, and continued until June of 1976 except for a few breaks

[2] Data on visitors' activities were recorded, but are not included here. The settlement of Toki is unique because it contains a resident population of thirty-five Yąnomamö, half of whom actually live within the village (in separate houses) while the other half live in a small settlement about ten minutes' walk away. The Yąnomamö were also included in my daily circuits and I have a set of data on them, identical with the set analyzed here for the Ye'kwana, which will be analyzed and compared with that on the Ye'kwana in a later publication.

[3] At first I was worried about the reliability of informant statements as to the location and activity of individuals outside the village. During the initial phase of my investigation, which lasted five weeks, I visited everyone who was outside the village during my circuits in order to see if they were doing what I had been told. I found informant statements to be extremely reliable and decided to use them. A longer discussion of this problem is found in Hames (1978).

when I left Toki to purchase supplies. During that time I made 360 sampling circuits resulting in approximately 29,000 observations; each observation consisted of an Ego, date, time, location, activity, and interactant(s).

Collecting genealogies in order to calculate coefficients of relatedness was quite easy. Most mature adults could give fairly accurate genealogies for every member of the village. My procedure was to interview each male and female head of household and ask them to trace their ancestry as far back as possible, and indicate how they were genealogically related to every other member of the village. All discrepancies were noted and cross-checked by re-interviewing until all errors were rectified to everybody's satisfaction.

Interaction may be defined as two or more individuals engaged in a coordinated activity. Thus the concept encompasses a multitude of human activities ranging from a mother nursing her child to a gang of children playing or to a team of men building a house. It is divisible into a variety of types and subtypes such as social, economic, or ritual, or any other combination that an observer can accurately define (such as Alexander's "nepotistic" and "reciprocal," 1974) and which suit some theoretical interest. Here we are concerned with any kind of interaction among the villagers of Toki, making no distinctions as to the kind of behavior they exhibited while interacting. While it is obvious that the kinds of interaction are very important, I focus on interaction per se since this report is only a preliminary approximation of the relationship between interaction and relatedness. Later work will break down interaction into a variety of types in order to see how each varies with relatedness, and with age and sex groups. The most common kinds of interaction observed in Toki were the sharing of meals, conversation, play, and a variety of economic activities such as male teams' hunting and female teams' gardening.

An 88 × 88 matrix was produced by computer, showing how many times each individual, regardless of age or sex, interacted with every other individual in the village of Toki. The column indicated the interactor and the row the interactee, and their corresponding cell displayed the number of times each dyad was observed to interact. If an individual was interacting with more than one person at a time, then interaction was scored with each of the other individual interactees.

Also, genealogies collected in the field were analyzed by computer (see Chagnon 1974 and this volume for discussion) to produce an 88 × 88 matrix of relatedness for each individual living in Toki against every other individual.

In order to graph the relationship between interaction and relatedness, a FORTRAN computer program was designed to select all dyads in the relatedness matrix related to each other by the highest degree (0.5: i.e., parent, offspring, full sibling) and then search for all those dyads in the interaction matrix and record the number of times they interacted. The number of times these dyads of the same degree of relatedness interacted was totaled and then divided by the number of unique dyads. Thus the first plot of the scattergram was created consisting of an "X" axis indicating the degree of relatedness, and a "Y" axis indicating the mean number of times the dyads interacted. The computer subsequently searched out all other degrees of relatedness and the mean of their interactions, ending with those individuals who were totally unrelated. A scattergram of 16 plots, shown in figure 9–1, was produced.

By inspection, figure 9–1 demonstrates that interaction increases with the degree of relatedness. Pearson's product-moment correlation coefficient was found to be highly significant at "r^2" $= 0.88$, as was an F-test at 0.001.[4]

Discussion

I have shown above that relatedness is a very important determinant of interaction in one human society. Furthermore, it parallels predictions made by Alexander (1974, 1975a, in press b) and others who have program matically applied kin selection theory to human society. Demonstrating that an Ego interacts more with his parents and siblings (people related to him at the 0.5 level) than with his half-siblings, aunts, uncles, and grandparents (people related to him at the 0.25 level) should surprise no one; after all, the nuclear family is a fundamental component of any society's social organization. What I think is important is this: at and below the 0.25 level, interaction steadily decreases with respect to the degree of re-

[4] Using this method two other scattergrams were produced. In the first the interaction-dependent variable was replaced with another dependent variable called proximity. Proximity was operationally defined for the data set as two or more people observed at the same date, time, and in the same location regardless of whether they were interacting or not. A proximity matrix was produced, identical in form with the interaction matrix, and correlated with the relatedness matrix, yielding a correlation coefficient of "r^2" $= 0.92$. Second, instead of averaging the amount of interaction for all dyads at each degree of relatedness, as is done in figure 9–1, a second scattergram was made using the unaveraged scores. This program created a scattergram of 7,832 plots with a correlation coefficient of "r" $= 0.516$.

Figure 9–1   Relatedness and Interaction   Relatedness, represented by the horizontal axis, is defined as the fraction of genes shared by two individuals that are identical by descent, averaged .over all loci. Interaction, represented by the vertical axis, is measured as the mean number of times all dyads at each degree of relatedness were observed to interact. In order to give a clearer picture of how degrees of relatedness correspond to American kinship terminology, the following list of degrees of relatedness and kin terms relative to Ego is presented: (a) 0.5 = parent, offspring, and sibling; (b) 0.375 = three-quarter sibling (this relationship is common in societies which practice sororal polygyny and may be defined as that of siblings who have the same father but different mothers who are sisters); (c) 0.25 = half-sibling, aunt, uncle, nephew, niece, grandparent, or grandchild; (d) 0.125 = full cousin, great-grandparent, great-grandchild, granduncle, grandaunt, grandnephew, or grandniece; 0.0936 = half cousin (an Ego's parent's half-sibling's offspring) ; (e) 0.0625 = first cousin once removed, great-great-grandchild, great-great-grandparent.

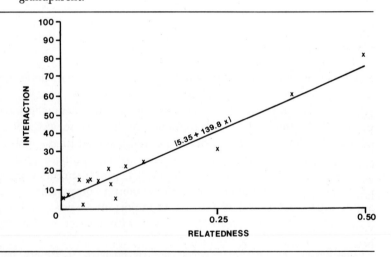

latedness. Nevertheless, one might argue that interaction is a function of residential propinquity, in that people who are closely related to one another, such as nuclear family members, tend to live in the same house, and therefore their rates of interaction would be greater than those with people who live in different houses.

There are two ways of dealing with this problem. First, one could argue that people who live in close propinquity (in the same house or sec-

II. Kinship

tion of the village) do so because they are closely related, and therefore residential propinquity and interaction are both functions of relatedness. To cite only one example of many, Lévi-Strauss (1967b, 1967c) has pointed out for New World aboriginal cultures that the residential organization of camps and villages is governed by kinship so that moieties, lineages, and marriage sections group closely related people into separate locales; an Ego lives nearest to those who are most closely related to him and furthest from those distantly related to him. Indeed, the residential organization of Toki follows this pattern, and it is evident in other Ye'kwana villages (Arvelo-Jiménez 1971). The issue of whether propinquity or relatedness is the cause of frequency of interaction is best put in the perspective of proximate and ultimate causation. I believe that residential propinquity is the proximate mechanism that accounts for *how* high levels of interaction are maintained while relatedness and reciprocity are the ultimate causes of *why* such interaction is adaptive. A village is organized with closely related individuals living near to each other so that they may interact more easily and frequently.

Second, it would be desirable to negate or control the effects of propinquity on interaction in order to test the effects of relatedness alone on interaction. To some extent, although not systematically, part of the data presented in figure 9–1 controls for the effects of proximity. All individuals related by 0.5 (Ego's parents and siblings) and by 0.375 (3/4 siblings, or the offspring of sisters married to the same man) live in the same house. The scattergram suggests that despite the fact of cohabitation, Ego, on the average, interacts more with those people who are related to him at 0.5 than at 0.375. Furthermore, many people related to him at 0.25 (especially half-siblings, but also aunts, uncles, and grand-parents), reside with Ego, yet he interacts with them less than he does with individuals related to him at the other two levels. Proximate mechanisms are notoriously difficult to understand. Residential propinquity, which leads to greater visibility, habituation to another's presence, and the facilitation of interaction between individuals, is likely to be a major proximate mechanism but it is not the only one; even when the effects of propinquity are controlled, interaction still varies predictably with relatedness. I suggest that the Ye'kwana are taught to recognize kin of various degrees of relatedness and vary their interaction accordingly.[5] This brings us to Sahlins' contention that kin termi-

[5] Due to the partly Hawaiian or generational nature of Ye'kwana kinship terminology, real genealogical differences between individuals are often merged under a single term. However, the Ye'kwana, when necessary, distinguish genealogical differences between individuals who share the same kin term.

nology and the attitudes appropriate to particular kin are better predictors of behavior than relatedness. Among the Ye'kwana, most individuals related at the 0.5, 0.375, 0.25, and 0.125 levels are called "brother" (*udui*) or "sister" (*yaya*). Therefore, it is evident that if we used Ye'kwana kinship terminology we could not predict interaction within these categories. In a later publication I shall systematically compare the utility of using native terminology and biological relatedness in predicting interaction.

As mentioned in the introduction, the factors of age and sex also determine rates as well as kinds of interaction between individuals. For example, an uncle thirty-five years old and his niece seven years old are related by 0.25. Given this amount of relatedness one would expect them to interact a great deal. However, this is frequently not the case; individuals of the opposite sex and such disparate ages usually have very little to do with one another, even if they live in the same house. But I would predict that this uncle and niece would interact more often with each other than they would with others who are equally different in terms of age and sex but more distantly related. Before the scattergram (figure 9–1) was produced I had expected the relationship between relatedness and interaction to be much weaker than it was, because of the uncontrolled effects of age and sex (and also marriage of unrelated individuals) on interaction. The better-than-expected goodness of fit is largely a result of a fortuitous balance of age-sex groups in each degree of relatedness.

One might legitimately ask what kind of connection there is between Ye'kwana interaction and the sociobiological concepts of nepotism and reciprocity. Most interactions are social (e.g., meal sharing, conversation, and play) and their intensities, as demonstrated above, are a partial function of relatedness. One would be hard put to prove that these interactions affect fitness in any direct way, but I think that frequent and long-term social interaction indicates a proportional degree of solidarity, affection, and willingness for mutual aid in times of difficulty. In daily life, economic interaction is probably the most crucial test of kin selection theory because activities such as the exchange of meat, babysitting, and assistance in house or canoe construction do affect the quality of one's life. Elsewhere (Hames 1978), I have shown that reciprocal garden labor is determined by relatedness. Perhaps the ultimate test of kin selection comes in times of political confrontation when one must literally decide to risk his life by joining one side of a conflict or the other; Chagnon and Bugos (this volume) have shown that this kind of decision is in accord with the theory of kin selection.

The data presented here are only the start of a more comprehensive analysis of interaction in two different tribal societies, the Ye'kwana and Yanomamö. In future work, I shall attempt to show how different kinds of interaction, such as nepotism and reciprocity, vary with relatedness and age and sex, and how the exchange of goods, especially meat, is governed by those same factors. In short, I shall be able to evaluate some of the models suggested by kin selection theoreticians. Because of my fortunate field situation among the Ye'kwana and Yąnomamö, I shall be able to evaluate kin selection models in two culturally distinct societies and determine whether both of them operate on similar principles.

III. Individual and Group Strategies

In one major respect Darwin's basic idea was operationally imprecise for the analysis of natural history. As hinted in 1930 by Fisher (1958), and extensively clarified by Williams (1957, 1966) and subsequent authors, in all evolutionary analyses we are forced continually to address a question Darwin largely avoided: "Survival of the fittest *what*?" The axis of consideration is the hierarchy of organization of life forms (Lewontin 1970). Darwin was at least vaguely aware of this problem (Alexander 1974:325), and Fisher alluded to it explicitly in the 1958 revision of his 1930 volume (p. 49). Darwin, however, ignorant of genetics, had only a few alternatives to consider in answering this question: individuals, groups of individuals, populations, and species. Our knowledge of genetics and ecology requires us to think now in terms of genes, supergenes, chromosomes, genotypes, and families as well as social groups, demes, populations, species, communities, and ecosystems. Williams (1966) convincingly eliminated from most (but not all) considerations all of these levels above that of the individual, or, as he put it, the parent(s) and their brood of offspring. He did not extensively contrast individuals and subunits such as genes. Lewontin (1970), however, did so, and he concluded that "the primary focus of evolution by natural selection is the individual." More recent authors have tended to focus almost exclusively on the gene (e.g., Trivers 1974; Dawkins 1976). Williams' modification of the concept of natural selection, actually initiated in his 1957 paper on senescence, is a crucial permanent refinement of Darwinian theory.

The new idea this refinement of theory offers to anthropology is that human social behavior should be adaptive (at least in the context of past if not present environments) for the individuals exhibiting the behavior, but not for the group to which these individuals belong. There is some difficulty in transferring into anthropology the notion that function/purpose/adaptation can be expected at the individual level, but not at the group level. The idea that frequently repeated patterns of behavior, and the cultural elements associated with them, have a function is not new to anthropology. The idea, although not universally accepted by anthropologists, is familiar to all, and has a respectable history going back to such eminent theoreticians as Durkheim, Radcliffe-Brown, and Malinowski. It is also clearly an important element in the thinking of many present-day ecological anthropologists, e.g., M. Harris and R. A. Rappaport. Yet function as it appears in the work of these authors is most often function at the level of some social group, or culturally delineated population.

Sociobiology, in contrast, is built on the assumption that function is expectable only at the individual level and that cultural patterns and social organization are epiphenomena of individuals striving for genetic survival (cf. Vayda and McCay 1975). In various styles the papers in this section explore ways in which anthropological data can be interpreted from this point of view.

In chapter 10, I present a hypothesis which can serve as a starting point for looking at institutionalized human behavior as individual-level adaptation. The hypothesis states that in every society there are pragmatic standards of success. Individuals evaluate the outcomes of efforts by various other individuals and coalitions of individuals as varying in desirability. Individuals themselves can also be ranked, at least to some extent, by the extent to which their efforts in a particular sphere of activity have, on the whole, led to results near the more preferable extremes. In short, within specific spheres of activity there are more or less successful individuals. Further, individuals strive to be successful. The paper hypothesizes that the effect of success, in this conscious pragmatic sense, on inclusive fitness (whether cognized or not) tends to be positive. Thus striving for economic, political, or other culturally defined forms of success are, in effect, strivings to increase inclusive fitness. The hypothesis is tested in the paper with positive results using data from the Turkmen of Persia. Another recent paper dealing with the same variables from a sociobiological perspective is Hartung (1976).

The second chapter in this section, by Bates and Lees, approaches the issue of the level at which adaptation is expectable from a different angle. They examine the methodological and theoretical difficulties surrounding the common assumption in ecological anthropology that various institutionalized patterns of behavior have the group-level function of preventing overpopulation and environmental degradation. They make the criticism that attempts to test this assumption have been rare even though acceptance of it has been widespread. Their critique is largely methodological. They point out the types of data and analyses that would be needed to test population-regulation hypotheses and show that in general those advocating such hypotheses have failed to produce appropriate data. They

III. Individual and Group Strategies

pay particular attention to recent work by Divale and Harris which purports to show that male chauvinism and warfare are adaptive at the population level because they cause female infanticide, which in turn leads to a population equilibrium. This is the most elaborately argued and most thoroughly tested of recently published population-regulation hypotheses. Bates and Lees show, however, that the data, which consist mainly of sex ratios drawn from census material, by no means prove that the populations in question had achieved equilibrium. They further point out that the data presented fail to dispel a number of other sources of doubt about the Divale and Harris hypothesis. Their paper clearly establishes three things which are important. First, they demonstrate that there is, at least at present, no strong empirical support for the proposition that human populations have group-level adaptations designed to achieve population equilibrium. Second, they point out that there are good theoretical reasons for doubting the existence of such adaptations. Third, they emphasize that there are alternate explanations of the various social practices—such as female-biased infanticide—which have been seen as adaptations for population regulation and that these alternative explanations need to be tested.

This sets the stage for chapter 12, by Chagnon, Flinn, and Melancon, and chapter 13, by Dickemann. These chapters explore alternate explanations of male-biased sex ratios, starting with the assumption that they are the outcome of individual-level strategies for maximizing inclusive fitness.

In addition to having direct implications for the question of group-versus individual-level function, these two chapters deal with the arcane subject of sex-ratio theory (reviewed in chapter 1:29–31). They build specifically on Fisher's basic insight into sex ratio and recent refinements of this insight (Trivers and Willard 1973; Alexander 1974). As Dickemann points out at the beginning of her paper, Trivers and Willard (1973) hypothesize that under certain conditions females should evolve the ability to vary the sex ratio of their offspring. They suggest two conditions as necessary for the evolution of this ability. The first is a higher variance in male reproductive success than in female reproductive success; that is, a situation in which the most successful males have more offspring than the most successful females, and the least successful males have fewer offspring than the least successful females. Such conditions are most pronounced in highly polygynous breeding systems, but could also exist in human populations in a smaller degree as a result of serial monogamy (see Alexander et al., this volume, chapter 15). The second condition is an element of predictability such that a female can "predict" from her own condition (or circumstance) whether her offspring will fall at the high or low end of the variance. Given these conditions, a female whose offspring can be predicted to fall near the high end of variance in RS would gain in the number of her grandoffspring if she produced more male than female offspring. One whose offspring can be predicted to fall near the low end of the variance in reproductive success would have more grandoffspring if she produced more female offspring. Natural selection would, therefore, favor any mechanism which caused a female to have more male offspring when her condition or circumstance indicate highly successful offspring, and caused her to have more females when her condition indicated that her offspring will fall at the low end of the variance in reproductive success. Trivers and Willard confine their discussion for the most part to physiological mechanisms. Alexander (1974) suggested that infanticide in human populations could be a behavioral mechanism serving this same function, and predicted that where this is the case female infanticide would be more common among the more successful segment of the population. This is the hypothesis which Bates and Lees suggest as an alternative to the Divale and Harris hypothesis, and which is tested in chapters 12 and 13.

The test of this hypothesis with Yąnomamö data by Chagnon, Flinn, and Melancon yields negative results. The authors suggest two possible reasons for this outcome: lack of the required condition of predictability of offspring's reproductive success, or the importance of marriage exchange as a means of mate acquisition. Either condition alone would be adequate to make the Trivers and Willard hypothesis inapplicable.

The data presented by Dickemann form an interesting contrast to the Yąnomamö, since in these societies the conditions which would make female infanticide adaptive are much more clearly met and the evidence for the presence of female-biased infanticide is much stronger. The Yąnomamö fall in the category of societies which anthropologists label egalitarian, whereas those with which Dickemann deals fall in the category of stratified societies. Chagnon in a later section of this volume presents data indicating that reproductive success is not equal among the Yąnomamö. His earlier data summarized in this section should also make it clear that many other things, such as political power and the size of kin networks one can call on for support, are also unequal in egalitarian societies.

This is not meant to suggest that the contrast between egalitarian and stratified societies is unreal, but rather that one should be careful not to exaggerate this contrast. Alexander (1978a) has suggested that in the societies which anthropologists classify as egalitarian, the primary resource for reproduction which is unequally distributed is *kin*. Societies in which other resources also become unequally distributed are different in important ways. In societies like the Yąnomamö which lack the state, and in which inheritance of wealth does not play an important role in determining a person's social status, there are limits on the extent and nature of the inequalities that arise (Alexander 1977a). The most significant limit, for the question of the applicability of Alexander's (1974) predictions, is the fact that changes in social status over generations are great enough to make the status of offspring unpredictable from their parents' status. In the societies studied by Dickemann, changes in social status over generations are much more gradual, and the social status and associated reproductive success of offspring are predictable from parents' social status. Both the importance of inherited forms of property and the greater and more stable difference in political power found in state societies are responsible for this element of predictability of offspring's status.

The Yąnomamö and the stratified societies studied by Dickemann also differ in the nature of marriage exchange. Among the Yąnomamö, women are acquired either by using violence or the threat of violence to appropriate them from unwilling parties, or by exchanging women for women or promises of women for women. The second means is sufficiently important to place men without sisters at a disadvantage in mate competition. Given this situation, there may be no advantage to intentionally biasing the sex ratio of investment in one's offspring in favor of males. The societies examined by Dickemann, in contrast, exchange property for mates. Because of the tendency for females to marry men of higher status, high-status women do not have enough potential mates, and low-status men face a similar situation. In both cases, property is used in exchange for what is scarce: high-status females pay dowries for scarce husbands and low-status males pay bridewealth for scarce wives.

In contrast to the Yąnomamö situation, men without sisters suffer no disadvantage in mate acquisition, and high-status parents can improve the expected reproductive success of their offspring by curtailing investment in daughters through female infanticide. Female celibacy which represents a limitation of parental investment in female offspring is also adaptive under these conditions. The predicted patterns of female infanticide and celibacy occurred in the societies examined, bearing out Alexander's (1974) prediction. The situation, however, is not reversed among the lower strata of the societies studied by Dickemann. Although Dickemann does not suggest it, the reason for the absence of male infanticide among lower strata may derive from the economic value of males at lower social levels. Among these groups male offspring may, indeed, have a lower expected reproductive success than their sisters, but nevertheless they are able to assist parents economically and presumably enhance their parents' ability to invest in daughters who have a higher reproductive expectation.

Underlying much of the discussion of infanticide is the issue of individual-versus-group-level advantage. This may be debated well into the future. Meanwhile, the contrasts in these societies should not be minimized: they vividly illuminate the behavioral plasticity of humankind. For anthropology, the reasons for, and nature of, this plasticity are as central an issue as that of the level at which behavior is adaptive, and often particular forms of behavior can only be understood if both of these issues are kept in mind.

W. I.

10. Cultural and Biological Success[1]

William Irons

This paper proposes a research strategy for testing the proposition that human beings tend to behave in such a way as to maximize their genetic representation in future generations. A general method for testing this theoretical principle is outlined, and then applied to data drawn from a particular population, the Turkmen of Persia. It is suggested that replication of this research procedure on data from a large number of human societies will provide a good test of the validity of this theoretical proposition.

Conscious Goals and Reproductive Success

One of the more obvious features of human behavior is that it is goal-directed. Human beings set for themselves conscious goals and then choose courses of action which they believe will lead to the accomplishment of those goals. The specific goals involved vary widely from one society to another. For example, among the Yąnomamö Indians of the Amazon basin, men strive to be fierce, that is, formidable in wielding violence against other men. Fierce men are able to acquire larger numbers of mates and male allies than less fierce men. These are aspirations that men consciously try to fulfill, and fulfilling them can be designated cultural success among the Yąnomamö. Alternate terms might be emic success or perceived success. The

[1] The collection and analysis of data reported in this paper was supported by National Science Foundation Grant GS-37888 (1973–1974) and a grant from the Ford and Rockefeller Foundations Program in Support of Social Science and Legal Research on Population Policy (1974–1975). Continuing analysis is currently supported by National Science Foundation Grant BN576–11904 (1976–1978) and a grant from the Harry Frank Guggenheim Foundation (1976–1978). My wife, Marjorie Rogasner, accompanied me during the 1973–1974 field season and worked full time as a research assistant doing both participant observation and survey research. Following the field season, she assisted in the initial coding of field data. *Khoday shokr wa hileyime sogh bol diyen.* Richard Alexander, Napoleon Chagnon, Clifford Clogg, Mark Flinn, Nancy Howell, and Jeffrey Kurland read earlier drafts of this paper and made helpful suggestions. I alone am responsible for its flaws. The original title of this paper, now cited in some places, was "Emic and Reproductive Success."

Nuer value cattle and strive to increase the sizes of their herds, and a man with many cattle is judged successful. Tiwi men strive to acquire large numbers of wives, and, preferring a single quantitative measure of a man's success, measure it in terms of his wife list which includes all the living and deceased wives he has ever had, much as academics measure success in terms of the number of citations in an individual's bibliography. Middle-class Americans aim for a combination of interesting work, moderate economic prosperity (by the standards of their society), and financial security. Most of the examples offered here are of male goals. It is unfortunately the state of the ethnographic literature that female goals, which are analytically as important as those of males, are less frequently described.

Although some ethnographies tell us little about the common aspirations of the people they purport to describe, or local standards of success and failure, it is reasonable to assume that such things can be found in any human society. Conscious goals and generally agreed upon measures of success can be identified by participant observation, and quantitative tests can be applied to determine whether a particular goal is actually pursued in a particular society. It is possible that certain stated goals are merely verbal preferences which never affect behavior. It is only those which can be shown to motivate behavior which are important for the sort of analysis discussed here.

I suggest as a hypothesis that in most human societies cultural success consists in accomplishing those things which make biological success (that is, a high inclusive fitness) probable. While cultural success is by definition something people are conscious of, they may often be unaware of the biological consequences of their behavior. This paper does not inquire into the nature of the proximate psychological mechanisms which cause people to consciously strive for things which have evolutionary consequences beyond their recognition, although it is not difficult to suggest what some of these might be (see for example Dawkins 1976:60–64). As a result of environmental change, what has been defined in the past in a particular society as worth achieving may cease to make a high inclusive fitness probable. When this happens, I hypothesize, members of the society gradually redefine their goals to make them correspond with those things which will increase the probability of a high inclusive fitness. This hypothesis is derived from the following more general theoretical principle: Human beings track their environments and behave in ways which, given the specific environment in which they find themselves, maximize inclusive fitness; what is observed as culture and social structure is the outcome of this process (cf Chapter 1:5–10 and 34–37).

Empirical Testing

The proposition that cultural, or emic, success makes a high inclusive fitness probable can be tested by collecting demographic data in combination with data on degrees of success by the standards defined by the population under study. One can then analyze the data to determine whether individuals who are emically successful have a higher inclusive fitness. This is a somewhat laborious procedure since it necessitates collecting large enough amounts of demographic data to estimate age-specific birth and death rates for different categories of individuals corresponding to different degrees of successfulness.[2] There is, however, much to recommend a procedure of this sort despite its difficulties, since predictions about the effect of social behavior on vital rates are central to sociobiology. Indeed, it can be said that it is a basic principle of sociobiology that the evolutionary significance of an individual is completely contained in his or her effect on vital statistics (Williams 1966:3–4). Direct measurement of these effects is, I suggest, a very effective way of testing sociobiological predictions. Testing for a positive association of cultural and biological success is a first step toward testing for causation. Often, given the association, the interpretation that cultural success increases the probability of biological success will be the most reasonable one in the ethnographic context in question. In other cases, an association may not justify such an inference, and additional tests may be necessary to permit a strong inference of cause. This issue is discussed in reference to a specific ethnographic context below.

Following is an illustration of the method proposed, using data I collected among the Turkmen of Persia in 1973–1974. These data are still being analyzed, so future papers will carry the analysis farther than this one and if they do not falsify the above hypothesis they will allow stronger inferential support (see Irons, in prep. b, for some additional results). Nevertheless, the analysis presented here is a type of test which would falsify the hypothesis that striving for cultural success equates with striving for biological success, if the predicted relationship among variables did not emerge. It is suggested that replication of this type of test in many human societies would yield either strong support for the hypothesis, or would falsify it, depending on the outcome.

The most significant emic measure of success among the Turkmen is

---

[2] It might be possible in some instances to utilize census data, but such data must be accurate (which often is not the case for the populations anthropologists study) and must allow for the association of variation in vital rates with variation in emic success.

wealth. A large part of the daily activities of Turkmen is devoted to economic production, and participant observation suggests that their basic economic strategy approximates one of maximizing wealth (Irons 1975:155–170). The most reasonable alternative hypothesis is that the Turkmen have a sufficing strategy in which they strive to meet their needs for consumption, but once these needs are met prefer to refrain from further labor (cf. Sahlins 1972). Such strategies are common among populations which have no means of storage of produce beyond what is immediately required for consumption—that is, no dependable ways of saving. The Turkmen, like all other Middle Eastern and Central tribal peoples, have long been tied into a market economy that reaches beyond their tribal boundaries. A significant portion of production is for consumption by the producing household, but production for trade is something they have depended on for at least a millennium. Savings in the form of money, jewelry, and consumable goods such as cloth, are common. Acquisition of capital in agricultural land, and in livestock which provide produce and capital well beyond what is required for immediate consumption, is also common. Such savings and capital are valuable in many ways. They can be used for consumption in years of low rainfall, when crops fail and herds are decimated, to meet needs not met by current income. Bridewealth is necessary for marriage, and is exorbitant. In the community in which I resided in 1966 and 1967, it took a family of median wealth from two to four years to acquire enough capital to be ready to give the hundred sheep necessary to obtain a bride for a son. The number of years necessary in any specific case varied widely because crop yields and the increase of flocks varied widely from year to year. Increasing capital was also necessary to carry out the common practice of eventually setting up one's sons as independent heads of households. Extra wealth could also be used to enjoy a higher standard of living, including better food and medical care. Faced with a situation of this sort, the economically rational thing to do would be to try to increase income beyond immediate needs in terms of consumption and to accumulate capital beyond what is necessary for consumption alone.

If economic activities are governed by a sufficing strategy one would expect per capita wealth to be roughly equal among households, since consumptive needs are approximately equal from one individual to another. If strategies of increasing wealth beyond consumptive needs govern the economy, one would expect those who are more able to acquire wealth to in fact have more capital. One factor influencing the ability of a household to accumulate wealth is the number of able-bodied adults in the household. Wealth (measured in the form of the monetary value of all capital owned) and the number of able-bodied adults in a household show a Pearson correlation coefficient of .39 (p < .001, N = 566). The same statistic for per capita wealth and number of adult laborers is .21 (p < .001, N = 566). Future analysis will focus on diachronic trends in capital holdings for households with different labor resources, to control for the influence of such factors as the initial patrimony with which a household starts and bridal payments (see Irons, in prep. b).

The next step in the analysis is to demonstrate that vital rates vary with differences in wealth. The vital rates presented here were calculated from data collected in a survey of 566 Turkmen households. The relevant data include complete fertility records for all individuals in the households surveyed, complete survivorship records for all children born to these individuals, and a record of all capital in the form of land and livestock owned by each household. Since among the Turkmen all forms of wealth have a monetary value, the value of each household's capital can be expressed in terms of a single quantity. The households in the sample were ranked in terms of this quantity, which represents a good measure of the wealth enjoyed by all members of the household, and the sample population was then divided into wealthier and poorer halves.

Separate age-specific fertility rates were then calculated from the male and female birth records for each half of the population. The calculation of mortality records is somewhat more complex because the sample of deaths and person years at risk of death was large enough to yield a good estimate of mortality probabilities only for the earlier years of life. Mortality rates were computed for the first twenty years of life and the estimated survivorship curve yielded by these calculations was matched to model survivorship curves from Coale and Demeny (1966) using a chi-square goodness-of-fit test.

The p-values for differences in fertility rates were calculated from the chi-square values computed for the difference between actual numbers of births recorded during each age interval for each group and the expected number of births if the difference in number of births between the two groups were solely a result of the different number of person years recorded for each group in each interval. After I completed this paper, Clifford Clogg, acting as a statistical consultant, devised a more powerful test of difference in fertility (see Irons, in prep. b). The p-value for death rates in the age interval 0–20, was calculated by assuming that deaths have a Poisson distribution and assuming a South 12 age-sex structure from Coale and Demeny (1966). The estimated death rates and variance of death rates were age standardized and a z test was used to calculate the p-value for a one-tailed

Table 10-1 Summary of Male Fertility Data

| Age | Wealthier Half of Population | | | Poorer Half of Population | | |
	Person Years	Births	Age-Specific Birth Rate	Person Years	Births	Age-Specific Birth Rate
15–19	1889	83	.044	2189	49	.022
20–24	1468	293	.200	1842	228	.124
25–29	1125	345	.307	1516	335	.221
30–34	909	297	.327	1265	337	.266
35–39	723	257	.356	1008	275	.273
40–44	546	178	.326	735	178	.242
45–49	417	105	.252	528	123	.233
50–54	277	58	.209	338	51	.151
55–59	169	38	.225	223	18	.081
60–64	100	17	.170	156	11	.071
65–69	35	5	.143	86	4	.047
70–74	17	2	.118	39	1	.026

$$df = 12 \qquad \chi^2 = 113.36 \qquad p < .001$$

alternative. The predictions tested are specific and directional, so that, in order to increase the power of my tests, one-sided p-values were calculated. These p-values are the probability of results equal to those reported or more extreme in the predicted direction than those reported if there were

Table 10-2 Summary of Female Fertility Data

| Age | Wealthier Half of Population | | | Poorer Half of Population | | |
	Person Years	Births	Age-Specific Birth Rate	Person Years	Births	Age-Specific Birth Rate
15–19	1925	253	.131	2254	292	.129
20–24	1476	492	.333	1868	547	.293
25–29	1166	391	.335	1366	428	.313
30–34	958	301	.314	1032	303	.294
35–39	775	213	.275	804	218	.291
40–44	575	95	.165	587	92	.157
45–49	393	17	.048	395	16	.040
50–54	217	2	.009	202	0	.000

$$df = 12 \qquad \chi^2 = 113.36 \qquad .3 < p < 5$$

Table 10–3 Summary of Male Mortality Data for the First Twenty Years of Life

| Age | Wealthier Half of Population | | | Poorer Half of Population | | |
	Person Years	Deaths	Age-Specific Death Rate	Person Years	Deaths	Age-Specific Death Rate
Less than 1	981	131	.133	953	154	.162
1	781	43	.055	744	64	.086
2	703	31	.044	640	29	.045
3	634	9	.014	577	27	.047
4	598	9	.015	512	4	.008
5–9	2116	14	.007	2075	18	.009
10–14	1695	5	.003	1480	3	.002
15–19	1071	1	.001	994	3	.003

$$z = 2.223 \qquad p = .013$$

no difference between the two groups. The difference in fertility rates was significant only for males, but the difference in mortality rates was significant for both sexes. The data from which these rates are computed are presented in tables 10–1 to 10–4. The empirical fertility rates are represented

Table 10–4 Summary of Female Mortality Data for the First Twenty Years of Life

| Age | Wealthier Half of Population | | | Poorer Half of Population | | |
	Person Years	Deaths	Age-Specific Death Rate	Person Years	Deaths	Age-Specific Death Rate
Less than 1	850	117	.138	881	108	.123
1	694	28	.040	714	56	.078
2	639	26	.041	634	35	.055
3	568	15	.026	559	13	.023
4	516	0	.000	502	6	.012
5–9	2360	8	.003	2088	23	.011
10–14	1473	1	.001	1425	4	.003
15–19	946	2	.002	924	7	.008

$$z = 2.548 \qquad p = .005$$

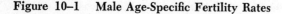

Figure 10–1   Male Age-Specific Fertility Rates

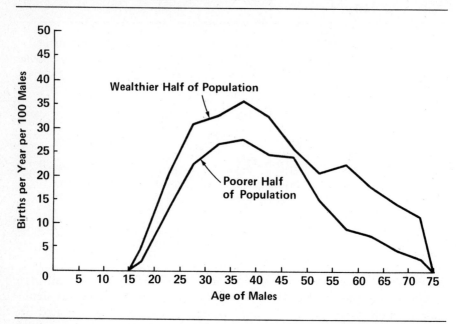

graphically in figures 10–1 and 10–2, and the model survivorship curves yielding best fit to the empirical data are presented in figures 10–3 and 10–4. Figures 10–1 and 10–2 present average births per year per hundred individuals in each age interval. Figures 10–3 and 10–4 present percentages of individuals surviving from birth.

An estimate of the average Darwinian fitness of individuals of each sex in each half of the population can be made by combining these vital rates. Assuming that rates are uniform within five-year age intervals, the following relationship allows computation of the number of children produced during any five-year age interval.

$$\text{Number of Children Born} = \left[l_i - \left(\frac{l_i - l_{(i + 5)}}{2} \right) \right] \cdot {}_5f_i \cdot 5 \qquad 1$$

In this relationship l_i represents the proportion of individuals surviving from birth to the beginning of the interval which is equated with the point at which the individual has completed the ith year of life. $l_{i + 5}$ represents the proportion surviving at the end of the interval which is reached with

III. Individual and Group Strategies

Figure 10–2   Female Age-Specific Fertility Rates   The empirical difference shown in this figure is not statistically significant. Fertility rates for women should be considered the same for both groups.

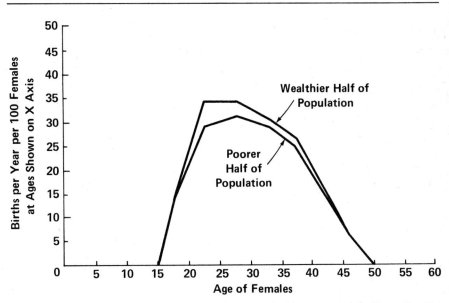

Note: The empirical difference shown in this diagram is not statistically significant. Fertility rates for women should be considered the same for both groups.

completion of year $(i + 5)^{th}$ year of life. The symbol $_5f_i$ represents the average number of births per year to individuals in the age cohort which begins with age i. The total number of offspring produced by the end of any five-year interval can be calculated by summing those produced during each completed interval:

$$\text{Total Children Born} = \sum_{i=0}^{n=\text{max age}} \left[l_i - \left(\frac{l_i - l_{(i+5)}}{2} \right) \right] \cdot {_5f_i} \cdot 5 \qquad 2$$

These quantities for males and females in each half of the population are presented graphically in figures 10–5 and 10–6. The number of children of each sex can also be computed by multiplying the total number of births by the proportion of births that are of each sex for each wealth stratum.

Figure 10–3   Male Survivorship by Wealth Stratum

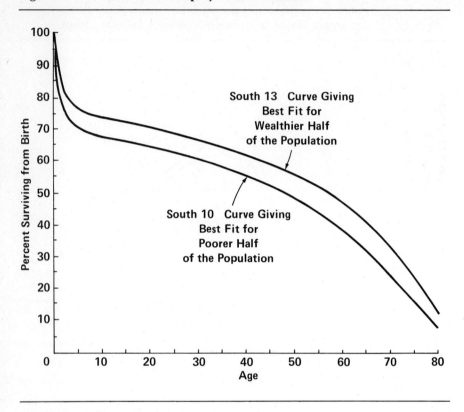

When equation (2) is adjusted to give the total female offspring of a female, then the quantity is the well known "net reproduction rate" developed by Fisher, Lotka, and others. Table 10–5 contains the total number of children of each sex that would be born in generation $n + 1$ by maximum reproductive age as a consequence of 100 hypothetical births in generation n, by using the vital rates above in combination with formula (2). The sex ratio at birth is different for the wealthier and poorer halves of the population, and empirical ratios drawn from the data were used in calculating the figures in table 10–5.

    The data in table 10–5 indicate that on the average individuals of both sexes in the wealthier half of the population enjoy a higher Darwinian fitness than do individuals of the same sex in the poorer half of the population. Moreover, the variation in male fitness is greater than in fe-

266   III. Individual and Group Strategies

Figure 10–4 Female Survivorship by Wealth Stratum

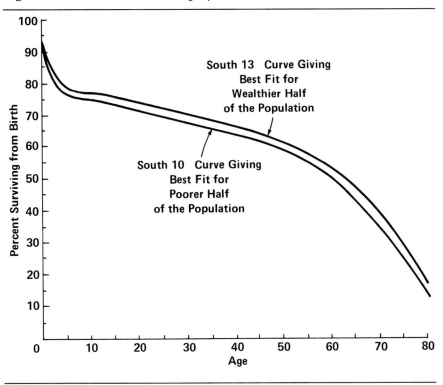

male fitness. Males in the wealthier half of the population enjoy a higher average fitness than do females in the wealthier half. For the poorer half the situation is reversed. The higher variance in male reproductive success and the positive association of wealth and fitness support the theoretical model developed by Hartung (1976).

Some of the reasons for the variation in vital rates in response to variation in wealth can be seen in the descriptive ethnographic data on the Turkmen. Wealthier individuals of both sexes enjoy better diets and medical care and devote less time to forms of labor which are strenuous or involve high risks. This in turn affects survivorship rates. Wealthier males have higher fertility because their families can afford to acquire brides for them at an earlier-than-average age, because they remarry more quickly after a wife dies, and because they are more frequently polygynous. Polygyny among the Turkmen is a rich man's luxury. The bridewealth necessary to

Figure 10–5 **Variation in Male Fitness** Figure is based on empirical fertility rates and model mortality tables.

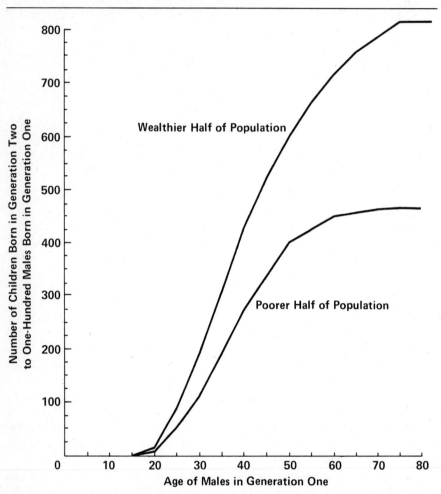

acquire a second or third wife is three times what one must pay for a first wife. This privilege of the upper stratum accounts for the wide divergence of male fertility rates in the later years of life visible in figure 10–1. Wealthy women in contrast do not have an extensive advantage over their poorer sisters in fertility. Better health probably does lead to a small gain in fertility, but the data show only a small statistically insignificant trend in this

III. Individual and Group Strategies

Figure 10–6   Variation in Female Fitness   Figure is based on empirical fertility rates and model mortality tables.

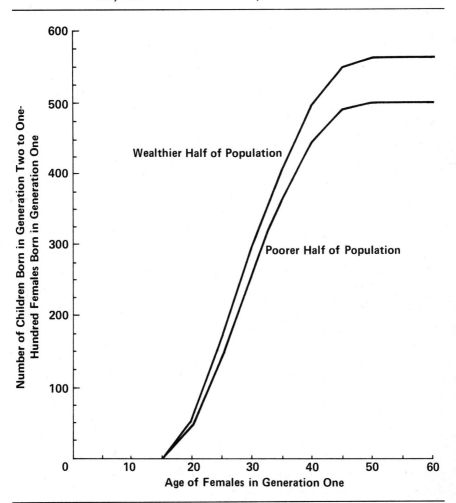

direction. Limitation of fertility through contraceptive techniques is extremely rare in this population and cannot explain the lack of a significant variation in female fertility with wealth.

One could suggest that the positive association of wealth and Darwinian fitness occurs because high accumulation of wealth is *purely* the effect of high survivorship and fertility. Given the ethnographic context, it

Table 10–5 Numbers of Descendants in Generation Two of One-Hundred Individuals in Generation One *

| | Descendants of 100 Males in Generation One | | Descendants of 100 Females in Generation One | |
	Sons	Daughters	Sons	Daughters
Wealthier Half of Population	442	371	305	256
Poorer Half of Population	239	225	257	242

* Calculated using empirical fertility rates and model mortality tables

is reasonable to assume that mortality—especially adult mortality—has a negative effect on household wealth, but it is improbable that this is the only relationship of cause and effect between these two variables. Better diet, better medical care, less need to perform heavy labor in the heat of a summer day, less need to sleep on the open steppe without a tent while tending sheep during the winter, more adequate shelter in general, and a number of other advantages conferred by wealth—I assume in this paper that all these have a positive effect on survivorship rates. I would not want to defend the assumption that they do not. The relationship between male fertility and wealth is also reasonably assumed to entail a similar two-way causation. High fertility does have a positive effect on wealth after a time lag of some fifteen to twenty years. (Child labor is not economically important in this society.) But it would be unreasonable to assume that earlier marriage, quicker remarriage after a wife's death, and more frequent polygyny do not have a positive effect on fertility—and only wealth makes them possible. The extent to which an association of emic success and high reproductive success allows inference in favor of the hypothesis explored in this paper depends on the form emic success assumes in a specific society. In the case discussed, I believe, an association of wealth and Darwinian fitness allows reasonably strong inferential support for the hypothesis. Future analysis of the Yomut material will use diachronic data to make more refined tests of the question of causation (see Irons, in prep. b).

Generally it is reasonable to assume that an individual's behavior is biologically successful if it leads to a high Darwinian fitness. Such behavior can be maladaptive only if it has the side effect of lowering the Darwinian fitness of close relatives. In Yomut society, since adult women do not interact extensively with parents or siblings (cf. chapter 7), it is unlikely that female behavior has any such effect. Male behavior could be conceived of as having this effect only when men achieve wealth by cheating their brothers out of their patrimony. Since variance in male fitness is greater than variance in female fitness, this effect might be consequential. The crucial question is this: do the brothers of wealthy men tend to be wealthy also? It can be answered with the 1973–1974 survey data. They do indicate such a tendency: the brothers of wealthy men are often wealthy themselves.

During their early reproductive years brothers are usually members of the same patrilateral extended family. As such the products of their labor are pooled in a common household budget, and each draws on the household's resources according to his need as interpreted by the household head (chapter 7:200–203 discussed this aspect of Yomut social organization in greater depth). Normally the head of such an extended family is the father of the brothers in question, although it may be the oldest brother if the father is deceased. Thus during their early reproductive years brothers enjoy the same level of economic prosperity. As a rule, somewhere between the ages of thirty and forty, a man separates from his natal household and establishes an independent domestic household of his own. Brothers are supposed to separate according to their birth order, and each is supposed to receive an equal share of his natal household's capital as his patrimony. There appear to be only rare deviations from these expectations. After becoming the heads of separate households, brothers have different economic experiences. Nevertheless, the fact of starting with approximately equal patrimonies leads to a variance in wealth among economically independent brothers which is smaller than the variance in wealth among the population as a whole. The intraclass correlation coefficient for wealth of economically independent brothers is .17 with a significance level of .05 (for 65 sets of brothers ranging in size from 2 to 5 brothers).[3]

The effect of the reproductive success of sisters on their siblings has not yet been analyzed, but as noted above this source of variation in inclu-

---

[3] This correlation coefficient was calculated on the basis of natural logarithms of wealth values, since the wealth values themselves violate the assumption of homogeneity of variance underlying the computation of the intraclass correlation coefficient. The analysis of variance was first performed on raw wealth scores, with sets of brothers constituting the groups in the one-way ANOVA, and it was found that the variances among groups were heteroscedastic, as judged by the Bartlett test of homogeneity of variances. Taking log-wealth as the dependent variable, Clifford Clogg found that the variance among the groups was stable enough to warrant calculation of the intraclass correlation coefficient.

sive fitness should be small compared to that of brothers. Figures 10–5 and 10–6 give an indication of the relative contribution of brother and sister to variation in inclusive fitness.

The analysis presented here supports the conclusion that emic success among the Turkmen makes a high inclusive fitness more probable.

Application to Other Populations

The populations which are most likely to produce evidence falsifying the hypothesis explored in this paper are post-demographic-transition populations. It would not be surprising if the pattern found in the Turkmen data emerged in the analysis of data from other societies characterized by high fertility and high mortality. However, in modern industrial societies the pattern of higher fertility among more successful individuals tends not to occur because of modern contraceptive practices. Lower mortality among higher-status individuals, however, does occur. Whether or not lower fertility and lower mortality result in higher or lower fitness depends on the precise vital rates involved. It may turn out that the hypothesis above holds only for pre-industrial populations. If this should turn out to be the case, it may indicate that the novelty of modern social environments is such that the proximate behavioral mechanisms which were adaptive in pre-industrial societies are no longer adaptive (see Irons, in prep. a, for further discussion of this). On the other hand, careful study of the connection between demography and social status in modern societies may indicate that the fertility limitation characteristic of industrial societies does contribute to a higher fitness. It is a common hypothesis that fertility limitation is part of a strategy either of upward social mobility or of the avoidance of downward mobility. This combined with lower mortality among individuals of higher social status could mean that maximum reproductive success in modern societies is achieved by limiting fertility. It is important to note that the more specific form of this hypothesis—that striving for wealth equates with striving for reproductive success—appropriate to the Yomut could have been falsified here in one of two ways: by showing that wealth has no effect on fitness, or by showing that Yomut do not, in fact, strive to increase wealth. In general, the research strategy suggested here consists of two broad steps: showing that people strive for a particular thing, and showing that this thing (whatever it may be) makes a high inclusive fitness more probable.

11. The Myth of Population Regulation[1]

Daniel G. Bates and Susan H. Lees

Current developments in evolutionary and behavioral biology, often subsumed under the label "sociobiology," have presented some interesting challenges to anthropological theory and practice. Among these are challenges of particular relevance to those of us concerned with studies of humans from an ecological perspective. The developments to which we refer have provided us with alternative approaches to the explanation of human behavior in evolutionary and environmental contexts, as well as alternative ways of perceiving the phenomena to be explained. Having been presented with such alternatives, we are clearly obliged to respond to the issues they raise. This entails a re-examination of some of our common basic assumptions and our established ways of gathering information about the relationships between human populations, their social behavior, and their environmental circumstances.

This paper attempts to open up discussion of these matters by exploring the methodological implications of one kind of assumption which has commonly formed the starting point of ecological investigation by anthropologists. In particular, we examine the assumption that vital rates of human populations are adjusted to maintain constancy in total numbers at levels appropriate to local environmental resources—that is, that populations are internally "regulated" with regard to the maintenance of their own resources. Our discussion will begin with an effort to explain the basis of this assumption, the concept of adaptation which it presupposes, and our reasons for believing it inadequate. We shall then go on to discuss the kinds of research procedures inspired by this assumption and the kinds of data systematically neglected as a consequence of adherence to its implications. In order to illustrate our points, we shall take a case from the recent anthropological literature to show how recourse to "population regulation" has been used as an explanatory device for a specific social practice—in this case, preferential female infanticide—and then discuss a contrasting explanation for the same phenomenon, derived from an alternative set of as-

[1] We are grateful to Francis Conant, Melvin Ember, Carol Ember, David Grass, Stephen Kowalewski, Gregory Johnson, and Burton Pasternak for their useful criticisms and suggestions. We thank Carol Hirsch for her bibliographic assistance.

sumptions. We shall conclude our discussion with a return to more general points related to problems of empirical observation of demographic and evolutionary units, particularly problems of scale in space and time.

The Myth of Population Regulation

An important segment of the contemporary ecological literature dealing with humans has as a central theme the notion that the successful local population is one which adjusts its numbers in such a way as to maintain local resource stability. (For example, see Rappaport 1968, Irons 1975, Thomas 1975, Little and Morren 1976, Gross 1975, Hayden 1975, Harris 1977a, 1977b, Divale and Harris 1976). The process and/or outcome of this adjustment is generally termed "population regulation" (see Harris 1975: 70–71). The assumed importance of population equilibrium via self-regulation has led some researchers to the conclusion that a wide variety of human behaviors can be related to this end (for popular examples, see Harris 1977a, 1977b). So pervasive are explanations based on this notion, and yet so lacking is it in empirical documentation, that we feel justified in calling it "the myth of population regulation."

Anthropologists subscribing to the notion that populations must be regulated with respect to resources have shown considerable concern with factors which are assumed or asserted to limit population increases in anticipation of the harmful effects which are thought to follow "overpopulation" (see Hayden 1975 for discussion). These effects appear to relate primarily to the threat of environmental degradation as a consequence of the overuse of resources by overcrowded groups of people. The common assumption is that mechanisms maintaining local population stability constitute a primary adaptive device: local populations which fail to regulate themselves, destroy their resource bases, or experience unnecessary stress, and hence fail in competition with other human groups which do not (Divale and Harris 1976: 531; Thomas 1975). Framed in these terms, this view of adaptation resembles closely "group selection" models of evolutionary process (Wynne-Edwards 1962; see Williams (1966, 1971) for critical discussion: for a brief summary see chapter 1:10–13). Research on specific populations within this perspective has dealt with social practices as diverse as brideprice and marriage (Irons 1975), warfare (Vayda 1969, Harris 1977b), ritual (Rappaport 1969), village ceremonials and warfare (Gross 1975), division of labor (Stott 1969), and infanticide (Birdsell 1958, 1968, Harris 1975, Divale 1972, Divale and Harris 1976), to name a few.

In order to weigh the usefulness of the assumptions underlying these approaches it is necessary to look to their basis in theory and to such empirical justification as may exist. Concisely stated, the theoretical justification for the assumption of local population regulation derives from the fact, early noted by Malthus and Darwin, that while all animal populations have the potential for exponential increase, they rarely ever attain their full potential growth rates. To be sure, any species experiencing such rates of increase would soon outstrip all conceivably available resources. Since species do not tend to behave this way, it must be assumed that they are "regulated" in some sense.

Over long periods of time the populations of all species display average rates of growth or change approaching zero (Wilson and Bossert 1971:102). There is logical and empirical justification for assuming that the human population of the earth since the Pleistocene has experienced long periods of relative stability, suggesting controls on population increase (see Weiss 1976: 353–354).

However, it remains to be shown what factors have limited population growth and by what mechanisms their effects are achieved. In the literature on the regulation of animal populations it is customary to distinguish density-dependent environmental resistance from other factors, such as climatic changes, which may occur regardless of the state of the population in question. It is also usual to distinguish extrinsic limits such as available food, from behaviors which can limit growth and which are intrinsic to the population, as would be the case with warfare, infanticide, and other cultural practices which can affect birthrates and survivorship. Any local population might be expected to be limited by a number of factors, affecting the population in different ways. Perhaps because anthropologists have long emphasized the uniqueness of humans they have been particularly attracted to the idea that human populations are internally self-regulated through social practices which consciously or unconsciously are directed to this purpose. Wynne-Edwards (1962), whose works have influenced such anthropological thought in this regard, proposes an evolutionary model in which population stability is achieved through a process of internal social adjustment to available resources.

In this he closely parallels the earlier work of Carr-Saunders (1922) but more directly addresses the question of how the interests of the population might be promoted over the immediate advantage of the individuals in it. In the Wynne-Edwards model, groups whose growth is limited internally by their own social behavior succeed in competition with other groups of the same species which do not. This is because "regulated" groups can avoid population crashes due to depletion of resources which non-regulated groups would eventually experience. This model has come to be termed "group selection" (see Irons, chapter 1:10–13).

In order to document this hypothetical process empirically, a number of points must be established. First, whether some form of social behavior in the groups in question is, in fact, maintaining population stability. Local population dynamics cannot be inferred from the simple fact that exponential growth is impossible over the long run, nor does the demonstration of local equilibrium indicate the probable causes. Even where we can demonstrate the effects of social behavior on population stability, it is necessary to show that this social behavior emerges to benefit the group *rather than* the individuals within it, in order to document the process of group selection.

Many anthropologists choose to ignore this latter question in the belief that it is immaterial. It is immaterial if one is concerned only with describing the immediate effects of some practice on population parameters. However, if one is concerned either with variability among populations or with how populations might respond to changed circumstances, it is necessary to begin with clear assumptions related to the evolutionary process.

If one views adaptation as the outcome of group selection, it is necessary either to stipulate or empirically document the level of risk a population would experience in depleting its resources, or to calculate the chance that a population might experience local extinction due to exhausting its resource base. This is a critical question, given the abundant examples of human population growth and successful readjustment to the disruption of traditional food resources, as witnessed in modern European and Asian history.

Two recent attempts have proposed operational models for the homeostatic adjustment of human populations to resource-related stress. Both of these emphasize the population or group as the adaptive unit. Hayden (1975) suggests how one might calculate the amount of stress experienced by populations in the past as a means of systematically relating social behavior to future risks. Thomas (1975:67–77) outlines a way in which cultural systems could constitute a homeostatic adaptive system, emphasizing the role of social behavior in regulating group size, density, and composition (see especially p. 71). These formal models are useful in that they clearly indicate the assumptions and the sort of data needed to test hypotheses arising from a view of cultures as adaptive systems. What they also indicate is that ecological anthropologists by and large have not collected nor even sought the appropriate data about specified populations measured over sufficient time to establish homeostatic behavioral regulation.

While the human population of the earth may indeed have been regulated for much of its existence, it has rarely, if ever, been established for the particular groups that ecological anthropologists study, that population regulation exists or is brought about by any particular social practice. Documentation is lacking because ecological anthropologists rarely, if ever, refer to demographic data on populations defined in a way appropriate to answering the question. Nor do we control data over sufficient time spans to be able to say what precisely is going on in the population. And while we might observe local social practices and estimate what effect these practices could conceivably have on a population, we usually have no empirical basis for saying that these practices confer selective advantages on groups because of those effects.

Employing an explicit group-selection model, for example, Irons has tested the hypothesis that certain social practices among the Yomut Turkmen—practices which affect the ages at which men and women marry and the likelihood of remarriage—serve as mechanisms adjusting the rate of population growth to the abundance of food resources. He further hoped to show that groups among the Turkmen most successful in limiting growth to appropriate levels would be advantaged in comparison to those experiencing resource-related stress. The practices in question were selected because of their obvious potential for reducing the number of fecund women actually exposed to the risk of pregnancy—and because the Turkmen behavior closely paralleled the stipulated cultural rules. The data, in what is probably the only anthropological field test of the Wynne-Edwards hypothesis, do not support the idea that social constraints adjust rates of population growth to the maintenance of a given resource base. Rather, Turkmen seemed primarily concerned with turning resources into people (Irons, in prep. b; cf. also Irons, chapter 10).

Even granting that a particular population of a species is regulated at some particular point in time, it remains to be shown that the population is regulated or controlled in some particular way. There is a considerable body of historical demographic data demonstrating regional population stability over often very impressive periods of time. In this regard we might note Renfrew's study of population growth in the prehistoric Aegean (1972: 383–399), Johnson's analysis of population trends in IVth millennium Khuzistan (1973), Kowalewski's Oaxaca study (1976;ms.), and Sumner's documentation of regular population oscillation in Southern Iran over a

6000-year period (1972), to name a few. But the dynamic stability of these and other regional populations does not show that either the larger regional population or its constituent groups were being controlled through any particular intrinsic mechanism. More important, it does not follow that a "self-regulated" population need regulate itself with respect to maintaining the quality of its habitat. And, finally, it by no means follows that particular behaviors or social practices, even those such as infanticide that seem directly related to population variables, are directed toward the end of population regulation, even though limits to growth may be a consequence of that behavior or practice (see Dickeman 1975:116–121).

That is to say, the selective advantage of a particular behavior pattern may very well not be related to population stability in any way. If stability is its result, the pattern may be selected for *despite,* rather than because of, this side effect. Resource over-utilization itself, despite its prominent place in contemporary ecological discussions, is apparently rarely responsible for more than cyclical oscillations among natural populations of animals and rarely for local extinction (McLaren 1971:14–15). This is because populations can generally turn to alternative resources and strategies before extinction occurs.

The historical studies mentioned above often document impressive short-term shifts in population size and distribution. However, the historical literature rarely documents the local extinction of human breeding populations. In fact, cases of local extinction as a result of resource depletion are very hard to document; the few we might anticipate would be exceedingly small groups who were seasonally isolated in confined areas by extreme weather conditions (e.g., Eskimos), who might be considered segments of the breeding populations.

Let us now consider why and how ecological anthropology has come to rely on the idea of population homeostasis as a means of explaining social behavior. This will entail some discussion of the concept of "carrying capacity" as employed in describing human populations.

Assumptions and Research Strategies

A world view providing the intellectual framework for much contemporary research in ecological inquiry derives from Malinowski's functionalism. In this view, relatively small, primitive groups of people are regarded as having cultures which are systematically organized in such a way that their component parts neatly buttress one another to serve the biological, psychological, and social necessities of the human population. The implied strategy of research is to discover how these component parts do indeed serve these purposes, and to explain the forms they take in terms of their own interlocking in a system. In the absence of written records, these systems are viewed as timeless, or at least assumed to have existed in the state at which the anthropologist is describing them, for quite a long time.

In a slightly circular twist, the next assumption follows: that if the observed pattern of behavior has existed for some time, it must be "successful" in the sense that it has allowed the group to persist by adequately serving their needs. In other words, these people *must* be doing "something right." Thus Malinowski and his successors set about showing how exotic behaviors "make sense," serve useful purposes.

The contribution of the new functionalists, the ecological anthropologists, to the Malinowskian scheme, was to draw attention to the relationships between people, their behavior patterns, and their environmental resources. While the older functionalist assumptions continued to hold, new ones were added on. As mentioned above, it was assumed that adaptive success depended upon close adjustments of population size and density to available resources. Since the size and density of groups at the time of ethnographic observation served as the starting point of research (i.e., were assumed to be at levels that had persisted, hence were environmentally appropriate), these variables were assumed explicable in terms of existing "regulatory mechanisms" (see Friedman 1974:457–460 for a similar critique of ecological anthropology). That is, various social practices, such as periodic warfare, residence relocation, postpartum sexual taboos, and infanticide, were seen as devices for maintaining population levels within boundaries which were appropriate with regard to environmental resources (i.e., would not lead to over-exploitation, hence degradation, hence deprivation). (See Stott 1969: 102–116.)

But since it is clear that some environmental resources are more plentiful than others, it is often felt that another step has to be taken. The strategy of research, then, is to search for an environmental resource which is available in the most limited quantities (such as protein), to establish that the population at current levels does not suffer from a lack of *that* resource, and then to show how social practices (e.g., warfare [Harris: 1977a]) within the population might serve to maintain the population at levels below which deprivation would be experienced. The assumption is that these social practices are somehow linked to the presumed limiting factor. That is, they have arisen or have been selected for because they serve to prevent the population from experiencing shortages of a critical resource.

This approach involves a limitless task. Not only are populations affected by a nearly infinite array of possible and changing problems, but their solutions to these depend on the evolved—and changing—characteristics of the members of the population itself. Moreover, where such self-regulation is postulated in anticipation of resource over-utilization, the social traits must seemingly manifest themselves before the environmental limitation in question is actually experienced as a problem (Friedman 1974: 457–460). Other environmental problems which are in fact being experienced by the population, on the other hand, are often not assumed to have anything to do with the social practices observed; since they are problems, the social practices are not assumed to have evolved to solve *them*. Finally, a limited resources may not itself be a problem (see Vayda and McCay 1975 for discussion).

The central analytic tool in both biological and anthropological discussions of population regulation is the concept of "carrying capacity." The usage of this concept in most anthropological references to human populations differs substantially from that in population biology. For anthropologists, the concept may be defined as by Hayden (p. 11): "The maximum ability of an environment to continuously provide subsistence at the level of culture provided by the inhabitants (Allan 1949; Cook 1972:25.)" This concept generally incorporates a notion of environmental degradation; carrying capacity is the point before which environmental degradation occurs. As such it is an assertion that there is an *appropriate* number of people for a given ecological setting. The origins of the concept in anthropology are closely tied up with a practical problem of benevolent colonial administration: how much land must be reserved for native cultivators in order to sustain them in an established system of land use (Allan 1949)? Ecological anthropologists dealing with living populations most commonly treat local carrying capacity primarily as a characteristic of the habitat and only secondarily as a function of the behavior of the group concerned and its exchanges with other human populations. This is fostered, no doubt, by a tendency to view traditional societies as static.

Population biologists and most ecologists, on the other hand, think of "carrying capacity" as a logistic model predicting the point at which growth reaches its limits. That is, carrying capacity is the point at which the rate of increase of a population equals zero due to environmental resistance. In order to establish the "carrying capacity" of a particular environmental setting, then, one would need first to establish retrospectively or specify such population parameters as death and birthrates as well as factors affecting them. This view, in a sense, begins from a different point from that of ecological anthropology. Where the anthropological definition is in terms of the quality of living, the ecological definition involves an after-the-fact observation. It attempts to model the observed behavior of many populations. Consequently, ecological and anthropological discussions of carrying capacity are rarely comparable; the demographic data necessary to establish ecological carrying capacity are not generally provided. One rarely, if ever, for example, has the time depth necessary to establish whether a population is growing, declining, or in equilibrium over time. This is itself a critical shortcoming, compounded by the tendency to assume what is in fact under investigation: population parameters and vital rates. Further, the ecological usage of carrying capacity refers simply to the balance established between environmental resistance and achieved growth rates. It is not assumed that such environmental factors are fixed: rather, it is more cautiously assumed that a particular population level will hold for a relatively short period of time.

Even where density dependent self-regulation is assumed, as where actual population dynamics closely fits the logistic model, there is no reason to infer that this is a result of "social" interactions or even responses intrinsic to the population, such as competition. It may be the outcome of any number of factors working singly or together. The empirical documentation of density-dependent self-regulation, while sufficient to warrant continued use and perfection of the logistic model, does not suggest by any means that one must assume a priori that any given local population will conform to it simply because of the impossibility of sustained uncontrolled growth.

The problem of scale frequently faces the anthropologist who would employ ecological models. The demographic unit generally described by anthropologists, the village population, is probably too small a unit to figure effectively in significant calculations of rates of growth or decline, let alone regulation. Then too, the local environment described by anthropologists is probably far too small a segment of the local breeding population's environmental setting to be seen as a determinant of population parameters such as birth, death, growth or decline rates. Thus, for example, the familiar ethnographic units, small villages or groups of villages, may be too small to provide an appropriate basis for the purpose of determining significant demographic parameters. Similarly, their local environments may be an inappropriate basis for determining available resources and the sources of environmental pressures. This latter problem is an important one for the ecological study of humans. Local human populations, including hunter-gatherers and horticulturists, engage in and depend on a wide range of social and economic exchanges with other populations. The anthropological obsession with local resources as fixed and limiting features of the landscape has obscured this aspect of human adaptation.

Population Regulation Versus Parental Investment: Two Explanatory Approaches

In order to illustrate what we believe are some of the shortcomings of the "population regulation" approach, and to suggest alternative approaches derived from evolutionary theory, we have selected a problem recently discussed in the anthropological literature and in the popular media: selective female infanticide.

In the most recent of a series of articles on this subject, Divale and Harris (1976)—see also Harris 1974, 1977a, 1977b—argue that preferential female infanticide is a device for regulating population growth, and that warfare (and other related social practices subsumed under the label "male supremacist complex") serves to promote female infanticide.

> . . . the most parsimonious explanation for the prevalence of warfare in band and village societies is that war was formerly part of a distinctively human system of population control. The principal component in this system was the limitation of the number of females reared to reproductive age through female infanticide, the benign and malign neglect of female infants, and the preferential treatment of male children. Warfare functions in this system to sustain the male supremacist complex and thereby provide the practical exigencies and ideological imperatives for postpartum cultural selection against female infants [p. 527. See also Harner 1977].

They go on to argue that selective advantages were conferred upon populations practicing warfare because of its effectiveness as a population-control device:

> Because of war's adaptively advantageous demographic and ecological feedback, war was self-perpetuating. Once introduced, its diffusion could not be resisted. Band and village societies which failed to attain stationary populations suffered cuts in their standard of living and were threatened by hunger and disease. Societies which achieved stationary populations by means other than the male su-

premacist-warfare complex were routed and destroyed by their more aggressive neighbors. Note that we are not suggesting that once in existence warfare simply perpetuated and propagated itself by inertia. Rather, we are saying that warfare perpetuated and propagated itself because it was an effective method for sustaining the material and ideological restrictions on the rearing of female infants [p. 531].[2]

The strategy of research here involves a cross-cultural survey of societies from which census figures are available. The supporting evidence for the Harris-and-Divale argument consists of sex-ratio information from indigenous band and tribal societies around the world. The data seem to show that where warfare is "present" or was "stopped" as recently as five years before observation, there tends to be a significantly higher ratio of males to females in the under-14 age group. This appears to suggest that female infanticide or preferential treatment of male children correlates with the practice of warfare. (However, the validity of Divale and Harris' statistical tests has been challenged by Hirschfeld, Howe, and Levin [1978]. See also Divale, Harris, and Williams' [1978] response to Hirschfeld, Howe, and Levin.)

What the figures do not show is what the rates of growth are, or whether the "populations" in question (which appear to be either ethnically designated groups such as Omaha, Walbiri, and Jivaro, or "local populations" which might be villages) are actually "stationary" or in equilibrium. In fact, the sex ratios, even if accurate, suggest little about the actual growth rate of the populations, nor do they indicate the causes of mortality that result in imbalanced sex ratios. There is no evidence to show that the population levels attained are in any way being adjusted to the maintenance of any particular "standard of living" or that they result in ecosystemic stability.

Moreover, one might easily challenge the notion that it is somehow advantageous for a *local* population to maintain itself in equilibrium. Although it is often asserted that there are advantages to population stability, one rarely sees any attempt to establish how social mechanisms could contribute to limited growth given the clear economic and political advantages to individuals and small groups with high rates of reproduction.

[2] Divale, W. and M. Harris. 1976. Population, Warfare and the Male Supremacist Complex. Reproduced by permission of the American Anthropological Association from the *American Anthropologist* 78:527 and 531, 1976.

11. The Myth of Population Regulation

Human groups are often in competition; under most circumstances, the obvious advantage would lie with the expanding local population.

The argument that warfare evolved because it was an effective device to promote preferential female infanticide in order to attain population stability is a tenuous one. It suggests that populations which engage in warfare and female infanticide should be relatively stable; yet there is no ethnographic support for such a conclusion, and every reason to believe that warfare is most marked among expanding (rather than stable) populations (e.g., Tiv, Nuer). There is no reason to conclude that population regulation itself *requires* warfare, which would be an extremely costly and risky means of promoting female infanticide. Warfare would thus seem to be an extremely unlikely "adaptive" device if its primary purpose were that of promoting infanticide.

It seems safe to conclude that female infanticide, however occasioned, is an improbable mechanism for the adjustment of populations to resources. Populations experiencing overcrowding could more effectively limit their numbers by non-sex-specific infanticide, and thus would not risk a potential shortage of females in the subsequent generation. If female infanticide arose as a means of regulating population, it must certainly have evolved under conditions of long-term resource and climatic predictability. The data cited, however, indicate the opposite condition for most groups reported to practice female infanticide.

Yet there is no reason to doubt that preferential treatment of males is widespread and that female infanticide, if less frequent than reported, is also widespread. It is also easy to accept that these practices are found more frequently in societies which engage in warfare. It should be possible to account for the existence and distribution of these practices without resorting to an assumption of population equilibrium or an explanation of their persistence as population-regulating devices.

The extensive debate in the literature on Eskimo female infanticide (Riches 1974; Freeman 1971; Hippler 1972; Schrire and Steiger 1974; Acker and Townsend 1975; Schrire and Steiger 1975) illustrates considerable disagreement and uncertainty with regard not only to explanation but also to the actual rate of occurrence of this practice. Schrire and Steiger (1974) provide a valuable lesson in their computer-simulated projection of what could happen to Eskimo populations if they engaged in varying rates of female infanticide. While the adequacy of their simulation has been challenged by Acker and Townsend (1975), their efforts show in any case that we must be very cautious in our interpretation of ethnographic reports about both the rates of infanticide and male:female ratios in juvenile and adult segments of a population (cf. also Chagnon et al., chapter 12). Other things being equal, certain rates of infanticide will obviously result in rather rapid extinction of the population; systematic tracking of adult male:female ratios by infanticidal measures is a highly risky, perhaps impossible "population control policy." Schrire and Steiger suggest that the female infanticide rate which would result in extinction for a typically small Eskimo population is quite low (anything over 8 percent) and that therefore systematic tracking (which might require a minimal rate of 15 percent) would be impossible over the long run. Ethnographic reports suggesting infanticide rates well beyond 8 percent would be highly suspect, and explanations in terms of demographic sex ratio adjustment in small populations would be similarly suspect. Most important, we can learn from Schrire and Steiger the value of actually working out the *implications* of certain demographic assumptions and "data" on certain types of behavior.

In fact, an alternative interpretation of preferential female infanticide has been proposed by Alexander (1974). This interpretation does not assume population equilibrium or group selection, but is derived from Trivers and Willard (1973) which is reviewed at the beginning of chapter 12. This alternative hypothesis, and other refinements of R. Fisher's (1958 [1930]) general theory of sex ratio (see Wilson 1975: 317) are tested by Chagnon, chapter 11, and Dickemann, chapter 12.

Rather than depending upon group selection or population equilibrium assumptions, this alternative approach assumes that parents are attempting to maximize their genetic contribution to the next and subsequent generations. Emphasizing the individuals' point of view rather than the group perspective exemplified by Divale and Harris, one is immediately confronted with the problem of differentiating between members of groups, as well as between groups. One does not assume that all parents of a society are in the same position with regard to parental investment strategies, nor that they will continue to be in the same position throughout their life cycles. Consequently, we are led by this perspective to investigate more precisely what the social behaviors in question entail. Who, for example, engages in infanticide; what are the implications of investment for parents; are parents in conflict with one another or with grandparents; and most important, what conditions account for intra-group and inter-group variations?

It should be clear, particularly from the kinds of questions we have asked, that this approach does not by any means suggest an abandonment of an ecological perspective. Quite the contrary. Rather, it is anticipated that specification of ecological factors which favor the persistence of certain behavioral patterns and the alteration of others will be facilitated by regarding such activities as female infanticide as efforts at family planning developed in response to specific environments.

Parental investment decisions are influenced by environmental and other problems confronting people as members of groups. Conditions of warfare, then, may well affect family planning strategies, as Divale and Harris suggest, but for quite different reasons. Alexander (1974) sees decisions involving female infanticide not as arising from a need to regulate populations in the face of potentially scarce resources, but as a consequence of a particular kind of social and reproductive context. He is led by his and others' observations on parental investment strategies to a variety of hypotheses to explain yet other common phenomena which Divale and Harris included under the rubric "male supremacist complex." Humans are not treated as unique, but rather as special cases of more general evolutionary patterns. We understand humans as "special" only to the extent that their behaviors are conditioned by learned experience, hence flexible. While a propensity for humans to behave in certain ways is not genetic in origin, human behavior is hypothesized to reflect strategies of inclusive fitness maximization—and more specifically, preferential female infanticide is assumed to reflect strategies shaped by sexual selection. The extent to which this may be correct for human populations can only be determined by an investigation into the social and environmental problems affecting the behaviors of particular individuals and groups in response to specific sets of environmental circumstances.

Conclusions

We are confronted here with two alternative explanations for the practice of preferential female infanticide among humans, one from the perspective of Harris' "cultural materialism" and the other from the perspective of behavioral evolutionism. The first, proposed by Divale and Harris, explains preferential female infanticide as a device for population control in the face of limited resources. Divale and Harris' explanation has some valuable contributions to make: it considers infanticide as part of a continuum involving a variety of "family planning" measures; it attempts to consider some social conditions which favor the behavior pattern; and it attempts to delineate implications for other behaviors associated with the practice.

Its shortcomings, however, are serious. It assumes what needs to be established—that is, that population regulation is the outcome of the infanticidal behavior. Second, it does not account for differential behaviors of individuals within groups. And third, it appears to apply only to humans, rather than to encompass similar behaviors of other animals. Humans are not unique in practicing infanticide, nor are they unique in having male dominance.

The alternative explanation to which we referred, that argued by Alexander (1974), is derived from an evolutionary theory of the family. This explanation does not assume population regulation as an outcome. Alexander argues, rather, that parental behavior with regard to offspring can best be understood in terms of investment strategies by individuals for reproducing their own genetic material. Because of the biology of sexual reproduction, we can sometimes expect male investment strategies to differ from those of females. The consequent behavioral differential has implications for both sexual dimorphism and social differentiation (see chapter 15). Male "dominance" can best be understood in this view as a product or part of this differentiation. In light of evolutionary theory, differential treatment of male and female offspring under certain circumstances can also be understood as one possible outcome of parental investment strategies.

Many anthropologists will find the perspective argued here reminiscent of other economic or political maximization models, often criticized for their reductionist implications. The utility of these models, however, is that their stipulation of ends makes it possible to compare observed with predicted behaviors. In this way hypotheses can be falsified (or supported); therefore an understanding of behavior will rest on firmer ground. Reduction of human behaviors to terms inclusive of other animal behavior patterns is only a first step in the determination of the extent to which expectations based on the observation of a number of species are borne out. This is a useful precursor to models predicated on the uniqueness of humans in nature.

We began this paper by suggesting that adequate discussion of human social practices in ecological perspective must, like accounts of other animal behavior, take into account the measurable demographic parameters of local populations, not simply assume population stability as the outcome of prevailing practices. Surely we cannot continue to assume that demographic stability is always an adaptive advantage, nor that populations are limited or regulated with respect to one particular and localized feature such as protein availability. To do so would reduce ecology to an oversimplified discovery procedure, in which the anthropologist merely attempts to discover what is the most likely "limiting factor" among the infinite array of possibilities.

In fact, if we reject the assumption of population regulation as a starting point for ecological research, we must adopt a new view of what ecology is all about. That is to say, our questions would not be phrased in terms of how populations regulate their numbers with regard to resources, but in terms of their actual, demonstrated problems, and how they cope with them (Vayda and McCay 1975).

If our questions relate to human demography in particular, we might begin by ascertaining the existing population parameters for the group under study. This would involve a regional analysis rather than mere collection of data about a few local groups. We could not assume that the local populations had achieved stable age structure or that they had zero growth rates. Only after the parameters of the population are known or clearly stipulated, could we make inferences about the relationship of social behavior to population dynamics and environmental resources.

In practice, we might begin our study of local populations by asking an admittedly difficult question: what determines the local abundance of people? This is in contrast to focusing on qualitatively defined carrying capacity, or asking "what constitutes the over-filling or under-filling of some local unit of ecological space?" The latter question is probably impossible to answer, while the former is at least amenable to empirical investigation.

The former question suggests regional comparisons of the dynamics of populations pursuing different modes of production and engaging in different cultural practices. The study of population and settlement through archeological time in a defined geographic region might be very useful as a means of relating actual population dynamics to resource availability, internal organization of exchange, and production. This means, of course, that population characteristics rather than offering a simple explanation of social phenomena would instead be the object of inquiry.

The anthropological usage of carrying capacity has obscured one important element in the relationship of humans to their resources: the extent to which local numbers are shaped by conditions and events outside the locality. Anthropologists might profit considerably by focusing more attention on intraspecific exchange. In particular, we should examine sources of variability in rates of exchange—a factor that is likely to be important in determining large scale population adjustments. The term exchange may well apply to objects, resources, information, people or genes.

Strategies related to the determination of optimal family size, sex and age ratios of local populations and rates of immigration may well be examined by taking into consideration the role of such exchange relationships. For example, population parameters may be adjusted in nomadic

III. Individual and Group Strategies

pastoralist populations in response to a changing exchange rate of herd products for imported necessities such as grain (Bates and Lees 1977). Rates of emigration of young men from the local population, age at marriage, and frequency of polygynous marriage may be altered as the price of wool, for example, goes up in relation to the price of grain.

The ecological study of such transactions, and the specification of their demographic implications and context, call for a change in research strategies. Some of these strategies have been discussed by Vayda and Mc-Cay (1975). They recommend paying attention to a variety of problems faced by human populations, investigating a variety of dimensions of hazards and human responses to them, abandoning an equilibrium-centered view, and studying responses by individuals as well as by groups (p. 302). Two changes that they do not emphasize strike us as important. One involves a more substantial effort in incorporating the time scale necessary to describe population dynamics. At the very least, ethnologists should be aware of the limited inferences one can make about population-related processes in the absence of temporal data. Another research strategy that has been relatively neglected in ethnology is the study of regional systems of human land use and population. Anthropological ecology is all too often restricted to the study of extremely localized populations. The treatment of small ethnically defined groups as local populations can be misleading. The recent volumes on regional analysis, edited by C. A. Smith (1976), reflect an increasing anthropological awareness of the utility of a regional perspective in the analysis of economic and social systems. We urge that this regional perspective be similarly adopted in the ecological investigation of population dynamics.

12. Sex-Ratio Variation among the Yąnomamö Indians[1]

Napoleon A. Chagnon, Mark V. Flinn,
and Thomas F. Melancon

The purpose of this paper is to explore the possibility that sex-ratio variations among the Yąnomamö Indians of southern Venezuela and northern Brazil conform to predictions from evolutionary biology. The issue to be addressed is the observed preponderance of males in the population, particularly in the junior age categories. We shall attempt to explain how sex-ratio imbalances in this population initially occur, and how they change through time. Earlier discussions and explanations of the sex-ratio variations among the Yąnomamö have been expressed, by the senior author of this paper, as the consequence of preferential female infanticide (Chagnon 1966, 1968a, 1968b, 1968c, 1972, 1974; Neel and Chagnon 1968; MacCluer, Neel, and Chagnon 1971). These earlier discussions were made on the basis of a less complete set of demographic data and in terms of the known practice of infanticide among the Yąnomamö in most areas of the tribal distribution. We must now entertain the possibility that factors other than *preferential* female infanticide can account for the major fraction, perhaps even all, of the statistical differences in the age/sex distribution in this population. This paper is prompted both by the accumulation of additional demographic data stemming from the senior author's recent field research and by the implications of recent developments in the general theory of behavioral biology. We believe that our treatment of sex-ratio variations in the Yąnomamö population has important theoretical implications for the widespread interpretation by our colleagues of male-biased

[1] The senior author's research was supported by grants from the Harry Frank Guggenheim Foundation, the National Institute of Mental Health (Grant No. MH26008) and the National Science Foundation (Grant No. SOC75–14262). Thomas Melancon's support came from the National Institute of Mental Health through the grant cited above. We would like to thank a number of our colleagues who read earlier drafts of this paper and commented critically on them; while we took many of their criticisms to heart and modified the text accordingly, we alone are responsible for the final product. In alphabetical order, we wish to thank Richard D. Alexander, William Irons, and Jeffrey Kurland for their numerous and helpful criticisms. We thank Bruce Levin for suggesting statistical improvements.

sex ratios reported for other tribal populations as the direct consequence of systematic preferential female infanticide.

Sex ratio measures the relative distribution of the sexes and is conventionally expressed as a male to female ratio; i.e., it is calculated by dividing the number of males in a given age category by the number of females in the same category and multiplying by one hundred. Sex ratios of common interest include the overall population sex ratio, the sex ratio at conception (primary sex ratio), the sex ratio at birth (secondary sex ratio), the sex ratio at maturity (tertiary sex ratio), and the sex ratio of adults in the population (quaternary sex ratio). Under stable population conditions, changes in the sex ratio between life-history stages give a measure of the differential mortality experienced by the sexes during that period (cf. Teitelbaum 1972).

In humans, as in other mammals, males are the heterogametic sex, and therefore sperm determine the sex of offspring. The control of early variations in the sex ratio is considered to be determined by females by (1) differential fertilization of ova by type of sperm (X- or Y-bearing chromosomes) at the point of conception, (2) fetal wastage during the period of gestation, (3) infanticide of newborns, or (4) differential patterns of postnatal care. It is clear that infanticide is only one of a number of physiological and behavioral factors that may affect sex ratios. As such, it must be considered within the overall context of an adaptive explanation for differential mortality by sex.

The practice of infanticide is frequently reported in the anthropological literature, and is known to occur in many different physical and social environments. Recently infanticide has attracted the attention of biologists (Alexander 1974), anthropologists (Dickeman 1975; Harris 1974; Divale and Harris 1976), and primatologists (Blaffer Hrdy 1974, 1977). This theoretical interest comes at a peculiar time in the history of both evolutionary biology and cultural anthropology, for a fundamental rethinking of major issues is taking place and far-reaching theoretical developments are leading to the rejection of formerly tenable hypotheses in a number of disciplines.

Anthropological explanations of many cultural phenomena have traditionally been based on group, population, or even ecosystem adaptation. Cultural practices which might impede population growth, such as infanticide, are therefore frequently interpreted as "adaptive" in an ecological, structural, and evolutionary sense, because such practices are believed to maintain "population equilibrium" or otherwise contribute to the stability of the cultural or ecological "system." Preferential female infanticide has been generally regarded as particularly effective to accomplish this because it not only limits the immediate size of the population by removing individuals but also diminishes the population's potential for continued growth. The rationale for this belief is the operation of what biologists now refer to as "group selection" (Williams 1966).

Briefly stated, a group-selection argument assumes or suggests that individuals forego their own reproductive interests in order to enhance the perpetuation of their group or local population—or even their cultural system. A typical example is expressed by Marvin Harris: "As in the case of other adaptive evolutionary novelties, groups that invented or adopted growth cutoff institutions survived more consistently than those that blundered across the limits of carrying capacity" (Harris 1974:66).

A similar position was, until recently, accepted by most biologists. However, largely as a consequence of G.C. Williams' (1966) seminal discussion of the levels of selection, most biologists now agree that "adaptations" at levels higher than the individual are *fortuitous effects* and not evolved functions. The focus on individual adaptation within biology during the past several years, and the emergent skepticism about the potency of selection above the level of the individual or clusters of related individuals, have resulted in a peculiar and somewhat unfortunate dilemma within anthropology. Generally, biological models that have found their way into the theoretical armaments used by contemporary anthropologists were borrowed from biology before the shift from group-selection to individual-selection emphasis in biology, and many of them are now inconsistent with recently developed biological theory.

In this paper, therefore, we adopt the perspective that selection operates most potently at the level of the individual. We are exploring the possibility that sex-ratio variation observed in populations of Yąnomamö Indians and infanticide practices are adaptive for individuals, and that "population-regulating" arguments are not satisfactory explanations of the observed sex-ratio variations. We are testing theories from evolutionary biology with one of the few large bodies of data available for a tribal population that is relatively unacculturated and that is known to engage in infanticide. As will soon be apparent, we only scratch the surface of an immense problem, for the data required to arrive at definitive conclusions would be of a quality and quantity not readily secured in a population such as the one discussed here. Still, there is enough to warrant some cautious conclusions. We have limited our analysis of Yąnomamö infanticide practices and sex-ratio variation to the following theories: R. A.

Fisher's general theory of sex ratio (1958), and the more recent extensions of that theory made by R. L. Trivers and D. E. Willard (1973).[2]

The recent dissemination of theories from evolutionary biology into the arena of anthropology has been attended by enthusiastic skepticism from a number of anthropologists. Some have even asserted that anthropologists know in advance that these biological arguments do not apply to human social behavior, since, as the argument runs, there are no genes for 'infanticide,' 'the nuclear family,' 'clans,' etc. (see, for example, Sahlins 1976a). We agree wholeheartedly that there are no such genes and that cultural differences in infanticide or any other human social practices are not likely to be the result of genetic differences. We do assume, however, that human beings are part of nature and subject to the same selective forces that operate on all other living organisms. We also assume that the highly plastic behavioral repertoire characterizing humans has evolved by the process of natural selection, adaptively responds to the environment, and is modified by experience and learning. Finally, we believe that it is legitimate and fruitful to examine human reproductive behavior in terms of predictions based on recently developed theories in evolutionary biology.

Infanticide and Adaptation

Two basic types of infanticide are relevant to an evolutionary biology perspective: 1) adjustment of parental effort through the destruction of offspring by parents, and 2) destruction of infants by unrelated individuals against parental wishes. Both types have been cited for many species (Blaffer Hrdy 1974, 1977; van Lawick-Goodall 1971; H. van Lawick and J. van Lawick-Goodall 1971; Wilson 1971, 1975; Chagnon 1968a; Biocca 1969; Sherman 1976). The first type of infanticide is of greater interest here: it is generally accepted by anthropologists (e.g., Divale and Harris 1976) as a group adaptation for maintaining populations below their carrying capacities. On superficial inspection and intuitive assessment, the purposeful destruction of offspring certainly seems contrary to the tenet of individual adaptation. Darwin, however, noted two conditions in which increased fertility would be opposed by natural selection: (1) where the cost to the parent through an increased risk of mortality and thus a poten-

[2] We also considered W. D. Hamilton's (1967) theory of "local mate competition" in our analysis of Yạnomamö sex-ratio data, but were unable to come to any substantial conclusions for both empirical and theoretical reasons.

tial loss in future reproduction outweighed the reproductive benefits to be gained by an immediate increase in fertility, and (2) where an increase in the total number of offspring reduced the overall ability of the offspring to survive (Darwin 1967 [1858]). Thus, R. D. Alexander (1974) has suggested several circumstances in which infanticide might *not* be maladaptive for the individual. These may be generally regarded as leading to adaptive adjustments of parental effort [3] and can be summarized as follows:

a Environmental flux
b Malformed or otherwise defective infants
c Spacing and parental care distribution
d Sex-ratio adjustments.

Ethnographic discussions of infanticide in all these contexts can be readily found in the anthropological literature (cf. Alexander 1974; Dickeman 1975). For example, droughts (environmental flux) are commonly cited as a reason for infanticide practices (the Australian aborigines; Basedow 1925; Bates 1944). The destruction of malformed infants occurs among the Yąnomamö (infra) and has been widely reported in the anthropological literature (cf. Dickeman 1975 and references there, as well as Dickemann, this volume, chapter 13).[4] Optimal distribution of parental expenditure may require the spacing of offspring beyond the human physiological potential. With multiple births the destruction of one or more of the newborn is commonly reported (Métraux 1946; Grantzberg 1973; see bibliography in Dickeman 1975 and Dickemann's references, this volume; Alexander 1974). Other anthropologists have noted the taxing problems of parental care and the difficulties in rearing more children than local domestic and economic conditions might permit: Birdsell (1968) has argued that ". . . children who cannot be reared are frequently conceived and born. The solution is systematic infanticide" (p. 236).

One of the more critical and perplexing problems for anthropologists, however, is the frequently reported occurrence of sex-preferential

[3] The concepts of "parental effort," "parental expenditure," and "parental investment" have been used interchangeably in some publications, but are distinguished from each other in others. We have basically adopted the usage of Low (1978), who suggests that "parental effort (PE: comparable to part of the parental expenditure of Fisher [1958:204]), is any expenditure of nutrient or effort or taking of risks in the production and raising of offspring or other kin. Parental investment (PI: Trivers [1972]) is that portion of the parental effort received by such offspring such that $\Sigma PI = PE$ for any period under consideration" (Low 1978: 198–199).

[4] The change in spelling is at Dr. Dickemann's request.

infanticide, usually the destruction of more female offspring than male. Divale and Harris (1976) have proposed a model which addresses this issue. Because their model is particularly representative of the 'group selectionist' position, and because Divale and Harris offer only one of the weakest of alternative explanations—"simple biological determinism" due to "innate aggression"—in contrast to their model, we feel it is worthwhile to examine their model in some depth.

Divale and Harris argue for the existence of a functional association between warfare and male-biased sex ratios, which they assume to result from female preferential infanticide. They assert that "because of war's adaptively advantageous demographic and ecological feedback, war was self-perpetuating . . . because it was an effective method for sustaining the material and ideological restrictions on the rearing of female infants" (p. 531). Warfare is more 'adaptive' than abortion or other means of controlling population growth because "male combat deaths were less costly emotionally and structurally than female deaths associated with abortion techniques" (p. 531). Thus, Divale and Harris claim to "explain the perpetuation of warfare in band and village society and its interaction with selective female infanticide as a response to the need to regulate population growth in the absence of less effective or less costly alternatives" (p. 531).

We contend that these claims are simply assertions, advocated on (1) the assumption that male-biased sex ratios in band and tribal societies are sufficient evidence that sex-preferential infanticide has produced the discrepancies and (2) on the belief that the alleged preferential infanticide practices result from the "group's need" to regulate population density. Much of the data they have used is confusing and highly suspect (Hirschfeld, Howe, and Levin 1978), no attempt was made to document population growth patterns in the societies included in their sample (probably impossible empirically), no measurements of "carrying capacity" for any of the societies discussed were given or even estimated. Thus, they have failed to demonstrate the crux of their model: the feedback between the approach to carrying capacity and the intensity, or even the very existence, of the cultural phenomena they purport to explain. They do not present any data demonstrating that these phenomena are, in fact, "a response to the need to regulate population growth"; they rely instead on the assumption—contrary to current biological theory—that individuals will voluntarily refrain from producing or rearing their own offspring in order to serve the group's or the environment's interests.

Besides failing to provide positive data for the assumed population-regulation function, Divale and Harris have overlooked a considerable amount of empirical data that suggest something contrary to their model. For instance, among the Yąnomamö, biomedically one of the most extensively studied tribal populations, there is no evidence of a protein deficiency or any other indication that ecological carrying capacity is being approached (Lizot 1977a, 1977b; Chagnon and Hames, 1979). On the contrary, the Yąnomamö appear to be getting five times the minimum daily protein requirement established by the World Health Organization. Divale and Harris fail to demonstrate that the asserted infanticide practices in the populations they list have operated to maintain these populations in equilibrium. The Yąnomamö, for example, are expanding at the rate of perhaps 1 to 2 percent per year (Chagnon 1974; Lizot 1977b). Moreover, population density in Yąnomamö populations does not appear to be correlated with the intensity of warfare: the Shamatari population, while engaging in a higher level of intergroup conflict than the Namoweiteri population, has a lower population density (Chagnon 1974, 1975; Chagnon and Hames 1979; Lizot 1977a, 1977b). Furthermore, vast areas of uninhabited land are readily available to the Yąnomamö. If the need for population regulation existed because of a protein (or some other "strategic resource") deficiency, why do the Yąnomamö not just disperse into these uninhabited areas that are adjacent and similar to the land they presently occupy? There is no evidence that Yąnomamö groups are in any danger of "blundering forward across the limit of carrying capacity." In short, we do not believe that Divale and Harris have adequately demonstrated the validity of their model.

An alternative explanation for sex-ratio variation, based on individual adaptation, was suggested in 1930 by R. A. Fisher (1958). Fisher's principle, in brief, states that *on a population-wide basis,* parental expenditure will tend to be equally divided between offspring of both sexes, since each contributes equally to the next generation's gene pool. Fisher noted that if parental expenditure is biased towards male offspring in a population, the genetic representation in the next generation of those parents with female-biased expenditure patterns would increase relative to that of parents with male-biased expenditure patterns, because the ratio of expenditure/genetic representation would be lower for female offspring. If, on average, the sexes receive equal expenditure per offspring, then the population's sex ratio of individuals within the period of parental expenditure will tend toward 50/50, i.e., 100. However, it is important to note that it is parental expenditure that will be equally divided: it does not necessarily follow that equal numbers of each sex will be produced or be present at the age of reproduction. If one sex receives twice as much expenditure per individual offspring, then Fisher's principle predicts an inversely proportional sex ratio, 2:1 in favor of the sex requiring less parental expenditure.

Fisher argued that as a result of higher male mortality during the period of parental expenditure ". . . the average expenditure is therefore greater for each boy reared, but less for each boy born . . ." because more males will perish before receiving their full complement of parental expenditure. It is worth emphasizing, at this juncture, that different mortality patterns between the sexes are most appropriately interpreted as the outcome of sexual selection (Darwin 1871; Fisher 1958; Trivers 1972; Alexander et al., this volume, chapter 15). The reproductively more variable sex is likely to incur a higher mortality rate because of more intense sexual competition. Thus, because males are the reproductively more variable sex among the Yąnomamö (see Chagnon, this volume, chapter 14), male/male competition for mates is therefore likely to result in a higher male mortality rate. Different mortality patterns for the two sexes may result in different amounts of parental expenditure for different-sexed offspring (infra).

Fisher's arguments, continuing, relate to sex ratio at birth: "We may therefore infer that the condition towards which natural selection will tend will be one in which boys will be the more numerous at birth, owing to their higher death rate" (1958:159). One way of expressing this argument is in terms of a graphic model (figure 12–1 below). If male offspring die, on the average, after receiving half of the full complement of parental expenditure, and females never die before receiving a full complement, then males are receiving half as much as expenditure per offspring as are females. Thus, according to Fisher's principle, selection would favor an initial sex ratio in favor of males. Because of higher male mortality, the sex ratio would balance at the "half-expenditure" stage; i.e., the sexes would be equally represented in the population at this point, and ultimately the ratio would change to favor females at the end of the period of parental expenditure as shown in figure 12–1 below.

The extension of Fisher's theory by Trivers and Willard (1973) deals with sex-ratio variations *within* populations. In essence, they outlined the advantages of variations in sex ratio in terms of the potential reproductive values of offspring of both sexes. If the reproductive success of a male offspring is more dependent on a given variable than is the reproductive success of a female offspring, the Trivers and Willard theory postulates that parents will alter sex ratios of progeny accordingly. For example, if male reproductive success is more dependent on maternal

Figure 12–1   Model of Fisher's Theory of Sex Ratio Selection   The vertical axis indicates the number of offspring of either sex and the horizontal axis indicates *both* the period of parental expenditure and the sex ratio among the offspring at any point in time during the period of parental expenditure. Male offspring die, on the average, after receiving one-half of the full complement of parental expenditure, whereas female offspring never die until receiving the full complement. Thus, the sloped line represents the number of males receiving parental expenditure and the horizontal line represents the number of females receiving parental expenditure. According to Fisher's principle, selection will favor an initial sex ratio that is biased in favor of males (shown as sex ratio = 150), a balanced sex ratio at the point of ½ expenditure, and, finally, a female-biased sex ratio (shown as sex ratio = 50), at the end of the period of parental expenditure.

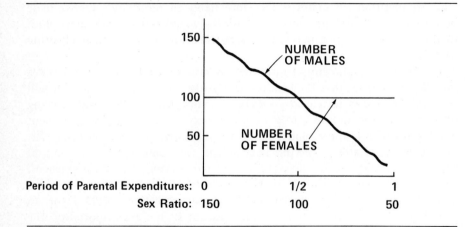

condition, then mothers in good condition are expected to tend toward male-biased sex ratios among their offspring relative to mothers in poor condition. The converse is expected if female reproductive success is more dependent on maternal condition. In human societies, social stratification or status has been suggested as a relevant variable comparable to variables like maternal condition (Alexander 1974; Trivers and Willard 1973). Thus, in a stable hypergynous system, such as those discussed by Dickemann (this volume, chapter 13), social strata that receive more females through upward mobility might be expected to practice female preferential infanticide because the reproductive value of a male offspring will be greater than that of a female. It is crucial to understand that this aspect of sex-ratio

298   III. Individual and Group Strategies

theory does not explain overall population sex-ratio bias: it only predicts sex-ratio variations *within* the populations. The practice of female infanticide, to the degree that it leads to a male-biased sex ratio in the junior age grades over the entire population, is a different problem. It is the kind of problem that Fisher's theory is able to shed light on. Both kinds of sex-ratio selection can, however, be concurrent.

An additional concern is the potential for indirect parental expenditure in offspring of one sex by offspring of the other sex (Trivers and Willard 1973). For instance, if males return parental expenditure to their sisters (or other female relatives), initial biases in parental expenditure toward males can be adaptive. The influence of males upon the reproductive success of their female relatives among the Yąnomamö (Chagnon, this volume, chapter 14, figure 14–5) might be an indication that an initially male-biased expenditure pattern would be adaptive. This could be a consequence of the greater political influence of males, or possibly of patrilocal residence, which results in a tendency for males to live closer to their relatives than do females. We shall explore the implications of this argument in another paper (Chagnon and Flinn, in preparation).

The theoretical aspects of sex-ratio selection that we have considered can be summarized as in figure 12–2.

What these biological theories of sex-ratio selection suggest is *not* that the practice of infanticide is determined by the presence or absence of certain genes, or that cultural differences in the practice of infanticide

Figure 12–2 Theories of Sex Ratio Considered in This Chapter This model shows how they relate to each other and to selected variables.

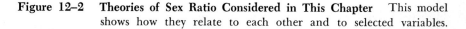

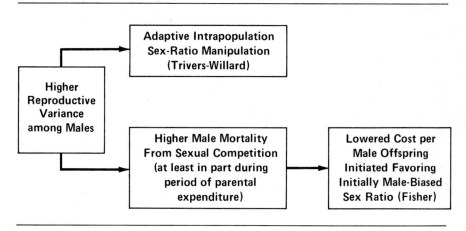

are a result of genetic differences. Rather, it is assumed that abilities to survive and reproduce optimally under a wide variety of social and environmental circumstances are basic to the human genotype *and that they are flexible.* Parental effort is one of these assumed abilities, and these theories are attempts to predict the variation of parental effort in different environmental and social situations. The predictions are based on individual, not group, adaptations. The variation of parental effort, of which infanticide is one aspect, is posited to be consistent with the survival and reproductive interests of the individual, rather than the group, because the individual is the level at which natural selection is primarily operative in evolution.

This briefly summarizes the relevant theories of interest to us in this paper. We find the Trivers and Willard theory to be of particular interest because the Yąnomamö are a relatively egalitarian society, and offer a contrast to the societies examined by Dickemann (this volume, chapter 13). Further, we suspect that the politics of marital exchange, which are especially critical among the Yąnomamö, produce complexities that are apposite not only to anthropological theory, but to biological theory as well.

With these interests in mind, we shall first discuss the practice of infanticide among the Yąnomamö and the empirical and theoretical problems relevant to understanding this practice, and then explore alternative theoretical explanations of the sex-ratio data.

Statistical data and Yąnomamö infant mortality

The information on which this paper is based has been drawn from the field data gathered among the Yąnomamö by the senior author between 1964 and 1975. The data consist primarily of information on two clusters of villages, six in the "Shamatari" population bloc and seven in the "Namowei-teri" bloc, which were the focus of the senior author's most intensive field research, and for which the demographic data are most reliable and complete (see Chagnon, chapter 4). Demographic information exists for 1336 individuals currently living in this segment of the population as well as similar information on their deceased relatives with the total census of both living and dead numbering 3270 individuals. Information collected by the senior author during the same period of time on some fifty additional villages is not included in this paper (see Chagnon 1974 for discussion of data reliability and data quantity).

It is extremely difficult to obtain statistically reliable information on the pattern of infant mortality for any population whose members do not keep written records of such vital events as birth and death (Howell 1973; Weiss 1975). This problem is compounded in the case of the Yąnomamö, who consider it extremely offensive to discuss dead kinsmen (Chagnon 1968a) and who systematically suppress as much of the memory of dead relatives as possible. Infant deaths, under such conditions, are more readily pushed from memory than the deaths of adults, whose lifetime activities and personal characteristics become widely known, even to members of other villages, and who therefore can be "discovered" more readily through the collection of genealogies by interviews. Complicating the matter even further is the limited nature of the Yąnomamö verbal enumeration system ("one," "two," and "more-than-two") and the consequent imprecision of native estimates of anything involving numbers, whether they be number of arrows the headman has or the number of offspring his first wife has had to date.

The several attempts made by the senior author to establish directly, in the field, the frequency with which infanticide was occurring all proved to be unsatisfactory because of these difficulties. For example, after rapport was established with the residents of particular villages, a process that could take months or years in the numerous villages under study, an attempt was made, working with female informants, to collect pregnancy histories of all females in the village. The informants in most cases were willing to discuss deceased infants of co-villagers in private, provided the women in question were not very close relatives, and they reported that specific women in the village had, at some time or other, destroyed children at birth—some women having done so 'more-than-two' times. They would even venture to recall the sex of the child. After exhausting the knowledge of one set of informants, the investigator attempted to verify the information using other female informants. Working in the same fashion, and without revealing to the second informants what the first had reported, he found that while there was good agreement on the identity of women who had destroyed children at birth, there was very little agreement on either the number or the sex of the infants destroyed. The first informant might indicate that a particular woman had killed "four" female babies during her recent reproductive life (indicating the number by holding up four fingers), but the second informant might indicate "six" or "eight" and claim that several were males.

It would, of course, be desirable to collect reproductive life histories directly from each informant personally, but because of the Yąnomamö attitudes about deceased relatives and their anger and frustration at being reminded of dead kin, such a procedure is odious, impolite, and in some cases, dangerous (see Chagnon 1968a:12–13 for an example).

A second kind of information regarding the practice of infanticide came from reports by individuals in the village that a particular woman had just destroyed a newborn. These accounts could be verified immediately by cross-checking with other informants and by verifying the report through the use of pregnancy records. Field notes were kept on the pregnancy status of all nubile women in some villages and it was known if a woman was pregnant on a particular date and what her estimated time of delivery was. The woman's rumored birth and infanticide could be checked directly by observation to see if she was pregnant, and if not, if she was nursing a newborn. Information about infanticide and infant mortality accruing in this fashion shed light only on recent reproductive histories of women, and then only in villages that constituted the focus of a particular year's field investigation.

Occasional visits to other villages where mission posts were established also yielded supplementary information on the practice of infanticide elsewhere in the tribe—outside the core thirteen villages of the study. In at least two mission villages along the upper Orinoco River, the local missionaries intervened in attempted infanticides and saved the lives of the babies. In both these cases the babies were females. One was later adopted by the (Protestant) missionary family and the other was given in adoption to an Italian family living in Caracas. The senior author also visited a large number of other Yąnomamö villages as a member of a multidisciplinary research project, and reports from local missionaries in those areas confirmed the practice of infanticide in large areas of the tribe. However, such visits were brief and never resulted in systematic collection of reliable supportive demographic data that would permit meaningful interpretation of local infanticide practices and rates, for there is enough demographic variation within villages of the same population bloc to suggest that pooling partial information from other villages in nonadjacent areas is inadvisable.

In view of these difficulties, let us hazard a rough approximation of the rate at which infanticide occurs in Yąnomamö villages in this area, using information obtained in just one of the villages. For example, twelve women in Village 05 were identified as having destroyed at least one child between 1957 and 1970, determined through interviews conducted in 1971 with a number of female informants from that village. Some of these women were alleged to have destroyed other babies earlier. There were, in 1971, about twenty-two women in the age category from which these twelve came—i.e., about half the women in the village destroyed one child during the approximate thirteen-year period. No attempt was made to improve this estimate by determining how many women who died during that period of time also destroyed newborns. The sexes of the destroyed newborns were seven females and five males; there was no great difference between the numbers of females versus the number of males destroyed. That is, one could not persuasively argue that there was a systematic bias toward destruction of female offspring versus male offspring in *this* village. The sex ratio of the village is consistent with this observation: between 0 and 13 years the present sex ratio is 107, and for the village as a whole it is 103. Thus there is no compelling evidence that the infanticide practices by women in this village are female-preferential, nor is the sex ratio biased in favor of males. Whether or not the male-biased sex ratios in other villages in this area of the tribe reflect sex-preferential infanticide practices cannot be demonstrated with similar data of comparable completeness—nor can it be disconfirmed. While some women in the other villages were identified as having destroyed newborns, we simply cannot say, because of the data-collection problems, what fraction of the women in these villages destroyed newborns, nor can we determine the sex ratio of the destroyed newborns.

In brief, while we know that the Yąnomamö practice infanticide over much of their tribal distribution and that infants are subject to a relatively high incidence of mortality from other causes, it is not possible to directly quantify the rates through traditional field investigative procedures based on interviews with the mothers or other knowledgeable women in the village. Furthermore, because of these difficulties, all measures of reproductive performance used in this paper must be considered as "reported" births and should not be construed necessarily as adequate measures of the complete life histories of all parents.

Variations in the Pattern of Infanticide and Infant Mortality

Yąnomamö infants, both male and female, are likely to be destroyed at birth or to suffer a higher risk of mortality due to systematic neglect, conscious or unconscious, for a variety of reasons other than a parent's preference for a child of one sex or the other. These include cases of physical abnormality, paternity uncertainty, and problems in the spacing of births.

The Yąnomamö will usually kill a child of either sex at birth if there are any obvious physical defects, such as polydactly, dwarfism, hydro-cephaly, etc. They justify such infanticides in terms of the argument that ". . . the baby was 'ugly' and deformed so she killed it!" If a child manifests obvious defects after several months of life, it might be permitted to live, for by then the mother has developed very strong emotional ties to the baby. However, life for such a child is extremely harsh, for the Yąnomamö are very inconsiderate about physical defects of any kind—inherited or the result of accidents—and joke about an individual's misfortunes. The contempt in which a crippled or otherwise defective child is generally held by all members of the village is ultimately expressed by differences in parental care for the child. Most crippled children the senior author has seen are underfed, infrequently bathed and frequently tormented by co-residents. One young man, for example, was born an achondroplastic dwarf and permitted to live. Even his closest kin tease and abuse him. As an adult he sexually shared his brother's wife for some time; one of her babies was born a dwarf and was immediately destroyed.

Another incident reveals that parents will destroy malformed children long after they are born, although this is unusual. One woman, with a six- or seven-year-old child who had become crippled well after birth, grew weary of carrying the child on the long visiting or camping trips the Yąnomamö customarily take, and she eventually killed it. Another crippled boy died in 1975 after years of harsh and abusive treatment; it is believed that this particular child died simply of malnutrition, the result of systematic neglect.

The extent to which a man's influence over his wife's decision to destroy a newborn is predicated on paternity uncertainties would be difficult to document, but it cannot be entirely dismissed. Several instances were reported in which a husband, suspecting that his wife's child was not his own, forced the pregnant woman to abort the child. Moreover, a woman and her son were abducted from a distant village and, after a few weeks in their captors' village, the son—a boy of ten or eleven years—was killed by one of the local men ". . . because he reminded me of his father, who is my enemy. . . ." The man had taken the captured woman as his own wife. On the other hand, the dramatic description by Valero of raiders systematically destroying all the babies in their enemy's village (Biocca 1969) is, so far as the senior author is concerned, a unique event: he has never heard of a similar instance anywhere in the tribe.

Yąnomamö infants, like all infants, require intense maternal attention, and a number of Yąnomamö 'explanations' for specific infanticides are phrased in terms of the mother's inability to nurse or care for children too closely spaced and to rear both of them successfully. The arrival of a new infant before an existing one has already made it through the initial hazardous years leads some Yąnomamö mothers to destroy the newborn in order to enhance the survival chances of an older, but still heavily dependent, child. Such considerations are reflected in the fact that Yąnomamö mothers often destroy one of a pair of twins, although there is no inflexible prescription to do so. Indeed, a number of mothers have successfully raised both of a pair of twins. More often, one of the twins is destroyed because the labor and inconvenience of rearing two babies simultaneously is considered too great a burden for a mother to bear.

Yąnomamö mothers pamper their babies for so long that even a three- or four-year-old can be an inconvenience if the mother delivers and elects to keep a new infant. Part of the difficulty in caring for two small children has to do with the myriad domestic obligations a Yąnomamö mother has. The long trips that the Yąnomamö regularly take through the jungle, to visit distant villages or to exploit seasonally abundant foods, require an enormous expenditure of energy and effort on the part of the women (see Lee 1972; cf. Blurton Jones and Sibly, 1978). Women must not only carry the edible supplies and household goods that the family will use, they must also carry their infants as well. We suspect that quite a few infants die during such extended trips, and that this is due largely to the mother's inability to provide adequate care under these circumstances. Thus, the spacing of children becomes an important practical consideration.

The inability of Yąnomamö women to rear successfully all of the children which they might be physiologically capable of producing is reflected in the average interval between reported births, which is close to three and a half years (3.4) in duration (table 12–1). This figure is consistent with estimates presented elsewhere (Neel and Chagnon 1968; Neel and Weiss 1975) based on a less complete set of Chagnon's demographic findings and supplementary biomedical information collected by Neel and his colleagues (urine specimen analysis and palpatation of the uterus during physical examination). Although factors other than infanticide, such as abortion, extended lactation, and coital taboos during lactation, undoubtedly contribute to this result, infanticide is implicated as one of the means by which Yąnomamö mothers space their children, so that the health and potential survival of a living child is not jeopardized by the birth of a new infant. These spacing practices are consistent with explanations from biological theory.

Table 12–1   **Birth Interval and Mother's Age, by Sex of Newborns, 1964–1974**
The interval between the birth of males and the previous birth (left side) and the interval between the birth of females and the previous birth (right side) is nearly the same, as is the mother's mean age at the births of male and female offspring. If female neonates were being eliminated more often than males through preferential female infanticide or suffered a higher post-natal mortality through systematic sex-preferential neglect, we would expect the interval between the birth of a male and the previous birth to be significantly smaller compared to the interval for female births in this population. These data do not support the arguments that (1) preferential female infanticide or (2) systematic neglect of female neonates, leading to higher female infant mortality, occur.

	Males			Females		
	N	$\overline{X}$	S.D.	N	$\overline{X}$	S.D.
Birth Interval	280	3.43	2.35	223	3.37	2.35
Mother's Age	386	26.0	7.6	299	25.69	7.18

Variance in reproductive success and differential mortality

As noted earlier, differential mortality by sex as a life-history phenomenon suggests a correlation between differential variance in adult reproductive success and deviations from equality in mean population sex ratio at birth. Differential variation in adult reproductive success is determined in the mechanics of the mating system. First, the practice of polygyny by the Yąnomamö results in some men having a disproportionate access to mates. Second, older and politically prominent widowers are likely to take young women as new wives, excluding younger men from early opportunities to reproduce. The net result is that while the sexes are nearly equally represented as adults (see below), male-male competition for wives ensures that only a fraction of adult males will dominate the reproductive contribution made from one generation to the next by females.

    The demographic consequences of the Yąnomamö mating system are reflected by substantial differences between the sexes in expectations of reproductive success. Yąnomamö males begin to reproduce later in life than do females. The mean age at first parenthood for a male is 24 years compared to 19 years for a female. On the other hand, Yąnomamö males are able to continue reproducing much later in life than are females (see Chagnon, this volume, chapter 14, table 14–3). As a result, the more successful males who manage to survive have nearly twice as many children as the more successful females. According to figures presented elsewhere (Chagnon, ibid, table 14–3) for example, males in the current population over the age of 59, and thus close to completing their reproductive lives, have averaged 9.72 offspring each compared to an average of 4.64 children per female for women over the age of 44. The most successful living male in the current population has had 22 children compared to 11 for the most fertile living female. Table 12–2 gives the distribution of individuals in the population who have reproduced at least once in their lifetime according to their age at the time of the last census (1975). Fifty-three percent of all females compared to 32 percent of all males have had at least one off-

Table 12–2   **Number of Males and Females in Current (Living) Population To Have Ever Reproduced, by Age and Sex**   While males suffer a higher pre-reproductive mortality than females, those males who do reproduce make, on the average, a greater reproductive contribution to the next generation than do reproductive females. Females suffer a lower pre-reproductive mortality; thus, a larger fraction of them reproduce, but their individual reproductive contribution to the next generation is, on the average, lower than that of reproductive males.

Age	Total Males	Ever Reproducing Males	Cumulative Percent	Total Females	Ever Reproducing Females	Cumulative Percent
0	140	0	0.0	119	0	0.0
5	109	0	0.0	77	0	0.0
10	101	1	0.1	69	5	0.8
15	80	10	1.5	47	32	6.0
20	65	26	5.1	55	48	13.9
25	51	37	10.2	57	56	23.0
30	50	42	16.0	57	55	32.0
35	52	49	22.8	44	43	39.1
40	25	23	26.0	21	21	42.5
45	21	18	28.5	27	25	46.6
50	10	8	29.6	17	17	49.3
55	9	9	30.8	10	10	51.0
60	6	6	31.6	4	4	51.6
65+	5	5	32.3	8	8	52.9
Total	724	234	32.3	612	324	52.9

spring. (This figure includes children not yet old enough to have reproduced). Overall, the figures show that 234 males compared to 324 females have had at least one child; i.e., among reproducers, there is a predominantly female-biased sex ratio of 72. Thus, while Yąnomamö males suffer higher pre-reproductive mortality than females, those males who do reproduce average a greater contribution per individual to the next generation than do reproductive females. These figures give an indication of the much higher variation in male reproductive success than female.

The variations in adult reproductive success and subsequent higher male mortality lead to the expectation of a correspondingly male-biased sex ratio at birth. Males are represented in the sex ratio at birth reported by the Yąnomamö in a ratio of 129 for every 100 female "births." If it is assumed that the true sex ratio of offspring at birth is consistent with the worldwide average of 105 (Colombo 1957), it can be estimated that some twenty percent of all female children actually born were destroyed for reasons having to do with parental preferences for male offspring (cf. Neel and Weiss 1975). This estimate, however, may be somewhat high with respect to the rate at which Yąnomamö mothers take the life of a child because of its sex. It may be that males are conceived at a higher rate than are females—i.e., the sex ratio at conception may be higher than 105, physiological factors may affect the sex ratio between conception and birth, or female offspring may be suffering a greater mortality in infancy due to differences in postnatal care and are subsequently not being "reported" as births by their mothers or other informants. There is no way of knowing for certain. Regardless of the proximate cause, however, more males than females enter the observable population. In short, it is possible that the true sex ratio at birth is of the order of 129—i.e., deviates substantially from the world average of 105.[5]

Some far-reaching problems of interpretation arise in the at-birth sex-ratio data (table 12–3) from the enlarged (post-1972) data set. Restricting the sample to just those villages studied most intensively by the senior author and looking only at births during the past ten years (i.e., during most of the period the senior author was studying the population), the best estimate of the at-birth sex ratio for firstborn children is 143, substantially higher (more male-biased) than the assumed 105 ratio used by the senior author in previous discussions of sex ratio and infanticide. If we assume that the 143 figure is the consequence of repeatedly "missing" female births in this restricted population (for example, female infants who

[5] A 0.95 confidence interval for the sex ratio at birth would fall between 111 and 152.

III. Individual and Group Strategies

Table 12–3   Sex Ratio of Firstborn Compared to Other Births   First births during the period 1964 through 1974 to women in selected villages were compared to births other than first births among women in the same villages during the same time period. The difference between the sex ratio of 143 for first births and that of 126 for the remaining births is not statistically significant ($\chi^2 = 0.54$, p $>$ 0.50). The difference between the overall sex ratio at birth of 129 and a "theoretically expected" sex ratio of 105 is statistically significant ($\chi^2 = 3.85$, p $<$ 0.05) with a 95% certainty that the "true" sex ratio at birth for the population falls between 111 and 152. Note that there is a slight discrepancy in the total number of births given in tables 12–3 and 12–1, a discrepancy that results from a few instances in which the year of birth of a few infants in some sibships could not be determined (estimated) in the field.

Sex	First Birth	Remaining Births	Combined
Male	103	280	383
Female	72	223	295
S.R.	143	126	129

were destroyed at birth and whose existence was never reported to the senior author), and if we further assume that the Yąnomamö have a "true" at-birth sex ratio of 105, then it is possible to continue interpreting the markedly biased sex ratios in the junior age categories as the probable consequence of preferential female infanticide. It is also possible that the Yąnomamö realize, through infanticide practices, their ideal that 'males are more valuable than females' and their stated preferences for a male as a firstborn. Moreover, births following the first child (sex ratio 126, table 12–1) would also reflect this, on the assumption that the at-birth sex-ratio is 105.

On the other hand, if the more restricted sample drawn from recent births in the villages most often censused by the senior author yields the most reliable estimate of at-birth sex ratio, then a wholly different interpretation is necessary. We believe that our estimate for the at-birth sex ratio of 129 is probably a more accurate estimate than the assumed 105 ratio. That is to say, the discrepancies in the sex ratios in junior age categories—the bias toward males—might be only the consequence of the male bias in the at-birth sex ratio. Differential female mortality among newborns could also account for the male-biased sex ratios in junior age categories, but an examination of the sexes of deceased neonates in the same villages for the same time period reveals no statistically significant differences in the numbers of female versus male infant deaths.

Assuming that our at-birth sex ratio estimate of 129 is more accurate than an assumed 105, a number of theoretical issues are raised and these, in turn, potentially have far-reaching implications for the anthropological and biological understanding of human infanticide. First, if we assume that infanticide practices are 'adaptive' for individuals, then it is difficult to make a convincing case that a female is enhancing her fitness by destroying a newborn daughter after having expended investment in carrying the fetus for nine months, if she does this only to have a male as a firstborn. The situations in which this *could* be adaptive are discussed in more detail below. Second, in a marriage exchange system of the kind characterizing the Yąnomamö (see Chagnon, chapter 4), it is advantageous for parents to produce both male and female offspring, since in order to operate effectively in the mating system, parents must produce daughters to give in reciprocal exchanges in order to acquire wives for their sons. Third, if it is desirable for members of villages to have large numbers of able-bodied warriors to defend the group and preferential female infanticide is the means used by individuals to bring this desirable condition about, then we are left with the difficult problem of explaining the "planning" dimensions of this, given that villages grow and fission at relatively high rates. We would have to assume, following this argument, that mothers are willing to gamble immediate reproductive success against the future contingency that they will be living in a village comprised of essentially the same members, and assume that they practice infanticide with the interests of that future group in mind. While this is not beyond the range of imagination, it essentially amounts to a group-selection argument of a most dubious kind. In view of the theoretical and empirical difficulties associated with such an argument, we feel that it is much more parsimonious and defensible to examine infanticide practices in terms of possible adaptive functions for individuals; and we invite our critics to demonstrate the group-selection dimensions of this problem.

The disproportionate representation of males at birth (assuming a true sex ratio of 129) is balanced by a correspondingly greater risk of mortality. As Fisher posited, ". . . boys are more numerous at birth but become less numerous owing to their higher death rate." The current (based on 1975 census data collected by the senior author) age-sex structure of the Yąnomamö population is given in figure 12–3. The overall sex ratio for the population (members of the thirteen core villages pooled) is 118, a

Figure 12–3   Yanomamö Age/Sex Pyramid in Five-Year Intervals

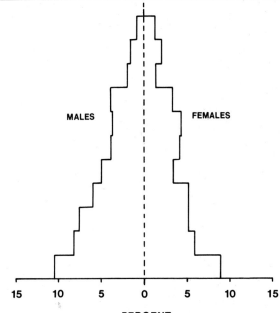

Age Categories	MALES		FEMALES		Sex Ratio
	Number	Percent	Number	Percent	
0–4	140	10.5	119	8.9	118
5–9	109	8.2	77	5.8	142
10–14	101	7.6	69	5.2	146
15–19	80	6.0	47	3.5	170
20–24	65	4.9	55	4.1	118
25–29	51	3.8	57	4.3	89
30–34	50	3.7	57	4.3	88
35–39	52	3.9	44	3.3	118
40–44	25	1.9	21	1.6	119
45–49	21	1.6	27	2.0	78
50–54	10	0.8	17	1.3	59
55–59	9	0.7	10	0.8	90
60–64	6	0.4	4	0.3	150
65–69	0	0.0	5	0.4	—
70–74	5	0.4	3	0.2	167
TOTALS:	724	54.2	612	45.8	118

Age/sex distribution of the Yanomamö population considered in this paper, based on the senior author's most recent (1975) census data in that population. (Cf. Chagnon 1974: 158–159 for comparative figures based on data from 1972 census.)

deviation from equality that is very largely due to the disproportionate number of males in the younger age categories. The sex ratio of the population between the ages of 0 and 14 is 132, while that for the portion which is 15 years of age and older is 108. These changes in the relative distribution of the sexes probably reflect a differential mortality experienced by males in the younger age categories. If differential male mortality occurs during the period of parental expenditure, the Yąnomamö sex ratio at birth can be viewed as a response to the differential variance in adult reproductive success. That is to say, the pattern of male mortality and the sex-ratio data conform to predictions from Fisher's general theory of sex-ratio selection.

As described in the introductory section of this paper, within-population variations in sex ratio may be adaptive in certain definable circumstances (Trivers and Willard 1973). Differences in social status might constitute conditions in which the potential reproductive value of offspring of each sex could vary (see Dickemann, chapter 13). The Yąnomamö are, according to commonly accepted anthropological definitions of status, an 'egalitarian' society insofar as specific kinds of relationship between individuals and resources are concerned (see Chagnon, chapter 14, for a critical discussion of egalitarianism). Egalitarian societies are those in which status positions are allocated on essentially just three criteria: age, sex, and personal characteristics (Service 1971; Fried 1967). Egalitarian societies are all those that generally lack positions of formal political status within which differential power, authority, and influence inhere irrespective of the qualifications of the human occupants of those positions. The status differentials that arise in egalitarian societies are based on the accomplishments of individuals; they tend to be nonhereditary, even ephemeral. There are, as Fried eloquently put it, as many positions of prestige as there are people capable of filling them. Yąnomamö status differentials are of this type; they do not arise out of formal political institutions but are largely a function of (a) an individual's kinship, descent, and marriage relationships, and (b) achieved, demonstrated charisma.

It should be mentioned at this juncture that anthropological discussions of differential status have often focused on questions about the evolution of social stratification (e.g., Fried 1967). The reproductive consequences of differential rank or status, on the other hand, have received relatively little attention, although it is generally known to anthropologists that political leadership and high prestige are often associated with polygynous marriage. This theme is discussed in chapter 14.

The context of reproductive competition between males in egalitarian societies also differs from the context of competition in economically stratified societies. Success in the competition for mates among the Yąno-mamö is not intimately bound to the individual's or family's accumulation and exclusive possession of scarce material goods. "Wealth" as the term is commonly understood does not exist as such, and therefore the acquisition of wives does not depend on the differential access of individuals or families to environmental resources. Males obtain wives through a process of direct exchange between kin groups (see Chagnon, this volume, chapter 4) in which eligible females of one group are given to the other and vice versa. In a very real sense, females are a strategic resource over which individual males and kin groups compete, and to acquire them in systems of direct exchange one must also produce them. While some groups may, because of their transient political influence, temporarily enjoy an advantage in acquiring wives from other groups by withholding their sisters and daughters, over the long term such imbalances even out (Chagnon 1968b). The ability to succeed in the competition for mates ultimately rests on the number of co-resident supporters an individual has, usually closely related kinsmen, and how groups of these enter into marriage-exchange obligations that last several generations. That is, the "fund of power" on which individuals can draw is ultimately a fund of kinsmen, not a collection of material resources and economic goods: successful competition for mates by males thus becomes a function of rights in the reproductive capacities of females, and these emerge from the marriage coalitions and the interpersonal relationships of kinship.

As one indicator of an individual's relative social status and political power we have used local descent group (lineage) size, focusing on the number of adult males fifteen years old and older. Male members of large lineages have a greater influence in village political affairs than do males from comparatively small lineages in the same village. Much of the support a Yąnomamö leader receives is from his male agnates—the adult males of his lineage. In addition, headmanship is almost invariably associated with the largest lineage of the village. Should there be two relatively large lineages in a village, there will be prominent men from the second lineage as well and even "dual" headmanship. Adult male agnates, of course, are not the individual's only source of political support. For example, if the immediately deceased patrilineal ancestors of two lineage heads have exchanged marriageable females, each lineage leader (brother-in-law) expects and usually receives support from the other (Chagnon 1968a, 1974, this volume, chapter 4). Marriage ties are therefore significant sources of political support to the members of matrimonially bound lineages. Here, however, we will focus primarily on the effects of agnatic kinship.

Table 12–4 **Lineage Ranks by Population and Villages-within-Population for Males 15 years or Older** The largest lineage in each village is given Rank 1 in that village: it contains the largest number of adult males in that village. The same lineage might have a different rank in another village. Thus, the largest fraction of adult males in Village 09 belongs to lineage 1222, but in Village 14 the adult males of lineage 1222 are outnumbered by the males of lineage 2936, etc. See tables 12–4 and 12–5 and the discussion in the text.

Shama-tari Village	1	2	3	4	5	6	7	8	9	10	11	12
09	1222	2700	2967	1443	2936	794	3204					
14	2936	1222	200	2967	916	2886						
16	1222	1443	2700	2876	2936							
21	2967	2936	81	200	1222							
49	2967	1222	2936	1443								
99	200	1414	2936	1443	2967	2985						
Namo-weiteri Village												
01	1598	1805	2250	3566	2856	2936	2954	3138	3445	3456	3466	
05	2954	2886	1443	916	2856	236	313	1598	2006	2814	2967	
06	2886	2954	916	2967	2856	2936	458	1222	1681	3557		
07	2954	2886	1829	1222	1598	2914	3559					
08	1598	3466	2250	3445	2888	2954	450	815	818	1805	2055	2936
18	2886	2954	2856	3445	81	1598						
19	2954	2886	1598	2967								

Table 12–4 gives the distribution of lineages ranked in terms of the number of living adult male members, arranged according to population bloc and village. Lineages are identified by the four-digit identification number assigned to the most remote patrilineal ancestor of the lineage. Most lineages are represented in a number of different villages, and the higher ranks in each village tend to be occupied by only a few of the possible lineages. Also, Shamatari villages (09, 14, 16, 21, 49, and 99) tend to have fewer, albeit larger, lineages dominating their composition than do the Namoweiteri villages.

Because of the nature of Yąnomamö village fissioning, some lineages become concentrated in óne or two villages and have very poor numerical representation in others. The men of a small but highly localized

III. Individual and Group Strategies

lineage might have considerable power in the local politics of their village, but be relatively insignificant in the supralocal distribution over the entire subpopulation (Chagnon 1968a, 1974, 1975, 1976, chapter 4, table 4–2).

We have tested the relationship between social status and variation in the sex ratio of offspring in three ways, using relative lineage size and headmanship as the basis for classifying differential social status. We have examined the reproductive performance of individuals in terms of (1) the rank size of their lineage in their village of residence and (2) the rank size of their lineage in the entire subpopulation of which they are members. Further, we have examined (3) the reproductive performance of headmen compared to the remaining males of equivalent age in the total population.

The results of the first comparison are given in table 12–5. For this comparison all adult males from the largest lineage in each village have been grouped together into "rank one," all males from the second largest lineage in each village into "rank two," and so on. As a consequence of the distribution of lineages throughout the population, individuals grouped in each rank will often be from different lineages while individuals from the same lineage will often be grouped into different ranks. For example, individuals from lineage 1222 in villages 09 and 16 would be in "rank one"

Table 12–5 Completed Family Size and Sex Ratio of Offspring per Adult Males by Rank of Lineage in Village of Residence of Each Male
If membership in larger lineages within villages correlated with high, predictable male fertility (Trivers and Willard extension), we would expect the sex ratio of offspring born to males who were members of the larger lineages to be male biased. This is not the case, according to the data presented here and assuming that membership in larger lineages is equivalent to higher status.

Village Rank	Adult Males	Sons	Daughters	Mean Offspring	S.D.	Sex Ratio
1	157	207	195	2.6	3.7	106
2	84	106	75	2.2	2.7	141
3	48	84	71	3.2	3.5	118
4	32	37	27	2.0	2.5	137
5	16	17	15	2.0	2.6	113
6	12	11	10	1.8	1.8	110
Other	25	33	19	2.1	2.3	174
TOTALS	274	495	412	2.4	3.2	120

while individuals from lineage 1222 in villages 14 and 19 would be in "rank two," and so on (table 12–5).

As can be seen in table 12–5, there is no evident trend for the sex ratio of offspring and the rank of an individual's lineage in his village of residence to co-vary. Nor is there a linear association indicated between rank and mean number of offspring, or sex ratio and mean number of offspring. These results are even more striking when individuals from the top two ranks are grouped together and compared to those from the remaining ranks. The mean number of offspring per individual and the average sex ratio of offspring for the top two ranks are virtually identical with those for individuals in the remaining ranks. For the two top-ranked groups, the average number of offspring was 2.41 and the sex ratio among them 115; among the remaining, the average number of offspring was 2.42 and the sex ratio 121. Hence, the reproductive value of male offspring does not seem significantly different and equivalent sex ratios are expected.

The results from the second comparison (of individual adult males grouped on the basis of lineage rank in the entire subpopulation) are given in table 12–6. For this comparison, all adult males from the largest line-

Table 12–6   Completed Family Size and Sex Ratio of Offspring for Adult Males by Rank of Lineage in Subpopulation of Residence   This table differs from table 12–4 in that the largest lineage in each subpopulation (Population 1 and/or Population 2) was given the highest rank, irrespective of how that lineage ranked in size in each village of the subpopulation (see table 12–4 for rank size by subpopulation and village). As the data in table 12–4 suggest, there is no obvious trend for sex ratio of offspring to covary with size rank of father's lineage.

Subpopulation Rank	Adult Males	Sons	Daughters	Mean Offspring	S.D.	Sex Ratio
1	95	122	96	2.3	3.3	127
2	91	141	126	2.9	3.6	112
3	58	51	41	1.6	2.5	124
4	28	40	44	3.0	3.5	91
5	18	38	42	4.4	3.9	91
6	15	15	6	1.4	1.5	250
Other	69	88	57	2.1	2.6	154
TOTALS	374	495	412	2.4	3.2	120

III. Individual and Group Strategies

age in each subpopulation are grouped into rank one, those from the
second largest lineage into rank two, and so on. Individuals are grouped
on the basis of *overall* lineage size irrespective of the rank of their lineage
in their particular village of residence. Again, there is no obvious trend
for the sex ratio of offspring to co-vary with the relative size of lineage.
When individuals from the top two lineages in each subpopulation are
grouped together, the average sex ratio of their offspring is 117.8, that for
the individuals in the remaining lineages 117.3.

Headmen

Another way to examine the impact of differential status on the sex ratio
of offspring is to investigate the reproductive performance of headmen (cf.
Irons, chapter 10). Table 12–7 summarizes this information for all current

Table 12–7 Reproductive Performance of Current Yąnomamö Headmen in All
Villages, Arranged in Order of Decreasing Reproductive Success
as of 1975

I.D.	Number Offspring	Sex Ratio	Number Males	Number Females	Number Wives	Age	Village
826	18	259	13	5	7	49	5
1660	16	128	9	7	4	60	14
471	16	100	8	8	3	48	21
1427	12	300	9	3	4	59	6
1880	11	266	8	3	2	54	14
379	11	37	3	8	4	44	21
1447	10	150	6	4	4	55	6
734	10	42	3	7	6	46	21
163	9	79	4	5	4	39	7
891	8	100	4	4	4	64	7
1474	8	100	4	4	2	46	18
778	7	75	3	4	3	46	18
1035	7	75	3	4	3	46	18
1140	7	39	2	5	3	35	99
1240	6	50	2	4	8	38	16
178	5	150	3	2	4	40	49
1327	5	150	3	2	1	46	19
3316	4	100	2	2	3	39	1
1551	2	100	1	1	1	37	9
3386	0	0	0	0	1	47	8
Total	172		90	82	71	938	
Mean	8.6	110	4.5	4.1	3.6	46.9	

Table 12–8 **Reproductive Performance of Headmen Compared to All Other Males Age 35 or Older in (Pooled) Population** Headmen average more than twice as many children (8.6 versus 4.2) as men of comparable age, but the sex ratio among their children is not significantly different from the sex ratio among the children of non-headmen as might be predicted from the Trivers and Willard theory. This assumes that headmanship is equivalent to variables such as mother's condition, discussed by Trivers and Willard (1973), insofar as predicting reproductive success of offspring according to their status and sex is concerned.

	Number	Sons	Daughters	Sex Ratio	Mean Offspring
Headmen	20	90	82	110	8.6 ± 4.6
Non-headmen	108	246	203	121	4.16 ± 3.4
					$p > .001$

(1975) Yąnomamö headmen, arranged according to their completed family size to date. In some villages there are several "headmen" as described above, a situation that often emerges when a village's composition includes several large descent groups. This is consistent with the pattern found in other egalitarian societies.

Tables 12–8 and 12–9 compare the reproductive performance of headmen against non-headmen in the population who are 35 years of age and older, using only these (non-headmen) for comparison controls for the effects of age on fertility. Headmen average more than twice as many offspring (8.6)

Table 12–9 **Marital Performance of Headmen Compared to Other Males Age 35 or Older** The greater reproductive success of headmen appears to be due to their greater success at acquiring multiple spouses rather than to a higher rate of reproduction per spouse. (Statistical tests: for number of wives, $t = 3.2546$, $p = .0015$; for offspring per wife, $t = -1.6942$, $p = .0927$).

	Number	Wives	Average Number Wives	Offspring per Wife
Headmen	20	71	3.6 ± 1.9	2.65 ± 2.5
Non-headmen	108	258	2.4 ± 1.4	1.99 ± 2.0

as non-headmen (4.2) of comparable age (cf. Chagnon, chapter 10.) However, the average sex ratio of offspring produced by headmen (110) is not significantly different than non-headmen's (121). The average sex ratio of offspring for headmen does not vary with social status as might be predicted by the Trivers-Willard theory.

Table 12–9 indicates that the probable basis for the greater than average reproductive success of headmen is their greater ability to acquire wives. The number of wives given in the table is the total number that men have had over the course of their lifetime, including deceased and divorced wives as well as polygynous marriages. Headmen have had an average of 3.6 wives compared to an average of only 2.4 for men of comparable age. However, while the difference in the number of wives per headman is significant below the .05 level, the difference in the number of offspring per marriage is not. Therefore it seems reasonable to conclude that the greater than average reproductive success of headmen is due primarily to their disproportionate ability to acquire multiple wives.

Conclusions

The temptation to interpret male-biased sex ratios in tribal and other populations as the logical and necessary consequences of sex-preferential infanticide results from two assumptions, both of them questionable. The first assumption is that such populations conform to the standard often reported for large, well-censused national populations: that the sex ratio at birth is approximately 105. The second assumption is that where sex ratios are demonstrably male-biased and where the population is known or suspected to engage in infanticide the male bias in the living population results necessarily from a sex bias in the infanticide practices. The temptation to make such assumptions and interpretations is very attractive, and the senior author of this paper has done so in a number of earlier publications. More extensive field research and a more careful examination of the data now point to the probability that Yąnomamö sex ratios at birth are substantially higher than the previously assumed 105 and may be closer to 130. While we still can not rule out the possibility that some portion of the male bias results from a tendency for the infanticide practices to be slightly female-biased, it is clear that alternative explanations for the observed male bias in junior age grades must be considered.

Previous and commonly-encountered theoretical treatments of sex-ratio variations, based on the assumption that they are due to female infanticide, have been couched in group adaptation terms; they generally argue that humans destroy female infants in order to regulate population density and growth rates and thereby prevent the degradation of the environment and conserve strategic resources. We have argued that this position is of dubious scientific utility on both empirical and theoretical grounds, and have shown that sex-ratio variations among the Yąnomamö can be adequately understood in terms of individual adaptation and by Fisher's general theory of sex-ratio selection.

The Trivers and Willard hypothesis does not appear to apply to the data we have considered. There are two possible reasons for this. First, it may be that the crucial element—predictability of offspring's reproductive success from parent's condition—is lacking. That is, there may be very little correlation between the social status and associated reproductive success of parent and offspring. This situation contrasts with those characterizing the societies studied by Dickemann (chapter 13), in which the social status of offspring and their associated reproductive success are predictable from their parents' social status. The second reason may stem from the fact that among the Yąnomamö, males usually gain wives as a result of reciprocal exchanges of kinswomen among closely related groups of males. Given this situation, any bias of the sex ratio of offspring in favor of males would leave these males at a disadvantage in terms of mate acquisition. Here again the contrast with the societies studied by Dickemann is sharp. The Yąnomamö exchange women for women; in the stratified societies Dickemann examines, spouses are obtained in return for wealth (brideprice or dowry). It is important to note that these two possible conditions vitiating adaptation of the sort hypothesized by Trivers and Willard are not mutually exclusive. Both conditions may hold, even though either by itself would exclude the kind of adaptive manipulation of sex ratio suggested by Trivers and Willard (1973).

The circumstances in which infanticide occurs are consistent with individual adaptation and it is not necessary to invoke group-selection arguments to explain these practices. They are, in general, situations in which parents destroy offspring for (1) spacing purposes and (2) obvious deformities.

It is clear to us that much more substantial documentation of sex-ratio variations and infanticide reports is required before a convincing demonstration can be made that male-biased sex ratios are the consequence of sex-preferential infanticide. It is not sufficient to assume such a relationship.

13. Female Infanticide, Reproductive Strategies, and Social Stratification: A Preliminary Model[1]

Mildred Dickemann

> Let us take the most common case in which the rule prescribes marriage with a woman of an immediately inferior status. How do women of the highest class get married? ... There must be a solution to this problem.
>
> Claude Lévi-Strauss. 1969.
> *The Elementary Structures of Kinship.* 474.

> The same motive which studded Europe with convents, in which youth and beauty were immured until liberated by death, first prompted the Rajpoot to infanticide.
>
> Lieut.-Col. James Tod. 1829.
> *Annals and Antiquities of Rajast'han,*
> v.1: 635.

Introduction

Trivers and Willard (1973) have demonstrated that under certain conditions the ability of parents to vary the sex ratio of their offspring will be advantageous to their own reproductive success (RS). Where males compete for access to females, variation in their condition will have greater reproductive consequences than will variation in the condition of females. If such variance is a "predictable attribute of adults in a species," then females should evolve the capacity to vary the sex ratio of their offspring, increasing the ratio when in good condition and decreasing it in adversity,

[1] Thanks to R. D. Alexander, G. Berreman, F. Boucher, L. A. Brownrigg, K. Gould-Martin, J. Hartung, K. Pakrasi and A. Wexler for helpful discussion and assistance with sources, and especially to S. Parker for calling my attention to Trivers and Willard 1973, the inspiration for this attempt. Thanks also to J. B. Birdsell, N. A. Chagnon, R. L. Trivers, and E. O. Wilson for encouragement. The many errors are of course my own. An earlier version of this paper was presented at the 74th Annual Meeting of the American Anthropological Association, December, 1975.

thus guaranteeing an excess of that sex of offspring which will most likely succeed reproductively in that state. Since in mammals it is males who are heterogametic, females cannot determine the sex of progeny directly, but must of necessity rely on some means involving differential selection of gametes at fertilization or differential mortality of the two sexes after conception.

Trivers and Willard proposed that this model applies to *Homo sapiens,* as evidenced by the fact that sex ratio at birth correlates with socioeconomic status. While they noted that the "application of the model to humans is complicated by the tendency for males to invest parental effort in their young (which reduces variance in male RS), and by the importance of kin interactions among adults," that is, the operation of altruistic behavior among kin, nevertheless they maintained that:

> the model can be applied to humans differentiated on a socio-economic scale, as long as the RS of a male at the upper end of the scale exceeds his sister's, while that of a female at the lower end of the scale exceeds her brother's. A tendency for the female to marry a male whose socioeconomic status is higher than hers will, other things being equal, tend to bring about such a correlation, and there is evidence of such a bias in female choice in the United States.[2]

While Trivers and Willard did not discuss cultural, as opposed to directly physiological, manipulation of the sex ratio in humans, Alexander (1974:369), in a discussion of parental investment of effort in offspring, predicted that in polygynous human societies (that is, those in which males compete for access to females, with consequent greater male than female variance in RS), "female-preferential infanticide is more likely among women married to high-ranking men and less likely among women married to low-ranking men or not legitimately married at all." However, he had at the time no status-differentiated data against which to test this prediction.

I present here evidence in support both of the hypergynous model of Trivers and Willard, and of Alexander's predicted correlation between preferential female infanticide and socioeconomic status, in three stratified

---

[2] Trivers, Robert L. and D. E. Willard. Natural Selection of Parental Ability to Vary the Sex Ratio of Offspring. *Science* 179:91, January 1973. Copyright 1973 by the American Association for the Advancement of Science.

human societies where variance in the conditions of adults is a "predictable attribute." These data, from feudal and post-feudal, but pre-industrial north India, China, and Europe, are generalized to form an initial model of human reproductive-demographic structure which identifies such widespread cultural phenomena as female infanticide and forms of celibacy, dowry and brideprice, and the seclusion and incapacitation of women as components of the reproductive strategies of members of a universally hierarchical and facultatively polygynous species. In conclusion, suggestions are made regarding the likely universality of this model, in which the societies reviewed here may be seen as extreme variants of a general human system.[3] Before reviewing the evidence, the model hypothesized here may be briefly summarized. (See figure 13–1.)

In certain stratified societies, characterized by intense competition for scarce resources, male reproductive success shows extreme variance, men of high rank acquiring access to a disproportion of females through polygyny, and in addition enjoying greater health and earlier entry into reproduction, while those at the bottom are disproportionately excluded from reproduction through delayed marriage, heavy mortalities, and the imposition of celibate roles, while their RS is further reduced through heavy mortalities among their progeny.[4] Further, the relative probable RS of males and females at different levels of the social hierarchy is culturally exacerbated through female preferential infanticide, suicide, and celibacy (including prohibitions against widow remarriage or against sexual intercourse by mothers of reproductive offspring), all reaching greatest intensity at the top of the social pyramid. Middle- and upper-class marriage systems are hypergynous, with competition between families (mostly patrilineal in these societies) for higher-status grooms possessing greater access to scarce resources. The symbolic and economic index of competitive effectiveness is dowry, or bridegroom price, which with other ceremonial dis-

---

[3] For other relevant discussions of human reproductive strategies, see Alexander 1974 and 1977a; Crook, Fox, and Trivers in Campbell, ed., 1972; Fox, ed., 1975; and West Eberhard 1975.

[4] RS of low ranking males is reduced not only directly through reduced access to females, but indirectly through lowered parental investment, as a result of economic disability, shorter average length of marriage due to higher rates of rupture and parental mortality, and earlier age of economic independence of offspring. In contrast, child betrothal in high-status families may result in investment in the betrothed's genes prior to the birth of her offspring, on the part both of her father and male siblings, and of her husband's kin group, a form of "anticipatory altruism." I am indebted to F. Boucher for these observations.

tributions of wealth demonstrates the winning family's superior fitness, buying increased RS for its shared genes in the next generation, through transfer of a female offspring to a more favorable milieu. Dowry initiates a series of financial and social obligations on the part of the bride's natal family to her conjugal family and her offspring. Flow of wealth from subordinate to superordinate affines maintains political dominance in a system of asymmetrical alliances (Fox 1967:208–239), while attempting to ensure preference for the bride and her progeny in competition with other females in a polygynous household. This function is often phrased in terms of the bride's brother ("mother's brother") who plays a competitive-defensive male role as representative of those genes shared by himself, his father, and the preferred sister. Predictably, his strongest obligations are toward his sister's son, exactly that descendant who will enjoy the increased RS of this reproductive strategy.[5]

At the bottom of the socioeconomic scale, in contrast, where female progeny enjoy greater probability of survival and reproduction than do males, their biological value is reinforced by the provision of economic roles for women which are equally or more rewarding than those for men (hence matrifocal families). Here brideprice prevails: males compete directly for the purchase of females. Where intense polygyny and female infanticide at the top create severe shortages of available females at the bottom, institutionalized systems of sale and capture of women occur. Thus individuals at all levels of the social hierarchy attempt to maximize RS through cultural strategies, though in general the relative success of those in high status is presumed to be greater than that of those below (cf. Hartung 1976; Irons, chapter 10; Trivers 1972:138–139).

At the top of the social hierarchy, competition involves larger kin units and greater investment of effort in both parental and sibling RS by more distant kin, that is, more extended forms of familism or nepotism. Hamiltonian altruism is here at its most intense, in contrast to the restricted and fragile kin units and limited extensions of altruism at the

---

[5] The analysis of the mother's brother's role presented here differs from that developed by Alexander (1974, 1977a), which emphasizes concern for confidence of paternity. In high-status families, confidence of paternity is high due to female seclusion and incapacitation. Here, however, male investment in sister's progeny may be better rewarded than investment in one's own, if hypergyny results in markedly increased probable RS for one's sister's son, as opposed to one's own. Ethnographic data on the relative contributions to sister's and to own sons in both egalitarian and stratified societies are needed to refine these hypothesis. Cf. Kurland, chapter 6.

bottom. This is probably because political systems of resource control increase environmental stability at the top, while at the bottom, greater environmental uncertainty makes altruism less rewarding and selfishness more so (cf. Alexander 1974:345).

In a variety of invertebrates and vertebrates, sexual selection has evolved means whereby the successful male ensures greater confidence of paternity (Wilson 1975:321–324), for example, through copulatory plugs (Devine 1975), pregnancy block (Macrides et al. 1975), or the killing of previously sired offspring (Blaffer Hrdy 1974, 1976). Parallel cultural mechanisms operate in *Homo sapiens*. Here, however, long-term paternal investment of effort in progeny, through provision of economic and political security to the reproductive units, is involved. Predictably, since high-ranking males invest more paternal care in their progeny than do those of lower rank, they also invest more in the protection of that paternal effort,[6] to ensure its expenditure only on their own genes as opposed to those of competing males. Hence, the intensity of a variety of cultural codes guaranteeing control over female reproduction is status-graded. These customs, often subsumed under the term "double standard," comprising differential enforcement of female chastity and fidelity, reduction of female choice in mating, and institutional seclusion and incapacitation of women, all reach greatest intensity at the top of the pyramid, contrasting with greater female freedom of choice, promiscuity,[7] relative economic independence, and freedom of physical and social movement at the bottom.

Although this model appears superficially symmetrical, the strategy of removal of high-status females from reproduction differs fundamentally from that directed against low-status males. Whereas rates of female infanticide approaching 100 percent of all female livebirths may occur at the top, no such intensity of male infanticide appears at the bottom (although male infanticide does occur). Similarly, where female reproductive careers are curtailed, rather than prevented through outright removal at birth, this shortening occurs late in the reproductive span, guaranteeing that what-

[6] Parental effort refers to all those aspects of parental care which increase the rates of survival and reproduction of one's offspring, relative amounts of which will vary both between individual parents and between individual offspring of the same parent, and does not refer to "parental investment" *sensu* Trivers 1972. For a recent discussion of these and related concepts see Alexander and Borgia 1978.

[7] Female promiscuity here is a product of the male's limited parental investment. Where male PE is low, the female gains nothing by fidelity, and may increase her RS through polyandrous or serial alliances with several minimally investing males.

ever reproduction occurs will fall during the period of maximum physiological potential. Thus, in either case, limitation on female reproduction falls outside the period of maximum reproductive value.[8] In contrast, many low-status males experience delayed entry into reproduction due to poverty, incarceration and other constraints, while access primarily to older females or those of poor physical status further reduces their RS. This contrast in reproductive fates must proceed from the fundamentally different roles of males and females, the one primarily aggressive-defensive, the other primarily reproductive-nurturant. In consequence, such human cultural forms as polygyny-polyandry or dowry-brideprice, often conceived as symmetrical opposites, are in fact profoundly asymmetric in demographic meaning and cannot be understood without appreciation of this fact.[9]

The model proposed above presumes that all human demographic structures rest on certain universal sociobiological potentials. Thus, while all human societies are hierarchical systems involving male dominance, the extreme intensity of competition achieved in the class-caste societies reviewed below must be a function of very particular combinations of ecological stress, technological capacity, and political history.

Likewise, while the human species must be conceived as everywhere facultatively polygynous, the degree of polygynous marriage regularly

[8] Although the prohibition against widow remarriage, and that against sex by women with married or breeding offspring, are clearly status-correlated, and hence conform to the general asymmetrical model presented here, their sociobiological functions are unclear. While ensuring that male competition centers around females of greatest reproductive value and with greatest probability of bearing healthy offspring, they may also increase the sex ratio by preventing higher order births, but this effect is probably trivial. When applied to mature females, these prohibitions operate as forms of "cultural menopause" guaranteeing parental investment in previously conceived offspring (cf. Alexander 1974:370–371). However, in the societies reviewed, high mortalities result in significant numbers of females betrothed and brides widowed before reproduction. It is difficult to understand the benefits of the prohibition to these widows and their kin. For the patriline of the deceased spouse, remarriage of the woman into another patriline is impossible, as it would involve (in these hypergynous societies) expenditure of dowry to no benefit of the deceased's genes. Only widow inheritance, celibate helper at the nest, or perhaps suicide (sati) are acceptable alternatives from the patriline's viewpoint. The question then becomes why some such groups do, and some do not, practice widow inheritance. Thanks to R. D. Alexander and J. Hartung for calling attention to this unclarity.

[9] Another discussion of demographic asymmetry is in Divale and Harris (1976). As the authors state, "groom price" in the sense of compensation to the groom's family for his removal is nonexistent. In the reproductive sense, however, dowry buys association with a male of higher probable RS: it is in this sense that I employ the term.

Figure 13–1   A Model of the Stratified Human Breeding System

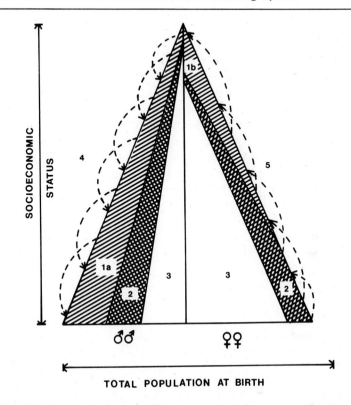

1 Removed from breeding population through cultural means: (a) masculine homicide, warfare, accident, celibacy imposed through poverty, incarceration, etc.; (b) female infanticide, celibacy, suicide.
2 Removed from breeding population through natural means.
3 Remaining breeding population.
4 Male downward mobility (through disinheritance, outcasting, economic failure, etc.)
5 Female hypergyny (through marriage, concubinage, prostitution, sale, capture).

achieved must again reflect specific transects of ecosystem, economy, and polity. The ultimate test of the applicability of this model must depend, then, not only on a larger sample of more refined demographic data than I possess, but also on specification of the interactions between demographic structures and their ecological and historical contexts, something which is not attempted here.

13. Female Infanticide, Reproductive Strategies, and Social Stratification   327

India [10]

Jharejas

In discussing India, I review in detail one case for which there are more complete demographic data available to me; I turn then to a general discussion of the system, especially in reference to Northern India.

The British discovery of female infanticide in India is familiar to readers of Darwin and Malthus. It was first noted in 1789, among the Rajkumar Rajputs near Varanasi (Benares): a campaign was launched against it, and in 1802 the Government of India declared the practice illegal. In 1804, the Governor of Bombay discovered the practice among the Jhareja Rajputs of Kathiawar, Gujarat, and instituted a campaign lasting fifty years, resulting in numerous government reports and some of the first annual censuses in the British Empire. It is this case which I summarize here, relying heavily on the publications of Pakrasi (especially 1968, 1970a) and excerpts from official documents which he provides.

The British were informed that the Jhareja subcaste killed all female infants at birth; as the campaign proceeded, other Rajput subcastes were also implicated. Early estimates, ranging from 3,000 to 20,000 infants killed annually, are no doubt exaggerated; but however inaccurate, censuses do support the contention that almost 100 percent of female live-births were removed. Censusing began in 1805 and was carried out again in 1817, 1824, 1827, and yearly thereafter. I place reliance on these early census results for my purposes for the following reasons. First, as the cam-

[10] I am acutely aware of the deficiencies in this broad survey. They arise in part from inadequacies in the sources: unreliable and noncomparable data, inconsistent classifications of cultural forms, lack of data on economic correlations of social behaviors, and poor samples; and in part from my own insufficient control of the demographic, political, and historical literatures of three great civilizations. Heavy reliance on secondary sources and individual anecdotes, and much temporal and regional overgeneralization are the consequence. The choice of the three cultures is historical accident: the Indian case first presented itself as a confirmation of Trivers and Willard's and Alexander's predictions; the other two seemed most likely to replicate its features. Another feudal society which seems to conform to the model at least on the peasant level is Tokugawa Japan. Relevant data are summarized in Dickeman 1975; my inability to locate data on the samurai and noble classes has led me to exclude it here. The development of variant models appropriate to such social forms as matriliny and polyandry, and the investigation of other civilizations such as those of Subsaharan Africa, the Arabic Near East, and modern industrial society must await further research. With apologies to the specialist, then, this idiosyncratic and uneven initial presentation will have served its purpose if it generates correction and improved formulation of the general theory of human behavior to which it contributes.

III. Individual and Group Strategies

paign intensified, with fines and prison sentences imposed, it is hard to imagine motives sufficient for the massive selective concealment of female offspring. Second, inspection of the censuses and the reports of observers reveal that the first response of Jharejas to the campaign was to preserve one female per family. When this failed to satisfy the new rulers, under-reporting of males, and in some cases of all livebirths, began. Also, numbers of females under two years of age failed to appear in the appropriate age groups in subsequent censuses, suggesting that the practice of female infanticide continued between census visits. Census results coincide with statements of Jhareja leaders regarding the extent of the practice. Through-out the campaign, open resistance of subcaste chiefs was coupled with bribing of census-takers and assassination of British-paid informers; chiefs who were fined became martyrs. Understandably, other Rajput subcastes in the area supported Jhareja resistance, as it was they who supplied brides to the infanticide-practicing group.

Some census results follow. By the end of 1808, in spite of public renunciations by chiefs, public meetings and cash awards to fathers of daughters, only 20 Jhareja females could be identified in the districts then censused; in 1817, in all of Kathiawar, only 63, of whom all but 3 had been born after the initiation of the campaign. The total Jhareja popula-tion of the area at the time must have been at least 4000 to 5000. By 1824, 266 females were identified, only 24 of whom were 13 years or older, and a little less than half of whom were under 3 years of age. The 1834 census identified both males and females by age group. The numbers of the living under 1 year of age were: males 1422, females 571. A reanalysis of this census on the basis of the 1837 figures revealed a large underreporting of males. The 1840 census, with new districts included, gave a total population of 5760 males and 1370 females, or a sex ratio of 420:100. In the group under one year the ratio was 225:100, although for newborns there was parity. In this year, the first census of the Jetwas Rajputs of Poorbunder district gave a sex ratio of 452:100 (77 males and 17 females). Subsequent censuses of 1842 and 1843 again reveal deceptions in the low numbers of male births. Obviously, subcaste members had deduced that the basis of the British campaign was the analysis of sex ratios. In conclusion, figures for the 1850 and 1854 censuses were as follows:

	1850		1854	
	M	F	M	F
Jharejas:	7520	3423	8144	3999
Jetwas:	242	126	253	155
Soomras:	493	326	529	360

These figures reveal two things: one is a trend toward greater proportions of females reared, and the other is rates of female infanticide of at least 30–80 percent during the campaign. The large underreporting of males suggests that this estimate is too low. As Pakrasi and Sasmal's (1971) data show, during the late 1840s and early 1850s, the sex ratio stabilized at a new lower level of about 240:100, probably in response both to the degree of British surveillance and to changing economic conditions. While outmigration of females could conceivably produce these results, the testimony of both Jharejas and observers precludes such an explanation. Thus, from 1837 reports (Pakrasi 1968: 129), ". . . the Jam's family having saved only two daughters since their arrival in Kattywar . . . spoke volumes. The Raos of Kutch [Jhareja Kings of Northwest India] never preserved one legitimate daughter in their families till the present Chief did. As a matter of fact, Jam Tumachee saved a daughter sixty-six years ago. . . ." And "only one daughter of Jam Lakajee's has been preserved for these ten generations . . ." (Pakrasi 1968:142). Jhareja chiefs emphasized that they were unable to find mates for their daughters, and hence destroyed them.

The system of hypergyny which formed the context for these practices prevailed widely in Indian society, and was perhaps most elaborated among Rajputs. While castes were rigidly endogamous (as regards legitimate marriages), subcastes, as well as family lines and in some cases villages, were often rigidly exogamous. In the usual case, residence among Rajputs was patrilocal. Thus, each subcaste sought marriage mates with other subcastes, but subcastes and sometimes villages were ranked in relation to one another, and the rule of hypergyny required that females could be accepted only from subcastes equal to or lower than one's own. The pyramidal nature of hierarchical societies meant that the higher the status of the subcaste, the fewer options for its daughters: the operation of hypergyny in a pyramidal structure guarantees competition for a resource which is always scarce in relation to demand. The economic expression of this competition was the provision of dowries of greater value in higher subcastes.

Among wealthier Rajputs polygyny was also common, aggravating the shortage of females at lower levels. Thus, Erskine reported in 1837 that "the present Jam has six wives, several concubines, besides his assuming to himself the privilege of cohabiting with any female whom his caprice points out; it can be supposed what a scene exists of female murder in his palace and environs" (quoted in Pakrasi 1970a:139–140). In fact, though many illegitimate offspring were destroyed, some entered into concubinage or into marriage with Muslim rulers.

The Jhareja case can be understood in terms of the general system of hypergyny and of their own history. Entering Gujarat from the west about five hundred years previously, they were the latest of several Rajput invaders to impose themselves on the resident population. In this politically unstable area of Northwest India, military superiority resulted in feudal control, district chieftains (*talukdars*) of the dominant subcastes and their relatives holding land, with other dependent groups in relations of tenancy. Most Rajputs other than the ruling houses were agriculturalists. When Jharejas displaced previously dominant Rajput subcastes, they took their brides from these groups (Jetwas, Jhallas, Waghelas, etc.). But the passage of their own brides to higher Rajput subcastes in the region proved in most cases impossible. While this may have been due in part to the relative poverty of Gujarat, I suspect it was also a reflection of the recency of their claim to high political status.

Thus the situation was especially severe for the highest-ranking families, who had of necessity to seek husbands in the households of Rajput rulers outside Gujarat. British success in encouraging the preservation of daughters began among the poorer Jharejas when provided with funds for payment of dowries (disbursed from an Infanticide Fund composed of fines levied against violators). But the upper classes were little affected until finally the Rao of Kutch agreed that in future his daughters might marry into lower-ranking subcastes. In fact, this was an expression of the ultimate cause of British success, the imposition of political control over the area, including removal of taxation powers from the chiefs and destruction of the feudal system.

Northern India in general

As the British soon realized, preferential female infanticide was not restricted to Rajkumars and Jharejas, nor to the Rajput caste alone. Subsequent inquiries uncovered the practice in numerous castes of middle and high rank, especially in Northern India, including Brahmins, Rajputs, Khatris, Jats, Gujars, Ahirs, Sikhs, and Muslims, as well as some tribal groups. Throughout the early nineteenth century, local campaigns were carried on against the practice; their failure led to the passage of an Infanticide Act by Parliament in 1870, which involved the identification and regular census of Proclaimed clans and villages, and the analysis of sex ratios as an index of compliance. In the Northwest Provinces alone, where females constituted only 30 percent of all children, a total of 4,959 villages, with a population of 485,000, fell under the provisions of the Act, which remained in force until 1906. As a result of local resistance, early censuses contain many inaccuracies but the direction of results is consistent and overwhelming. Nor need they stand alone: frank testimony regarding the custom was freely given by caste leaders until British suppression drove them to deceit and denial. (For general reviews see Balfour 1885; *Calcutta Review*, 1844a; Cave-Browne 1857; Das 1956, 1957; Pakrasi 1970a, 1970b, 1972; Wilson 1855).

Most surprising to the British was the intensity of female infanticide among the highest-ranking castes and subcastes. So great was British fascination with this aspect of the problem that data on infanticide among lower classes, or against males, are hard to find (but see Burnes 1834:198). I here ignore as well the operation of female infanticide among tribal groups, for which some data exist, which would repay separate study.

Even without access to primary data in the Parliamentary Papers and other Government sources, it is clear that a positive correlation existed between the rank of the group and the incidence of female infanticide. Many North Indian castes were composed of ranked exogamous subcastes for whom hypergyny was either preferred or mandatory, and hypogyny strongly disapproved. Those at the bottom of local or regional hypergynous systems practiced little or no female infanticide, while those at the top often destroyed all females at birth. There is no question that this generalization is accurate, but since it has been greeted with skepticism I offer a few examples.

The Kulin Brahmins of Bengal, one of only two Brahmin groups in my sources practicing female infanticide, were the highest ranking of four exogamous subcastes observing strict hypergyny (Calcutta Review, 1844b:16). The other, Moyal Brahmins of the Punjab, practiced female infanticide in the Jhelum Division, where they were the "most aristocratic" group but not in Multan Division where they were considered inferior [Panigrahi 1972:26–29].

In Agra Division, Northwest Provinces, the three highest Bhadauri Rajput "clans" gave their daughters to other Rajput groups including those in neighboring Rajputana. Among them, female infanticide was so extensive that in some villages no daughter had ever been married off within living memory. The lower-rank Bhadauri groups did not engage in the practice [Cave-Browne 1857:99–102].

III. Individual and Group Strategies

In Mainpuri, the Chauhan Rajputs were one of the highest-ranking subcastes; the Raja was a member of this group. While they gave brides to four other high-ranking Rajput groups in the region, a sample census in 1843 could find no female children in the district, and the Raja's family had preserved no females for centuries [Cave-Browne 1857:79–80; Raikes 1852:14, 18–19, 30].

In Kangra District, Punjab, in 1852, the whole Hindu population had a sex ratio among children of 119:100. The Rajput ratio was 125:100, but that of the three leading Rajput subcastes was 302:100 or only about 33 percent females [Cave-Browne 1857: 184–186].

Likewise among Sikhs, female infanticide was universally practiced by the Bedi Sikhs of the Punjab, highest-ranking priestly subcaste and descendants of the founder, Baba Nanuk. In 1846, the Commissioner of Jullundhur Division stated that there were no female children among 2000 Bedi families. Investigations in 1852 uncovered the case of one Bedi who had preserved two daughters prior to the institution of British rule. In consequence, he was outcasted and treated as a sweeper. Throughout Punjab, the Bedi Sikhs were known by the epithet Kuri-Mar ("daughter-slayer"). The Sodhi Sikhs, rivals of the Bedis for highest rank, and the source of later religious leaders, also practiced female infanticide, as neither group would give its daughters to the other [Cave-Browne 1857: 192–3, 283; Panigrahi 1972:25–28].

These examples could be multiplied at length.

These infanticidal castes were primarily dominant military elites in a feudal structure, imposing their rule through conquest. Their preferred roles were military and administrative, although in poverty they were sometimes forced to farm. They controlled land through patrilineal inheritance: farmland and protection were made available to dependent families and groups through a variety of forms of tenancy, serfdom and donation, in return for tribute, labor, and loyalty. These patron-client relations existed both within and between castes, although unfortunately the anthropological literature has focused primarily on the relations between endogamous castes (the so-called jajmani system) which do not involve legitimate marriage. As we shall see below, however, hypergyny is not entirely absent from intercaste relations. In addition to the landlord castes, extreme rates of female infanticide occurred in higher-status agricultural and pastoral castes. Almost all, including even the Brahmins, had traditions of militarism and conquest (Rivers 1921).

Emphasis on hypergyny in North India was phrased ideologically in a variety of ways. Hindu scriptures refer to hypergynous marriage as *anuloma* ("with the hair"), and hypogynous marriage as *pratiloma* ("against the hair") (Mandelbaum 1970 (1):236). Among Rajputs, higher-ranking groups clustered in the Northwest, hence the saying "the girl from the east, the boy from the west" (Karve 1965:169; Mahar 1966:176–179; Opler and Singh 1948: 180). Phrasing in terms of preferential matrilateral cross-cousin marriage was also widespread (Karve 1965:168–170, 172). The mother's brother "is an especially supportive kinsman. . . . As a brother, a man characteristically wants to help his sister in her married house . . . by aiding her husband, by backing his family, by giving gifts and favors to her children. A father also seeks to help his married daughter . . ., but he usually leaves the direct participation to his sons" (Mandelbaum 1970 (1):148–149). Shame and avoidance on the part of the bride's father vis-à-vis the groom's family, customarily expressed, symbolized his relative rank in the hypergynous alliance (Risley 1915:168; Karve 1965:170; Mandelbaum 1970 (1):69). The persistence of this pattern is attested by the review of ethnographic sources in Mandelbaum (1970 (1):112–114, 236–239).

Central to hypergynous marriage systems is the dowry, or bride-groom price, characteristic of high-ranking North Indian groups. That female infanticide was rationalized as a consequence of competitive demand for large dowries and other wedding expenses from the bride's father, and the small number of available sons at the top of the hierarchy, is clear from testimony of native leaders. The higher the status of the groom's family, the greater the dowry demanded (Burnes 1834:285–288; Cave-Browne 1857:31–34; Pakrasi 1970a:73; Wilson 1855:342–343). Subsequently, a "continuous flow of gifts" passed from the male relatives of the bride to her new conjugal family (Mandelbaum 1970 (1):148). Intensity of competition for sons-in-law resulted in child betrothal and early marriage, especially in higher-status groups (Risley 1915:186-206; Blunt 1931:75–84).

The complementary roles of superordinate and subordinate families linked in asymmetrical alliance are not entirely clear from the ethnographic literature, which has been devoted primarily to investigation of intercaste (jajmani) relations. While Karve (1965:169) speaks of "material gains in indirect ways," and "a girl married into a ruling family tries to get her relatives appointed in different posts," most sources fail to objectivize such terms as "prestige," or "status," in economic or behavioral terms. Mandelbaum (1970 [1]:100) states: "Status mobility . . . requires a solid economic base. Wealth is not a sufficient condition for attaining a higher rating, but it is usually a necessary precondition." Surveying available data on the mobilization of affinal networks (although most sources do not refer to Northern India), he specifies exchange of labor, goods, and cash, and use of the affinal home as a refuge when in trouble (Mandelbaum 1970 (1):148–151), and more generally, the use of kin networks to arrange marriages for others, and as a source of allies in power struggles with other families (Mandelbaum 1970 (1):152–158). Surely hypergyny must function to secure both economic and political protection. Human intuition tells us that a rise in status must correlate with economic and survival gains. Nevertheless, more specific data are needed regarding the advantage both of higher status and of the particular alliance created, if we are to be able to specify the degree to which perceived economic, political, and psychological benefits are necessary to empower the breeding strategies of human beings.

Still, Mandelbaum's analysis supports the contention made above that dowry functions as an economic index of competitive success. In his discussion of "Marriage as a Test of Status," he indicates that "marriage provides the prime opportunity for demonstrating and validating family status."

Temporal assets do not automatically bestow higher status. They must be used in ways that confer status, and one of the main avenues is through establishing a marriage alliance with a family of unquestioned higher standing. . . . What an advantageous marriage accomplishes for a status-ambitious family is to put its members into the same bracket of rank as the higher family. . . . [T]he marriage demonstrates for all to see that the lowlier family has risen far enough for the higher to accept one of its daughters. The higher family, in North India, gains by this match through the lavish gifts that the lower gives to its daughter in her married home. The bride's family, in a Muslim village of Punjab where this gift flow has been closely studied, gives about ten times as much in gifts to the groom's family as they receive from them (Eglar, 1960, pp. 108–115; Marriott, 1962, p. 265) [Mandelbaum 1970 (1):98–99].

Geographically the centuries-long operation of this system in North India has interesting consequences. Wherever, as in the case of the Rajputs, a caste had wide geographic distribution, hypergyny acquired a geographic character, with brides flowing from lower-status, politically weaker regions to those of higher status; hence the Rajput saying quoted above, "the girl from the east, the boy from the west." Elsewhere geographic hypergyny was phrased in terms of flow up- and downriver. These folk sayings are not fictions, but accurate descriptions of intercaste relations. One may suspect that the direction of flow is a consequence of the repeated intrusion of conquest societies into the Indian subcontinent from the Northwest since perhaps 2500 BC.

Female infanticide correlates with other familiar aspects of Indian culture. Mahar (1966:228) records the common North Indian joke about the "plight of a man wandering about the countryside in search of a husband for his daughter." This is clearly an expression of anxiety over failure in the competition for marital alliances. Intensity of competition resulted in child betrothal and early marriage (Risley 1915:186–206; Blunt 1931: 75–84). Flow of females upward was aggravated by polygyny, which occurred among wealthy and ruling houses of both Hindus and Muslims. In addition to formal marriage, high-status males had access to females of lower castes, gathering large numbers of concubines in their households. In some cases, such concubines served to create alliances with groups to whom formal marriage was forbidden, as between Hindu and Muslim ruling houses. Illegitimate offspring of such unions were often, but not invariably, destroyed (Panigrahi 1972: 181–182; Pakrasi 1970a:35, 136–142; Wilson 1855:74). Removal of females from the reproductive pool, and consequent continued demand for brides from below, was also achieved by prohibitions against widow remarriage in high-ranking groups, and by the practice of sati, both widely discussed (Jacobson 1974:136–137; Luschinsky 1975 (2):609–618; Minturn and Hitchcock 1966:27–29).

The seclusion of women in the zenana, or women's quarters, and their assumption of veiling when in public, is intense in North India, and not restricted to Muslims. For example, Wiser and Wiser (1971:85–86) describe a Brahmin village wife who knew no other Brahmin women, as they were separated from her house by a lane: her total knowledge of the village came from male members of her family and from servants. This system of concealment, although practiced by all who can afford it as a sign of status, is directly correlated with caste rank, lower-caste women moving freely at their occupations and doing agricultural labor alongside men. Restrictions on mobility not only contribute to female subservience to men, they also support and depend for their maintenance on the jajmani system of intercaste occupational dependence, which transfers traditionally female activities to low-status castes. The association of seclusion with high status rests directly on the economic cost of servants, as in our own society (Wiser and Wiser 1971:72–86; Jacobson 1974:133–138, 150–159; Luschinsky 1975 (1):336–344; (2):609–618; Minturn and Hitchcock 1966:27–29).[11]

The scarcity of available women among lower castes, and among the poorest members of middle- and upper-caste groups, resulted in the payment of brideprice, and even the purchase of daughters from other castes. Kidnapping and the sale of women and girls were institutionalized in North India, involving professional child-thieves and middlemen. Lower-caste females were sold to men of higher castes, often with their true caste status disguised (Panigrahi 1972:133–134). Mandelbaum (1970 (1):107–8) summarizes a modern case in which two-thirds of the wives of landowning Patidars are in fact of lower-caste origin, although the public fiction that they are Patidars is maintained. Sale of females from poor families into urban prostitution continues in modern times. And many unsuccessful men of high-caste status formed illegal liaisons with low-caste women, often resulting in outcasting (Blunt 1931:70; Crooke 1897:136–139; Karve 1965: 132; Luschinsky 1975 (1):292–293; Panigrahi 1972:133–137; Risley 1915: 198–199; Wilson 1855:47). In the very lowest castes, women experienced little or no seclusion, and greater economic equality with men. Sati was not practiced, and even today remarriage, which remains rare in top castes, occurs for 60 percent or more of low-caste widows (Agarwala 1972:53, 95–101).

There is some evidence on the fate of males excluded from matrimony. In spite of universal encouragement to marriage, many sources report that poor males have higher rates of celibacy than do poor females (Blunt 1931:47; Carstairs 1958:30–37; Crooke 1897:138–139; Luschinsky [1975] (1):292–293; Mahar 1966:174–175; Jacobson 1974:157). Fortunate men from poor families might contract adoptive-groom marriages with families of higher status who lacked male heirs, though this hyperandrous marriage was viewed with disfavor (Mandelbaum 1970 (1):99). In addition, criminal outcastes, ascetic castes, and the caste of professional male prostitutes recruited membership from higher-caste males who, failing in marital competition, moved downward in the system (Carstairs 1958:58–60; Crooke 1897:138–139; Panigrahi 1972:136–137). Many ascetic and celibate groups recruited males primarily from other castes, showing a consequent excess of males (Crooke 1897:253–254; Ibbetson 1916:225–230). Hence the pro-

---

[11] This system of role specialization forms a striking parallel, even to the delegation of wetnursing, to specialist roles of reproductive queen bee and helper at the nest found in eusocial insects (Wilson, 1975: 397ff).

13. Female Infanticide, Reproductive Strategies, and Social Stratification   337

verb, "A wifeless man takes to religion" (Blunt 1931:85). Finally, high-caste males served as warriors in conquest and feuding between North Indian groups, a role they continued in the British army. Unfortunately, I have no quantitative data either on numbers or mortalities.

Data and sources reviewed above indicate the complexity of a hypergynous model operating in societies composed of strongly endogamous units (castes). Hypergyny is most intense within endogamous units, where approved marriage systems with formal economic exchanges occur. Nonetheless, no endogamous barriers are complete: both illegal liaisons and occasional formal marriages occur across castes. What is striking in all stratified societies, and strong confirmation of the biological model proposed here, is the conformance of illegal matings on the average to the hypergynous system (cf. "interracial" matings in the U.S.), as likewise the downward movement of males across caste boundaries. Consequently, a macrosystem of female (upward) and male (downward) movement replicates that of each formally endogamous subunit, although at much lower rates of gene flow.

A historical note

Pakrasi's analysis of the Indian data indicates that the practice of female infanticide had largely declined by about 1881; however, the failure of the census to report by subcaste rather than caste may have masked its existence to some degree. It is known to have continued in local areas until a generation or so ago, and there is much indirect evidence that it still persists.

India remains today (with Pakistan and China) one of the three modern nations with the greatest excess of males, and this masculinity has been increasing since the turn of the century (from 103:100 in 1901 to 107:100 in 1971). This distortion can probably be explained by the operation of preferential female infanticide or aggressive neglect, and indeed Risley (1915:175–178) reported an increase in aggressive neglect of female children in the 1880s and 1890s as a consequence of the infanticide campaigns. Gould (1960:487) attributed a sex ratio of 166:100 in an Uttar Pradesh community in the 1950s to aggressive neglect. This explanation is strengthened when it is recalled that high levels of disease and famine should reduce masculine excess. Moreover, the all-India census which provides the overall figure includes many areas in south India which have significant female excess, such as Kerala, Madras, and Orissa. In fact the masculinity which characterized Northern India under British rule persists today in the Punjab, Assam, Jammu and Kashmir, and West Bengal, where

III. Individual and Group Strategies

it averages around 115:100 (Desai 1969:5–9; Agarwala 1972: 45–47; Pakrasi 1964). Datta (1957) has analyzed census figures in Bengal from 1838 through 1941 and uncovered a peculiar picture of increasing femininity up to about 1881, and a consistent decline thereafter, both by district and religion. Migration does not seem to be involved, and Datta can offer no explanation: the chronological concordance with the impact of the Infanticide Act as analyzed by Pakrasi is suggestive. Likewise, an unexplained high sex ratio (113:100) is reported by Gustafson (1969) for Karachi Parsis.

The geographic cline in masculinity in India-Pakistan has persisted for seven generations and probably far longer. It correlates with a shift from patrilineal systems in the north to more frequent matrilineal systems in the south. The latter has generally been explained primarily in historical terms, as a reflection of differing cultural traditions in North and South. Yet the geography, ecology, and political history of the Indian subcontinent suggest that an analysis of these clines in terms of social demography might be fruitful. The relationship will, however, not be simple, as systems of hypergyny with and without female infanticide occur in southern India as well, among patrilineal societies such as the Toda (sex ratio ca. 130:100 in the first decades of this century) and matrilineal groups such as the Nayar (Balfour 1885:343–345; Karve 1965:285 ff.; Pakrasi 1964; Pakrasi 1970c:270; Mandelbaum 1970 (1):238–239).

In the context of these observations on the demography of modern India, a historical note may be made. As Pakrasi (1970) has indicated, it was Risley, in the Census of India, 1901, who first identified the relationship between hypergyny and female infanticide in India. He proposed:

> *Husbands are at a premium in the upper groups and become the object of vigorous competition . . . [T]he rich get their daughters married above their proper rank, poorer people are driven to reckless borrowing or in the last resort to other means if they would avoid the disgrace of letting their daughters grow up unmarried. There are unhappily several ways . . . [of] putting artificially straight what has been artificially made crooked. One approved way is for the parents to kill, or to make no attempt to keep alive, all female infants except those for whom they can make sure of finding husbands [quoted in Pakrasi 1970c:273].*

Risley's great early survey, *The People of India* (1915:163–181), contained an extensive discussion of the interaction between hypergyny,

13. Female Infanticide, Reproductive Strategies, and Social Stratification   339

dowry, and female infanticide, and Rivers followed Risley in an essay describing

> some of the consequences which necessarily result from the action of this system. Since women of the highest group can only marry men of their own rank, women of high rank will either remain unmarried or the inequality must be redressed in some manner, as by the practice of polygyny, or by means of female infanticide, and as a matter of fact both these practices are widely associated with hypergamy. On the other hand, since men of the lowest grade may only marry women of their own rank, while women of this rank are taken by men of the higher groups, there will be a shortage of women in place of the excess of the highest rank [1921:11–12].

In spite of these clear statements of the essentials of the system, reference to female infanticide disappears almost completely from the anthropological literature after about 1920. Although Mandelbaum (1970 (1):106–107) notes the correlation between dowry and hypergyny, contrasting with the occurrence of brideprice where women are scarce and have greater economic importance, he does not mention infanticide in this connection. Exceptions to this statement are both rare and recent (cf. Minturn and Hitchcock 1966:58; Jacobson 1974:112–113). And this in spite of the fact that the same cases (castes) which early sources established as notorious for infanticide are cited over and over again in recent discussions of hypergyny, and in spite of the fact that the same chain of primary and secondary sources is employed by modern authors, from Risley and Rivers through Blunt (1931) and Hutton (1963) down to modern surveys such as that of Karve (1965). Indeed, by the early twentieth century, obscure genetic theories were offered to explain the persistent masculinity of North Indian upper-status groups (Risley 1915:177–178), and it was these that were perpetuated (cf. Hutton 1963:131–132, first edition, 1946).

I believe there is a moral here for anthropology. While avoidance of this subject in the literature may in part be an expression of sympathy for the embarrassment of a modern nation about a practice which its former colonial rulers abhorred, it would appear to me more central that the neglect of infanticide in anthropological literature occurred at the time when the field was becoming a profession, self-defined as defender and spokesman for the embattled "primitive." Neglect of this subject parallels the neglect of such practices as cannibalism, wife capture, and even warfare, similarly abhorrent to most Westerners, and similarly relevant to an accurate definition of our species. Recent attention to all these behaviors suggests the growth of a less ethnocentric and less romantic perspective in the discipline.

Traditional China

Extensive female infanticide in Imperial China is attested by Western and Chinese reports. While earlier census data are unreliable, nineteenth-century surveys report childhood sex ratios up to 430:100, and adult ratios of almost 200:100 as late as the 1870s (Ho 1959:8–62; Lamson 1935:560–562). A Roman Catholic foundling hospital in Peking collected over 8000 abandoned infants from the streets in the decade 1871–81 (Fielde 1887:23). Highest frequencies of infanticide among the peasantry occurred where there was greatest rural poverty and tenancy, especially in the lower Yangtze River Valley, Amoy, and Fukien. In these areas, women seldom allowed more than two daughters to live (Geddes 1963:15–17; Ho 1959:217ff.; Smith 1899:259; Nevius 1869:205). Fielde (1887:19–26) interviewed 40 postparous Swatow women who had destroyed 28 daughters out of 183 male and 175 female livebirths; other combined small postparous samples from various regions totaled 160 women who had borne 631 sons and 538 daughters; 360 sons (60 percent) had survived to ten years of age, but only 205 daughters (ca. 38 percent). No male children had ever been destroyed, but 158 daughters had admittedly been killed, a figure probably "considerably below the truth," even at a time when foundling homes were beginning to provide an alternative. Nineteenth-century surveys of Amoy gave average rates of removal of 30–40 percent of female livebirths for the province as a whole, village frequencies ranging from 10–80 percent (Smith 1899:308–309; Gordon Cumming 1900:134–137, 272–276; Martin 1847:48–49). In a Yangtze River farming village in the 1930s, infanticide was practiced primarily but not exclusively against females, resulting in a sex ratio of 135:100 in the 0–6 years cohort (Fei 1939:33–34, 51–52). In this area and elsewhere, the practice persisted into the twentieth century with ratios as high as 375:100 in the first year of life (Geddes 1963:12–17; Lang 1946:150–151).

At least in some areas, the practice was less common in towns, or perhaps urban frequencies were offset by the immigration of rural females; in any case, urban sex ratios sometimes showed a female excess (Fei 1939: 33–34, 52–53; Lang 1946:151; Nevius 1869:205). Female infanticide was not limited to peasants, however, but occurred among the wealthy in the seventeenth through nineteenth centuries as a result of concern over dowries

(Ho 1959:60; Nevius 1869:207). A serious deficiency in my Chinese sources is a lack of data on the intensity of infanticide in the gentry.

As in India, female infanticide occurred in the context of hypergyny and dowry, both marital ideals. A Chinese axiom states, "the family of the married daughter holds its head down, while the family of the man whom she has married holds its head up" (Smith 1899:286), and a clan history of a Hopei village family advises, "in promising a daughter in marriage, one should see that her future husband's family is superior" (Gamble 1963:245–246). In Shantung, "frequently the girl's family is of poorer social and economic status" (Yang 1965:106), while on Taiwan, families "seldom take a daughter-in-law from a family whose social status is higher than their own" (A. P. Wolf 1968:70, footnote). In a Yangtze River village, hypergyny and hypogyny were referred to as "going uphill" and "going downhill"; the former was associated with family prosperity, the latter with ruin. Repeated matrilineal cross-cousin marriage was the ideal here (Fei 1939:51–52; Geddes 1963:28–29), as in other provinces (Fried 1953:64; Hsu 1967:80–82). Among the very poor, however, where women played important agricultural and other laboring roles, there is no mention of hypergyny (Fei and Chang 1945:65–66, 30–32, 62–63). Among the upper classes the extent of hypergyny is unclear, although it is known to have served as an expression of fealty in feudal China (Ch'u 1965:154) and the continuing role of familism in creating alliances and preferment is well known. Whether hypergyny and female infanticide operated significantly among the gentry is a question critical to the development of this model, as this class was not entirely dependent upon landholding for economic and political influence, being both more meritocratic and probably more socially mobile than its peasant subordinates. Unfortunately, this question cannot be answered from my sources. Nevertheless, some correlation between social status and dowry is apparent, as in India. Many sources agree that brideprice prevailed among the poor and in south China, and Lang states that middle and upper classes never paid brideprice but provided dowry (Lang 1946:37, 126–27; Smith 1899:27–71); this, however, seems not to apply to the urban mercantile class (Hsu 1967:65–74, 84–103). That dowry was the elite ideal is well demonstrated by the fact that it was this portion of the marital exchange which was publicly displayed, not the groom's gifts (Ball 1903:421), in almost all regions. Throughout China, social fictions resulted in covert adjustments of the relative payments of each family to the social status of the parties, so that de facto net payment had no necessary relation to public display. Thus, "brideprice" was regularly devoted to the purchase of mobile wealth which was returned to the groom's family as "dowry," along with an equivalent or greater amount contributed by the bride's family.[12] For the latter family to retain a portion of the "brideprice" for its own use was cause for shame (Fei 1939:43–53, 123, 133; Nevius 1869:207; Diamond 1969:51–59; Lang 1946:37; Yang 1965:108–109). But in adverse conditions, as during a depression, and in the lowest laboring class, reduction in the contribution of the woman's family could result in the payment of net brideprice. Cases from two Yunnan villages reported by Fei and Chang (1945:102, 110, 256–259) are exemplary: a middle-class marriage in a village of moderate economic health involved net outlay by the groom's family of $1205, as compared to $4195 by the bride's. Among peasant landowners, the average bride's family spent $30 to $60 on dowry, but transactions of landless laborers consisted, in one case, of $180 and food gifts from the groom, and in another of a hen, also from the groom's family. Studies of twentieth-century Chinese communities on Taiwan do not always show this correlation between socioeconomic status, hypergyny, and flow of marriage wealth. Although I suspect that effects of modern urbanism are involved, I make no attempt here to unravel the Taiwanese systems (A. P. Wolf 1966, 1968; Ahern 1974).

As in India, alternative forms of low-status marriage existed. Most common was adoptive-bride marriage, in which a female child as young as three years was purchased for minimal brideprice, and reared in the groom's family until of marriage age, wedding ceremony and dowry being entirely dispensed with. Although a variant seems to occur among wealthy families of north Taiwan, mainland sources are unanimous in describing this form as motivated by poverty, often despised and abandoned when economic conditions improved, as witness Mao Tse-Tung's "a poor man who doesn't have a *tung-yang-hsi* (adoptive bride) must be satisfied with an old woman" (Fei 1939:53–55; A. P. Wolf 1966, 1968, 1970). In some cases, this form operated functionally as bride exchange (Ball 1903:419; A. P. Wolf 1968). In addition, adoptive-groom marriage was available for families lacking male heirs. As in India and Japan, the man involved in this hyperandrous marriage was of low status, either a landless laborer without inheritance, or the second son of a landed family (A. P. Wolf, 1966; Fei 1939:70–72; Fei and Chang 1945:66, 112–114; Fried 1953:113–114). While unexplained

[12] Here I place the terms "brideprice" and "dowry" within quotation marks, because close examination indicates that some of this "brideprice" in fact became "dowry" and therefore was not brideprice at all in the strict sense but an element in a circular wealth exchange.

regional variations in the frequency of this form occur, in each locale for which data are given, frequency correlated positively with declining social status (Ball 1903:424; Fei and Chang 1945:112–114, 258).

The role of hypergyny in creating complementary relations between dominant and dependent families is suggested in some sources, but in general data are weaker here than in India. Instances of favoritism and reliance on affinal kin for support in both mercantile and agricultural classes, as well as the role of the mother's brother, are provided by Fried (1953:95–96, 139–140, 154–160): in the Yangtze River village, certain affines, as well as close patrilineal relatives, have an obligation to assist in financial aid associations which have been organized by their in-laws. Sister's husband, mother's brother, and wife's father must join or find a surrogate affine. Larger kin networks provide better security against financial crises; hence the disadvantage of adoptive-bride marriage which creates no lasting affinal ties (Fei 1939:132, 267–269).

The traditional role of the mother's brother is not limited to hypergynous marriage systems. It is described in detail by Ahern (1974) for a hypogynous Taiwan community, where the flow of wealth with women to the groom's patriline and the role of mother's brother as mediator parallel Indian accounts. In the hypergynous mainland systems, the mother's brother's role involves lasting obligations to the sister's son, including provision of gifts, protection, and mediation in property division (Fei 1939:43–44, 87), but lacks the shame and distance attached to the Indian role.

Other predictable aspects of the model appear in China as well. Child betrothal and early marriage are reported in some cases as a consequence of competition for mates. The intensity of hypergyny is revealed in many accounts of well-to-do families whose crippled, insane, or idiot sons could contract marriages with healthy girls of poorer families (Smith 1899:292). In Fei's Yangtze River village (1939:40–41) arrangements were usually made when the girl was six or seven. Evidence for the upward flow of females, and for consequent shortage of wives at the very bottom of the social pyramid, is abundant. Concubinage was a functional equivalent of polygny (hence the term "small wife"), highly valued as an index of status as well as a means to assure male heirs. While concubines and their offspring might be kept within the household, some men established mistresses in separate villages or towns (Ch'u 1965:123–127; Lamson 1935: 513–518; A. P. Wolf 1966:890; Fried 1953:41). During the Han dynasty, conventions governed the number of concubines permissible for those of specific ranks (Loewe 1970:61–62). A survey by Lamson (1935:514) reveals status correlations in recent times: middle-school students from 1,781 families in Eastern China reported that from 10 to 16 percent of fathers who were military men, lawyers, businessmen, officials, and independently wealthy gentlemen had one or more concubines, but only 5 to 6 percent of fathers who were agriculturalists, educators, or physicians.

By defining second and later wives as concubines, the Chinese system excluded their offspring from the inheritance of major real estate, though not from other economic advantages; it should therefore be understood as an alternate form of primogeniture. This function is evidenced by the tolerance for legal second marriages on the part of men who were heirs to two family estates (Ch'u 1965:124). Concubines were drawn from the families of the poorest commoners, and from the ranks of bondservants, prostitutes, entertainers and slaves, thus providing an important means of upward mobility for the landless peasantry and for those outcaste groups (so-called "mean people") below commoner status. While the concubine's status within her mate's household was often no better than that of a servant, her increased security and wealth as compared to those of alternate available roles must surely have enhanced her reproductive success on the average (Ch'u 1965:125).

In addition, pawned or bound servants and slaves were held in great numbers in upper-status households. While many were men, the predominance was clearly female: edicts against child slavery from the 1920s and '30s refer only to "slave-girls" (Lamson 1935:564–566). In the nineteenth century a wealthy household might have held thirty or more such servants and slaves, many of whom would later become wives and concubines of the master's sons and retainers, since both law and custom encouraged the marrying off of dependents and their replacement with new youthful labor, thus ensuring a continuous flow of members of the lowest socioeconomic groups through wealthy households.

For the very poor, sale of children, especially daughters, and in extreme cases even wives, was an alternative to infanticide. Sales of women to become concubines, courtesans, prostitutes, bondservants, or slaves occurred most frequently in those poorer provinces where both female infanticide and oppressive landlordism were intense (Martin 1847:46–48; Nevius 1869:206, 209–213; Lamson 1935:497, 562–563; Smith 1899:259, 295–296, 307). Kidnapping of young women and wives for sale suggests the existence of a regularized traffic (Smith 1899:292–295). While slaves were forbidden to commoners during the Ming dynasty, in fact the practice was widespread. In addition, the government held large numbers of its own and awarded them to nobles and officials. One source of government slaves was the families of condemned criminals, regularly enslaved during the Ming and Ch'ing dynasties (Ch'u 1965:188; for a discussion of categories of slaves see Ch'u 1965:159). Fielde (1887:24–25) describes the peddling of babies from foundling homes by hawkers; the description suggests that these new institutions had lowered the price of female slaves.

The degree to which clustering of lower-status females in the households of high-status males implied reproductive control cannot be determined exactly. However, legal sources make clear the master's right of sexual access to his female slaves, their daughters, and (until 1673) the wives of his male servants and slaves, through at least four dynasties of Chinese history. In contrast, reverse relations often resulted in death for the male slave, and sometimes for the guilty wife or concubine as well (Ch'u 1965:66, 199). By Ch'ing times officials could no longer marry prostitutes or female entertainers, although the latter remained an important source of concubines. Commoners, however, could do so, while in contrast no male member of the entertainer class could marry a commoner female. Hypergamy was an escape from the "mean" outcaste group apparently only available to females (Lamson 1935:447, 518–522; Ch'u 1965:161; Fried 1953:42; A. P. Wolf 1966:889).

The consequent shortage of spouses for the very poorest males, and resultant high rate of bachelorhood, is not surprising. In every village and town there were bachelors too poor to marry, many of them laborers and coolies (Lang 1946:39, 127). Not a single woman over 25 in Fei's Yangtze River village remained unmarried, while 43 men over that age were still single (Fei 1939:52). In Gamble's Hopei county study, out of 5255 families there remained only 5 unmarried females over 21 years of age, but 1177 males, or 13.7 percent of those over 21 (Gamble 1954:7). Unfortunately, no status correlations are given. In Anhui province, many beggars, itinerant workers, poor farm laborers and hired hands, as well as some few shop clerks, artisan's apprentices and government workers, remained too poor to marry (Fried 1953:66–67). In the south, where the percentage of landless peasants and hired laborers was highest, "wandering souls" lived a hand-to-mouth existence with no prospect of marriage. In both north and south, de facto primogeniture operated among poor landed peasants, second and later sons being ejected to find roles as artisans and shop clerks, if fortunate, or as servants and in the military. In Yunnan, the poorest families sent their excess sons into the army, police, peddling, coolie and agricultural labor, or into child labor in the mines, where life expectancy was short (Fei 1939:178–179, 183; Fei and Chang 1945:58–60, 266–276; Fried

1953:63, 66–67, 166). Reproductive success of low status males was reduced not only by lifelong celibacy, but by delayed and intermittent sexual access. Demand for brideprice in the lowest social levels functioned to delay entry into marriage, relative to higher-status males; on the average this delay meant a female partner of reduced reproductive potential as well, as increasing numbers of widows, older women, and those with severe physical disabilities were paired in late marriages. Likewise, many of the roles open to the poor male imposed long periods of isolation from the spouse or from other females (Fried 1953:43–44, 114, 154–156), a factor of significance given the positive correlation between frequency of intercourse and rates of conception (Nag 1972:231–233). As in other stratified societies, criminal sanctions must have operated differentially against lower-status males. Legal mortalities must have been high, banishment to the poorer and marginal provinces was common, while official connections made possible more lenient treatment. Slavery and banishment were imposed on the immediate families of criminals (Ch'u 1965:15–127, 187; Loewe 1970:68); during the Ch'ing dynasty, male relatives of rebels were killed if over sixteen years, or castrated and taken into imperial service if under that age (Martin 1847:48).

In some cases, downward mobility resulted in outcasting. Bound servants unable to redeem themselves at termination of their contracts fell into permanent slavery. While some outcaste groups were closed breeding populations, many were rather statuses of downward mobility, upon which many legal disabilities fell. (For invaluable discussion of outcaste groups, see Ch'u 1965:128–200.) I am unable so far to estimate the role of warfare in male mortalities. Banditry was apparently a fact of life, drawing members from the dispossessed and disaffected. The army, however, seems not to have played a significant role; during most of this period it was small and composed primarily of married men and a rotating levy of draftees (Loewe 1970:75–87; Martin 1847:116–121).

While female seclusion was, as in India, correlated with social rank, the means by which it was achieved differed. Enforced segregation from men, for example while eating, and use of the sedan chair when traveling, were status-linked, contrasting with the regular outdoor labor and cross-sexual interactions of farm women, artisans' wives, slavegirls, beggars, and entertainers. Yet the imposition of seclusion was by all accounts less extreme than in the North Indian case (Fielde 1887:2–3; Ball 1903:762–767). Rather, the custom of footbinding served to impose on women both the restriction of movement and of productive capacity (Lang 1946:45–46) and served simultaneously as a central mark of a woman's social status, as did purdah in India. Granting regional differences in the practice, in most areas women of agricultural and other manual laboring classes and castes did not bind their feet (Davin 1975:248). Both Fielde and Nevius make clear that the correlation involved not only the presence but the intensity of the practice, as measured by the age at which it was begun and the degree of reduction in the size of the foot. Well-to-do women's tightly bound feet prevented them from walking more than a few steps at a time; they were carried for moderate distances by natural-footed slave women. Middle-class women, with feet less tightly bound, might walk several miles, while many rural women with natural feet dressed them to appear bound only when attending festivals or in town. Female slaves and bondservants were in general possessed of natural feet (Fielde 1887:27–32; Nevius 1869: 201–203; A. P. Wolf 1975:98–99); indeed certain outcaste groups were legally barred from footbinding (Ch'u 1965:130). The differential mortality and productivity thus enforced were clearly dependent on the number of servants which the household was able to employ (Fried 1953:44–45).

As in India, many upper- and middle-class women were removed from reproduction early in life. The universal cultural ideal was that widows never remarried. According to Fielde (1887:5) none did so if they had the property necessary to support themselves. The poor did so but with a loss of status (Martin 1847:39; Lang 1946:52–53, 126; Hsu 1967: 103–104; Yang 1965: 117–118). Laws restricting remarriage only to certain relatives of the deceased applied to concubines as well as formal wives Ch'u 1965:96–97) and even betrothed girls widowed before marriage often completed the marriage ceremony and lived as celibate members of the deceased's family (Ball 1903:765). Fried (1953:45–46) describes the positive correlation between social class and attitude toward remarriage in his Anhui study. In remarrying, the widow would generally be taken only by a very poor or an elderly man. Needless to add, these restrictions did not apply to males. In Gamble's county survey (Gamble 1954:38), 61 percent of the men who had been widowed had remarried, but only 14 percent of the widowed women.

Sati of widows was likewise considered virtuous, even for the widowed fiancée, and was a regular imperial practice until the eighteenth century (Douglas 1901:227; Gordon Cumming 1900:441). The practice was most common among young widows of the gentry class, who might have stone memorials erected in their honor by the government (Ball 1903:766; M. Wolf 1975:111). In addition, religious celibacy played a greater role than in India. Buddhist and Taoist nunneries existed in great numbers, as did other sectarian institutions for celibate laymen in some areas

(Douglas 1901:214; Gordon Cumming 1900:327–328). They seem to have been especially common in Swatow and Kwangtung: Fielde (1887:72–74) reports for Swatow, "one may see a dozen nunneries within a day's journey; and in one forenoon I visited three nunneries, having a hundred nuns in them," while Topley (1975:67–68) describes the "vegetarian halls" common in some parts of Kwangtung during the last century. The Swatow nuns replicated themselves by the purchase of female orphans two or three years old, each nun supporting as many as possible. Fielde reports that their lives were easy compared to those of the peasantry. While I have no data on social class origins, it is clear that female monasticism in China would repay further study.

In addition to religious celibacy, other forms existed, involving formal vows never to marry. Topley (1975:67–88) has analyzed in detail these customary forms of celibacy among girls in the silk-producing regions of Kwangtung during the last two centuries. Here the importance of female labor was intensified by the growth of silk factories in the last century: both infanticide and footbinding were less frequent in the area, and not only Buddhist nunneries but also semisecret sisterhoods became common. The high value on celibacy and consequent lower birth rate in this area, relative to other regions, persist to this day.

Suicide of both unmarried and young married women removed significant numbers from the breeding population in China.[13] In many places, the semi-clandestine sisterhoods which vowed never to marry preserved their vows through individual or mass suicide; the rate of suicide among wives was also high (Douglas 1901:214–215; Smith 1899:287–309; Ball 1903:427–429; Fielde 1887:7–8). M Wolf (1975:111–141) has analyzed in detail available data on female suicide rates in Taiwan and China. Modern Taiwanese rates are still as high as 25 per 100,000 in some areas, equaling or exceeding those of males, and peaking in the 20–24 age group. This accords well with anecdotal and journalistic accounts from nineteenth-century mainland China. Wolf's study also provides some support for the assumption that such suicide was status-correlated, which the model would predict. She predicts that the psychological pressures of various forms of marriage would lead to a greater frequency of female suicide in major marriages rather than in the low-status alternatives reviewed above. Indeed,

[13] As in the case of prohibitions against widow remarriage, the apparent correlation of intensity of female suicide with status agrees with the structural model presented here. However, its benefit either to the kin of the suicide or to the spouse and his patriline is unclear, unless it resulted in the acquisition of additional dowry (when the widower remarried) for a family who could not afford to support a secondary wife.

the rates among Hakka-speaking women, members of a low-status minority group whose women engaged in construction labor, never bound their feet, and retained significant economic independence after marriage, are predictably lower (e.g., Taiwan, 1905: Hokkien-speaking: 21.5 per 100,000 vs. Hakka-speaking: 6.5 per 100,000).

In summary, while Chinese sources suffer from overconcentration on the peasantry and neglect of the gentry and the landless poor, there seems to be a general conformity to the hypergynous model proposed—at least within the peasantry and probably beyond it. Undoubtedly, sources in Chinese could expand both the social coverage and the time depth of this survey.

Western Europe

Lastly, historical data from medieval and early modern Western Europe suggest the existence of a variant of the model proposed above. That infanticide was practiced in Europe continuously from Greco-Roman times to the 1870s is now well known. (See reviews in Langer 1972, 1974; and Kellum 1974). Massive infant abandonment encouraged the growth of rural wet-nursing ("baby farms"), foundling institutions, and ecclesiastical and legal obsession with the crimes of infanticide and overlaying (smothering in the parental bed), especially in the later Middle Ages and Renaissance. In England, Parliament began investigations in the 1870s, at the very time when legislation was enacted against infanticide in British India (cf. Ryan 1862). We may ask, then, to what degree the European practice was preferentially female, and whether there is indication of its relation to hypergynous marriage systems.

Evidence for preferential removal of females is strong enough to have convinced several demographers, and comes from all periods down to the eighteenth century. Medieval British data analyzed by Russell show normal adult sex ratios until the mid-thirteenth century, rising during the fourteenth to a high of 133:100, when the Great Plague epidemic equalized them again, thereafter rising again during the fifteenth century. These figures refer to landholding members of the population; one sample of serfs maintained a ratio of 170:100 even during the plague years (Russell 1948:167–168). Scattered sex ratios from villages and towns in France and Germany in the eighth and ninth centuries range from 107 to 132 males per 100 females (Russell 1958:13–15). Such figures refer to adult or to total populations, however, and consequently do not allow the separation of preferential female infanticide from other relevant variables, especially differential migration, hypergyny, and differential mortality. The great masculinity of serf ratios, which occurs in several samples, is most likely the result of a high proportion of bachelor males in this lowest-status group, as much as or more than the product of female infanticide.

Recently, however, historical demographers have begun analyses of census data by age and social status, which allow for a better understanding of distortions in sex ratios. A census of eighth-century dependents of the monastery of Farfa, Italy, yields a "scarcely creditable" childhood sex ratio of 135:100, and an adult ratio (excluding landless slaves) of 112, producing an overall ratio of 122 (Herlihy 1975:6). On the other hand, the Carolingian dependents of the monastery of St. Victor, Marseilles, had a childhood ratio of 93.4, but an adult ratio of 102:100. While Herlihy (1975:7) sees this shift in ratios as a product of greater female mortality after infancy, he concedes that female children especially "seem to be underreported in most Carolingian surveys."

A more detailed study of the ninth-century dependents of the Abbey of Saint-Germain-des-Prés, near Paris (Coleman 1976), reveals that the greater the amount of arable land, or the larger the total population of the *manse* (dependent farm unit), the more depressed the sex ratio. However, a greater number of individuals per household correlates with a higher sex ratio (with the exception of single-person households). Again, these overall ratios do not allow the identification of female emigration or male immigration as factors. Some distortion is, as Coleman says, the product of a high incidence of bachelors on the smallest farms, as is probably the case with Russell's plague-year serf ratios cited above. In addition, since some of the adult sex ratios of the estates censused are higher than the total child/adult ratios (average adult sex ratio 127:100 [range 110–253]; total ratio 136 [range 116–156]), other factors besides female infanticide are clearly operative. However, Coleman reviews the historical and literary evidence for the practice during the early Middle Ages, and concludes that it is implicated in the childhood distortions.

While Coleman demonstrates a positive correlation between number of children and amount of arable land, the sex ratios show a more complicated relationship. The negative correlation between childhood sex ratio and *manse* population, which is stronger than that between adult ratio and total *manse* population, is a product of the inclusion of two- and three-person farms. Excluding these, a more interesting picture emerges, of similar children's ratios at both ends of the population size continuum (4 persons per *manse*: childhood ratio 136.5; 19 per *manse* and over: 134), with the lowest ratio falling slightly above the median (15 per *manse*: ratio 103). The same curvilinear relationship occurs in the adult sex ratio as well, as it does in Coleman's chart of total and childhood sex ratios by amount of *manse* arable (*manse* arable 1 *bunuarium*: childhood ratio 128; 17 *bu.*: 107; 22 *bu.* and over: 170). Such correlations suggest the combined operation of high bachelorhood on the very smallest farms, and female emigration, hypergyny, and female infanticide, both on poor and on the very largest, presumably most prosperous, farms. Elsewhere, Coleman (1973) has reported the sex ratios of this census by social class. Among *servi* (slaves) it was 297, while among *coloni* (free tenants) it was 117.

Five hundred years later, Renaissance Florentine sex ratios have the same character. In 1427, the city's overall sex ratio was 114:100 (for infants, 118:100), while the dominion as a whole had a ratio of 119:100. Thus the specifically rural ratio must have been even higher. However, the city's wealthy class had a ratio of 124:100 (Trexler 1973a:100–101). Slightly different computations from the same census (Herlihy 1975) give sex ratios for the city and county of Florence (excluding much of the rural dominion) of 124.5 for infants 0–4 years old, but a decline to 105 by the age group 53–57. This census does not include any clergy of either sex, however. An even higher ratio, 162:100, is reported for the offspring of the French nobility in the late Middle Ages (Russell 1958:19). Thus it appears that high masculinity may have widely characterized both ends of the social scale in medieval and Renaissance Europe.

While these suggestions of class differentials in sex ratio are local and meager, and do not tell us the degree to which preferential female infanticide was involved, some other demographic data suggest the means by which distortions in sex ratio were achieved. Demographers have long recognized that a high rate of female celibacy is a component of the specifically European demographic pattern. Thus, up to 1900, while fewer than 5 percent of females remained unmarried at age 50 in Eastern Europe, from 10 to 20 percent did so in the West (Hajnal 1965:101–104). This high rate of celibacy combines with a significant percentage of widows to produce female excesses which, while not restricted to cities, occur first in urban censuses. For example, tax data from England in 1377 reveal a correlation between size of place and degree of sex-ratio distortion, ranging from 111:100 for places of 25 or fewer inhabitants to 93–95:100 for those over 1000 population. This correlation is offset only by higher masculinity in parts of the boroughs of London, Oxford, Rochester, and York (Russell 1948:149–156; 1958:17). Urban populations on the continent, especially in northern Europe, also show consistent distortions in favor of females as early as the fourteenth century. The 1449 Nürnberg census reveals a female surplus in both burgher and servant classes, resulting in a total sex ratio of 88:100, contrasting with 109 for the surrounding countryside (Russell 1958:16–17). Zürich censuses from the fourteenth, fifteenth, and seventeenth centuries reveal an excess of single and widowed women, especially the former. Female surpluses also occurred in Frankfurt and Basle during the Middle Ages (Hajnal 1965:117, 124), and at Rheims, Freiburg, Bologna, and elsewhere during the fourteenth century (Herlihy 1975:12–13, 20). Herlihy attributes these feminine sex ratios to increasing female life expectancy in urban environments after the eleventh century, but it is clear that other factors were operative as well.

From the late Middle Ages onward, cities drew large numbers of females from the countryside, as slaves, servants and laborers. By the twelfth century, agrarian slavery had largely disappeared except in a few Mediterranean regions. Where slaves occurred, they were primarily domestic servants and concubines, attached to manors or urban households (Bloch 1966:94–95). Women outnumbered men by over three to one as household manorial slaves in Carolingian Farfa (Herlihy 1975:7). Most of the black slaves employed in sixteenth-century Seville and Lisbon were female household servants and nursemaids. Down to the eighteenth century, significant numbers of rural and small-town women were absorbed into upper-class households in these cities as domestics and wet-nurses, "for seldom did upper class females nurse their children" (Pescatello 1976:26, 30). Celibacy was almost always enjoined upon these females. Their presence in the homes and on the estates of the well-to-do contributed to a distinctly European reproductive complex (Langer 1974:357; Pescatello 1976:30): rather than engaging in formal polygyny, their employers sired large numbers of illegitimates by them, who were in some cases reared in the homes of their fathers, but more often destroyed, abandoned, or placed to wet-nurses in the country or in foundling homes, where early mortality for most was assured. In addition, the demand for wet-nurses caused poor country women to destroy their own offspring. Thus in both city and country responsibility for the removal of infants was passed in large part to the lower class. Trexler's (1973a, 1973b) impressive analysis of fourteenth- and fifteenth-century Florentine data makes clear that females were disproportionately destroyed in almost all decades by both wet-nursing and foundling care.

The female excess in urban European populations was not, however, limited to the lower classes. Perhaps the most distinctive feature of West European demographic structure is the development of female celibacy as an alternative to preferential female infanticide in the middle and upper classes. An increase in the number of celibate females in ruling families is identifiable in Geneva where, by 1650, 25 percent of females over 50 years had remained single (Hajnal 1965:114; Henry 1965:452–453), and in the British nobility around 1650, rising to 20 percent in both sexes at age 50 among those born from 1830 to 1879 (Hollingsworth 1965:304–305; Hajnal 1965:113). Other censuses showing a high rate of female celibacy are the Zürich censuses from three centuries referred to above, and those from certain regions of France in the eighteenth and nineteenth centuries (Hajnal 1965:114–117; Henry 1965:452–453).

One factor permitting the preservation of females was the greater number of economic opportunities open to them, especially in the emerging mercantile class, as compared to India and China. While, as elsewhere, lower-status women labored in field and factory alongside men (Power 1975:11), some opportunity for independent earning existed even in the artisan class. While in England guild restrictions limited female industry to wives, widows, and daughters of craftsmen, unmarried daughters were apprenticed as were sons, and could continue in crafts and trades as single women. Power provides a long list of the crafts engaged in by women. On the continent, women were in some cases organized into all-female guilds, and in others participated as members equally with men (Power 1922:5; 1975:53–65).

Paralleling the opportunity for independent female labor was the right of women to control land in their own names, whether as free tenants or serfs, or as members of the gentry and nobility, to administer it in the deceased or absent husband's name, and to transmit it through testament (Power 1975:71). While the degree of independent control varied from region to region, landowning and mercantile classes often gave to the woman control over all or some portion of the dowry, whether land or mobile wealth, brought to the marriage, or granted her some fraction of her husband's land at his death (dower) (Power 1975:38–40). It is the regional and temporal variation in these practices in medieval and modern Europe, in contrast to the simple passage of wealth from one lineage to another in so many other patrilineal societies, which has produced such semantic confusion in regard to the concept of dowry in anthropological literature.

There were several important consequences of the economic roles for women. In the largely urban craft and burgher classes, secular celibacy was a real alternative for many women. In the nobility and gentry, marriage was the preferred state, and, as we shall see, religious celibacy the only approved alternative. But in both groups, economic independence meant a higher rate of widow survival, a higher frequency of widow remarriage, and the absence of any formal pattern of widow suicide. This is in striking contrast to India and China, where the high-status widow was essentially without role or status. Still, this difference in the fate of widows, however significant, is only a matter of degree. Postan (1975:37) reports that in England, marriage to landed widows of the villein class became increasingly common as a result of land shortages in the later thirteenth century. Even in Europe, the aristocracy was characterized by lower rates of widow remarriage than other classes. Thus, in the sixteenth century it was only one-twentieth as common among female as among male aristocrats on the continent (Peller 1965:89). It was not uncommon for a widow to take a vow of chastity, or to enter a nunnery (Power 1922:38–39). And the association of celibacy and widowhood with accusations of witchcraft in Europe as elsewhere suggests some degree of statuslessness for widows there.

If independent administration of estates was an appropriate role for widows in the landed class, for the young woman the only accepted alternative to marriage was the nunnery. The contribution of the clergy to rates of celibacy in Western Europe has long been a matter of dispute. While its importance has been dismissed by some on the basis of its low proportion to the total population, this overlooks its significance in relation to specific classes. Coulton (1949:265–266) estimates that there were about 8,000 priests, monks, and nuns in Tudor England out of a total population of four and a half million, increasing to about 12,000 by A.D. 1200. Russell (1948:162) states that in 1086, perhaps half of the "more substantial class" in England was in the clergy. There were always more male than female members, and they were drawn from a wider spectrum of society. While free tenants (villeins) could send their sons to monasteries on payment of a fine to the lord, this was not the practice with daughters, whose only association could be as lay sisters or servants attached to a nunnery.

The means by which this class discrimination in female access to the religious life was enforced was the dowry. In spite of long-continued opposition by the Church, both in England and on the Continent, dowry was demanded as a condition of entry. In consequence, entry was restricted to members of the nobility, landed gentry, and increasingly from the fourteenth century onward, the upper mercantile class. The analysis of wills makes clear the parallel of religious to marital transaction: fathers granted a dowry to surviving daughters for use either in marriage or to enter religious life. However, since the dowry demanded by the nunnery was less than that required to achieve an acceptable marriage, it was excess daughters, beyond the financial capacity of the father to marry them, who were regularly sent during the father's lifetime. Often, a single nunnery received several members of a noble family from several generations, thus replicating the patron-client relationship of asymmetric marriage systems. Nor did the parallel end there. New entrants often brought with them mobile property for their support, including furniture, linens, plate, jewelry, and utensils. Continuing gifts to the nun or her house, and wills providing annuities or other grants from her family members, were common (Chojnacki 1976:176; Hajnal 1965:118; Henry 1965:452; Pescatello 1976:25; Power 1922:4–24, 324–327, 658–660, 674).

The role of the Church as a "dumping-ground" for excess daughters evolved in parallel with the growth of the feudal manorial system after the Carolingian era, and with it the institutionalization of dowry, patriliny, and primogeniture. Until about the eleventh century, nunneries served primarily as refuges for widows and women divorced by their noble husbands, sometimes accompanied by their daughters. After that period, young girls began to enter independently, with dowries. During the late twelfth and early thirteenth centuries, large numbers of women, primarily of noble origin, formed voluntary religious associations, vowing chastity and poverty, or petitioned for attachment to masculine orders. There was intense opposition by the Church to the recognition of female orders under vow of poverty—vows which necessitated refusal by such orders of property for their support. In spite of its opposition to the dowry per se, the Church never opposed secular donations to its houses. The Church's position on this issue reveals clearly its intent to ensure that female celibacy remain an upper-class institution. The appearance of this largely spontaneous movement of women into religious life, increasingly urban after 1200, has been seen as a result of the increasing emphasis on primogeniture, competition for large dowries, and consequent loss of female status, in short, increasing feudalization of the upper classes during this period (Bolton 1976; Brownrigg, personal communication). By 1350, Power (1975:89) estimates, there were 3,500 nuns in England. On the continent there were surely over 10,000. What proportion of the upper class this represented is not clear, but the analysis of wills suggests that a significant number of females from large families were included (Power 1922:14–15). Trexler (1973b:262) maintains that nunneries came to replace infanticide as a means of disposal of upper-class females in fifteenth- and sixteenth-century Florence: in consequence, 13 percent of the city's females were religious celibates by the sixteenth century.

Not only were girls vowed to a religious life in infancy, entering the nunneries as early as seven years of age, or more commonly in the early teens (thus paralleling the early marriage of the upper classes), but in addition, nunneries served as refuges for other unwanted females from the upper class: widows, young girls escaping marriage, orphans whose patrimonies were coveted by their relatives, wives and daughters of defeated enemies of kings, old concubines, illegitimate daughters of nobles and clergy, and the disabled and mentally defective. Lay boarders, temporary and permanent, were attached to the nunneries as pensioners or temporary refugees: illegitimates, concubines, and widows of the king's dependents, though not all of these were women (Power 1922:25–40, 189–198). The overcrowding of late medieval nunneries as upper-class welfare institutions is not surprising.

This pattern of disposal of females among the landed classes is accompanied by other demographic practices which would be anticipated from previous cases. Among the French aristocracy rates of male celibacy remained higher than those of the French population as a whole down to the eighteenth century (17 to 27 percent of males over 50 as opposed to 10 percent for the general population). (Unfortunately there are no comparable figures for the female nobility). Hollingsworth's study (1965:304–305) of British ducal families also reveals far higher rates of celibacy for younger sons (29 percent of those born from 1680 to 1828 at age 50, as contrasted with only 10 percent of eldest sons at the same age). Large numbers of males were removed through violent death from warfare (including the Crusades), civil disturbances, and treason. In Hollingsworth's ducal male cohort born from 1330 to 1479, 46 percent of all males dying over the age of 15 suffered violent deaths. This figure declined during succeeding eras but rose again to 48 percent for the cohort born from 1880–1939. In consequence, survivorship curves do not approach equality with those of females until the cohort enters its forties (Hollingsworth 1965:358–362), a pattern not unfamiliar to ethnographers. This pattern is replicated on the continent, with far higher violent mortalities for celibates than for married males. Thus the rate of violent death of the bachelor nobility, aged 25–29, for all cohorts from the sixteenth to nineteenth century was 203 per thousand (Peller 1965:94–95). My sources provide only hints regarding the fates of low-ranking males: the high rate of bachelorhood among serfs and their exclusion from religious orders, the large numbers of monks, friars, and scholars, often poor and often engaged in begging and in crime, drawn from all ranks of enfranchised society—these suggest a picture not unlike the Indian, although with more reliance on celibacy than on outcasting as a means of exclusion of excess males. Indeed, the great increase in religious, and especially mendicant, orders beginning in the twelfth century was very likely a consequence of the existence of large numbers of middle- and low-status men with reduced marital and economic opportunities.

My information on polygyny and concubinage is also less satisfactory. Polygyny was common in the upper class in the early Middle Ages, continuing among the Franks until the seventh century, but was replaced by the Carolingian period by serial monogamy and concubinage (cf. Charlemagne's five successive wives and four concubines: McNamara and Wemple 1976:98–99, 104–105; Pescatello 1976:33). Sacerdotal polygyny likewise did not entirely disappear until the ninth or tenth century, while sacerdotal monogamy continued far longer. In addition, many women were concubines of clerics and bore offspring from these unions (Brownrigg, personal communication; Herlihy 1976:20–26; Pescatello 1976:33).

In addition to the heavy reliance on celibacy, a late age at marriage (generally above 23 years) has long been cited by demographers as a component of the specifically West European demographic pattern. However, this seems to be a later phenomenon, not appearing until the fifteenth century. During the Middle Ages, child betrothal and early marriage were the rule for all classes. Marriages of those as young as eight years old occurred. The aristocracy preserved the custom of early arranged marriage longer than the urban mercantile or rural populations did; the French aristocracy, whose feudal role in local agrarian matters persisted longer, continued the custom into the eighteenth century (Hajnal 1965:116–120; Pescatello 1976:33; Power 1975:39–40; Russell 1948:148–156). Ideologically, however, the evolution of late marriage may well have been dependent upon the pre-existing tolerance for celibacy in European society.

While my sources provide little insight into the operation of hypergyny, the predicted relation between social class and type of marriage exchange occurs widely. Western Europe underwent a transition from earlier Germanic brideprice to dowry as the ideal, beginning in the sixth century and reaching completion by perhaps A.D. 1150, at the same time that dowries came to be requisite for nunnery entrance (Herlihy 1975:9, 12; Power 1922:17). Herlihy has attributed this shift to an excess of women in the later Middle Ages, but it is more likely an index of the increasingly rigid feudal structure of the second period of European feudalism. Numerous sources attest to the concern of fathers for the provision of dowries, lest their daughters be socially degraded (Power 1975:41), and the inflation in dowry size as a result of competition for grooms (Herlihy 1975:12, 16): the concern of fathers at the birth of baby girls clearly parallels that

III. Individual and Group Strategies

of Northern India. Trexler (1973b:262) cites high dowry as a motive for female abandonment in fourteenth-century Florence, while Chojnacki (1976) reviews attempts to control and adapt to dowry inflation in thirteenth- to fifteenth-century Venice, the product of competition for favorable marital alliances among patrician families. (See also Stuard 1976 on fourteenth- and fifteenth-century Ragusa.) Chojnacki provides interesting data on the role of the maternal kin group in providing dowries to the daughters of married sisters. With women retaining control over much of their own dowry wealth, as in the rest of Europe, not only uncles and brothers but aunts and mothers themselves were engaged in this transfer of wealth. But while the mediators in the process here include females, the outcome seems to be the same: long-term transmission of wealth from the maternal to the paternal patriline. The persistence of hypergyny associated with dowry has been documented ethnographically in several traditional local-level class structures (Anderson 1973:65; Friedl 1962:48–70; Wylie, ed., 1966:144–148, 305–306).

However, hypergyny was not universal in Europe: Coleman's analysis of ninth-century Saint-Germain-des-Prés reveals significant hyperandry (one-sixth of the married population) from the *servi* (slaves) to the *coloni* (free tenants), resulting in an increase in the proportion of higher-status *coloni* on the estates over the number of generations covered by the census, a mobility made possible by the inheritance of status through the mother among these low-ranking agrarian dependents. This pattern existed in conjunction with the extremely masculine sex ratio reported above. While its appearance in these low-status groups is not surprising, its magnitude may also reflect the agrarian expansion and population growth of the Carolingian period (Coleman 1973). Much later, with the rise of the burgher class, hyperandry was not unknown as a means of gaining noble status, but hypergyny was equally common (Bloch 1966:125; Pescatello 1976:24–25). I have little information on the practice of brideprice, but it persisted in some places among the lower classes, as did the outright sale of wives by the desperately poor, into the nineteenth century; indeed during the eighteenth century the market price of wives was regularly quoted in the London *Times* (Henriques 1960:194–197).

The less exact conformance of European society to the theoretical model is reflected as well in a difference in the degree of claustration and incapacitation of women. While class bias in the degree of involvement of women in active labor and in the outer, masculine world occurs here as elsewhere, medieval women of noble and gentle origin were never as enclosed as those of India and China. The lady of the manor moved freely in her own social world outside the bounds of her own estates, carried in a palanquin perhaps, but with face unveiled. Her physical competence included riding and hawking (Power 1975; Herlihy 1976). Within the religious domain, claustration was an ideal often honored in the breach. While chastity, the veil, and claustration are elsewhere imposed on secular women, here they were difficult to impose even within the Church, as Power's study of English nunneries dramatically demonstrates. Gadding about the countryside on social visits and pilgrimages, attending parties, dances, and taverns, dispensing hospitality both before and after hours to noblemen and women, priests, monks and scholars, surrounded often by the luxuries to which their noble origin had accustomed them, and even in some small but not insignificant proportion engaging in illicit relations, bearing and rearing and endowing some of their illegitimate offspring: these nuns epitomize a long-standing European conflict between the feudal ideal and the realities of feminine independence. Yet this latter can be exaggerated. Surely religious claustration (and the consequent reduction in births) was far more effective against women than against men: the wandering "ecclesiastical proletariat" of friars and scholars had no feminine counterpart (Power 1922:341–474, 660–674).

Imperfect claustration was a concomitant of the greater right of women to control and administer estates, to inherit, own and earn, in noble, married clerical, burgher, and artisan classes. It has often been suggested that this enhanced female economic role (and the related feminine sex ratios) was a consequence of the loss of manorial males during the period of the Crusades, but the eleventh century is far too late to serve in a causal role, nor do these events explain its appearance in other social groups. One evidence of greater feminine self-sufficiency is the use of the matronymic in Europe, not only among the poor but in significant numbers in all social classes, as analyzed by Herlihy (1976), especially after the ninth century and reaching a peak in the eleventh century. A product of the female right to inherit and dispose of wealth, this custom reflects as well the peculiarly European frequency of, and tolerance for, illegitimacy which, though more common in the lower classes, occurred as well in the highest levels of secular and religious society (Herlihy 1976:21–23).

In summarizing those aspects of European social structure which make up a distinctive variant of the general reproductive model here proposed, it should be apparent that the differences compose, not a contrasting demographic system per se, but variation in degree and in means. The increasing emphasis on dowry in middle- and high-status groups, as a means of contracting and maintaining alliances, is as predicted. Heavy reliance on both secular and religious celibacy as a means of removing excess females from the reproductive pool serves as an alternate to preferential female infanticide, no doubt related in some way as yet unclear to the greater assignment of economic roles to women. In consequence, claustration, although still status-correlated, is far milder. The demographic expression of these differences is the frequent appearance of depressed sex ratios in European censuses. It need scarcely be noted that many aspects of this European variant persist to this day.

Two final comments, ideological and ecological, may be made on the European case. Coming to European history with a sociobiological model in mind, one is struck by the great consistency with which the Church plays its role in medieval and pre-modern society. Evolving its function as the highest-status patron in the social hierarchy, absorbing women and their familial wealth into its institutional control, its legal obsessions have been, since the early Middle Ages, predictably focused. The struggle to acquire control over the regulation of marriage, to limit polygyny, clerical marriage, divorce, adultery, infanticide, to enforce the claustration of nuns: from the Gregorian reforms to the Council of Trent and beyond, the overwhelming content of these great disputes was frankly demographic. An institution at once economic and ideological, the Church, it appears, had as its primary goal, often in conflict with other strains in European history, the regulation of reproduction in European society. Perhaps in no other case does the opportunity exist, as it does here, for historical demography in the largest sense to unravel the role of ideological institutions in the evolution and maintenance of human demographic structures.[14]

This leads, of course, to the larger question: which events, economic, military, technological, may be identified as playing causal roles in the development of the European variant outlined above? Nowhere else does the wealth of documentation, the temporal depth, the amount of previous investigation provide equal opportunity to speculate on the relations between ecology, economy and demography, an opportunity to which modern historical demographers have begun to respond (see especially Bloch 1961; Bloch 1966; Postan 1975; Stuard, ed., 1976b:1–12). At the risk of violent oversimplification, some of the relations between demographic

[14] Demography in the narrow sense refers to what demographers call the "rates" and their study: natality, mortality, migration, etc. In the largest sense it has referred to the attempt to integrate those rates with theories of family structure and of economic and ecological conditions and processes. I recommend the inclusion of biological theory in this "largest sense" of demography.

13. Female Infanticide, Reproductive Strategies, and Social Stratification   361

and other events may be suggested. By the end of the Carolingian era, continental Europe, as a consequence of invasions and internal wars, was markedly depopulated. This period saw an increase in female inheritance, in the use of matronyms, and an end to secular and sacerdotal polygyny. Slow but steady growth in population resulted, beginning about A.D. 1050, in a period of demographic and economic expansion lasting through the thirteenth century. Colonization of reconquest Spain and the Slavonic plains, forest clearance and the expansion of arable lands was accompanied by rapid population increase leading by about 1300 to excess population, land hunger, and a period of recurrent famines and plagues. (The period of clearance began earlier in England, or more accurately perhaps, continued with less interruption, from the sixth to the twelfth century, resulting in overpopulation by about A.D. 1200.) A consequence of this increasing population pressure on land was the consolidation of the feudal system into its classic late medieval form, with greater judicial and economic control by the manorial lord, fewer free peasants independent of feudal ties, and the evolution of the classic forms of serfdom and vassalage as states of personal dependence. Demographic responses to these developments took predictably feudal forms. Both the growth of the masculine clergy and the Crusades served to siphon off excess males. By 1100, nunneries had acquired their classic role as a means of disposal of upper-status females. At the same time, the intensification of patron-client relations institutionalized the dowry as the acceptable form of marital exchange for middle and upper classes, both in secular and religious transfers of women. A decline in female status and increasing emphasis on patriliny occurred. The Gregorian Reforms of the eleventh century were, among other things, an attempt (not entirely successful) to establish the Church as most dominant patron in the feudal hierarchy, and to define its membership as chaste celibates, excluded from the reproductive pool.

The subsequent period of population stagnation and decline, of intermittent famines and plagues, during the fourteenth and fifteenth centuries, was nevertheless one of urban growth. As urban female excess began to appear in the fourteenth century, it was accompanied by the development of urban foundling homes and nunneries, and dowry inflation began to occur in the Renaissance communes. By the fifteenth century, rural serfdom and feudal organization were in decline, the focus of economic competition having shifted to mercantile centers. Accompanying these developments was a new burst of Church effort to regulate demographic processes.

There is no need to extend this tentative sketch further. If any validity may be attached to it, it will be apparent that European data offer a unique invitation to the study of interactions between demography, economy, and polity in diachronic terms, in short, to the understanding of both the causes and functions of human demographic systems.

Conclusion

In spite of gaps in the data reviewed above, resulting in lack of comparability and specificity, it appears that a fundamentally similar reproductive system characterized all three of the stratified societies discussed. All the traits dealt with, female infanticide or celibacy, polygynous breeding, hypergyny, status-correlated marital wealth exchange, matrilateral cross-cousin marriage, seclusion of women, are predictable from a model involving male competition for mates. However, at least some components of this system are not restricted to stratified societies. Increased interest of anthropologists and biologists in the demography of smaller, unstratified societies has provided some materials which suggest a much more widespread distribution of this reproductive system, and encourage the search for a universal human reproductive paradigm. Some of the most salient of these materials will be briefly reviewed here.

Eskimo groups have long been noted for high rates of preferential female infanticide. Although not universal, it occurred from Alaska to Greenland, producing childhood sex ratios up to 200:100. These rates were offset by heavy adult male mortalities from hunting, homicide, and suicide, resulting in most cases in parity in middle age, and sometimes a disproportion of females in older cohorts. Optional polygyny was widespread (Balikci 1967, 1970; Freeman 1971; Riches 1974; Weyer 1932). Most discussed in recent literature are the Netsilik of Canada, whose adult sex ratio was almost 150:100. Male competition over mates was here intense, with "the desire to steal a certain woman . . . the most frequent cause for attempted or successful murder" (Balikci 1970:179). Only the best hunters could afford to support more than one wife (3 out of 61 unions were polygynous in Rasmussen's 1923 census), and the shortage of women resulted in some polyandrous unions (though the status of participants is not indicated). Most females were betrothed at or soon after birth (Balikci 1970:147–179). Riches (1974) has proposed a correlation between the intensity of child betrothal and the rate of female infanticide in four Canadian Eskimo groups, including the Netsilik, as a function of increasing degrees of environmental stress.

Similar structures, involving high rates of adult male mortality, accompanied by polygyny of successful males, female infanticide, child betrothal and wife capture, have been reported for some parts of Highland New Guinea (Langness 1967; Lindenbaum 1972; Harris 1975). Many years ago, Firth and coworkers reported the existence of preferential female infanticide (maximum sex ratio of cohorts under age 27, 153:100) on Tikopia, with male and female celibacy, especially involving younger sons, and high rates of male suicide (Borrie et al. 1957; Firth 1957, 1959, 1965; Spillius 1957). (The Tikopian data are summarized in Dickeman 1975; I have not, however, reviewed these materials with reference to hypergyny).

However, the best support for the existence of the model under discussion in unstratified societies comes from recent ethnographic and demographic investigations of Amazon Basin societies (Chagnon 1968a, 1968b, 1968c, 1974; De Oliveira and Salzano 1969; Johnston et al., 1969; Neel 1969; Neel and Chagnon 1968; Neel et al. 1964; Neel and Weiss 1975; Salzano and Cardoso de Oliveira 1970; Salzano et al. 1967; Siskind 1973).[15] Among these horticulturalists, preferential female infanticide is known for the Yąnomamö and Cashinahua and suspected for the Xavante (sex ratios, 0–14 years cohort: Yąnomamö 129, Xavante 124, Peruvian Cashinahua 148). For the first two years of life, the Yąnomamö sex ratio is 140:100, with individual villages much higher. Inter- and intragroup conflict produces 24 percent of all male mortalities, concentrated in the young adult age group. Polygyny aggravates male competition over females, resulting in child betrothal and wife capture. Alliances between groups involve exchange of brides; temporarily powerless groups gain protection from more dominant ones at the cost of yielding their women to their protectors.

Most valuable in regard to demographic aspects of the model are Chagnon's (1974; and chapters 4 and 14) data on reproductive variance. Not only is polygyny concentrated within the larger, more dominant lineages, but it characterizes headmen, who tend to be members of these larger groups. Variance in male reproductive success is extreme, as revealed by census and genealogy, as a result of polygyny, serial monogamy and extramarital liaisons, in both the Yąnomamö and Xavante (Salzano et al. 1967).

In these societies lacking formal class or caste stratification, hypergyny exists only temporarily in reference to the current statuses of individual families, patrilineages and villages. Since the shifting fortunes of specific groups result in changes of status over time from predominantly wife-giving to predominantly wife-taking, hypergyny is never institutionalized. Symmetrical marriage exchange is the long-term model, and the

[15] See new interpretation by Chagnon, Flinn, and Melancon, chapter 14.

culturally phrased ideal. But that apparently symmetric system consists, on closer examination, of oscillations in a fundamentally asymmetric system, produced ultimately by male competition over mates.

In contrast, stratified societies are characterized by the crystallization of dominant-subordinate relationships. Consequently, the direction of hypergynous flow is also stabilized, and comes to be expressed, with dowry, as a cultural ideal. Upending of formerly more equable competitive relations into a stable hierarchy results in a shift to asymmetric marriage systems, as Lévi-Strauss (1969) long ago observed. Female infanticide, or celibacy if economically feasible,[16] may be intensified at the top, as is male control over mates through female seclusion, incapacitation, and differential enforcement of fidelity, and the elaboration of new ideologies of feminine purity and chastity.[17] But other aspects of the former symmetric system persist: polygynous breeding systems, child betrothal, wife capture and sale. This intensification is also expressed at the bottom of the social scale, in the fates of males with low reproductive opportunities. Whereas permanent bachelorhood may occur in small horticultural societies, it does so at low frequencies. There, exclusion of males occurs primarily through early mortality and lesser success at polygynous breeding. In stratified societies, the ejection of low-status men from the breeding pool is more intense, more formalized, and more often lifelong. Just as formal systems of female celibacy evolve at the top, so formal systems of male celibacy develop at the bottom, through religious roles, incarceration, or other means. The dominance of elder over junior males, so often a feature of marriage systems in unstratified societies (Fox 1972:322–323), now becomes the lifelong dominance of high-status males over those below. It appears, then,

---

[16] Long-term celibacy for wealthy females requires the economic support of their kin, or independent access to income. Unanswered here, however, is the question of kin benefit from preserving the celibate daughter. As elsewhere, data on the political and economic strategies of individual families are sorely needed.

[17] It may be suggested here that the widespread equation of "feminine" with "promiscuous" in human cognitive systems can best be understood as a product of masculine concern with confidence of paternity and control of female reproduction. In stratified societies, the evolution of contrasting roles for women at the top and the bottom of the hierarchy, one emphasizing, fidelity, chastity, and celibacy and the other emphasizing promiscuity as a means to upward mobility, is associated with the development of contrasting feminine ideal types (virgin and promiscuous Marys) and the appearance of a new equation of "feminine" with the preservation of family and class morality. These thoughts lead to the conclusion that recent research on sexual dualisms would be greatly enriched by attention to the status context of the ideologies studied, and to their sociobiological functions (cf. Trivers 1972 on the "mixed strategy" of males in societies with paternal care of young).

13. Female Infanticide, Reproductive Strategies, and Social Stratification

that at least some forms of repression in complex societies have important reproductive functions.

These remarks on the evolution of stratified breeding systems are not intended to gloss over the many problems, aside from the inadequacies in the data presented, which attend the application of this model to human societies. Limiting ourselves to the variables which have been chosen as the subject of this review, there is obviously no clear understanding of the degree to which they are tied to each other (as the alternatives of female celibacy and infanticide demonstrate). Recently, Divale and Harris (1976) have presented evidence for the correlation of warfare with preferential female infanticide, and in addition proposed its association with a long list of other cultural traits, including patrilocality, polygyny, marriage by capture, brideprice and postmarital sex restrictions on women, in band and village societies.[18] My understanding of the functions of these traits differs from theirs; in addition the widespread, indeed near-universal, distribution of some of these variables may make correlative tests of any validity extremely difficult. Nevertheless, it is evident that this kind of search for degree of association between variables is a requisite for the definition of a human sociogram, its invariant qualities and the range and limits of its flexibility.

In terms of a larger theoretical framework, if human demographic patterns are more than epiphenomena, and indeed have reproductive meaning, they must be linked on the one hand to competition over scarce resources imposed by ecological and technological imperatives, and on the

---

[18] The assumption of the authors that the primary function of warfare is to encourage female infanticide and hence population limitation is ingenious but probably unnecessary. Both territoriality and aggressive conflict in man are fundamentally means of ensuring reproductive success. Direct competition for mates and indirect competition for territory (control over resources) both occur at interindividual, interclass and intersocietal levels. All these agonistic forms are engaged in primarily by the masculine sex, as in other mammals, but in some human societies, masculine excess and hence agonism is enhanced by the manipulation of sex ratios (cf. Alexander and Noonan, chapter 16). Physiological and morphological sexual dimorphism are best seen as a consequence, not as a cause, of the involvement of males in agonistic roles. Female infanticide, then, is not necessarily a means of limiting population, but a strategy to ensure increased RS to those who practice it. This strategy involves increased efficiency of investment of parental effort at the level of individual or familially shared genomes, rather than total populations. The greater economy of this sociobiological explanation resides, first, in the fact that the behaviors here discussed are commonplace in other vertebrates, and with the same functions here attributed to them. It is only the cultural manipulation of the sex ratio and the use of other learned means in reproductive strategies which is distinctive of our species. Second, no appeal to unsupported levels of group selection is necessary with this analysis.

other to formal learned cultural systems of approved economic investment and prestige reward. The difficulties involved in defining and quantifying these external variables need no underlining here, but the application of Darwinian theory to the human species emphasizes our need to overcome them. A start has been made here as well, however. Irons (chapter 10) has now demonstrated for the Turkmen of North Persia not only greater male than female variance in reproductive success, as reflected in numbers of offspring, but also greater variance in male than female survivorship. Importantly, these variances have been correlated with differences in socioeconomic status. Not only the better diet and medical care which greater wealth make possible, but the higher rates of polygyny, earlier marriage, and remarriage of upper-class males are involved. Thus, in this one case, the relation between culturally defined status and reproductive success has been demonstrated.

Recognizing the enormous amount of testing which remains to be done, nevertheless in this provisional exercise the close fit of familiar human social structures to that theoretical structure which would be predicted by sociobiology is striking. Behind the surface complexity of human cultural forms, a general mammalian model, maximizing reproductive success through male competition and the manipulation of sex ratios, is clearly visible. Human cultural history, as Alexander (1974:368–370; and chapter 3) has noted, is by no means independent of, but closely bound to, the biological history of human reproduction.

IV. Male and Female Strategies

The papers in this section deal in various ways with the subject of sexual selection and the closely related subject of parental investment (see chapter 1, pp. 27–29). In many interesting ways the papers in this section bridge the gap between social anthropology and biology. The paper by Alexander et al., for example, uses an interspecific comparison of a wide range of mammalian species in order to broaden our understanding of human breeding systems and some of their concomitants. A belief in the value of some sorts of comparisons between human beings and other primates has long been established in anthropology. One of the values of this paper is its implicit suggestion that such a belief is unnecessarily restrained, and that broader comparisons are likely to be fruitful. The paper also bridges the gap between social anthropology and biology by examining the relationship between variables that are conventionally thought of as biological (such as sexual dimorphism of stature) and ones that are conventionally thought of as behavioral or cultural (such as the extent of polygyny). The second paper in this section, by Alexander and Noonan, similarly combines concern with the conventionally biological and with the conventionally cultural. Part of the power of natural selection theory lies in the breadth of phenomena—genetic, morphological, physiological, behavioral—which can be understood in terms of a single paradigm. If the new form of natural selection theory—sociobiology—does prove generally successful, the now-conventional distinction between what is cultural and what is biological will probably be reformulated to include cultural things as a special subcategory of biological things.

In view of this, readers should not be surprised to discover in this section a paper like that of Bernds and Barash which uses the theoretical paradigm of sociobiology to shed light on a phenomenon, spontaneous abortion, which most social scientists would view as "biological in nature" and totally beyond the domain to which any "social theory" is relevant.

The papers in this section are also interesting in that they focus attention on aspects of the conventionally cultural/social/behavioral which anthropologists have by and large ignored. Low's paper on ornamentation,

Chagnon's paper on differential reproductive success, Spuhler's treatment of continual sexual receptivity, and Alexander and Noonan's discussion of concealment of ovulation and sexual receptivity are all examples of this, as much as the papers discussed above. For readers unfamiliar with sociobiology the papers in this section should be especially informative.

The first chapter in this section, by Chagnon, addresses the very basic question of whether reproductive success is equal among the Yąnomamö, a society which falls in the anthropologically defined category of egalitarian societies. He examines his impressive body of data on reproductive success within this group and shows that it conforms to the general mammalian pattern of a higher variance in male reproductive success than in female reproductive success. This demographic characteristic, of a higher variance in reproductive success among males than among females, underlies those aspects of their social organization which derive from mate competition. These features of social organization were discussed at length in chapter 4. It is unfortunate that comparable data are not available for a larger number of egalitarian societies. Data on the Bushmen, gathered and analyzed by N. Howell (1976), indicate a similar pattern of variance in reproductive success among this egalitarian group, and there may be a few other egalitarian societies for which data on fertility and mortality are sufficient to determine variances in male and female reproductive successes. My data in chapter 10 show a similar pattern although the status of the Yomut as an egalitarian society is arguable. Their political system is egalitarian (Irons 1971), but heritable wealth is unequally distributed. Despite the lack of data, it seems unlikely that variance in male reproductive success would be equal to, or less than, variance in female reproductive success in any human society. Chagnon notes that intense mate competition in egalitarian societies casts doubt on their "egalitarian" nature.

The chapter by Alexander et al. begins with a test of the basic proposition that the extent of sexual dimorphism correlates with the degree to which the breeding system deviates from monogamy. The expected correlation appears in the available data on interspecific variation among several mammalian families. Human beings as a species appear to fit the interspecific pattern, with a low degree of polygyny and sexual dimorphism. Intraspecific variation among human populations, in contrast, runs contrary to the expected pattern, with the most polygynous populations showing the least sexual dimorphism (measured in terms of stature). Further analysis reveals that the anomaly is removed if societies with socially imposed (rather than ecologically imposed) monogamy are put in the polygynous category. This observation leads to some interesting hypotheses about the

IV. Male and Female Strategies

functions of socially imposed monogamy as a means of creating solidarity within social units that compete as groups with other similar groups.

The third chapter in this section, by Alexander and Noonan, is theoretical in nature. It explores possible functions of concealment of ovulation and continual sexual receptivity in human females, and suggests, as the most promising hypothesis, that they have served in human evolution as means of ensuring male investment in their offspring. This hypothesis, if it stands the test of empirical data, should be an especially important one since the increasing importance of paternal investment is an important trend in human evolution which is divergent from the usual primate pattern. The discussion in this chapter relates to the numerous human social institutions, associated with paternity confidence and male nurturance of members of the next generation, which were discussed earlier in this volume (Kurland, chapter 6).

The fourth chapter in this section, by Spuhler, provides an interesting contrast to the Alexander and Noonan chapter by suggesting a different explanation of the evolution of continual sexual receptivity in human females. Spuhler explains this phenomenon not as an adaptation but as a secondary effect of an adaptation: that is, as the side effect of an increase in the production of thyroid and adrenal hormones as an adaptation to endurance in muscle activity. The contrast between these papers is important because they represent two very distinct ways of theorizing about evolution. The difference lies in the importance attributed to natural selection and adaptation. The authors of both papers see natural selection as the force giving direction to evolution, and they also agree that adaptations can have secondary effects which are not themselves adaptive.

The difference lies in the extent to which it is seen as possible for an organism to develop elaborate characteristics which are side effects of adaptations, without having these secondary effects become themselves subject to modification by selection. The issue hinges on two questions: are these secondary effects neutral in their effect on reproductive success, and if not, is it probable that mutation will introduce new genetic material modifying the secondary effect without changing the primary adaptive effect? Phrased in terms of the specifics of the issue on which these papers differ, these questions become the following. Was the difference between periodic and continual sexual receptivity adaptively neutral in human evolution? If not, and if periodic receptivity is adaptively superior, are mutations probable which would eliminate continual receptivity as a secondary effect of increased thyroid and adrenal hormones without eliminating the primary adaptive effect of increased muscle endurance?

Spuhler's hypothesis rests either on the assumption that this difference is neutral, or that mutations modifying it without modifying the primary effect are improbable. The Alexander and Noonan hypothesis rests on the assumption that a difference such as that between continual and periodic sexual receptivity is unlikely to be neutral in view of the cost in terms of energy and risks involved in continual sexual activity, and that mutations modifying it in the way described above are probable.

The theoretical difference represented by these two papers is an important one. Many biologists and biological anthropologists differ as do these authors in the importance they attribute to adaptation as opposed to other explanations of the persistence of traits. This difference of theoretical emphasis frequently leads to widely different interpretations of the characteristics of organisms. The theoretical developments which have led to the new interest in sociobiology and which have motivated most of the papers in this volume are based on assumptions similar to those underlying the Alexander and Noonan hypothesis. Which of these theoretical views is preferable should be determined by the relative value of each as a predictor of observable phenomena.

Low's chapter uses sexual-selection theory to derive a number of hypotheses about ornamentation in human societies and tests these hypotheses with data from the Human Relations Area File. The results of the tests indicate that sexual selection theory can greatly increase our understanding of human ornamentation. The fact that such a clearly cultural phenomenon as human ornamentation fits predictions made from sexual-selection theory is a good indication of the value of this kind of theory for understanding cultural phenomena. It is interesting to observe that this paper, like many of the papers in this volume, leads us to look at an aspect of human behavior, ornamentation, which many anthropologists would not think of as relevant to important theoretical issues.

The paper by Bernds and Barash, as noted earlier, uses sociobiological theory to explain a phenomenon far beyond the range of what has traditionally been thought of by social scientists as "social." They suggest that spontaneous abortion serves the function of terminating parental investment in unborn offspring which have a low probability of reproductive success. They even extend the argument to explain some aspects of the behavior of gametes. Although they do not explore it at length, they also point out that the same theoretical considerations could explain infanticide. This would be especially obvious in the case of the elimination of malformed offspring but logically would also be true of the other types of infanticide discussed in this volume especially that documented by

Dickemann in chapter 13. Female infanticide among high-caste Hindus would represent termination of investment in offspring with low chances of success. This is one of many cases in which human beings exhibit both physiological and behavioral mechanisms for dealing with the same problem.

W. I.

14. Is Reproductive Success Equal in Egalitarian Societies?[1]

Napoleon A. Chagnon

Status in Egalitarian Society

During his brief sojourn among the Nambikuara Indians of Brazil in the late 1930s, Claude Lévi-Strauss (1944) was struck by the fact that a society so simple should have "chiefs" and leadership. He made two suggestions that are relevant to the theme of this paper. The first had to do with individual motivation and the tendency for men to seek out and strive for what appeared to be burdensome, thankless tasks that fell to all leaders. This tendency or striving, he argued, did not emanate from culture itself, but had its fount in what, for want of a better word, we might call human nature:

> . . . I feel imperiously led to this answer: there are chiefs because there are, in any human group, men who, unlike most of their companions, enjoy prestige for its own sake, feel a strong appeal to responsibility, and to whom the burden of public affairs brings its own reward. These individual differences are certainly emphasized and "played up" by the different cultures, and to unequal degrees. But their clear-cut existence in a society as little competitive as the Nambikuara strongly suggests to my mind that their origin itself is not cultural. They are rather part of those psychological raw materials out of which any given culture is made. Men are not all alike. . . .[2]

The second observation by Lévi-Strauss that is central to the theme of this paper has to do with the rewards of chiefly status. The Nambikuara

[1] I wish to express my gratitude to the officers of the Harry Frank Guggenheim Foundation who generously supported my research efforts during 1974–7. I am also indebted to the National Science Foundation (Grant No. SOC75–14262) and the National Institute of Mental Health (Grant No. MH26008) for additional support during the same period of time.

[2] Citations to Lévi-Strauss' 1944 article on Nambikuara chiefs are from the reprinted version in Cohen and Middleton, 1967.

leaders were compensated, in large measure, for their burdensome tasks through the unequal distribution of marriageable females: chiefs were polygynous. Multiple spouses, argued Lévi-Strauss, were ". . . at the same time, leadership's prize and instrument." (ibid. p. 59) If we consider polygyny to be a perquisite of leaders and a mark or measure of inequality, then in the world's so-called "egalitarian" societies not all men are in fact equal, at least insofar as their reproductive potential and ultimate biological success are concerned. Polygyny is widespread in the tribal world and has probably characterized human mating and reproduction for the greater fraction of our species' history (cf. Alexander et al., chapter 15). Given that natural selection by definition entails the differential reproduction and survival of individuals, this fact of life—this inequality—is of considerable importance. This raises the question of the utility of viewing human status differentials largely, if not exclusively, in terms of *material* resources and the relationships that individuals in different societies have to such resources. That the relationship between people and control over strategic resources is central to understanding status differences in our own highly industrialized, materialist culture is insufficient reason to project these relationships back in evolutionary time and to suggest that all human status systems derive from struggles over the means and ends of production. Struggles in the Stone Age were more likely over the means and ends of reproduction.

Students of tribal politics often distinguish "egalitarian" forms of political organization from "ranked" or "stratified" forms (e.g., Fried 1967), usually with an attempt to demonstrate how economic transactions and relationships are related to those of a political order. Egalitarian societies are generally those in which strategic material resources are available to all for the asking and nobody has privileged access to land, water, wood, game, etc. insofar as they are members of a particular local group. Status distinctions in these societies are based almost entirely on age, sex, and ephemeral charisma, generated through periodic admirable deeds—luck in the hunt, turning the predator away, or bargaining effectively during crises with those in other groups. In a word, for each sex and age category, members of egalitarian societies are, so the analyses argue, almost freely interchangeable with each other. As Professor Fried aptly put it, there are as many positions of prestige as there are capable individuals to fill them (ibid., p. 33). Society, in short, has no mechanisms or institutions for limiting the number of prestigious positions.

Viewed as a system of role and status differentiation, based on the relationship of people to material resources on the one hand, and how differential *access* to resources translates into political power on the other, such a view of egalitarianism is meaningful for comparative studies of socio-political forms. One can clearly understand and perceive that during the evolution of culture from hunting and gathering times, through agricultural adaptations and the emergence of states and nations, the relationships of people to resources change, and the systems of differential status and rank—the extraordinary economic and political privileges of few—gradually become an expression of the relationship between individuals and the strategic resources that are central to and vital aspects of the society.

But positions of prestige and status thus considered function largely to enable us as members of highly stratified societies to understand how central the material want-satisfying objects and resources are to our own relative position in the hierarchy of social things, and to emphasize the degree to which material considerations are implicated in the general evolution of political forms. The relationships that emerge between people and material things as culture evolves, and how these, in turn, affect status differentials are not perceptible to tribesmen. But it would be misleading, if not erroneous, to conclude that important status differentials do not exist in egalitarian societies. It would also be misleading to believe that competition for status is absent on the argument that there is no differential access to strategic resources. Competition does exist, and a common preoccupation among tribesmen has to do with regulating sexuality and acquiring mates. In this competition, not all individuals are equal: those with large numbers of kin, more powerful kin, or greater ability to manipulate kin, acquire both higher status and greater reproductive success.

I was struck with the difference between our materialist mentality about the relative importance and value of things and relationships in the external world and the perceptions held by the Yąnomamö Indians, from whom I had just returned, in an exchange I had a few years ago with a distinguished anthropologist. He was puzzled and amazed by the preoccupations of Yąnomamö men concerning sex and women as described in some of my publications: "Why in the world would they fight over women?" he asked rhetorically. He added, puckishly: "Diamonds and gold I can understand, but women? Never." The obverse revelation—i.e., the perception of the Yąnomamö about the preoccupations we have in much of our behavior—was made indelibly clear to me when I explained to them that some of my colleagues, Professor Marvin Harris for example (Harris 1974, 1975, 1977a), refuse to believe that they fight over women, status, or for revenge. I told them that by his assertion the "true" cause of their warfare is a shortage of protein in their diet. They laughed and retorted: "Even though we enjoy eating meat, we like women a whole lot more!" (Chagnon 1977: 145–146; see also Chagnon and Hames 1979).

Egalitarianism in social anthropology is a concept that often involves describing or characterizing relationships between humans to resources and these relationships, in turn, to positions of prestige, rank, and privilege. It is, as such, more a function of the preoccupations of industrialized citizens who bear the status "anthropologist" and who are concerned with the manners, processes, and means by which the status differentials familiar to them arose in the course of human social evolution.

It would also appear that tribesmen, for whom relationships between men and resources of that dimension are totally foreign, are concerned about other things and other problems. In a word, thinkers from industrialized communities are concerned with sticks, stones, and the means of production—with material resources. Actors in tribal societies are concerned about sex, quality of mates, and the means of reproduction—and how best to achieve this, if not maximize their opportunities to do so.

Reproductive success necessarily entails costs, and it is here that material resources become critical elements in our understanding of primitive social organization. But a new approach to economics is required to demonstrate the relationship between provisioning and reproductive potential (Goody 1976). The major issues have very little to do with differential *access* to strategic resources, but much to do with differential *utilization* of such resources. The critical variables have to do with a fundamental asymmetry in reproductive potential between males and females (Katchadourian and Lunde 1975; Trivers 1972), and the degree to which parental investment by males is required to successfully rear all offspring sired by males. One basic fact has to do with the male's imposing potential to produce sperm and, hence, offspring. A male can, theoretically, sire billions of offspring during the course of his lifetime, whereas a female's potential is much more restricted by reproductive physiology. Females produce few gametes by comparison, are fertile for very brief periods each month, carry fetuses for nine months during which additional reproductive acts cannot enhance reproductive success, and, after the birth of the offspring, nurse the highly dependent infant for as long as three years or more. During lactation, fertility is suppressed. If a male's ability to mate and reproduce is limited by the degree to which he is expected to materially invest in the care and well-being of a pregnant mate and her dependent offspring, then his reproductive potential is limited by the extent to which he can assemble the material wherewithal required for that investment. Assuming that competition for mates by males is so limited, it is absolutely essential to discover the processes and means by which the necessary flow of material goods takes place in those situations where there is differential reproductive success by some males. It follows that if it takes ten units of material investment by a male to raise one offspring, a male with ten offspring will have to command and assemble 100 such units of wherewithal. Thus, a male with ten offspring necessarily must command ten times as much of the resources available as a man with only one offspring. This can only be accomplished through two mechanisms. Either he alone works ten times as hard as his peers, or he controls the productive efforts of others around him who assist him. In most tribal societies, some combination of the two strategies probably occurs, but until empirical demonstrations of this are provided by anthropologists, the best guess is that highly successful reproducers attain the resources they need mainly through the labor contributed by kinsmen and affines. Such a view of primitive economy is consistent with the "substantivist" view (Polanyi 1957; Sahlins 1972; Dalton 1961), but in effect turns the Marxist perspective entirely on its head: there is necessarily an asymmetry in utilization of material resources in primitive societies characterized by high variation in male reproductive success and obligatory paternal investment. That strategic resources are freely available to all, insofar as access to them is concerned, is simply beside the point and totally irrelevant to an understanding of status differentials and reproduction. The crucial issue is consumption and utilization of resources, and not everybody is equal in these regards. Out of the reproductive inequalities also come economic inequalities. We have thus come full circle in our argument about status and material considerations in primitive society. The prevalent materialist view (e.g., Harris 1975) is that primitive societies are egalitarian because there is unimpeded access by all to environmental resources that are central to and critical dimensions of any given culture. This is misleading on two counts: status differences among primitive peoples are probably more a function of differential reproductive accomplishments on the one hand, and differential utilization of strategic resources on the other. Economic realities derive out of reproductive realities; differential reproductive success creates differential status, which, in turn, requires differential utilization of strategic resources.

If we concern ourselves, for a moment, with the preoccupations of tribesmen and think of what appears to be important to them in terms of differential success and status, it is clear that some individuals, particularly among males, have more success than others in either acquiring wives or

IV. Male and Female Strategies

producing large numbers of children. In tribal societies, the former usually translates into the latter.

Let us, then, consider egalitarianism in terms of differential reproductive success and explore the degree to which variations can and do occur, both within each sex and between the sexes. Such a view is not only consistent with viewing human marriage systems as mating systems, but more consistent with native views of what, to them, is of considerable importance. Our anthropological preoccupation with kinship and marriage for the past thirty years suggests—or should suggest—that these are truly important dimensions of tribal society. What follows, therefore, is a view of Yąnomamö society in terms of the extent to which differential reproductive success occurs and is organized by members of a typical egalitarian society. Defined in terms of differential reproductive success, egalitarianism does not prevail, but quite the opposite obtains: not everyone is in fact equal.

Descendants of Shinbone

Let us begin with an example. According to my Yąnomamö informants in the village of Bisaasi-teri, all the Yąnomamö living in the villages to the south were called "Shamatari" and had descended from a man whose name was Matakuwä—"Shinbone." [3] Shinbone's people—probably his father's generation—originated in a village just north of the Orinoco, near its headwaters. The ancestors of my Bisaasi-teri informants also originated in that same area and had chronic, and often hostile, contacts with Shinbone's people. Over time, and because of a series of wars, Shinbone's people gradually moved south and spread out over a vast area as their population grew and their villages fissioned (Chagnon 1966, 1968b, 1974; this volume, chapter 4). Despite the fact there were many Shamatari villages to the south of the Bisaasi-teri, the latter persistently referred to all of them as 'descendants' of Shinbone. As my field research eventually drew me south into the Shamatari villages (Chagnon 1974), it became clear, through my genealogical and demographic research, why the Bisaasi-teri thought of the entire Shamatari population as 'descendants' of Shinbone: a very large fraction of them were. More accurately, the members of the Shamatari population were largely the descendants of Shinbone *and* his siblings, although Shinbone himself made the most dramatic reproductive contribution to the Shamatari population

[3] Matakuwä, literally, means "shin."

through his 43 children. Shinbone's father had 14 children, 143 grandchildren, 335 great grandchildren and, at the time of my last census (1975), 401 great-great grandchildren. The sizes of the latter two categories will continue to grow, since many of the individuals in the antecedent categories are still reproducing.

Although Shinbone and several of his direct descendants (sons and grandsons, see figure 14–4, p. 396) enjoyed rather dramatic reproductive success, most of his peers did not. There was (and still is) very marked variation in the degree to which individuals, particularly males, in the Shamatari and other subpopulations of Yąnomamö managed to reproduce. Much of this variation is the direct result of mate competition and the success that particular men have at attracting and keeping multiple wives (Chagnon 1974; this volume, chapter 4). Let us consider, briefly, the long-term consequences of such facts in terms of inclusive fitness.[4] Table 14–1 provides an indication of the degree to which particular individuals—men like Shinbone's father—are genetically represented in the Yąnomamö population under consideration.[5]

The impact of Shinbone's father on the Shamatari population, measured in terms of lineal and non-lineal descendants presently alive in the Shamatari villages, can be seen in the first column: his identification number is 1222. Over 3/4 (.76) of all residents (see BLOC TOTAL) of the seven Shamatari villages summarized in table 14–1 are descended in some way from 1222, i.e., carry his genes. In some villages (Villages 09, 16, and 21), over 90 percent of all residents are his descendants. Despite the fact that individual 1222 was a "Shamatari" and therefore a founder of a different population than the one from which villages in the bottom half of table 14–1 derive, abductions, migration and intermarriage have introduced a large number of Shamatari into villages of that population bloc. Founder 1222 thus has many descendants in non-Shamatari villages: 20 percent of all Namoweiteri are descendants of 1222. When all the residents of both populations are considered, we find that nearly half (48 percent) of all Yąnomamö in this area are, in some way, descended from a single individual. This is an impressive fact about inclusive fitness.

The table also shows that other founders (individuals 2954, 2936,

---

[4] By inclusive fitness I mean the number of descendant and nondescendant relatives of an individual, i.e., the magnitude of the genetic representation of an individual in a population as a consequence of his or her own reproductive success and the reproductive success of relatives (Hamilton 1964).

[5] See Chagnon, this volume, chapter 4, for a definition of the population considered here.

Table 14–1 **Cognatic Descendants of Selected Founders** The founders of the five largest patrilineages (individuals 1222, etc.) are listed across the top of the table. The number of living descendants for each founder is given for each village, as well as the percentage of that founder's descendants in the total population of each village. Population 1 (Shamatari) villages are given in the top half of the table and Population 2 (Namoweiteri) villages are given in the bottom half. Sub-bloc totals are given after each population and pooled at the bottom.

Villages	Size	1222	%	2954	%	2936	%	2967	%	2886	%
09	97	92	.95	29	.30	52	.54	52	.54	0	.00
10	215	124	.58	1	.00	45	.21	36	.17	2	.01
14	119	91	.77	14	.12	97	.82	93	.78	6	.05
16	116	107	.92	50	.43	39	.34	50	.43	0	.00
21	95	92	.98	5	.04	80	.84	89	.94	0	.00
49	77	52	.68	16	.14	38	.49	58	.75	0	.00
99	37	18	.49	1	.00	33	.89	21	.57	2	.05
Bloc Total	756	576	(.76)	116	(.15)	384	(.51)	399	(.53)	10	(.01)
01	100	3	.03	38	.38	7	.07	0	.00	9	.09
05	127	37	.29	103	.81	41	.32	19	.15	83	.65
06	94	25	.27	62	.66	29	.31	22	.23	55	.59
07	116	40	.34	95	.82	36	.31	21	.18	63	.54
08	122	9	.07	58	.48	32	.26	2	.02	39	.32
18	147	22	.15	126	.86	51	.35	16	.11	110	.75
19	78	21	.27	67	.86	45	.58	16	.21	69	.88
Bloc Total	784	157	(.20)	549	(.70)	241	(.31)	96	(.12)	428	(.55)
Population Total	1,540	733	(.48)	665	(.43)	625	(.41)	495	(.32)	438	(.28)

Population 1 labels the top seven villages (09–99) and the first Bloc Total; Population 2 labels the middle seven villages (01–19) and the second Bloc Total.

et al.) have likewise had a large impact on the population, although not as dramatic as individual 1222's. Thus, 70 percent of all Namoweiteri are descendants of 2954, 55 percent are descendants of 2886, etc. It is not surprising, in view of these facts, that the levels of interpersonal relatedness described in a previous paper (Chagnon, this volume, chapter 4) are relatively high in Yąnomamö villages, for marriages frequently take place there between individuals who have several ancestors in common.

14. Is Reproductive Success Equal in Egalitarian Societies? 381

Moreover, the structure of relatedness within particular villages is very complex. In Village 21, for example, there are three different ancestors from whom 98 percent, 94 percent, and 84 percent of the residents, respectively, are able to trace (cognatic) descent. This kind of situation emerges through the systematic exchanges of marriageable females among closely-bound lineage groups as described in chapter 4 (this volume). Sociopolitically, however, the members of Village 21 have some impending marriage difficulties. Their village is composed of several lineage groups, all of which are exogamic; i.e., individuals within them must seek mates outside that lineage (See chapter 4, table 4–2, this volume, for the distribution of lineages in this and other Yąnomamö villages). Seventy-four of the 95 residents of Village 21 (78 percent) are members of the same lineage, so legitimate marriage arrangements will grow increasingly more difficult in the future unless the village is joined by members of other lineages. More likely, the villages will increase the frequency of incestuous, illegitimate marriages (Chagnon 1972; Chagnon and Fredlund, in prep.)

Table 14–1 clearly indicates that some males enjoy rather impressive levels of inclusive fitness. The mechanics and machinations of mate competition described in chapter 4 (this volume) result in a situation in which males assist their agnates and brothers-in-law in acquiring mates through systematic exchanges of marriageable females. Therefore the degree to which males are ultimately differentiated into ancestral founders of high and low levels of inclusive fitness is a consequence of their political roles in the marriage system itself. Descent through the male line is used by the Yąnomamö to classify and define groups of relatives for the purposes of marriage arrangements and political action. Coupled with a situation in which there is high variability in male reproductive success, these agnatic groups in turn can vary in size, as figure 14–1 (p. 386) will show, and their members take advantage of the simple biological fact that males can produce prodigious quantities of offspring.

Variation and Variability in Reproductive Success

It is a fundamental fact of biology that males, because they are less parental, potentially have higher variability in reproductive success than females (Trivers 1972; Alexander 1974; Alexander et al., chapter 15, this volume). While there is variation among females in fertility, the variation is much less marked compared to males. The most fertile male in my sample, for

IV. Male and Female Strategies

Table 14–2   Reproductive Performance of Males and Females in Population 1 (Shamatari) and Population 2 (Namoweiteri) Based on Deceased and Currently Living Reproducers

| | Deceased | | | | Living | | | |
| | Shamatari | | Namoweiteri | | Shamatari | | Namoweiteri | |
	M	F	M	F	M	F	M	F
No. of Parents	140	181	161	156	137	182	142	198
No. Children (Both Sexes)	695	782	664	708	533	484	589	542
Average	5.59	3.67	4.40	3.42	3.53	3.24	3.82	3.51
Variance	37.64	8.02	12.15	6.01	12.40	5.19	7.82	3.63
Standard Deviation	6.14	2.83	3.40	2.45	3.52	2.28	2.80	1.91

instance, sired 43 children whereas the most fertile female had only 14.[6]

Differences in the variation of reproductive success by males and females can be more fully appreciated by considering the data in table 14–2.[7] A number of significant facts are apparent. First, there is high variation in male reproductive success, especially among the individuals of Population 1. Second, the variation in female reproductive success is much lower by comparison. Finally, the variation among both males and females is higher in Population 1 than it is in Population 2.

Table 14–2 only partially reveals the significance of biological limitations to reproductive potential for males and females. Whereas males can theoretically continue to reproduce until they are very old, the effective reproductive life span of females is much shorter. Table 14–3 brings this out more clearly. A male in this population (table 14–3) can expect to produce about five more children than a female if both live a full life (see mean column for age 60–64: 9.7 − 4.8 = 4.9).

Table 14–3 provides age-specific completed family size for males and females, the members of both Populations 1 and 2 being pooled to-

[6] It would be more accurate to say that the most fertile male "thought" he had 43 offspring and the most fertile female *knew* she had fourteen offspring.

[7] These figures are slightly different from those published in Chagnon 1974:131. The major differences stem from (a) an enlargement of the sample size as a result of additional field research and (b) recent changes in the mortality patterns, especially the occurrence of an epidemic in 1973–4 in some of the villages of Population 1 (see Chagnon 1977, chapter 6).

14. Is Reproductive Success Equal in Egalitarian Societies?   383

Table 14–3   **Age-Specific Completed Family Size for Males and Females**   In general, variation in reproductive success (S. D. column) increases during a man's life, but remains relatively uniform for females.

	Males				Females		
Age	Total	Mean	S.D.	Age	Total	Mean	S.D.
10–14	1.0	0.0	0.1	10–14	4.0	0.1	0.3
15–19	13.0	0.2	0.5	15–19	48.0	1.0	0.9
20–24	38.0	0.6	0.8	20–24	100.0	1.8	1.2
25–29	112.0	2.2	2.0	25–29	185.0	3.2	1.3
30–34	123.0	2.5	2.0	30–34	205.0	3.6	2.0
35–39	180.0	3.5	2.5	35–39	213.0	4.8	2.4
40–44	116.0	4.6	3.0	40–44	108.0	5.1	2.5
45–49	120.0	5.7	4.9	45–49	114.0	4.2	2.3
50–54	44.0	4.4	3.9	50–54	79.0	4.6	1.9
55–59	54.0	6.0	3.5	55–59	39.0	3.9	1.8
60–64	107.0	9.7	6.1	60–64	58.0	4.8	1.6

gether. While females begin producing earlier than males, males continue to produce for a longer time, and with age, the variation in reproductive success of males generally increases. Headmen, in particular, continue to acquire wives in their later life and tend to produce significantly larger numbers of offspring than other males (for data, see Chagnon, Flinn, and Melancon, this volume, chapter 12). Note how the variation in male reproductive success (S.D. column) generally continues to increase with increasing age of males. The opposite is true for females.

Lineal Descent and Fertility

While the Yąnomamö clearly have ideas and convictions about the importance of agnatic (through males) links and patrilineal descent, they do not exploit the agnatic principle as extensively or as elaborately as, for example, members of African societies (see discussion of lineal descent in African societies in Fortes 1953). Thus Yąnomamö lineages tend to be significant at the local level (villages) only, and primarily in the area of regulation of marriages. Agnation is recognized beyond the village—and in some areas the Yąnomamö seem to conceive of the residents of other villages as essentially members of a single patrilineal descent group—but there are no formal attributes of supra-local descent groupings. They do not, for ex-

IV. Male and Female Strategies

ample, periodically come together to worship an ancestor or meet at some lineage shrine. Indeed, depending on the immediate political circumstances between two villages with a common origin, they might even deny common descent with current enemies to justify continued raiding against them (Chagnon 1974). An "African" model of lineage organization, in short, is inappropriate when considering Yąnomamö descent principles and organization, just as it is inappropriate for many New Guinea societies (Barnes 1962). While there is variation in the details of the organization of descent groups from one Yąnomamö region to another, an ideology of lineal descent is found elsewhere in the tribe (Ramos 1972; Ramos and Albert 1976; Lizot, 1976).

Yąnomamö lineages are not even named, although at least one student of the culture argues that auto designations for 'clans' are identified in the northern region of the tribal distribution (Ramos 1972).[8] In the villages under discussion here, however, the lineages have no names; at most, the Yąnomamö will make references to the *mashi, nodiwä* or *shee* (agnatic relatives and descendants) of some particularly prominent man. For purposes of analysis, I have "named" the lineages by using the four-digit identification number of the genealogically most remote identifiable male ancestor of the descent group as described in chapter 4, this volume.

While the lineages are not given higher or lower status with respect to one another—i.e., they are not ranked according to a pattern of inherited status—the members of particularly large lineages have somewhat more authority over domestic and political activities in the villages. The village headman, if there should be only a single headman, invariably comes from the single largest lineal descent group in the village. If there are two comparatively large lineages in the village, it is common to find two headmen, one from each descent group, and quite common for most of the village social activities to reflect the interests and desires of the two leaders. Very often these men are cross-cousins to each other and married to each other's sister(s). In many cases, the two lineages have been bound to each other over several generations through reciprocal marriage exchanges, as explained in chapter 4, this volume. In a de facto political sense, then, in all villages some lineages are more important than others, the relative importance or "dominance" being largely a function of size of group, especially the number of adult males represented in that group.

[8] Lizot (1976) also argues that the lineages in the area north of the Orinoco are likewise named. I suspect that in the former case Ramos has interpreted old village names as clan names and Lizot has used alter-ego animal names as lineage names. I doubt that they are "clan" names in either case.

14. Is Reproductive Success Equal in Egalitarian Societies?

Since the process of village fissioning (see chapter 4, this volume) separates less-related individuals from each other and leads to their dispersal in newly founded villages, some lineages have a relatively wide distribution over the entire region occupied by villages of the same population bloc. (For data see table 4–2, chapter 4, this volume.) It follows that lineages will have a distribution largely confined to villages of the same bloc; i.e., they will tend to be concentrated in villages with a common origin. However, marriage alliances do take place between villages of historically unrelated population blocs and some lineages are therefore found in villages outside their original population bloc. Moreover, abduction and migration occur in some areas of the tribe, likewise leading to further dispersal of lineages. In the following discussion, lineages will be identified as belonging primarily to Population 1 or Population 2.

The 3,270 individuals in the sample under consideration fall into a large number of patrilineal lineages. These have been arranged in figure

Figure 14–1 **Lineage Rank Arranged by Decreasing Size** Each column of the histogram includes the total number of living and deceased individuals who belong to that lineage; the population of origin (Population 1 or 2) is indicated inside the histogram bars for the largest 15 lineages.

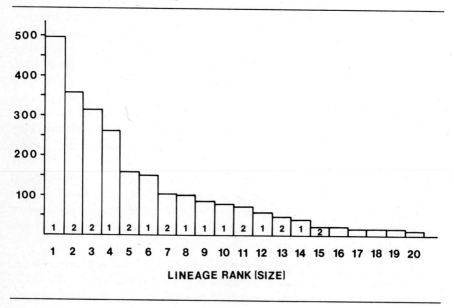

14–1, in descending order of size, for the twenty largest patrilineages, each identified as belonging primarily to Population 1 or 2. The most striking fact of the distribution is that a few large lineages account for a very large fraction of the entire population. In particular, lineage size diminishes rapidly beyond the fourth-ranked lineage, and beyond the fifteenth there is very little variation at all: they are all small and contain fewer than twenty individuals (living and dead are included).

A more forceful way to illustrate the numerical significance of a few lineages in the entire population is to calculate the fraction of the population each lineage represents, and then plot the cumulative percent as in figures 14–2 and 14–3, which give the distributions for (1) living in-

Figure 14–2   **Cumulative Percent Living Residents, Core Villages**   The data on lineage size show that a relatively small number of large patrilineages (Curve A) embraces a large fraction of the total living population. If the Yąnomamö population were "redefined" as matrilineal for purposes of comparison (see text), variation in female reproductive success and a relatively weak association of fertility between mothers/daughters would yield a situation in which lineages (matrilineages) would be relatively uniform in size and, therefore, many of them would be required to embrace (include) a large fraction of the total population (Curve B).

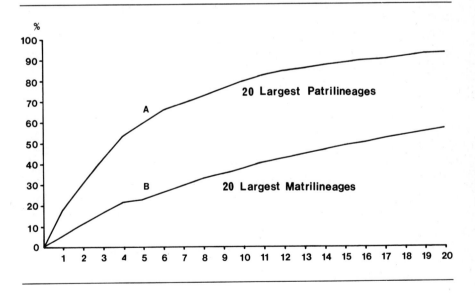

Figure 14–3 Cumulative Percent Living and Dead Members, Twenty Largest Lineages in the Core Villages Figure 14–3 differs from Figure 14–2 only in that both living and dead lineage members are given.

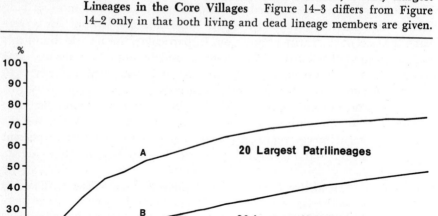

dividuals and (2) living-and-dead individuals respectively (curve 'A').[9] The twenty largest lineages include 75 percent of all living and dead individuals in the sample (all members of Populations 1 and 2), and 93 percent of all living members. Even more striking is the fact that nearly one-fifth (0.19) of the population of living individuals belong to the single largest lineage, nearly one-third (0.31) to the two largest lineages, and more than half of the population falls into just four lineages. As we shall see in a moment, the relative dominance of particular lineages is even more pronounced when each population is considered separately. For the moment, let me emphasize that the biological impact of just a few individuals is very apparent in the Yąnomamö population even when only the patrilineal (as distinct from cognatic) descendants of founders are considered. But the distribution of lineages according to size very poorly underrepresents the *actual* genetic impact of lineage founders. When the total number of descendants, i.e., descendants through both male *and* female links, is considered, the results are very impressive. Table 14–1, above, gave the distribution of

[9] Curve B shows the distribution of lineage size based on descent through the female line. That is, *if* the Yąnomamö were matrilineal and reproduced in the same pattern as they have done in the "real" world, then their matrilineage sizes would be as shown in Curve 'B'. See below for discussion.

IV. Male and Female Strategies

total living cognatic descendants of the "founders" of the four largest lineages and their distribution by village.

The difference between variation in male reproductive success compared to the same kinds of variations in female reproductive success, as it might reflect itself sociopolitically, can be appreciated by "redefining" the Yąnomamö as a matrilineal society for analytical purposes. Thereby we can examine the variation in sizes of matrilineal lineage groups—on the assumption that reproduction would occur in a matrilineal system much as it does in a patrilineal system. That is, the transformation should aid us in understanding how variation in male reproductive success works to the advantage of patrilineal systems in a way that it cannot for a matrilineal system. This assumes, of course, that we can conceive of "advantage" as somehow or other being a function of group size (see Chagnon 1975 for a discussion of group size and kinship relatedness).

This arbitrary transformation led to some new insights that I had not previously considered, and it was well worth the effort from the point of view of ethnology as well as biology. For example, if the Yąnomamö were in fact matrilineal, their political system would have to undergo some far-reaching organizational changes, particularly in the arranging of marriages by lineal descent groups. The limits on a female's reproductive success lead to a situation in which matrilineages are not highly variable in size and, accordingly, would probably lead to a political situation in local villages very different from what exists in the real villages: it is unlikely that villages would be dominated, numerically, by single lineages. If matrilineal organization did exist, most villages would be extremely heterogeneous in lineage composition and the competition for marriageable females would probably be very different when compared to the patrilineal situation, in which large size gives considerable advantage to the larger groups.

Moreover, multiple spouses by females (polyandry) could not have the same kind of effect in increasing lineage size through offspring as polygyny does for males in a patrilineal society: the possibility for a matrilineage to grow rapidly is much more limited when compared to patrilineage growth potentials. Figures 14–2 and 14–3 (above) gave the distribution (curve B) of matrilineage size by cumulative percent of population for comparison to the patrilineal version. The most obvious differences, when the comparison is examined, are that the matrilineages are quite small, do not vary much in size, and that many of them are required to encompass the entire population.

The simple facts of biological limitations to reproduction could possibly have some interesting sociopolitical consequences in such "egalitarian" societies. It is clear that high reproductive success by males could be exploited to advantage in the political system of patrilineally organized societies: the more offspring a male has, the larger his lineage grows. The same is true for females in matrilineally organized societies, but the limits are much more restrictive. If, for example, the long-term capacity of a group to compete effectively with other groups is a function of the size of that group, then patrilineally organized societies could have an advantage over matrilineally organized societies. The conditions under which this could occur would be, for example, pioneering situations in which one group is penetrating a territory held by another, and the groups are competing. If the two groups are composed of several local populations and the success of particular confrontations is determined by the size of the military group that can be mustered for that confrontation, and if the principle of recruitment to the offensive and defensive groups is largely based on descent, it is likely that the patrilineal group would have an advantage and would prevail. In the long run, the "massing effect" (Sahlins 1961) might be sufficient to enable the patrilineal group to displace their matrilineal competitors. It is tempting to speculate that the relative frequency of patriliny and matriliny in the ethnographic world might have emerged as a consequence of the relatively greater ease with which high variation in male reproductive success can be translated into rapid growth of politically significant social groups, and that in a competitive milieu, patriliny might have military advantages over matriliny.[10]

Extraordinary Fertility among Males and Females

To examine in more detail the impact of high fertility on the lineage composition of villages and the putative genetic contribution of particular individuals to future generations, the thirty most fertile males and females in the entire population were identified and their marriage and reproductive histories examined.

Table 14–4 (below) presents the data on the thirty most fertile males and females, giving their rank in terms of number of offspring produced, their identification number, the number of children produced, their patrilineal lineage, whether or not they produced any of their children by the thirty most fertile of the opposite sex, their "matrilineal lineage," and

---

[10] Murdock (1967) classifies 588 societies as patrilineal and 164 societies as matrilineal.

IV. Male and Female Strategies

the size-rank of both their "matrilineal" and patrilineal lineages respectively. A number of striking facts emerge from this comparison.

First, if we examine the details of male reproduction and separate the several wives of the individual thirty most productive males into "non-dominant" and "dominant" (patrilineal) lineages,[11] a very interesting pattern emerges. Where a man's wives have come from one of the numerically dominant (patrilineal) lineages, the average number of children per wife is much higher, especially for the more fertile of the thirty males. Table 14–5 shows the distribution. While the overall pattern suggests that highly fertile males produce more (total) children by wives from dominant lineages (4.59 per marriage with wives from dominant lineages compared to 3.82 with wives from non-dominant lineages), the higher fertility is only true for the top two-thirds of the males. Thus, the ten most fertile males produced 5.43 children by wives from dominant lineages compared to only 3.30 with wives from non-dominant lineages. This pattern continues through the next ten males (the "Mid 10 Males") where the averages per wife are 4.35 and 3.41 respectively. However, in the next ten most fertile males (the "Low 10 Males") the pattern reverses: there are more children per marriage with women from the non-dominant lineages.

A factor that might account for these striking facts is the manner in which numerical dominance was defined. As implied above, the "dominance" of a lineage has been defined in terms of its numerical representation in the *total* population. But, because of the way in which kinsmen remain together during the process of village fissioning, small lineages (small in the sense that they are not widely found throughout the entire population) may in fact have an extremely confined geographic distribution and be very heavily represented in just one or two villages. In those villages the "smaller" lineages may in fact be numerically dominant at the local level. Village 07, for example, contains 100 percent of all the members of Lineage 1829 (23 individuals in total), and in that village it is the second largest lineage and politically one of the most important. Indeed, virtually all of the women of that lineage married into one of the other prominent lineages represented in the village. Therefore, the prominence of Lineage 1829 in the *total* population is not a good indicator of its actual numerical and political significance at the *local level*. The pattern of reproduction among the lower ten most fertile men may in fact be more similar to that of the upper twenty: they may be marrying into locally dominant lineages and in fact demonstrating the same reproductive pattern found among the top twenty.

[11] "Dominance" here means numerical preponderance.

Table 14-4 Correlation of High Fertility to Lineage Identity and Spouse's Lineage

30 Most Fertile Males

Rank	Ego	Off	Pat Lin	Fer Sps	Mat Lin	Rank Mlin	Rank Plin
1	1221	43	1222	Yes	2038	0	1
2	1650	32	1222	Yes	2709	11	1
3	0341	30	2967	Yes	2966	15	4
4	1461	26	2700	Yes	0865	0	12
5	*1739	22	1222	No	0435	6	1
6	1905	22	1222	Yes	2038	0	1
7	1856	21	2967	Yes	0274	0	4
8	1505	19	1222	Yes	2966	15	1
9	1005	19	1222	No	2038	0	1
10	*0826	18	2954	Yes	0645	3	2
11	*0471	16	2967	Yes	0977	7	4
12	*1660	16	0200	Yes	2836	9	9
13	1603	16	2936	Yes	2155	0	6
14	1515	15	1598	No	3448	0	5

30 Most Fertile Females

Rank	Ego	Off	Pat Lin	Fer Sps	Mat Lin	Rank Mlin	Rank Plin
1	0896	14	2867	Yes	1832	0	0
2	0558	12	2936	Yes	2676	2	6
3	0631	11	0869	Yes	0645	3	0
4	1199	11	2954	Yes	2841	1	2
5	1008	11	0	Yes	1008	14	0
6	1529	11	1222	Yes	0745	19	1
7	*1467	11	1222	Yes	2960	13	1
8	1643	10	1222	Yes	0977	7	1
9	*0371	10	0	No	0371	0	0
10	*0311	10	2967	No	0455	5	4
11	0162	10	1222	Yes	0455	5	1
12	*0156	10	1226	Yes	3569	0	0
13	2038	10	0	Yes	2038	0	0
14	*2072	9	2967	No	2709	11	4

Left portion (rows 15–30):

Rank	Ego	Size	Pat Lin	Fer Sps		Off	Rank Plin
15	0463	15	2886	Yes	0645	3	3
16	*0340	15	1443	No	1078	17	10
17	0222	14	1443	Yes	2841	1	10
18	1407	14	0916	Yes	1728	0	11
19	1602	14	2954	No	2955	0	2
20	1222	14	1222	Yes	0	0	1
21	1598	13	1598	No	0	17	5
22	*0777	13	1443	No	1078	0	10
23	0806	12	2856	No	2857	0	7
24	0628	12	2886	Yes	2887	0	3
25	0199	12	0200	No	2178	0	9
26	2048	12	1222	Yes	1959	0	1
27	2267	12	2886	No	2955	0	3
28	1533	12	2954	Yes	2955	0	2
29	*1427	12	2886	No	2841	1	3
30	0962	12	2967	Yes	2676	2	4

Right portion (rows 15–30):

Rank	Mat Lin	Size		Fer Sps			Rank Mlin
15	1804	9	1222	Yes	0977	7	1
16	*2636	9	1222	No	0907	0	1
17	2803	9	0	Yes	2803	0	0
18	0181	9	2700	Yes	1394	4	12
19	0197	9	2967	Yes	2966	15	4
20	*0117	9	2846	Yes	0751	0	0
21	*0063	9	3204	Yes	0049	10	0
22	0699	9	1222	Yes	2709	11	1
23	1711	9	1222	Yes	0435	6	1
24	0977	9	0	Yes	0977	7	0
25	1078	9	0	Yes	1078	17	0
26	1182	9	0192	Yes	0193	0	0
27	1259	8	2967	Yes	2676	2	4
28	1251	8	0	No	1251	0	0
29	1136	8	2886	No	1081	0	3
30	1045	8	2967	Yes	2966	15	4

* Individuals presently living

Rank = size of lineage; Ego = identification number of individual; Off = number of offspring Ego produced by all spouses; Pat Lin = identification number of Patrilineage; Fer Sps = spouses, at least one, are among the 30 most fertile of the opposite sex; Mat Lin = identification number of matrilineage (see text for discussion of this hypothetical transformation); Rank Mlin = numerical rank of matrilineage of Ego; Rank Plin = numerical rank of patrilineage of Ego.

Table 14–5 Reproductive Performance of 30 Most Fertile Males

	Wives from Dominant Lineages			Wives from Non-Dominant Lineages		
	Children	Wives	Avg.	Children	Wives	Avg.
Top 10 Males	163	30	5.43	89	29	3.30
Mid 10 Males	74	17	4.35	75	22	3.41
Low 10 Males	57	17	3.35	65	11	5.91
	294	64	4.59	229	60	3.82

The more intriguing question, of course, is why the most fertile men produce more offspring when they marry women from numerically dominant lineages. I suspect that the answer has to do with marriage stability: they probably remain married to these women longer than they do to other women, or marry them earlier in their reproductive careers.[12] This might be related to the political implications of marriages between individuals from dominant lineages. The dissolution of a marriage where both spouses represent major political factions of the village has more political consequences than the dissolution of a marriage where only one spouse comes from a politically significant group. An example illustrates the point. Several years ago in Village 18, the wife of one of the village headmen began having a sexual affair with another man. She came from the other large lineage in the village, and her brother, also one of the village headmen, attempted to persuade her to stop the affair. The two headmen were brothers-in-law and had exchanged sisters in marriage. The woman in question refused to follow her brother's advice, so he killed her with an ax. The recalcitrant woman's brother acted in such a way as to demonstrate to his brother-in-law that he considered the marriage alliance between them and their respective groups of kin to be more important than the life of his sister. The two men were the most important leaders in the village and the fount of that village's solidarity and cohesion and there was, therefore, considerable political pressure on them to keep these bonds strong. There appears to be, in short, more social pressure to make marriages between dominant lineages last longer.

A second remarkable fact, related to the first, is the high correlation of reproductive success of the thirty most fertile females with either their

[12] A more comprehensive analysis of these intriguing data is required and will be the subject of a separate publication.

IV. Male and Female Strategies

own patrilineage or their marriage to individuals among the thirty most fertile males. Twenty-four of the thirty women (80 percent) produced most of their children by individuals who are among the thirty most fertile males. Of the six women who did not produce their children by men of the thirty-most-fertile group, four of them were members of the largest four patrilineages. Conversely, only nine of the thirty most fertile men produced any of their children by females of the thirty most fertile group.

A third important fact is the correlation of fertility with descent through the male line. All of the males belong to the twenty largest patrilineal lineages (table 14–4, column "RANK PLIN") and, with just one exception, to the ten largest patrilineages. Moreover, most of these males belong to the five largest patrilineages (21 of 30, or 70 percent) and eight of them (27 percent) belong to the single largest lineage. Equally striking is the fact that eight of the thirty most fertile females also belong to the largest single patrilineage.

If we examine the effects of matrilineal descent on fertility, it is clear that matriliny is much less effective in "concentrating" fertility through the female line. Only five of the most fertile men belong to the five largest matrilineages (see column "RANK MLIN") and only thirteen of them have a matrilineage identity at all.[13] Nevertheless, these thirteen men have made very substantial contributions to the reproductive success of the thirty most fertile women, and most of the nonlineal descendants of their wives (some of the wives married other men as well) are descendants of these men.

The correlation of fertility of females with their matrilineal descent line is less striking by comparison. Whereas all of the thirty most fertile men belonged to the largest patrilineages, only twenty of the thirty females belong to the largest matrilineages, and in eight cases of these, they belonged to matrilineages that ranked among the ten smallest. This underscores the point made above (see figures 14–2 and 14–3) that the high variation in male reproductive success leads to a potentially rapid growth of patrilineages whereas the limitations on a woman's reproductive ability serve as a limiting factor on the growth of matrilineages. One should expect that high variation in male reproductive success, even in a matrilineal society, would result in the situation where the inclusive fitness of a female is much more a function of her sons' reproductive success than of her daughters'.

The simplest way to illustrate the significance of these data is to

13 For purposes of simplification, I did not assign a matrilineage identity to individuals belonging to small matrilineages.

14. Is Reproductive Success Equal in Egalitarian Societies?

Figure 14–4 **Genealogical Relationships Between Fertile Males in Major Patrilineages** Number of children is given below the four-digit I.D. number, here and in figure 14–5.

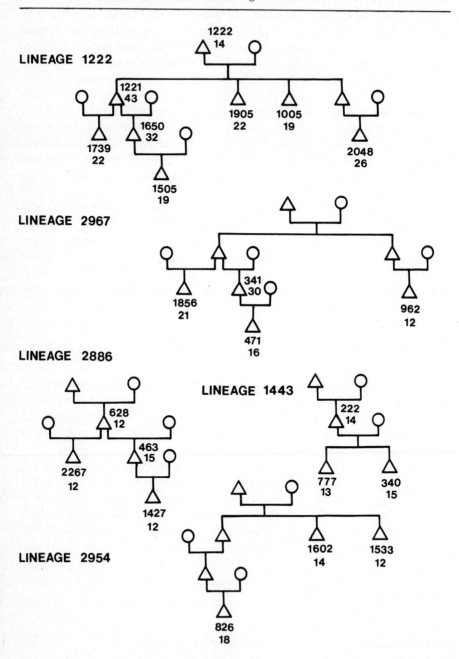

show, in genealogical format, how high male fertility and patrilineal descent are associated with each other. Figures 14–4 and 14–5 give the genealogical connections among the most fertile individuals discussed above. Figure 14–4 demonstrates the association between founders of the larger five patrilineages and their highly fertile male offspring. The discussion of mate competition (chapter 4, this volume) should make it clear that reciprocal giving of females between larger lineages results in the differential growth of the larger lineages—numerical preponderance in the village leads to high degrees of polygyny, which, in turn, translates into high male fertility and the increased growth of the larger descent groups. This sets ideal conditions in a society whose marriage rules prescribe marriage with cross-cousins; the grandchildren of any highly fertile male are related, among themselves, as cousins. Should there be long-term reciprocity between two large lineages, then the grandchildren of the initial male "founders" would fall into two categories from the point of view of any individual one of them: parallel cousins, who are classified with siblings and are unmarriageable, and cross-cousins, who are legitimate and desirable mates. In brief, high fertility among males makes it easy for grandchildren to marry according to rules that prescribe cross-cousin marriage.

Figure 14–5, finally, shows the genealogical relationships among the highly fertile male and female descendants of individual 1222—Shinbone's father. Recall that eight of the thirty most fertile females come from this

Figure 14–5   Highly Fertile Males and Females, Lineage 1222

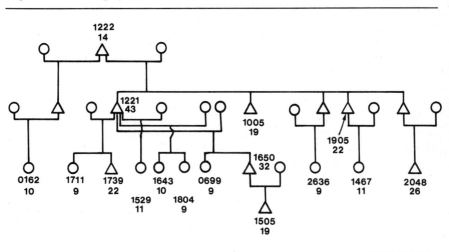

patrilineage, and eight of the thirty most fertile males come from this patrilineage. Given the probability that Yąnomamö women are all exposed to the risk of pregnancy to the same degree, it is puzzling that females from the dominant lineages appear to be more fertile.[14]

Discussion

Viewing human marriage systems as mating systems necessarily requires a detailed understanding of variations in fertility. Natural selection, by definition, entails the differential reproduction and survival of genotypes from one generation to the next. While chance alone, or "stochastic" processes as some might call them, can produce some of the variation in fertility that I have documented for the Yąnomamö, it is clear that the competition for mates and the political maneuverings associated with that competition (Chagnon, this volume, chapter 4) probably account for the major fraction of the extraordinary variation in male reproductive success. The marriage system among the Yąnomamö appears to take much of its form and substance from the fact that males are capable of producing large numbers of offspring. This gives rise to considerable political power for some men, who build upon a fund of relatives—descendants and potential marriage partners—that results from the previous generation's polygyny and high fertility. In a literal sense, high fertility begets large differences in inclusive fitness, since extraordinarily fertile males are more able than others to arrange marriages for their sons. Thus, we find an association of high male fertility in one generation with high male fertility in the next. In a patrilineally organized society like the Yąnomamö, this eventually results in the numerical preponderance of a few lineages in the overall population. We find men like Shinbone who sire 43 children . . . and thereby augment the reproductive potentials of their offspring. It is no accident that a high proportion of the population's most fertile individuals are direct descendants of Shinbone. Two of his sons together have produced 54 children, and one of these men is still in the prime of his reproductive career, headman of his village, and attended by several young wives who will probably continue to reproduce in the immediate future.

Viewing patriliny and matriliny in terms of the inherent biological

[14] This might be related to a possibly higher quality of subsistence and, thus, a more reliable level of investment from both mates and male kin: it is quite possible that females from dominant lineages receive more assistance from brothers and husbands, assistance that affects their survival and reproductive success.

limitations on fertility for males and females respectively, it is clear that in patrilineal systems the high variation in male reproductive success works—or can work—to the benefit of the political objectives of males in patri-lineages in a way that it can not for either males or females in matrilineal societies. In a competitive milieu where the outcome might depend on both size of lineage and the ability of lineages to "mass" large numbers of supporters, patriliny would appear to have a built-in advantage over matriliny. I suspect that the known ethnographic preponderance of patrilineal systems derives from the political advantages of patriliny, advantages that are ultimately predicated on the sexual asymmetry of human reproductive potential.

Finally, recent demographic data collected in Yąnomamö villages that are now exposed to missionary influence and pressures to abandon polygyny suggest that the variation in male reproductive success is declining in those villages. It is still too early to tell how this will affect the nature of the marriage system in those villages, but it seems likely that the frequency of cross-cousin marriages will decline in subsequent generations. The politics of marriage will undoubtedly change when this happens—whether or not the Mission influence persists, since individuals will produce fewer children and, hence, grandchildren, and they will have less comparative advantage in marriage negotiations. Something closer to egalitarianism in reproduction will emerge and the variation in male reproductive success will begin approaching that of female. It is tempting to suggest that the Yąnomamö of the immediate future will constitute a kind of paradigm represented in the theoretical debates of the recent past: they will have a prescriptive marriage rule, but, like the Purum, practice actual cross-cousin marriage to a negligible statistical degree (Ackerman 1964). Then we shall have only the rules to observe, with very little idea about how such rules ultimately relate to reproduction. I suspect that, divorced from the kind of biodemographic pattern in which they once functioned, the marriage rules themselves will begin to vary. One might even speculate that where reproductive egalitarianism prevails in societies with "positive" marriage rules, there will always be a wide discrepancy between "statistical" models of the marriage system and "formal" models based only on rules and ideology. I venture to say that systems of cousin marriage depend in very large measure on the reproductive variations that characterize polygynous systems. As polygyny diminishes, so also does the goodness of fit between the statistical facts of marriage and the ideal rules about how marriage should or does take place.

This brings us to a view of status and egalitarianism that is somewhat ironic. What brings about the demise of polygyny or reduces its attractiveness as an institutionalized form of marriage? The answer, I would suggest, is the degree of parental investment required by males. Let me contrast two polar extremes. The first cultural condition is one in which resources are abundant, predictable, and require very little time or effort to amass. Some males, especially those with large numbers of close kin, are able to assemble the necessary material wherewithal required as paternal investment for their polygynous families through the system of kinship economy . . . they can finesse their dependent and obligated younger male kin to contribute labor and the fruits of that labor to the consumption requirements of the polygynous household. The numbers of hours of labor to "make a living" is very small in most primitive societies (Sahlins 1972; Lee 1969) and the discrepancy between "means" and "ends" is so negligible that primitive cultures have been characterized as the original affluent societies: their members in general *have* what they perceive as *wants* and do not go on overproducing when those wants are met. To a limited degree, the heads of polygynous households might even have to work somewhat harder than other, monogamous, men to assemble the material components of paternal investment. When highly polygynous men make marriage coalitions and enter into long-term marriage agreements, they constitute a major political, moral, and matrimonial force in small communities whose membership consists largely of their dependent younger agnates and potential (cognatic) sons-in-law. The future reproductive careers of the younger men are in large measure determinable by decisions of the older, polygynous men—and they generally appear willing to contribute a fraction of their labor's fruit in exchange for favor. It is thus to the advantage of the older men to continue to attract additional spouses to the extent that the economics of parental investment work in their favor.

The opposite extreme is one in which resources are scarce, unpredictable, and require considerable effort to exploit, where the margin of sufficiency is precarious. Here, the economic activities of younger kin do not lend themselves readily to the amassing of predictable supra-sufficient produce, and the polygynous household is a less viable institution. Here, larger fractions of the wherewithal of paternal investment must necessarily come from the direct efforts of male household heads, who may indeed work no harder than their highly polygynous counterparts in better-endowed environs, but who can depend far less on their nexus of kinship followings for material support. The logical consequence would be that with lower frequencies of polygyny, there would be lower degrees of variation in male reproductive success—and fewer highly successful men whose grandchildren

IV. Male and Female Strategies

are all related among themselves as siblings or cousins. Thus, a rule of cross-cousin marriage would be satisfied, statistically, less often than in the previous example.

But in neither case is egalitarian status, defined in terms of differential access to strategic resources, an important issue. What is different is that polygynous men in the resource-abundant situation differentially *utilize* material resources and convert them into reproductive success. They are equal to their peers neither as economic consumers nor as potential reproducers.

There are, of course, other factors that reduce the attractiveness and viability of polygyny. Acculturation frequently is accompanied by demands on tribesmen to cease polygyny for "moral" reasons. The introduction of cash cropping or any form of cash economy makes it attractive for younger, unmarried males to divert fractions of their economic efforts to amass, for personal use, exogenous material items. Employment outside the community removes a potential source of the polygynous males' material support. As male heads of households must rely increasingly on their own efforts to provide parental investment in their wives and children, polygyny becomes less attractive to both males and females: it can only be maintained when the quality and predictability of paternal investment is high.

Ironically, as "gold and diamonds"—material items—become increasingly important in definitions of status, i.e., as society becomes less egalitarian economically, polygyny probably wanes in statistical frequency and becomes characteristic of the elite alone. On a society-wide basis, reproductive variation probably wanes also and the variation in male reproductive success begins to approach the variation in female reproductive success. Society becomes more egalitarian insofar as opportunities to reproduce are concerned, but less egalitarian in a material sense. Variance in male fertility, and probably overall reproductive success (which includes survivorship of offspring as well as fertility), decline. However, it should be noted that differences in reproductive success still appear to remain central to what people concern themselves with. Some evidence suggests that differences in economic success are associated with differences in survivorship, as well as a more limited variation in fertility (Irons, chapter 10, this volume). Many of these ideas remain yet to be documented, but most of them lend themselves readily to rigorous testing through field research.

15. Sexual Dimorphisms and Breeding Systems in Pinnipeds, Ungulates, Primates, and Humans[1]

Richard D. Alexander, John L. Hoogland, Richard D. Howard, Katharine M. Noonan, and Paul W. Sherman

Introduction

A positive correlation is generally assumed between the amount of sexual dimorphism in a species and the deviation of the breeding system from monogamy. This relationship may be predicted on the following grounds: with certain qualifications that we discuss later, sex-ratio selection in populations not affected in sexually asymmetrical fashions by local mate competition tends to yield adult sex ratios approximating 1:1 (Fisher 1958; Hamilton 1967). Consequently, if individual males are able to father the offspring of several females or if individual females are able to monopolize the reproductive effort of several males, then sexual competition will be relatively more severe in the sex which includes the disproportionately successful individuals. In other words, it will be difficult for any individual to reproduce successfully in the sex in which some individuals are unusually successful.

Thus, in a polygynous species (for example, one in which some males have harems and in which the adult sex ratio approximates 1:1) reproductive success will vary more among males than among females, and, in all likelihood, fewer males than females will contribute genetically to succeeding generations (Bateman 1948; Trivers 1972). In a polyandrous species the reverse will be true. Observations supporting these arguments have recently been carried out on a variety of polygynous species—Bateman 1948 (*Drosophila melanogaster*); Downhower and Armitage 1971 (marmots); Le Boeuf 1974 (elephant seals); Robel and Ballard 1974 (prairie chickens); Haigh 1968 (redwinged blackbirds); Cronin and Sherman 1976 (honeyguides); Trivers 1976a, Ruby 1976 (lizards); Chagnon 1974, chapter 14, and

[1] For assistance we thank Sydney Anderson, A. T. Bergerud, Terry Bowyer, John F. Eisenberg, Helmut Hemmer, Carl B. Koford, William Z. Lidicker, Tracy Mengerinck, George Miller, Joan Miller, Martin Moynihan, Nancy Olds, James L. Patton, Philip Myers, and Kenneth J. Raedeke.

Chagnon, Flinn, and Melancon, chapter 12; (Yąnomamö Indians); Irons, chapter 10 (Turkmen); Borgia 1977 (dungflies); Howard 1977 (bullfrogs); Sherman 1976 (ground squirrels); and a few polyandrous species—Jenni 1974 (jacanas); and Taber and Wendel 1958, Adams et al., 1977 (honeybees).

Greater intensity of sexual competition will enhance selection for attributes leading to success in that context. In all except monogamous species there will be asymmetry in this regard, leading to a divergence of selective action on the male and the female. As a result sexual dimorphism will be exaggerated, except in cases in which there was an initial sexual dimorphism in the opposite direction. For example, if males were smaller than females at the outset, then sexual competition favoring larger males would, for a while, at least, decrease rather than increase sexual dimorphism in size.

Except for Clutton-Brock and Harvey (1977a and 1977b), no extensive systematic effort has previously been undertaken to demonstrate correlations between breeding systems and sexual dimorphisms (but see Crook 1972; Jarman 1974; Gautier-Hion 1975; Ralls 1976). In figures 15-1-15-6 we demonstrate the predicted correlations (see also tables 15-1 through 15-6, pp. 424-433). In figures 15-1 and 15-2, we compare sexual dimorphism with both mean and maximum degrees of polygyny for pinnipeds; in figures 15-3 and 15-4, for ungulates (Artiodactyla and Perissodactyla), and

Figure 15-1   Dimorphism Data for Pinnipeds

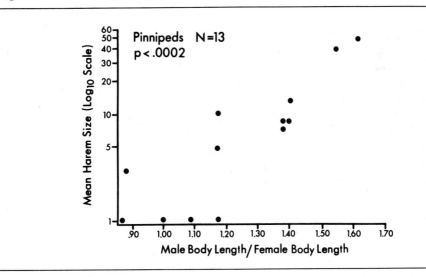

Figure 15–2   Dimorphism Data for Pinnipeds

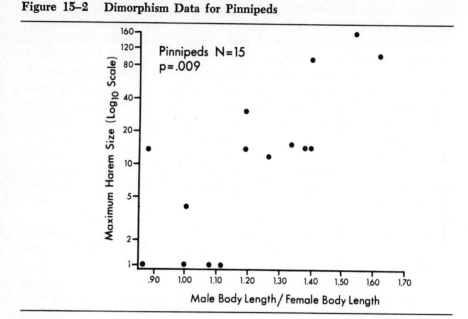

in figures 15–5 and 15–6, for primates. We chose these three groups because each includes both monogamous and variously polygynous species for which sufficient data were available.

Materials and Methods

Most data are from the literature, although some ungulate and primate information is unpublished (see tables). For each species we used all data that seemed reliable. As the measure of sexual dimorphism we used body lengths (including head) rather than body weights because lengths are less subject to variation due to nutritional status, health, age, or reproductive condition (e.g., pregnancy). (See also Ralls 1976). We accepted only dimensions from males and females that were described as fully adult.

We based estimates of polygyny exclusively on field studies. We used laboratory or zoo data on body lengths only when adequate field data were unavailable. When data were available from different populations or subspecies we combined them. For primate data we used only those species which apparently live in bisexual groups containing only one adult male more than half the time.

IV. Male and Female Strategies

Figure 15–3   Dimorphism Data for Ungulates

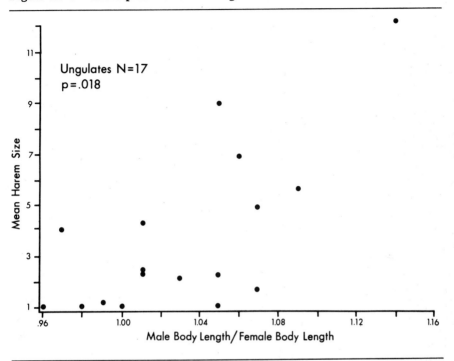

We searched extensively for accurate harem counts for each species, and for data on body length when the data for any species were few. When large sample sizes were provided by one or a few studies, the search for more data was abandoned. When an investigator specifically reported an absence of sexual dimorphism we used a dimorphism ratio of 1.0. For primates, males judged by investigators to be senile were excluded from breeding data (n = 2). Investigators of primates generally use the term "subadult female" to refer to females capable of successful breeding, but not yet fully grown. Subadult females were therefore included in harem size calculations; the only exceptional cases were species of the genus *Presbytis*, for which subadult females, as defined, apparently cannot breed. In several cases, successive studies of primates were conducted in the same areas; in these cases we excluded group counts that were obviously repeats. Comparisons of male-female standing heights of *Gorilla gorilla* (Schaller 1963) and sitting heights of *Hylobates lar* (Carpenter 1940) and *Papio*

Figure 15–4   Dimorphism Data for Ungulates

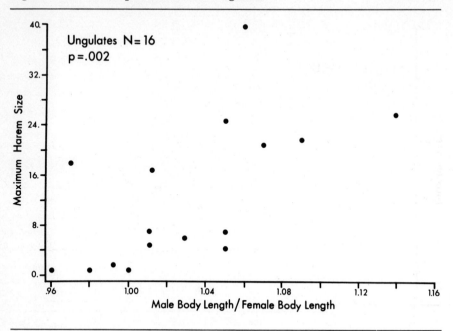

Ungulates N = 16
p = .002

Maximum Harem Size

Male Body Length/Female Body Length

Figure 15–5   Dimorphism Data for Primates

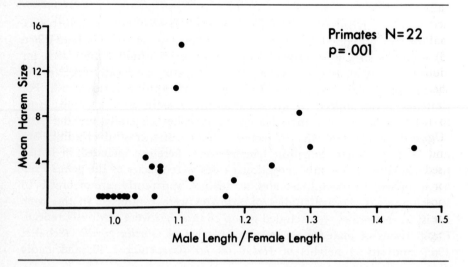

Primates N = 22
p = .001

Mean Harem Size

Male Length/Female Length

Figure 15-6   Dimorphism Data for Primates

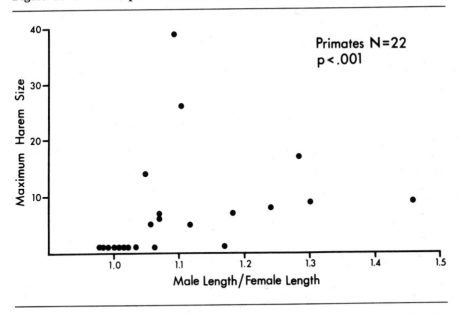

hamadryas (Kummer 1968a) were considered equivalent to comparisons of body lengths of the sexes in other species.

The polygyny data rest on several assumptions: (1) percents of sexually receptive females within harems, and of individuals correctly identified as "adult females," do not vary systematically with harem size; (2) adult males potentially have sexual access to all adult females in their groups; (3) observed harem sizes do not fluctuate during the mating period (obviously not always true: Le Boeuf 1974; du Plessis 1972); (4) males retain the same groups of females during the mating period rather than sequentially tending groups of similar sizes; (5) females do not move from harem to harem or mate with more than one male during the mating period (Uganda kob females do move from male to male for mating: Buechner and Schloeth 1965). For species of ungulates, and for elephant seals, we used male copulatory success rather than harem size. We excluded ungulates for which copulatory success was known for only part of the mating period, those in which males were not individually identified, and those in which the investigator believed that considerable copulation occurred out of sight (e.g., bighorn sheep and stone sheep: V. Geist, personal communication). We assumed that the following possible sources of error did not vary systematically with the degree of polygyny: (a) accuracy of measurements, (b) relevance of size as a measure of sexual dimorphism, (c) accuracy of classifying males and females as fully adult, and (d) accuracy of data on degrees of polygyny. There are occasional problems. For example, *Callicebus moloch* females, which are treated as monogamous, sometimes copulate with more than one male (Mason 1966). Males of *Presbytis entellus* commonly do not successfully inseminate all the females within their harems, because of frequent takeovers by other males (Blaffer Hrdy 1974; Mohnot 1971; Sugiyama 1964).

For humans the sample included all societies for which there were data in the University of Michigan Human Relations Area Files (HRAF) on both marriage system and sexual dimorphism in stature. Societies were also included for which there was information on the marriage system in HRAF and data on sexual dimorphism in stature in other sources. Societies whose marriage systems in our view could not be classified reliably according to the criteria were excluded. No attempt was made to gather a representative sample of societies (Murdock 1967).

Stature measurements for human males and females were always obtained from the same study. Data for different societies varied widely in sample size, and in some cases sample size was not reported. If data from two studies were used sexual dimorphism was calculated separately for each study and the two averaged. Nutrition and age distribution varied in different populations; no attempt was made to control for these variations.

For the most part, human societies were considered to be polygynous if Murdock (1967) classified them as having either general or limited polygyny; most of the societies so classified also distinguish cross- and parallel cousins, implying a history of polygyny (Alexander 1974, 1977a). Societies were classified as monogamous if they included only monogamous units or very few polygynous units; most also did not distinguish cross- and parallel cousins, implying a history of monogamy (Alexander 1974, 1977a). Circumstantial and sometimes subjective criteria were used to classify societies as "ecologically" or "socially" monogamous. For example, all societies showing occasional polyandry, indicating a marginal habitat, were classified as ecologically monogamous (Coorg, Ladak, Tibetans, and Toda: Murdock 1967; Central Thai: Phillips 1965; Thompson 1941; Copper Eskimo: Jenness 1917, 1922; Lepcha: Morris 1938; Pygmies: Turnbull 1965a; Semang: Schebesta 1954; Vedda: Seligman and Seligman 1911). Dispersed social units consisting of single families (Lepcha and Senoi) or groups of fewer than fifty (Copper Eskimo, Chilcotin, Labrador Eskimo, Lapps, Pygmies, Semang, Toda, Vedda, and Yahgan) with no prominent social ties above the group

IV. Male and Female Strategies

level were also considered to be indicative of a poor habitat and ecologically imposed monogamy. Long postpartum sex taboos, combined with the other factors above, (Pygmies, Senoi, and Semang) were also regarded as indicating marginal habitat. The Chilcotin, Copper Eskimo, Labrador Eskimo, Lapps, Ona, Senoi, and Yahgan were classified as ecologically monogamous on the subjective grounds that the environment was judged to be harsh and polygyny was described as extremely rare. All monogamous societies not meeting the above criteria were classified as "socially" monogamous; in other words, they were regarded as imposing monogamy by rule. In at least a few of the societies judged to be ecologically monogamous there are also indications of social pressure against polygyny.

The data for different groups were assembled chiefly as follows: pinnipeds, Howard; ungulates, Sherman; nonhuman primates, Hoogland; humans, Noonan.

Results with Nonhuman Groups

Every correlation of body length with degree of polygyny in nonhuman mammals was significant (see pages 403–407). Moreover, except for ungulates, the degree of sexual dimorphism was significantly different between monogamous and polygynous species compared simply as two different groups. This was true for both mean and maximum harem sizes. For mean harem sizes the results were as follows: for pinnipeds, $p = 0.002$; for ungulates, $p = 0.018$; for primates, $p = 0.001$ (Mann-Whitney U test). In pinnipeds and ungulates, the correlations between degree of sexual dimorphism and harem size were significant even when all of the monogamous species were excluded (using mean harem sizes: for pinnipeds, $r = 0.74$, $p < 0.05$; for ungulates, $\tau = 0.35$; $p < 0.02$; df $= 12$; Kendall rank correlation test). That is, among polygynous species alone, degree of sexual dimorphism in size correlates directly with either mean or maximum harem size.

Alternative Hypotheses

Contexts other than asymmetry in sexual competition in which sexual dimorphisms might evolve include (1) division of labor in parental effort (Ralls 1976, Myers 1978), (2) differential use of resources by members of mated pairs (Selander 1966, 1972), or (3) intrasexual competition in three-dimensional environments. The last of these cases requires explanation. Among the cases of sexual dimorphism we examined, Weddell's seal is distinctive. In this species males are smaller than females even though the maximum reported harem size is 12 and the mean is 3.0. Such "reverse" dimorphism is actually not rare in the animal kingdom, occurring in thousands of apparently polygynous insects and fish, and also in frogs, lizards, birds, and bats (Ralls 1976, Myers 1978). In insects it is often associated with a narrowly defined breeding season, amounting to semelparity (one-time breeding) whenever adults do not survive between seasons. The smaller sizes of males in such species may be owing to the advantage of maturing earlier than females, rather than a season or a year later, as is possible in polygynous, iteroparous vertebrates (for an exception, see Howard 1977).

Most of the groups mentioned above live partly in three-dimensional environments, in the air, in water, or on vegetation. In such environments agility may be relatively more useful in combat (H. W. Power, personal communication) and large size may be relatively more detrimental for other reasons. In view of this correlation, it may be significant that in Weddell's seal, male combat occurs underwater, for females descending through separate holes from the surface of the ice where they have just given birth (Cline et al., 1971).

Effects like those above could either dilute or enhance differences in amounts of sexual dimorphism between monogamous and nonmonogamous species deriving from differences in sexual competition. They are, however, unlikely to explain widespread correlations between degrees of sexual dimorphism and degrees of polygyny in two-dimensional environments. The significance of the comparisons in three different taxonomic groups, together with the theoretical predictions described above, strongly suggest that the relevant variable is the greater pressure of sexual competition among males, associated with their generally low parental effort and high mating effort.

We tested for the possibility that increases in sexual dimorphism are partly a function of increasing body size and we found no relationship. Clutton-Brock and Harvey (1977a; 1977b), however, found a positive correlation between body weight and sexual dimorphism in body weight in primates, and between "socionomic sex ratio" and sexual dimorphism in body weight. They found no correlation between socionomic sex ratio and body weight. Unlike our test, they included both single-male and multi-male groups, but their data for the two kinds of groups are not significantly different (Harvey, personal communication). They also found that the correlation of sexual dimorphism with body weight in primates is better than the correlation of sexual dimorphism with harem size as deduced from "breeding sex ratio." Errors in estimating degree of polygyny in multi-male groups should tend to be underestimates: socionomic sex ratios (number of adult females divided by number of adult males) are almost certain to include adult males who breed little or not at all and others disproportionately successful. Thus, Clutton-Brock and Harvey's socionomic sex ratios may not be precisely comparable with our estimates of harem sizes in single-male groups. There is also a possibility of correlation between the size of this discrepancy and the numbers of adult males in groups.

Ultimately, whether or not polygyny is possible depends on the distribution of females. Pinniped males in polygynous species compete for females during brief breeding seasons in localities where females give birth. These locales are on land or on ice, and in polygynous species they are always restricted localities, probably defined chiefly by inaccessibility to predators. Males are able to defend harems because the females must crowd together during the breeding season. Most polygynous ungulate and primate bands, in contrast, are mobile or nomadic, even during the breeding season, and many of the larger groups live in grasslands or other open habitats where they are more or less continually susceptible to predation. To some extent, the herd rather than features of the habitat is each individual's cover (Hamilton 1971). Predators are outrun or outmaneuvered.

Monogamous ungulates and primates, on the other hand, tend to live in forests, or habitats with considerable cover. It seems reasonable to assume that more of their defense against predators involves concealment or escape into trees. This suggestion is supported by the sedentary nature of some species, sometimes involving territoriality, and also by the presence of cryptic coloration and behavior. Monogamous ungulates and primates are generally smaller than their polygynous relatives (see figures 15–3 and 15–4, pages 405–406), and we speculate that the cause is related to their generally different methods of escaping predation. To elude predators in open habitats almost surely favors larger sizes in many instances, while concealment or escape in a forest situation seems less likely to do so. Large herds of ungulates and primates, living in open habitats and escaping predators by outmaneuvering and outrunning them, represent greater clumping of females, giving some males the potential for dramatically increasing their mating success. The resulting polygyny would tend to favor larger size in males.

As body size and sexual dimorphism increased through evolution in grassland herding species, we can expect that size thresholds would be passed, first by males then by both sexes, in which group members could confront certain smaller predators rather than flee from them. This situation would in turn select for still larger size, and sometimes, at least, would tend to exaggerate sexual dimorphism as well. In some species aggressive defense against predators has acquired a group cooperative effect (e.g., savannah baboons: Washburn and DeVore 1961a). In other species increasing body size and the capability of aggressive defense against predators may have led to secondary reductions of group size, perhaps causing the re-emergence of one-male groups in particularly large species. This situation, associated with different kinds of predators in different regions, may be involved in the varying degrees of separation of harems of individual males in different baboon species (Crook 1966; Kummer 1968a). In one-male bands, because of the higher confidence of paternity, male parental care is likely to be more strongly favored, and this could lead to still more dramatic size increases and greater dimorphism between the sexes (that is, somewhat independently of, or only indirectly linked to, mating competition—see page 409, Alternative Hypotheses). Unusual size dimorphism occurs in some primate species living in single-male bands (e.g., Gorillas).

Thus one might speculate that in both ungulates and primates the largest groups would involve species intermediate in size, living in grasslands or other open habitat. The largest species in turn should be polygynous forms living in one-male bands. Among primates such species are not restricted to open habitats (e.g., gorillas). Chimpanzees also appear to be an exception, since they are large, polygynous primates living in open forest habitats. However, gorilla and chimpanzee males defend against predators (e.g., Schaller 1963; Kortland 1967). Also, there is evidence that chimpanzee males (that are genetically related) defend territories in groups (Bygott, in press; Wrangham, in press) and therefore that females rather than males may move between groups, unlike all other primates except gorillas (Harcourt, Steward, and Fossey 1976) and humans.

The hypotheses developed here imply that predators have been largely responsible for shaping the grouping tendencies of primates, ungulates, and pinnipeds, thus for shaping their forms of sociality, breeding systems, and patterns of parental investment as well. Abundance and distribution of edible plants—for example, in baboon habitats—may influence the costs of living in groups of particular sizes or densities. Thus, hamadryas baboons, because of the relative sparseness of vegetation, may be under greater pressure than cynocephalus baboons to spread out while foraging. But it does not seem easy to use food distribution or abundance to account for group-living in any primate, ungulate, or pinniped (Alexander 1974).

Cause of Polygyny

In mammals polygyny seems to replace monogamy when the distribution of females, for whatever reason, is such that some males are able to monopolize the reproductive effort of disproportionate numbers of females. This observation leaves unanswered the more basic question of why asymmetries from monogamy tend toward polygyny rather than polyandry. This question has received attention recently (Orians 1969; Trivers 1972; Dawkins and Carlisle 1976). We suggest an answer somewhat different from those of earlier authors (see also Alexander and Borgia, 1978).

For organisms in general, the significant factor in the history of differential parental effort by the two sexes, and therefore differential mating effort and occurrence of polygyny or polyandry, may have been a consistent asymmetry in confidence of parenthood—in other words, a difference in the degree of genetic relatedness of the adult male or female to its putative offspring. This asymmetry would subsequently be affected by grouping tendencies and other aspects of social life, in turn influenced by predators and resource distribution. Once differential parental investment between the sexes is initiated, subsequent specialization of the two sexes will cause the sex that invests less to become more able to gain by alternatives such as multiple matings, and the sex that invests more to become less capable of gaining by such alternatives.

In the early evolution of mammals, internalizing of the embryo by females and lengthening of gestation probably correlated with unusually high loss of probability of parenthood by males. Female parental effort, as might be expected, is extreme in mammals, and monogamy and large male parental effort are secondary specializations in modern mammals, nearly always in association with habitats that allow isolation of mated pairs—hence, effective sequestering of the female and high confidence of paternity. Probably the entire mammal line has always been polygynous, in the sense that male variance in reproductive success has exceeded that of females.

Effects of Polygyny

Several effects deriving from the increased competition of males in polygynous mating systems influence adult sex ratios, and are important in understanding the general influence of a history of polygyny on patterns of social behavior.

First, in the species studied here, males of polygynous species are not only larger as adults than are females, but they almost surely take longer to mature. This means that if parental effort is expended equally on male and female offspring—a tendency predicted from the theory and facts of sex-ratio selection (Fisher 1958; Hamilton 1967)—then males will be added to the breeding population at a somewhat lower rate than females. This effect of polygyny will tend to lower the adult sex ratio.

Second, larger males requiring longer to mature may be expected to suffer a higher overall mortality during immaturity than females. The contributing factors are the greater time involved and the risks associated with activities involved in maximizing one's growth rate. This effect of polygyny, which has been suggested by direct observations on some species (e.g., LeBoeuf 1974), will also reduce somewhat the proportion of adult males.

Third, adult males, contesting more vigorously for reproductive success in a polygynous system, are likely to suffer a higher mortality than adult females for this reason. This mortality, coming after the reproductive maturity, is likely to lead to an evolutionary acceleration of senescence in males as compared to females, aggravating the already higher rate of male mortality. This effect is predicted because consistently higher mortality after the onset of reproduction lowers the value of any gene effects occurring late in life which reduce the effects of senescence. The lowered value of such effects occurs partly because fewer individuals remain to be assisted by them and partly because of the lowered residual reproductive value of older individuals. As Williams (1957) and Hamilton (1966) have both pointed out, the result of the combined effects of increased mortality and accelerating senescence is that a greater accumulation or "piling on" of deleterious effects on older males may be expected than for older females (there may also be effects deriving from differences in the pattern of reproductive opportunities for the two sexes).

Fourth, only juvenile males that are quite likely to be successful are sound parental investments, which probably largely explains the existence of the generally male-biased primary sex ratio coupled with a higher rate of mortality of juvenile males than females, especially among embryos. In parental terms, more males than females are conceived, or started under parental care; and more are terminated because of higher likelihood of failure later on.

Fifth, individual males reared to the normal termination of pa-

414   IV. Male and Female Strategies

rental care are likely to receive, on average, slightly more parental care than individual female offspring. This effect would result from tendencies to equalize the investment in males and females, while both starting and terminating more males as a result of selective pressure to rear only males likely to succeed in the competitive polygynous situation.

Sixth, high-ranking or very healthy or capable parents are likely to favor male offspring more than do low-ranking or less healthy and capable parents, since their male offspring have a greater chance of success in the highly competitive male situation (Trivers and Willard 1973; Alexander 1974; Dickemann, chapter 13; Chagnon, Flinn, and Melancon, chapter 12).

These biological predictions about species with polygynous breeding systems are solidly based on a group of interconnecting theories from evolutionary biology, deriving from what is known of the effects of selection on sex ratios, senescence, and patterns of expenditure of mating and parental effort. They are all results, not causes, of polygyny, and by returning effects to the polygynous system, they represent an essential part of the characterization of life cycles, sexual differences and similarities, and the general biological substrate upon which social systems develop in all polygynous species.

Humans

We may now ask whether or not anything useful is to be gained from considering humans in the general biological terms so far used to characterize other mammalian groups. We assume at the outset that humans possess no special features invalidating such a comparison.

In regard to sexual dimorphism humans tend to fall in the region of mildly polygynous species, with males taller than females by about 5-12 percent—slightly less dimorphic, for example, than chimpanzees (Clutton-Brock and Harvey, 1977a, 1977b). This is not surprising, since harem polygyny occurs in many human societies in many parts of the world, and has been even more prevalent within recorded history (Murdock 1967). Moreover, tendencies to promiscuity, even in the absence of harems as such, would lead, as in most mammals, to a polygynous effect, meaning that fewer males than females would be likely to contribute genetically to each generation and some males would likely be more successful than any females. A similar although probably weaker effect would be realized as a result of a greater frequency of sequential marriages (yielding offspring) by men than by women in societies which do not allow harem polygyny. In other words, either on the basis of human marriage or mating systems, or on the basis of the human degree of sexual dimorphism in comparison with other primate species, we would have classified humans as mildly polygynous and identified the selective forces acting on humans throughout much of their history as similar to those acting on polygynous species in other groups.

This view tends to be confirmed by the fact that all of the six kinds of selection we have described as occurring under polygyny are evidenced for human history by the current human condition. Thus, human males are not only larger than females, but also take longer to mature (Tanner 1962; Eveleth and Tanner 1976). In most situations they suffer higher mortality both before and after the onset of reproductive age and they tend to senesce more rapidly (Stern 1960; Hamilton 1966). They are conceived in greater numbers than females, and they die in greater numbers as embryos (Stern 1960). Based on gestation periods and weights at birth (references in Meredith 1970) and later (Tanner 1962; Eveleth and Tanner 1976), males individually receive somewhat more parental effort than do individual females. Data gathered by Dickemann (this volume) indicate that sons are favored in high-ranking families in highly stratified polygynous societies (e.g., those with caste systems).

In other words, the strong evidence of greater variance in reproductive success among human males than among human females, now and in all likelihood throughout human history, is sufficient to account for (1) the higher proportions of males conceived and born, (2) the longer gestation periods and higher birth weights of males, (3) the higher mortality rates of male embryos, (4) longer periods of suckling of male children (e.g., Cowgill and Hutchinson 1963), (5) the apparently more widespread occurrence of female-biased infanticide and child neglect (Dickemann, this volume), (6) the slower rates of sexual maturation of human males, (7) the existence and the general direction of adult sexual dimorphism, (8) the generally higher mortality rates of human males, especially from the late teens onward, and (9) the more rapid senescence and shorter life spans of males. Moreover, from the same set of considerations testable solutions can be generated for a large number of questions deriving from established facts about human societies. Examples are (1) greater rigidity of "sex-typing" of boys (Luria, in press), (2) the rise of rates of lawbreaking among males around ages 17–22 (Sutherland and Cressey 1966; Mulvihill and Tumin 1969), coinciding with the rates of highest mortality from war—e.g., Chagnon et al., chapter 12), and (3) greater rates of delinquency among lower-class and

416

minority males (Clark and Wenninger 1962; Himelhoch 1972; Cortés and Gatti 1972; Ferracuti and Dinitz 1974).

To this point we have considered the effects of polygyny only on attributes characteristic of the human species as a whole. Now we may ask whether variations in breeding or marriage systems within the human species correlate with variations in the phenomena here regarded as consequences of polygyny.

Marriage Systems and Sex Differences

Unlike any other species, the various populations of humans exhibit all of the kinds of breeding systems known: monogamous, promiscuous-polygynous, harem-polygynous, and polyandrous (Murdock 1967). Comparing human societies with one another, as we have done for different species in various mammal groups, is a more complicated task. Maximum harem size seems an almost useless statistic for humans, since, unlike other primate species, certain kinds of male leaders sometimes have very large numbers of wives, many more than any other males in the society. Maximum harem size in humans is thus an unreliable indicator of the variance in male reproductive success compared to female reproductive success in a population. Nonhuman species probably do not have such leaders. Mean harem size, which would probably be the most useful statistic, is usually not available for human societies for which degrees of dimorphism are known. So we are limited to comparing monogamous and polygynous societies.

Two approaches are possible. First, extensive comparisons have already been made of sexual dimorphism between human populations of different geographic origins. These populations could also be compared with respect to breeding-system differences. Eveleth (1975) and Eveleth and Tanner (1976), for example, compare a large number of populations of Europeans, Africans, Amerindians, Asians, and inhabitants of New Guinea in regard to sexual dimorphism in stature. Their conclusions are that Amerindians are the most dimorphic, followed by Asians and Europeans, with inhabitants of Africa and New Guinea more or less alike and the least dimorphic. Using recent history as the criterion, it would appear that African and New Guinea populations are the most polygynous of these five groups rather than the least as the dimorphism data would suggest from comparisons with other mammal groups.

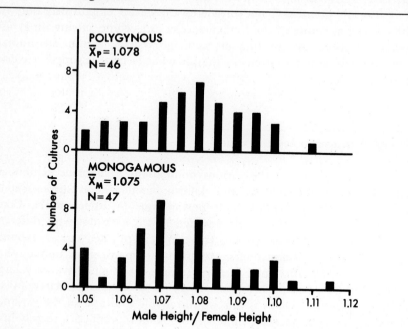

The second approach involves comparing societies with different marriage systems, regardless of geographic origins. For this purpose we used data on marriage systems from the Human Relations Area File and Murdock's (1967) Ethnographic Atlas. Considering, first, monogamous and polygynous societies, we found no significant difference in regard to stature differences in males and females (figure 15–7). This result may seem explainable on the grounds that human societies, classified solely by existing marriage systems and without regard to geographic location or origin, are unlikely to have differed consistently in degree of polygyny long enough for the kinds of genetic changes to occur that are almost certain to lie behind species differences in nonhuman mammals.

Before we accept the conclusion implied by these two approaches, we should distinguish between what seem to be two kinds of monogamy in human societies. The first might be termed "ecologically imposed" monogamy, meaning that monogamy is universal or prevalent apparently because, owing to the ecological situation, individual men are typically unable to gain by attempting to provide for offspring of more than one wife. This kind of monogamy we might expect in extreme or marginal habitats, correlated with (1) occasional polyandry, (2) wide spacing of offspring, (3) high rates of abortion or infanticide, (4) long periods of nursing, and, perhaps, (5) extended postpartum abstention from sexual activity. Thus, what we are calling ecologically imposed monogamy in humans is roughly equivalent to monogamy wherever it occurs in other mammals. We might speculate that, in societies characterized for a very long time by ecologically imposed monogamy, sexual dimorphism would be minimal. Figure 15–8 suggests that this is so.

There is probably no good reason yet for accepting that differences in degrees of sexual dimorphism between ecologically monogamous and

Figure 15–8   Dimorphism Data; Mann-Whitney U Comparison, Significant Difference: E & S .03, E & P .03, P & S Not Significant

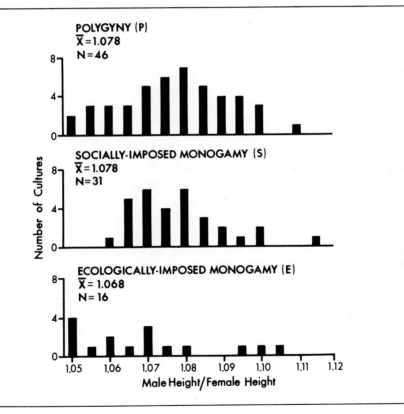

other humans actually reflect genetic differences between populations with different marriage systems. Ecologically imposed monogamy seems to occur in what would usually be termed marginal habitats such as the Arctic or the edges of deserts. Nutrition is likely to be less than optimal, and improved nutrition may increase sexual dimorphism. To the extent that such effects are caused by males responding more dramatically to increased nutrition (Tobias 1962), a polygynous background is implied. The reason is that, when male reproductive success varies more than that of females, parental care to males should vary more than that extended to females; hence, males should have been afforded more opportunities to evolve abilities to take advantage of unusually lavish parental care.

The second kind of monogamy, which we refer to as "socially imposed monogamy," is unique to humans. It is a cultural phenomenon deriving from systems of laws or rules. American society, for example, imposes monogamy on its members, and societies similar in this regard, of European and Asian origin, have evidently contributed to a spread of socially imposed monogamy within recorded history. Although concubinage, extramarital liaisons, and promiscuity of various sorts occur in such societies, the net effect of rules prescribing monogamy is almost certainly a significant depression in the variance of male reproductive success relative to that in stratified societies which do not prescribe monogamy. Some societies have become socially monogamous because of domination by societies imposing monogamy. Others seem to have begun the change under the influence of missionaries. Perhaps there are historical records of societies which changed from polygyny to socially imposed monogamy for reasons other than contact with societies imposing monogamy on their members, but we are not aware of such cases. At least until recently, socially imposed monogamy appears to have spread chiefly as a result of conquest.

It is not immediately clear what one should predict in regard to amounts of sexual dimorphism between polygynous societies and those with socially imposed monogamy. In societies with these two kinds of marriage systems, sexual dimorphism appears to be the same (figure 15–8). The data of Eveleth (1975) and Eveleth and Tanner (1976), on the other hand, imply that sexual dimorphism may be exaggerated under socially imposed monogamy.

To test the question whether breeding-system differences among populations of different geographic organisms may have occurred consistently in the right direction to explain the evident variations in sexual dimorphism uncovered by Eveleth and Tanner (1976), we could seek other

IV. Male and Female Strategies

biological correlates of the breeding-system differences described earlier in this paper. The only one for which sufficient data exists in regard to humans is sex ratios, and here we are immediately impressed with the finding, long unexplained and regarded as remarkable, that significant variations in sex ratios at birth exist among the same populations for which Eveleth and Tanner found differences in sexual dimorphism (e.g., Stern 1960; Kang and Cho 1962; Hunt, Lessa, and Hicking 1965; Lyster 1968; Cowgill and Hutchinson 1963; Crew 1937; Dahlberg 1951; Bernstein 1954; Ciocco 1938; Colombo 1957; Bernstein 1958; Edwards 1958). Surprisingly, however, the findings also seem opposite to what might have been expected. Populations of African origin, whether located today in Africa or the New World, tend to have significantly lower sex ratios at birth, with the highest sex ratios at birth and the greatest degree of adult sexual dimorphism recorded in Amerindian, Asian, and European populations.

How are these correlations to be explained? First, we can take account of the apparent coincidence in certain societies of very high sex ratios among young children and very high mortality of pre-adult and young-adult males (e.g., Eskimos: Hoebel 1954; Freeman 1971; and Central and South American Indians: Cowgill and Hutchinson 1963; Chagnon 1968a). Assuming that males in the high mortality ages (17–22: Chagnon 1968a) are still receiving parental investment, upward adjustments of the sex ratios of very young offspring, even through the expensive practice of female-biased infanticide (reported by the above authors in both Eskimos and Amerindians), could lead to a maximizing of biological reproduction by individual parents through a manipulation of investment in the two sexes. This individual-level function could be served even if it exacerbated the often-cited "shortage" of women, increasing sexual competition among males and leading to further increases in mortality among young males. In both Eskimos and Yąnomamö Indians, the high mortality of young males occurs mostly during competition for females (including warfare in the Yąnomamö). (See also Chagnon, Flinn, and Melancon, this volume, chapter 12.)

Thus, it is at least possible that the cultural practice of female-biased infanticide is employed in a fashion that maximizes the biological reproduction of its practitioners by altering the sex ratio of offspring, which likely does not change fast enough through natural selection on the genetic materials to keep pace with changes in cultural practices like war and other mortality-causing social behaviors. The following quotation from Cowgill and Hutchinson (1963) is relevant:

The sex ratio among children under 15 years of Indian families is approximately 178 males per 100 females while in Ladino families in the same region it is 86 per 100. There is no significant difference in family size. . . . The neonate sex ratio is not responsible . . . although, outside our area in Tabasco, a very high ratio is reported. The disproportionate number of males in Indian families is established by the fourth year.

During infancy a cultural tendency to favor males in Indian families is apparently expressed by breast-feeding male infants for a longer period than females. It is in fact possible to find male children still breast-fed while younger female siblings have already been weaned. Living with the people, one gets the impression that, after weaning also, boys are better cared for than girls.[2]

Sex ratios at birth reported by Cowgill and Hutchinson for eleven states of Mexico varied from 1.023 to 1.223 and averaged 1.077. Even without the high ratio from Tabasco, which the authors regarded as reliable, the overall ratio is 1.063. Ratios from Guatemala reported by the same authors average 1.053 for Indians and 1.047 for "Ladinos."

Infanticide remains an expensive method of adjusting parental investment in the two sexes, so its practice would not eliminate selection to alter the primary and secondary sex ratios; under conditions of high mortality among young men, the sex ratio at birth should continue to climb. High sex ratios at birth, then, could reflect long histories of high mortality of males while they are still under parental care. In human societies, males in particular (who in most societies are not likely to move away from their parental home or village) are not deprived of parental care upon maturity, indeed often not until the parents are either dead or without any means of delivering benefits to descendants. Very speculatively, one may wonder if pockets of high neonate sex ratios as in Tabasco (Cowgill and Hutchinson 1963) and Korea (Kang and Cho 1962), should they prove real, reflect local genetic changes actually yielding sex ratios much closer to those favored by selection in the absence of the reproductively expensive practice of female infanticide. In any case, it is clear that sex ratios at birth and degrees of sexual dimorphism in height among adults are ordered in essentially the same fashion in the several groups compared by Eveleth (1975). It is reasonable to hypothesize that their causes are related, and that these two dif-

[2] Reprinted from Cowgill, Ursula M. and G. E. Hutchinson. Sex Ratio in Childhood and Depopulation in Peten, Guatemala. *Human Biology*, 35(1963):90–103, by permission of the Wayne State University Press. © 1963 by the Wayne State University Press.

IV. Male and Female Strategies

ferences reflect genetic differences among those populations deriving from that set of related causes.

At this point we return to the significance of the uniquely human phenomenon of socially imposed monogamy. One of its effects is to prevent any males from achieving enormous reproductive success by acquiring harems, thereby depriving other males of any wives, and also depriving females of the ability to secure all or nearly all of the reproductive effort of their mates in the form of parental effort. Another effect is to assure parents of the ability to dispense heritable goods and property to daughters without the risk that such resources will be distributed among the offspring of their son-in-law by other wives.

Socially imposed monogamy is characteristic of Europeans and many Asian societies, as well as some Amerindian groups, and it is rare in Africa and New Guinea. High sexual dimorphism and high neonate sex ratios thus correlate with socially imposed monogamy, probably because socially imposed monogamy has correlated with high rates of mortality among late juvenile males (still under parental care—Fisher 1958). In the usual nonhuman polygynous species we associate the mortality of young males with efforts to secure mates and succeed in reproduction. To the extent that the various forms of military service are a part of the process of sexual competition and the attainment of reproductive success through social, political, and economic affluence, war-related mortality of young males in either polygynous or monogamous societies parallels mortality connected with sexual competition in nonhuman species. Either socially imposed monogamy or polygyny, should they correlate closely with high mortality of young men as a result of intergroup aggression, may be predictable correlates of increased sexual dimorphism and high neonate sex ratios.

Alexander (1978a) argues that the general function of laws, such as that forbidding polygyny, is to regulate the reproductive striving of individuals and subgroups within societies, in the interests of preserving unity in the larger group. Because of the importance of mate competition, socially imposed monogamy exemplifies the essence of societal laws—the restricting of the ability of societal members to exercise fully their different capabilities for reproductive competition and success, and enhancing the security and potential reproductive success of the individuals who collaborate to conceive and enforce the laws.

Elsewhere (Alexander 1974, 1975, 1977a, 1978a) the argument has been developed that the absence of justification for group selection means

Text continues on p. 432.

Table 15-1 Pinniped Data

Species	Length Dimorphism	Weight Dimorphism	Mean Harem	Max Harem	References
Steller sea lion (*Eumetopias jubata*)	1.19	3.67	10	30	Fiscus 1961; Mathison, Baade, Lopp 1962; Orr 1972; Pike, Maxwell 1958; Rand 1972; Scheffer 1945, 1958.
California sea lion (*Zalophus californianus*)	1.33	3.09		15	Orr 1967, 1972; Scheffer 1958.
Southern sea lion (*Otaria byronia*)	1.26			12	Hamilton 1934; Harrison and Kooyman 1968; Scheffer 1958.
Australian sea lion (*Neophoca cinerea*)		1.80		13	Scheffer 1958; Stirling 1972.
Northern fur seal (*Callorhinus ursinus*)	1.54	6.00	40	153	Bartholomew, Hoel 1953; Dorofev, Bychkov 1964; Orr 1972; Scheffer 1958; Scheffer, Wilke 1953.
South American fur seal (*Arctocephalus australis*)	1.38	2.83	8.4		Bonner 1958; King 1954.
South African fur seal (*Arctocephalus pusillus*)	1.38	2.67	7.5	14	Rand 1959, 1967, 1972.
Kerguelen fur seal (*Arctocephalus tropicalis*)	1.39	3.20	8.85	14	Bonner 1968; Paulian 1964.
Guadalupe fur seal (*Arctocephalus philippii*)		3.0		10	Nishiwaki 1972; Orr 1972; Peterson, Hubbs, Gentry, DeLong 1968.
New Zealand fur seal (*Arctocephalus forsteri*)		2.40	7	8	Stirling 1970, 1971a; Stirling Warneke 1971.

Species				References
Grey seal (*Halichoerus grypus*)	1.19	1.16	5	12	Cameron 1967; Harrison and Kooyman 1968; Harrison 1972; Hewer 1964; Scheffer 1958.
Common seal (*Phoca vitulina*)	1.09	1.34	1	1	Bigg 1969; Harrison, Tomlinson 1960; Lockley 1966; Mansfield 1963; Venables, Venables 1959.
Harp seal (*Pagophilus gröenlandicus*)	1.00	1.00	1	1	Harrison 1972; Scheffer 1958; Sergeant 1965; Sivertsen 1941.
Weddell seal (*Leptonychotes weddelli*)	.88	.97	3	12	Lindsey 1937; Mansfield 1958; Stirling 1969, 1971b.
Crabeater seal (*Lobodon carcinophagus*)	1.00	1.00	1	4	Bertram 1940; Laws 1958; Nel 1965, 1966; Scheffer 1958.
Leopard seal (*Hydrurga leptonyx*)	.87	.61	1	1	Harrison 1972; Marlow 1967; Scheffer 1958.
Hooded seal (*Cystophora cristata*)	1.17	1.52	1	1	Carrick, Csordas, Ingham, Keith 1962; Mansfield 1963; Oritsland 1970; Scheffer 1958; Wirtz 1968.
Southern elephant seal (*Mirounga leonina*)	1.62	7.76	48	100	Bryden 1969; Carrick, Csordas, Ingham, Keith 1962; Harrison and Kooyman 1968; Laws 1953.
Northern Elephant seal (*Mirounga augustirostris*)	1.39	4.00	13	90	Bartholomew 1952; Le Boeuf 1971; LeBoeuf, Peterson 1969; Orr 1972; Townsend 1912.

Table 15-2 Ungulate Data

Species	Length Dimorphism	Weight Dimorphism	Mean Harem	Max Harem	References
Common Duiker (*Sylvicapra grimmia*)	0.96		1.00	1.00	Baudenon 1952; Smithers 1971; Wilson, Clarke 1962.
Kirk's Dikdik (*Madoqua kirki*)	1.00		1.00	1.00	Hendrichs 1975b; Hendrichs, Hendrichs 1971; Kellas 1955; Ralls 1976; Sachs 1967; Tinley 1969.
Klipspringer (*Oreotragus oreotragus*)	0.99		1.12	2.00	Ansell 1959; Dunbar, Dunbar 1974a; Jarman 1968; Roberts 1951; Shortridge 1934; Smithers 1971; Wilson, Child 1965.
Steenbok (*Raphicerus campestris*)	0.98		1.00	1.00	Hendrichs 1972; Shortridge 1934; Smithers 1971.
Reedbuck (*Redunca arundinium*)	1.05		1.00	4.00	Jungius 1970, 1971; Roberts 1951; Shortridge 1934; Smithers 1971.
Guanaco (*Lama guanaco*)	.97		4.00	18.00	de la Tour 1954; Herre, Thiede 1965; Krumbeigel 1944; Raedeke 1976, pers. comm.; Röhrs 1958.
Vicuña (*Vicugna vicugna*)	1.01		4.30	17.00	Herre, Thiede 1965; Koford 1957; Röhrs 1958.
Hartmann's Zebra (*Equus zebra hartmannae*) (Perissodactyla)	1.03		2.20	6.00	Joubert 1972, 1974b; Klingel 1968; Roberts 1951.
Plains Zebra (*Equus quagga*) (Perissodactyla)	1.01		2.50	5.00	Klingel 1965, 1967, 1969a, 1969b; Roberts 1951; Sachs 1967.

Species				References
Bohor Reedbuck (*Redunca redunca*)	1.05	2.32	7.00	Anderson, Olds, pers. comm.; Hendrichs 1975a; Meinertzhagen 1938.
Blesbok (*Damaliscus dorcas phillipsi*)	1.05	9.00	25.00	Anderson, Olds, pers. comm.; du Plessis 1972; Harper 1939; Roberts 1951.
Pronghorn (*Antilocapra americana*)	1.01	2.47	7.00	Kitchen 1974; Mitchell 1971; Wright, Dow 1962.
Saiga (*Capra tatarica*)	1.14	12.23	26.00	Bannikov 1967.
Sun River Elk (*Cervus canadensis nelsoni*)	1.07	5.00	21.00	Knight 1970; Murie 1951; Quimby, Johnson 1951.
Uganda Kob (*Adenota kob*)	1.09	5.82	22.00	Buechner 1974; Buechner, Morrison, Leuthold 1966; Floody, Arnold 1975; Ledger, Smith 1964.
Newfoundland Caribou (*Rangifer tarandus*) (Questionable)	1.07	1.75		Banfield 1974; Bergerud 1971, 1974; Dauphine 1976; Skoog 1968.
Soay Sheep (*Ovis musimon*) (Questionable)	1.06	7.00	40.00	Boyd, Doney, Gunn, Jewell 1964; Grubb 1971.

Table 15–3 Primate Data

Species	Length Dimorphism	Weight Dimorphism	Mean Harem	Max Harem	References
Aotus trivirgatus	1.167	1.138	1.000	1	Schultz 1956; Napier and Napier 1967; Hill 1960; Moynihan 1964, pers. comm.
Callicebus moloch	1.031	1.000	1.000	1	Mason 1966; Hershkovitz 1963; Krieg 1930; Mason 1968.
Hylobates agilis	0.990	1.053	1.000	1	Groves 1972; Schultz 1933, 1944; Lyon 1908; Pocock 1927; Carpenter 1940; Ellefson 1974.
Hylobates hoolock	1.062	1.070	1.000	1	Groves 1972; McCann 1933; Wroughton 1916; Pocock 1927; Schultz 1933.
Hylobates klossii	1.015	0.961	1.000	1	Groves 1972; Miller 1903; Chasen and Kloss 1927; Schultz 1933; Tenaza and Hamilton 1971; Tenaza 1975.
Hylobates lar	1.019	1.078	1.000	1	Groves 1972; Schultz 1944; Lyon 1908; Carpenter 1940; Pocock 1927, 1939; Chivers 1972; Kawabe 1970; Marshall et al. 1972; Ellefson 1968; McClure 1964.
*Hylobates moloch**	0.984	1.029	1.000	1	Davis 1962; Groves 1972; Schultz 1944, 1956.
Hylobates pileatus	1.010	no data	1.000	1	Groves 1972; Schultz 1944; Kloss and Anderson 1916; Pfeffer 1969; Marshall et al. 1972.

Species				References
Indri indri	1.000	1.000	1.000	1	Napier and Napier 1967; Petter 1962a, 1962b, 1962c, 1965; pers. comm.; Petter and Peyrieras 1974; Pollock 1975.
Symphalangus syndactylus	0.983	1.088	1.000	1	Groves 1972; Napier and Napier 1967; Schultz 1933; McClure 1964; Ellefson 1974; Chivers 1971, 1972, 1974; Kawabe 1970; Carpenter 1940.
Alouatta seniculus	1.119	1.434	2.684	5	Hill 1962; Hershkovitz 1949; Sanderson 1949; Neville 1972.
Cebus capucinus	1.057	1.297	3.714	5	Oppenheimer 1969; Schultz 1956; Hill 1960.
Colobus guereza	1.070	no data	3.385	6	Allen 1925; Dunbar and Dunbar 1974; Marler 1968; Napier and Napier 1967; Koford 1973; Leskes and Acheson 1971; Schenkel and Schenkel-Hulliger 1967; Ullrich 1961.
Erythrocebus patas	1.284	1.827	8.417	17	Hall 1965; Napier and Napier 1967; Hill 1966; Struhsaker and Gartlan 1970.
Gorilla gorilla	1.300	1.952	5.400	9	Schaller 1963; Fossey 1971; Imanishi 1965.
Papio hamadryas	1.182	1.952	2.442	7	Crook 1972; Napier and Napier 1967; Kummer 1968a; Kummer and Kurt 1963.
Presbytis cristatus	1.107	1.127	14.417	26	Bernstein 1968; Furuya 1962; Schultz 1956; Washburn 1942.

Table 15-3 (*cont.*)

Species	Length Dimorphism	Weight Dimorphism	Mean Harem	Max Harem	References
Presbytis entellus	1.098	1.314	10.617	39	Sugiyama 1964; Pocock 1928; Jay 1965; Yoshiba 1968; Mohnot 1971; Sugiyama et al. 1965; Napier and Napier 1967.
Presbytis geei	1.458	no data	5.250	9	Khajuria 1956; Mukherjee and Saha 1974.
Presbytis johnii	1.048	1.090	4.545	14	Hill 1934; Poirier 1969, 1970; Leigh 1926; Pocock 1928; Prater 1971; Tanaka 1965.
Presbytis senex	1.071	1.250	3.773	7	Hill 1934; Pocock 1939; Eisenberg et al., 1972; Eisenberg pers. comm.; Rudran 1973.
Theropithecus gelada	1.243	1.505	3.900	8	Crook 1966, 1972; Dunbar and Dunbar 1975.

* *Hylobates moloch* is sometimes considered a subspecies of *Hylobates lar* (e.g., see Groves 1972).

Table 15–4   Societies Classified as Polygynous

Society	Dimorphism in Stature (♀♂)	Reference
Aguaruna	1.059	Karsten 1935; Salzano 1971
Ainu	1.070	Landor 1893
Akha	1.055	Bernatzik 1947
Apache	1.079	Hrdlicka 1931
Arawak	1.084	Gillin 1936
Ashanti	1.061	Rattray 1923
Australian	1.077	Howells 1937
Azande	1.064	Culwick 1950
Bedouin Arab	1.080	Seltzer 1940
Cahuilla	1.057	Gifford 1926
Carib	1.075	Taylor 1938; Salzano 1971
Chiriguan	1.082	Harris 1926
Choctaw	1.099	Collins 1925, 1928
Comanche	1.079	Hrdlicka 1931
Cuna	1.076	Hrdlicka 1926
Fang	1.056	Dugast 1949
Ganda	1.064	Roscoe 1911
Havasupai	1.068	Spier 1928
Hottentot: Nama	1.085	Schapera 1930
Hupa	1.093	Gifford 1926
Kamarakoto	1.089	Simpson 1939–1940
Khmer	1.072	Morizon 1936
Kikuyu	1.079	Schebesta 1954
Kurd	1.088	Field 1952
Loyalty Islands	1.072	Sarasin 1916
Luiseño	1.077	Gifford 1926
Maidu	1.066	Gifford 1926
Manu	1.078	Heath and Carter 1971
Maricopa	1.090	Harris 1926
Masai	1.090	Orr and Gilkes 1931
Motilon	1.059	Salzano 1971
Murngin	1.083	Chaseling 1957
Nambicuara	1.100	Roquette-Pinto 1938
Nootka	1.053	Birkbeck and Lee 1973
Papago	1.083	Salzano 1971
Pima	1.096	Salzano 1971
Populucca	1.096	Salzano 1971
Seminole	1.075	Pollitzer et al. 1970
Shilluk	1.080	Riad 1955
Sioux	1.075	Hrdlicka 1931
Teda	1.086	Briggs 1958
Trumai	1.048	Murphy and Quain 1955
Turu	1.111	Davenport 1925
Yokuts	1.084	Gifford 1926
Yurok	1.073	Gifford 1926
Western Apache	1.110	Kraus 1961

Table 15–5 Societies Having Socially-Imposed Monogamy

Society	Dimorphism in Stature ($♀♂$)	Reference
Andaman	1.068	Man 1942; Temple 1903
Armenian	1.063	Field 1952
Aztec	1.087	Hrdlicka 1935; Salzano 1971
Bulgar	1.063	Niederle 1911
Caraja	1.100	Krause 1911a
Cayapo	1.075	DaRocha and Salzano 1972
Chinantec	1.080	Salzano 1971
Choco	1.076	Hrdlicka 1926
Czech	1.076	Niederle 1948
English	1.097	Heath, Hopkins, and Miller 1961
Finn	1.063	Minn 1955
Hopi	1.087	Harris 1926
Irish	1.084	Hooten and Dupertuis 1955
Japanese	1.080	Harris 1926
Karen	1.066	Marshall 1922
Magyar	1.070	Hanzeli 1955
Miao	1.069	Bernatzik 1947
Nahua	1.079	Salzano 1971
Okinawan Gunto	1.070	Newman and Eng 1947
Quiche	1.074	Salzano 1971
Shoshoni	1.089	Hrdlicka 1931
Tarahumara	1.116	Salzano 1971
Tewa	1.070	Hrdlicka 1935
Thai nonaboriginals	1.059	Zimmerman 1937
Toba	1.064	Salzano 1971
Tuareg	1.100	Briggs 1958
Ukrainians	1.068	Ivanofsky 1923
U.S. Whites of N.W. European ancestry	1.079	Greulich 1951
Yucatec Maya	1.092	Steggerda 1941
Yaqui	1.081	Salzano 1971
Zuni	1.082	Hrdlicka 1935

that group-living calls for special, extrinsic explanations—in most cases predator effects (Hamilton 1971). The larger the group the more intense must be that selective force maintaining it. There can be no doubt that there is strong correlation between nations' becoming very large and the imposition of monogamy on their citizens. It is almost as if no nation can become both quite large and quite unified except under socially imposed

IV. Male and Female Strategies

Table 15–6   Societies Classified as Ecologically Monogamous

Society	Dimorphism in Stature ($\female\male$)	Reference
Central Thai	1.049	Hauck 1956
Chilcotin	1.093	Birkbeck and Lee 1973
Coorg	1.106	Krishna Iyer 1948
Copper Eskimo	1.054	Jenness 1923
Labrador Eskimo	1.075	Harris 1926
Ladak	1.049	Cunningham 1854
Lapp (Norway)	1.070	Harris 1926
Lepcha	1.063	Gorer 1938
Pygmy	1.047	Harris 1926; Vallois 1940
Semang	1.061	Evans 1937
Senoi	1.068	Cerruti 1904
Tibetan	1.082	Hermanns 1948
Toda	1.050	Breeks 1873
Vedda	1.069	Seligman and Seligman 1911
Yahgan	1.062	Lothrop 1928
Ona	1.100	Lothrop 1928

monogamy. This is not to say that large polygynous polities have not existed, (e.g., under Islam, the Ottoman Empire) but that their numbers, sizes, unity, and durability have been less than those of large nations with socially imposed monogamy. Socially imposed monogamy inhibits the rise of the kind of disproportionately large and powerful lineages of close relatives shown by Chagnon (1975 and chapter 14) to be involved in the fissioning of Yąnomamö groups, and responsible for the development of their own sets of laws and the avenging of kin. One of the correlates of the rise of nations, and a function of systems of law, is to suppress the right or responsibility to avenge wrongs done to kin, and to prevent subgroups and clans from attaining undue power (Flannery 1972).

Several authors have proposed some form of the idea that the force behind the rise of nations has been the maintenance of balances of power among neighboring or interacting groups (especially Fried 1961, 1967; Carneiro 1961, 1970; Durham 1976a; Alexander 1971, 1974, 1975a, 1977a, 1978a). Keith (1949), Bigelow (1969), Alexander and Tinkle (1968), Alexander (1971), and Wilson (1973) have proposed that intergroup aggression has even been responsible for the divergence of humans from other primates. Carneiro's (1970) argument for the primacy of war in the development of the state would appear consistent not only with socially imposed monogamy but also with high sex ratios at birth and increased sexual dimorphism in stature. It is only necessary to assume that these things stem from the effects of more or less continual aggression, with high death rates among young men and selection for increased fighting or survival ability correlated with height or body size, as it appears to be in other mammals.

Summary

A close correlation exists between sexual dimorphism in body size and breeding system in pinnipeds, ungulates, and primates: with larger harem sizes sexual dimorphism increases. This effect is here interpreted as resulting from the greater intensity of sexual competition among males because, in the absence of effects from local mate competition (Hamilton 1967), sex-ratio selection does not compensate for the relative shortages of one or the other sex as a result of breeding systems (Fisher 1958).

In mammals greater reproductive variance among males is a concomitant not only of harem polygyny, but of promiscuity and usually at least sequential monogamy as well; we use the term polygyny for this outcome, regardless of its basis, because many of the effects are similar. So defined, polygyny not only influences direction and degree of sexual dimorphism, but leads to several other common features of mammals such as larger numbers of males conceived and born, higher mortality rates among male embryos, more parental care for individual males, longer juvenile periods in males, higher mortality rates among young adult males, more rapid senescence of males, and shorter life spans of males, as compared to females. All of these attributes appear in the human species, together constituting a quite powerful indication of a history of greater reproductive variance among human males than among human females.

Significant differences in amounts of sexual dimorphism have been demonstrated for human populations with physical differences and other indications of long-term geographic isolation (Eveleth 1975; Eveleth and Tanner 1976). If geographic origins and physical differences are ignored, populations with monogamous and polygynous marriage systems (data mostly from HRAF) appear not to differ from one another in amounts of sexual dimorphism. If, however, societies which impose monogamy upon their members by rules or law are separated from those in which, as with nonhuman monogamous species, monogamy appears to be voluntary (and the most efficient reproductive arrangement for individual males and females), then societies with such "ecologically imposed" monogamy appear to be less sexually dimorphic than others. This is the result that studies of other mammals would predict.

For only one of the several correlates of polygyny, sex ratios at birth, have sufficient data apparently been amassed to test for a correlation with marriage or breeding system. In regard to degrees of sexual dimorphism and amounts of male-bias in the neonate sex ratio, the human populations studied by Eveleth and Tanner (1976) rank alike —that is, (1) Amerindians, (2) Asians, (3) Europeans, and (4) Africans. This correspondence, in view of the selective effects of polygyny described earlier, raises the possibility that both sets of data may reflect genetic differences. In humans, males competing for mates and resources as young adults are not beyond parental care. This means that high mortality in such enterprises may affect not only sexual dimorphism but also sex ratios at conception, and probably sex ratios at birth; this sex-ratio effect is absent in most other mammals because of the earlier termination of parental care (Fisher 1958).

We speculate that the high neonate sex ratio and high sexual dimorphism of socially monogamous human populations, and some human populations permitting harem polygyny, reflect a long history of high mortality of young males, either in interindividual sexual and other reproductive competition, or as a result of intergroup combat. Large, unified nations have apparently always imposed monogamy upon their members, at least to a token degree. Intergroup aggression in humans thus introduces into monogamous human societies effects that in nonhuman mammals occur only in strongly polygynous species. The biological correlates of human sociality suggested here support the notion that at least a substantial portion of culture is directed at maximizing the reproductive success of the individual members of societies. They are also consistent with the arguments of various authors that intergroup aggression and balances of power have been centrally involved in the rise of nations, and perhaps in the evolutionary divergence of the human species from other primates.

16. Concealment of Ovulation, Parental Care, and Human Social Evolution

Richard D. Alexander and Katharine M. Noonan

Alexander et al. (this volume, chapter 15) describe reasons for assuming, from its current attributes, that the human species has been polygynous during much of its recent evolutionary history (i.e., that, generally speaking, fewer males than females have contributed genetically to each generation, although not necessarily that harems have been involved). Considerable evidence already indicates that humans have essentially always lived in bands of close kin, probably containing more than a single adult male (e.g., Lee and DeVore 1968). These two characteristics, however, fit a large number of nonhuman primate species. Alone they tell us nothing about how the human species came to possess its numerous distinctive and social attributes.

Here we approach this question by first listing and discussing a number of distinctive human attributes. Surprisingly, most of these attributes are sexually asymmetrical or involve the interactions of the sexes. They suggest that the human male is not particularly unusual among primate males, except that he is generally more parental than the males of other group-living species. On the other hand, the human female is distinctive in several regards, most dramatically in undergoing menopause and in the concealment of ovulation. Menopause has been associated with parental care by the female (Williams 1957; Alexander 1974; Dawkins 1976), and we shall argue that concealment of ovulation is associated with the unusual amount of parental care by the male. Several other distinctively human attributes, such as length of juvenile life and helplessness of young juveniles, indicate that an increase in the prominence of parental care was one of the most dramatic changes during evolution of the human line.

Concealment of ovulation, as a strategy for obtaining parental care, seems likely to evolve only in certain kinds of social situations. We believe that by considering the nature of these situations, together with circumstances that could lead to the evolution of increased parental care, it is possible to gain insights into the very general question of how humans evolved their distinctive sexual and social attributes.

Distinctively Human Attributes

Most lists of distinctively human attributes include, in some form, the following and little else:

1 Consciousness (self-awareness)
2 Foresight (deliberate planning, hope, purpose, death-awareness)
3 Facility in the development and use of tools (implying consciousness and foresight)
4 Facility in the use of language and symbols in communication (implying consciousness and foresight)
5 Culture (a cumulative body of traditionally transmitted learning—including language and tools, and involving the use of consciousness and foresight)

As suggested by the parenthetical comments, these five attributes are closely related to one another, perhaps inseparable. They are also not strictly comparable to one another: thus, consciousness and foresight are aspects of the human *capacity* for culture, while language and tools are simultaneously *vehicles* and *aspects* of culture. Culture in turn, by its existence and nature, and through its changes, becomes a central aspect of the environment in which the capacities of individuals to acquire and use consciousness, foresight, and facility in the development and use of language and tools have been selected.

Although these five attributes may once have been regarded as uniquely human, it now seems likely that all occur in other primate species, and chimpanzees alone may possess all five, though not in the form or to the degree that they are expressed in humans (Lawick-Goodall 1967; Gallup 1970; Premack 1971; Fouts 1973; Rumbaugh et al. 1973; Gardner and Gardner 1969, 1971; Mason 1976). The problem in understanding this set of related attributes, and why humans possess them, is to determine their relationship to the reproductive success of individuals during human history, when the capacities and tendencies to express them were originating and being elaborated. Despite the attention paid to them, these attributes have not been extensively analyzed as contributors to reproductive success.

Numerous other traits are also distinctive to humans (d, in the list below) or distinctively expressed in humans, as compared to their primate relatives (de). They may be either cultural (c) or noncultural (nc) in origin, and universal (u) or not universal (nu) among humans. We first list these additional attributes, then discuss their significance in trying to reconstruct the evolutionary background of human sociality. Our reason for presenting this list, in developing an argument about the relationship of parental care and the concealment of ovulation during human social history, is to emphasize how many distinctive human attributes are somehow sexually asymmetrical (as) rather than symmetrical (s) in their expression (probably all but 6 and 30 in the following list), and how many involve: (1) interactions of the sexes in connection with parental care (especially 9–16) and (2) group-living (especially 17–30). We shall argue that concealment of ovulation could only evolve in a group-living situation in which the importance of parental care in offspring reproductive success was increasing, and that these two circumstances together describe a large part of the uniqueness of the social environment of humans during their divergence from other primates. We make no pretense that the following list is a complete set of attributes unique to humans.

6 Upright locomotion usual (de, nc, u, s)

7 Frontal copulation usual (de, c & nc, u, as)

8 Relative hairlessness (de, nc, u, as)

9 Longer juvenile life (d, nc, u, as)

10 Greater infantile helplessness (de, nc, u, as)

11 Parental care frequently extending into and even across the offspring's adult life (d, c, u?, as)

12 Unusually extensive paternal care for a group-living primate (de, c?, nu?, as)

13 Concealed ovulation in females (sometimes described as continuous sexual receptivity, continuous estrus, "sham" estrus, or lack of estrus (d, nc, u, as)

14 Greater prominence of female orgasm (perhaps—but see Lancaster, in press) (d, nc?, u, as)

15 Unusually copious menstrual discharge (d, nc, u, as)

16 Menopause (d, nc, u, as)

17 Close association of close kin of both sexes, sometimes throughout adulthood (de, c, u?, as)

18 Extensive extrafamilial nepotism (de, c, u?, as)

19 Extensive extrafamilial mating restrictions (de, c, u?, as)

20 Socially imposed monogamy (d, c, nu, as)

21 Extreme flexibility in rates of forming and dissolving coalitions (d, c, u, as)

22 Systems of laws imposed by the many (or powerful) against the few (or weak) (d, c, nu, as)

23 Extensive, organized, intergroup aggression; war (d, c, u?, as)

24 Group-against-group competition in play (d, c, u?, as)

25 Ancestor worship (d, c, nu, as)

26 Political and other kinds of appointed, elected, or hereditarily succeeding leaders (d, c, nu, as)

27 The concepts of gods and life-after-death (d, c, nu, as)

28 Organized religion (d, c, nu, as)

29 Nationalism; patriotism (d, c, nu, as)

30 Polities of thousands or millions of nuclear families (d, c, nu, s)

What challenges, in the form of differential reproduction, caused the emphasis on (1) consciousness and foresight, (2) social living, and (3) parental activities, revealed in the above list of human attributes (cultural and physiological)? If we assume that the above combination of attributes arose as a result of physical or nonhuman biotic selective forces, such as climate, predators, or food shortages, then an evolutionary sequence diverging humans so far from other species in the particular directions they have taken, with all the intermediate stages becoming extinct, appears difficult to reconstruct (Alexander 1971). In the absence of any clear evidence of a massively unique selective environment in these respects for humans, we would have to postulate that our uniqueness as a prehuman primate preadapted us to respond uniquely to some not-so-unique concatenation of environmental conditions, thereby evolving humanness. We regard this hypothesis as unlikely.

The alternative is that something about the evolving human species itself explains the differential reproduction that led to the divergence of the human line, and the extinction of close relatives along the way. This possibility is immediately tantalizing, since it suggests a solution to the problem of human uniqueness. Once set in motion, such a selective force could be self-propelling and, simultaneously, capable of suppressing similar trends in closely related lines. It further implies a reason for the continuing elaboration of cultural patterns, outracing genetic changes so dramatically as to render them trivial in regard to rates of behavior change.

The attribute that could cause differential reproduction leading to human uniqueness, we believe, is an increasing prominence of direct intergroup competition, leading to an overriding significance in balances of power among competing social groups, in which social cooperativeness and eventually culture became the chief vehicle of competition. The probable relevance of complex social competition to human intelligence, consciousness, and foresight—and elaborate social tendencies—has been emphasized before (Darwin 1871; Keith 1949; Fisher 1958; Alexander 1969, 1971, 1974, 1975a, 1975b, 1977a, 1978a, in press a; Bigelow 1969; Alexander and Tinkle 1968; Carneiro 1970; Flannery 1972; Wilson 1973). Intergroup competition has not, however, been linked to the human emphasis on parental care or the unusual sexual attributes of humans.

If intergroup competition was a principal guiding force in human evolution and if groups as a result grew in size and in social unity among the individuals comprising them, then parental care would have increased in value in two general ways. First, larger group sizes inevitably meant intensified competition for resources within groups. Juveniles, lacking the strength and sophistication to compete successfully for themselves, would have benefited increasingly from parental protection and assistance in securing resources for growth and future reproduction. Second, the intensification of both within- and between-group competition implies a growing conflict in individual reproductive strategies by pitting the value of direct competition with other group members against potential gain from their cooperation in inter-group competition (or within-group alliances). Individual reproductive success would depend increasingly on making the right decisions in complex social situations involving self, relatives, friends, and enemies. Critical choices would be aided by experience, and an intimate knowledge of the particular social environment. Parents who could impart to their offspring this information and the social skills for using and expanding it, while providing guidance during the vulnerable years of learning, would have realized increasing reproductive advantages over parents who failed to so equip their offspring. Buffered against physical and social disaster by parental protection, the human juvenile may have evolved to abandon efforts at serious direct competition, becoming increasingly helpless over longer periods, while evolving extraordinary abilities to absorb and retain information and develop skills through attachment, identification, imitation, and more formal learning in early years. In other words, because of the existence of groups intensely competitive against one another, and because of the complexity of social competition within groups evolving to be effective in inter-group competition, the human species in some sense became its own most important selective environment, and the pressure of evolutionary change focused increasingly on parental care.

Tendencies to infanticide or enforced desertion of infants would benefit males to the extent that such practices hastened ovulation in females

IV. Male and Female Strategies

and preserved female reproductive effort for the male's own offspring. The increased parental care of human mothers, its greater duration, and the wider spacing of babies associated with more intensive early parental care and infant helplessness would enhance the benefits of infanticide and enforced desertion of children to males acquiring females from other males. Thus, an important aspect of male parental care may have been protection of the child against other group males competing for the female as a reproductive resource. Observations by Bygott (1972) suggest that if a chimpanzee mother with an infant joins a new group, the infant is vulnerable to infanticide by group males. Accounts of men (or women) killing children made fatherless by inter-community warfare and exchange of women, such as among the Yąnomamö (Biocca 1969), imply that this may have been an important selective context for paternal care in human history as well, and another indirect consequence of the extension of juvenile dependence.

In ancestral humans, then, an orphan, even at an advanced juvenile stage, was probably doomed to social impotence and reproductive failure, if not pre-reproductive death, unless it was a female old enough to interest a mature male; the extremely derogatory connotation of words for "fatherless" juveniles in nontechnological societies supports this inference (see Alexander 1977a). On the other hand, juveniles with powerful parents and other relatives must have been essentially certain of high success. Indeed, the unstratified or egalitarian bands presumed to represent the ancestral kind of human sociality can almost be defined by saying that in them the major resource by which reproductive competition could be maximized is kinspeople (see also Chagnon chapter 14).

To clarify these circumstances we first examine the social situations in which concealment of ovulation might evolve and compare the resulting model with extant nonhuman primates, then consider the situations in which increases in parental care leading to the human condition might be favored.

Why Conceal Ovulation?

The human female has commonly been described as "continually sexually receptive" because she may willingly mate at any time during the menstrual cycle (James 1971). Most other female mammals mate only during a brief estrus period occurring around the ovulatory period. To refer to the human female's sexual behavior simply as "continuous receptivity," however, seems a gross oversimplification. First, this "receptivity" is unlike the relatively uninhibited receptivity of some estrous female mammals, which may accept essentially any male. By comparison, the human female's behavior might best be described as a kind of selective or low-key receptivity, commonly tuned to a single male, or at least to one male at a time. From the point of view of males not bonded to a particular female, it might just as well be termed "continuous nonreceptivity." It is a truly remarkable attribute of human females that their ovulation is often essentially impossible to detect, even, in some cases, through medical technology (Sturgis and Pommerenke 1960; Behrman 1960; Cohen and Hanken 1960).

Conditions in nonhuman primates that seem to approach those of the human female are: (1) sham estrus in langurs (Blaffer Hrdy 1974, 1977), (2) sexual receptivity outside the ovulatory period, especially in rhesus (Loy 1970) and chimpanzees (van Lawick-Goodall, 1971; Lancaster, in press, reviews other primate cases of mating outside the usual estrus period around ovulation), and (3) relatively few external signs of ovulation in gibbons (Carpenter 1941), orangutans (Rijksen 1975), gorillas (Schaller 1963; Hess 1973; Nadler 1975), and possibly bonnet macaques (Simonds 1965; Rahaman and Parthasarathy 1969; MacArthur et al. 1972). In the last case we are assuming that advertisement of estrus by pheromones is not unusually exaggerated in species with few visual signs; any efforts to quantify advertisement of estrus among species are necessarily restricted to visual signs because no effort has been made to accomplish this with pheromones.

In nonhuman primates the general period of ovulation always appears to be more or less dramatically signaled to males (even if only by pheromones or other means not obvious to human observers). All of the nonhuman primates in which females are known to show "pseudo-estrus" are group-living species, while the least obvious signs of ovulation seem to occur in monogamous species like gibbons, or polygynous species, like gorillas, which tend to live in single-male bands. Human females are thus unique in that they give little or no evidence of ovulation and may be receptive during any part of the ovulatory cycle. Although some women have discovered ways to determine the time of their own ovulation, it is clear that selection has reduced the obviousness of ovulation during human evolution, apparently to women themselves as well as to others.

Emphasis on the so-called continuous responsiveness of the human female, in trying to model its history, has focused attention on the proximate effect that the male is able to enjoy copulation more or less whenever he desires it. Thus, it has been argued that sexual competition is reduced among human males, allowing larger group sizes and more extensive cooperation (Etkin 1963; Washburn and Lancaster 1968; Pfeiffer 1969), or, that females keep their males at home by supplying constant sex (Washburn and DeVore 1961b; Campbell 1966; Morris 1967; Crook 1972). Those approaches have not provoked explanations for the male's retaining his interest in frequent copulation with his mate when fertilization of her ovum is unlikely—that is, when she is not ovulating or when she is pregnant. Focusing on concealment of ovulation within the essentially continuous receptivity of the female, on the other hand, raises the question of the value to the female of this concealment. Evidently it deceives all males in the female's vicinity, both those with whom she is copulating and those with whom she is not copulating. Such deceit would be valuable to the female only if recognition of the ovulatory period somehow caused males to gain at her expense. In the absence of parental investment by males, advertisement of ovulation would both assure the female of copulation at times appropriate to fertilization and increase the likelihood of competition among males, thus increasing her likelihood of securing a male of unusual competitive ability (e.g., Cox and Le Boeuf 1977). Concealment of ovulation and more or less continuous receptivity would have little value in this circumstance, although some tolerance of mating may be expected to appear if male insistence was quite deleterious to resisting females (e.g., McKinney 1975, on ducks). Conversely, if males invest parentally, sexual advertisement of ovulation might cost a female her mate's parental care in two ways: (1) by attracting competing males who threaten his confidence of paternity, and (2) by freeing him, after a brief consort period, to seek copulations with other fertile females who would compete later with her for his parental care.

We suggest that concealment of ovulation evolved in humans because it enabled females to force desirable males into consort relationships long enough to reduce their likelihood of success in seeking other matings, and simultaneously raised the male's confidence of paternity by failing to inform other, potentially competing males of the timing of ovulation. If these events occurred in a situation in which paternal care was valuable, but not sufficiently valuable to males to offset philandering (Trivers 1972), and in which desertion was frequent when confidence of paternity was low, they could tip the balance, making increased paternal investment profitable to males. This strategy would be most likely to be successful for females perceived by males to be of unusual value as mates. Thus, its effectiveness would have been magnified during human history first by abilities and tendencies of males to kill or enforce abandonment of fatherless offspring, and, second, by the rise of differences in heritable wealth and status.

To explore the significance of concealed ovulation, we shall now consider variations in the advertisement of ovulation among female primates living in different kinds of social groups, which might be considered to parallel certain aspects of the social environment in which human sexuality evolved. We shall begin with the most monogamous forms, such as the white-handed gibbon. The male and female form an isolated, territorial pair and raise their offspring alone. There are indications that adults are hostile to strangers of the same sex, and their territorial tendencies would seem to minimize direct sexual competition (Ellefson 1974). Males are virtually certain of their paternity because, usually, no other males are around to compromise it, and females are relatively free of competition from other females for their mate's parental care. It might be supposed that the human species lived in this fashion during much of its evolutionary history, and that the so-called "continuous receptivity" of the human female evolved because such females tended to keep their husbands home while other husbands went roving, presumably to satisfy persistent sexual cravings. Such an argument, however, does not describe the behavior of modern gibbons, which mate only when the female ovulates, and it is difficult to defend on a logical basis. If males that stayed at home, tending their mates and their offspring, outreproduced faithless males, their doing so would surely not depend on whether or not their mates provided them with constant sex. Indeed, in such circumstances, constant sex would be no more than a useless and potentially dangerous distraction from the business of staying alive and healthy and rearing one's offspring. Rather than being continuously receptive, females in such families should evolve to be receptive only during a brief period associated with ovulation—just long enough, in other words, to maximize the likelihood of fertilization at the appropriate times. They should not be gaudy or extravagant about their responsiveness, communicating no further than the mate. The male, likewise, should evolve to be interested in sex only during the same period and only with his mate. Gibbons, which appear to behave as these arguments suggest they should, do not provide a suitable model for the history which determined the nature of present human sexuality. Only if continuous sexuality in the male consistently yielded opportunities for philandering should it be maintained by selection and defenses against philandering be evolved by females because of the value of male parental effort; these conditions are likely only when families are either polygynous or in relatively close proximity.

In orangutans one male often controls a territory containing more than one female (Rijksen 1975). It is not clear how effectively such males exclude other males, and males move about, sometimes in groups, and apparently rape females (Rijksen 1975; MacKinnon 1971). Females sometimes

IV. Male and Female Strategies

approach males for copulation and are said to prefer "high-ranking" males (Rijksen 1975). Males evidently provide no parental care. From these reports, we might predict that orangutan females advertise ovulation more than gibbon females, and are sexually responsive only at ovulation time. Females may also be receptive when approached by strange males, if such males might benefit from killing an offspring sired by another male or when resistance to rape would be detrimental (infanticide, however, has not been observed in orangutans). To the extent that orangutan females select males, they might profit from concealing ovulation altogether and ovulating reflexively. Males would then gain by copulating with any available female whenever they could. But the orangutan situation, which is still known only very sketchily, appears not to have led to extensive male parental care, nor does it involve extensive group-living, both of which seem essential to a model of human social and sexual history.

Considering single-male primate bands next, such as gorillas,[1] we might again predict a relatively low rate of sexual activity, and a relatively nonobvious estrus period. Although females in a band must compete with one another to some extent for the single dominant male's attention, male competition apparently consists largely in securing and maintaining a harem of females. To the extent that this is true, females would gain little by advertising estrus more than is necessary to secure the male's attention at ovulation time, unless other potentially better males are constantly in range of their signals, and able to use them to usurp ownership of the band. As with gibbons, the male's confidence of paternity is probably high—at least in species in which harems are held for long periods—and some paternal care should thus be evident. Because males are essentially certain of their paternity, females would gain little in terms of a larger share of paternal care by concealing ovulation and prolonging receptivity. Sexual behavior in gorillas is indeed infrequent, estrus is not sharply advertised, and the silverback male's evident willingness to repel potential predators could be interpreted as paternal effort (Schaller 1963; Fossey 1970, 1971).

[1] Although blackback, younger males occur with gorilla bands including but one silverback male, and some bands have two silverback males, we believe gorilla bands are appropriately termed single-male, or at least are different from such species as chimpanzees, cynocephalus baboons, and rhesus macaques, because of the evident dominance of one male and the fact that one silverback male generally determines band movements (Schaller 1963; Fossey 1970, 1971). Harcourt, Stewart, and Fossey (1976) argue that the dominant silverback gorilla male inhibits other males from mating more effectively than do dominant baboon or chimpanzee males and suggest that some blackbacks are offspring of the silverback male.

In multi-male bands of nonhuman primates one finds the most dramatic advertisements of sexual receptivity, the most obvious and intense sexual competitiveness, and—aside from single-male harems for which ownership changes frequently (e.g., langurs, Blaffer Hrdy 1974, 1977)[2]—the most striking cases of receptivity outside the ovulation period. In baboons, macaques, chimpanzees, and a few other forms that live in multi-male troops, the females develop bright-colored swollen rumps during estrus. It is difficult to explain these gaudy swellings except on the assumption that females in such groups gain by competing for the attention of the dominant males. Paternal care is evidently minimal in such groups, compared to one-male bands and isolated monogamous pairs, and one apparent correlate is a low confidence of paternity. The gaudy females appear to be competing for the attention of the males most capable of physically monopolizing them at ovulation. There is no necessary correlation between a male's ability to monopolize a female and his ability to provide paternal care; such a correlation might evolve, for example, if females consistently gained from protection against predators (or other males) during the period of sexual receptivity. If monopoly gives a male high confidence of paternity, his willingness to invest parentally may be raised; in contrast, if a female copulates with a subordinate male, and he is quickly supplanted after copulation, neither male is likely to be willing to provide paternal care.

The trend in the three kinds of social situations just discussed—isolated, territorial pairs, single-male bands, and multi-male bands—seems opposite to that which gave rise to the human condition, at least in regard to advertisement of ovulation by the females and the extent of paternal care. Yet it is commonly accepted that humans evolved in multi-male bands. On the other hand, it is difficult to see how concealment of ovulation could evolve in either isolated monogamous families or single-male harem groups, since there would be no "extramarital" males from which to conceal ovulation. Nor does the evolution of tendencies toward regular and continual sexuality in mated human males and females seem likely in either single-male groups or monogamous families unless takeovers by new males occur frequently enough (Blaffer Hrdy 1974, 1977).

[2] Langurs are probably most appropriately compared to multi-male troops because their rapid changes of ownership by males, and the sham estrus of females by which even pregnant females mate with the new owner of a troop, suggest that rapid shifts of ownership are not a novel or recent phenomenon, as has been argued in criticisms of Blaffer Hrdy's (1977) conclusions, presaged by Mohnot (1971) and Sugiyama (1967)—see Alexander (1974).

IV. Male and Female Strategies

It might be argued that humans were extensively group-living, or multi-male in social structure, when the distinctive attributes of the human female evolved. Perhaps our ancestors lived in isolated monogamous families or in single-male harem-polygynous groups, with initially extensive male parental care followed by expanded group size in response to predator pressure. For two reasons, this alternative seems a less likely route to human sociality than the prevalent view that prehumans lived in relatively large multi-male bands. First, humans are thought to have evolved in open woodland or savannah (e.g., Lee and DeVore 1968; Kolata 1977) where, today, there are no monogamous primates and few single-male, harem-polygynous ones. Moreover, primate species in such habitats today (e.g., langurs, vervets, patas) show anti-predator behavior which seems counter to the trend in human evolution—hiding, secretiveness, and little direct confrontation of predators. Man's most similar relatives, chimpanzees, which inhabit woodland and savannah, have a multi-male, polygynous social structure. Second, the selective pressures generally thought to have been important in human social evolution—cooperative defense, hunting, and inter-group competition—favor group sizes probably greater than one male and his harem. So, even if humans began in small harem groups, they obviously (and probably early) achieved multi-male situations which tend to threaten pair bonds. Cooperation by males against predators occurs both in multi-male bands with harems (hamadryas and gelada baboons) and in so-called "promiscuous" multi-male bands (cynocephalus baboons). In both types of social structure a male's confidence of paternity is threatened to some degree, probably more in the latter case.

In summary, we believe that two coincident circumstances can explain the evolution of concealment of ovulation. The first is a social situation in which females of reproductive age are not completely inaccessible to males other than their mates or consorts (e.g., multi-male groups or defensible multi-female territories). The second is a growing importance of parental care such that the value to a female of a male's prowess in monopolizing her at ovulation time would be overshadowed by the value of male prowess and willingness as a providing or protective parent. Gradual evolution of concealment of ovulation by females behaving so as to maximize their mate's confidence of paternity—hence his likelihood of behaving paternally—would with each step toward concealment improve the female's ability to secure her mate's parental care. Because no male could tell when a female was ovulating, only a male who tended her more or less continuously could be sure of the paternity of her offspring. Occasional forced or clandestine matings outside the pair bond, in the absence of information about ovulation, would have a very low likelihood of resulting in pregnancy (e.g., Tietze 1960).

According to what sequence of changes might the human female have evolved her current uniqueness in regard to the cycling of sexual receptivity and external signs of ovulation? One might consider three possibilities: either (1) external evidence of estrus diminished first, with receptivity later increasing in duration; (2) receptivity became more or less continuous, with external evidence of ovulation later diminishing; or (3) these two changes occurred together. Since we favor the hypothesis of a human ancestor living in multi-male groups we tend initially to eliminate the first of these three possibilities.

Presumably sham estrus, or receptivity outside the ovulatory period, is effective only if it actually mimics estrus. It can only do this by becoming elaborate like true estrus, or by a reduction in the elaboration of true estrus. One might imagine that females gained directly from damping signs of ovulation, if pairing and some male parental behavior preceded concealment of ovulation, as they must have. In an extensively group-living species, however, at this stage, opportunities for males to be polygynous must have been numerous, detracting from the value of the pair bond to males, but not to females. It is difficult to see how a female could keep her mate by damping sexual signals. Rather, a gradual extension of signals beyond the ovulatory period seems a more likely way to lure the male into giving more parental care than he would give if he based his effort on a correct determination of the time of ovulation.

Steep differentials in female quality would enhance the effectiveness of this deception. The highest-quality females (in terms of ability to bear and rear offspring, and, perhaps, to enhance their status or other correlates of reproductive success), would be in demand by the highest-quality males most prone to polygyny; such females could afford to prolong estrus longer than others without risk of desertion by the male. Low-quality females would be at least partially excluded from mating with the highest-quality males by this ploy. Competition for matings by lower-quality males would be reduced (because top-quality males are already committed), making concealment of ovulation advantageous to low-ranking females in securing at least some parental care for their offspring. Once sham estrus became prevalent, reduction of external signs of ovulation seems inevitable if only on the basis of cost reduction. So we postulate that sham estrus evolved for a time to mimic true estrus, and subsequently the elaborateness of both true and sham estrus was reduced.

IV. Male and Female Strategies

Bright sexual skins in hamadryas and gelada baboon females at first seem to contradict our hypothesis because these species have harem-polygynous breeding systems. Paternity is more certain here than in the promiscuous polygynous bands of savannah baboons, and one might therefore expect the evolution of paternal care and concealed ovulation in females. However, observations by Kummer (1968b) suggest that hamadryas females, too, may be competing for the attention of high-quality males. Although harem-masters do not fight over estrous females or mate extramaritally they do battle over anestrous females so that females occasionally pass between harems. Females are more "spatially independent" while in estrus, perhaps inviting competition between their harem-masters and extramarital males, primarily bachelors. Fighting takes place frequently between harem-masters and bachelors, and occasionally between two or more harem-masters. Mating occurs in crowded areas near sleeping cliffs, and adulterous matings with bachelors are common, reducing the confidence of parenthood of harem-masters. Males in this system provide little direct parental care to their offspring, and the willingness of females to stray and mate with other males suggests that securing the best possible mating is more central to their reproductive strategy than maintaining a high confidence of paternity.

Concealed Ovulation and Rape

When females do not reveal their ovulations, unmated males no longer have the opportunity to compete for ovulating females. If our interpretation that human females are better viewed as continuously *nonreceptive* or continuously *selectively* receptive is correct, then males not bonded to a female have no way of obtaining reproductively effective matings except by increasing their numbers of matings, more or less randomly with respect to ovulation. Moreover, since female receptivity does not correlate with ovulation, there is no reason, except convenience and lowered risk, for males to seek only receptive females. A forced mating might even be as likely to lead to actual success in reproduction, since unwillingness sometimes would imply a pair bond, hence the possibility of paternal care for the resulting offspring from a cuckolded male. In this sense, then, concealed ovulation and some aspects of rape in humans may be historically related. As females evolved to deny males the opportunity to compete at ovulation time, copulation with unwilling females became a feasible strategy for achieving some reproduction. A raped female, moreover, might sometimes lose too much by revealing the event to her mate, and this would increase the likelihood of rapists' going unpunished. Compared to other primates, then, a mating with a willing human female is less likely to lead to reproduction (because she is less likely than a willing nonhuman primate female to be ovulating). A mating with an unwilling female is more likely to do so (because she is more likely than an unwilling nonhuman primate female to be ovulating, also more likely to have a male who gives paternal care and whom, on that account, she is unlikely to inform of the rape).

In many societies in which rape occurs rather frequently, women submit to avoid being hurt and usually do not complain later (e.g., New Guinea: Matthiessen 1962; Kenya: LeVine 1977). Such rapes are not necessarily associated with psychological pathology in the males or murder, characteristic of a significant proportion of rapes in the U.S. (but see Amir 1971). The association of rape with murder and psychological pathology in males in the United States may reflect the severe penalties traditionally incurred for violating socially imposed monogamy. Only the most deprived males (in actuality or by delusion) would be inclined to behave as though viewing rape as a viable reproductive strategy in relation to other reproductive alternatives; having committed such a crime, fear of discovery might lead such males to murder their victims—canceling any reproductive gain, but escaping certain death if caught.

Concealed Ovulation and Female Orgasm

Female orgasm was once regarded as unique to humans. Although recent studies suggest that this is untrue (see review by Lancaster, in press) the frequency of orgasm in the human female, and perhaps its intensity or outward signs, may still be unique. To examine the significance of this situation we may note first that orgasms in other primate females have been described in species such as rhesus macaques which live in multi-male groups and rather consistently show sexual receptivity outside the ovulatory period (Lindburg 1971).

Orgasm in the human female, and perhaps other primates as well, may increase the likelihood of fertilization (Fox et al. 1970; but see Masters and Johnson 1966: 122–124). But when should there be external signs of orgasm? We suggest two possibilities: (1) orgasms may sometimes increase the likelihood of abortion, thus decreasing the likelihood of paternity mistakes in some circumstances, and (2) external signs of orgasm may communicate the female's sexual satisfaction to the male. In the latter case the

IV. Male and Female Strategies

apparent tendency of female orgasm, in humans at least, to resemble male orgasm, in the apparent absence of a correlation with an event paralleling release of gametes (Masters and Johnson 1966), may suggest (1) that the correlation is to some extent with the pleasure or satisfaction of male orgasm to the male (so that the external signs of a female's orgasm suggest to the male pleasure on her part similar to his own), and (2) that this aspect of the female orgasm may be a communicative device which tends to raise her male's confidence that the female is disinclined to seek sexual satisfaction with other males.

To the extent that this interpretation is correct, the obvious outward signs of female orgasms should (1) mimic male orgasms and (2) frequently involve deception, with females pretending to have orgasms when they do not. Moreover, both this function and effects on likelihood of fertilization suggest that orgasms should (1) occur most frequently in (a) deeply satisfying or long-term interactions with males committed to the female and her offspring (Gebhard 1966), and (b) with dominant males or males with obviously superior ability to deliver parental benefits, and (2) occur least frequently in brief or casual encounters, or in copulation with a partner unsatisfactory in the above regards. All of these contingencies seem compatible with what is known about orgasm in human females, while few of them seem to characterize male orgasm. All appear to be consistent with the information reported by Lancaster, except possibly for the suggestion that female macaques in the laboratory achieve orgasms sooner if they have been deprived of sexual activity. According to our speculation, female orgasms would perhaps be more likely in females trying to obtain or keep a "good" male, identified as a male with much parental investment to offer. Thus, we believe that this feature of human female sexuality too may be linked to male parental care and the threat of desertion.

Parental Care and Hairlessness

A possible relationship exists between the relative hairlessness of humans and their emphasis on parental care. In the several published arguments on this question it seems to have been overlooked that the least hairy of all humans are their juveniles. Hairlessness in young mammals otherwise seems to correlate with multiple births and a helpless period in the nest. Humans may be the only mammal giving birth to a naked single offspring. We suggest that the selective value of being a juvenile, or of giving that impression, should be investigated in efforts to explain the gradual evolution of hairlessness in humans, and its present distribution among humans of different ages and sexes.

Upright Locomotion and Parental Care

Upright locomotion has been associated with the evolution of hunting and tool use (Eimerl and DeVore 1965; Morris 1967). Washburn and DeVore (1961b) suggest that parental care may be implicated in the evolution of bipedalism, as well. They argue that, as the human infant became more and more helpless, and the human mother more hairless, the baby was no longer able to cling unassisted, as nonhuman primate babies do from a few days after birth. Upright posture may, in fact, have tended to evolve first in females in the context of carrying infants. If so, then with the possible exception of frontal copulation (7) and unusually copious menstrual discharge (25), all of the attributes which we have identified as uniquely expressed in humans appear to be related in some rather direct fashion to parental care and other forms of nepotism.

Self-Awareness and Concealed Ovulation

Whether or not the above hypotheses about concealed ovulation are precisely correct, any argument from adaptiveness must take into account that the human female has evolved to conceal her ovulation not only from others in her vicinity but evidently from herself as well. The timing of her own ovulation is not commonly a part of a woman's conscious knowledge. Unless one assumes that other primate females, such as chimpanzees, are also not aware of their extensive behavioral and physiological changes at ovulation, this fact suggests that it has somehow been reproductive for human females actually to lose awareness of their own ovulation.

If disappearance of outward signs of ovulation was favored because they deceived other individuals, suppression of self-awareness of ovulation, unless merely incidental, may appropriately be hypothesized to have furthered the deception. What is implied is that social deception may sometimes be more successful if the deceiver is unaware of it (Alexander 1975b).

Evolutionists can scarcely fail to be puzzled and intrigued that with all the complexity of human consciousness, and its apparent pervasion of all of our social interactions, humans nevertheless express surprise, disbelief, or even outright anger at the suggestion that their behavior has evolved to

IV. Male and Female Strategies

maximize their genetic reproduction. Unless one rejects the primacy of differential reproduction this response indicates that it has been advantageous for us to think that we have other goals. Perhaps what has actually been advantageous is for us to be able continually to deceive others in regard to the nature and extents of our likely gains as a result of particular activities with effects on them. That is, except for avowed enemies such as members of alien or competitive groups, it may have been more detrimental, during human history, to us as individuals to have others construe continually that our immediate motivations for each social act were personal gains relative to those with whom we are interacting or for them to know exactly how much we are likely to gain from the interaction. Yet these are the precise criteria of success in differential reproduction.

It is difficult to avoid the conclusion that we are better at convincing others that our acts are truly beneficial to them and theirs, as opposed to ourselves, if we believe it ourselves. Righteousness is a valuable aid and effective deceiver. Deliberate lying is notoriously difficult as a social strategy; we are extraordinarily clever at detecting it, vindictive and grudge-holding in our response to it, and much more likely to be fooled by the selfish person with a sincere belief in his own altruism and integrity.

The ability to deceive, partly by self-deception as to motives, we here suggest to be a central part of human sociality, and of consciousness and self-awareness in the human individual (see also Alexander 1975a). Concealed ovulation we view as a particularly powerful and instructive case of deception of others, linked with self-deception and made more effective by it.*

---

* Beverly Strassman has remarked to us that nowhere in this chapter have we emphasized that concealment of ovulation would tend to favor subordinate males, inferior in direct physical competition for oestrus females but usually willing and capable in regard to parental effort. We think her point is well taken.

17. Continuities and Discontinuities in Anthropoid-Hominid Behavioral Evolution: Bipedal Locomotion and Sexual Receptivity[1]

James N. Spuhler

The paths of hominid behavioral and biological evolution are correlated through time but not completely so, because biological inheritance involves the transfer of gametes and a distinctive hominid behavioral inheritance involves the transmission of learned actions, which are affected by, but not determined by, genes although the capacity for man's symbolic language has a genetic basis and all symbolates are learned (Lenneberg 1967). In 29 population samples from 20 primate species, the correlation between biological distances observed on the living and paleontological distances estimated for their ancestors, ranged between $+ 0.62$ and 0.97, but correlations between 18 ecological, demographic, and social variables and the paleontological distances ranged only between $+ 0.35$ and 0.42 (Spuhler and Jorde 1975).

This chapter will discuss some biological and behavioral aspects of two continuities-discontinuities in the history of hominid behavior—that is, important differences arising by evolutionary change in gene frequencies *and* in environmental factors: 1) persistent bipedal locomotion, and 2) continual sexual receptivity. In these behaviors both continuities and discontinuities are important. The chapter will end with the position that both modes of evolution are also important in 3) persistent tool making and use, 4) symbolic language of the strictly human sort, and 5) social interactions based on symboling, including kinship systems and incest taboos.

Continuity-Discontinuity

There seems to be an increasing interest among anthropologists and biologists in studying the continuities in the evolution of human behavior. The question of animal awareness—do animals have intentions or mental

[1] I am grateful to Drs. Jeffrey W. Froehlich and Peter L. Workman and Ms. Frances Purifoy, Department of Anthropology, University of New Mexico, for helpful criticism of the first draft of this paper.

images?—is seriously considered once again (Griffin 1976). Of course, there are still staunch champions for strict discontinuity—a difference of kind, not of degree, separating man from other animals absolutely and discontinuously—for instance, Noam Chomsky, Susanne Langer, and Leslie White regarding the capacity for language and symboling.

Is the difference between a difference of kind and of degree, itself a difference of kind or of degree? A philosopher colleague recently remarked: "Every difference of degree is a degree of difference of kind and every difference of kind is a kind of difference of degree" (Alexander, personal communication). Mathematicians and philosophers have long recognized that nature exhibits continuities without requiring infinitesimals (Russell 1943). Whitehead wrote: "Continuity concerns what is potential; whereas, actuality is incurably atomic" (1930:95). The potential of biological evolution is astronomically vast and continuous; the fundamental actuality of biological evolution (at least on our planet) rests on the sequence of four kinds of nucleotides in the DNA double helix. There is increasing evidence that the atoms of memory and symboling will turn out to depend on the structure of nucleic acids and proteins. Whitehead also remarked: "The distinction between man and animals is in one sense only a difference in degree. But the extent of the degree makes all the difference. The Rubicon has been crossed" (1938:38).

Persistent Bipedalism

Starting with Anaxagoras 2500 years ago (Durant 1966:340), scholars have recognized that man's bipedal locomotion freed the hands for carrying tools and loads and for other manipulations and thus opened a new potential for extrasomatic artifacts and for enhanced social behavior. Here, I want to speculate that hominid bipedalism also led to the degree of continual sexual receptivity that distinguishes our species.

The empirical evidence is clear that men and women walk further and endure running longer without rest or feeding than most other mammals. The data are not as full as a biometrician would want, but Watanabe's (1971) survey of the literature shows that, while game animals are faster runners over short times and distances, in general, they have less staying power. Scores of different peoples are known to run down and take large prey by a dogged pursuit often lasting one or two days. Perhaps the Tarahumara and Yukaghir are best known, but many other hunters accomplish the same capture of prey by endurance running—for example, the

Navajo take deer and turkey in this way without weapons other than ceremonial corn meal and pollen. Women also show excellent endurance in walking and running while carrying a load, or, as in Australia, joining the men in emu hunting. Tarahumara and Yukaghir women enjoy foot races of five or six miles. Man can keep running until his prey dies of exhaustion.

In general, modern European women adapt to endurance running as well as, and in some respects better than, men (Ullyot 1976). The male leading finisher in the 1976 Boston Marathon ran the 26 miles 385 yards in 2 hours 20 minutes 19 seconds, the female leading finisher in 2 hours 47 minutes 10 seconds, a difference of about 1 minute per mile (Delury 1976: 843). The 1975 world record for the Marathon is 2:08:33.6 for men and 2:38:19 for women, a difference of 1.14 minutes per mile (Ullyot 1976: 41–42). Other endurance records include a reputed run in 1836 covering 5558 miles from Istanbul to Calcutta and back in 59 days at an improbable average of 94.2 miles per day. The record nonstop run is 121 miles 440 yards in 22 hours 27 minutes. The 24-hour running record set in 1973 is 162 miles 175 yards. In 1888, a man ran 623.75 miles in 139 hours 1 minute. (McWhirter and McWhirter 1974:441).

Of course, it is not necessary that primitive men and women run enduringly every day of their reproductive years in order that natural selection increase the frequency of genes resulting in greater capacity for endurance running. Selection often adapts a genotype to extreme rather than to common conditions (Simpson 1953).

By regressing oxygen consumption against movement per gram per kilometer in five species of nonprimate quadrupedal mammals ranging in body size from a mouse to an 18-kg. dog, Taylor et al. (1970) estimated that a 70-kg. man running bipedally at the equivalent energy cost would use 0.098 ml. of oxygen per gram per kilometer, which is less than one-half of the observed value of 0.212 ml. The observed value for a 22-kg. rhea running bipedally was 0.34 ml., also about double the oxygen consumption for quadrupedal mammals of equal body weight. However, Taylor and Rowntree (1973) found no measurable difference in oxygen consumption by a chimpanzee, a rhesus, and a spider monkey (that often walk bipedally while on the ground) when running at any speed on two or on four legs. The cost of bipedal locomotion in the chimpanzee was about 50 percent higher than predicted for a quadrupedal nonprimate mammal of equal body weight, but the observed bipedal cost in the two monkeys was not higher than the predicted. Thus, some non-human primates expend the same amount of energy whether they move on two or four legs. Although it is dangerous to extrapolate from non-human primates running on a laboratory treadmill

IV. Male and Female Strategies

to early hominids running in high grass over rough terrain, seemingly the change from four- to two-footed locomotion in early man was not at a prohibitively high cost in physiological efficiency. In retrospect, the gain from the ability to carry tools and supplies outweighed whatever increased energy cost.

Oxygen was not in short supply and needed no carrying. Man could run and hunt for many hours without stopping to rest, drink, or feed, provided he could store biologically enough food and water, was equipped with the required metabolic machinery to use these stores, and had the means to keep his core temperature steady during long-term muscle action.

When a human hunter is running down a prey animal, he metabolizes up to 10,000 kcals/day, or ten to eleven times his basal metabolic rate (Balke and Snow 1965; Edholm 1967), and about two or three times the usual rate of fuel consumption for man doing hard labor for 8 hours.

Some physiological differences that account for man's capacity for endurance running include loss of body hair, an increase in sweat output (to keep his core temperature steady while burning the extra 6,000 kcal.) and an increase in production of thyroid and adrenal hormones to catalyze the steady release of energy in the muscles for endurance running. Also, man differs from the faster-moving less-enduring mammals in the physiology of certain deep leg muscles that have more sarcoplasm per fiber, longer duration of twitch, and reach the condition of tetanus at a lower twitch frequency (Young 1957).

Androgens have a general anabolic effect. They reduce nitrogen excretion in many species. They promote growth of muscle. The uptake of glucose and glycogen synthesis in muscle is androgen-dependent. Men who have the genes for pattern baldness do not lose their head hair unless they have circulating androgens. Androgens increase sweat secretion rates (Wagner and Hughes 1974).

Carnivores in general have relatively large *adrenal* glands in terms of body weight; herbivores in general have *thyroid* glands relatively large in terms of body weight. The adrenals in adult women are about 70 percent larger relative to body weight than in adult female chimpanzees (Crile and Quiring 1940). Later studies of chimpanzees and rhesus monkeys confirm the relatively great size of the human adrenal glands (Bourne and Golarz de Bourne 1972; Bourne 1975; Graham 1970). Since there is no significant storage of androgens in the primate body, a fresh supply must be synthesized as it is used. The production rate of testosterone in nonpregnant adult human females is 0.29–0.35 mg/day and that of androstenedione 3.3–3.7 mg/day, the production of androgens by the adrenals being twice that of the ovaries (Reid, Ryan, and Benirschke 1972). Mean values of androgen excretion in the urine of normal women are 40 to 47 IU/day, or approximately two-thirds the amount excreted by males. Means of two adult female chimpanzees were 3.1 and 3.7 IU/day and those for ten adult female rhesus macaques ranged from 1.2 to 2.6 IU/day (Dorfman 1948:501–502, 516). If we let 1 IU represent the biological activity of 0.1 mg. of androsterone, the values in mg/kg/day are 0.7 for adult female chimpanzees and 8 for women. In a review of the literature, Graham (1970:203) noted that in chimpanzees male and female daily output of androgens was many times lower than the values obtained for man and close to values obtained for rhesus monkeys.

Probably as a result of natural selection for endurance bipedal running, men and women have greatly larger thyroid glands, and significantly larger adrenal glands and consequently greater hormone output than do rhesus monkeys and chimpanzees. In general, the story of hormone evolution involves changes in target organ response rather than in the chemical structure of the hormones. Females of our species have a higher blood level of androgens than do rhesus monkeys and chimpanzees because natural selection has adapted men and women for endurance bipedal walking and running. And, as we shall find, the increased androgen production had a side effect in women and men.

Continual Sexual Receptivity

The assertion that since the divergence of man from the pongids there was a change in kind from periodic estrous receptivity to continual sexual receptivity in the human female is oversimple and misleading. The heterosexual mating patterns of all catarrhine primates may be divided into attractive, appetitive, consummatory, and postconsummatory phases each engaged in by both sexes. I follow Beach (1976) in distinguishing *attractivity* as "the female's stimulus value in evoking sexual responses by the male," *proceptivity* as "reactions by the female toward the male which constitute her assumption of initiative in establishing or maintaining sexual interaction," and *receptivity* as "female responses necessary and sufficient for the male's success in achieving intravaginal ejaculation."

Experimental evidence with ovariectomized females, hormone injection, and pheromone application shows that female rhesus monkeys are sexually receptive throughout their sexual cycle, but they are sexually attractive to the males *only* when estrogens are keying changes in the sexual skin and vaginal pheromone (copulin) composed of six simple aliphatic acids (Michael et al. 1971). It should be noted that rhesus monkeys tend to lose seasonal estrus in captivity.

There is considerable evidence for a phylogenetic increase in the relative importance of the central nervous system in control of most phases of sexual behavior—experience, conditioning, and individual differences may mask or modulate hormonal influences in rhesus monkeys, chimpanzees, and humans (Beach 1969, 1976).

All major physiological and morphological changes in the ovaries, the uterus, and the vagina taking place in the estrous cycles of nonprimate eutherian mammals and the menstrual cycles of Old World primates including women, are identical (excepting a quantification given below) except that nonprimate mammals show periodic peaks of sexual receptivity and attractiveness (estrus) whereas women and some other primates do not (Nalbandov 1976). In eutherian mammals, the uterine endometrium is shed between ovulations. Old World monkeys and apes have coiled (or spiral) arteries in the endometrium. Menstrual bleeding results from local necrosis of these spiral arteries lasting 30–60 minutes eventually involving the entire uterine inner surface. New World monkeys lack spiral arteries, and shedding the endometrium is accompanied by only microscopic bleeding. In most other mammals the shed uterine cast is composed mostly of epithelial tissues and is not associated with necrosis of endometrial arteries.

The conspicuous uterine bleeding in cows and dogs, and the microscopic uterine bleeding in other mammals from elephant shrews to sheep, differs from menstrual bleeding in that it is triggered by high estrogen levels and occurs just prior to ovulation (in dogs) or just after (in cows) due to diapedesis of blood cells through intact vessel walls from an estrogen-stimulated endometrium. In catarrhine primates, menstrual bleeding is triggered by low estrogen and progesterone levels and occurs from a progesterone-stimulated endometrium (Nalbandov 1976).

The true menstrual cycles of women, Old World monkeys, and apes are physiologically similar and involve homologous anatomical structures in the uterus. Some Old World primates have both menstrual and estrous cycles. But the difference in sexual receptivity in our species—whatever its biological and environmental components—is *not* based on the difference between a menstrual *versus* an estrous cycle.

The duration of heat as a percentage of the time interval between successive ovulations varies considerably in mammals, for example 10.4 percent in the white mouse, 36.8 percent in the mare, 47.6–60.0 percent in the cat, if no mating occurs, (Nalbandov 1976:133), but only 0.2 percent (i.e., only one day per year) in the ringtail lemur (Jolly 1966), and 4–5 percent in the dog.

The chimpanzee menstrual cycle is about 30 days in length, and sexual skin swelling is maximal during the middle 10 days of the cycle when the females are most attractive and receptive and proceptive to males. A captive gorilla had a menstrual cycle of about 31 days and a well-circumscribed period of receptivity of 2–3 days duration, presumably near midcycle (Michael et al. 1973:262–263). Michael et al. (1972) found that treatment of ovariectomized rhesus macaques with physiological doses of estrogen can reproduce the sexual behavior seen during the menstrual cycles of intact females. A low dose (1 g. of estradiol per day) is without effect in both female and attending males; with 2 g., female attractiveness is above threshold but proceptivity is below; with 5 g., the normal course of mating and ejaculation takes place. Although androgens increase sexual receptivity in female rhesus macaques, their mode of physiological action is unknown. The results of Michael and his colleagues show that olfactory signals are more important than visual signals in increasing female sexual attractiveness to males. During the later follicular phase, rhesus vaginal secretions contain a mixture of six short-chain aliphatic acids that stimulates male sexual activity even when an artificial mixture of five of the acids is rubbed on the bottoms of ovariectomized females without recent estradiol injections.

These aliphatic acid pheromones are present in estrogen-induced vaginal secretions of several primate species including ours. Goldfoot et al. (1976) suggested that primate sex pheromones may be only one cue, among several including some that are learned, that informs the male rhesus something about the attractivity, proceptivity, and receptivity of a potential sex partner. Doty et al. (1975) concluded that human beings cannot tell accurately the time of ovulation on the basis of the odor of vaginal secretions. In human sexual behavior visual, acoustic, and tactile signals are more important than olfactory signals (Money 1961).

It is well established that androgens are libido hormones in male primates. Since they are present in both sexes, and since the Y chromosome carries only a small fraction of the total genome in higher primates, it is not surprising that androgens should be libido hormones in women and some other female catarrhines. In *Homo sapiens,* erotic imagery, sensations, and actions are influenced in both males and females by androgens; in males the androgens are of both testicular and adrenal origin, in females mostly of adrenal secretion. The removal of the ovaries in mature women, chimpanzees, and some rhesus monkeys does not stop sexual drive, activity, and responses. Although castrated rhesus monkeys are not sexually attractive to males (unless copulin is artificially supplied), ovariectomized chimpanzees and women are still sexually attractive. The androgens probably increase sex drive, attractivity, proceptivity, and receptivity by increasing target-organ sensitivity. Women who receive injections of testosterone experience increased libido (Money 1961). Adrenalectomized females in *Homo, Pan*, and *Macacca* show reduction of sex drive which may be restored by androgen injections (Waxenburg et al. 1959, 1960; Everitt et al. 1972).

Conclusion

In conclusion, both persistent bipedal locomotion and continual sexual receptivity in hominids differ in degree and not in kind from locomotor and sexual patterns in macaques and chimpanzees. The evolution of bipedalism and of continual sexual receptivity probably resulted from gradual changes in gene frequency; we need not postulate a Goldschmidtian macro-mutation. Nor can environmental changes acting alone account for the observed facts. Hominids responded to the selective challenge of endurance walking and running in order to take large game animals by developing hypertrophied thyroid and relatively larger adrenal glands. A side effect was the higher degree of continual sexual receptivity in hominid females.

Although there is not space here to give the evidence, I think that similar conclusions hold for the gradual evolution of tool use, language, kinship systems, and social federation of groups larger than the biological family, all based on a complex interplay of genetic and nongenetic factors.

Man differs from the higher living primates and from his primate ancestors in degree rather than in kind, but the extent of the degree makes all the difference.

18. Sexual Selection and Human Ornamentation[1]

Bobbi S. Low

Ornaments as Sexual Signals

As Darwin (1871) first noted, sexual selection frequently leads to sexual dimorphism. Competition for the best mates favors heightened development of features increasing mating success: size, weapons, modified plumage, mating calls, and behavioral displays, for instance. In general, then, males of polygynous species and females of polyandrous species are larger and more colorful or more ornamented than the opposite sex;[*] in monogamous species, in which the reproductive interests of male and female show more overlap and roles in parental care are likely to be more similar, monomorphism is more frequent (Williams 1966; Alexander et al., chapter 15). In systems of strong sexual selection, variance in reproductive success tends to be high (Bateman 1948; MacCluer et al. 1971; Trivers 1972; Chagnon chapter 14), and sexual selection may override conflicting selective forces in the environment (Fisher 1958: 152).

Sexual dimorphism resulting from sexual selection may involve size, strength, or weapons used against individuals of the same sex in gaining dominance or resources, such as antlers in numerous ungulates; or it may involve ornaments functioning as sexual attractants (Darwin 1871:I, 258). Ornaments as sexual attractants appear to signal to the opposite sex either (1) genetic ability to produce vigorous, highly competitive, and successful offspring or (2) availability or quality of parental effort on the part of the bearer.

[1] I am grateful to a number of people for assistance. D. Silverman, E. Rockwell, B. Newell, K. Landauer, and S. Cahn helped with the gathering of data and the preparation of manuscript. R. D. Alexander, W. D. Hamilton, K. M. Noonan, and E. Barrows read the manuscript in various stages and made helpful comments. Any errors are, of course, entirely my own.

[*] Webster's Collegiate Dictionary defines "ornament" as "an embellishment; a decoration" and "a quality which serves to adorn." Thus we may speak of either physical or behavioral traits as adornments in some sense. In humans, these are frequently nonbiological, manmade, cultural ornaments.

Female Ornamentation in Polygynous Systems

Because polygyny heightens male-male competition, we expect to see ornamentation of males in polygynous species. But in humans, ornamentation is more likely to be associated with females rather than males. Further, females are sexually ornamented in numerous polygynous nonhuman primates such as chimpanzees, baboons, and other primates (e.g. Lancaster, in press). What are the correlates of female ornamentation in such systems?

Darwin did not explore the conditions under which female-female, as well as male-male, competition will occur in polygynous systems and female as well as male ornamentation will be favored by selection. He noted (1871:II, 371) that there were exceptional cases in which "males are the selectors rather than the selected," and reported that this was the case for rhesus monkeys (1871:II, 371) and man: "there can be little doubt that such men (the strongest and most vigorous) would generally be able to select the more attractive women" (1871:II, 369).

In primates, there exists a spectrum of female ornamentation (Lancaster, in press), from monogamous territorial gibbons with little female ornamentation to multi-male group-living species like chimpanzees, macaques, and baboons, in which females develop brightly colored rump patches during estrus. The correlation appears to be with the range of variation available in male quality, and the availability of dominant males; Alexander and Noonan (chapter 16) speculate that sexual ornamentation in these females results from their competition for the attention of the dominant males.

In species in which male quality varies greatly, or male parental care strongly influences offspring success, male quality may become "limiting" for females—that is, best males may become difficult to obtain as mates—so that female-female competition rises, and female ornamentation may be favored.

Two conditions would appear to intensify female-female competition in either single- or multi-male polygynous systems. If males, in order to increase certainty of paternity, form consort pairs with the females with whom they mate, as in many primates, then if (1) the group is large or (2) females have developed synchronous estrus, the degree of competition is heightened between females for the attention of the male in a single-male group, and for the attention of the dominant male in a multi-male group. Synchronous estrus appears worth examining as a female reproductive strategy: any female who comes into estrus *slightly ahead* of other females not only gains the male's attention, but effectively precludes other females' securing it. The result of such competition would be an apparent synchrony of estrus among females of a group. There is evidence that synchrony of estrus occurs in hamadryas baboons (Kummer 1968b), which live in large multi-male bands, and also in rhesus monkeys (Lindburg 1971) and humans (McClintock 1971), the last two species there is evidence of male, rather than female, choice in a polygynous system.

Humans apparently evolved in polygynous multi-male bands (Lee and DeVore 1968; Bigelow 1969; Alexander 1971; Flannery 1972) which in most parts of the world have tended toward increasing size (Flannery 1972; Carneiro 1970). Unlike other group-living primates, humans have also evolved extensive male parental care (Alexander and Noonan, chapter 16). Since a crucial correlate of male parental care is male confidence of paternity (i.e., males will be favored who give parental care to their own offspring), females in such groups would be under strong selective pressure to (1) retain a male's attention on a relatively constant basis, because only then is he available for parental care, and (2) behave in ways which will tend to increase the male's confidence of paternity. At an extreme, female-female competition to gain and monopolize a male's attentions might yield continuous receptivity and concealed ovulation (Alexander and Noonan, chapter 16).

Cultural Modification of Sexual Signals in Humans

The use of sexual signals to serve the functions given above is widespread, but humans alone augment or change sexual signals by cultural means. Ornaments mimicking natural signals of sexual fitness, readiness, and availability differ from natural signals in that they not only imitate the most fit state, but also hide the real condition. A female, for example, may be able through cultural augmentation to signal sexual responsiveness to her mate continuously, while simultaneously concealing even the slightest hint of interest in other males; such ability, like outward signs of female orgasm (Alexander and Noonan, this volume) should be favored once ovulation becomes difficult to detect. Ornaments will be favored in males who can use them to enhance their prowess sexually or paternally.

Cultural augmentation of sexual signals in males appears to fall into two categories analogous to those in other species:

1 sexual fitness ornaments, which may be of several types:
   a those signaling status—right group, right sex, sexual maturity, accepted member of a group (cicatrice scars in Australian aboriginals; evidence of circumcision);
   b mimics of physical vigor, such as shoulder pads and perhaps penis sheaths;
   c tokens of physical prowess, such as judo belts or football sweaters;
   d ferocity, mimics like war paint (Darwin 1871: II, 342) and ornamental weapons. Both appear analogous to displays by other vertebrates, which may show teeth or other weapons, or increase apparent size by erecting hair;
2 success tokens which indicate the individual's ability as a good provider (and thus imply potential available parental care), such as expensive cars, homes, and clothing. In fact, any display of conspicuous consumption may become an appropriate ornament in this category (see Veblen 1899; Molloy 1975; and others).

Four categories of ornamentation in human females may be recognized; three of them signal sexual availability, sexual and maternal fitness, and a fourth may represent male-female conflict of interest:

1 mimics of maternal fitness, such as uplift or padded brassieres, girdles, or, as an extreme, surgical procedures which change or accentuate breast size or waist/pelvic width ratio (e.g., current practices of mammoplasty, or the Victorian operation to remove women's lower ribs for the wasp-waisted look [Kinzer 1974]);
2 signals of sexual receptivity or nonreceptivity, like various sorts of makeup; the use of belladonna to dilate the pupils; rouge and lipstick, which mimic the heightened cheek or lip color of sexual excitation or interest; eye makeup, which makes eyes appear "larger," as do dilated pupils. Some experimental evidence suggests that males respond more positively to photographs of the same female when her pupils are dilated than when they are contracted (Hess 1975). Tests of male response to different degrees of other female sexual signals like cheek and lip color would be appropriate;
3 signals of sexual availability or unavailability, like engagement or wedding rings, differing hair- or dress styles for girls, available women, or married women (e.g., the trimming of braids at marriage in parts of the Caucasus [Grigolia 1939]; obligatory Japanese hair-

styles for girls and women of different marital status; the Tahitian custom of a flower behind the left ear to signal availability and behind the right ear to signal prior commitment, and so on);

4 ornaments, usually expensive, traditionally given by males to females in any society, like mink coats and diamond rings. Such ornaments may raise a female's status; they simultaneously advertise a (potentially polygynous) male's ability to raise a female's status, or to provide for offspring.

Dowries, brideprices, and potlatches may represent another category of cultural signals falling into the broad definition of "ornamentation," but their significance is difficult to limit to signals of fitness, since most "signals" in this category appear to function more broadly in systems of nepotism and reciprocity.

Deception

Even in a system without cultural augmentation of sexual signals, there are still possibilities for deception. For example, if amount of mammary tissue correlates with maternal fitness (Macey et al. 1930, 1945; see also Alexander 1971), females with large breasts and males who prefer large-breasted females will be favored. Females who have large breasts due to fatty rather than mammary tissue might benefit initially. Fatty breasts, however, are probably a "cheat," mimicking fitness without providing it. If so, selection should favor males able to discriminate between large breasts due to mammary tissue and large breasts due to fatty tissue. Thus one might predict that men would be especially attracted to large-breasted but otherwise slender women.

Cultural augmentation of sexual signals multiplies the possibilities for deception. Further, because cultural ornamentation not only hides some conditions, but is a mimic and can be changed, ornamentation trends, not surprisingly, differ among societies (see the examples in the categorization of ornaments), and may be very subtle and difficult for outsiders to interpret.

Symbols

The cultural ornaments treated so far have been in the category of *signals* or *signs*, which communicate directly. A further category of ornamentation

IV. Male and Female Strategies

might be classed as *symbols,* which are both more abstract and more reversible in meaning than signals. Signals such as dilated pupils or heightened cheek color are unlikely in any society or at any time to be interpreted as signs of sexual indifference, or indeed as anything but signs of sexual interest or excitation. This is so even though the cultural ways we augment these signals (rouge, mascara) may be applied or not applied, or applied in varying degrees and fashions. On the other hand, more abstract symbols, such as hair shades, for example, do not seem to relate directly to sexual fitness, suitability, or availability, and can have opposite meanings in the same circumstance, either in different societies or in the same society at different times. We may regard blonds as pure and virginal, or as wicked and likely to "have more fun" (cf. Fiedler 1958).

The use of symbols can augment the display of conspicuousness. In some non-human organisms individuals with conspicuous, extreme displays are frequently favored (Fisher 1958: 152)—in many ungulates, for example, larger, older bucks with large antlers have larger harems or simply get more matings than smaller, less ornamented males.

In humans, conspicuousness or extremeness may be accentuated culturally. Women may acquire conspicuousness by extreme display, being first to wear new or novel fashions; further, the converse is also true—women who can successfully ignore fashion dictates, and, for example, retain long hair in a year of short haircuts, also become conspicuous. This substitution of simple conspicuousness for extremeness in a particular direction is unique in cultural systems. In genetic systems, the direction of selection is unlikely to reverse frequently; once a correlation exists between fitness and some signal like antler size, sexual selection will continue to favor increased antler size. In cultural systems, the correlation is not with any particular hairstyle or skirt length, but with *any* conspicuous display which signals ability to read fashion trends. Because of this shift in correlation, novelty in either direction may become an effective signal.

Richardson and Kroeber (1940; see also Kroeber 1919) found that certain fashions (skirt length and width, waist height) showed long-term trends, with about a hundred-year cycling period, in which variance increased when the fashions approached what appeared to be their limits of extremeness; despite the fact that fashions were "felt to be satisfying" (Richardson and Kroeber 1940:144) when in conformity with a "basic ideal or pattern" (Richardson and Kroeber 1940: 145), fashion never rested, but always appeared to be in the process of change. Viewed from the perspective of sexual selection, these observations are extremely interesting. If conspicuous displays are favored, it follows that (1) fashions will always be in flux rather than stabilized, and (2) variance will increase at extreme points. Once skirt lengths have reached the floor, for example, how can a woman make her display more conspicuous? Skirts longer than floor length may so constrict movement as to represent a limit. Skirts a little shorter than floor length are not conspicuous or extreme, but reminiscent of a couple of years ago, and thus a negative signal (unless some other sign such as skirt shape can be significantly altered). Short skirts represent both a conspicuous and extreme display; however, because they also represent a reversal in trend, they may be difficult for all but the most confident and secure woman to adopt. In consequence, variance in skirt length will increase at such times, and trends will reverse.

The extent to which the abstractness and reversibility of symbols meet environmental contingencies relevant to reproductive success, better than irreversible signals or rapid phenotype modification, determines the extent to which reversibility or plasticity will represent the prevailing phenotypic characteristics. The presence of abstract and apparently arbitrary symbols in human communication seems to reflect the complexity and unpredictability of human social environments. A difficult, but central, problem is to evaluate the extent to which selection has been refining facility in the kinds of flexibility and reversibility that characterize use of symbols (and thus trends toward the "blank slate" representation of human intellect), as against the extent to which it has been maintaining or exaggerating trends toward behavioral tendencies correlated with certain environmental circumstances.

Cultural Ornamentation and Sexual Selection: Some Predictions

As Fisher (1958: 152) noted, modification of any character involved in sexual selection proceeds under two selective influences: (1) any initial advantage (not due to sexual preference), and (2) any additional advantage conferred by preference exerted by the choosing sex. So long as ornamented individuals of the competing sex have an advantage over other competitors, selection will tend to increase not only the degree of ornamentation, but also the intensity of preference for ornaments. These principles apply equally well whether we are considering sexual selection on biological or culturally augmented ornamentation.

Even when selection other than sexual selection opposes further modification of ornaments, modification can proceed so long as the sexual advantage exceeds the other disadvantages. Consider the peacock, or, in humans, the binding of feet in ancient China, and the use of cosmetics containing mercury or lead. These could hardly have increased fitness except in sexual contexts. Fisher (1958:153) observed that the "runaway" aspects of sexual selection must have been checked in existing species, and that because of the potential opposition of sexual and other natural selection, we are likely to see an evolutionary progress of spurts of change rather than gradual accumulation of change.

If, then, human cultural augmentation of sexual signals functions in the ways suggested above, we can derive some testable predictions about patterns of ornamentation in human societies:

1 Because cultural augmentation should be favored by selection in ways analogous to biological ornamentation, some ornamentation is likely in all societies.

2 Because ornamentation serves different functions in males and females, trends in ornamentation between the two sexes should often diverge.

3 Male-male competition should be most intense, and the degree of male ornamentation correspondingly greatest, in harem-polygynous and promiscuous-polygynous societies.

4 Male ornamentation should be reasonably extensive in societies in which monogamy is socially imposed (Alexander et al. chapter 15) and least extensive in ecologically monogamous societies.

5 Within any society, ornamentation should be gaudiest or most extreme (but not most expensive) in both males and females of subgroups which are unlikely to be able to amass much real wealth or available parental effort. Similarly, within any class, ornamentation should be more extreme in younger but otherwise comparable (with regard to marital status) males.

6 In general, mated females should be less ornamented than unmated females, or wear ornaments of unavailability (category 3) or ornaments of "excess" male parental effort (category 4), while differences in male ornamentation should relate to puberty or wealth or power, rather than marital ("availability") status.

7 In ecologically monogamous societies, in which selective pressures are most like those on nonhuman monogamous species, female ornamentation, like male ornamentation, should be low.

8 In socially imposed monogamous systems with high male parental care, especially those in which serial monogamy is seen, female-female competition should be high, and female ornamentation correspondingly high.

9 In harem-polygynous systems with high male parental care, female ornamentation before marriage should be high to compete for high-ranking males. After marriage, ornamentation should switch to ornaments of categories 3 and 4 (see Prediction 6).

10 In promiscuous-polygynous systems, females seem always to be in a competitive state, suggesting that female ornamentation should be high (unless males invest only nepotistically, as in 11).

11 In societies in which male confidence of paternity is low, and males spend their parental effort nepotistically (as in societies in which "mother's brother" is the important male [see Alexander 1974, 1977a]), female ornamentation should be low, since females in such situations are unlikely to gain parental effort from other males because confidence of paternity is low.

12 Use of abstract symbols with reversible meanings as sexual symbols should be most intense in cultures or societies which have the most turbulent or unpredictably fluctuating social environments.

Testing Predictions

Although these predictions are theoretically testable from currently available data, using sources such as the Human Relations Area File (HRAF), reliable tests may require fieldwork for comparisons. Using previously gathered data raises two problems. First is the matter of observer bias: to what extent do apparent differences in ornamentation reflect real differences, and to what extent do they represent differences in the interest of the observer, and thus observer bias? Even graphic and visual analyses do not eliminate this problem. The second, more subtle, problem derives from the fact that the observations we make depend on the questions we wish to test, so that even though earlier workers have made observations on ornamentation, the crucial data to test these predictions may not have been recorded. Of the predictions given above, numbers 1 and 2 appear to be the most amenable to testing with current data; numbers 3 and 4, and 6 through 11 require more subtle within-society comparisons which may make them more difficult to test than the first two, and numbers 5 and 12 appear to be the most difficult to test.

Data related to ornamentation and social system were gathered for 138 societies from sources in the HRAF, using the categories Ornaments, Toilette, Mutilation, Everyday Garments, Special Garments, Nuptials, and Polygamy (tables 18–1 and 18–2; figures 18–1 and 18–2; pp. 472–483). The sample approximated Murdock's (1961) World Ethnographic Sample, with from one to four societies sampled from each of his sixty groupings. The modal number of societies sampled from each group was two.

It is difficult to assess with any confidence the relative amount of ornamentation, because different cultures work with different materials (Does gold constitute "more" ornamentation than leather? If only leather is available, does it count equally with gold?), and because it was impossible to determine the degree of observer bias (Does the naming of many categories of rings worn by Bedouin women reflect a high degree of ornamentation in the Bedouin, or an interest by the observer in rings, language, or women?). Therefore, another measure which appeared to be functionally similar in sexual signaling was substituted: to what extent do the ornaments worn distinguish either sexual availability or status (usually wealth or political rank, occasionally some feature such as bravery in war)? In general, sexual availability was signaled by such ornamentation as different hair styles for women of different sexual categories, the wearing of certain garments by women of different categories, the scarring of males at initiation rites, and similar decoration. Rank or status was more difficult to assess accurately. A culture was counted as differentiating rank within a sex if the author commented that rich or powerful persons wore certain garments or ornaments. When no such comment was made, the society was scored as negative, although I consider it likely that in many societies for which no such comment was made by the observer, marks of status exist. Because I was concerned with rank or status in the general sense, reflecting individual power or wealth (and thus available parental effort), no score was made in this category for ornamentation of special status of *categories* of people—if shamans or soldiers wore special garments, for example. If *individual* awards for extraordinary bravery, for instance, were awarded, these were counted, since they would signal an individual's increased status above that of others in his category. The only exception to this rule was the Creeks (table 18–1). Swanton (1928) reported special prostitutes garb, and since this category is a direct reflection of sexual availability, it was counted as such.

Ornamentation was ranked with regard to the degree to which it distinguished either sexual availability (puberty, marital status) or status (wealth or power). The lowest score was assigned to societies in which neither sex was ornamented, or both sexes were ornamented, but for which the observer remarked that there was little or no difference between ornamentation of both sexes; and the highest score to societies in which *both* sexes distinguished by ornament both sexual availability and status. In

Text continues on p. 483.

Figure 18–1   Ornamentation Scores from Table 18–1   Societies are defined as: EM, ecologically monogamous; SM, socially imposed monogamous; M/P, monogamous with rare polygyny; P, polygynous; RP, rank-correlated polygynous; PA, polyandrous.

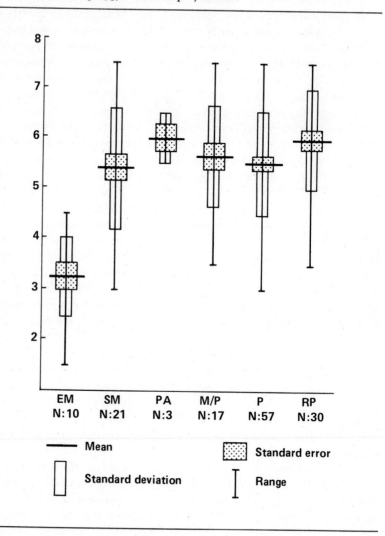

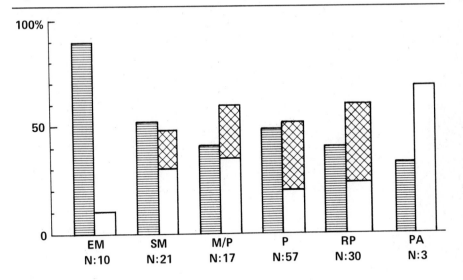

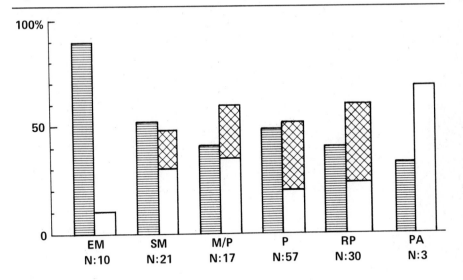
percent of societies in which male and female ornaments distinguish within-sex status equally (both males and females distinguish neither pubertal/marital status nor wealth/power status, or both sexes distinguish one category, or both sexes distinguish both categories).

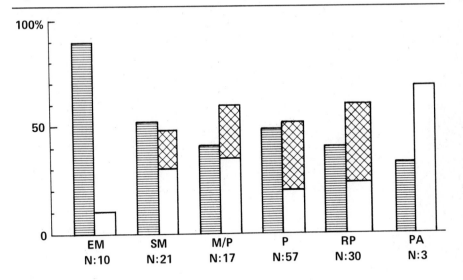
percent of societies in which female ornaments distinguish more categories than male ornaments.

percent of societies in which male ornaments distinguish more than female ornaments. For further explanation, see text.

Table 18–1 Patterns of Ornamentation in 138 Societies

Culture	Orn[1] m	Orn[1] f	Diff[2] m/f	Diff[3] f/f	Diff[3] m/m	Cerem[4] Orn	Score[5] Orn	Marr[6] Syst	References
Abipon	+	+	+		#	−	6	3	Dobritzhofer 1822
Afghanistan	+	+	+	+,#	+,#	+	7.5	4a	Caspani and Cagnacci 1951; Niedermayer 1924; Bell 1948; UNESCO 1952; Ikbal 1928; Fox 1943; Vavilov and Bukinich 1929; Cervinka 1950; Benawa 1946
Ainu	+	+	+	+	#		5	4b	Munro 1963; Landor 1893; Batchelor 1927
Akha	+	+	+	+	+	(+)	5	4a	Bernatzik 1947
Albania	++	++	++	+,#	#		6	4b	Durham 1928
Aleut	++	++	++				3	4b	Coxe 1804; Veniaminov 1840
Alor	+	+	++	++	+,#	+	5.5	4a	Du Bois 1944
Amhara	+	+	+	++	+,#		6	1b	Alvarez 1881; Messing 1957; Levine 1965
Andaman	+	+	(+)	+	−	+	4.5	4b	Radcliffe-Brown 1922; Man 1932 (1885)
Ashanti	+	+	+		#	+	4.5	4b	Rattray 1923; Danquah 1928; Christensen 1954
Arunta	+	+	+	+	+	+	5.5	4b	Spencer and Gillen 1927; Strehlow 1947
Azande	+	+	+	+			4	4b	Larken 1926; Anderson 1911; Baxter and Butt 1953; Seligman and Seligman 1932a
Aztec	+	+	+	(+)	#	+	5.5	1b	Vaillant 1941
Brazilians (Bahia)	+	+	+	+	+	+	5.5	1b	de Azevedo 1953; Hutchinson 1957; Pierson 1967

Society									References
Bali	+	+++	+		+	+	4.5	3	Franken 1960; Belo 1949
Bedouin Arab	++	+++	++		+	+	4.5	4b	Dickson 1949; Harrison 1924
Bella Coola	++	+++	+	+	#		5	4b	McIlwraith 1948
Bemba	+	+	+	+,#	+,#	+	4.5	4b	Richards 1935, 1939, 1940; Slaski 1950; Labrecque 1931
Bhil	++	++	(+)	+,#	+,#	+	7.5	4b	Koppers 1948; Fuchs 1942; Naik 1956; Nath 1960
Buka	++	(+)	+	+,#	+,#	+	6.5	4a	Blackwood 1935; Parkinson 1899
Burmese	++	+	+	+,#	+,#	+	7.5	3	Mi Mi Khaing 1946; Scott 1910; Brant 1950, 1951; Orr 1951; Htin Aung 1937; Ferrars 1901; Slater 1951
Buryat	+++	+++	++	+	+	−	5	4b	Vyatkina 1964; Wash. St. Univ. 1956
Cagaba	(+)	++	(+)	+	#	(+)	4	4b	Park 1946; Brettes 1903
Caraja	+	(+)	+	+	#	+	5.5	1b	Lipkind 1948; Ehrenreich 1891; Krause 1911a, b
Carib	+	+	+	+		(+)	3	4b	Gillin 1936; Thurn 1883
Caucasia (Georgia)	++	++				+	4.5	4b	Grigolia 1939; Allen 1932; Columbia University 1956
Cayapa	+	+	+	+	+	+,−	5	3	Heimann 1932; Barrett 1925; Altschuler 1965
Chagga	+	+	(+)	+,#	+,#		7	4b	Abbott 1891; Dundas 1924; Raum 1940; Gutmann 1926, 1932; Marealle 1963
Chiricahua	++	++	++	+,#	+	+	4.5	4a	Opler 1941
Chiriguano	++	++	+	+,#	+,#	+	7.5	4a	Métraux 1930, 1948; Nordenskiöld 1912, 1920; Schmidt 1938; Nino 1912; Rosen 1924
Chuckchee	++	+++	++	+,#	#	+	5.5	4b	Bogoras 1904–9
Comanche	+++	++++	++	+,#	#	+	5.5	4b	Hoebel 1940; Wallace and Hoebel 1952
Creek	+	+	+	#	#	+	5.5	4b	Swanton 1928
Cuna	+	+	+	+,#	#	+	6.5	3	Nordenskiöld 1938; Wafer 1934; McKim 1947; Marshall 1950; Coope 1917
Czech	+	+	+	+	+	+	5.5	3	Jirasek 1894

Table 18–1 (cont.)

Culture	Orn[1] m f	Diff[2] m/f	Diff[3] f/f	Diff[3] m/m	Cerem[4] Orn	Score[5] Orn	Marr[6] Syst	References
Dorobo	+ +	+	+	#		5	4a	Huntingford 1929, 1951, 1953, 1955; Maguire 1928; Merker 1910
Easter Island	+ +	(+)	+,#	+,#		7	4b	Routledge 1919; Behrens 1908; anonymous 1908; Cooke 1899; Métraux 1940
Eskimo,								
Copper	+ +	+	−	−	(+)	3	1a	Jenness 1946, 1959; Stefansson 1914
S. Alaska	+ +	+	+	−	(+)	4	4b	Birket-Smith 1953; Hrdlicka 1975; Bancroft 1875
Fang	+ +	+ +	−	−	+	3.5	3	Tessman 1913
Fellahin	+ +	+ +	+,#	#		6	4a	Ammar 1954; Blackman 1927
Ganda	+ +	+ +	+,#	#	(+)	6.5	3	Southwold 1965; Kagwa 1934; Roscoe 1911
Garo	+ + +	+ + +	+	+,#	(+)	6	4b	Burling 1963, 1964; Playfair 1909
Gilyak	+ + +	+ + +	+		+	4.5	4b	Schrenck 1881
Goajiro	+ + +	+ + +	+,#		(+)	5	4b	Gutiérrez de Pineda 1950
Gros Ventre	+ +	+ +	+,#	+	+	5.5	4a	Flannery 1944, 1953; Flannery and Cooper 1946; Cooper 1944, 1956; Kroeber 1908
Hausa	+	+	+,#	+,#		7	4a	Greenberg 1941; Rattray 1913; Hassan and Shuaibu 1952; Smith 1954, 1955; Forde 1946; Hill 1972
Havasupai	+	+ +	+		+	4.5	3	Spier 1928; Smithson 1959
Hopi	+ +	+ +	+	+	+	5.5	1b	Titiev 1971, 1972; Voth 1905, 1912; Talayesva 1942
Hottentot	+ +	+ +	+ +	+,#		6	4b	Schapera 1930; Schultz 1907
Hungarian	+ +	+ +	+ +	+	+	5.5	1b	Hanzeli 1955; Karolyi 1939; Viski 1932

Society								References
Iban	+	+	+	+,#	+,#	7.5	3	Freeman 1955, 1958a, 1958b; Howell 1910; Low 1848; Roth 1892, 1893; Gomes 1911; Haddon and Start 1936; Sutlive 1973
Ifugao	+	+	+	+	+,#	6.5	3	Barton 1919, 1922, 1930; Beyer and Barton 1911; Lambrecht 1932, 1958; Vanoverbergh 1929; Daguio 1952
Ila	+	+	+	+,#	#	6.5	4b	Smith and Dale 1920; Smith 1949
Innis Beag	+	+	+	+		1.5	1a	O'Suilleabhain 1956; Messenger 1969
Iranian	+	+	+	+,#	+,#	7.5	4a	Field 1939; Lambton 1953; Masse 1938; Bawer 1954; Sykes 1910; Nweeya 1916
Jivaro	+	+	+	+	+,#	6.5	4b	Karsten 1935; Rivet 1907, 1908; Harner 1973a; Stirling 1938; Vigna 1945; Reiss 1880; Anthony 1921
Kapauku	+	+	+	+	+,#	6.5	4b	Pospisil 1958, 1963
Karen	+	+	+	+	+	5.5	1b	Scherman 1915; Marshall 1922
Kerala	+	+	+	+,#	#	6.5	4b	Gough 1954, 1955, 1961a; Peter 1963; Thurston and Rangachari 1909; Panikkar 1918; Fawcett 1915
Khmer	+	+	+	+	#	5.5	4b	Porée and Maspéro-Porée 1938; Franck 1926; Vincent 1874
Kikuyu	+	+	+	+	+,#	6	4b	Lambert 1956; Kenyatta 1953; Routledge and Routledge 1910
Kol	+	+	+	+	#	5.5	4a	Griffiths 1946
Koryak	+	+	+	+,#		3.5	4b	Jochelson 1908
Kurd	+	+	+	+,#	+,#	7	4b	Garnett 1891; Masters 1954
Ladak	+	+	+	#	#	6.5	4b	Douglass 1953; Ramsay 1890; Tyndale-Biscoe 1922; Ribbach 1940; Heber and Heber 1926
Lapp	+	+	+	+	+	4.5	1a	Pehrson 1957; Bernatzik 1938; Minn 1955
Lau	+	+	+	+,#	+,#	7.5	4b	Hocart 1929; Thompson 1940a, 1940b

Table 18–1 (cont.)

Culture	Orn[1] m	Orn[1] f	Diff[2] m/f	Diff[3] f/f	Diff[3] m/m	Cerem[4] Orn	Score[5] Orn	Marr[6] Syst	References
Lepcha	+	+	(+)	#	#	+	3.5	1a	Gorer 1938; Morris 1938
Lolo	+	+	+	+,#	+,#	+	7.5	4a	Lin 1947; Ma 1944; Lei 1944; Pollard 1921; Tseng 1945
Lovedu	+	+	+	+	#	+	5.5	4b	Kruger 1936; Krige 1938, 1964; Krige and Krige 1943
Magyar	+	+	+	+	+	+	5.5	1b	Hanzeli 1955; Karolyi 1939
Makassan	+	+	+	+,#	+,#	+	7.5	1b	Chabot 1950
Malekula	+	+	+	#	+,#	+	6.5	4b	Layard 1942; Harrisson 1936
Manus	+	+	+	+,#	#		6	4b	Mead 1930b
Maricopa	+	+	+	+	+,#		6	4b	Spier 1933; Bartlett 1854
Marquesas	+		+	+,#	#	+	6.5	2	Linton 1923b, 1939; Handy 1923; Suggs 1966; Lisianskii 1814
Marshallese	+		+	#	+,#	+	6.5	4a	Spoehr 1949; Mason 1954; Wedgwood 1943; Senfft 1903; Erdland 1914; Finsch 1893; Krämer 1906; Knappe 1888; Krämer and Nevermann 1938
Masai	+	+	+	+,#	#		6.0	4b	Bernardi 1955; Hollis 1905
Maya	+	+	+	+,#	#		6	1b	Villa Rojas 1945; Redfield and Villa Rojas 1934
Mende	+	+	+	+,#	+,#		7	4b	Staub 1936; Little 1951; Crosby 1937; Bockani 1945
Miao	+	+	(+)	+	+,#	+	6.5	1b	Wang 1948; Ling and Ruey 1947; Wallis and Wallis 1953, 1955; LeClercq 1910; Speck 1951; Johnson 1943; Denys 1908; Parsons 1926
Micmac	+	+	+	+	+,#	+	6.5	4a	

Society						Number	Code	References
Mongolia, Inner	+ +	+ +	+	+,#	+	6.5	4a	Washington State University 1956
Mosquito	+ +	+ +	+	+,#	+	5.5	4a	Kirchhoff 1948; Conzemius 1932; Pijoan 1946
Mossi	+	(+)	#	+,#	+	6.5	4b	Dim Delobsom 1932; Mangin 1921; Tauxier 1912, 1917; Skinner 1964
Murngin	+ +	+ +		+		4.5	4b	Chaseling 1957; Warner 1937
Nambicuara	+ +	+ +	+	+,#	+	6	4b	Lévi-Strauss 1948; Roquette-Pinto 1938; Oberg 1953
Nootka	+	+	#	#		5.5	4b	Drucker 1951; Swan 1870
Okinawan	+ + +	+ + +	+	+	+	4.5	1b	Pitts, Lebra, and Suttles 1955
Ona	+ + +	+ + +	+	+		4	1a	Gusinde 1931
Orokaiva	+ + +	+ + +	+,#	+,#	+	6.5	4a	Williams 1928, 1930; Reay 1954
Paez	+,—	+	+			3	1a	Nachtigall 1955; Hernandez de Alba 1946
Paiute	+	+	+,#	#	+	6.5	4a	Kelly 1934; Lowie 1924; Angulo and Freeland 1929; Stewart 1937, 1941; Park 1934, 1937, 1938; Whiting 1950; Loud 1931
Papago	+	+	+	+,#	+	6.5	4a	Underhill 1936, 1939, 1946; Lumholtz 1902, 1912; Davis 1920; Hayden 1937; Castetter and Underhill 1935; Densmore 1929; Spicer and Chesky 1949; Bartlett 1854
Pawnee	+	+	+,#	+,#	+	7.5	4a	Fletcher 1904; Lesser 1933; Murie 1914; Dorsey and Murie 1940; Linton 1922, 1923a; Wedel 1936; Grinnell 1961; Weltfish 1965
Pomo	+ + + +	+ + + +	+	+	+	5.5	4b	Kroeber 1953; Loeb 1926
Pukapukan	+	+	+	+,#	+	6.5	1b	Beaglehole and Beaglehole 1938
Pygmy (Mbutu)		+	+		+	3.5	1a	Turnbull 1965a, 1965b
Rif	+	+		+	+	4.5	4a	Coon 1931
Samoan	+ + + +	+ + + +	+,#	+,#	+	7.5	4a	Mead 1928, 1930a; Grattan 1948; Keesing 1938; Turner 1884; Handy and Handy 1924; Buck 1930; Stair 1897

Table 18-1 (cont.)

Culture	Orn[1] m	f	Diff[2] m/f	Diff[3] f/f	Diff[3] m/m	Cerem[4] Orn	Score[5] Orn	Marr[6] Syst	References
Samoyed	+	+	(+)	+,−			3	1a	Hajdu 1963; Islavin 1847; Popov 1966
Semang	+	+	+	+,#			5	4b	Schebesta 1954; Evans 1937
Seri	+	+	+	#		+	4.5	4a	Davis 1965; Davis and Dawson 1945; McGee 1898; Kroeber 1931
Shilluk	+	+	+		+,#		5	4b	Westerman 1912; Dempsey 1955; Seligman and Seligman 1932b; Oyler 1926; Howell and Thompson 1946; Pumphrey 1941
Sinhalese	+	+	+	+	#	(+)	5	4b	Yalman 1971; Beaglehole and Beaglehole 1938; Leach 1961
Siriono	+	+	+				3	4b	Holmberg 1946, 1950; Ryden 1941; Métraux 1942
Siwans	+	+	+	+,#	#	−	6	3	Radwan 1929
Somali	+	+	+	+	+,#		6	4a	Puccioni 1936; Steindorf 1904; Belgrave 1923; Lewis 1955; Swane 1900; Cerulli 1959
Talamanca	+	+	+				3	4b	Stone 1949; Skinner 1920; Gabb 1876
Tallensi	+	+	+	−	#	+	4.5	4a	Fortes 1938, 1945; Rattray 1932
Tamil	+	+	+	+	+	+	3.5	1b	Yalman 1971
Tapirap	+	+	+	+	+,#	+	5.5	3	Baldus 1937, 1949; Wagley 1945, 1960
Tarasco	+	+	+	#	#		6.5	4a	Beals 1946; Kaplan 1951; Boyd 1958
Tarahumara	+	+	+		#	+	5.5	3	Bennett and Zingg 1935; Lumholtz 1902; Passin 1943
Tehuelcha	+	+	+	+,#			5	3	Cooper 1946; Musters 1873; Viedma 1837; Bourne 1874
Tewa	+	+	+		+	+	4.5	1b	Parsons 1929; Robbins et al. 1916

Society									References
Thai (central)	+	+	+		+		3	1a	Hauck et al. 1958
Thonga	+	+	+	+	+,#	+	6.5	4a	Junod 1927
Tibetan	+	+	+	#	#	+	5.5	2	Shen and Liu 1953
Tikopia	+	+	+	+	+,#	+	6.5	4b	Firth 1914, 1936, 1940, 1959, 1970; Rivers 1914
Timbira	+	+	+	−	+,#	+	5.5	1b	Nimuendajú 1946; Kissenbirth 1912
Tiv	+	+	+	+	+,#	+	6.5	4b	Akiga 1939; Abraham 1940; Temple 1922; Bohannan and Bohannan 1953, 1969
Toda	+	+	(+)	+,#	#	(+)	6	2	Peter 1963; Rivers 1906; Marshall 1873; Thurston 1909
Trukese	+	+	+	+	+,#	+	6.5	3	Goodenough 1951; Gladwin and Sarason 1953; LeBar 1964; Matsumura 1918; Hall and Pelzer 1946; Bollig 1927; Krämer 1932; Mahony 1970
Tuareg	+	+	+	+	#	+	5.5	1b	Lhote 1944; Nicolaisen 1963; Benhazera 1908
Tubatulaba	+	+	+	−	−	+	3.5	1a	Voegelin 1935, 1938; Gayton 1948
Turkoman	+	+	+	+	#	+	5.5	4b	Leix 1941
U.S. whites (Northern European descent)	+	+	(+)	+,#	+,#	+	7.5	1b	Seligman and Seligman 1911
Vedda	+	+	+	+	+		5	1b	Coughlin 1950; De Soudack 1916; Tran-Nuong Hahn 1882; Gourou 1936; Richard 1867; Coulet 1926; Vassal 1910; Vincent 1874; Tran-Van-Trai 1942; Brodrick 1942; Laborde 1918; Orléans 1894
Vietnamese	+	+	+	+,#	+,#	+	7	4b	
Winnebago	+	+	+	+	#	+	5.5	4b	Lurie 1953; Radin 1916; Michelson 1935; Crashing Thunder 1926
Wogeo	+	+	+	+	+,#	+	6.5	4b	Hogbin 1935a, 1935b, 1938, 1939, 1945, 1946, 1970

Table 18-1 (cont.)

Culture	Orn[1] m	Orn[1] f	Diff[2] m/f	Diff[3] f/f	Diff[3] m/m	Cerem[4] Orn	Score[5] Orn	Marr[6] Syst	References
Wolof	+	+	+	+,#	#	(+)	6	4a	Gamble 1957; Gorer 1935; Bérenger-Féraud 1879
Xavanti	+	+	+		#	+	4.5	3	Severin 1973
Yaruru	+	+	+			+	3.5	4a	Petrullo 1939
Yoruba	+	+	+	+,#	+,#	+	7.5	4b	Johnson 1921; Prince 1964; Lloyd 1965; Forde 1951; Ajisafe 1924; Parrinder 1949
Zuñi	+	+	+	#		+	4.5	1b	Kroeber 1972; Stevenson 1902

[1] Ornamentation was scored as + if the observer mentioned ornaments, or described them; scored as − if the observer noted that no ornamentation was worn; scored as a blank if the observer made no mention of ornamentation.

[2] Scored as a + if the observer noted differences, as a − if the observer noted that there were no differences, as a (+) if the observer noted differences but counted the differences as slight, and as a blank if the observer gave no information relating to differences in ornamentation.

[3] Scored as a + if the observer commented on ornamentation which differentiated either pubertal or marital status, as a # if ornamentation differentiated wealth, rank or status, as a − if the observer claimed that there were no within-sex distinctions of ornament.

[4] Scored as a + if special garments or paraphernalia were used in ceremonies, as − if the observer reported no special garb for ceremonies, and as (+) if no special garb was reported, but the observer noted that all wore their best garments.

[5] Scoring for ornamentation: (1) = no ornamentation reported for either sex, or ornamentation reported for both sexes, but with little difference between the sexes, (2) = ornamentation reported for one sex only, (3) = ornamentation reported for both sexes, with moderate to extreme differences between sexes, (4) = within either sex, ornamentation differs either between (a) marital or pubertal status or (b) wealth, rank, or status, (5) = in both sexes, either marital or wealth/rank status is differentiated, or in one sex, both are differentiated, (6) = in one sex, either marital or wealth status is differentiated, and in the other sex, both are differentiated, (7) = in both sexes, both marital and wealth status are differentiated. A value of 0.5 was added to the base score if special ornaments or apparel were worn for ceremonial occasions.

[6] Marriage system: 1a = ecologically monogamous; 1b = socially imposed monogamy (see text); 2 = polyandry; 3 = monogamy with rare polygyny; 4a = polygyny associated with male rank or status; 4b = polygyny reported without comment that it was rank-correlated

Table 18–2 Statistical Summary of Ornamentation Scores

A. Statistical Descriptors for the Ornamentation Scores

Society	N	Min	Max	Mean	S.D.	Skewness	Kurtosis
EM	10	1.5	4.5	3.25	0.791	−0.711	0.844
SM	21	3.0	7.5	5.40	1.241	−0.380	−0.231
M/P	17	3.5	7.5	5.65	1.086	−0.013	−0.520
P	57	3.0	7.5	3.52	1.154	−0.379	−0.339
RP	30	3.5	7.5	6.10	1.062	−0.464	−0.394
PA	3	5.5	6.5	6.00	0.500	0	−1.500

B. One-Way Scheffe Analysis of Variance Pairwise Comparison of Means

	Diff	Signif
EM		
SM	−2.155	p < .01
M/P	−2.397	p < .01
P	−2.267	p < .01
RP	−2.850	p < .01
PA	−2.750	p < .025
SM		
M/P	−0.242	NS
P	−0.112	NS
RP	−0.695	NS
PA	−0.595	NS
M/P		
P	0.129	NS
RP	−0.453	NS
PA	−0.353	NS
P		
RP	−0.583	NS
PA	−0.483	NS
RP		
PA	0.100	NS

EM = "ecologically" monogamous, SM = "socially" monogamous (see text), M/P = monogamous with rare polygyny reported, P = polygyny reported without comment by the observer that polygyny was associated with rank, RP = polygyny in which the number of wives correlated with a man's status or wealth, PA = polyandrous.

addition, rank score was raised slightly if special ornaments or garments were worn for ceremonial occasions, but not if the observer simply remarked that for a given occasion all participants wore their best garments.

Data on marriage systems were also taken from the HRAF. If an observer reported a society as monogamous and listed no exceptions, the society was counted as monogamous. In general, these societies tended to be small groups living in resource-poor environments, usually hunter-gatherers or subsistence agriculturalists.

Because I was interested in the question of ornaments as sexual signals, the degree of polygyny (as a crude reflection of the variance in reproductive success) was important. Many societies usually called "monogamous" actually have some polygyny, or a high rate of second marriages. If a society was called monogamous but the observer reported rare polygyny, or if the observer reported that polygyny was allowed but that almost no one could afford more than one wife, the society was listed as "monogamous with rare polygyny." Another category of society usually called monogamous includes large national groups in which monogamy is not necessarily advantageous at the individual level, but in which monogamy appears to be socially imposed. Frequently such societies are effectively polygynous or promiscuous-polygynous because of second (or more) marriages.

When the ornamentation scores for these two kinds of societies, monogamous with rare polygyny and "socially" monogamous, are compared with the ornamentation scores for "ecologically" monogamous societies, the scores of the societies in which polygyny or serial marriages occur are significantly higher than the scores of the "ecologically" monogamous societies ($p < .01$; table 18–2), and not significantly different ($p > .2$) from those of polygynous societies. Alexander et al. (this volume, chapter 15), who first made the distinction between ecologically and socially imposed monogamy, found similar patterns in sexual dimorphism in humans: patterns in the socially imposed monogamous systems approximated those of polygynous systems, and differed from those of ecologically imposed systems. An important difference should be noted, however. Cultural responses are more quickly made and more quickly reversed than physical responses such as sexual dimorphism. Thus in a society which has social strictures against polygyny but is only relatively recently in a resource-poor environment which makes polygyny disadvantageous to individuals (in table 18–1, Innis Beag is perhaps an example), one might expect cultural aspects to respond much more quickly than physical aspects.

Societies for which the reporter recorded polygyny as frequent, but without specifying that the number of wives correlated with a man's status or power, were classed as polygynous. Societies in which polygyny was reported as rank-correlated were classed as rank-associated polygyny.

In three societies, polyandry was reported as more than a rare occurrence in a society otherwise monogamous or polygynous; these were counted as polyandrous.

The data gathered in the way just described (tables 18–1, 18–2; figures 18–1, 18–2) provided information relevant to predictions 1, 2, 3, 6, and 7. Predictions 1 and 2 appeared fulfilled: no society, even those in harsh conditions with material for ornaments, lacked ornamentation entirely, and ornamentation patterns differed between the sexes. The patterns of ornamentation between societies, between sexes within societies, and within each sex within societies, provide information relevant to predictions 3, 6, and 7.

Ecologically monogamous societies had a mean ornamentation score significantly lower than all other societies ($p < .025$ when compared with polyandrous, $p < .01$ for all others; table 18–2); the ornamentation scores of societies with all other kinds of marriage systems did not differ significantly ($p > .2$) from each other (figure 18–1, table 18–2). Further, there are differences among societies in the degree to which male ornaments and female ornaments distinguish something about the wearer's within-sex status: pubertal or marital status (+ in table 18–1) or wealth or power status (♯ in table 18–1). As figure 18–2 shows, in nine out of ten ecologically monogamous societies, male and female ornaments were equally discriminating about within-sex status, with both sexes discriminating neither "+" nor "♯" status, or both sexes discriminating one, or both sexes discriminating both kinds of status. In one out of ten, female ornaments distinguished more about within-sex status than did male ornaments.

Polyandrous societies had a relatively high ornamentation score (figure 18–1, table 18–2), and in two of the three societies, female ornaments distinguished more about a woman than male ornament did about a man (figure 18–2).

The only societies in which male ornament signaled more about within-sex status than did female ornaments were societies which appear to be effectively polygynous: polygynous societies (32 percent of polygynous societies fell in this category), rank-associated polygynous societies (37 percent), monogamous societies in which rare polygyny was reported (24 percent), and "socially imposed" monogamous systems (19 percent).

Of the 138 societies, 102 distinguish by ornament or garment the marital or pubertal status of females. Of these, only 3 distinguish puberty without distinguishing marital status. Forty-nine societies distinguish wealth by female ornamentation, though no society appears to distinguish power as a separate entity by female ornament. Thirty-three of these societies are polygynous or rank-associated polygynous, 8 are monogamous with rare polygyny, and 4 are socially monogamous; in these cases it is difficult to tell whether the distinction of wealth by ornament is a distinction relating to the female herself, or merely a reflection of her husband's wealth (see category 4 of female ornaments).

Eighty-seven societies distinguish male status by ornament, 39 of them without distinguishing pubertal or marital status. Of the 70 societies in which marital or pubertal status is distinguished (whether or not rank or status is distinguished), only four (two of the four are ecologically monogamous) distinguish marital status; the others distinguish puberty but not marital status. Thus there is a trend for female ornamentation to distinguish sexual availability (pubertal or marital status), while male ornamentation tends to distinguish rank and frequently puberty, but seldom marital status.

Discussion

The above tests suggest that further testing should be done as fuller information becomes available both on degree and kind of ornamentation, and other parameters not measured here. This is true not only for predictions I have given but not tested here, but for other hypotheses as well. For example, group size, which may provide a crude estimate of societal complexity, should be tested for correlation with the degree of differentiation in ornamentation.

The predictions tested here further suggest that selection theory is useful in phrasing questions about ornamentation in a testable manner. It predicts the general categories of ornaments likely to be perpetuated—signals of youth, vigor, available parental effort, and so on. With some knowledge of the environment in which a culture exists, selection theory may predict further aspects of what constitutes "fitness" in that environment. For example, we would never predict that a thin woman would be considered beautiful in an Eskimo society. In a Western industrial society with some class distinctions, and some general dietary correlates with class or income, the matter of what a woman's weight might signal about her reproductive potential appears more complex. Emaciation implies extremely low income (or a pathological condition), overweight may signal low income with considerable starch in the diet, or middle-class over-consumption of food. There is a category of weight sometimes close to emaciation, but without other signals attendant on poverty or malnutrition, in which thinness may signal a woman of the leisure class, associated with a powerful male, and able to return periodically to an expensive health farm. Veblen (1899:107) gives an interesting insight into this phenomenon at the turn of the century.

IV. Male and Female Strategies

Selection theory further predicts, by analogy with selection on biological sexual signals, that culturally augmented sexual signals may be favored when they represent a novelty; and that they should be favored when they exist in a somewhat exaggerated form. These predictions have existed in some form for considerable time. As Darwin noted:

> As the great anatomist Bichat long ago said, if everyone were cast in the same mold, there would be no such thing as beauty. If all our women were to become as the Venus de Medici, we should for a time be charmed; but we should soon wish for variety; and as soon as we had obtained variety, we should wish to see certain characters in our women a little exaggerated beyond the then existing standard [1871: II, 354]

Currently, selection theory seems unlikely to predict finely enough to suggest *exactly* what will constitute beauty in any society, or *exactly* which novelty will be currently favored—whether this will be the year of the short skirt, or the year of slacks. Nonetheless, selection theory is extremely useful in posing predictions against which observations may be tested, and in giving direction to the observations we make.

19. Early Termination of Parental Investment in Mammals, Including Humans

William P. Bernds and David P. Barash

Both Williams (1957) and Hamilton (1966) have argued that senescence may have evolved as a result of selection for those control genes which would cause the expression of debilitating traits after the conclusion of the reproductive period. In addition, they have proposed that the same process may be responsible for the evolution of mechanisms which would end investment in a defective offspring at an early stage. However, neither author has been explicit about methods and mechanisms which might be involved in the early termination of parental investment. In this paper we propose a general theory for the early termination of parental investment in mammals, including humans—i.e., a glimpse at the other side of senility.

A mammal may refuse to initiate parental investment (Trivers 1972) by failing to form viable gametes (aspermia and anovulation). Furthermore, parental investment may be terminated by failure to fertilize an ovum, failure to implant, resorbtion, mummification, spontaneous abortion, and early infanticide or cannibalism. These are given in the chronological order that they may be employed by a parent or developing organism. Up to "spontaneous abortion," this order also reflects increasing *direct cost* to the parent, in that risk to the parent's health varies directly with the step of offspring development at which parental investment is terminated: anovulation and failure to implant cause lesser maternal risk than does abortion following implantation. Furthermore, the *indirect cost* of terminating parental investment also increases with delay in such termination, because a parent's reproductive value decreases after its age at first reproduction.

Embryologists commonly consider these alternatives not as methods used to end investment, but as an inevitable response to inadequate morphogenesis or maternal incompetence. This proximate explanation not only fails to account for observed variation in which method may be employed, given a specific defect of the offspring, but also fails to explain why morphogenesis is so often inadequate. In contrast, an evolutionary interpretation suggests that living things may well be possessed of considerable "enlightened self-interest." If we grant that living things are selected for maximization of their inclusive fitness (Hamilton 1964), the situation may well arise in which gametic altruism, fetal altruism, and/or parental manipulation (Alexander 1974) may produce early termination of parental investment. We therefore propose that living things may be considerably more than passive recipients of the vagaries of gametogenesis and embryogenesis. Rather, to an extent hitherto unappreciated by biologists, we may be the "masters of our fate" and the captains of our embryos, if not our souls!

In the following discussion, the term "abortion" will be used to signify all of the methods for early termination of parental investment prior to normal birth at term. There may be two ultimate explanations for the evolution of the methods of abortion. These are parental manipulation and gametic or fetal altruism. If it would increase the fitness of a parent to terminate the development of an offspring, mechanisms should evolve which enable the parent to do this. However, abortion may also be seen as an altruistic act. Both gametes which form the zygote are in an ideal position to determine the genetic integrity of the complementary gametes and the probable viability of the newly formed or developing zygote. Likewise, the fetus may be in a better position to monitor its development than the parent. If either the gametes or the fetus can determine that the individual which will develop will be reproductively inefficient, unable to aid fellow offspring, or will utilize parental or environmental resources to the detriment of parents and sibs (more than its own personal gain if it persists), methods should evolve which would allow it to halt its own development.

Gametic Altruism: a Possibility

Regarding possible gametic altruism, consider that a gamete is related to the parents from which it was derived by $r = 1$, while the parent's relation to that gamete is only $r = \frac{1}{2}$. (This calculation is made in exactly the same manner as for traditional coefficients of relationship: by determining the proportion of alleles in a focal individual identical by common descent with the other individual in question. The results are somewhat novel, however, because the two entities in question differ in ploidy—gametes haploid and the parent diploid. Such disparities will always result in asymmetric coefficients of relationship, although their evolutionary implications remain unchanged.)

In addition to this asymmetry in r, parents can produce additional gametes much more readily than gametes can produce additional parents. Thus, gametes should tend to be more altruistic toward the parent than the parent should be toward them. Note that a sperm is expected to be altruistic with respect to the male from which it was derived, not the female with whom the male mated. However, some time prior to implantation, the relevant altruism becomes that of the developing organism. Unless one is willing to assume that the genetic complexes derived from each parent still adhere to that strategy which will maximize the inclusive fitness of the given parent, some composite and unified strategy must be considered. In general, this will be altruism toward the mother: that parent with the greatest present rate of parental investment. But since each offspring is related to itself by an $r = 1$ and only related to its sibs of the same parents by an average $r = \frac{1}{2}$, while the parents are related to all offspring equally ($r = \frac{1}{2}$, exactly), we would expect more conflict between parent and offspring than parent and gamete with respect to the desirability of an abortion (Trivers 1974).

The interests, options, and hence strategies of females differ from those of males. This difference should be apparent not only in parental manipulation, but also in the abortion-related altruism manifested by their gametes. Females may be defined as that sex which produces a relatively small number of gametes, each of which is costly in energy. Conversely, males produce a relatively large number of inexpensive small gametes. This implies that females may be more concerned about the quality of their gametes than are males. Thus, we may expect to find in the female more sophisticated mechanisms to determine the viability of a gamete as it is developing. Due to the higher parental investment that will be required *in the future* to replace a defective egg (Dawkins and Carlisle 1976), the developing gamete in the female is under stronger selection pressure to halt this investment as soon as the inviability of the resulting product can be determined. Similarly, the female parent should have more sophisticated mechanisms for testing the viability of a developing gamete. Possibilities for such mechanisms include responses to the physical state of the developing gamete, withholding metabolic investment until appropriate biochemical byproducts of development are detected, or subjecting the gametes to stress in such a way as to halt development of inadequate gametes. Indeed, it is an interesting and as yet unexplored question whether a fetus that would be defective as an adult would be different enough to be detectable biochemically. Parents who could do so would clearly have a selective advantage. Although we might expect to find comparable mechanisms in the male, we expect that those in the female will be more highly developed.

The pattern of meiosis in the two sexes may be evidence for this. In males, one primary cell yields four spermatozoa, while in the female one primary cell yields one ovum and three inactive polar bodies. The traditional explanation for this has been that the larger size of the ovum necessitates concentrating all of the cytoplasm into one cell. However, the polar bodies do not completely lack cytoplasm, as might be expected on this argument. It may be that only the most viable of the four possible daughter cells will develop into an ovum. It may be possible that the first division in a meiosis involves a competition between the two nonidentical chromosome sets for cytoplasmic material, the "winner" taking most, but not all. In the second division, altruistic restraint is possible in the set of chromosomes which eventually becomes a polar body, since its relation to the developing ovum is r = 1. It may also be significant that the genetically dissimilar first polar body does not develop; the development of another primary cell would surely result in an ovum which had a greater degree of relation to the first ovum than did the first polar body. For those ova in apolytocous species which were derived from a single primary cell the mean coefficient of relationship would be $\frac{1}{3}$. This would be true whether four, three, or two mature ova were derived from a single primary cell so long as nondevelopment by a particular ovum was an independent event. If the degree of genetic relationship between ova is decreased, it is probable that any altruism between them is also decreased. This would also decrease the mean genetic relatedness of any sibship. Since a parent usually desires more altruism between sibs than the sibs desire to have with each other (Trivers 1974) it is a particularly poor strategy for a parent to do anything to lower the genetic relatedness of a sibship.

We expect that the same strategies that generally distinguish the courtship of males and females will also apply to strategies at the time of fertilization. Thus, fertilization is probably not a passive process at all, but involves the sperm overcoming some resistance on the part of the ovum. In this case, the interests of male and female parents are identical, and since each gamete is totally related to its respective parent, such mechanisms are probably well developed. It is in the interests of both parents that a superior sperm fertilize a given egg, if attempted penetration does not render the ovum inviable. In addition, the average relationship of $\frac{1}{2}$ shared between sperm facilitates competition between them. Therefore, we might expect mobility and ability to penetrate an ovum to be correlated with functional integrity of a sperm, with barriers established by the ovum so as to ensure that the "best sperm wins."

Following penetration and fertilization, the interests of the two gametes or parents are not identical. In general, the female (or her genetic complement in her ovum) will be more sensitive to inadequacy of development; however, the magnitude of this difference will depend upon the nature of the species involved. In those species where the male supplies a significant proportion of parental care, and where selection is based upon quality rather than quantity of offspring, the interests of male and female will be most similar. It is expected that in such K-selected animals, as litter size increases, so will the number of abortions. This is because future parental investment, *per individual offspring,* is higher under a K-selected regime. This would select for increased reluctance to retain any offspring that represents a poor future investment—i.e., mechanisms should evolve for the early termination of parental investment in such cases. In any case, any termination of development caused by parental manipulation will be caused by that parent with the greatest present or future investment, extent of past investment not being a relevant factor (Dawkins and Carlisle 1976).

Such considerations are directly related to the mating system of the animal. It is expected that a promiscuous, r-selected species in which the female is responsible for some parental investment other than lactation will display maximum conflict between male and female as to whether abortion should occur at a particular stage. In such a case, the male would be relatively unconcerned with the future reproductive potential of the female unless the group was so small that revisits to the same female could be a selective factor. Thus selection may operate on small, isolated groups so that the sexes show more similarity than would a historically large and panmictic population of the same species. In this case, the lower the investment of the female following fertilization, the lower the rate of abortion should be. In monogamous K-selected species which mate for life, and where investment after fertilization is significant for both male and female, the correspondence of interests between the sexes and the rate of abortions at early stages of development should be high. In this case, the future reproductive capacity of the female is of concern to the male as well as the female; detection of inferior offspring and early abortion is of mutual benefit; and there should be little difference between large panmictic and isolated populations regarding the average age at which abortion occurs. Following the reasoning given for the difference in abortion rate of K and r-selected species, iteroparous species are expected to have a higher abortion rate than are semelparous species.

Similar considerations might also elucidate differences in reproductive strategies among different taxa. Thus, for example, Low (1978) has pointed out that marsupials differ from placentals in that the smaller *in utero* parental investment in marsupials facilitates terminating parental investment with minimal maternal loss. Such a system is likely to be especially advantageous in conditions of relatively great environmental uncertainty such as the deserts of central Australia.

Early Termination of Parental Investment in Humans

Its possible value

Among human physiologists, it has been recognized for some time that "waste, in the sense of loss without purpose, is not a feature of biological systems, for natural selection insures its continual elimination" (Bishop 1964). Embryonic death provides one of the means of eliminating unfit genotypes at a low biological cost. An additional means is selective mortality in the gametogenic cells. According to Hamilton (1966), it is only because there is a possibility of sibling replacement that infant or pre-infant mortality can be selected. "It is obvious that there is better chance of nearly full replacement if an offspring dies of a congenital disorder in infancy than at age 10, and better again if it dies in the earliest stages of pregnancy. Thus, modifiers of recurrent lethal mutations of any kind which cause them to express themselves earlier will be selected for."

In the human female, as in most mammals, one primary oocyte gives rise to one ovum and three polar bodies. The possibilities that this affords the female for producing a superior gamete have already been explored. Triple-X females are fertile, and one would expect them to have children in proportions $\frac{1}{4}XX:\frac{1}{4}XY:\frac{1}{4}XXX:\frac{1}{4}XXY$. However, the abnormal XXX and XXY karyotypes are rarely found. Ehrman and Parsons (1976) suggest that this may be due to directed meiotic segregation of two of the mother's X chromosomes into polar bodies with the remaining X chromosome in the ovum. At the beginning of each menstrual cycle a number of ovarian follicles begin to develop in each ovary, but normally only one of them grows into a mature graafian follicle destined to ovulate, while the rest at one stage or another stop growing and undergo atresia (Bulmer 1970). This situation is similar in all mammals and affords an even wider range of potential ova. The mechanism by which growth is suppressed in all but one follicle is unclear. If genetic altruism is involved it seems likely that this altruism will be more relevant to the inclusive fitness of the parent to which the gamete is related by $r = 1$, rather than altruism toward the developing gamete where the relationship is only an average $r = \frac{1}{2}$. This implies that a gamete may respond with great altruistic enthusiasm to a parental manipulation to suppress its growth.

If an oocyte lingers longer than day 14 in a follicle, it has an increasing chance of becoming a "bad egg" when fertilized. In any one month when conditions are optimal about 15 percent of the oocytes fail to become fertilized. Of those that are fertilized about 10–15 percent fail to implant, but only 42 percent are of such viability as to cause the female to miss her expected menstrual period. Of the women who actually miss a period, the probability of an abortion before term is 27.6 percent (Hertig 1967). Thus, only 30.4 percent of the ova which are afforded the opportunities of fertilization result in a live birth—and these are only the ova which are actually ovulated. If we accept the idea that this is not loss without purpose, it is perhaps evidence for an intricate system for eliminating all but the most fit genotypes from continued parental investment.

It has been suggested that female mammals may have internal mechanisms for testing the competence of sperm. Ehrman and Parsons

(1976) note that trisomic offspring of XYY males are quite rare. It is probable that the internal environment of a woman strongly selects against XY and YY sperm. However, male selection may also occur in this regard.

The nature of the uterine environment in mammals facilitates parental monitoring of fetal development. This environment is a highly reactive one with responses "varying in a most complex manner to provide for the special needs of the organism at each successive stage of development" (Anderson, personal communication). The intrauterine environment is less favorable in older than younger mothers, parity being held constant, due to aging; and it is less favorable in primiparae than in multiparae, age being held constant, due to the beneficial usage effect of the first pregnancy (Bulmer 1970). However, this situation is not true in all animals. Hamilton (1966) postulated another mechanism which might allow for selection of abortion, ". . . in which there is some sort of batching of the eggs which results in early competition mainly between siblings." The incidence of certain congenital abnormalities in polytocous species declines with maternal age. Carr (1967) suggests that the competition between individuals *in utero* increases with maternal age with the result that the abnormal embryos tend to die. Here aging diminishes the degree of uterine accommodation. Whether the aging human uterus provides similar selection against abnormal embryos is unclear since this is confounded by an increasing frequency of chromosomal abnormalities in the ova. It is interesting to speculate, though, that the intrauterine environment may provide a partial filter against these abnormalities, by screening out the more deleterious.

Its appropriate occasions

Anovulation in humans usually occurs in situations which reliably predict the unsuitability of parental investment. During the early years after menarche, girls show an excess of insufficient cycles. A maximal number of normal cycles usually does not occur until a woman is 26 to 30 years old (Doring 1969). This adolescent sterility may be adaptive in that it may allow a girl with developing secondary sexual characteristics the opportunity to learn her culture without a premature investment in offspring. This selective advantage has been alluded to in studies of several isolated cultures (Mead 1950). The incidence of insufficient cycles after age 40 can be considered in the same manner as a natural protection: older mothers are usually less suited to the task of bringing up small children and may raise their inclusive fitness to a greater degree by caring for their grandchildren. After the birth of a child, a woman usually experiences at least three insufficient cycles (Doring 1969) even if she is not lactating, and often many more if she is lactating (Hamilton 1966). The adaptive significance of this should be obvious. Masters and Johnson (1966) found that lactation was usually coupled with an increase in sexual desire. Since this occurs at a time when anovulation is more likely, a reasonable explanation may be that the female's increased sexuality at this time is adaptive in that it serves to strengthen the pair bond with the father or perhaps another male resulting in increased investment by that male in the mother-young dyad.

Another reliable predictor of a time of inappropriate investment would be one in which food was scarce. Thus the duration of fecundability is shorter in females of developing countries. Menarche occurs later and menopause earlier. During the past century, nutrition has improved in Europe and there has been progressively earlier puberty and deferred menopause in women. A study of 26 young Finnish women who starved themselves in order to lose weight showed their ovarian functions reduced to menopausal level. Severe nutritional deprivation during the Dutch famine of 1944–45 markedly reduced the number of conceptions resulting in births. There was a lag period of about two months before fertility was affected; upon relief of famine, however, recovery was immediate. Above 1500 calories no definite effect was apparent. Below this threshold, the estimated number of conceptions resulting in birth correlated $r = .92$ with average official daily rations. The reduction was greater among the manual than the nonmanual occupations. The most reasonable explanation for the class difference was differential access to food. The effect was probably due to anovulation since if abortion were involved it would be expected that an excess of females would be born (Stein and Sausser 1975).

The male contribution to fertility is also affected by starvation. In young American men who volunteered to undergo experimental starvation, sperm were fewer, less motile, and shorter-lived than normal (Klatskin et al. 1947, cited in Stein and Sausser 1975). High temperatures and high altitudes also tend to produce aspermia (Cowgill 1969).

It is also possible for a female to produce ova from a given ovary at a rate which is twice as high as normal. In uniparous species, one ovary may be inactive (as in bats); there may be strict alternation (in seals), or an increased chance of alternation (as in humans). In the latter case, and for most mammals, there is probably some sort of central control so that the presence of a graafian follicle in one ovary inhibits the development of a similar follicle in the other ovary. The additional implications for altruistic restraint have already been discussed. If one ovary is removed, however, there is a compensatory hypertrophy of the remaining ovary. Within two cycles following unilateral ovariectory, a human female will produce as many ova from a single ovary as were previously produced by two (Biggers 1969).

Just why a particular sperm will fertilize a given egg is not known. It is often assumed that the chance is equally great that any of the sperm which reach an ovum at a given moment will penetrate and fertilize to the exclusion of all others. However, with several hundred sperm surrounding an egg at the time of fertilization it is difficult to imagine how some mechanism which selected a superior sperm for fertilization would not evolve.

The next stage at which investment may be halted is prior to implantation. It is generally agreed that a relatively high proportion of fertilized ova disappear during the six days prior to implantation. Most of these are not dead, but their growth rate is abnormal. Mitoses have been observed in even the most defective-appearing ones. It is estimated that about one-half of the "bad" zygotes fail to implant (Hertig 1967). It is significant that mitoses continue in zygotes which fail to implant, for it weakens the argument that it is merely inadequate morphogenesis which is responsible. Indeed, why is morphogenesis apparently adequate in the hybrid offspring of many animals (some of whose parents even differ in chromosome number)? One possible mechanism for the evolution of means to prevent implantation is altruism of the offspring in the form of the zygote. Prior to implantation, the zygote would be the best, and perhaps the only, judge of its own fitness. But the "strength" of this altruism by the offspring is not as great as that of the gamete. While the gamete is related to the mother $r = 1$, the zygote is only related by $r = \frac{1}{2}$. A zygote is related to *all* future sibs by an average $r = \frac{1}{2}$ only if the same father is involved; if not, the relationship is an average $r = \frac{1}{4}$. Of course, at the time of implantation the parent may have means of testing the adequacy of the zygote, but the zygote is now expected to behave so as to maximize its new inclusive fitness.

Humans can and do resorb both ova and zygotes (Siegler 1944). The two most common forms of prenatal mortality occur before or immediately following implantation, as discussed above, and result in complete resorbtion of the conceptus (Hafez 1968). Just why this response has evolved in humans is not clear. Having only one young at a time, a human would gain nothing from not expelling the conceptus upon its death. It seems doubtful if the energy gained from resorbtion at such an early stage would offset the effort involved. Perhaps the resorbtion phenomenon is an ancient mammalian strategy which is not selected against so long as cost and benefit are nearly in balance.

Its higher stakes

Following implantation, the developing embryo represents new costs to the mother; costs which must be offset by the potential of the offspring to increase the mother's inclusive fitness. On the one hand, there is the obvious metabolic cost imposed by the embryo upon the mother: nourishment must be provided from the mother's own bloodstream. Second, there is cost due to the lack of an immune response to the embryo on the part of the mother. "The existence of two animals in a form of parabiosis during gestation, without immunological interaction detrimental to either participant, implies modification of certain normal properties of both individuals" (Anderson 1972). During pregnancy, not only are the mother and fetus normally free from deleterious immunological interaction, but neither is the mother sensitized to subsequent genetically similar pregnancies, even when the mother is artificially sensitized against paternally derived tissues. There is, however, ample evidence that a mammalian fetus may both initiate an immune response in other animals and also develop an immune response itself. This immunity does have a developmental sequence, and differs in different mammals. (See references in Anderson 1972).

The most frequent explanation for this situation is that the placenta acts as a nonantigenic layer preventing sensitization of the mother toward fetal tissues. But in humans, there is much evidence of cellular exchange with transplant antigens (Anderson 1972). In spite of this, Peer and Walker (1959, cited in Anderson 1972) found that if skin grafts from newborn armadillos were made to both parents, all grafts exchanged between fathers and their infants were rejected in less than 21 days, whereas $\frac{1}{4}$ of the mother-infant grafts survived longer than 30 days. The same results were obtained with human subjects. This must be considered a very real cost to the mother, for experiments indicate that the third trimester of human gestation is accompanied by a diminished response to grafts of skin from unrelated subjects (Anderson 1972). In the armadillo studies cited above, death of the mother occurred in three of the four animals within 32 days of transplant for reasons such as pneumonia, intestinal obstruction, and peritonitis.

The immune response in women accompanies approximately 25 percent of all instances of infertility. The most common condition is for the antibodies to agglutinate the sperm. If a mother is sensitized to seminal fluid or preparations of testis *prior to* gestation, fertility is diminished. Even among normally fertile women, 8 percent have antibodies which will agglutinate some sperm and there is an observed deficit of 25 percent in blood type A and B children among matings where the mother is type O and the father is either A, B, or AB (Anderson 1972). Biologists since Medawar (1954) have puzzled over the paradox of transplantation immunology created by the success of the fetus as an allograft. Recently it has been found that women who experience idiopathic spontaneous abortions lack serum levels of lymphocyte migration inhibitory factor to paternal alloantigens, whereas by contrast, normal multigravid women possess the serum blocking factor (Rocklin et al. 1976). Indeed, failure to suppress the maternal immune system may be a common proximate mechanism, activated when it maximizes maternal fitness.

Its Conspicuous Expressions:
Spontaneous Abortion and Perinatal Mortality

If one defines spontaneous abortion as the "observed expulsion of a dead fetus promptly following its death," it is preeminently a phenomenon of uniparae. Once a uniparous fetus has died, abortion is the safest route toward recovery of the affected female (Stander 1936). In humans, every fifth or sixth pregnancy ends in spontaneous abortion. If cases in which profuse loss of blood following delay of the menstrual period are taken into account, the incidence is much higher. In 17,224 pregnancies in New York City from 1947–1950, spontaneous abortion occurred at a frequency of 8.2 percent; immatures, 1.2 percent; prematures, 4.5 percent, and full-term pregnancies, 86.2 percent. So spontaneous abortion ranks next to full term-pregnancy and delivery (Javert 1957; Hertig 1967). A study by Hertig (1960, cited in Biggers 1969) suggested that a high incidence of early embryonic death may occur in normally fertile patients.

The hypothesis that spontaneous abortion may be of adaptive significance is supported by the observation that in more than 60 percent of spontaneous abortions one can demonstrate an anomaly of the products of conception, and the earlier the abortion, the more pronounced is its association with malformation (Kerr 1969). The incidence of abnormality in aborted embryos is high while that in aborted fetuses is much lower. Tupper and Weil (1968) suggest that abortions may be of two types: defective ova in a good environment, and good ova in a defective environment. Whether these types represent gametic altruism and parental manipulation respectively has not been investigated.

At least 30 percent of all first-trimester abortions show a gross chromosomal anomaly, and this is usually associated with defective embryogenesis (Kerr 1969). The selective advantage of eliminating chromosomally defective embryos at an early stage of development is obvious. Muller (1954, cited in Bishop 1964) estimates that at least 20 percent of human embryos die as a result of spontaneous mutation. An increase in maternal age appears to be related to the incidence of certain trisomies, while triploidy and XO abortions are not related to maternal age (Carr, 1967). That a process other than "inadequate morphogenesis" may be involved is evidenced by the fact that in the study in question, the mean gestational age of *spontaneous abortions with normal and abnormal karyotypes was 85.9 and 106.7 days, respectively*. However, chromosomal abnormalities are assumed to be the prime etiological factor in early abortions (Szulman 1968). Carr (1963, cited in Tupper and Weil 1968) found a 22 percent incidence of lethal chromosomes in 400 abortuses under 500 grams.

It is very rare for external physical trauma to cause spontaneous abortion. In a study of 2,000 abortions, Javert (1957) found that physical trauma *ex utero* was present in only 7 cases. The maternal mortality following spontaneous abortion is quite low. Javert (1957) noted only 1 instance of maternal mortality in 2,545 abortions. The overall rate is 5–10 maternal deaths following spontaneous abortion for every 10,000 live births (Taussig 1936). These data support the adaptive value of spontaneous abortion, as a technique whereby maternal fitness is preserved at the cost of zygotic survival.

Most spontaneous abortions occur in the second or third month of pregnancy (Taussig 1936): 30 percent of abortions occur between 1–8 weeks, 60 percent from 9–16 weeks, and 10 percent from 17–22 weeks. This distribution does not quite parallel the pathology of the ovofetus: pathogenic ovum, 20.6 percent; defective embryo, 11.9 percent; abnormal fetus, 2.4 percent (Javert 1957). Deaths before the onset of labor are higher than deaths during labor in the early months of pregnancy, and the opposite is true of those near term (Potter and Adair 1940). According to Trivers (1974), the time just before birth would represent one peak in biologically based parent-offspring conflict. It seems significant that death at this stage usually follows the onset of labor.

Stillborn fetuses delivered early in pregnancy are much more commonly male than female. In the first trimester, at least 78 percent are male (Potter and Adair 1940). Since only approximately 30 percent of fertilized ova result in live birth, the excessive antenatal wastage among males indicates that the sex ratio at conception must be at least 1.8 (Sutherland 1949). The high preponderance of females in trisomic live patients (Szulman 1968) and the fall in sex ratio in multiple births (Bulmer 1970) result from the increased prenatal mortality for males. Since abortion is correlated with maternal condition and with abnormality in the conceptus, we may speculate on the selective advantage of producing an imperfect female rather than an imperfect male. Trivers and Willard (1973) have reasoned that in times of scarcity, an adaptive parental strategy would be to produce females (in those species in which females have a higher probability of mating and a lower need for nutrition than males), when the condition of the mother is below normal. The tendency in humans to abort males sooner than females may have the same ultimate cause, and may not merely be the result of "an unguarded X-chromosome."

There is some circumstantial evidence that orgasm may induce abortion. Javert (1957) noted that Kinsey's data on percentage of coital orgasms by age correlated rather well with the age distribution of spontaneous abortions. Masters and Johnson (1966) state: ". . . if it is true that coitally induced orgasmic experience and the subsequent uterine contractile responses have a tendency to induce pregnancy wastage, particularly among susceptible women, it also must be considered probable that masturbatory activity will create the same tendency in the susceptible aborter. . . . There are legitimate clinical concerns with both coition and automanipulation at or near term. It is probably true that contractions of orgasm at or near term can send a woman into labor." Masters and Johnson found that more than three-fourths of nulliparous and two-thirds of parous women "experienced a significant reduction in eroticism and frequency of sexual performance as the estimated date of confinement approached." However, pregnant parous women were fully effective in their capacity for sexual performance when directly approached. (No data were given for the nulliparous group.) Thus, the data imply a possible selective disadvantage to women who are orgasmic in their third trimester of pregnancy.

Assuming that there is some genetic basis for orgasmic competence and some variance therein, it is legitimate to question what factors maintain the trait (or polymorphism) in the population. A female rat exposed to the scent of a strange male will commonly resorb her litter if she is pregnant (Bruce 1966). This response may be considered adaptive since it terminates investment in a litter which would probably be killed by the new male had it been carried to term, while initiating the sequence leading to receptivity of the female to the new male. Throughout human history it has not been unusual to take women as spoils of war (Mead 1950). If the subsequent offspring were subject to infanticide, those women who aborted as a consequence of orgasm would be at a selective advantage. A more consistent advantage would exist if males who demanded sexual performance of a third trimester woman were likely to abandon mother and infant at a later time.

Almost all behavioral responses in humans which have a strong biological basis can be modified to a considerable degree by learning, and abortion is probably no exception. A review of the data indicated that psychogenically induced abortion may be as adaptive as that induced by physiological mechanisms. Devereux (1955), a psychoanalytically trained anthropologist, has cited instances where the power of suggestion in a prescribed ritual elicits spontaneous abortion. Psychotherapeutic success in the cure of habitual abortion has been reported at rates up to 80 percent (Tupper and Weil 1968; Freedman et al. 1975). Two personality profiles in habitual aborters emerged from a large number of psychiatric histories. One was the predominantly immature woman who cannot accept the challenges of mature femininity and the responsibility of motherhood. The other was the "independent, frustrated woman who has adjusted to a man's world and whose main aspirations are beyond her feminine limits" (Tupper and Weil 1968). Habitual aborters commonly have been tied to their mothers from early infancy, never actually maturing as persons. Interpersonal relationships with adults are characterized by infantile dependence, and marriage is usually to a man who is very protective (Freedman et al. 1975). Specifically, habitual abortion has been associated with destructive tendencies (both self- and other-directed), fear of inability to become a mother, and association of the child with an undesired accomplishment (Deutsch 1945).

As the age of a woman increases so does the number of copulations at time of maximum fertility which are necessary to produce pregnancy. The following table is taken from Siegler (1944):

Age of Women (N)	Net Potentially Effective Copulations/Pregnancy
under 20 (69)	176
20–29 (184)	202
30–39 (138)	290
40–49 (75)	1,434

The number of spontaneous abortions per pregnancy is lowest at age 16 to 19 at about 4 percent and rises to 11.5 percent at age 35–39. The mean rate over 40 is 18 percent (Javert 1957). Thus a young woman experiencing a normal cycle conceives more easily and aborts less frequently than an older woman. However, the proportion of normal aborted fetuses drops from about 30 percent at age 25 to 3 percent over age 40 (Szulman 1968). So it appears that older women not only have lower fertility, but they are also more selective with respect to the fetus that they carry to term. It may be that an aging woman is increasingly unable to care for defective offspring, and in most human cultures approaching the time when her resources are more advantageously invested in grandchildren. This increasing selectivity may also partially buffer the increased frequency of such abnormalities as trisomies which are associated with increasing maternal age (Sutherland 1949).

The age of the father is not insignificant either. Sonneborne (1960, cited in Parsons 1964) found a significantly higher fetal death rate for offspring from old fathers from a sample of 330,000 births in New York City. Sutherland (1949) found that when the age of the mother was held constant, the variation in neonatal mortality with the age of the father was very marked. It started high for very young fathers, dropped to a minimum, and rose thereafter with the age of the father. These data are somewhat questionable, not being directly confirmed by other studies. However, due to the close-knit nature of human groups, it is not unlikely that a period of partial sterility following puberty would exist in males as well as females; but this should not approach the extent of adolescent sterility observed in girls. The increase of fetal death with paternal age could signify both senescence on the part of the male and selection by the female against conception with a male too old to provide sufficient support for herself and her offspring.

Selection of this sort could operate either by unconscious, psychologically mediated response of females to the age of their mates, or by maternal rejection of sperm or fetus that are somehow indicative of male senescence. Of course, selection in this case would also be expected to favor the elimination of spermatic characters that signal senescence on the part of the males that produce them. Such "deceit" would be adaptive so long as the elderly male has no genetic interest in the offspring of his female. If he does, as in the case of perennial monogamy, then males would not be selected to disguise their age, since they would enhance their fitness by adhering to the same strategy that is optimal for the female, especially if her alternative to bearing incompetent offspring is to provide additional investment in his offspring already produced. In such a situation, a more parsimonious evolutionary solution would be loss of libido in the male with increasing age.

Given that spontaneous abortion is adaptive, it would follow that women with a number of children could afford to be more selective about the quality of other offspring. If frequency of abortion is any indication of such a process, this may well be the case: when age is held constant, multigravidae and multiparae have twice the incidence of spontaneous abortion of primigravidae and primiparae (Javert 1957). Mothers in England and Wales with unusually large families for their age tended to have excessively high stillbirth rates (Sutherland 1949).

Nutrition also seems to affect stillbirth rate in an adaptive way. An unpublished study by Javert and Kuder (cited in Javert 1957) from 1932–1941 showed that among 27,405 pregnant patients the three highest months for spontaneous abortion per delivery were April, July, and November. In other words, the conceptions occurring in the spring and early summer had less chance of aborting. Summer diets are more sufficient to meet increased requirements of pregnancy. This same pattern has been observed in England and Wales (Sutherland 1949). As might be expected, this trend is greater in the poorer classes. The New Zealand pattern of birth frequency is the reverse of the European, with a major natal peak in October and a minor one in February and March (Cowgill 1969). There is a general tendency for underweight patients to have a higher incidence of premature infants (Kaltreider 1963).

The proximal reasons for the occurrence of prematurity in humans is largely unknown. There does seem to be a reliable increase in frequency of prematurity with the age of the mother (G. Sackett, personal communication). In general, abnormalities in premature infants are not due to a higher level of congenital factors, but to the developmental stage at which the infant was born. It is tempting to speculate that prematurity is a late form of spontaneous abortion caused by parental manipulation. This seems to be supported by the pattern of greater frequency of threatened abortion in mothers whose infants were born prematurely than in those who bore full-term babies (Kohl 1955). The infantile mortality rate due to prematurity is around 20 percent and is the most frequent cause of neonatal death (Javert 1957; Potter and Adair 1940).

Following arguments by Lack (1954), it is probable that the optimal litter size for humans is one. That is, throughout human history, a greater number of children from single births have survived to reproductive maturity than have children of multiple births. The number of ovarian follicles which ripen during each estrus is not an intrinsic property of the ovary but is regulated by the gonadotropic hormone of the anterior pituitary. Injection of gonadotropins into humans has resulted in a great excess of multiple births. The frequency of both dizygous (DZ) twinning and level of gonadotropins in the blood increase with maternal age. It is likely that the constancy of the monozygous (MZ) twinning rate in man is due to the constancy of the uterine environment. In fish eggs which develop outside the mother, the frequency of MZ twinning can be altered more easily by changes in the external environment (Bulmer 1970).

Since humans are quite able to have litters greater than one, the restraint shown in single births must be adaptive. Adaptive modification of litter size usually occurs as a result of DZ twins, while MZ twins appear at a fairly consistent rate in all age groups, cultures, and environmental conditions. Nutrition seems to influence DZ twinning rate in an adaptive manner. There was no change in the MZ twinning rate during World War II; however, the DZ rate decreased in France, Holland, and Norway during this period where undernutrition was common (Bulmer 1970). Jeanneret and MacMahon (1962, cited in Parkes 1969) found a substantial decrease in white twinning rate from 1920 to 1969. There was a very sharp drop in the five years up to 1943, followed by a peak in 1946. "The reasons for the drop is not obvious, but if one assumes that food conditions improved materially at the end of the war in 1945, the 1946 peak might be reminiscent of the shepherd's practice of 'flushing' his ewes at tupping time to increase the proportion of twin lambs." For nonwhites, the overall twinning rate is higher and the decrease less, but the decrease in the years before 1943 is even more marked and the subsequent recovery slower. The white triplet rate declined more steeply and on the whole more regularly than the twin rate.

The incidence of congenital abnormalities is higher in twins than in single births after correction is made for maternal age and increased stillbirth rate (Parsons 1964). This increase is due entirely to MZ twins, which show a frequency of congenital malformations twice that of single births (Bulmer 1970). This may be due to the fact that MZ twins are themselves a genetic anomaly (Hafez 1968).

Twin pregnancy is regarded by most observers as a contributing cause of spontaneous abortion. The incidence of premature labor is also higher in the case of twin pregnancy (Javert 1957). The combined stillbirth and infant mortality rate for England and Wales in recent years is 5 percent for singles, 17 percent for twins, and 38 percent for triplets. Survivors per pregnancy are .95 for singles, 1.66 for twins, and 1.86 for triplets. Thus, in recent years mothers of multiple births in industrial countries may enjoy a selective advantage. This would be true only if their survival and rate of pregnancy were the same as other women's and if sufficient resources existed to meet the needs of the young. In eighteenth-century Europe, and throughout most of human history, however, mothers of twins were almost certainly at a selective disadvantage (Bulmer 1970). From 1757 through 1784 in Dublin, perinatal mortality was 20 percent for children of single births and 39 percent for twins. During the period 1939–41, the rate of stillbirths among twins in England and Wales was twice as high as for single births (Sutherland 1949). The ratio of instances when only one twin was live-born to instances when both were stillborn is 2.3 for like-sexed twins and 4.39 for twins of different sexes. Since twins of different sexes must be DZ twins, while twins of the same sex may be either MZ or DZ, MZ twins are more likely to share the same fate. However, in both cases it is more likely that only one twin will be stillborn. It is not unreasonable to ask whether altruism is involved in the death of only one twin. Although MZ twins are genetically identical and we can expect altruism to be maximally likely, we can also expect identical genetic defects. They are also monochorionic, so the fate of one more easily affects the other. Significantly, when one twin dies in the uterus, there is a tendency for the living twin to be born first. Perinatal mortality is higher in the second twin than in the first (Bulmer 1970).

Such altruism among MZ twins would be most efficient in terms of fitness maximization, if the aborting twin did so as a result of information suggesting that the other twin was healthier, although the behavior could also evolve without communication of this sort. Because of the genetic identity of MZ twins, there would be no selection for sibling-sibling deceit *in utero* as to the condition of each. In contrast, although altruism mediated by kin selection could operate between DZ twins as well, their $\frac{1}{2}$ relatedness would select for signals indicating that the sender is healthier—i.e., more deserving of altruistic abortion by the receiver—than it really is. Of course, this would in turn select for enhanced ability to distinguish a false "I'm OK" message from an accurate one.

The final means of early termination of parental investment is infanticide. In many cultures, this occurs during periods of migration or famine, in response to the birth of a child with an obvious defect, the birth of twins, or the birth of a child of the "wrong" sex or one conceived outside of proper ritual.

Its Selective Power Evaluated

Taken together, the mechanisms considered here, working through various and not always interconnected proximate factors, form a well-integrated system to limit or discontinue parental investment at the most appropriate stage of development and the most appropriate environmental conditions, "appropriateness" here measured in units of fitness. To explain such a system by looking at each proximate factor or mechanism is like trying to explain Pompeii by looking only at each brick or building: interconnectedness, unity of form and purpose, are obscured, and the basic whys and hows of the system remain uninvestigated.

A recent study suggests that a system of early termination of parental investment may have real selective power. Of 268 female prison inmates, approximately one-fourth were prostitutes, one-fourth were both addicts and prostitutes, and one-fourth had committed other offenses. The histories of these women indicate that 136 had at least one unusual termination of pregnancy. Both the rate of stillbirth and spontaneous abortion were far in excess of normal. They had 373 live children; given the U.S. average, 27 children would be expected to be born with birth defects. However, in this case there were none (Avis Green, pers. comm.). This suggests that early termination of maternal investment is more likely to discriminate against incompetent fetuses when the rearing environment is likely to be more stressful.

In summary, we propose that animals are selected for termination of parental investment when such an occurrence increases inclusive fitness. Furthermore, fitness would generally be maximized by early termination, mediated by gametic altruism, fetal altruism and/or parental manipulation. We believe that the intimate relation between mother and young makes this most likely in mammals. Data have also been presented suggesting that a well-integrated system for early termination exists in human beings.

V. Prospect and Retrospect:
Some Viewpoints

This final short section looks at the emergence of interest in studying human behavior in terms of evolutionary biology as an historical phenomenon. In the last two decades, two approaches to the study of behavior have been developed by biologists as perspectives which might usefully be applied to social and cultural anthropological data: ethology and sociobiology. The works of European ethologists, especially Niko Tinbergen (1951, 1953, 1965) and Konrad Lorenz (1950, 1965, 1966), provided a promising new source of theory for anthropology by connecting the study of behavior with the principles of biological evolution. With their stress on studying a wide variety of species in more natural settings than earlier students of animal behavior and earlier learning theorists had done, they shed considerable light on the functions of behavior and the beneficial effects of their interests are still an important force in biology. Serious attempts to introduce this perspective into anthropology were made by Lionel Tiger and Robin Fox in their joint publications (1966, 1971) and also in a number of separate publications (see Fox 1971, 1972, 1975; and Tiger 1969, 1970, 1974).

The second biological perspective, sociobiology, which has motivated most of the articles in this volume, appeared more recently as a challenge to social anthropology. This discipline has built heavily on the earlier work of R. A. Fisher (1958 [1930]) and J. B. S. Haldane (1932), and its basic principles have been developed by G. C. Williams (1966, 1971, 1975), W. D. Hamilton (1964, 1967, 1971) and R. L. Trivers (1971, 1972, 1974). The gist of this approach is the explanation of the existence of the various characteristics of organisms, especially sociality, in terms of their functions—that is, in terms of the benefits they confer on their bearers which cause them to reproduce more successfully than would alternate characteristics. Attempts to apply this perspective to human behavior are recent and, like earlier attempts to bring biology to bear on human social behavior, they are controversial. However, despite the controversy, there is reason to hope that the more precisely defined expectations concerning the relationship between behavior and individual level, or lower level, selection associated with sociobiology will allow more decisive empirical testing with human data, than did earlier theories which attributed function to whichever level (gene, individual, breeding population, species) seemed convenient.

In addition to the papers in this volume and in the DeVore volume (see preface: p. x), recent attempts to apply sociobiology specifically to human behavior include the following: Alexander 1971, 1974, 1975, 1977a, 1978a, 1978b; Barkow 1978; Blurton Jones and Sibly, in press; Daly and Wilson 1978: 263–330; Dyson-Hudson and Smith 1978; Ember and Ember 1978; Greene 1978; Hartung 1976; van den Berghe and Barash 1977; Weinrich 1977; Wilson 1975: 547–575, 1978. These works all represent efforts to study human behavior in terms of its ultimate effect on differential reproduction, and they may be of value to readers who find this volume useful. It should be kept in mind, however, that this shared interest does not imply that the authors of these works all adhere to one monolithic theory of human behavior. They do not, and it is good that they do not. The progress of knowledge depends on, among other things, a diversity of theoretical views. We also wish to emphasize that pointing to these works as examples of human sociobiology does not imply any lack of value in other attempts to study humankind from other biological perspectives (such as the study of fossils as a means of reconstructing human evolution). The same can be said of approaches to the study of humankind which are not biological at all. Human behavior can best be understood if researchers seek multiple levels of explanation (see Daly and Wilson 1978:8–13 for a good discussion of this issue). Having said this, we remain convinced that studying human behavior in terms of its ultimate evolutionary causes is an especially promising and underexploited line of research. This last set of papers discusses some of the issues relevant to the introduction of this specific approach into anthropology in particular and the social sciences in general.

The paper by Tiger (1975) examines some of the historical reasons why individuals of liberal and radical political persuasion have felt more comfortable with positions of extreme environmentalism, and why biological theories of human behavior have been thought of as associated with political reaction. He makes the important point that these associations of political and scientific views are historical but not logical. He further makes the provocative suggestion that on logical grounds one might more easily defend an association of extreme environmentalism with arbitrary governmental manipulation of the governed and biological theories of behavior with defense of the rights of the governed vis-à-vis those who govern.

The short essay by Wilson makes an interesting prediction for the future of sociobiology in the social sciences. Drawing on a number of historical cases which parallel in certain ways the current attempt to incorporate sociobiology into the social sciences, he suggests that the two distinct areas of inquiry will merge and that in doing so both sociobiology and the social sciences will be transformed. He has developed the ideas presented here in a recent article in *Daedalus* (1976), and commented on them further in his book *On Human Nature* (1978).

In the final chapter, Chagnon discusses the place of natural-selection theory in anthropology, considering the philosophical traditions of the discipline as well as its historic setting and academic development. He emphasizes the logic of studying human sociality and culture in terms of natural selection if we accept the basic assumption that these phenomena evolved out of antecedent phenomena in conformity with natural law—that is, in accordance with the principles of biology, chemistry, and physics. Speaking as a practicing social anthropologist, he ponders the apparent anomaly of the general lack of interest in natural-selection theory among his colleagues. He points out that fieldwork designed to test sociobiological models is a promising line of future research.

The results presented in this volume, I believe, support this view. One could point out that the number of tests made, the number of human populations from which data were drawn, and the number of aspects of behavior examined, are all small. It is true that the work of empirical testing has only begun, and one cannot safely predict its outcome at present. Nevertheless, I and many others are convinced that the results of the sort presented in this volume justify the claim that research aimed at testing sociobiological models in human populations is well worth pursuing.

It seems a safe prediction that such research will become extensive in the near future. Anthropologists, and other social scientists, will turn to existing monographs and to the Human Relations Area Files for data to test one or another prediction. The results of such research, however, I expect, will be limited because often the data most needed will be absent. The real evaluation of the relevance of natural selection to human behavior will require the collection of new data. This is bad news for those who are anxious for a definitive answer. Collecting data is expensive and time-consuming. However, it is only by this laborious process that we can eventually arrive at a really good estimation of the extent to which our behavior is predictable from the evolutionary processes which produced us.

In addition to empirical work, new theoretical developments will probably also be required before we can really understand the effect of natural selection as the ultimate evolutionary cause of human behavior.

Any attempt to apply a theory developed in reference primarily to one type of data (nonhuman animal behavioral data) is almost certain to require rethinking and refinement as it is applied to a new area of data (human behavioral data). Human behavior in comparison to other forms of animal behavior has many unique or unusual features. These include language, the great elaboration of culture, and the extensive exploitation of reciprocal altruism as an adaptive strategy, the extension of parental investment to adult offspring, and the frequent arrangement of mate choices for offspring. Explaining these things in terms of natural selection will probably require some refinement of our understanding of processes of natural selection and their consequences. E. O. Wilson's essay suggests something of what can be expected here.

W. I.

20. Biology, Psychology, and Incorrect Assumptions of Cultural Relativism

Lionel Tiger

I want to make a brief comment about the ethnography of the assumptions behind ethnography, to suggest the derivation of some of these assumptions, and to note their links to some other sciences of social behavior. My basic point is that the regnant behavioral psychology underlying the characteristic cultural relativism of much of North American anthropology is simply wrong, and that the anthropology has yet to respond fully to changes in the information and theory of the psychology on which it is perforce if not inevitably based. I am not gainsaying the improvements in description, analysis, and explanation which have occurred recently (and which, interestingly enough, were amply reflected in the overall program of the annual meeting of anthropologists in Washington in 1976 in which the symposium leading to this volume was held). Nevertheless, there remains a general avoidance by anthropologists of what has become a major shift in the skill with which biologists can describe and analyze a genotypically-linked normative gregariousness for social animals—that is, that not only individual behavior but also social-structural behavior is to an important, though very variable, degree a response to genotype as well as to the specific environments the phenotype encounters.

The psychology upon which basic anthropological research depended was of the environmentalist variety and that in turn was based upon ambient biological notions about organisms and their social behavior; these biological notions were uninformed by any serious phylogeny of behavior, they were focused on relatively small-scale behavioral units, and they inadequately linked the ontogeny of organisms to their phylogeny. Now the biology has changed radically and the psychology is beginning to change as well. For example, it becomes clearer than ever that learning itself is subject to genotypically normative patterns. More and more psychologists ask David Hamburg's question, "What's easy for the animal to learn?", believing that such a question is likely to yield information about contemporary behavior which is further illuminated by data from the evolutionary history of the species (Hamburg 1963. See also Seligman and Hager 1972. For an up-to-date discussion of an ethological view of the learning of mental processes see Griffin 1976.)

Yet despite serious changes in the basic supporting structure of its *modus operandi*, ethnographic work continues to use assumptions formed in the early days of relatively naive environmentalism. Questions about human behavioral nature, or the mere possibility of the existence of propensities for specific behaviors organized and phased in predictable ways, remain uncomfortable ones. Such questions are set aside, at a distance; occasionally they are taken up by rare and intrepid synthesizers who are quickly defined as unsound or grandiose.

Even work with verve and explanatory scope such as Divale and Harris's recent study of male-female differences reflects this pattern; in effect, they remove from their concern the possibility that they are dealing with a genotypical matter and instead focus on the specific environmental and demographic circumstances which may compose the reason for the regularities they observe (1976).

Interestingly enough, it appears that one assumption of much traditional ecological research in anthropology has been that the organism is in a sense genotypically neutral or somehow canceled out—so that, in effect, what you put in as resources directly determines what you get out as behavior. The organism in this model is a black box which merely transfers resources into behavior with, it appears, predictable noninterference; at least, the form of the interference is scarcely defined. But this is of course a very strong theory of human nature—that it is irrelevant and that it will cause little or no interference in economic transactions. For the implicit and conscious self-interest Adam Smith employed as an assumption (he was wrong, of course) we have here a notion which replaces it: that the organism somehow knows how to allocate resources and to seize economic opportunities almost in an instinctive manner, although it has in this model, again, no instincts.

Of course this is a caricature drawn here, but I'm merely trying to point up the relationship of assumptions about human nature to data and theory. After all, the ecological assumption about the primacy of the economic variable is nothing less than a proposition that the factors of economy, protein consumption, etc., prevail over such factors as sexual dimorphism, the endocrines, and possible differences in cognitive and affective patterns associated with lateralization or other (as yet thoroughly arcane) sex-linked processes. Relatively hermetic as it is, the Divale-Harris position and those it represents and encompasses stop short of linking directly and willfully the process of eating, getting food, and exchanging it,

V. Prospect and Retrospect: Some Viewpoints

with other processes known or suspected of having formal connection to the human genotype. The Divale-Harris focus on the variable of gender without confronting the problem of genotype, when gender is obviously one of the genotypically-linked human phenomena, is par for the cultural-relativist course. My point is that the possibility of a "next-connection" is almost programmatically ignored. Nor, in all the espousal of protein as a cause for major social action, is it ever made clear just how the need for protein is recognized, presumably by the body, and then translated presumably through some cognitive manipulation into action. Nor is it made clear how protein comes to be favorably evaluated by communities so that it becomes prestigious to possess and consume it. We are never shown how, precisely, the organism affects its own behavior in confronting the socioeconomic environment.

Early Assumptions: Placed in Context

The cultural-relativist tradition emerges historically as a correlate of two scientific movements—the expansion of cross-cultural study, and Pavlovian behaviorist psychology. These two factors require only brief discussion.

The development of behaviorist psychology should be discussed first: alertness to the law of parsimony requires that initial assumptions about how the basic unit of behavior functions should be examined first. The Pavlovian assertion was that the behavior of an organism could be described and analyzed most responsibly and cumulatively by placing the individual in experimental situations which permitted manipulation of one or more variables related to the problem under review. Few investigators assumed that animals should be studied while interacting with conspecifics in their natural settings. Central to Pavlovian experiments was the expectation that the subjects would alter their behavior as a mathematical function of the variables under study rather than because of an internally produced or mediated stimulus. Of course, on any other assumption the experiment could show nothing directly, only that the researcher had misconstrued his subject animal and the repertoire of behaviors which could be studied by this method.

Broadly speaking, learning theory generated the preponderance of a vast amount of research on non-human animals (Beach 1950). With a readiness which may surprise those current workers who are firmly criticized for cross-specific comparisons, the principles of learning theory were extended from small rodents and mammals to humans. It is worth reformulating this: learning theories could be easily extrapolated to man from very distant animals without stirring up much discussion, whereas other theories concerned with genetic explanations met resistance when an effort was made to extrapolate from man's close relatives, the primates, to ourselves. To my knowledge this curious contrast has not been explicitly examined.

Of course not all research on learning was of the learning/nonsense-syllable type. Nevertheless, narrow-compass research dominated the field. A great volume of work appeared, however, and the assembling of so much material yielded what appeared to be a well-integrated and centralized theory about behavior, although what was chiefly invoked was a single principle. This process was accompanied by the rejection of instinct-type theories of behavior, and this was not accidental. The grandiose claims of instinct theories were firmly rebuffed as the level of specificity either increased bizarrely (e.g., in McDougall's escalating list of specific instincts) or became compounded beyond usefulness (e.g., Adler's instinct of "will to power" as general explanation for social processes).

Given the ambience of pyschology and the desuetude of the quest for "human nature" it is understandable that scientists of group social behavior should have turned from a focus on human similarities to an emphasis on variation; in anthropology, cultural relativism was not only supported by psychology but stimulated, perhaps even more powerfully, by the facist and racist ideologies of those who disputed it. The latter claimed that groups could be perceived as significantly different, almost in kind, and that this permitted a ranking of groups on first racial and then social-class criteria. These elusive criteria were alleged to have real effects, and sundry theories of human value were created in this scheme, culminating inexorably if not logically in the catastrophic Nazi madness. In the United States particularly, the formal and comprehensive passion against racism which marked so much of informed American sociopolitical thought was a formidable catalyst of the behaviorist movement; even now the struggle still occurs, often apparently with as much heat as decades ago. Nevertheless the subject matter of the debate in terms of substance has critically de-escalated. What were once full-blown arguments about master races and the like are now reduced to discussions of a few percentage points of difference in performance on artificially prepared and questionably realistic tests of what psychologists define as intellectual ability. Surely this involves the fallacy of misplaced concreteness. Yet the persistence of the considerable affect reveals the extent of concern about the nature-nurture problem and what a possible scientific solution may yield—or imply.

Throughout this period, with its emphatic rejection of genetic

V. Prospect and Retrospect: Some Viewpoints

theories, a positive process was taking shape: the accumulation of ethnographic evidence about human variation. The increasingly detailed ethnographic, mathematical, and statistical rendering of data about cultural differences offered additional justification for maintaining some reserve and distance from biology. After all, there was enough useful work to do, and earlier efforts to relate anthropological data to biology had proven futile and even ethically hazardous.

I stress the matter of biology not simply because it seems logical that a good social science find important links to biology—particularly a social science principally about an extremely gregarious animal boasting very complex societies. I stress it also because cultural relativism was—by virtue of its psychological assumptions—based on biology anyway. The fact that this was an incorrect biology necessitates a stern rethinking of basic principles. This need, however, is not obvious to many anthropologists because these incorrect assumptions are rarely examined explicitly.

For a variety of reasons two crude categorizations in the social system appear to bear reasonably clear if also extremely complex relations to biology. Paradoxical as it may seem, my suspicion is that a good deal of the renewed interest in sex roles, sex differences, and sex similarities is the product of an attention, after long neglect, to the possible biological components of gender-linked behavior. That is, as feminists and other writers have recently been telling us, and as I argued myself in 1969, the assumption is foolish and unfair that the study of society is basically the study of males and their actions. That assumption was possible only in an ambience which permitted social scientists to ignore the sexual variable. This was made possible at least in part by the assumption that genotype had a negligible effect on behavior, even upon behavior as genetically portentous as gender-linked behavior.

Early Assumptions: Under Current Review

Openly feminist and more conventional scientists are in rapid and ambitious fashion seeking to remedy this remarkable mis-emphasis in social science. Plainly, a good deal of the energy fueling this effort is born of political, economic, and social grievance and resentment about differences in the sexes' roles and rewards. But I think that another important source of change is the beginning of a shift in social science to a greater attention to, if not profit from, biology; and the current concern with gender is a revealing indication of how fundamental will be the consequences for current work of the impending revisions in the relationship of new biology to science about human social behavior. Anyone involved in the study of sex roles can affirm, often with considerable puzzlement, that controversies are severe and often conducted with weapons of disputation at once crude and effective.

Nevertheless, the important thing is that the matter is finally under stringent review and already reveals greater consensus about some general matters than would have seemed possible even six or seven years ago. For example, the recognition that genotypically based experiences connect all females with each other (as they may establish a bond among males) is at least a respectable hypothesis even in fairly radical feminism. At the same time, masculinity as an optional and variable matter has begun to receive discussion within a species-wide perspective. All this is not only a far cry from the inattention such subjects received, except in the broadly psychoanalytic fields, as recently as a decade ago, but also an indication that the way is being cleared for a full-scale effort to deal substantially with the overall problem of the relationship of gender to genotype. Since Darwin's elaborate start on this subject it has remained a central question in the field. Heretofore it has been answered with only a portion of the available cross-disciplinary tools. Inattention to the biological category of sex has not only yielded the curiosities of an economics, politics, history, and to a lesser extent, anthropology and sociology, which assume that the proper study of mankind was men. There are other immediate and real social consequences of these assumptions. For example, though they are controversial in many quarters, the so-called IQ and similar tests are in regular use in nearly all major bureaucracies especially educational ones—whose function in part is to encourage the development of inner "potential" in a socially constructive manner.

(The concept of "potential" seems to me to be an essentially neo-genetic one. It affirms the existence of an inherited range of possible available talents, propensities, enthusiasms, qualities, etc., which require only a suitable environment for their manifestation. This is an ironic twist, because here we find a genetic characteristic being thwarted·by an environmental circumstance. Yet means of developing this "potential" become the subject matter of a major aspect of environmentalist psychology. All this is of course a description of a very muddled situation, another indication of the confusion between assumption and facts which prevails in the discussion of these matters.)

How do test-makers deal with the question of gender? A basic assumption of makers of tests of general and widely applicable behaviors is

V. Prospect and Retrospect: Some Viewpoints

that responses to the tests will fall, in a large enough population, more or less along a normal curve of distribution. (A reasonable enough plan, of course, since it seems that normal curves are also largely natural—and hence useful reflections of genotypes. A good rule of thumb, which I for one find useful for students, is that in studying complex animals the shortest analytical distance between two points is a normal curve). So far so good. When a question is answered disproportionately well or badly by a particular group of individuals—blacks, whites, urbanites, males, females, Catholics, etc.,—it is rejected as defective because it is detecting characteristics of subcultures and not measuring "real" native (that is, genetic) ability. Fair enough. Since we know that the genetic differences between Catholics and Protestants, blacks and whites, surburbanites and farmers, are likely to be trivial, reflecting what Thiessen has called "genetic junk" (1974), then this procedure is surely reasonable. And the largest remaining problem about all this is that the cleansing process of all the questions does not go far enough.

But is not sex a different kind of category than the others? Does it not involve characteristics with presumptively more biological import than Methodism as distinct from Armenian Orthodoxy? Obviously I think it does, and the result of treating all diagnostic variables as of equal significance is that questions which are discriminatory at the ends of the curves of response of males and females are lopped off the test. What remains are questions which most males and most females can answer. What are not revealed are those questions distinguishing males and females as groups, questions which either sex can answer unusually well or unusually badly. Thus the unisexual emphasis of the question-making procedure—based on an assumption about the equivalence of all differentiating variables—yields a test which a priori cannot test for precisely those extremes that tests are frequently used to find.

This very factor, by the way, may account for a considerable portion of the differential responses to IQ tests of different racial and perhaps sociocultural groups; what may be under test here, as much as or more than IQ, is the way in which these racial or sociocultural groups relate to the "normal pattern" of sex-linked perceptions and performance. Clearly this could be a significant subject for analysis by those concerned with the relationship of human capabilities to social opportunities and the resultant social system; it is therefore surprising that so little attention has been paid to the different character of the array of variables controlled for in psychological tests. That IQ scores involve a relationship between performance and age, and that females everywhere as infants, children, and adolescents, mature more rapidly than males, should provide further point to an inquiry about the encounter of sociological assumption with biological reality.

Early Assumptions: the Unexpected Outcome

Other issues arise in like manner, which bear more or less relevance to social policy. I want to conclude these remarks with some brief efforts at an *exposé sommaire* about some underlying psychological assumptions of industrial societies, the relationship of these assumptions to anthropology, and their implications for ethical perceptions about the functions of the genotype and the behavioral implications of this.

The behaviorist psychology which begins with the Pavlovian discoveries makes its way into managerial processes in industrializing and centralizing societies—most prominently in the Soviet Union, through the impact of Lysenkoist thought on the social sciences, and in the U.S. through the industrial psychology of Frederick Taylor to the more general one of B. F. Skinner. Both of these nations are marked by great regional diversity, ambitious programs of industrialization, and highly elaborate and centralized military assertiveness. In both cases it has happened, and it has been convenient, that the regnant psychology has preoccupied itself with fitting individuals and even whole ethnic groups into the central industrial ideology—either in the guise of the "new Soviet man," or of the American "melting pot"—and the development in both cases of nationwide standards of financial and educational procedure. That all this happened to be to the advantage of the ruling cadre of the respective societies is presumably scarcely accidental. The impetus toward such centralization and homogenization has been reincarnated in the form of "modernization theories," the modern version of the Victorian notion of progress; in this general perception the relationship of people to systems has been extended to include peoples formerly excluded as hopelessly incompetent (primitive), or morally unsuitable (savage), for the benighted tasks of so-called civilized society.

It is ironic that the role of biology in social explanation has been frequently described as politically conservative and socially rigidifying. However, the contrary explanation, that there are no "natural" aspects of human social-structural behavior, opens the possibility that theories produce assertions about how people should behave—particularly theories which suit the political, moral, and economic interests of ruling groups. In other words, the environmentalist theory offers an extensive set of policy

V. Prospect and Retrospect: Some Viewpoints

options to governors, though of course the ones chosen need not be dictatorial or inequitable. Nevertheless there is more room for political maneuver than on the basis of a psychological theory defining a clear set of human needs, rights, and "natural" patterns. Naturally I do not wish to establish here an opposition for its own sake. I certainly do not attribute to persons committed to an environmentalist psychology any particular malice, manipulativeness, or disrespect for humane values. I want merely to say that for too long there has been an identification of biological-linked theory with political reaction which is not a logical identification. On the face of it the opposite interpretation about the relationship of politics and biology may be at least as logical, if not more so.

21. Biology and Anthropology: A Mutual Transformation?

Edward O. Wilson

Recent commentators have spoken almost exclusively of the potential impact of sociobiology on anthropology, but a reciprocal effect seems equally likely. Sociobiology is itself a malleable, growing subject rather than an immutable catalyst. Its future depends on the challenges created by its most difficult subjects and most especially anthropology. Both areas of science can expect to be enriched by a mutual transformation.

This prognosis is based to some extent on the existence of two historic parallels in the history of the biological sciences. The first occurred in conjunction with the rise of biochemistry. By 1900 this discipline was well established. Eduard Buchner's success as of 1897 in separating zymase, which could convert sugar to alcohol and carbon dioxide, was correctly viewed as a demonstration that basic processes of the cell are performed by organic molecules far simpler than the complex apparatus represented by the cell itself. Biochemists had moreover grown confident that protoplasm, already enshrined as the physical basis of life (to use Huxley's compelling phrase), could be similarly decomposed. At the same time cytologists had pushed light microscopy close to its limits to work out the gross architecture of the cell and the details of mitosis.

In spite of the broad overlap of their interests, practitioners of the two disciplines went largely separate ways. The biochemists were prone to ignore the findings of cytology, as later they were to neglect classical genetics. With no small amount of arrogance they stressed the fundamental importance of chemical and physical explanations of cellular phenomena. Cell biologists, on the other hand, could not believe that the complicated mesostructures they were discovering were entirely the result of elementary physiochemical reactions.

They were both right. The phenomena of cytology are being explained in exclusively physicochemical terms, but both cellular biology and biochemistry have had to undergo enormous technical and conceptual advances before the first convincing chains of explanation were completed. The two fields were mutually transforming each other. The broad area of their juncture is known as molecular biology—which can be defined as physiological chemistry constrained by the spatial arrangements of macromolecules. Joseph Fruton, a distinguished biochemist who recently reviewed the history of the subject, has noted that inevitably "such competition is attended by tensions among the participants. I venture to say that this competition and these tensions are the principal source of vitality of biochemistry and are likely to lead to unexpected and exciting novelties in the future, as they have in the past" (1976:327–334). There is a lesson here for sociobiologists and anthropologists.

A second example of a fruitful interaction of reductionist and holistic forces is to be found in the development of modern ecology. Model building in theoretical population ecology, the approximate reductionist equivalent of biochemical analysis, was given a strong impetus with the formulations of A. J. Lotka and Vito Volterra in the 1920s. Yet most of ecology developed in isolation of this event and continued its growth as a descriptive science. It can be fairly said that true deductive theory languished during the next thirty years. When it gathered new force in the late 1950s and 1960s, largely through the influence of the late Robert H. MacArthur, the reductionist approach met considerable resistance from traditional ecologists. Ecosystems, they declared, are much too complex to be dissected by elementary equations and graphical models. Each community of living organisms is a unique historical event, and generalizations,

V. Prospect and Retrospect: Some Viewpoints

they therefore concluded, must be honestly wrung from painstakingly close examination of such systems in nature.

Again, it turned out that both sides were partly right. Postulational-deductive theory, based to a large extent on mathematical models, has won a secure if still narrow beachhead in ecology (see, for example, May, ed. 1976). To enlarge its effectiveness, it is being molded into new forms and made more complex. Each fresh look at the "tangled bank"—Darwin's phrase for the real ecological world—invites a renovation in theory. The synthesis is not nearly so far along as it is in molecular biology, but the creative tensions of which Fruton wrote are equally in evidence.

I suggest that we are in the first stages of a comparable interaction between sociobiology and anthropology. Evolutionary theory and population biology, the foundation disciplines of sociobiology, are too crude to address any but the simplest problems in anthropology. Recently, I made a list of what I could perceive as the ten most central problems in theoretical sociobiology (Wilson 1976). Although my personal interests are in the social insects, half of the problems identified were inspired by human sociobiology. The reasons are the much greater complexity of the human species and the superior descriptive knowledge of the subject, permitting a clearer view of what is possible. The special challenges include the role and penetration of group selection and kin selection in the evolution of unilateral altruism (as opposed to reciprocal altruism); the effects of noncongruence of linguistic, political, and trade boundaries on population structure and gene flow; and the interaction of cultural evolution, which is a very rapid Lamarckian process, with genetic evolution, which is Darwinian and slower by at least an order of magnitude. Biological theory will have to be considerably extended to handle such problems.

It is healthful for anthropologists to tell the biologists that their ideas are too simple to explain the really important qualities of human social behavior, and for biologists to tell the anthropologists that they will never have a satisfying explanation of that behavior in the absence of evolutionary theory and population biology. I predict that we are about to repeat the history of molecular biology and ecology. For every Sahlins there will be a DeVore. Anthropology will become more biological, and biology will become more anthropological. The seam between the two subjects will disappear, and both will be richer in content.

22. Anthropology and the Nature of Things

Napoleon A. Chagnon

Anthropologists familiar with the history and tradition of the discipline might properly ask, at the end of this volume, what is so distinctive about considering human behavior in terms of evolutionary biology, viewing man and his behavior as a product of natural selection? After all, our craft began with the purpose of explaining both man's natural and cultural variations and has always held both social and biological questions as within its legitimate domain. Anthropology has always been, and will continue to be, what anthropologists do; and it is a prescient, if not presumptuous, soul who could hazard an accurate definition of what the future scope of the field will be.

One of my former teachers, Leslie A. White, was clearly aware of this. He whimsically advised his classes on the history of the discipline that "Anthropology is the study of anything that has to do with any primate at any point in time." On occasion White was dismayed by this prodigious scope, but he shared the vision of many of our academic forebears that anthropology by necessity incorporated and depended upon knowledge that other disciplines generated about the nature, history, and evolution of man. One of our distinguished intellectual ancestors, Edward B. Tylor, was more pointed and ebullient: he argued, with admirable confidence, that anthropology had a mission that entailed assembling all the knowledge about man and making it intelligible. In this enterprise, many of the other sciences, as Tylor expressly argued, served subordinate roles: "Various other sciences . . . must be regarded as subsidiary to anthropology, which yet hold their own independent places in the field of knowledge" (1910:109). Among these, Tylor explicitly included anatomy and physiology, psychology, philology, ethics, sociology, archaeology and geology. Tylor's boldly articulated vision presumably came unwelcomed to other scholars of his day, whose already mature disciplines were making notable advances in knowledge and shedding considerable light on the track of man. All the more, since anthropology was then a nascent discipline, just taking form and substance, yet rendering unto itself the supreme responsibility, if not privilege, of assuming the role of queen of the sciences.

All of this should remind us that anthropology has always concerned itself with the study of human behavior in a biological as well as a cultural sense, has always depended on the knowledge accumulated by other sciences to achieve this end, and has always represented itself as the most holistic of disciplines, destined to be supreme in a hierarchy of knowledge. Yet, one cannot help being amused by the fact that, despite Tylor's confident vision, there still exist as independent and vigorous disciplines all the "subsidiary" sciences he identified. Many of our colleagues seem to fear that evolutionary biology will aspire to the role that Tylor envisioned for anthropology. I am confident that their concerns are exaggerated. This is not because I share Tylor's view about the supremacy of anthropology but because, as the essays in this volume repeatedly show, man is at once a product of culture and nature and a comprehensive understanding of his behavior requires both a biology and an anthropology.

Claude Lévi-Strauss, who characteristically focuses his attention on enigmatic themes and who, for that reason, often determines major trends in anthropological inquiry, has always puzzled over a fundamental dichotomy characteristic of the intellectual concerns of most of the human species: the Nature/Culture opposition. The myths of peoples all over the globe reflect, elaborate upon, and attempt to reconcile the contradictions of an almost unacceptable Truth: that Man is at once part of Nature but yet, as distinct from other animals, independent of it because he has Culture— fire, tools, souls, language and immortality. Thus, in the *tristes tropiques* of Amazonas, Jaguar can successfully hunt and devour men unarmed and uncultured, but we deny this to him in our stories about him: in myth, he is a fool and invariably duped by Men. In a curious and amusing sense, the ideology of cultural anthropology is very much like the ambivalence of myth regarding Jaguar's nature: Yes, we say early in our textbooks, humans are primates and behave according to the laws of nature, but because humans can learn and have culture they are, in later sections of the textbook, almost immune to these laws and apart from nature. So prevalent is this attitude that Alexander (chapter 3, this volume) concludes that two of the major obstacles to accepting general notions of evolution as applicable to humans are organized religion on the one hand, and cultural anthropology on the other!

This remarkable outgrowth of our philosophical tradition stems in part from a zealous and uncritical adherence to Durkheim's general admonition that the proper explanation of social facts had necessarily to be sociology in its narrowest form, a perspective that Leslie White himself elaborated in his compelling works on the science of culture. Their views, in their most exclusivist expressions, were challenged and modified by the cultural-ecological works of the 1960s and 1970s, when the "environment" was painfully admitted into the functional scheme of things. The deterministic dimension emerging in the harder side of social anthropology could hardly be incompatible with arguments that humans, like all other organisms, had to subsist to survive, and that their subsistence regimes reflected ecological realities which necessarily had to be considered in explanations of both human behavior and cultural adaptations (although the latter were the primary focus of attention).

But the conspicuous opposition of social anthropologists to biological models of human behavior is, in another sense, a consequence of the history of anthropology itself. Social and cultural anthropology set off on a specialized course nearly one hundred years ago while physical anthropology and human biology went a different way—and few of the respective practitioners had much awareness of what the others were doing. The fiction of a holistic anthropology was largely maintained through introductory textbooks and by the fact that all "good" departments had to include both physical and cultural anthropologists. Thus, much of the lack of understanding, or even the suspicion, that characterizes the relationships between biologically oriented and culturally oriented anthropologists is built into the discipline itself, a product of increasing specialization and narrower and narrower focuses on smaller and smaller problems—coupled with stronger and stronger convictions about the symbolic nature of kinship, marriage, and even reproduction itself. Today it is commonplace for social and cultural anthropologists to scorn the very suggestion that kinship has biological attributes and functions, and that kinship behavior might make sense in terms of predictions from evolutionary biology. If in some quarters the significance of the "environment" has won a grudging acceptance, the possible significance of the "biogram" still incurs an apprehensive aversion.

Curiously, the reservations many of us in social anthropology have about the utility of biological models reflect in an uncanny way the theme that pervades the myths of tribesmen: Men are part of Culture and apart from Nature. Why is it so difficult, even repugnant, for humans to admit that they are as much a part of Nature as they are a part of Culture? We so willingly admit, both in scientific ideology and in myth, that humans and animals are one with each other and for many purposes interchangeable. We even permit them in fiction to beget each other, if not in enchanting stories of creation, then in evolutionary sequences. But in both instances we ultimately insist on a sharp break, a great divide, an insuperable gulf separating ourselves from the rest of the creatures. One is almost compelled to suggest that an idea so firmly entrenched in the minds of men has some adaptive function or meaning. Would admitting our "naturalness" reduce

V. Prospect and Retrospect: Some Viewpoints

our capacity to effectively adapt to our surroundings? Does the optimistic conviction that Nature is subordinate to Culture confer any advantage in dealing with—struggling with—the external world, in the past or in the present?

Probably if the essays in this volume had been published ten years ago, they would have appeared in the context of physical anthropology without stirring much of a ripple among cultural anthropologists, but they may provoke more discussion now because the concerns of most of the authors can be simply expressed as an attempt to see beyond a Culture/Nature opposition, to reaffirm the kind of holistic view of human behavior that distinguished many of our academic ancestors. We can imagine nothing more exciting or scientifically profound than the possibility that much of human behavior conforms to predictions from evolutionary biology—and nothing more legitimate as a field of anthropological inquiry. But we also know that premature conclusions are not good science—they are not science at all. The recent impact of evolutionary biology on anthropological studies has come at a time when biological theory itself has gained new, powerful, and far-reaching insights into the nature of all behavior. The number of critical concepts or new ideas is small—inclusive fitness, nepotism, reciprocal altruism, kin selection, mating strategies, parental investment—but their implications for many kinds of characteristically human behavior are great. And behavior is the key word, particularly as it is relatable to strategies of reproduction and differences in reproductive success. The sexual asymmetries in reproductive physiology widespread in nature are likewise characteristic of our species, and in that simple truth a great many profound questions about human nature must necessarily lie. Anthropologists have been studying human kinship and marriage for over one hundred years, and yet we are hardly able to claim more than Morgan did in 1870: systems of consanguinity and affinity in the human family vary. But how does reproduction within them vary, individual by individual, sex by sex?

It should be obvious by now that definitive answers to the key questions will require new and highly detailed information. Lamentably, anthropology, in its traditional concerns, stands in the twilight of a rapidly disappearing era, for the kinds of societies in which new work can be done—or previous work extended—are vanishing, and many of those remaining societies are inaccessible for political reasons. While the now-limited ethnographic cosmos may hinder us, it does not preclude new studies altogether. Indeed, valuable work in this vein can be done in any society, for the variations of which we speak lie not only in the exotic hinterlands of remote places and anywhere therein, but everywhere. We believe that new studies of human behavior from the vantage of both evolutionary biology and traditional anthropology should be initiated on a broad scale with tests of natural selection hypotheses in mind, not only because such inquiries have always been within the traditional scope of our science, but also because they are scientifically important. We may enter blind alleys on some or make new discoveries on others, for such is the fate of those who take new paths and fresh ideas into unknown domains. Almost no explicitly sociobiological fieldwork in human societies has yet been accomplished. But, as the essays in this volume suggest, some existing data give us reason to believe that the return for such efforts will be great. To make this step, future field researchers must set aside the cliché of Nature-opposed-to-Culture, hold in abeyance some of the preconceptions and prejudices that mark our profession's recent parochial history, and responsibly reflect on the kinds of questions that aroused an earlier generation of students of man. It is entirely fitting to end this volume with an attempt to capture some of the caution and optimism that marked the measured words of Tylor:

> *None will deny that, as each man knows by the evidence of his own consciousness, definite and natural cause does, to a great extent, determine human action. Then, keeping aside from considerations of extra-natural interference and causeless spontaneity, let us take this admitted existence of natural cause and effect as our standing-ground, and travel on it so far as it will bear us [1958(1871):3.]*

While Tylor had in mind the distinction between science and supernaturalism, which need not concern us here, his dismissal of causeless spontaneity surely applies to the question of the independence of man's behavior from his evolutionary and biological character. To deny any relationship or oppose any inquiry is to ignore the great aphorism of Lucretius: that nothing yet from nothing ever came.

Bibliography

Abbott, W. L. 1891. Ethnological Collections in the U.S. National Museum from Kilima-Njaro, East Africa. U.S. National Museum Report (1891):381–428.

Aberle, D. F. 1961. Navaho. *In* Matrilineal Kinship. D. M. Schneider and K. Gough, eds. Pp. 96–201. Berkeley: University of California Press.

Abraham, R. C. 1940. The Tiv People. London: Crown Agents for the Government of Nigeria. [1933. edition. Lagos: Government Printer. 1968 facsimile by Farnborough, Gregg.]

Acker, Cheryl, and Patricia Townsend. 1975. Demographic Models and Female Infanticide. Man 10(3):467–470.

Ackerman, Charles. 1964. Structure and Statistics: the Purum Case. American Anthropologist 66:53–65.

Adams, J., E. D. Rothman, W. E. Kerr, and Z. L. Paulino. 1977. Estimation of the Number of Sex Alleles and Queen Matings from Diploid Male Frequencies in a Population of *Apis mellifera*. Genetics 86(3):583–596.

Agarwala, S. N. 1972. India's Population Problems. Bombay: Tata McGraw-Hill.

Ahern, E. 1974. Affines and the Rituals of Kinship. *In* Religion and Ritual in Chinese Society. A. P. Wolf, ed. Pp. 279–307. Stanford: Stanford University Press.

———— 1975. The Power and Pollution of Chinese Women. *In* Women in Chinese Society. M. Wolf and R. Witke, eds. Pp. 193–214. Stanford: Stanford University Press.

Ajisafe, A. K. 1924. The Laws and Customs of the Yoruba People. London: G. Routledge & Sons.

Akiga. 1939. Akiga's Story: The Tiv Tribe as Seen by One of Its Members. Rupert East, trans. and ed. International Institute of African Languages and Authors. London: Oxford University Press.

Alexander, R. D. 1969. Comparative Animal Behavior and Systematics. *In* National Academy of Sciences. Publication 1692, Pp. 484–520.

———— 1971. The Search for an Evolutionary Philosophy of Man. Proceedings of the Royal Society of Victoria 84 (1):99–120.

———— 1974. The Evolution of Social Behavior. Annual Review of Ecology and Systematics 5:325–383.

———— 1975a. The Search for a General Theory of Behavior. Behavioral Science 10:77–100.

———— 1975b. Natural Selection and Specialized Chorusing Behavior in

———— 1977a. Natural Selection and the Analysis of Human Sociality. *In*

Acoustical Insects. *In* Insects, Science, and Society. D. Pimentel, ed. Pp. 35–77. New York: Academic Press.

Changing Scenes in the Natural Sciences, 1776–1976. C. E. Goulden, ed. Pp. 283–337. Academy of Natural Sciences, Special Publication 12, Philadelphia: the Academy.

———— 1977b. Evolution, Human Behavior, and Determinism. Proceedings of the Biennial Meeting of the Philadelphia Science Association (1976). Vol. 2:3–21.

———— 1977c. *Review of* The Use and Abuse of Biology: An Anthropological Critique of Sociobiology. American Anthropologist 79:917–920.

———— 1978a. Natural Selection and Societal Laws. *In* Science and the Foundations of Ethics. III. Morals, Science, and Society. T. Engelhardt and D. Callahan, eds. Hastings-on-Hudson, New York: Hastings Institute of Society, Ethics and the Life Sciences. Pp. 249–290.

———— 1978b. Evolution, Creation, and Biology Teaching. American Biology Teacher 4(2):91–104.

———— 1978c. The Challenge of Darwinism. Rockham Reports 4:1–2.

———— In press a. Evolution, Social Behavior, and Ethics. *In* Science and the Foundations of Ethics. IV. Hastings-on-Hudson, New York: Hastings Institute of Society, Ethics, and the Life Sciences.

———— In press b. Natural Selection and Social Exchange. *In* Social Exchange and Developing Relationships. R. L. Burgess and T. L. Huston, eds. New York: Academic Press.

Alexander, R. D., and G. Borgia. 1978. Group Selection, Altruism, and the Levels of Hierarchical Organization of Life. Annual Review of Education and Systems 9:449–474.

Alexander, R. D., and P. W. Sherman. 1977. Local Mate Competition and Parental Investment Patterns in the Social Insects. Science 196:495–500.

Alexander, R. D., and T. W. Tinkle. 1968. *Comparative Book Review of* On Aggression by Konrad Lorenz *and* the Territorial Imperative by Robert Ardrey. Bioscience 18:245–248.

Alexander, R. D., and G. Borgia. In press. On the Origin and Basis of the Male-Female Phenomenon. *In* Sexual Selection in Insects. M. F. Blum, ed. New York: Academic Press.

Allan, W. 1949. Studies in African Land Usage in Northern Rhodesia. The Rhodes-Livingston Institute. London: Oxford University Press.

Alland, Alexander. 1972. Cultural Evolution: The Darwinian Model. Social Biology 19:227–39.

Alland, Alexander, and Bonnie McCay. 1973. The Concept of Adaptation in Biological and Cultural Evolution. *In* Handbook of Social and Cultural Anthropology. J. Honigmann, ed. Pp. 142–178. Chicago: Rand McNally.

Allen, J. A. 1925. Primates Collected by the American Museum Congo Expedition. Bulletin of the American Museum of Natural History 47:283–499.

Allen, W. E. 1932. A History of the Georgian People from the Beginning down to the Russian Conquest in the Ninteenth Century. London: Treubner.

Altmann, J. 1974. Observational Study of Behaviour: Sampling Methods. Behaviour 49:227–267.

Altmann, S. A. 1968. Sociobiology of Rhesus Monkeys. III. The Basic Communication Network. Behaviour 32:17–32.

Altschuler, M. 1965. The Cayapa: A Study of Legal Behavior. Ph.D. dissertation, University of Minnesota, 1964. University Microfilms, Ann Arbor, Publication No. 65–995.

Alvarez, F. 1881. Narrative of the Portuguese Embassy to Abyssinia during the Years 1520–1527. Lord Stanley, ed. and trans. London: Hakluyt Society.

Amir, M. 1971. Patterns in Forcible Rape. Chicago: University of Chicago Press.

Ammar, H. 1954. Growing up in an Egyptian village, Silwa, Province of Aswan. London: Routledge and Paul.

Anderson, J. M. 1972. Nature's Transplant: The Transplant Immunology of Viviparity. London: Butterworths.

Anderson, R. G. 1911. Some Tribal Customs in Their Relation to Medicine and Morals of the Nyam-Nyam and Gour People Inhabiting the Eastern Bahr-El-Ghazal. Wellcome Tropical Research Lab at Gordon Memorial College, Khartoum 413:239–277.

Anderson, R. T. 1973. Modern Europe: An Anthropological Perspective. Pacific Palisades, Calif.: Goodyear.

Anderson, Sydney, and Nancy Olds. Data from the collection of the American Museum of Natural History, New York, personal communication.

Angulo, J. de, and L. S. Freeland. 1929. Notes on the Northern Paiute of California. Société des Américanistes de Paris. Journal, nouvelle série 21:313–335.

Anonymous. 1908. Journal of the Principal Occurrences During the Voyage of the Frigate Santa Rosalia from El Callao de Lima to the Island of David, and Thence to San Carlos de Chiloe, in the Year 1770; by an Officer of the Said Frigate. *In* The Voyage of Captain Don Felipe Gonzalez to Easter Island in 1770–1. B. G. Corney, trans. and ed. Pp. 83–110. Second series, no. 13. Cambridge: Hakluyt Society.

Ansell, W. F. 1959. Mammals of Northern Rhodesia. Lusaka: Government Printing Office.

Anthony, H. 1921. The Jivaro Indians of Eastern Ecuador. Natural History 21:147–160.

Ardrey, R. 1961. African Genesis; a Personal Investigation into the Animal Origins and Nature of Man. New York: Atheneum.

———— 1966. The Territorial Imperative: A Personal Inquiry into the Animal Origins of Property and Nation. New York: Atheneum.

———— 1970. The Social Contract: A Personal Inquiry into the Evolutionary Sources of Order and Disorder. New York: Atheneum.

Arvelo-Jiménez, N. 1971. Political Relations in a Tribal Society: The Ye'cuana Indians of Venezuela. Ph.D. dissertation, Cornell University. Dissertation Series No. 31, Latin American Studies Program. Ithaca, New York: Cornell University Press.

Asch, T., and N. A. Chagnon. 1975. The Ax Fight. 16mm film. Somerville, Mass.: Documentary Educational Resources.

Bailey, F. G. 1969. Stratagems and Spoils. New York: Schocken.

Baker, P., and J. Dutt. 1972. Demographic Variables as Measures of Biological Adaptation: A Case Study of High-Altitude Human Populations. *In* The Structure of Human Populations. G. Harrison and A. J. Boyce, eds. Pp. 352–378. Oxford: Clarendon Press.

Baldus, H. 1937. Os grupos de comer e os grupos de trabalho dos Tapirapé. *In* Ensaios de Etnología Brasiliera. Vol. 1:86–111. São Paulo: Companhia Editore Nacional. A. Brunel, trans. [Also in the Human Relations Area Files.]

———— 1949. Os Tapirapé, tribu Tupí no Brasil central. A. Brunel, trans. São Paulo: Revista do Arquivo Municipal. [Selected pages in the HRAF.]

Balfour, E. G. 1885. Cyclopaedia of India and of Eastern and Southern Asia. . . . 3rd ed. Vol. 2:342–345. London: Bernard Quaritch.

Balikci, A. 1967. Female Infanticide on the Arctic Coast. Man 2:615–625.

———— 1970. The Netsilik Eskimo. Garden City, New York: Natural History Press.

Balke, B., and C. Snow. 1965. Anthropological and Physiological Observations on Tarahumara Endurance Runners. American Journal of Physical Anthropology 23:293–301.

Ball, J. D. 1903. Things Chinese: Or, Notes Connected with China. 4th ed. Hong Kong: Kelly and Walsh.

Bancroft, H. H. 1875. The Native Races of the Pacific States of North America. Vol. 1. The Wild Tribes. New York: D. Appleton and Co.

Banfield, A. W. F. 1974. The Mammals of Canada. Toronto: University of Toronto Press.

Bannikov, A. G. 1967. The Biology of the Saiga. Jerusalem: Israel Program for Scientific Translations.

Barash, D. P. 1977. Sociobiology and Behavior. New York: Elsevier.

Barkow, J. H.   1978. Culture and Sociobiology. American Anthropologist 80(1): 5–20.

Barnes, J. A.   1962. African Models in the New Guinea Highlands. Man 62:5–9.

————— 1971. Three Styles in the Study of Kinship. Berkeley: University of California Press.

Barnett, H. G.   1953. Innovation: the Basis of Cultural Change. New York: McGraw-Hill.

Barrett, S. A.   1925. The Cayapa Indians of Ecuador. 2 vols. Heye Foundation, Museum of the American Indian. Indian notes and monographs. Miscellaneous series no. 40.

Barth, Fredrik.   1966. Models of Social Organization. Royal Anthropological Institute, Occasional Paper No. 23. London: Royal Anthropological Institute.

————— 1967. On the Study of Social Change. American Anthropologist 69: 661–669.

Bartholomew, G. A., Jr.   1952. Reproductive and Social Behavior of the Northern Elephant Seal. University of California Publications in Zoology 47(15):369–472.

Bartholomew, G. A., Jr., and P. G. Hoel.   1953. Reproductive Behavior of the Alaskan Fur Seal, *Callorhinus ursinus*. Journal of Mammalogy 34: 417–436.

Bartlett, J. R.   1854. Personal narrative of explorations and incidents in Texas, New Mexico, California, Sonora, and Chihuahua, connected with the U.S. and Mexico Boundary Commission, during the years 1850, '51, '52, and '53. New York: Appleton.

Barton, R.   1919. Ifugao Law. Berkeley: University of California Press. [Also in the HRAF, 1955.]

————— 1922. Ifugao Economics. Berkeley: University of California Press. [Also in the HRAF, 1955.]

————— 1930. The Half-way Sun: Life among the Head-hunters of the Philippines. New York: Brewer and Warren. [Also in the HRAF, 1956.]

Basedow, H.   1925. The Australian Aboriginal. Adelaide: F. W. Preece and Sons. [Also in the HRAF.]

Basehart, H. W.   1961. Ashanti. *In* Matrilineal Kinship. D. M. Schneider and K. Gough, eds. Pp. 270–297. Berkeley: University of California Press.

Batchelor, J. 1927. Ainu Life and Lore: Echoes of a Departing Race. Tokyo: Kyobunkwan.

Bateman, A. J.   1948. Intrasexual Selection in *Drosophila*. Heredity 2:349–368.

Bates, Daisy.   1944. The Passing of the Aborigines: A Lifetime Spent Among the Natives of Australia. London: J. Murray.

Bates, Daniel, and Susan Lees.   1977. The Role of Exchange in Productive Specialization. American Anthropologist 79:824–841.

Baudenon, P.   1952. Notes sur les Bovidés du Togo. Mammalia 16:109–121.

Bauer, H. R. 1976. Sex Differences in Aggregation and Sexual Selection in Gombe Chimpanzees. American Zoologist 16:209.

Bawer, M. 1954. The Kuhgalu of Iran. Unpublished manuscript. New Haven, Human Relations Area Files.

Baxter, P. T. W., and A. Butt. 1953. The Azande, and Related Peoples of the Anglo-Egyptian Sudan and Belgian Congo. London: International African Institute.

Beach, F. A. 1950. The Snark Was a Boojum. American Psychologist 5:115–124.

————— 1969. Locks and Beagles. American Psychologist 24:971–989.

————— 1976. Sexual Attractivity, Proceptivity, and Receptivity in Female Mammals. Hormones and Behavior 7:105–138.

Beaglehole, E., and P. Beaglehole. 1938. Ethnology of Pukapuka. Honolulu: Bernice P. Bishop Museum Bulletin 150.

Beals, R. L. 1946. Cheran, a Sierra Tarascan Village. Washington, D.C.: United States Government Printing Office.

Beckerman, S. 1976. An Unusual Live-Birth Sex Ratio in Ecuador. Social Biology 23:172–174.

Bedford, J. M. 1969. Limitations of the Uterus in the Development of the Fertilizing Ability (Capacitation) of Spermatozoa. Journal of Reproduction and Fertility Supplement 8:19–26.

Behrens, C. F. 1908. Another Narrative of Jacob Roggeveen's Visit. *In* The Voyage of Captain Don Felipe Gonzales to Easter Island, 1770–1. B. C. Corney, trans. and ed. Pp. 131–137. Cambridge: Hakluyt Society.

Behrman, S. J. 1960. Detection of Ovulation. Postgraduate Medicine 27:12–17.

Beidelman, T. O. 1971. The Kaguru: a Matrilineal People of East Africa. New York: Holt, Rinehart and Winston.

Belgrave, C. D. 1923. Siwa: the Oasis of Jupiter Ammon. London: John Lane.

Bell, M. J., ed. 1948. An American Engineer in Afghanistan. From the Letters and Notes of A. C. Jewett. Minneapolis: University of Minnesota Press.

Belo, J. 1949. Bali: Rangda and Barong. New York: J. J. Augustine.

Benawa, A. R. 1946. Native Literature, Poems on and about Marriage. Afghanistan 1(4):43–46.

Benedict, Ruth. 1934. Patterns of Culture. New York: Houghton Mifflin.

————— 1959. Patterns of Culture. New York: New American Library, Mentor books. [1st ed., 1934].

Benhazera, M. 1908. Six mois chez les Touareg du Ahaggar. Algiers: Typographie Adolphe Jourdan. [Translated for the Human Relations Area Files by A. R. Coleman, 1960.]

Bennett, John W. 1969. Northern Plainsmen; Adaptive Strategies and Agrarian Life. Chicago: Aldine.

————— 1976. The Ecological Transition: Cultural Anthropology and Human Adaptation. New York: Pergamon.

Bennett, W. C., and R. M. Zingg. 1935. The Tarahumara: an Indian Tribe of Northern Mexico. Chicago: University of Chicago Press.

Benshoof, L., and R. Thornhill. In press. The Evolution of Monogamy and Loss of Estrus in Humans.

Bérenger-Féraud, L.-J.-B. 1879. [The Wolof]. *In* Les Peuplades de la Sénégambie. Pp. 1–62. Paris: Ernest Leroux.

Bergerud, A. T. 1971. The Population Dynamics of Newfoundland Caribou. Wildlife Monographs 25:1–55.

————— 1974. Rutting Behavior of Newfoundland Caribou. *In* The Behaviour of Ungulates and Its Relation to Management. V. Geist and F. Walther, eds. Vol. 1:395–435. Morges, Switzerland: International Union for the Conservation of Nature and Natural Resources.

Bernardi, B. 1955. The Age-System of the Masai. Annali Lateranensi 18:257–318.

Bernatzik, H. A. 1938. Overland with the Nomad Lapps. Vivian Ogilvie, trans. New York: R. M. McBride and Co.

————— 1947. Akha und Meau, Probleme der angewandten Völkerkunde in Hinterindien. 2 vols. [Akha and Miao: Problems of Applied Ethnography in Farther India.] Innsbruck: Kommissionsverlag Wagnerische Universität.

Bernstein, I. S. 1968. The Lutong of Kuala Selangor. Behaviour 32:1–16.

Bernstein, M. E. 1954. Studies on the Human Sex Ratio. 4. Evidence of Genetic Variation of the Primary Sex Ratio in Man. Journal of Heredity 45:59–64.

————— 1958. Studies in the Human Sex Ratio. 5. A Genetic Explanation of the Wartime Increase in the Secondary Sex Ratio. American Journal of Human Genetics 10:68–70.

Bertram, G. C. L. 1940. The Biology of the Weddell and Crabeater Seals. British Graham Land Expedition 1934–1937, Scientific Reports 1:1–139.

Beyer, H., and R. F. Barton. 1911. An Ifugao Burial Ceremony. Philippine Journal of Science 6:227–252.

Bigelow, R. S. 1969. The Dawn Warriors. Boston: Little, Brown.

Bigg, Michael A. 1969. The Harbor Seal in British Columbia. Journal of the Fisheries Research Board of Canada Bulletin 172:1–33.

Biggers, J. D. 1969. Problems Concerning the Uterine Causes of Embryonic Death, with Special Reference to the Effects of Ageing of the Uterus. Journal of Reproduction and Fertility Supplement 8:27–43.

Biocca, E. 1969. Yanoama: the Narrative of a White Girl Kidnapped by Amazonian Indians. New York: Dutton.

Birdsell, Joseph. 1958. On Population Structure in Generalized Hunting and Collecting Populations. Evolution 12(2):189–205.

————— 1968. Some Predictions for the Pleistocene Based on Equilibrium Systems among Recent Hunter-Gatherers. *In* Man the Hunter. R. B. Lee and I. DeVore, eds. Pp. 229–240. Chicago: Aldine.

Birkbeck, J. A., and M. Lee. 1973. Growth and Skeletal Maturation in British Columbia Indian Populations. American Journal of Physical Anthropology 38:727–738.

Birket-Smith, K. 1953. The Chugach Eskimo. Copenhagen: Nationalmuseets Publikationsfond.

Bischof, Norbert. 1975. The Comparative Ethology of Incest Avoidance. *In* Biosocial Anthropology. R. Fox, ed. Pp. 37–67. London: Malaby Press.

Bishop, M. W. H. 1964. Paternal Contribution to Embryonic Death. Journal of Reproduction and Fertility Review 7:383–396.

Blackwood, B. 1935. Both Sides of Buka Passage: An Ethnographic Study of Social, Sexual and Economic Questions in the North-Western Solomon Islands. Oxford: Clarendon Press.

Blackman, W. S. 1927. The Fellahin of Upper Egypt. London: Harrap. [Also in the HRAF, 1962.]

Blaffer Hrdy, S. 1974. Male-male Competition and Infanticide among the Langurs (*Presbytis Entellus*) of Abu, Rajasthan. Folia Primatologica 22:19–58.

———— 1976. Care and Exploitation of Nonhuman Primate Infants by Conspecifics Other Than the Mother. *In* Advances in the Study of Behavior 6:101–158. J. S. Rosenblatt, R. A. Hinde, and E. S. Shaw, eds. New York: Academic Press.

———— 1977. Infanticide as a Primate Reproductive Strategy. American Scientist 65:40–49.

Blaney, P. H. 1976. *Comment on* Genetic Basis of Behavior—Especially of Altruism. American Psychologist 31:358.

Blanton, R. 1975. The Cybernetic Analysis of Human Population Growth. *In* Population Studies in Archaeology and Biological Anthropology: A Symposium. A. C. Swedlund, ed. Pp. 116–126. American Antiquity 40(2), Memoir 30.

Blau, P. M. 1964. Exchange and Power in Social Life. New York: John Wiley and Sons.

Bloch, M. 1961. Feudal Society. 2 vols. Chicago: University of Chicago Press.

———— 1966. French Rural History: An Essay on Its Basic Characteristics. Berkeley: University of California Press.

Blunt, E. A. H. 1931. The Caste System of Northern India: with Special Reference to the United Provinces of Agra and Oudh. London: Oxford University Press. [Also in the HRAF, 1955.]

Blurton Jones, N. G., ed. 1972. Ethnological Studies of Child Behaviour. London: Cambridge University Press.

———— 1976. Growing Points in Human Ethology: Another Link Between Ethology and the Social Sciences? *In* Growing Points in Ethology.

P. P. G. Bateson and R. A. Hinde, eds. Pp. 427–450. Cambridge: Cambridge University Press.

Blurton Jones, N. G., and M. J. Konner. 1973. Sex Differences in Behavior of London and Bushman Children. *In* Comparative Ecology and Behaviour of Primates. R. P. Michael and J. H. Crook, eds. Pp. 689–750. New York: Academic Press.

Blurton Jones, N. G., and R. Sibly. 1978. Testing Adaptiveness of Culturally Determined Behaviour: Do Bushmen Women Maximize Their Reproductive Success By Spacing Births Widely and Foraging Seldom? *In* Human Behavior and Adaptation. V. Reynolds and N. Blurton Jones, eds., pp. 135–157. Symposium No. 18, Society for Study of Human Biology. London: Taylor and Francis.

Bockani, J. 1945. Mende Warfare. Farm and Forest 6(2):104–105.

Boehm, Christopher. 1978. Rational Preselection from Hamadryas to *Homo sapiens:* The Place of Decisions in Adaptive Process. American Anthropologist 80:265–296.

Bogoras, W. G. 1904–9. The Chukchee. 2 vols. Memoirs of the American Museum of Natural History. New York: Stechert.

Bohannan, L., and P. Bohannan. 1953. The Tiv of Central Nigeria. London: International African Institute.

———— 1969. A Source Notebook on Tiv Religion. New Haven: Human Relations Area Files Press.

Bollig, L. 1927. Die Bewohner der Truk-Inseln. Religion, Leben, und kurze Grammatik eines Mikronesiervolkes. Münster in Westphalia: Aschendorffsche Verlagsbuchhandlung.

Bolton, Brenda M. 1976. Mulieres Sanctae. *In* Women in Medieval Society. S. M. Stuard, ed. Pp. 141–158. Philadelphia: University of Pennsylvania Press.

Bonner, W. N. 1958. Notes on the Southern Fur Seal in South Georgia. Proceedings of the Zoological Society of London 130(2):241–252.

———— 1968. The Fur Seal of South Georgia. Scientific Report of the British Antarctic Survey no. 56.

Boorman, S. A., and P. R. Levitt. 1972. Group Selection on the Boundary of a Stable Population. Proceedings of the National Academy of Sciences. U.S.A. 69(9):2711–2713.

———— 1973. Group Selection on the Boundary of a Stable Population. Theoretical Population Biology 4(1):85–128.

Borgia, G. 1977. Effects of Male-male Competition and Resource Structure on Male Mating Success in *Scatophaga stercocara*. Ph.D. dissertation, University of Michigan.

Borrie, W. D., R. Firth, and J. Spillius. 1957. The Population of Tikopia, 1929 and 1952. Population Studies 10(3):229–252.

Bourne, B. 1874. The Captive in Patagonia: or, Life among the Giants. A Personal Narrative. Boston: D. Lothrop.

Bourne, G. H. 1975. Collected Anatomical and Physiological Data from the Rhesus Monkey. *In* The Rhesus Monkey. G. H. Bourne, ed. Pp. 1–76. Baltimore: University Park Press.

Bourne, G. H., and M. Nelly Golarz de Bourne. 1972. The Histology and Histochemistry of the Chimpanzee. *In* The Chimpanzee, 5. Histology, Reproduction, and Restraint. G. H. Bourne, ed. Pp. 1–76. Baltimore: University Park Press.

Boyd, J. M., J. M. Doney, R. G. Gunn, and P. A. Jewell. 1964. The Soay Sheep of the Island of Hirta, St. Kilda. A Study of a Feral Population. Proceedings of the Zoological Society of London 142:129–163.

Boyd, M. 1958. Eight Tarascan Legends. Gainesville: Florida State Museum Press.

Boyd, R., and P. J. Richerson. Ms. A Dual Inheritance Model of the Human Evolutionary Process. II. Costly Culture and the Genetic Control of Cultural Fitness.

Brant, C. S. 1950. Tadagale: A Burmese Village. Cornell University, Southeast Asia Program, data paper 13. [Also in the HRAF, 1955.]

———— 1951. Burmese Kinship and the Life Cycle: An Outline. Southwestern Journal of Anthropology 7:437–454.

Breeks, James Wilkinson. 1873. An Account of the Primitive Tribes and Monuments of the Nilagiris. London: India Museum.

Brettes, J. de. 1903. Les Indiens Arhouaques-Kaggabas. Société d'Anthropologie de Paris, Bulletins et Mémoires 5(4):318–357.

Briggs, L. Cabot. 1958. The Living Races of the Sahara Desert. Papers of the Harvard University Peabody Museum of American Archaeology and Ethnology. Vol. 28, No. 2.

Britan, Gerald, and Bette S. Denich. 1976. Environment and Choice in Rapid Social Change. American Ethnologist 3(1):55–72.

Brodrick, A. H. 1942. Little China: The Annamese Lands. Oxford: Oxford University Press.

Bruce, H. M. 1966. Smell as an Exteroceptive Factor (Excluding Pregnancy Blocking in Mice). Journal of Animal Science Supplement 25:83–89.

Brüning, H. 1928. Reisen im Gebiet der Aguaruna. Bässler Archiv 12:46–85.

Bryden, M. M. 1969. Growth of the Southern Elephant Seal, *Mirounga leonina* (Linn.). Growth 33(1):69–82.

Buck, Peter. 1930. Samoan Material Culture. Honolulu: Bernice P. Bishop Museum Bulletin 75.

Buechner, H. K. 1974. Implications of Social Behavior in the Management of Uganda Kob. *In* The Behaviour of Ungulates and Its Relation to Management. V. Geist and F. Walther, eds. Vol. 1:853–870. Morges,

Switzerland: International Union for Conservation of Nature and Natural Resources.

Buechner, H. K., J. A. Morrison, and W. Leuthold. 1966. Reproduction in Uganda Kob with Special Reference to Behavior. Symposia of the Zoological Society of London 15:69–88.

Buechner, H. K., and R. Schloeth. 1965. Ceremonial Mating Behavior in Uganda Kob (*Adenota kob thomasi* Neumann). Zeitschrift für Tierpsychologie 22:209–225.

Bulmer, M. F. 1970. The Biology of Twinning in Man. Oxford: Clarendon Press.

Burling, R. 1963. Rengsanggri: Family and Kinship in a Garo Village. Philadelphia: University of Pennsylvania Press.

———— 1964. Garos. *In* Ethnic Groups of Mainland Southeast Asia. F. M. LeBar, G. C. Hickey, and J. K. Musgrave, eds. Pp. 55–57. New Haven: Human Relations Area Files Press.

Burnes, A. 1834. On Female Infanticide in Cutch. Journal of the Royal Asiatic Society of Great Britain and Ireland 1(2). Article 17:193–199; Article 23:285–288.

Burnham, P. 1973. The Explanatory Value of the Concept of Adaptation in Studies of Cultural Change. *In* The Explanation of Cultural Change. C. Renfrew, ed. Pp. 93–102. London: Duckworth.

Burton, F. D. 1971. Sexual Climax in Female *Macaca mulatta*. *In* Proceedings of the Third International Congress on Primatology. H. Kummer, ed. Vol. 3:180–191. Basel: S. Karger.

Bygott, J. D. 1972. Cannibalism among Wild Chimpanzees. Nature 238:410–411.

———— In press. *In* The Behaviour of Great Apes; Perspectives on Human Evolution. D. A. Hamburg and J. Goodall, eds. New York: Staples/W. A. Benjamin.

Calcutta Review. 1844a. Female Infanticide in Central and Western India. Calcutta Review 1(2), article 4:372–448.

———— 1844b. The Kulin Brahmins of Bengal. Calcutta Review 2(3,) article 1:1–31.

Cameron, A. W. 1967. Breeding Behavior in a Colony of Western Atlantic Grey Seals. Canadian Journal of Zoology 45(2):161–174.

Campbell, B. G. 1966. Human Evolution. Chicago: Aldine.

Campbell, B. G., ed. 1972. Sexual Selection and the Descent of Man, 1871–1971. Chicago: Aldine.

Campbell, D. T. 1960. Blind Variation and Selective Retention in Creative Thought as in Other Knowledge Processes. Psychological Review 67:380–400.

———— 1965. Variation and Selective Retention in Sociocultural Evolution.

In Social Change in Developing Areas: A Re-interpretation of Evolutionary Theory. H. R. Barringer, G. L. Blanksten, and R. W. Mack, eds. Pp. 19–49. Cambridge, Mass.: Schenckman.

———— 1975. On the Conflicts between Biological and Social Evolution and between Psychology and Moral Tradition. American Psychologist 30:1103–1126.

Carneiro, R. L.   1961. Slash-and-burn Cultivation among the Kuikuru and Its Implications for Cultural Development in the Amazon Basin. *In* The Evolution of Horticultural Systems in Native South America: Causes and Consequences; a Symposium. J. Wilbert, ed. Antropológica [Venezuela] Supplement 2:47–67.

———— 1970. A Theory of the Origin of the State. Science 169:733–738.

Carpenter, C. R.   1940. A Field Study in Siam of the Behavior and Social Relations of the Gibbon (*Hylobates lar*). Comparative Psychology Monograph 16:1–212.

———— 1941. The Menstrual Cycle and Body Temperature in Two Gibbons (*Hylobates lar*). Anatomical Record 79:291–296.

Carr, D. H.   1967. Cytogenetics of Abortions. *In* Comparative Aspects of Reproductive Failure. K. Benirschke, ed. Pp. 96–117. New York: Springer-Verlag.

Carr-Saunders, A. M.   1922. The Population Problem. London: Clarendon Press.

Carrick, R., S. E. Csordas, S. E. Ingham, and K. Keith.   1962. Studies on the Southern Elephant Seal, *Mirounga leonina* (L.). III. The Annual Cycle in Relation to Age and Sex. C.S.I.R.O. Wildlife Research [Australia] 7(2):119–160.

Carstairs, G. M.   1958. The Twice-Born: A Study of a Community of High-caste Hindus. Bloomington: Indiana University Press.

Caspani, E., and E. Cagnacci.   1951. Afghanistan, crocevia dell'Asia. Milano: A Vallardi.

Castetter, E. F., and R. M. Underhill.   1935. The Ethnobiology of the Papago Indians. Ethnobiological Studies in the American Southwest. University of New Mexico Bulletin. Albuquerque: University of New Mexico Press. [Also in the HRAF, 1959.]

Cave-Browne, J.   1857. Indian Infanticide; Its Origin, Progress, and Suppression. London: W. H. Allen.

Cerruti, G. B.   1904. The Sakais of Batang Pudong. Perak. Royal Asiatic Society, Journal of the Straits Branch 41:113–117.

Cerulli, E.   1959. The Consuetudinary Law of Northern Somalia. *In* Somalia, Scritti vari Editi ed. Inediti. vol. 2. A Cura dell'Amministrazione Fiduciaria Italiana della Somalia. Roma. Pp. 1–74, 382–384.

Cervinka, V.   1950. Afghanistan: Structure économique et sociale, commerce extérieur. Lausanne: Office suisse d'expansion commerciale. [Also in HRAF, 1955. A. Kalmyk, trans.]

Chabot, H. 1950. Verwantschap, stand en sexe en Zuid-Celebes. Groningen: J. B. Wolters.

Chagnon, N. A. Yąnomamö Warfare, Social Organization and Marriage Alliances. Ph.D. dissertation, University of Michigan. University Microfilms. Ann Arbor, Michigan.

———— 1967. Yąnomamö: The Fierce People. Natural History 76:22–31.

———— 1968a. Yąnomamö: The Fierce People. New York: Holt, Rinehart and Winston.

———— 1968b. Yąnomamö Social Organization and Warfare. *In* War: The Anthropology of Armed Conflict and Aggression. M. Fried, M. Harris, and R. Murphy, eds. Pp. 109–159. Garden City: Natural History Press.

———— 1968c. The Culture-ecology of Shifting (Pioneering) Cultivation Among the Yąnomamö Indians. Proceedings, III International Congress of Anthropological and Ethnological Sciences, Tokyo, 1968. Vol. 3: 249–255. *Also in* Peoples and Cultures of Native South America. D. R. Gross, ed. Pp. 126–142. Garden City: Natural History Press. 1973.

———— 1968d. The Feast. Natural History 77:34–41.

———— 1972. Social Causes for Population Fissioning: Tribal Social Organization and Genetic Microdifferentiation. *In* The Structure of Human Populations. G. A. Harrison and A. J. Boyce, eds. Pp. 252–282. Oxford: Clarendon Press.

———— 1974. Studying the Yąnomamö. New York: Holt, Rinehart and Winston.

———— 1975. Genealogy, Solidarity, and Relatedness: Limits to Local Group Size and Patterns of Fissioning in an Expanding Population. *In* Yearbook of Physical Anthropology, 1975. Vol. 19:95–110. Washington: American Association of Physical Anthropologists.

———— 1976a. Fission in an Amazonian Tribe. Sciences 16:14–18. New York Academy of Sciences.

———— 1976b. Marriage and Genealogical Relatedness among 3500 Yąnomamö Indians: Implications for Population Fissioning. Paper presented at the 1976 Meetings of the American Anthropological Association, Washington, D.C.

———— 1977. Yąnomamö: The Fierce People. 2nd ed. New York: Holt, Rinehart and Winston.

———— Ms. a. Terminological Kinship, Genealogical Relatedness and Village Fissioning among the Yąnomamö Indians. To appear in Natural Selection and Social Behavior. R. D. Alexander and D. Tinkl, eds.

———— Ms. b. Asymmetry of Local Group Composition after Village Fissions.

Chagnon, N. A., J. V. Neel, L. R. Weitkamp, H. Gershowitz, and M. Ayres. 1970. The Influence of Cultural Factors on The Demography and

Pattern of Gene Flow from the Makiritare to the Yąnomamö Indians. American Journal of Physical Anthropology 32:339–349.

Chagnon, N. A., and R. B. Hames. 1979. Protein Deficiency and Tribal Warfare in Amazonia: New Data. Science 203:910–913.

Chagnon, N. A., and M. Flinn. In preparation. Frequencies and Degrees of Cousin Types among the Yąnomamö.

Chagnon, N. A., and E. V. Fredlund. In preparation. Genealogical Dimensions of Yąnomamö Incest Practices.

Champion, J. R. 1963. A Study in Culture Persistence: The Tarahumara of Northwestern Mexico. Ph.D. dissertation, 1962. Columbia University. Ann Arbor: University Microfilms #63–06107.

Chang Chung-li. 1955. The Chinese Gentry: Studies on Their Role in Nineteenth-Century Chinese Society. Seattle: University of Washington Press.

Chaseling, Wilbur S. 1957. Yulengor: Nomads of Arnhem Land. London: The Epworth Press.

Chasen, F. N., and C. B. Kless. 1927. Spolia mentawiensia—mammals. Proceedings of the Zoological Society of London 2:797–840.

Chivers, D. J. 1971. Spatial Relations within the Siamang Group. Proceedings of the Third International Congress on Primatology, Zurich, 1970. H. Kummer, ed. 3:14–21. Basel: Karger.

———— 1972. The Siamang and the Gibbon in the Malay Peninsula. In Gibbon and Siamang 1. Evolution, Ecology, Behavior, and Captive Maintenance. D. M. Rumbaugh, ed. Pp. 103–135. Basel: Karger.

———— 1974. The Siamang in Malaya. Contributions to Primatology 4:1–335.

Chojnacki, S. 1976. Dowries and Kinsmen in Early Renaissance Vienna. In Women in Medieval Society. S. M. Stuard, ed. Pp. 173–198. Philadelphia: University of Pennsylvania Press.

Christensen, J. B. 1954. Double Descent among the Fanti. G. A. Highland, ed. New Haven: Human Relations Area Files.

Ch'u T'ung-tsu. 1965. Law and Society in Traditional China. Paris: Mouton. [Originally published in 1947].

Ciocco, A. 1938. Variation in the Sex Ratio at Birth in the United States. Human Biology 10:36–64.

Clark, J. P., and E. P. Wenninger. 1962. Socioeconomic Class and Area as Correlates of Illegal Behavior among Juveniles. American Sociological Review 27:826–834.

Cline, D. R., D. B. Siniff, and A. W. Erickson. 1971. Underwater Copulation of the Weddell Seal. Journal of Mammalogy 52:216–218.

Cline, W. B. 1936. Notes on the People of Siwah and El Garah in the Libyan Desert. Menasha, Wisc.: G. Banta. [Also in the HRAF, 1960.]

Cloak, F. T., Jr. 1975. Is a Cultural Ethology Possible? Human Ecology 3(3):161–182.

————— 1977. Comment on "The Adaptive Significance of Cultural Behavior." Human Ecology 5(1):49–52.

Clutton-Brock, T. H., and P. H. Harvey. 1977a. Primate Ecology and Social Organization. Journal of Zoology 183:1–39.

————— 1977b. Sexual Dimorphism, Socionomic Sex Ratio, and Body Weight in Primates. Nature 269:797–800.

Coale, A. J., and P. Demeny. 1966. Regional Model Life Tables and Stable Populations. Princeton, N.J.: Princeton University Press.

Cohen, M. R., and H. Hanken. 1960. Detecting Ovulation. Fertility and Sterility 11:497–507.

Cohen, R., and J. Middleton. 1967. Comparative Political Systems. Garden City: Natural History Press.

Coleman, E. R. 1973. Medieval Marriage Characteristics: A Neglected Factor in the History of Medieval Serfdom. In The Family in History: Interdisciplinary Essays. T. K. Rabb and R. I. Rotberg, eds. Pp. 1–15. New York: Harper and Row.

————— 1976. Infanticide in the Early Middle Ages. In Women in Medieval Society. S. M. Stuard, ed. Pp. 47–70. Philadelphia: University of Pennsylvania Press.

Collins, H. B., Jr. 1925. Anthropometric Observations on the Choctaw. American Journal of Physical Anthropology 8:425–436.

————— 1928. Additional Anthropometric Observations on the Choctaw. American Journal of Physical Anthropology 11:353–355.

Colombo, B. 1957. On the Sex Ratio in Man. Cold Spring Harbor Symposia on Quantitative Biology 22:193–202.

Colson, E. 1961. Plateau Tonga. In Matrilineal Kinship. D. M. Schneider and K. Gough, eds. Pp. 36–95. Berkeley: University of California Press.

Columbia University. Language and Communication Research Center. 1956. The Caucasus. Principal Investigators B. Geiger et al. New York: Columbia University Press. [Also in the HRAF.]

Conaway, C. H., and C. B. Koford. 1965. Estrous Cycles and Mating Behavior in a Free-Ranging Band of Rhesus Monkeys. Journal of Mammalogy 45(4):577–588.

Conzemius, E. 1932. Ethnographical Survey of the Miskito and Sumu Indians of Honduras and Nicaragua. Bureau of American Ethnology Bulletin 106.

Cook, S. F. 1972. Prehistoric Demography. Addison-Wesley Modular Publication, no. 16. Reading. Also in Current Topics in Anthropology 3:1–42.

Cooke, G. H. 1899. Te Pito te Henua, Known as Rapa Nui; Commonly Called Easter Island, South Pacific Ocean. U.S. National Museum Report pt. 1 (1896–7):689–723.

Coon, C. S. 1931. Tribes of the Rif. Cambridge, Mass: Peabody Museum of American Archaeology and Ethnology. [Kraus reprint, 1971].

Coope, A. 1917. Anna Coope, Sky Pilot of the San Blas Indians, an Autobiography. New York: American Tract Society.

Cooper, J. M. 1944. The Shaking Tent Rite Among Plains and Forest Algonquians. Primitive Man 17:60–84.

——— 1946. Patagonian and Pampean Hunters. *In* Handbook of South American Indians. J. H. Steward, ed. Vol. 2:127–168. Washington, D.C.: U.S. Government Printing Office.

——— 1956. The Gros Ventres of Montana, Pt. 2. Religion and Ritual. Washington, D.C.: Catholic University of America. [Also in the HRAF, 1961.]

Cortés, J. B., and F. M. Gatti. 1972. Delinquency and Crime: A Biopsychosocial Approach. New York: Seminar Press.

Coughlin, R. J. 1950. The Position of Women in Vietnam. Yale University Southeast Asia Studies 1:1–45. New Haven [Also in the HRAF, 1954.]

Coulet, G. 1926. Les sociétés secrètes en terre d'Annam. Saigon: Imprimerie Commerciale C. Ardin. [Also in the HRAF, 1952.]

Coulton, G. G. 1949. Medieval Panorama: The English Scene from Conquest to Reformation. Cambridge: Cambridge University Press.

Covarrubias, M. 1938. Island of Bali. New York: Knopf.

Cowgill, U. M. 1969. The Season of Birth and Its Biological Implications. Journal of Reproduction and Fertility Supplement 6:89–103.

Cowgill, U. M., and G. E. Hutchinson. 1963. Sex-ratio in Childhood and the Depopulation of the Petén, Guatemala. Human Biology 35:90–103.

Cox, C. R., and B. J. LeBoeuf. 1977. Female Incitation of Male Competition: A Mechanism in Sexual Selection. American Naturalist 111:317–335.

Coxe, W. 1804. Account of the Russian Discovery between Asia and America. To Which Are Added, the Conquest of Siberia and the History of the Transactions and Commerce Between Russia and China. London: Cadell and Davies.

Crashing Thunder. 1926. Crashing Thunder: the Autobiography of an American Indian. Paul Radin, ed. New York: D. Appleton.

Crew, F. A. E. 1937. The Sex Ratio. American Naturalist 71:529–559.

Crile, G., and D. P. Quiring. 1940. A Record of the Body Weight and Certain Organ and Gland Weights of 3690 Animals. Ohio Journal of Science 40:219–259.

Cronin, E. W., Jr., and P. W. Sherman. 1976. A Resource-based Mating System: The Orange-rumped Honeyguide. The Living Bird 15:5–32.

Crook, J. H. 1966. Gelada Baboon Herd Structure and Movement: A Comparative Report. Symposia of the Zoological Society of London 18:237–258.

——— 1972. Sexual Selection, Dimorphism, and Social Organization in the Primates. *In* Sexual Selection and the Descent of Man, 1871–1971. B. Campbell, ed. Pp. 231–281. Chicago: Aldine.

Crooke, William. 1897. The North-Western Provinces of India: Their History, Ethnology, and Administration. London: Methuen.

Crosby, K. H. 1937. Polygamy in Mende Country. Africa 10:249–264.

Culwick, G. M. 1950. A Dietary Survey among the Zande of the Southwestern Sudan. Khartoum, Agricultural Publications Committee for the Ministry of Agriculture, Sudan Government, 1950:1–155.

Cunningham, Alexander. 1854. Ladak, Physical, Statistical, and Historical; with Notices of the Surrounding Countries. London: W. H. Allen.

Daguio, A. 1952. Hudhud Hi Aliguyon, a Translation of an Ifugao Harvest Song. M.A. thesis, Stanford University. [Also in the HRAF, 1956.]

Dahlberg, G. 1951. The Primary Sex Ratio and Its Ratio at Birth. Acta Genetica et Statistica Medica 2:245–251.

Dalton, George. 1961. Economic Theory and Primitive Society. American Anthropologist 63:1–25.

Daly, Martin, and Margo Wilson. 1978. Sex, Evolution, and Behavior. N. Scituate: Duxbury Press.

Damas, David, ed. 1969. Contributions to Anthropology: Ecological Essays. National Museum of Canada, Bulletin No. 230, Anthropological Series no. 86. Ottawa: National Museum of Canada.

Danquah, J. B. 1928. Gold Coast: Akan Laws and Customs and the Akim Abuakwa Constitution. London: Routledge.

Da Rocha, F. J. and F. M. Salzano. 1972. Anthropometric Studies in Brazilian Cayapo Indians. American Journal of Physical Anthropology 36:95–102.

Darwin, Charles. 1871. The Descent of Man, and Selection in Relation to Sex. 2 vols. London: John Murray.

———— 1967. On the Origin of Species. Boston: Harvard University Press. [facsimile of the 1859 edition].

Das, M. N. 1956. Female Infanticide among the Bedees and the Chouhans: Motives and Modes. Man in India 36(4):261–266.

———— 1957. Movement to Suppress the Custom of Female Infanticide in the Punjab and Kashmir. Man in India 37(4)280–293.

Datta, J. M. 1957. Variation in Sex-Ratio in Bengal during 150 Years. Man in India 37(2):133–148.

Dauphiné, T. C., Jr. 1976. Biology of the Kaminuriak Population of Barrenground Caribou, Part 4: Growth, Reproduction, and Energy Reserves. Canadian Wildlife Services Report 38:1–71.

Davenport, C. 1925. Notes on Physical Anthropology of Australian Aborigines and Black-white Hybrids. American Journal of Physical Anthropology 8(1):73–94.

Davin, D. 1975. Women in the Countryside of China. In Women in Chinese

Society. M. Wolf and R. Witke, eds. Pp. 243–273. Stanford: Stanford University Press.

Davis, D. D. 1962. Mammals of the Lowland Rain-forest of North Borneo. Bulletin of the National Museum of the Straits of Malaya (Singapore) 31:1–129.

Davis, E. H. 1920. The Papago Ceremony of Vikita. Indian Notes and Monographs 3:153–178.

———— 1965. The Seri Indian. *In* E. H. Davis and the Indians of the Southwest United States and Northwest Mexico. Pp. 141–218. Lowrey, Calif.: Eilena Quina.

Davis, E. H., and E. T. Dawson. 1945. The Savage Seris of Sonora. Scientific Monthly 60:193–202, 261–268.

Dawkins, R. 1976. The Selfish Gene. Oxford: Oxford University Press.

Dawkins, R., and T. R. Carlisle. 1976. Parental Investment, Mate Desertion and a Fallacy. Nature 262:131–132.

de Azevedo, T. 1953. The Colored Elite in a Brazilian City. Paris: UNESCO.

De la Tour, G. D. 1954. The Guanaco. Oryx 2:273–279.

Delury, G. E., ed. 1976. The World Almanac and Book of Facts 1977. New York: Newspaper Enterprise Association, Inc.

Dempsey, J. 1955. Mission on the Nile. London: Burns, Oates, and Washborne.

Deng, F. M. 1972. The Dinka of the Sudan. New York: Holt, Rinehart and Winston.

Densmore, F. 1929. Papago Music. Smithsonian Institution: Bureau of American Ethnology Bulletin 90.

Denys, N. 1908. The Description and Natural History of the Coasts of North America (Acadia). W. F. Ganong, ed. and trans. Toronto: Champlain Society.

De Oliveira, A. E., and F. M. Salzano. 1969. Genetic Implications of the Demography of Brazilian Juruna Indians. Social Biology 16(3):209–215.

Desai, P. B. 1969. Size and Sex Composition of Population in India, 1901–1961. Bombay: Asia Publishing House.

De Soudack, J. 1916. [The Day of a Lady of Fashion at Hué.] Hanoi: Bulletin des Amis du Vieux Hué 3:27–39.

Deutsch, H. 1945. The Psychology of Women. New York: Grune and Stratton.

Devereux, G. 1955. A Study of Abortion in Primitive Societies. New York: Jullian.

Devine, M. C. 1975. Copulatory Plugs in Snakes: Enforced Chastity. Science 187:844–5.

DeVore, I., ed. In preparation. Sociobiology and the Social Sciences.

Diamond, N. 1969. K'un Shen: A Taiwan Village. New York: Holt, Rinehart and Winston.

Dickeman, M. 1975. Demographic Consequences of Infanticide in Man. Annual Review of Ecology and Systematics 6:107–37.

Dickson, V. 1949. Artistic House-decoration in Riyadh. Man 49:76–77.

Dim Delobsom, A. A. 1932. L'empire du moghonaba; coutumes des Mossi de la Haute-volta. Paris: Domat-Montchrestien.

Divale, W. T. 1972. Systemic Population Control in the Middle and Upper Paleolithic: Inferences Based on Contemporary Hunters-Gatherers. World Archaeology 4:22–43.

Divale, W. T., and M. Harris. 1976. Population, Warfare, and the Male Supremacist Complex. American Anthropologist 78:521–538.

Divale, W. T., M. Harris, and D. T. Williams. 1978. On the Misuse of Statistics: A Reply to Hirschfeld et al. American Anthropologist 80:379–386.

Dobritzhofer, M. 1822. An Account of the Abipones: an Equestrian People of Paraguay. vol. 2. From the Latin of Martin Dobritzhofer. Sara Coleridge, trans. London: J. Murray. [Also in the HRAF, 1960.]

Dobzhansky, T. 1951. Human Diversity and Adaptation. Cold Spring Symposia on Quantitative Biology 15(1950):385–400.

Doolittle, J. 1865. Social Life of the Chinese: With Some Account of Their Religious, Governmental, Educational, and Business Customs. Vol. 2. New York: Harper and Bros.

Dorfman, R. I. 1948. Biochemistry of Androgens. *In* The Hormones: Physiology, Chemistry and Applications. G. Pincus and K. V. Thiman, eds. Vol. 1:467–548. New York: Academic Press.

Doring, G. K. 1969. The Incidence of Anovular Cycles in Women. Journal of Reproduction and Fertility Supplement 6:77–81.

Dorofev, S. U., and U. A. Bychkov. 1964. Biological Grounds for Regulating the Population Size of the Mature Male Fur Seal (*Callorhinus ursinus*) on Tyuleni. Izvestiia Tikhookeanskogo Nauchno-isslededovatelskogo Instituta Rybnogo Khoziaistva I Okeanografii. [The Transactions of the Pacific Scientific Research Institute of Fisheries and Oceanography.] 54:83–90.

Dorsey, G. A., and J. R. Murie. 1940. Notes on Skidi Pawnee Society. Chicago Field: Museum of Natural History, Anthropological Series Vol. 27, no. 2.

Doty, R. L., M. Ford, G. Preti, and G. R. Huggins. 1975. Changes in the Intensity and Pleasantness of Human Vaginal Odors During the Menstrual Cycle. Science 190:1316–1319.

Douglas, R. K. 1901. Society in China. London: Ward, Lock and Co.

Douglass, W. O. 1953. Beyond the High Himalayas. Garden City: Doubleday.

Downhower, J. F., and K. B. Armitage. 1971. The Yellow-bellied Marmot and the Evolution of Polygamy. American Naturalist 105:355–370.

Draper, P.   1975. Cultural Pressure on Sex Differences. American Ethnologist 2(4):602–616.

———   1977. Social and Economic Constraints on Child Life among the !Kung. *In* The Kalahari Hunter-Gatherers. R. B. Lee and I. DeVore, eds. Pp. 199–217. Cambridge: Harvard University Press.

Drucker, P.   1951. The Northern and Central Nootkan Tribes. Washington, D.C.: U.S. Government Printing Office. [Also in the HRAF, 1960.]

Du Bois, C.   1944. The People of Alor: A Social-Psychological Study of an East-Indian Island. Minneapolis: University of Minnesota Press.

Dugast, Idelette.   1949. Beti et Pahorins. *In* Inventaire Ethnique du Sud-Cameroun. Pp. 57–94. Douala: French Institute of Black Africa.

Du Plessis, S. S.   1972. Ecology of Blesbok with Special Reference to Productivity. Wildlife Monographs 30:1–70.

Dunbar, R. I. M.   1977. Age-dependent Changes in Sexual Skin Color and Associated Phenomena of Female Gelada Baboons. Journal of Human Evolution 6:667–672.

Dunbar, R. I. M. and E. P. Dunbar.   1974a. Social Organization and Ecology of the Klipspringer (*Oreotragus oreotragus*) in Ethiopia. Zeitschrift für Tierpsychologie 35:481–493.

———   1974b. Ecology and Population Dynamics of *Colobus guereza* in Ethiopia. Folia Primatologica 21:188–208.

———   1975. Social Dynamics of Gelada Baboons. Contributions to Primatology 6:1–157.

Dundas, C.   1924. Kilimanjaro and Its People: A History of the Wachagga, Their Laws, Customs, and Legends Together with Some Account of the Highest Mountain in Africa. London: Witherby.

Durant, W.   1966. The Life of Greece. The Story of Civilization, Vol. II. New York: Simon and Schuster.

Durham, M. E.   1928. Some Tribal Origins, Laws, and Customs of the Balkans. London: Allen and Unwin.

Durham, W. H.   1976a. The Adaptive Significance of Cultural Behavior. Human Ecology 4(2):89–121.

———   1976b. Resource Competition and Human Aggression, Part 1: A Review of Primitive War. Quarterly Review of Biology 51(3):385–415.

———   1977. Reply to Comments on "The Adaptive Significance of Cultural Behavior." Human Ecology 5(1):59–68.

———   Ms. Resource Competition and Human Aggression, Part II: Dependence and Manipulation.

Durkheim, Emile.   1958. The Rules of Sociological Method. George E. C. Catlin, ed. John H. Mueller and Sarah A. Solovay, trans. Glencoe: Free Press. Original: Les reglès de la Méthode Sociologique, 1895.

Dyson-Hudson, Neville.   1970. Structure and Infrastructure in Primitive Society:

Lévi-Strauss and Radcliffe-Browne. *In* The Structuralist Controversy. Richard Macksey and Eugenio Donato, eds. Pp. 218–246.
Baltimore: The John Hopkins Press.

Dyson-Hudson, R., and E. A. Smith. 1978. Human Territoriality. American Anthropologist 80:21–42.

Edholm, O. G. 1967. The Biology of Work. New York: McGraw-Hill Book Co.

Edwards, A. W. F. 1958. An Analysis of Geissler's Data on the Human Sex
Ratio. Annals of Human Genetics 23:6–15.

Eggan, F. R. 1950. Social Organization of the Western Pueblos. Chicago: University of Chicago Press.

Eglar, Z. 1957. Panjabi Village Life. *In* Pakistan: Society and Culture. S. Maron,
ed. Pp. 62–80. New Haven: Human Relations Area Files Press.

Ehrenreich, P. 1891. Beiträge zur Völkerkunde Brasiliens. Berlin: W. Spemann.

Ehrman, L., and P. Parsons. 1976. The Genetics of Behavior. Sunderland, Mass.:
Sinauer Associates.

Eimerl, S., and I. DeVore. 1965. The Primates. New York: Time-Life Books.

Eisenberg, J. F., N. A. Muckenhirn, and R. Rudran. 1972. The Relation between Ecology and Social Structure in Primates. Science 176:863–
874.

Eisenberg, J. F., and W. S. Dillon, eds. 1971. Man and Beast: Comparative Social
Behavior. Washington: Smithsonian Institution Press.

Ellefson, J. O. 1968. Territorial Behavior in the Common White-handed Gibbon,
Hylobates lar Linn. *In* Primates. Studies in Adaptation and Varia-
bility. P. C. Jay, ed. Pp. 180–199. New York: Holt, Rinehart and
Winston.

————— 1974. A Natural History of White-handed Gibbons in the Malayan
Peninsula. *In* Gibbon and Siamang. 3. Natural History, Social Behavior, Reproduction, Vocalizations, Prehension. D. M. Rumbaugh,
ed. Pp. 2–134. Basel: Karger.

Ember, M., and C. R. Ember. 1978. Male-Female Bonding: A Cross-Species Study
of Mammals and Birds. Behavior Science Research, in press.

Erdland, A. 1914. Die Marshall-Insulaner: Leben und Sitte, Sinn und Religion
eines Südsee-volkes. Münster: Aschendorff. [Also in the HRAF,
1961.]

Etkin, W. 1963. Social Behavioral Factors in the Emergence of Man. Human
Biology 35:299–310.

Etter, Martin A. 1978. Sahlins and Sociobiology. *Review of* Marshall Sahlins, The
Use and Abuse of Biology. American Ethnologist 5:160–169.

Evans, Ivor H. N. 1937. The Negritos of Malaya. Cambridge: Cambridge University Press. [Also in the HRAF, 1955.]

Evans-Pritchard, E. E. 1940. The Nuer. Oxford: Oxford University Press.

———— 1956. Nuer Religion. Oxford: Oxford University Press.

Eveleth, P. B.   1975. Differences between Ethnic Groups in Sex Dimorphism of Adult Height. Annals of Human Biology 2:35–39.

Eveleth, P. B., and J. M. Tanner.   1976. World-wide Variation in Human Growth. International Biological Program no. 8. Cambridge: Cambridge University Press.

Everitt, B. J., J. Herbert, and J. D. Hamer.   1972. Sexual Receptivity of Bilaterally Adrenalectomized Female Rhesus Monkeys. Physiology and Behavior 8:409–415.

Fallers, L. A.   1973. Inequality: Social Stratification Reconsidered. Chicago: University of Chicago Press.

Fathauer, G. H.   1961. Trobriand. In Matrilineal Kinship. D. M. Schneider and K. Gough, eds. Pp. 234–269. Berkeley: University of Berkeley Press.

Fawcett, F.   1915. Nayars of Malabar. Madras Government Museum Bulletin 3, no. 3:185–323.

FBI Uniform Crime Reports. Washington, D.C.: U.S. Government Printing Office.

Fei Hsiao-T'ung.   1939. Peasant Life in China: A Field Study of Country Life in the Yangtze Valley. London: Routledge and Sons.

———— 1953. China's Gentry: Essays in Rural-Urban Relations. Chicago: University of Chicago Press.

Fei Hsiao-T'ung, and Chih-i, Chang.   1945. Earthbound China: A Study of Rural Economy in Yunnan. Chicago: University of Chicago Press.

Ferguson, A.   1976. Can Evolutionary Theory Predict? The American Naturalist 110:1101–1104.

Ferracuti, F., and S. Dinitz.   1974. Cross-Cultural Aspects of Delinquent and Criminal Behavior. In Crime and Delinquency: Dimensions of Deviance. M. Reidel and T. P. Thornberry, eds. Pp. 18–34. New York: Praeger.

Ferrars, M.   1901. Burma. 2nd ed. London: Low, Marston. [Also in the HRAF, 1956.]

Fiedler, L. A.   1958. Love and Death in the American Novel. New York: Criterion Books.

Field, H.   1939. Contributions to the Anthropology of Iran. Chicago: Field Museum of Natural History. Anthropological Series, Vol. 29, nos. 1 and 2. [Also in the HRAF, 1965.]

———— 1952. The Anthropology of Iraq. Papers of the Peabody Museum of American Archaeology and Ethnology, Harvard University Vol. 46, nos. 1 and 3.

Fielde, A. M.   1887. Pagoda Shadows: Studies from Life in China. London: T. Ogilvie Smith.

Finsch, O. 1893. [The Marshall Archipelago.] *In* Ethnologische Erfahrungen und Belegstücke aus der Südsee. Pp. 375–438. Wien: Alfred Hölder.

Firth, R. 1914. Tattooing in Tikopia. Man 36:173–177.

————— 1936. We, the Tikopia: A Sociological Study of Kinship in Primitive Polynesia. London: Allen and Unwin.

————— 1940. The Work of the Gods in Tikopia. London: London School of Economics and Political Science.

————— 1957. We, the Tikopia: A Sociological Study of Kinship in Primitive Polynesia. 2nd ed. London: Allen and Unwin.

————— 1959. Social Change in Tikopia: A Restudy of a Polynesian Community after a Generation. London: Allen and Unwin.

————— 1964. Essays on Social Organization and Values. London School of Economics Monographs on Social Anthropology, No. 28. Pp. 30–87. New York: Humanities Press.

————— 1965. Primitive Polynesian Economy. 2nd ed. London: Routledge and Kegan Paul.

————— 1970. Rank and Religion in Tikopia: A Study in Polynesian Paganism and Conversion to Christianity. Boston: Beacon Press.

Fiscus, Clifford H. 1961. Growth in the Steller Sea Lion. Journal of Mammalogy 42(2):218–223.

Fisher, R. A. 1958. The Genetical Theory of Natural Selection. New York: Dover Press. [Originally published in 1930].

Flannery, K. V. 1972. The Cultural Evolution of Civilizations. Annual Review of Ecology and Systematics 3:399–426.

Flannery, R. 1944. The Gros Ventre Shaking Tent. Primitive Man 17:54–59.

————— 1953. The Gros Ventres of Montana: Part 1, Social Life. Washington, D.C.: Catholic University of America. [Also in the HRAF, 1961.]

Flannery, R., and D. M. Cooper. 1946. Social Mechanism in Gros Ventre Gambling. Southwestern Journal of Anthropology 2:391–419.

Fletcher, A. C. 1904. The Hako: A Pawnee Ceremony. 22nd Annual Report of the Bureau of American Ethnology. [Also in the HRAF, 1960.]

Floody, O. R., and A. P. Arnold. 1975. Uganda Kob (*Adenota kob thomasi*): Territoriality and the Spatial Distributions of Sexual and Agonistic Behaviors at a Territorial Ground. Zeitschrift für Tierpsychologie 37:192–212.

Forde, C. D. 1946. The North: The Hausa. *In* The Native Economies of Nigeria. Vol. 1. The Rural Economics. C. D. Forde and R. Scott, eds. Pp. 119–179. London: Faber and Faber.

————— 1951. The Yoruba-Speaking Peoples of South-western Nigeria. London: International African Institute.

Fortes, M. 1938. Social and Psychological Aspects of Education in Taleland. London: Oxford University Press. [Also in the HRAF, 1957.]

————— 1945. The Dynamics of Clanship among the Tallensi: Being the First

Part of an Analysis of the Social Structure of a Trans-Volta Tribe. London: Oxford University Press.

———— 1950. Kinship and Marriage Among the Ashanti. *In* African Systems of Kinship and Marriage. A. R. Radcliffe-Brown and D. Forde, eds. Pp. 252–284. London: Oxford University Press.

———— 1953. The Structure of Unilineal Descent Groups. American Anthropologist 55:17–41.

———— 1959. Descent, Filiation, and Affinity: A Rejoinder to Dr. Leach. (2 parts) Man 59 (309):193–197 and 59(331):206–212.

———— 1969. Kinship and the Social Order. Chicago: Aldine.

Fortune, R. 1963. Sorcerers of Dobu. New York: E. P. Dutton and Co. [Originally published in 1932.]

Fossey, D. 1970. Making Friends with Mountain Gorillas. National Geographic Magazine 137:48–67.

———— 1971. More Years with Mountain Gorillas. National Geographic Magazine 140:574–585.

———— 1972. Vocalizations of the Mountain Gorilla (*Gorilla gorilla beringei*). Animal Behavior 20:36–53.

Fouts, R. S. 1973. Acquisition and Testing of Gestural Signals in Four Young Chimpanzees. Science 180:978–980.

Fox, C. A., H. S. Wolff, and J. A. Baker. 1970. Measurement of Intra-vaginal and Intra-uterine pressures during Human Coitus by Radiotelemetry. Journal of Reproduction and Fertility 22:243–251.

Fox, E. F. 1943. Travels in Afghanistan, 1937–1938. New York: MacMillan.

Fox, R. 1965. Demography and Social Anthropology. Man 65:86–87.

———— 1967. Kinship and Marriage: An Anthropological Perspective. London: Penguin.

———— 1971. The Cultural Animal. *In* Man and Beast: Comparative Social Behavior. J. E. Eisenberg and W. S. Dillon, eds. Pp. 273–296. Washington, D.C.: Smithsonian Institution Press.

———— 1972. Alliance and Constraint: Sexual Selection in the Evolution of Human Kinship Systems. *In* Sexual Selection and the Descent of Man, 1871–1971. B. Campbell, ed. Pp. 282–331. New York: Aldine.

———— 1973. Encounter with Anthropology. New York: Harcourt Brace Jovanovich.

———— 1975a. Primate Kin and Human Kinship. *In* Biosocial Anthropology. R. Fox, ed. Pp. 9–35. London: Malaby Press. New York: Wiley.

Fox, R., ed. 1975b. Biosocial Anthropology. London: Malaby Press. New York: Wiley.

———— In press. Crow-Omaha Systems and the Elementary-Complex Continuum: Where Next?

Fox, R., and U. Fleising. 1976. Human Ethology. *In* Annual Review of Anthropology. Vol. 5:265–288. B. J. Siegel, A. R. Beals, and S. A. Tyler, eds.

Franck, H. A. 1926. East of Siam: Ramblings in the Five Divisions of French Indo-China. New York: Century.

Franken, H. J. 1960. Bali: Studies in Life, Thought, and Ritual. Published for the Royal Tropical Institute. The Hague: W. van Hoeve. [Also in the HRAF.]

Freedman, A. M., H. K. Kaplin, and B. J. Sadock, eds. 1975. Comprehensive Textbook of Psychiatry. Vol. 2. Baltimore: Williams and Wilkins Co.

Freeman, Derek. 1966. Social Anthropology and the Scientific Study of Human Behaviour. Man 2:330–342.

Freeman, J. D. 1955. Iban Agriculture: A Report on the Shifting Cultivation of Hill Rice by the Iban of Sarawak. London: H. M. Stationery Office.

——— 1958a. The Family System of the Iban of Borneo. *In* The Developmental Cycle in Domestic Groups. J. Goody, ed. Pp. 15–52. Cambridge: Cambridge University Press.

——— 1958b. The Iban. Unpublished manuscript. The Australian National University, Department of Anthropology and Sociology, Canberra.

Freeman, M. M. R. 1971. A Social and Ecologic Analysis of Systematic Female Infanticide among the Netsilik Eskimo. American Anthropologist 73:1011–1018.

Fried, M. H. 1953. Fabric of Chinese Society: A Study of the Social Life of a Chinese County Seat. New York: Praeger.

——— 1961. Warfare, Military Organization, and the Evolution of Society. Anthropologica 3:134–147.

——— 1967. The Evolution of Political Society. New York: Random House.

Friedl, E. 1962. Vasilika: A Village in Modern Greece. New York: Holt, Rinehart and Winston.

Friedman, Jonathan. 1974. Marxism, Structuralism and Vulgar Materialism. Man 9:444–469.

Fruton, J. S. 1976. The Emergence of Biochemistry. Science 192:327–334.

Fuchs, H. 1962. La estructura residencial de los Maquiritare de el Corobal y las Ceibas. America Indigena 22:169–190.

Fuchs, S. 1942. The Marriage Rites of the Bhils in the Nimar District. Man in India 22:105–139.

Fuller, C. J. 1976. The Nayars Today. London: Cambridge University Press.

Furuya, Y. 1962. The Social Life of Silvered Leaf Monkeys, *Trachypithecus cristatus*. Primates 3:41–60.

Gabb, W. M. 1876. On the Indian Tribes and Languages of Costa Rica. Proceedings of the American Philosophical Society 14:483–602.

Gallup, G. G. 1970. Chimpanzees: Self-recognition. Science 167:86–87.

Gamble, D. P. 1957. The Wolof of Senegambia. London: International African Institute. [Also in the HRAF, 1959.]

Gamble, S. D. 1954. Ting Hsien: A North China Rural Community. Stanford: Stanford University Press.

———— 1963. North China Villages: Social, Political and Economic Activities before 1933. Berkeley: University of California Press.

Gardner, B. T., and R. A. Gardner. 1969. Teaching Sign Language to a Chimpanzee. Science 165:664–672.

———— 1971. Two-way Communication with an Infant Chimpanzee. In Behavior of Non-human Primates. A. M. Schrier and F. Stollnitz, eds. Pp. 117–184. New York: Academic Press.

Garnett, Lucy M. J. 1891. Kurdish Women. In Women of Turkey and Their Folk-lore. Vol. 2, The Jewish and Moslem Women. Pp. 113–189. London: David Nutt.

Gautier-Hion, A. 1975. Dimorphisme sexuel et organisation sociale chez les cercopithecinés forestiers africains. Mammalia 39:365–374.

Gayton, A. H. 1948. Yokuts and Western Mono Ethnography. 2 vols. Berkeley: University. Vol. 14, No. 2. [Also in the HRAF, 1955.]

Gladwin, T., and S. B. Sarason. 1953. Truk: Man in Paradise. New York:

Geddes, W. R. 1963. Peasant Life in Communist China. Monograph No. 6, Society for Applied Anthropology. Ithaca, New York.

Geertz, C. 1973. The Interpretation of Cultures. New York: Basic Books.

Ghiselin, M. T. 1974. The Economy of Nature and the Evolution of Sex. Berkeley: University of California Press.

Gifford, Edward Winslow. 1926. Californian Anthropometry. University of California Publications in American Archaeology and Ethnology 22:217–390.

Gillin, John. 1936. The Barama River Caribs of British Guiana. Papers of the Peabody Museum of American Archaeology and Ethnology, Harvard University. Vol. 14, No. 2 [Also in the HRAF, 1955.]

Gladwin, T., and S. B. Sarason. 1953. Truk: Man in Paradise. New York: Wenner-Gren Foundation for Anthropological Research.

Glass, D. V. and D. E. C. Eversley, eds. 1965. Population in History: Essays in Historical Demography. Chicago: Aldine.

Goethals, G. W. 1971. Factors Affecting Permissive and Nonpermissive Rules Regarding Premarital Sex. In Studies in the Sociology of Sex: A Book of Readings. J. M. Henslin, ed. New York: Appleton-Century Croft.

Goldfoot, D. A., M. A. Kravetz, R. W. Goy, and S. K. Freeman. 1976. Lack of Effect of Vaginal Lavages and Aliphatic Acids on Ejaculatory Responses in Rhesus Monkeys: Behavioral and Chemical Analyses. Hormones and Behavior 7:1–27.

Goldschmidt, W. R.   1965. Theory and Strategy in the Study of Cultural Adaptability. American Anthropologist 67:402–408.

——— 1966. Comparative Functionalism: An Essay in Anthropological Theory. Berkeley: University of California Press.

Gomes, E. H.   1911. Seventeen Years Among the Sea Dyaks of Borneo: A Record of Intimate Association with the Natives of the Bornean Jungles. London: Seeley.

Goodale, Jane C.   1971. Tiwi Wives. Seattle: University of Washington Press.

Goodenough, W. H.   1951. Property, Kin, and Community on Truk. New Haven: Yale University Press.

Goodman, L. A., N. Keyfitz, and T. W. Pullum.   1974. Family Formation and the Frequency of Various Kinship Relationships. Journal of Theoretical Population and Biology 5:1–27.

Goody, Jack.   1976. Production and Reproduction: A Comparative Study of the Domestic Domain. Cambridge Studies in Social Anthropology, 17. Cambridge: Cambridge University Press.

Gordon Cumming, C. F.   1900. Wanderings in China. Edinburgh: Wm. Blackwood.

Gorer, G.   1935. Book One: Senegalese. In Africa Dances: A Book about Western African Negroes. Pp. 25–79. London: Faber and Faber.

——— 1938. Himalayan Village: An Account of the Lepchas of Sikkim. London: Michael Joseph.

Gough, E. K.   1954. The Traditional Kinship System of the Nayars of Malabar. Unpublished manuscript. Prepared for the Social Science Research Council Summer Seminar on Kinship, Harvard University.

——— 1955. Female Initiation Rites on the Malabar Coast. Journal of the Royal Anthropological Institute of Great Britain and Ireland 85:45–80.

Gough, K.   1961a. Nayar: Central Kerala. In Matrilineal Kinship. D. M. Schneider and K. Gough, eds. Pp. 298–384, Berkeley: University of California Press.

——— 1961b. Nayar: North Kerala. In Matrilineal Kinship. D. M. Schneider and K. Gough, eds. Pp. 385–404, Berkeley: University of California Press.

——— 1961c. Variation in Interpersonal Kinship Relationships. In Matrilineal Kinship. D. M. Schneider and K. Gough, eds. Pp. 577–613. Berkeley: University of California Press.

——— 1961d. Variation in Residence. In Matrilineal Kinship. D. M. Schneider and K. Gough, eds. Pp. 545–576. Berkeley: University of California Press.

Gould, H. A.   1960. The Microdemography of Marriages in a North Indian Area. Southwestern Journal of Anthropology 16(4):476–491.

Gourou, P.   1936. Les paysans du delta tonkinois: étude de géographie humaine.

Paris: Editions d'art et d'histoire. [The Peasants of the Tonkin Delta: A Study in Human Geography. Translated for the HRAF, 1953, by R. R. Miller.]

Graham, C. E. 1970. Reproductive Physiology of the Chimpanzee. *In* The Chimpanzee. 3. Immunology, Infections, Hormones, Anatomy, and Behavior. G. H. Bourne, ed. Pp. 183–220. Baltimore: University Park Press.

Grantzberg, G. 1973. Twin Infanticide: A Cross-cultural Test of a Materialistic Explanation. Ethos 1(4):405–412.

Grattan, F. J. H. 1948. An Introduction to Samoan Custom. Apia: Samoa Printing and Publishing Co.

Greenberg, J. H. 1941. Some Aspects of Negro-Mohammedan Culture-Contact among the Hausa. American Anthropologist 43:51–61.

Greene, Penelope J. 1978. Promiscuity, Paternity, and Culture. American Ethnologist 5(1):151–159.

Greulich, William Walter. 1951. The Growth and Development Status of Guamanian School Children in 1947. American Journal of Physical Anthropology 9:55–70.

Griffin, D. R. 1976. The Question of Animal Awareness: Evolutionary Continuity of Mental Experience. New York: Rockefeller University Press.

Griffiths, W. 1946. The Kol Tribe of Central India. Calcutta: Royal Asiatic Society of Bengal, Monograph series, Vol. 2.

Grigolia, A. 1939. Custom and Justice in the Caucasus: The Georgian Highlanders. Philadelphia: University of Pennsylvania [privately printed].

Grinnell, G. B. 1961. Pawnee, Blackfoot, and Cheyenne. New York: Scribner and Sons.

Gross, Daniel. 1975. Protein Capture and Cultural Development in the Amazon Basin. American Anthropologist 77:526–549.

Groves, C. P. 1972. Systematics and Phylogeny of Gibbons. *In* Gibbon and Siamang 1. Evolution, Ecology, Behavior, and Captive Maintenance. D. M. Rumbaugh, ed. Pp. 1–89. Basel: Karger.

Grubb, P. 1971. Mating Activity and the Social Significance of Rams in a Feral Sheep Community. *In* The Behaviour of Ungulates and Its Relation to Management. V. Geist and F. Walther, eds. Vol. 1:457–487. Morges, Switzerland: International Union for Conservation of Nature and Natural Resources.

Gusinde, M. 1931. The Selk'nam: On the Life and Thought of a Hunting People of the Great Island of Tierra del Fuego. Mödling bei Wein: Verlag der Internationalen Zeitschrift "Anthropos."

Gustafson, E. B. 1969. A Demographic Dilemma: The Parsis of Karachi. Social Biology 16(2):115–127.

Gutiérrez de Pineda, V. 1950. Organizacion social en la Guajira. Bogota: Prensas del Ministerio de Educacion Nacional. [Translated for the HRAF by S. Muirden, 1960.]

Gutmann, B. 1926. Das Recht der Dschagga. München: C. H. Beck. [Translated for the HRAF by M. Nagler, 1953.]

———— 1932. The Tribal Teachings of the Chagga. Vol. 1. München: C. H. Beck. [Translated for the HRAF, 1958, by W. Goodenough and D. Crawford.]

Haddon, A. C., and L. E. Start. 1936. Iban Sea Dayak Fabrics and Their Patterns: A Descriptive Catalogue of the Iban Fabrics in the Museum of Archaeology and Ethnology. Cambridge: Cambridge University Press.

Hafez, E. S. E. 1968. The Trophoblast and Its Relationship to Infertility. *In* Progress in Infertility. S. H. Behrman and R. W. Kistner, eds. Boston: Little, Brown, and Co.

Haigh, C. H. 1968. Sexual Dimorphism, Sex Ratios, and Polygyny in the Red-Winged Blackbird. Ph.D. dissertation, University of Washington.

Hajdú, P. 1963. The Samoyed Peoples and Languages. M. Esztergar and A. P. Csanyi, trans. Bloomington: Indiana University Press.

Hajnal, J. 1963. Concepts of Random Mating and the Frequency of Consanguineous Marriages. Proceedings of the Royal Society of London, Series B 159:125–177.

———— 1965. European Marriage Patterns in Perspective. *In* Population in History: Essays in Historical Demography. D. V. Glass and D. E. C. Eversley, eds. Pp. 101–143. Chicago: Aldine.

Haldane, J. B. S. 1932. The Causes of Evolution. New York: Longmans, Green and Co.

———— 1956. The Argument from Animals to Man: An Examination of its Validity for Anthropology. Journal of the Royal Anthropological Institute 86:1–14.

Hall, E. T., and K. J. Pelzer. 1946. The Economy of the Truk Islands: An Anthropological and Economic Survey. U.S. Commercial Co., Economic Survey.

Hall, K. R. L. 1965. Behaviour and Ecology of the Wild Patas Monkey, *Erythrocebus patas*, in Uganda. Journal of Zoology 148:15–87.

Hamburg, D. A. 1963. Emotions in the Perspective of Human Evolution. *In* Expressions of the Emotions in Man. P. Knopp, ed. Pp. 300–317. New York: International Universities Press.

Hames, R. B. 1978. Behavioral Account of the Division of Labor among the Ye'kwana Indians of Southern Venezuela. Ph.D. dissertation, Department of Anthropology, University of California, Santa Barbara.

Hames, R. B., and I. L. Hames. 1976. Ye'kwana Basketry: Its Cultural Context. Antropologica 44:3–58.

Hamilton, J. E. 1934. The Southern Sea Lion, *Otaria byronia* (de Blainville). Discovery Reports 8:269–318.

Hamilton, W. D. 1964. The Genetical Evolution of Social Behaviour, Parts I and II. Journal of Theoretical Biology 7:1–52.

———— 1966. The Moulding of Senescence by Natural Selection. Journal of Theoretical Biology 12:12–45.

———— 1967. Extraordinary Sex Ratios. Science 156:477–488.

———— 1971. Geometry for the Selfish Herd. Journal of Theoretical Biology 31:295–311.

———— 1972. Altruism and Related Phenomena, Mainly in Social Insects. Annual Review of Ecology and Systematics 3:193–232.

———— 1975. Innate Social Aptitudes of Man: An Approach from Evolutionary Genetics. *In* Biosocial Anthropology. R. Fox, ed. Pp. 133–155. London: Malaby Press.

Hamilton, W. J., III, R. E. Buskirk, and W. H. Buskirk. 1975. Chacma Baboon Tactics During Intertroop Movements. Journal of Mammalogy 56:857–870.

Handy, E. S. C. 1923. The Native Culture in the Marquesas. Honolulu: Bernice P. Bishop Museum Bulletin 9.

Handy, E. S. C., and W. C. Handy. 1924. Samoan House Building, Cooking, and Tattooing. Honolulu: Bernice P. Bishop Museum Bulletin 15.

Hanzeli, V. E. 1955. The Hungarians. New Haven: Human Relations Area Files Press.

Harcourt, A. H., K. S. Stewart, and D. Fossey. 1976. Male Emigration and Female Transfer in Wild Mountain Gorilla. Nature 263:226–227.

Harner, M. J. 1973a. The Jívaro: People of the Sacred Waterfalls. Garden City: Anchor Press.

———— 1973b. Hallucinogens and Shamanism. New York: Oxford Press.

———— 1977. The Ecological Basis for Aztec Sacrifice. American Ethnologist 4:117–135.

Harper, F. 1939. The Name of the Blesbok. Proceedings of the Biological Society of Washington 52:89–92.

Harris, M. 1968. The Rise of Anthropological Theory. New York: T. Y. Crowell.

———— 1971. Culture, Man, and Nature: An Introduction to General Anthropology. 1st Edition. New York: Crowell.

———— 1974. Cows, Pigs, Wars, and Witches: The Riddles of Culture. New York: Random House.

———— 1975. Culture, People, and Nature: An Introduction to General Anthropology. 2nd Edition. New York: Crowell.

———— 1977a. Cannibals and Kings: The Origins of Cultures. New York: Random House.

———— 1977b. Why Men Dominate Women. New York Times Magazine, November 13, 1977, p. 46.

Harris, R. 1926. The San Blas Indians. American Journal of Physical Anthropology 9:17–63.

Harrison, P. W. 1924. The Arab at Home. New York: Thomas Crowell.

Harrison, R. J., ed. 1972. Functional Anatomy of Marine Mammals. New York: Academic Press.

Harrison, R. J., and J. D. W. Tomlinson. 1960. Normal and Experimental Diving in the Common Seal (*Phoca vitulina*). Mammalia 24:386–399.

Harrison, R. J., and G. L. Kooyman. 1968. General Behavior and Physiology of the Pinnipedia. *In* The Behavior and Physiology of Pinnipeds. R. J. Harrison et al., eds. Pp. 211–296. New York: Appleton-Century-Crofts.

Harrisson, T. 1936. The New Hebrides People and Culture. Geographical Journal (88):332–341.

Hart, C. W. M., and A. R. Pilling. 1960. The Tiwi of North Australia. New York: Holt, Rinehart and Winston.

Hartung, John. 1976. On Natural Selection and the Inheritance of Wealth. Current Anthropology 17:607–622.

Hassan, A., and S. Na'ibi. 1952. A Chronicle of Abuja. Translated and arranged from the Hausa of Malam. Ibadan: Ibadan University Press. Translated by F. Heath. [Also in the HRAF, 1959.]

Hatch, E. J. 1973. Theories of Man and Culture. New York: Columbia University Press.

Hauck, H. M. 1956. Aspects of Health, Sanitation and Nutritional Status in a Siamese Rice Village: Studies in Bang Chan, 1952–1954. Cornell University Department of Far Eastern Studies. Data Paper no. 22.

Hauck, H. M., S. Sudsaneh, and J. R. Hanks. 1958. Food Habits and Nutrient Intakes in a Siamese Rice Village. Cornell University Department of Far Eastern Studies. Data Paper no. 29.

Hayden, Brian. 1975. The Carrying Capacity Dilemma. *In* Population Studies in Archaeology and Biological Anthropology: A Symposium. A. C. Swedlund, ed. Pp. 11–21. American Antiquity 40(2), Part 2, Memoir 30.

Hayden, J. 1937. The Vikita Ceremony of the Papago. Southwestern Monuments Monthly Report. Supplement for April, 1937, pp. 263–277.

Heath, Barbara Honeyman, and J. E. Lindsay Carter. 1971. Growth and Somatotype Patterns of Manus Children, Territory of Papua and New Guinea. Application of a Modified Somatotype Method to the Study of Growth Patterns. American Journal of Physical Anthropology 35:49–68.

Heath, Barbara Honeyman, C. E. Hopkins, and C. D. Miller. 1961. Physiques of Hawaii-born Young Men and Women of Japanese Ancestry,

Compared with College Men and Women of the United States and England. American Journal of Physical Anthropology 19:173–184.

Heber, A. R., and K. M. Heber. 1926. In Himalayan Tibet. Philadelphia: Lippincott.

Heimann, M. 1932. Die Cayapa-Indianer. Zeitschrift für Ethnologie 63:281–287. [Also in the HRAF, 1957.]

Hendrichs, H. 1972. Beobachtungen und Untersuchungen zur Ökologie und Ethologie, insbesondere zur sozialen Organisation ostafrikanischer Säugetiere. Zeitschrift für Tierpsychologie 30:146–189.

———— 1975a. Observations on a Population of Bohor Reedbuck, *Redunca redunca* (Pallas 1767). Zeitschrift für Tierpsychologie 38:44–54.

———— 1975b. Changes in a Population of Dikdik, *Madoqua (Rhynchotragus) kirki* (Günther 1880). Zeitschrift für Tierpsychologie 38:55–69.

Hendrichs, H., and U. Hendrichs. 1971. Dikdik und Elefanten. Ökologie und soziologie zweier afrikanischer Huftiere. München: R. Piper.

Henriques, F. 1960. Love in Action: The Sociology of Sex. New York: E. P. Dutton.

Henry, L. 1965. The Population of France in the Eighteenth Century. *In* Population in History: Essays in Historical Demography. D. V. Glass and D. E. C. Eversley, eds. Pp. 434–456. Chicago: Aldine.

Herlihy, D. 1975. Life Expectancies for Women in Medieval Society. *In* The Role of Women in the Middle Ages. R. T. Morewedge, ed. Pp. 1–22. Albany: State University of New York Press.

———— 1976. Land, Family, and Women in Continental Europe, 701–1200. *In* Women in Medieval Society. S. M. Stuard, ed. Pp. 13–45. Philadelphia: University of Pennsylvania Press.

Hermanns, Matthias. 1948. Die a Mdo pa Grosstibeter: die sozial-wirtschaftlichen Grundlagen der Hirtenkulturen Innerasiens [The A Mdo Pa Greater Tibetans: The Socio-economic Bases of the Pastoral Cultures of Inner Asia]. Frieburg: Philosophische Fakultät der Universität Freiburg in der Schweig. [Translated for the HRAF by F. Schutze, 1961.]

Hernandez de Alba, G. 1946. The Highland Tribes of Southern Colombia. *In* Handbook of South American Indians. J. H. Steward, ed. Vol. 2:915–927, 937–956. Washington, D.C.: United States Government Printing Office.

Herre, W., and U. Thiede. 1965. Studien an gehirnen Südamerikanischer Tylopoden. Zoologische Jahrbucher. Abteilung für Anatomie und Ontologie der Tier 82:177–188.

Hershkovitz, P. 1949. Mammals of Northern Colombia. Preliminary Report No. 4: Monkeys (Primates), with Some Taxonomic Revisions of Some Forms. Proceedings of the United States National Museum 98:323–427.

——————— 1963. A Systematic and Zoogeographic Account of the Monkeys of the Genus *Callicebus* (Cebidae) of the Amazonas and Orinoco River Basins. Mammalia 27:1–79.

Hertig, A. T. 1967. Human Trophoblast: Normal and Abnormal. American Journal of Clinical Pathology 47:249–260.

Hess, E. H. 1975. The Role of Pupil Size in Communication. Scientific American 233(5):110–149.

Hess, J. P. 1973. Some Observations on the Sexual Behavior of Captive Lowland Gorillas, *Gorilla gorilla gorilla*. *In* Comparative Ecology and Behavior of Primates. R. P. Michael and J. H. Crook, eds. Pp. 508–581. New York: Academic Press.

Hewer, H. R. 1964. The Determination of Age, Sexual Maturity, Longevity and a Life Table in the Grey Seal (*Halichoerus grypus*). Proceedings of the Zoological Society of London 142(4):593–624.

Hiatt, L. R. 1965. Kinship and Conflict: A Study of an Aboriginal Community in Northern Arnhem Land. Canberra: Australian National University Press.

Hill, P. 1972. Rural Hausa: A Village and a Setting. Cambridge: Cambridge University Press.

Hill, W. C. O. 1934. A Monograph on the Purple-faced Leaf-monkeys (*Pithecus vetulus*). The Ceylon Journal of Science, Sec. B (Zoology and Geology) 19:23–89.

——————— 1960. Primates. Comparative Anatomy and Taxonomy. Vol. 4 (Cebidae), Part A. Edinburgh: Edinburgh University Press.

——————— 1962. Primates. Comparative Anatomy and Taxonomy. Vol. 5 (Cebidae), Part B. Edinburgh: Edinburgh University Press.

——————— 1966. Primates. Comparative Anatomy and Taxonomy. Vol. 6 (Catarrhini). Edinburgh: Edinburgh University Press.

Himelhoch, J. 1972. A Psychosocial Model for the Reduction of Lower-class Youth Crime. *In* Crime Prevention and Social Control. R. L. Akers and E. Sagarin, eds. Pp. 3–14. New York: Praeger Publications.

Hinde, R. A. 1970. Animal Behaviour: A Synthesis of Ethology and Comparative Psychology. 2nd ed. New York: McGraw-Hill Book Co.

Hinde, R. A., and J. Stevenson-Hinde, eds. 1973. Constraints on Learning: Limitations and Predispositions. New York: Academic Press.

Hippler, A. E. 1972. Additional Perspective on Eskimo Female Infanticide. American Anthropologist 74:1318–1319.

Hirschfeld, Lawrence, James Howe, and Bruce Levin. 1978. Warfare, Infanticide, and Statistical Inference: A Comment on Divale and Harris. American Anthropologist 80:110–115.

Hirshfield, M., and D. W. Tinkle. 1975. Natural Selection and the Evolution of Reproductive Effort. *In* Proceedings of the National Academy of Sciences 72:2227–2231.

Ho Ping-Ti. 1959. Studies on the Population of China, 1368–1953. Cambridge, Mass.: Harvard University Press.

Hocart, A. 1929. Lau Islands, Fiji. Honolulu: Bernice P. Bishop Museum Bulletin 62. [Also in the HRAF, 1959.]

Hodson, T. C. 1914. Female Infanticide in India. Man 14(44):91–92.

Hoebel, E. A. 1940. The Political Organization and Law-ways of the Comanche Indians. American Anthropological Association, Memoir no. 54. Contributions from the Santa Fe Laboratory of Anthropology, Vol. 4.

———— 1954. The Law of Primitive Man: A Study of Comparative Legal Dynamics. Cambridge: Harvard University Press.

Hogbin, H. Ian. 1935a. Native Culture of Wogeo: Report of Field Work in New Guinea. Oceania 5:308–337.

———— 1935b. Trading Expeditions in Northern New Guinea. Oceania 5:375–407.

———— 1938. Tillage and Collection: A New Guinea Economy. Oceania 9:127–151, 286–325.

———— 1939. Native Land Tenure in New Guinea. Oceania 10:113–165.

———— 1945. Marriage in Wogeo, New Guinea. Oceania 15:324–352.

———— 1946. Puberty to Marriage: A Study of the Sexual Life of the Natives of Wogeo, New Guinea. Oceania 16:185–209.

———— 1970. The Island of Menstruating Men: Religion in Wogeo. Scranton: Chandler Publishing Co.

Hollingsworth, T. H. 1965. A Demographic Study of the British Ducal Families. *In* Population in History: Essays in Historical Demography. D. V. Glass and D. E. C. Eversley, eds. Pp. 354–378. Chicago: Aldine.

Hollis, A. C. 1905. The Masai: Their Language and Folklore. Oxford: Clarendon Press. [Also in the HRAF, 1965.]

Holm, C. H. 1973. Breeding Sex Ratios, Territoriality, and Reproductive Success in the Red-Winged Blackbird (*Agelaius phoeniceus*). Ecology 54:356–365.

Holmberg, A. R. 1946. The Siriono: A Study of the Effect of Hunger Frustration on the Culture of a Semi-nomadic Bolivian Indian Society. Ph.D. dissertation, Yale University, New Haven.

———— 1950. Nomads of the Long Bow: The Siriono of Eastern Bolivia. Washington, D.C.: United States Government Printing Office.

Homans, G. C. 1961. Social Behavior: Its Elementary Forms. New York: Harcourt, Brace, and World.

Homans, G. C., and D. M. Schneider. 1955. Marriage, Authority, and Final Causes. Glencoe: Free Press.

Hooten, Earnest A., and C. Wesley Dupertuis. 1955. The Physical Anthropology of Ireland. Papers of the Peabody Museum of American Archaeology and Ethnology, Harvard University, Vol. 30, no. 2.

Howard, R. 1977. The Evolution of Mating Strategies and Resource Utilization in Bullfrogs, *Rana catesbeiana*. Ph.D. dissertation, University of Michigan.

Howell, Nancy. 1973. The Feasibility of Demographic Studies in "Anthropological" Populations. *In* Methods and Theories of Anthropological Genetics. M. H. Crawford and P. L. Workman, eds. Pp. 249–262. Albuquerque: University of New Mexico Press.

———— 1976. Normal Selection Rates of the Demographic Patterns of the !Kung San. Paper presented at the 1976 meetings of the American Anthropological Association, Washington, D.C., 1976.

Howell, P. P., and W. P. G. Thomson. 1946. The Death of a Reth of the Shilluk and the Installation of His Successor. Sudan Notes and Records 27:4–85.

Howell, W. 1910. A Collection of Articles on the Sea Dyak. Sarawak Gazette Vols. 38–40.

Howells, W. W. 1937. Anthropometry of the Natives of Arnhemland and the Australian Race Problem. Papers of the Peabody Museum of American Archaeology and Ethnology, Harvard University, Vol. 16(1).

Hrdlicka, A. 1926. The Indians of Panama: Their Physical Relation to the Mayas. American Journal of Physical Anthropology 9:1–15.

———— 1931. Anthropology of the Sioux. American Journal of Physical Anthropology 16:123–170.

———— 1935. The Pueblos: With Comparative Data on the Bulk of the Tribes of the Southwest and Northern Mexico. American Journal of Physical Anthropology 20:235–460.

———— 1975. The Anthropology of Kodiak Island. New York: Amspress. [Originally published in 1944.]

Hrdy, S. *See* Blaffer Hrdy, S.

Hsu, F. L. K. 1967. Under the Ancestors' Shadow: Kinship, Personality, and Social Mobility in Village China. Garden City: Natural History Press.

Htin Aung, U. 1937. Burmese Drama, a Study, with Translations, of Burmese Plays. London: Oxford University Press [Also in the HRAF, 1955.]

Humphrey, N. K. 1976. The Social Function of Intellect. *In* Growing Points in Ethology. P. P. G. Bateson and R. A. Hinde, ed. Pp. 303–317. Cambridge: Cambridge University Press.

Hunt, E. E., W. A. Lessa, and A. Hicking. 1965. The Sex Ratio of Live Births in Three Pacific Island Populations (Yap, Samoa, and New Guinea). Human Biology 37:148–155.

Huntingford, G. W. B. 1929. Modern Hunters: Some Accounts of the Ka'melilokopchepkende Dorobo (Okiek) of Kenya Colony. Journal of the

Royal Anthropological Institute of Great Britain and Ireland 59: 333–378.

———— 1951. The Social Institutions of the Dorobo. Anthropos 46:1–48.

———— 1953. The Southern Nilo-Hamites. London: International African Institute.

———— 1955. The Economic Life of the Dorobo. Anthropos 50:602–634.

Hutchinson, H. W. 1957. Village and Plantation Life in Northeastern Brazil. Seattle: University of Washington Press.

Hutton, J. H. 1963. Caste in India: Its Nature, Function, and Origins. 4th ed. London: Oxford University Press.

Ibbetson, D. 1916. Panjab Castes: Being a Reprint of the Chapter on "The Races, Castes, and Tribes of the People" in the . . . Census of the Punjab . . . 1883 . . . . Lahore: Superintendent of Government Printing, Punjab.

Ikbal, A. S. S. 1928. Afghanistan of the Afghans. London: Diamond Press. [Also in the HRAF, 1955.]

Imanishi, K. 1965. The Origin of the Human Family: A Primatological Approach. In Japanese Monkeys. A Collection of Translations. S. A. Altmann, ed. Pp. 113–140. Atlanta: Published by the editor.

Irons, William. 1971. Variation in Political Stratification among the Yomut Turkmen. Anthropological Quarterly 44:143–156.

———— 1975. The Yomut Turkmen: A Study of Social Organization among a Central Asian Turkic Speaking Population. Anthropological Paper No. 58, Museum of Anthropology, University of Michigan.

———— In preparation a. Evolutionary Biology and Human Fertility. (Paper presented at the annual meetings of the American Anthropological Association, 1977.)

———— In preparation b. Is Yomut Behavior Adaptive? (Paper presented at the annual meeting of the American Association for the Advancement of Science, Washington, D.C., 1978).

Islavin, V. 1847. [The Samoyed in Their Domestic and Social Life.] St. Petersburg: Ministerstva Gosudarstvennykh.

Ivanovsky, A. A. 1923. Physical Modifications of the Population of Russia under Famine. American Journal of Physical Anthropology 6:331–353.

Jacobson, D. 1974. The Women of North and Central India: Goddesses and Wives. In Many Sisters: Women in Cross-Cultural Perspective. C. J. Matthiasson, ed. Pp. 99–175. New York: The Free Press.

James, W. H. 1971. The Distribution of Coitus within the Human Inter-menstruum. Journal of Biosocial Science 3:159–171.

Jarman, P. J. 1974. The Social Organization of Antelope in Relation to Their Ecology. Behaviour 58:215–267.

———— 1968. Unpublished thesis, Manchester University, cited in P. J. Jarman. The Social Organization of Antelope in Relation to Their Ecology. Behaviour 58:215–267.

Jarvie, I. C.   1975. Epistle to the Anthropologists. American Anthropologist 77: 253–266.

Javert, C. T.   1957. Spontaneous and Habitual Abortion. New York: McGraw-Hill.

Jay, P. C.   1965. The Common Langur of North India. In Primate Behavior: Field Studies of Monkeys and Apes. I. DeVore, ed. Pp. 197–249. New York: Holt, Rinehart and Winston.

Jenness, Diamond.   1917. The Copper Eskimos. The Geographical Review 4:81–91.

———— 1922. The Life of the Copper Eskimos. Report of the Canadian Arctic Expedition, 1913–18. Vol. 12, pt. 2. Ottawa: F. A. Acland.

———— 1923. The Physical Characteristics of the Copper Eskimos. Report of the Canadian Arctic Expedition, 1913–18. Vol. 12. Part B. Ottawa: E. Cloutier.

———— 1946. Material Culture of the Copper Eskimo. Report of the Canadian Arctic Expedition, 1913–1918. Vol. 26. Ottawa: E. Cloutier.

———— 1959. The People of the Twilight. Chicago: University of Chicago Press.

Jenni, D. A.   1974. Evolution of Polyandry in Birds. American Zoologist 14:129–144.

Jirasek, A.   1894. Some Aspects of Czech Culture. In Die oesterreich-ungarische Monarchie in Wort und Bild: Boehmen, Pt. 1. R. Neuse, trans. Pp. 392–437. Wein: Kaiserlich-Königliche Hof und Staatsdruckerei.

Jochelson, W.   1908. Material Culture and Social Organization of the Koryak. New York: American Museum of Natural History.

Johnson, F.   1943. Notes on Micmac Shamanism. Primitive Man 16:53–80.

Johnson, G. A.   1973. Local Exchange and Early State Development in Southwestern Iran. Anthropological Paper No. 51, Museum of Anthropology, University of Michigan.

Johnson, S.   1921. The History of the Yorubas from the Earliest Times to the Beginning of the British Protectorate. London: Routledge.

Johnston, F. E., and K. M. Kensinger.   1971. Fertility and Mortality Differentials and Their Implications for Microevolutionary Change among the Cashinahua. Human Biology 43:356–364.

Johnston, F. E., K. M. Kensinger, R. L. Jantz, and G. F. Walker.   1969. The Population Structure of the Peruvian Cashinahua: Demographic, Genetic and Cultural Interrelationships. Human Biology 41:29–41.

Jolly, A.   1966. Lemur Behavior: A Madagascar Field Study. Chicago: University of Chicago Press.

Joubert, E. 1972. The Social Organization and Associated Behavior in the Hartmann Zebra *Equus zebra hartmannae*. Madoqua 6:17–56.

———— 1974. Size and Growth as Shown by Pre- and Post-natal Development of the Hartmann Zebra *Equus zebra hartmannae*. Madoqua 8:55–58.

Jungius, H. 1970. Studies on the Breeding Biology of the Reedbuck (*Redunca arundinium* Boddaert, 1785) in the Krüger National Park. Zeitschrift für Saiigetierkunde 35:129–146.

———— 1971. The Biology and Behavior of the Reedbuck (*Redunca arundinium* Boddaert, 1785) in the Krüger National Park. Mammalia Depicta. Hamburg: P. Parey.

Junod, H. 1927. The Life of a South African Tribe. 2nd ed. 2 vols. London: Macmillan. [Also in the HRAF, 1953.]

Kagwa, A. 1934. The Customs of the Baganda. New York: Columbia University Press. [Also in the HRAF, 1962.]

Kaltreider, D. F. 1963. Effects of Height and Weight on Pregnancy and the Newborn. Springfield, Ill.: Charles C. Thomas.

Kang, Y. S., and W. K. Cho. 1962. The Sex Ratio at Birth and Other Attributes of the Newborn from Maternity Hospitals in Korea. Human Biology 34:38–48.

Kapferer, B., ed. 1976. Transaction and Meaning. ASA Essays in Social Anthropology, Vol. 1. Philadelphia: Institute for the Study of Human Issues.

Kaplan, B. A. 1951. Changing Functions of the Quanancha Dance at the Corpus Christi Festival in Paracho, Michoacan, Mexico. Journal of American Folklore 64:383–392.

Kaplan, D., and R. A. Manners. 1972. Culture Theory. Englewood Cliffs, N.J.: Prentice-Hall.

Karolyi, A. F. 1939. Hungarian Pageant. Budapest: G. Vajna and Co.

Karsten, Y. R. 1935. The Head-hunters of Western Amazonas: The Life and Culture of the Jibaro Indians of Eastern Ecuador and Peru. Helsingfors: Centraltryckevet.

Karve, I. 1965. Kinship Organization in India. 2nd ed. Bombay: Asia Publishing House.

Katchadourian, Herant A., and Donald T. Lunde. 1975. Fundamentals of Human Sexuality. 2nd ed. New York: Holt, Rinehart and Winston.

Kawabe, M. 1970. A Preliminary Study of the Wild Siamang Gibbon (*Hylobates syndactylus*) at Fraser's Hill, Malaysia. Primates 11:285–291.

Kawai, M. 1965. Newly Acquired Precultural Behavior of the Natural Troop of Japanese Monkeys on Koshima Islet. Primates 6:1–30.

Kawamura, S. 1965. Matriarchal Social Ranks in the Minoo-B Troop: A Study of the Rank System of Japanese Monkeys. *In* Japanese Monkeys. S. Altmann, ed. Pp. 105–112. Atlanta: published by the editor.

Keesing, F. 1938. The Taupo System of Samoa: A Study of Institutional Change. Oceania 8:1–14.

Keesing, R. M. 1975. Kin Groups and Social Structure. New York: Holt, Rinehart and Winston.

Keith, S. 1949. A New Theory of Human Evolution. New York: Philosophy Library Inc.

Kellas, L. M. 1955. Observations on the Reproductive Abilities and Growth Rates of the Dikdik. Proceedings of the Zoological Society of London 124: 751–784.

Kellum, B. A. 1974. Infanticide in England in the Later Middle Ages. History of Childhood Quarterly 1(3):367–388.

Kelly, I. T. 1934. Ethnography of the Surprise Valley Paiute. Berkeley: University of California Press.

Kenyatta, J. 1953. Facing Mount Kenya: The Tribal Life of the Kikuyu. London: Secker and Warburg. [Originally published in 1938.]

Kerr, M. G. 1969. Infertility in Women Clinically Attributed to Uterine Factors. Journal of Reproduction and Fertility Supplement 8:1–8.

Khajuria, H. 1956. A New Langur (Primates: Colobidae) from Goalpara District, Assam. Annals and Magazine of Natural History 9:86–88.

King, Judith E. 1954. The Otariid Seals of the Pacific Coast of America. Bulletin of the British Museum (Natural History) Zoology 2:309–337.

Kinzer, N. S. 1974. The Beauty Cult. The Center Magazine, Nov./Dec. 1974:2–9.

Kirchhoff, P. 1948. The Caribbean Lowland Tribes: The Mosquito, Sumo, Paya, and Jicaque. *In* Handbook of South American Indians. J. H. Steward, ed. Vol. 2:219–229. Washington, D.C.: United States Government Printing Office.

Kissenberth, W. 1912. Among the Canella Indians in Central Menanhao. Bässler Archiv 2(1):45–54.

Kitchen, D. W. 1974. Social Behavior and Ecology of the Pronghorn. Wildlife Monographs 38:1–96.

Klingel, H. 1965. Notes on the Biology of the Plains Zebra, *Equus quagga boehmi* Matschie. East African Wildlife Journal 3:86–88.

———— 1967. Soziale Organisation und Verhalten freilebender Steppenzebras (*Equus quagga*). Zeitschrift für Tierpsychologie 24:580–624.

———— 1968. Soziale Organisation und Verhaltensweisen von Hartmann-und Berg-zebras (*Equus zebra hartmannae* und *E. z. zebra*). Zeitschrift für Tierpsychologie 25:76–88.

———— 1969a. The Social Organization and Population Ecology of the Plains Zebra (*Equus quagga*). Zoological Africana 4:249–263.

———— 1969b. Reproduction in the Plains Zebra, *Equus burchelli boehmi*: Behaviour and Ecological Factors. Journal of Reproduction and Fertility Supplement 6:339–345.

Kloss, C. B., and K. Andersen. 1916. On a Collection of Mammals from the

Coast and Islands of Southeast Siam. With an Account of the Fruit-bats. Proceedings of the Zoological Society of London 1:27–75.

Knappe, C. 1888. Religiöse Anschauungen der Marshall-Insulaner. Mittheilungen von Forschungsreisenden und Gelehrten aus den Deutschen Schutzgebieten 1:63–81.

Knight, R. R. 1970. The Sun River Elk Herd. Wildlife Monographs 23:1–66.

Koford, C. B. 1957. The Vicuña and the Puna. Ecological Monographs 27:153–219.

———— [1973] Guereza Monkeys of Kibale Forest, Western Uganda: *Colobus guereza uellensis* Matschie, 1913. Unpublished manuscript.

Kohl, S. G. 1955. Perinatal Mortality in New York City. Cambridge: Harvard University Press.

Kolata, G. B. 1977. Human Evolution. Hominids of the Miocene. Science 197:244–245, 294.

Koppers, W. 1948. Die Bhil in Zentralindien. Wien: Verlag Ferdinand Berger.

Kortlandt, A. 1967. Experimentation with Chimpanzees in the Wild. *In* Progress in Primatology. R. Schneider and H. J. Kuhn, eds. Pp. 208–224. Stuttgart: Fischer.

Kowalewski, Stephen. 1976. Prehispanic Settlement Patterns of the Central Part of the Valley of Oaxaca, Mexico. Ann Arbor University Microfilms.

———— Ms. Population Growth Trends from Ancient Oaxaca.

Koyama, N. 1967. On Dominance Rank and Kinship of a Wild Japanese Monkey Troop in Arahiyama. Primates 8:182–216.

Krämer, A. 1906. Hawaii, Ostmikronesien, und Samoa. Stuttgart: Strecker und Schröder.

———— 1932. Truk. Hamburg: Friederichsen.

Krämer, A., and H. Nevermann. 1938. Ralik-Ratak (Marshall Inseln). Hamburg: Friederichsen.

Kraus, Bertram S. 1961. The Western Apache: Some Anthropometric Observations. American Journal of Physical Anthropology 19:227–236.

Krause, Fritz. 1911a. In den Wildnissen Brasiliens: Bericht und Ergebnisse der Leipziger Araguaya-Expedition, 1908. Leipzig: R. Voigtländer.

———— 1911b. Die Kunst der Karaja-Indianer. Bässler Archiv 2:1–31.

Krieg, H. 1930. Biologische Reisestudien in Südamerika. XVI. Die Affen des Gran Chaco und Seiner Grenzgebiete. Zeitschrift für Wissenschaftliche Biologie. Abt. A Morphologie und Ökologie der Tiere 18:759–785. (Quoted by Hershkovitz, 1963).

Krige, E. 1938. The Place of the North-eastern Transvaal Sotho in the South Bantu Complex. Africa 10:265–293.

———— 1964. Property, Cross-Cousin Marriage, and the Family Cycle among the Lovedu. *In* The Family Estate in Africa. R. F. Gray and P. H. Gulliver, eds. Pp. 155–195. Boston: Boston University Press.

Krige, E., and J. D. Krige. 1943. The Realm of a Rain Queen: A Study of the Pattern of Lovedu Society. London: Oxford University Press. [Also in the HRAF, 1958.]

Krishna Iyer, L. A. 1948. The Coorg Tribes and Castes. Madras: Gordon Press.

——— 1962. The Sudras of Cochin. *In* The Cochin Tribes and Castes. Vol. 2, Pp. 1–102. London: Higginbotham.

Kroeber, A. L. 1908. Ethnology of the Gros Ventre. American Museum of Natural History. Anthropological Papers, vol. 1, part 4.

——— 1917. The Superorganic. American Anthropologist 19:163–213.

——— 1919. On the Principle of Order in Civilization as Exemplified by Changes of Fashion. American Anthropologist 21:253–263.

——— 1931. The Seri. Los Angeles: Southwest Museum.

——— 1944. Configurations of Culture Growth. Berkeley: University of California Press.

——— 1953. Handbook of the Indians of California. Berkeley: University of California Press.

——— 1972 [1917]. Zuni Kin and Clans. New York: American Museum of Natural History.

Kruger, F. 1936. The Lovedu. Bantu Studies 10:89–105.

Krumbeigel, I. von. 1944. Die neuweltlichen Tylopoden. Zool. Anzeiger 145:45–70.

Kummer, H. 1968a. Two Variations in the Social Organization of Baboons. *In* Primates: Studies in Adaptation and Variability. P. Jay, ed. Pp. 293–312. New York: Holt, Rinehart and Winston.

——— 1968b. Social Organization of Hamadryas Baboons. A Field Study. Bibliotheca Primatologica, No. 6, pp. 1–189. Basel: S. Karger.

——— 1971. Primate Societies: Group Techniques of Ecological Adaptation. Chicago: Aldine.

Kummer, H., and F. Kurt. 1963. Social Units of a Free-living Population of Hamadryas Baboons. Folia Primatologica 1:4–19.

Kurland, J. A. 1976. Sisterhood in Primates: What to Do with Human Males. Paper presented at the 1976 meetings of the American Anthropological Association. Washington, D.C., 1976.

——— 1977. Kin Selection in the Japanese Monkey. Contributions to Primatology 12. Basel: Karger.

——— In press. Can Sociality Have a Favorite Sex Chromosome? American Naturalist.

Kurland, J. A., and Steven J. C. Gaulin. In preparation. Aspects of Sexual Selection. I: Parental Certainty and Reproductive Effort.

Laborde, A. 1918. [The Eunuchs at the Court at Hué.] Hanoi: Bulletin des Amis du Vieux Hué 5:107–125.

Labrecque, E. 1931. Le Mariage chez les Babemba. Africa 4:209–221.

Lack, D. 1954. The Natural Regulation of Animal Numbers. Oxford: Clarendon Press.

———— 1968. Ecological Adaptations for Breeding in Birds. London: Methuen.

Lambert, H. E. 1956. Kikuyu Social and Political Institutions. London: Oxford University Press.

Lambrecht, F. 1932. The Mayawyaw Ritual. Proceedings of the Catholic Anthropological Conference, Washington, D.C., Dec. 1932. Vol. 4(1):1–167.

———— 1958. Ifugao Weaving. Folklore Studies 17:1–53.

Lambton, A. K. S. 1953. Landlord and Peasant in Persia. London: Oxford University Press.

Lamson, H. D. 1935. Social Pathology in China: A Source Book for the Study of Problems of Livelihood, Health, and the Family. Shanghai: Commercial Press.

Lancaster, J. B. In press. Sex and Gender in Evolutionary Perspective. *In* Sex and Its Psychosocial Derivatives. H. Katchadourian and J. Martin, eds.

Landor, A. H. S. 1893. Alone with the Hairy Ainu; or, 3,800 Miles on a Pack Saddle in Yezo and a Cruise to the Kurile Islands. London: J. Murray [Johnson Reprint, 1970.]

Lang, O. 1946. Chinese Family and Society. New Haven: Yale University Press.

Langer, W. L. 1972. Checks on Population Growth, 1750–1850. Scientific American 226(2):92–9.

———— 1974. Infanticide: A Historical Survey. History of Childhood Quarterly 1(3):353–365.

Langness, L. L. 1967. Sexual Antagonism in the New Guinea Highlands: A Bena Bena Example. Oceania 37(3):161–177.

Larken, P. M. 1926. An Account of the Zande. Sudan Notes and Records 9:1–55.

Laski, V. 1958. Seeking Life. Memoirs of the American Folklore Society 50:1–176.

Laughlin, C. D., and E. G. d'Aquili. 1974. Biogenetic Structuralism. New York: Columbia University Press.

Lawick-Goodall, J. van. 1967. Mother-offspring Relationships in Free-ranging Chimpanzees. *In* Primate Ethnology. D. Morris, ed. Pp. 287–346. Chicago: Aldine.

———— 1971. In the Shadow of Man. Boston: Houghton Mifflin.

Lawick, H. van, and J. van Lawick-Goodall. 1971. Innocent Killers. Boston: Houghton Mifflin Co.

Laws, R. M. 1953. The Elephant Seal (*Mirounga leonina* Linn.) I. Growth and Age. Falkland Islands Dependencies Survey Scientific Reports, No. 8:1–62.

———— 1958. Growth Rates and Ages of Crabeater Seals. *Lobodon carcinophagus* Jacquinot and Purcheran. Proceedings of the Zoological Society of London 130:275–288.

Layard, J. W.   1942. Stone Men of Malekula. London: Chatto and Windus.

Leach, E.   1961. Pul Eliya, a Village in Ceylon: A Study of Land Tenure and Kinship. Cambridge: Cambridge University Press.

———— 1962. Rethinking Anthropology. London: Athlone.

LeBar, F. M.   1964. The Material Culture of Truk. Yale University Department of Anthropology Publications in Anthropology, no. 68.

LeBoeuf, B. J.   1971. The Aggression of the Breeding Bulls. Natural History 130(2):82–97.

———— 1974. Male-male Competition and Reproductive Success in Elephant Seals. American Zoologist 14:163–167.

LeBoeuf, B. J., and R. S. Peterson.   1969. Social Status and Mating Activity in Elephant Seals. Science 163:91–93.

Le Clercq, C.   1910 [1691]. New Relation of Gaspesia. . . . W. F. Ganong, ed. and trans. Toronto: Champlain Society.

Ledger, H. P., and N. S. Smith.   1964. The Carcass and Body Composition of the Uganda Kob. Journal of Wildlife Management 28:827–839.

Lee, C.   1944. See Lei, Chin-Ilu.

Lee, Richard B.   1969. !Kung Bushman Subsistence: An Input-Output Analysis. In Environment and Cultural Behavior. A. P. Vayda, ed. Pp. 47–79. New York: Natural History Press.

———— 1972. !Kung Spatial Organization: An Ecological and Historical Perspective. Human Ecology 1:125–147.

Lee, Richard B., and Irven DeVore, eds.   1968. Man the Hunter. Chicago: Aldine.

Lei, Chin-Ilu.   1944. Ancestor Worship of the Lolo in Ch'eng-cheang, Yunnan. Frontier Affairs 3(9):31–36.

Leigh, C.   1926. Weights and Measurements of the Nilgiri Langur (Pithecus johnii). Journal of the Bombay Natural History Society 31:223.

Leigh, E. G.   1970. Sex Ratio and Differential Mortality Between the Sexes. American Naturalist 104(936): 205–210.

Leix, A.   1941. Turkestan and its Textile Crafts. Ciba Review 4:1433–1465.

Lenneberg, E. H.   1967. Biological Foundations of Language. New York: John Wiley and Sons.

Leskes, A., and N. H. Acheson.   1971. Social Organization of a Free-Ranging Troop of Black and White Colobus Monkeys (Colobus abyssinicus). Proceedings of the Third International Congress on Primatology, Zurich, 1970.

Lesser, A.   1933. The Pawnee Ghost Dance Hand Game. New York: Columbia University Press.

Levine, D. N.   1965. Wax and Gold; Tradition and Innovation in Ethiopian Culture. Chicago: University of Chicago Press.

LeVine, R. A.   1973. Culture, Behavior, and Personality. Chicago: Aldine.

———— 1977. Gusii Sex Offenses. In Forcible Rape: The Crime, the Victim, the Offender. D. Chappell, R. Geis and G. Geis, eds. Pp. 189–226. New York: Columbia University Press.

Levins, Richard. 1966. The Strategy of Model Building in Population Biology. American Scientist 54:421–431.

———— 1970. Extinction. *In* Some Mathematical Questions in Biology. M. Gerstenhaber, ed. Pp. 77–107. Lectures on Mathematics in the Life Sciences, Vol. 2. Providence: The American Mathematical Society.

Lévi-Strauss, C. 1944. The Social and Psychological Aspects of Chieftainship in a Primitive Tribe: The Nambikuara of Northwestern Matto Grosso. Transactions of the New York Academy of Sciences 7:16–32.

———— 1948. La Vie familiale et sociale des Indiens Nambikwara. Paris: Société des Américanistes. [Family and Social Life of the Nambikuara Indians. Translated for HRAF by Eileen Sittler.]

———— 1949. Les Structures élémentaires de la parenté. Paris: Plon.

———— 1962. La Pensée sauvage. Paris: Plon.

———— 1967a. Structural Anthropology. C. Jacobson and B. G. Schoepf, trans. New York: Doubleday/Anchor.

———— 1967b. Social Structures of Central and Eastern Brazil. *In* Structural Anthropology. Pp. 116–127. New York: Doubleday/Anchor.

———— 1967c. Do Dual Organizations Exist? *In* Structural Anthropology. Pp. 128–160. New York: Doubleday/Anchor.

———— 1969. The Elementary Structures of Kinship. Translated by J. H. Bell and J. R. von Sturmer. R. Needham, ed. Boston: Beacon Press.

Lewis, I. M. 1955. Peoples of the Horn of Africa. London: International African Institute.

Lewontin, R. C. 1970. The Units of Selection. Annual Review of Ecology and Systematics 1:1–18.

Lhote, H. 1944. Les Touaregs du Hoggar. Paris: Payot. [Translated for the HRAF, 1956, by M. A. Sipfle.]

Lin Yüeh-hwa. 1947. The Lola of Liangshan. Shanghai: Shanghai Commercial Press.

Lindburg, D. G. 1971. The Rhesus Monkey in North India: An Ecological and Behavioral Study. *In* Primate Behavior. Developments in Field and Laboratory Research. L. A. Rosenblum, ed. Pp. 1–106. New York: Academic Press.

Lindenbaum, S. 1972. Sorcerers, Ghosts, and Polluting Women: An Analysis of Religious Belief and Population Control. Ethnology 11(3):241–253.

Lindsey, A. A. 1937. The Weddell Seal in the Bay of Whales, Antarctica. Journal of Mammalogy 18(2):127–144.

Ling, S., and Y. Ruey. 1947. A Report on an Investigation of the Miao of Western Hunan. National Research Institute of History and Philology, Academia Sinica, Shanghai. Monographs Series A, no. 18.

Linton, R. 1922. The Thunder Ceremony of the Pawnee. Chicago: Field Museum of Natural History.

———— 1923a. Annual Ceremony of the Pawnee Medicine Men. Chicago: Field Museum of Natural History.

———— 1923b. The Material Culture of the Marquesas Islands. Honolulu: Bernice P. Bishop Museum Memoirs 8(5):263–471.

———— 1939. Marquesan Culture. *In* The Individual and His Society. A. Kardine, ed. Pp. 138–196. New York: Columbia University Press.

Lipkind, W. 1948. The Caraja. *In* Handbook of South American Indians. J. H. Steward, ed. Vol. 3:179–191. Washington: United States Government Printing Office.

Lisianskii, U. 1814. A Voyage around the World in the Years 1803, 1804, 1805, and 1806. London: John Booth and Longman, et al. [1968 reprint, Ridgewood, N.J.: Gregg Press.]

Little, K. L. 1951. The Mende of Sierra Leone: A West African People in Transition. London: Routledge and Kegan Paul.

Little, M., and G. Morren. 1976. Ecology, Energetics, and Human Variability. Dubuque, Iowa: William C. Brown Co.

Lizot, J. 1971. Remarques sur le vocabulaire de parenté Yanomami. L'homme 11:25–38.

———— 1976. Descendance et affinité chez les Yanomami: antinomie et complémentarité. Acts du XLIIeme Congrès International des Américanistes. Vol. II:55–70. Paris.

———— 1977a. Population, resources et guerre chez les Yanomami. Libre 2:110–145. Paris: Petite Bibliothèque Payot.

———— 1977b. Population, Resources and Warfare among the Yanomami. Man 12(3/4):497–517.

Lloyd, P. 1965. The Yoruba of Nigeria. *In* Peoples of Africa. J. L. Gibbs, Jr., ed. Pp. 549–582. New York: Holt, Rinehart and Winston.

Lockley, R. M. 1966. Grey Seal, Common Seal. New York: October House.

Loeb, E. M. 1926. Pomo Folkways. University of California Publications in American Archaeology and Ethnology 19(2):149–408.

Loewe, M. 1970. Everyday Life in Early Imperial China: During the Han Period 20 B.C.—A.D. 220. New York: Harper and Row.

Lorenz, K. 1950. The Comparative Method in Studying Behaviour Patterns. Symposia of the Society for Experimental Biology 4:221–268.

———— 1965. Evolution and Modification of Behavior. Chicago: University of Chicago Press.

———— 1966. On Aggression. New York: Harcourt, Brace, and World.

Lothrop, Samuel Kirkland. 1928. The Indians of Tierra de Fuego. Note on Anthropometry by E. A. Hooten. New York: Museum of the American Indian, Heye Foundation.

Loud, L. L. 1931. Notes on the Northern Paiute. University of California Publications in American Archaeology and Ethnology 25(1):152–164.

Low, Bobbi S. 1978. Environmental Uncertainty and the Parental Strategies of Marsupials and Placentals. American Naturalist 112:197–213.

Low, H. 1848. Sarawak, Its Inhabitants and Productions. London: Richard Bentley.

Lowie, R. H. 1924. Notes on Shoshonean Ethnography. Anthropological Papers of the American Museum of Natural History 20:185–314.

Loy, J. 1970. Perimenstrual Sexual Behavior among Rhesus Monkeys. Folia Primatologica 13:286–297.

———— 1971. Estrous Behavior of Free-ranging Rhesus Monkeys (*Macaca mulatta*). Primates 12:1–31.

Lumholtz, K. S. 1902. Unknown Mexico. New York: Scribner's.

———— 1912. New Trails in Mexico. New York: Scribner's.

Luria, Z. In press. Psychosocial Determinants of Gender Identity, Role, and Orientation. *In* Sex and Its Psychosocial Derivatives. H. Katchadourian and J. Martins, eds. Berkeley: University of California Press.

Lurie, N. O. 1953. Winnebago Berdache. American Anthropologist 55:708–712.

Luschinsky, M. S. [1975.] The Life of Women in a Village of North India: A Study of Role and Status. Unpublished Ph.D. dissertation. 1962. Cornell University, Department of Anthropology, Ithaca, New York. Ann Arbor: University Microfilms No. 63–749. 2 vols.

Lyon, M. W. 1908. Mammals Collected in Eastern Sumatra by Dr. W. L. Abbott during 1903, 1906, and 1907, with Descriptions of New Species and Subspecies. Proceedings of the United States National Museum 34:619–679.

Lyster, W. R. 1968. The Sex Ratio of Live Births in Integrated But Racially Different Populations, U.S.A. and Fiji. Human Biology 40:63–68.

Ma, Ho-t-ien. 1944. Exorcism, a Custom of the Black Lolo. Frontier Affairs 3(9):27–30.

MacArthur, J. W., J. Ovadia, O. W. Smith, and J. Bashir-Farahmond. 1972. The Menstrual Cycle of the Bonnet Monkey (*Macaca radiata*). Changes in Secretion of Cervical Mucus, Vaginal Cytology, Sex Skin and Urinary Estrogen Secretion. Folia Primatologica 17:107–121.

MacArthur, R. H. 1965. Ecological consequences of Natural Selection. *In* Theoretical and Mathematical Biology. T. H. Waterman and H. J. Morewitz, eds. Pp. 388–397. New York: Blaisdell Publishing Co.

MacCluer, J. W., J. V. Neel, and N. A. Chagnon. 1971. Demographic Structure of a Primitive Population: A Simulation. American Journal of Physical Anthropology 35:193–207.

Macey, I. G., H. A. Hunscher, E. D. Donelson, and B. Nims. 1930. Human Milk Flow. American Journal of Diseases of Children 39:1186–1204.

Macey, I. G., H. H. Williams, J. P. Pratt, and B. M. Hamil. 1945. Human Milk Studies XIX. Implications of Breast Feeding and Their Investigations. American Journal of Diseases of Children 70:135–141.

MacKinnon, J. R. 1971. The Orang-utans in Sabah Today. Oryx 11:141–191.

Macrides, F., A. Bartke, and S. Dalterio. 1975. Strange Females Increase Plasma Testosterone Levels in Male Mice. Science 189:1104–1106.

Maguire, R. A. 1928. Il Torobo. Journal of the African Society 27:127–141, 244–268.

Mahar, J. M. 1966. Marriage Networks in the Northern Gangetic Plain. Ph.D. dissertation, Cornell University, Department of Anthropology, Ithaca, New York.

Mahony, F. J. 1970. A Trukese Theory of Medicine. Ph.D. dissertation, Stanford University. Ann Arbor: University Microfilms No. 70–18439.

Mair, L. P. 1934. An African People in the Twentieth Century. London: G. Routledge and Sons.

Malinowski, B. 1926. Crime and Custom in Savage Society. New York: Harcourt Brace & Co.

———— 1929. The Sexual Life of Savages. New York: Harcourt, Brace, and World.

Man, Edward Horace. 1932. On the Aboriginal Inhabitants of the Andaman Islands. London: Royal Anthropological Institute of Great Britain and Ireland. [Also in the HRAF, 1957.]

Mandelbaum, D. G. 1970. Society in India. Vol. 1: Continuity and Change. Berkeley: University of California Press.

Mangin, E. 1921. Les Mossi: essai sur les moeurs et coutumes du peuple Mossi au Soudan Occidental. Paris: Augustin Challamel. [Translated for the HRAF by A. Brunel and E. Skinner.]

Mansfield, A. W. 1958. The Breeding Behaviour and Reproductive Cycle of the Weddell Seal (Leptonychotes weddelli Lesson). Falkland Islands Dependencies Survey Scientific Reports 18:1–41.

———— 1963. Seals of Arctic and Eastern Canada. Bulletin of the Canadian Fisheries Research Board 137:1–30.

Marealle, P. I. 1963. Notes on Chagga Customs. Tanganyika Notes and Records (1963):67–90.

Marler, P. 1969. Colobus quereza: Territoriality and Group Composition. Science 163:93–95.

Marlow, B. J. 1967. Mating Behaviour in the Leopard Seal, Hydrurga leptonyx (Mammalia: Phocidae) in Captivity. Australian Journal of Zoology 15(1):1–5.

Marshall, D. S. 1950. Cuna Folk: A Conceptual Scheme Involving the Dynamic Factors of Culture, as Applied to the Cuna Indians of Darien. Manuscript, Harvard University.

Marshall, Harry Ignatius. 1922. The Karen People of Burma: A Study in Anthropology and Ethnology. Columbus: Ohio State University Press.

Marshall, J. T., B. A. Ross, and S. Chantharojvong. 1972. The Species of Gibbons in Thailand. Journal of Mammalogy 53:479–489.

Marshall, W. E. 1873. A Phrenologist amongst the Todas, or the Study of a Primitive Tribe in South India: History, Character, Customs, Religion, Infanticide, Polyandry, Language. London: Longmans, Green & Co. [Also in the HRAF, 1954.]

Martin, R. D. 1972. Concepts of Human Territoriality. In Man, Settlement, and Urbanism. P. J. Ucko, R. Tringham, and G. W. Dimbleby, eds. Pp. 427–446. Cambridge, Mass.: Schenkman.

Martin, R. M. 1847. China: Political, Commercial, and Social; in an Official Report to Her Majesty's Government. Vol. 1. London: James Madden.

Mason, L. 1954. Relocation of the Bikini Marshallese: A Study in Group Migration. Ph.D. dissertation. Yale University.

Mason, W. A. 1966. Social Organization of the South American Monkey, *Callicebus moloch:* A Preliminary Report. Tulane Studies in Zoology and Botany 13:23–28.

———— 1968. Use of Space by *Callicebus* Groups. In Primates: Studies in Adaptation and Variability. P. C. Jay, ed. Pp. 200–216. New York: Holt, Rinehart, and Winston.

———— 1976. Environmental Models and Mental Modes. Representational Processes in the Great Apes and Man. American Psychologist 31: 284–294.

Masse, H. 1938. Croyances et coutumes persanes. C. A. Messner, trans. Paris: Librairie Orientale et Américaine. [Also in the HRAF, 1954.]

Massey, A. 1975. Kin Selection in Macaques. Master's thesis. University of Georgia, Athens.

———— 1977. Agonistic Aids and Kinship in a Group of Pigtail Macaques. Behavioral Ecology and Sociobiology 2:31–40.

Masters, W. H., and V. E. Johnson. 1966. Human Sexual Response. Boston: Little, Brown.

Masters, W. M. 1954. Rowanduz: A Kurdish Administration and Mercantile Center. Ph.D. dissertation, University of Michigan. Ann Arbor: University Microfilms. [Also in the HRAF, 1962.]

Mathison, O. A., R. T. Baade, and R. J. Lopp. 1962. Breeding Habits, Growth and Stomach Contents of the Steller Sea Lion in Alaska. Journal of Mammalogy 43:469–477.

Matsumura, A. 1918. Contribution to the Ethnography of Micronesia. Imperial University, Tokyo, College of Science Journal 40(7):1–174.

Matthiessen, P. 1962. Under the Mountain Wall: A Chronicle of Two Seasons in the Stone Age. New York: Viking.

Mauss, M. 1967. The Gift. New York: W. W. Norton. [I. Cunnison, trans. Glencoe, Ill.: Free Press, 1954. Originally published 1925.]

May, R. M., ed. 1976. Theoretical Ecology: Principles and Applications. Philadelphia: W. B. Saunders Co.

Maybury-Lewis, D. H. P. 1965. Prescriptive Marriage Systems. Southwestern Journal of Anthropology 21:207–230.

————— 1967. Akwe-Shavante Society. Oxford Clarendon Press.

Maynard Smith, J. 1964. Group Selection and Kin Selection. Nature 20(4924): 1145–1147.

————— 1972. On Evolution. Edinburgh: Edinburgh University Press.

————— 1975. The Theory of Evolution. 3rd edition. Harmondsworth: Penguin Books Ltd.

————— 1976. Commentary: Group Selection. Quarterly Review of Biology 51(2):277–283.

Mayr, E. 1963. Animal Species and Evolution. Cambridge: Harvard University Press.

McCann, C. 1933. Notes on the Colouration and Habits of the White-browed Gibbon or Hoolock (*Hylobates hoolock* Harl.) Journal of the Bombay Natural History Society 36(2): 395–405.

McClintock, M. K. 1971. Menstrual Synchrony and Suppression. Nature 229:244–245.

McClure, H. E. 1964. Some Observation of Primates in Climax Diptocarp Forest near Kuala Lumpur, Malaya. Primates 5:39–58.

McGee, H. J. 1898. The Seri Indians. 17th Annual Report of the Bureau of Ethnology. Washington, D.C.: United States Government Printing Office.

McIlwraith, T. F. 1948. The Bella Coola Indians. 2 vols. Toronto: University of Toronto Press. [Also in the HRAF.]

McKim, F. 1947. San Blas: An Account of the Cuna Indians of Panama. Göteborg: Etnografiska Museet.

McKinney, F. 1975. The Evolution of Duck Displays. *In* Function and Evolution in Behaviour. G. Baerends, C. Beer, and A. Manning, eds. Pp. 331–357. Oxford: Clarendon Press.

McLaren, I. A. 1971. Introduction. *In* Natural Regulation of Animal Populations. I. A. McLaren, ed. Pp. 1–21. New York: Atherton.

McNamara, J., and S. F. Wemple. 1976. Marriage and Divorce in the Frankish Kingdom. *In* Women in Medieval Society. S. M. Stuard, ed. Pp. 95–124. Philadelphia: University of Pennsylvania Press.

McWhirter, N. and R. McWhirter. 1974. Guinness Book of World Records. New York: Sterling Publishing Company, Inc.

Mead, M. 1928. Coming of Age in Samoa: A Psychological Study of Primitive Youth for Western Civilization. New York: Morrow.

———— 1930a. Social Organization of Manu'a. Honolulu: Bernice P. Bishop Museum Bulletin 76.

———— 1930b. Growing up in New Guinea: A Comparative Study of Primitive Education. New York: Morrow.

———— 1950. Male and Female. Harmondsworth: Penguin Books.

Medawar, P. B. 1954. Evolution of Viviparity in Vertebrates. Symposium, Society for Experimental Biology 7:320.

Meinertzhagen, R. 1938. Some Weights and Measurements of Large Mammals. Proceedings of the Zoological Society of London (Series A) 108:433–439.

Meredith, H. B. 1970. Body Weight at Birth of Viable Human Infants. A World-wide Comprehensive Treatise. Human Biology 42:217–264.

Merker, M. 1910. Die Masai: Etnographische monographie eines östafrikanischen semitenvolkes. Berlin: D. Reimer.

Messenger, J. C. 1969. Inis Beag: Isle of Ireland. New York: Holt, Rinehart and Winston.

Messing, S. D. 1957. The Highland Plateau Amhara of Ethiopia. Ph.D. dissertation, University of Pennsylvania, University Microfilms No. 23619, Ann Arbor. [Also in the HRAF.]

Métraux, A. 1930. Etudes sur la civilisation des Indiens. Revista del Instituto de Etnologia de la Universidad Nacional de Tucuman 1:295–493.

———— 1940. Ethnology of Easter Island. Honolulu: Bernice P. Bishop Museum Bulletin 160. [Also in the HRAF, 1961.]

———— 1942. Siriono: Tribal Divisions and History. In The Native Tribes of Eastern Bolivia and Western Matto Grosso. Bureau of American Ethnology Bulletin 134:110–114, 171–182.

———— 1946. Ethnography of the Chaco. In Handbook of South American Indians. J. H. Steward, ed. Vol. 1:197–370. Washington, D.C.: United States Government Printing Office.

———— 1948. Tribes of the Eastern Slopes of the Bolivian Andes. In Handbook of South American Indians. J. H. Steward, ed. Vol. 3:465–506. Washington, D.C.: United States Government Printing Office.

Mi Mi Khaing. 1946. Burmese Family. New York: Longmans, Green and Co.

Michael, R. P., E. B. Keverne, and R. W. Bonsall. 1971. Pheromones: Isolation of Male Sex Attractants from a Female Primate. Science 172:964–966.

Michael, R. P., M. Wilson, and T. M. Wilson. 1973. Sexual Behaviour of Male Primates and the Role of Testosterone. In Comparative Ecology and Behaviour of Primates. R. P. Michael and J. H. Crook, eds. Pp. 235–313. New York: Academic Press.

Michael, R. P., D. Zumpe, E. B. Keverne, and R. W. Bonsall. 1972. Neuroendocrine Factors in the Control of Primate Behavior. Recent Progress in Hormone Research 28:665–706.

Michelson, T. 1935. Some Notes on Winnebago Social and Political Organization. American Anthropologist 37:446–449.

Miller, G. S. 1903. Seventy New Malayan Mammals. Smithsonian Miscellaneous Collection. 45:1–73.

Minn, E. K. 1955. The Lapps. Indiana University Graduate Program in Uralic and Asian Studies. New Haven: Human Relations Area Files Press.

Minturn, L., and J. T. Hitchcock. 1966. The Rajputs of Khalapur, India. (Six Cultures Series, vol. 3). New York: John Wiley.

Mitchell, G. J. 1971. Measurements, Weights, and Carcass Yields of Pronghorns in Alberta. Journal of Wildlife Management 35:76–85.

Mohnot, S. M. 1971. Some Aspects of Social Change and Infant-killing in the Hanuman Langur, Presbytis entellus (Primates: Cercopithecidae) in Western India. Mammalia 35:175–198.

Molloy, J. T. 1975. Dressing for Success. New York: Wyden.

Money, J. 1961. Sex Hormones and Other Variables in Human Eroticism. In Sex and Internal Secretions. 3rd ed. W. C. Young, ed. 2:1382–1400. Baltimore: Williams and Wilkins Company.

Moore, J. N., and H. S. Slusher, eds. 1970. Biology: A Search for Order in Complexity. Grand Rapids, Mich.: Zondervan Publishing House.

Morewedge, R. T., ed. 1975. The Role of Women in the Middle Ages. Albany: State University of New York Press.

Morgan, L. H. 1870. Systems of Consanguinity and Affinity of the Human Family. Washington: Smithsonian Institution.

———— 1877. Ancient Society. New York: World Publishing Co.

Morison, J. E. 1963. Foetal and Neonatal Pathology. London: Butterworth.

Morizon, R. 1936. La province cambodgienne de Pursat. Paris: Les Editions Internationales.

Morris, C. J. 1938. Living with Lepchas: A Book about the Sikkim Himalayas. London: W. Heinemann. [Also in the HRAF, 1958.]

Morris, D. 1967. The Naked Ape. New York: Dell Publishing Co.

———— 1969. The Human Zoo. New York: McGraw Hill.

Moynihan, M. 1964. Some Behavior Patterns of Platyrrhine Monkeys: I. The Night Monkey (Aotus trivirgatus). Smithsonian Miscellaneous Collection 146(5):1–84.

Mukherjee, R. P., and S. S. Saha. 1974. The Golden Langurs (Presbytis geei Khajuria, 1956) of Assam. Primates 15:327–340.

Mulvihill, D. J., and M. M. Tumin. 1969. Crimes of Violence. 3 vols. Washington, D.C.: United States Government Printing Office.

Munro, N. G. 1963. Ainu Creed and Cult. New York: Columbia University Press.

Murdock, G. P. 1945. The Common Denominator of Cultures. *In* The Science of Man in the World Crisis. Ralph Linton, ed. Pp. 123–142. New York: Columbia University Press.

———— 1949. Social Structure. New York: Macmillan.

———— 1957. World Ethnographic Sample. American Anthropologist 59:664–687.

———— 1960a. Cognatic Forms of Social Organization. *In* Social Structure in Southeast Asia. G. P. Murdock, ed. Pp. 1–14. Chicago: Quadrangle.

———— 1960b. How Culture Changes. *In* Man, Culture, and Society. H. L. Shapiro, ed. Pp. 247–260. New York: Oxford University Press.

———— 1961. World Ethnographic Sample. *In* Readings in Cross-Cultural Methodology. F. W. Moore, ed. Pp. 195–220. New Haven: Human Relations Area Files Press.

———— 1967. Ethnographic Atlas. Pittsburgh: University of Pittsburgh Press.

Murie, J. R. 1914. Pawnee Indian Societies. American Museum of Natural History, Anthropological Papers 11 (part 8):543–644.

Murie, O. J. 1951. The Elk of North America. Washington, D.C.: Wildlife Management Institute.

Murphy, R. F., and B. Quain. 1955. The Trumai Indians of Central Brazil. American Ethnological Society Monograph no. 24.

Musters, G. 1873. At Home with the Patagonians. London: Murray. [Also in the HRAF, 1958.]

Myers, P. 1978. Sexual Dimorphism in Size of Vespertilionid Bats. American Naturalist 12:701–711.

Nachtigall, H. 1955. Tierradentro: Archäologie und Ethnographie einer Kolumbianischen Landschaft. Zurich: Origo.

Nadler, R. D. 1975. Cyclicity in Tumescence of the Perineal Labia of Female Lowland Gorillas. Anatomical Record 18:791–797.

Nag, M. 1972. Sex, Culture and Human Fertility: India and the United States. Current Anthropology 13(2):231–237.

Naik, T. B. [1956.] The Bhils, A Study. Delhi: Bharatiya Adimjati Sewak Sang. [Also in the HRAF, 1959.]

Nalbandov, A. V. 1976. Reproductive Physiology of Mammals and Birds: The Comparative Physiology of Domestic and Laboratory Animals and Man. 3rd ed. San Francisco: W. H. Freeman and Co.

Napier, J. R., and P. H. Napier. 1967. A Handbook of Living Primates. New York: Academic Press.

Nath, Y. V. S.   1960. Bhils of Ratanmal: An Analysis of the Social Structure of a Western Indian Community. Baroda: Maharaja Sayajrao University.

Needham, R.   1962. Structure and Sentiment. Chicago: University of Chicago Press.

———— 1971. Remarks on the Analysis of Kinship and Marriage. *In* Rethinking Kinship and Marriage. R. Needham, ed. London: Tavistock.

Neel, J. V.   1969. Some Aspects of Differential Fertility in Two American Indian Tribes. Proceedings, 8th International Congress of Anthropological and Ethnological Sciences, Tokyo, 1968. Vol. 1:356–361. Tokyo: Science Council of Japan.

Neel, J. V., and N. A. Chagnon.   1968. The Demography of Two Tribes of Primitive Relatively Unacculturated American Indians. Proceedings of the National Academy of Sciences 59(3):680–689.

Neel, J. V., F. M. Salzano, P. C. Junqueira, F. Keiter, and D. Maybury-Lewis.   1964. Studies on the Xavante Indians of the Brazilian Mato Grosso. American Journal of Human Genetics 16(1):52–140.

Neel, J. V., and K. M. Weiss.   1975. The Genetic Structure of a Tribal Population, The Yanomama Indians. XII. Biodemographic Studies. American Journal of Physical Anthropology 42(1):25–51.

Nel, J. A. J.   1965. Body Lengths and Temperatures of the Crabeater Seal. *Lobodon carcinophagus.* Zoologica Africana 1(1):319–320.

———— 1966. On the Behaviour of the Crabeater Seal *Lobodon carcinophagus* (Hombron and Jacquinot). Zoologica Africana 1(2):91–93.

Netting, Robert M. C.   1968. Hill Farmers of Nigeria; Cultural Ecology of the Kofyar of the Jos Plateau. American Ethnological Society Monograph 46.

———— 1971. The Ecological Approach in Cultural Study. McCaleb Modules in Anthropology. Reading, Mass.: Addison-Wesley Publishing Co.

Neville, M. K.   1968. A Free-ranging Rhesus Troop Lacking Adult Males. Journal of Mammalogy 49:771–773.

———— 1972. The Population Structure of Red Howler Monkeys (*Alouatta seniculus*) in Trinidad and Venezuela. Folia Primatologica 17:56–86.

Nevius, J. L.   1869. China and the Chinese: a General Description of the Country and Its Inhabitants. . . . New York: Harper and Bros.

Newman, M. T., and R. L. Eng.   1947. The Ryuku People: A Biological Appraisal. American Journal of Physical Anthropology 5:113–157.

Nicolaisen, J.   1963. Ecology and Culture of the Pastoral Tuareg. National Museum of Copenhagen.

Niederle, Lubor.   1911. La race slave: statistique, démographie-anthropologie. L. Leger, trans. Paris: F. Alcan.

Niedermayer, O. von.   1924. Afghanistan. Leipzig: K. W. Hiersemann. [Translated for the HRAF by W. Chafe, 1955.]

Nimuendajú, C. 1946. The Eastern Timbira. R. H. Lowie, trans. and ed. Berkeley: University of California Press.

Nino, B. 1912. Etnografía Chiriguano. La Paz: Tipografía Comercial de Ismael Argote.

Nishiwaki, Masaharu. 1972. General Biology. *In* Mammals of the Sea; Biology and Medicine. S. H. Ridgway, ed. Pp. 3–204. Springfield, Ill.: Charles C. Thomas.

Nordenskiöld, E. 1912. Indianerleben: El Gran Chaco, Südamerika. Leipzig: Bonnier.

————— 1920. An Historical and Ethnological Survey of the Cuna Indians. Göteborg: Göteborgs Museum, Ethnografiska Avdelningen. [Also in the HRAF, 1966.]

————— 1938. An Historical and Ethnological Survey of the Cuna Indians. Comparative Ethnographical Studies, Vol. 10. H. Wassen, ed. Göteborg, Sweden, Göteborg Museum.

Nweeya, S. K. 1916. Persia, The Land of the Magi. Philadelphia: Winston.

Oberg, K. 1953. Indian Tribes of Northern Mato Grosso, Brazil. Washington, D.C.: United States Government Printing Office.

Oliver, D. L. 1955. A Solomon Island Society. Cambridge: Harvard University Press.

Opler, M. E. 1941. An Apache Life-way: The Economic, Social and Religious Institutions of the Chiricahua Indians. Chicago: University of Chicago Press.

Opler, M. E., and R. D. Singh. 1948. The Division of Labor in an Indian Village. *In* A Reader in General Anthropology. C. S. Coon, ed. Pp. 464–496. New York: Holt, Rinehart and Winston.

Oppenheimer, J. R. 1969. Changes in Forehead Patterns and Group Composition of the White-faced monkey (*Cebus capucinus*). Proceedings of the Second International Congress of Primatology, 1. Behavior. C. R. Carpenter, ed. Pp. 36–42. Basel: Karger.

Orians, G. H. 1969. On the Evolution of Mating Systems in Birds and Mammals. American Naturalist 103:589–603.

Oritsland, T. 1970. Sealing and Seal Research in the South-west Atlantic Pack Ice, Sept.-Oct. 1964. *In* Antarctic Ecology. M. W. Holdgate, ed. Pp. 367–376. Vol. I. New York: Academic Press.

Orléans, Henri, Prince d'. 1894. Around Tonkin and Siam. C. B. Pitman, trans. London: Chapman and Hall.

Orr, J. B., and J. L. Gilkes. 1931. Studies of Nutrition: The Physique and Health of Two African Tribes. London: H. M. Stationery Office. [Also in the HRAF, 1965.]

Orr, K. G. 1951. Field Notes on the Burmese Standard of Living as Seen in the Case of a Fisherman-Refugee Family. Notes of the Burma Community Research Project, Department of Anthropology. Rangoon: University of Rangoon.

Orr, Robert T.   1967. The Galapagos Sea Lion. Journal of Mammalogy 48(1):62–69.

——— 1972. Marine Mammals of California. Berkeley: University of California Press.

O'Suilleabnain, Sean.   1956. Two Death Customs in Ireland. Studia Ethnographica Upsaliensia XI; Arctica: 208–215.

Oyler, P. S.   1926. Shilluk Notes. Sudan Notes and Records 4:57–68.

Packer, C.   1975. Male Transfer in Olive Baboons. Nature 225:219–220.

Pakrasi, K. B.   1964. A Note on Differential Sex-Ratios and Polyandrous People in India. Man in India 44(2):161–174.

——— 1968. Infanticide in India—A Century Ago. Bulletin, Socio-Economic Research Institute (Calcutta) 2(2):21–30.

——— 1970a. Female Infanticide in India. Calcutta: Editions Indian.

——— 1970b. Infanticide, Vital Statistics and Proclaimed Castes in India. Bulletin, Socio-Economic Research Institute (Calcutta) 4(1–2):81–98.

——— 1970c. The Genesis of Female Infanticide. Humanist Review (Bombay) 2(3):255–281.

——— 1972. On the Antecedents of Infanticide Act of 1870 in India. Bulletin, Cultural Research Institute (Calcutta) 9(1–2):20–30.

Pakrasi, K. B., and B. Sasmal.   1971. Infanticide and Variation of Sex-Ratio in a Caste Population of India. Acta Medica Auxologica (Italy) 3(3): 217–228.

Panigrahi, L.   1972. British Social Policy and Female Infanticide in India. New Delhi: Munshuram Manoharlal.

Panikkar, K. M.   1918. Some Aspects of Nayar Life. Journal of the Royal Anthropological Institute of Great Britain and Ireland 48:254–292.

Park, W. Z.   1934. Paviotso Shamanism. American Anthropologist 36:98–113.

——— 1937. Paviotso Polyandry. American Anthropologist 39:366–368.

——— 1938. Shamanism in Western North America: A Study in Cultural Relationships. Evanston: Northwestern University.

——— 1946. Tribes of the Sierra Nevada de Santa Marta, Columbia. In Handbook of South American Indians. J. H. Steward, ed. Vol. 2: 865–886. Washington, D.C.: United States Government Printing Office.

Parkes, A. S.   1969. Multiple Births in Man. Journal of Reproduction and Fertility Supplement 6:105–116.

Parkinson, R.   1899. On the Ethnography of the Northwestern Solomon Islands. Königliche Zoologische und Anthropologische-Ethnographische Museum.

Parrinder, G.   1949. West African Religion Illustrated from the Beliefs and

Practice of the Yoruba, Ewe Akan, and Kindred Peoples. Journal of Yoruba and Related Studies 2:20–28.

Parsons, E. C. 1926. Micmac Notes. Journal of American Folklore 39:460–485.

———— 1929. The Social Organization of the Tewa of New Mexico. Memoirs of the American Anthropological Association 36:1–309.

Parsons, P. A. 1964. Parental Age and the Offspring. Quarterly Review of Biology 39:258–275.

Passin, H. 1943. The Place of Kinship in Tarahumara Social Organization. Acta Americana, Vol. 1.

Paulian, P. 1964. Contribution a l'étude de l'otarie de l'île Amsterdam. Mammalia 28 (Supplement 1):1–146.

Pehrson, R. N. 1957. The Bilateral Network of Social Relations in Könkämä Lapp District. Bloomington: Indiana University Press.

Peller, S. 1965. Births and Deaths Among Europe's Ruling Families Since 1500. *In* Population in History: Essays in Historical Demography. D. V. Glass and D. E. C. Eversley, eds. Pp. 87–100. Chicago: Aldine.

Pennington, C. W. 1963. The Tarahumara of Mexico: Their Environment and Material Culture. Salt Lake City: University of Utah Press.

Pescatello, A. M. 1976. Power and Pawn: The Female in Iberian Families, Societies, and Cultures. Westport, Conn.: Greenwood.

Peter, Prince of Greece and Denmark. 1963. A Study in Polyandry. The Hague: Mouton.

Peters, R. H. 1976. Tautology in Evolution and Ecology. American Naturalist 110:1–12.

Peterson, R. S., C. L. Hubbs, R. L. Gentry, and R. L. De Long. 1968. The Guadalupe Fur Seal: Habitat, Behavior, Population Size and Field Identification. Journal of Mammalogy 49(4):665–675.

Petrullo, V. 1939. The Yaruros of the Capanaparo River, Venezuela. Bureau of American Ethnology Bulletin 123.

Petter, J. J. 1962a. Ecological and Behavioral Studies of Madagascar Lemurs in the Field. Annals of the New York Academy of Sciences 102:267–281.

———— 1962b. Remarques sur l'écologie et l'ethologie comparées des lémuriens malgaches. La Terre et la Vie 109:394–416.

———— 1962c. Recherches sur l'écologie et l'ethologie des lémuriens malgaches. Mémoires du Muséum National d'Histoire Naturelle, Séries A (Zoology) 27:1–146.

———— 1965. The Lemurs of Madagascar. *In* Primate Behavior: Field Studies of Monkeys and Apes. I. DeVore, ed. Pp. 292–319. New York: Holt, Rinehart and Winston.

Petter, J. J., and A. Peyrieras. 1974. A Study of Population Density and Home Ranges of *Indri indri* in Madagascar. *In* Prosimian Biology. R. D. Martin, G. A. Doyle, and A. C. Walker, eds. Pp. 39–48. London: Duckworth.

Pfeffer, P. 1969. Considérations sur l'écologie des forêts claires du Cambodge oriental. La Terre et la Vie 116:3–24.

Pfeiffer, J. E. 1969. The Emergence of Man. New York: Harper and Row.

Phillips, Herbert P. 1965. The Thai Peasant Personality: The Patterning of Interpersonal Behavior in the Village of Bang Chan. Berkeley: University of California Press.

Pierson, D. 1967. Negros in Brazil: A Study of Race Contact at Bahia. Carbondale: Southern Illinois University Press. [Originally published 1942]

Pijoan, M. 1946. The Health and Customs of the Miskito Indians of Northern Nicaragua: Interrelationships in a Medical Program. Mexico: Instituto Indigenista Interamericano. [Also in the HRAF, 1958.]

Pike, Gordon C., and Brian E. Maxwell. 1958. The Abundance and Distribution of the Northern Sea Lion (Eumetopias jubata) on the Coast of British Columbia. Journal of the Fisheries Research Board of Canada 15(1):5–17.

Pitts, F. R., W. P. Lebra, and W. P. Suttles. 1955. Post-war Okinawa. Washington, D.C.: Pacific Science Board, National Research Council.

Playfair, A. 1909. The Garos. London: Hutt.

Pocock, R. I. 1927. The Gibbons of the genus Hylobates. Proceedings of the Zoological Society of London: [pt. II] 719–741.

———— 1928. The Langurs, or Leaf monkeys, of British India. Journal of the Bombay Natural History Society 32:472–504.

———— 1939. The Fauna of British India. Mammalia, Vol. 1. London: Taylor and Francis.

Poirier, F. E. 1969. The Nilgiri Langur (Presbytis johnii) Troop: Its Composition, Structure, Function and Change. Folia Primatologica 10:20–47.

———— 1970. The Nilgiri Langur (Presbytis johnii) of South India. In Primate Behavior: Developments in Field and Laboratory Research. L. A. Rosenblum, ed. 1:254–383. New York: Academic Press.

Polanyi, Karl. 1957. The Economy as an Instituted Process. In Trade and Market in the Early Empires. K. Polanyi, C. Arensberg and H. Pearson, eds. Pp. 243–270. Glencoe: The Free Press.

Pollard, S. 1921. In Unknown China. Philadelphia: Lippincott.

Pollitzer, W. S., D. Rucknagel, R. Tashian, D. C. Schreffler, W. C. Leyshon, K. Namboordiri, and R. C. Elston. 1970. The Seminole Indians of Florida: Morphology and Serology. American Journal of Physical Anthropology 32:65–82.

Pollock, J. I. 1975. Field Observations on Indri indri: A Preliminary Report. In Lemur Biology. I. Tattersall and R. W. Sussman, eds. Pp. 287–311. New York: Plenum Press.

Popov, A. A. 1966. The Nganasan: The Material Culture of the Tavgi Samoyeds. E. K. Ristinen, trans. Bloomington: Indiana University Press.

Porée, G., and E. Maspéro-Porée. 1938. Moeurs et coutumes des Khmèrs: origines, histoire, religions, croyances, rites [et] évolution. Paris: Payot. [Translated for the HRAF by K. Botsford, 1952.]

Pospisil, L. 1958. Kapauku Papuans and Their Law. New Haven: Yale University Publications in Anthropology, no. 54.

———— 1963. Kapauku Papuan Economy. New Haven: Yale University Publications in Anthropology, no. 67.

Postan, M. M. 1975. The Medieval Economy and Society: An Economic History of Britain in the Middle Ages. Harmondsworth: Penguin.

Potter, E. L., and F. L. Adair. 1940. Fetal and Neonatal Death. Chicago: University of Chicago Press.

Potter, R. G. 1963. Birth Intervals: Structure and Change. Population Studies 17:155–166.

Power, E. E. 1922. Medieval English Nunneries, c. 1275 to 1535. Cambridge: Cambridge University Press.

———— 1975. Medieval Women. M. M. Postan, ed. Cambridge: Cambridge University Press.

Prater, S. H. 1971. The Book of Indian Animals. Bombay: Leaders Press.

Premack, D. 1971. On the Assessment of Language Competence in the Chimpanzee. *In* Behavior of Nonhuman Primates. A. M. Schrier and F. Stollnitz, eds. Pp. 185–228. New York: Academic Press.

Prince, R. 1964. Indigenous Yoruba Psychiatry. *In* Magic, Faith and Healing. A. Kiev, ed. Pp. 84–120. New York: Free Press of Glencoe.

Puccioni, Nello. 1936. Resultati delle Missioni Stefanini-Paoli (1913) e Stefanini Puccioni (1942). *In* Somalia. Vol. 3. Real Società Geographica Italiana. [Anthropology and Ethnography of the Peoples of Somalia]. K. A. Looney, trans. [Also in the HRAF, 1960.]

Pumphrey, M. E. C. 1941. The Shilluk Tribe. Sudan Notes and Records 24:1–45.

Quimby, D. C., and D. E. Johnson. 1951. Weights and Measurements of Rocky Mountain Elk. Journal of Wildlife Management 15:57–62.

Rabb, T. K., and R. I. Rotberg, eds. 1973. The Family in History: Interdisciplinary Essays. New York: Harper and Row.

Radcliffe-Brown, A. R. 1922. The Andaman Islanders. Cambridge: Cambridge University Press.

———— 1924. The Mother's Brother in South Africa. South African Journal of Science 21:541–545.

———— 1931. The Social Organization of Australian Tribes. Oceania 1:426–456.

———— 1950. Introduction. *In* African Systems of Kinship and Marriage. A. R. Radcliffe-Brown and D. Forde, eds. Pp. 1–85. London: Oxford University Press.

———— 1965. Structure and Function in Primitive Society. Glencoe: Free Press. [Originally published in 1952.].

Radin, P. 1916. The Winnebago Tribe. 37th Annual Report of the Bureau of American Ethnology, pp. 35–560.

Radwan, E. 1929. Einiges über die Sirionos. Zeitschrift für Ethnologie 60:291–296.

Raedeke, K. J. In press. La Distribution, dinamica de la poblacion, y ecologia del guanaco (Lama guanacoe) de Magallanes, Chile.

Rahaman, H., and M. D. Parthasarathy. 1969. Studies on the Social Behavior of the Bonnet Monkeys. Primates 10:149–162.

Raikes, C. 1852. Notes on the North-Western Provinces of India. London: Chapman and Hall.

Ralls, K. 1976. Mammals in Which Females Are Larger Than Males. Quarterly Review of Biology 51:245–276.

Ramos, Alcida. 1972. The Social System of the Sanumá of Northern Brazil. Ph.D. dissertation. University of Wisconsin, 1972.

———— 1974. How the Sanumá Acquire Their Names. Ethnology 12(2):171–185.

Ramos, Alcida, and Bruce Albert. 1976. Yanomama Descent and Affinity: The Sanumá/Yanomam Contrast. Actes du XLIIeme Congrès International des Américanistes. Vol. II: 71–90. Paris.

Ramsay, H. 1890. Western Tibet: A Practical Dictionary of the Language and Customs of the Districts Included in the Ladak Wazarat. Lahore: W. Ball, Government Printers.

Rand, R. W. 1959. The Cape Fur Seal (Arctocephalus pusillus). Distribution, Abundance and Feeding Habits Off the Southwestern Coast of the Cape Province. Union of South Africa. Department of Commercial Industries. Division of Fisheries Investment Report 34:1–74.

———— 1967. The Cape Fur Seal (Arctocephalus pusillus). III. General Behavior on Land and Sea. Union of South Africa Division of Fisheries Investment Report 60.

———— 1972. The Cape Fur Seal Arctocephalus pusillus. IV. Estimates of Population Size. Union of South Africa Div. Sea Fish. Invest. Rep. 89:1–28.

Rappaport, Roy A. 1968. Pigs for the Ancestors: Ritual in The Ecology of a New Guinea People. New Haven: Yale University Press.

———— 1969. Ritual Regulation of Environmental Relations among a New Guinea People. In Environment and Cultural Behavior. A. P. Vayda, ed. Pp. 181–201. Garden City: Doubleday.

Rattray, R. S. 1913. Hausa Folk-lore, Customs, Proverbs, Etc. Vol. 2. Oxford: Clarendon Press. [O.U.P. facsimile 1969.]

———— 1923. Ashanti. Oxford: Clarendon Press.

———— 1932. The Tribes of the Ashanti Hinterland. Vol. 2:293–364. Oxford: Clarendon Press.

Raum, O. F. 1940. Chagga Childhood: A Description of Indigenous Education in an East African Tribe. London: Oxford University Press.

Reay, M. 1954. Social Control Amongst the Orokaiva. Oceania 24:110–118.

Redfield, R., and A. Villa Rojas. 1934. Chan Kom, A Maya Village. Chicago: University of Chicago Press.

Reid, D. E., K. J. Ryan, and K. Benirschke. 1972. Principles and Management of Human Reproduction. Philadelphia: W. B. Saunders Company.

Reiss, W. 1880. Ein besuch bei den Jivaros-Indianern. Verhandlungen der Gesellschaft für Erdkunde 7:325–337.

Renfrew, Colin. 1972. Patterns of Population Growth in the Prehistoric Aegean. *In* Man, Settlement, and Urbanism. P. J. Ucko, R. Tringham, and G. Dimbleby, eds. Pp. 383–399. Cambridge, Mass.: Schenkman.

Reynolds, Vernon. 1972. Ethology of Urban Life. *In* Man, Settlement and Urbanism. P. J. Ucko, R. Tringham and G. W. Dimbleby, eds. Pp. 401–408. Cambridge, Mass.: Schenkman.

Riad, Mohamed. 1955. Some Observations of a Field Trip Among the Shilluk. Wiener Volkerkundliche Mitterlunger 3:70–78.

Ribbach, S. H. 1940. Drogpa Namgyal, ein tibeterleben. München-Palnegg: Wilhelm Barth.

Richard, P. C. 1867. [Notes on the Ethnography of Cochinchina]. Revue Maritime et Coloniale 21: 92–133.

Richards, A. 1935. A Modern Movement of Witch Finders. Africa (8):448–460.

———— 1939. Land, Labour and Diet in Northern Rhodesia: An Economic Study of the Bemba Tribe. London: Oxford University Press.

———— 1940. The Political System of the Bemba Tribe—Northeastern Rhodesia. *In* African Political Systems. M. Fortes and E. E. Evans-Pritchard, eds. Pp. 83–120. London: Oxford University Press.

———— 1950. Some Types of Family Structure Amongst the Central Bantu. *In* African Systems of Kinship and Marriage. A. R. Radcliffe-Brown and D. Forde, eds. Pp. 207–251. London: Oxford University Press.

Richardson, J., and A. L. Kroeber. 1940. Three Centuries of Women's Dress Fashions: A Quantitative Analysis. University of California Anthropological Records 5(2):110–154.

Richerson, P. J. 1977. Ecology and Human Ecology: A Comparison of Theories in the Biological and Social Sciences. American Ethnologist 4(1): 1–26.

Richerson, P. J., and R. Boyd. 1978. A Dual Inheritance Model of the Human Evolutionary Process I: Basic Postulates and a Simple Model. Journal of Social Biological Structure 1:127–154.

Riches, D. 1974. The Netsilik Eskimo: A Special Case of Selective Female Infanticide. Ethnology 13(4):351–361.

Riddell, F. A. 1960. Honeylake Paiute Ethnography. Nevada State Museum Anthropological Papers No. 4.

Rijksen, H. D.   1975. Social Structure in a Wild Orangutan Population in Sumatra. *In* Contemporary Primatology: Fifth International Congress of Primatology, Nagoya, Japan. S. Kondo, M. Kawai and A. Ehara, eds. Pp. 373–379. Basel: S. Karger.

Risley, H. H.   1915. The People of India. 2nd ed. Calcutta: Thacker, Spinck and Company.

Rivers, W. H. R.   1906. The Todas. New York: Macmillan and Company.

———— 1914. Tikopia. *In* The History of Melanesian Society. W. H. R. Rivers, ed. Pp. 298–362. Cambridge: Cambridge University Press.

———— 1921. The Origin of Hypergamy. Journal, Bihar and Orissa Research Society. 7 (Pt. 1):9–24.

Rivet, P.   1907/8. Les Indiens Jibaros: étude géographique, historique, et ethnographique. L'Anthropologie 18:333–368, 583–618; 19:69–87, 235–259.

Robbins, W. W., J. P. Harrington, and B. Freire-Marreco.   1916. Ethnobotany of the Tewa Indians. Bureau of American Ethnology Bulletin 55:1–124. [Also in the HRAF, 1961.]

Robel, R. J. and W. B. Ballard, Jr.   1974. Lek Social Organization and Reproductive Success in the Greater Prairie Chicken. American Zoologist 14(1):121–128.

Roberts, A.   1951. The Mammals of South Africa. New York: Hafner Publishing Company.

Robinson, M. S.   1962. Complementary Filiation and Marriage in the Trobriand Islands: A Reexamination of Malinowski's Material. *In* Marriage in Tribal Societies, M. Fortes, ed. Pp. 121–157. Cambridge: Cambridge University Press.

Rocklin, R. E., J. L. Kitzmiller, C. B. Carpenter, M. R. Garovoy, and J. R. David.   1976. Absence of an Immunologic Blocking Factor from the Serum of Women with Chronic Abortions. New England Journal of Medicine 295(22):1209–1213.

Röhrs, M.   1958. Ökologische beobachtungen an wildebenden Tylopoden Südamerikas. Verhandlungen der Deutschen zoologischen Gesellschaft. Supplement 21:538–554.

Roquette-Pinto, E.   1938. Redonia. 4th Ed. São Paulo: Companhia Editora Nacional.

Roscoe, John.   1911. The Baganda. An Account of Their Native Customs and Beliefs. London: Macmillan. [Also in the HRAF, 1959.]

Rose, F. G. G.   1960. Classification of Kin, Age Structure and Marriage amongst the Groote Eylandt Aborigines; A Study in Method and A Theory of Australian Kinship. Berlin: Akademic Verlag.

Rosen, E.   1924. The Chiriguano. *In* Ethnographical Research Work During the Swedish Chaco-Cordillera Expedition 1901–1902. Pp. 187–225; 269–275. Stockholm: Fritze Booksellers.

Rossi, Alice.   1977. A Biosocial Perspective on Parenting. Daedalus 106:1–31.

———— 1978. Essay: The Biosocial Side of Parenthood. Human Nature 1(6): 72–79.

Roth, H. L.   1892. The Natives of Borneo. Edited From the Papers of the Late Brooks Low, Esq. Journal of the Royal Anthropological Institute of Great Britain and Ireland 21:110–137.

———— 1893. The Natives of Borneo. Edited from the Papers of the late Brooks Low, Esq. Journal of the Royal Anthropological Institute of Great Britain and Ireland 22:22–64.

Routledge, K.   [1919]. The Mystery of Easter Island. London: Sifton, Praed.

Routledge, W. S., and K. Routledge.   1910. With a Prehistoric People: The Akikuyu of British East Africa. London: Edward Arnold.

Rowell, T. E.   1972. Female Reproductive Cycles and Social Behavior in Primates. Advances in the Study of Behavior 4:69–105.

———— 1977. Variation in Age at Puberty in Monkeys. Folia Primatologica 27: 284–296.

Ruby, D.   1976. The Behavioral Ecology of the Viviparous Lizard, *Sceloporous jerrovi*. Ph.D. dissertation, University of Michigan.

Rudran, R.   1973. Adult Male Replacement in One-male Troops of Purple-faced Langurs (*Presbytis senex senex*) and Its Effect on Population Structure. Folia Primatologica 19:166–192.

Rumbaugh, D. M., T. V. Gill, and E. C. von Glaserfeld.   1973. Reading and Sentence Completion by a Chimpanzee (*Pan*). Science 182:731–733.

Russell, B.   1943. The Principles of Mathematics. New York: W. W. Norton. [Originally published in 1903.]

———— 1945. A History of Western Philosophy. New York: Simon and Schuster.

Russell, J. C.   1948. British Medieval Population. Albuquerque: University of New Mexico Press.

———— 1958. Late Ancient and Medieval Population. Transactions of the American Philosophical Society, N. S. 48(3):1–152.

Ruyle, E. E.   1973. Genetic and Cultural Pools: Some Suggestions for a Unified Theory of Biocultural Evolution. Human Ecology 1(3):201–215.

———— 1977. Comment on "The Adaptive Significance of Cultural Behavior." Human Ecology 5(1):53–55.

Ryan, W. B.   1862. Infanticide: Its Laws, Prevalence, Prevention, and History. London: J. Churchill.

Ryden, S.   1941. A Study of the Siriono Indians. Göteberg: Elanders Boktryckeri.

Sachs, R.   1967. Liveweights and Body Measurements of Serengeti Game Animals. East African Wildlife Journal 5:24–36.

Sade, D. S.   1972a. Sociometrics of *Macaca mulatta* I. Linkages and Cliques in Grooming Matrices. Folia Primatologica 18:196–223.

————— 1972b. A Longitudinal Study of Social Behavior of Rhesus Monkeys. *In* The Functional and Evolutionary Biology of the Primates. R. Tuttle. ed. Pp. 378–398. Chicago: Aldine-Atherton.

Sahlins, M. D. 1961. The Segmentary Lineage: An Organization of Predatory Expansion. American Anthropologist 63:322–345.

————— 1968. On the Sociology of Primitive Exchange. *In* The Relevance of Models for Social Anthropology. M. Banton, ed. Pp. 139–227. London: Tavistock. [Originally published in 1965.]

————— 1972. Stone Age Economics. Chicago: Aldine Atherton.

————— 1976a. The Use and Abuse of Biology: An Anthropological Critique of Sociobiology. Ann Arbor: University of Michigan Press.

————— 1976b. Culture and Practical Reason. Chicago: University of Chicago Press.

Salzano, F. M., ed. 1971. The Ongoing Evolution of Latin American Populations. Springfield, Ill.: Charles C. Thomas.

Salzano, F. M., J. V. Neel, and D. Maybury-Lewis. 1967. Further Studies on the Xavante Indians. I. Demographic Data on Two Additional Villages: Genetic Structure of the Tribe. American Journal of Human Genetics 19(4):463–489.

Salzano, F. M., and R. Cardoso de Oliveira. 1970. Genetic Aspects of the Demography of Brazilian Terena Indians. Social Biology 17(3):217–223.

Sanderson, I. T. 1949. A Brief Review of the Mammals of Suriname (Dutch Guiana), Based on a Collection made in 1938. Proceedings of the Zoological Society of London 119:755–789.

Sarasin, F. 1916. Étude anthropologique sur les néo-caledoniens et les loyaltiens. Archives suisses d'anthropologie générale. 2(1–2):83–103.

Schaller, G. B. 1963. The Mountain Gorilla: Ecology and Behavior. Chicago: University of Chicago Press.

Schapera, Isaac. 1930. The Khoisan Peoples of South Africa: Bushmen and Hottentots. London: George Routledge and Sons.

Schebesta, Paul. 1954. Die Negrito Asiens, II. Band, Ethnographie der Negrito. Studia Instituti Anthropos vol. 6:12–13. [Translation of Vol. 2, parts 1–2, by F. F. Schütze for the HRAF, 1962.]

Scheffer, V. B. 1945. Growth and Behavior of Young Sea Lions. Journal of Mammalogy 26:390–392.

————— 1958. Seals, Sea Lions, and Walruses. A Review of the Pinnipedia. Stanford: Stanford University Press.

Scheffer, V. B., and F. Wilke. 1953. Relative Growth in the Northern Fur Seal. Growth 17:129–145.

Schenkel, R. and L. Schenkel-Hulliger. 1967. On the Sociology of Free-ranging Colobus, (*Colobus quereza caudatus*). *In* Progress in Primatology. D. Starck, R. Schneider and H. J. Kuhn, eds. Stuttgart: Fischer.

Scherman, L. 1915. Wohnhaustypen in Burma und Assam. Archiv für Anthropologie 14:203–234.

Schmalhaulsen, I. I. 1949. Factors in Evolution, The Theory of Stabilizing Selection. Philadelphia: Blakiston.

Schmidt, M. 1938. Los Chiriguanos e Izozos. Revista de la Sociedad Cientifica del Paraguay 4(3):1–115.

Schneider, D. M. 1961a. Introduction: The Distinctive Features of Matrilineal Descent Groups. *In* Matrilineal Kinship. D. M. Schneider and K. Gough, eds. Pp. 1–29. Berkeley: University of California Press.

———— 1961b. Truk. *In* Matrilineal Kinship. D. M. Schneider and K. Gough, eds. Pp. 202–233. Berkeley: University of California Press.

———— 1964. The Nature of Kinship. Man 217:180–181.

———— 1965. Kinship and Biology. *In* Aspects of the Analysis of Family Structure. A. J. Coale et al., eds. Pp. 83–101. Princeton: Princeton University Press.

Schrenck, L. von. 1881. Die Völker des Amurlandes. (His "Reisen und Forschungen in Amur-Lande in den Jahren 1854–6.") 2 vols. in 1. St. Petersburg: Kaiserlich Akademie der Wissenschaften.

Schrire, Carmel, and William Lee Steiger. 1974. A Matter of Life and Death: An Investigation Into the Practice of Female Infanticide in the Arctic. Man 9(2):161–184.

———— 1975. Reply to Acker and Townsend. Man 10(3):470–472.

Schultz, A. H. 1933. Observations on the Growth, Classification and Evolutionary Specializations of Gibbons and Siamangs. Human Biology 5:212–255.

———— 1944. Age Changes and Variability in Gibbons. American Journal of Physical Anthropology, New Series 2:1–129.

———— 1956. Postembryonic Age Changes. *In* Primatologica. I. H. Hofer, A. H. Schultz, and D. Starck, eds. Pp. 887–964. Basel: Karger.

Schultz, L. 1907. In Namaland and the Kalahari. Jena: Gustav Fischer.

Science for the People. *See* Sociobiology Study Group of Science for the People.

[Scott, J. G.] 1910. The Burman, His Life and Notions. 3rd ed. London: Macmillan.

Seger, John. [1976]. Genetic Indeterminism and the Inheritance of Behavior. Paper presented at the 1976 meetings of the American Anthropological Association, Washington, D.C., 1976. [In preparation. *In* I. DeVore, ed. Sociobiology & the Social Sciences.]

Selander, R. K. 1966. Sexual Dimorphism and Differential Niche Utilization in Birds. Condor 68:113–151.

———— 1972. Sexual Selection and Dimorphism in Birds. *In* Sexual Selection and the Descent of Man, 1871–1971. B. Campbell, ed. Pp. 180–230. Chicago: Aldine.

Bibliography

Seligman, C. G., and B. Z. Seligman. 1911. The Veddas. Cambridge: Cambridge University Press. [Also in the HRAF, 1961.]

———— 1932a. The Azande. *In* Pagan Tribes of the Nilotic Sudan. C. G. Seligman and B. Z. Seligman, eds. Pp. 495–539. London: Routledge.

———— 1932b. The Shilluk. *In* Pagan Tribes of the Nilotic Sudan. C. G. Seligman and B. Z. Seligman, eds. Pp. 37–135. London: Routledge.

Seligman, M. 1971. Phobias and Preparedness. Behavior Therapy 2:307–320.

Seligman, M. E. P., and J. L. Hager. 1972. Biological Boundaries of Learning. New York: Appleton-Century Crofts.

Seltzer, Carl C. 1940. Contributions to the Racial Anthropology of the Near East. Papers of the Peabody Museum of American Archaeology and Ethnology, Harvard University. Vol. 16. (2).

Senfft, A. 1903. Die Marshall-Insulaner. *In* Rechsverhältnisse von eingeborenen Völkern in Afrika und Ozeanien. S. R. Steinmetz, ed. Pp. 425–455. Berlin: Julius Springer.

Sergeant, D. E. 1965. Migrations of Harp Seals, *Pagophilus groenlandicus* (Erxleben), in the Northwest Atlantic. Journal of the Fisheries Research Board of Canada 22(2):433–464.

Service, Elman R. 1971. Primitive Social Organization. 2nd edn. New York: Random House.

Severin, T. 1973. Vanishing Primitive Man. New York: American Heritage Publishing Company.

Sheldon, W. H. 1961. The Criterion of the Good and the Right. *In* Experience, Existence, and the Good. I. C. Lieb, ed. Pp. 275–284. Carbondale: Southern Illinois University Press.

Shen, Tsung-lien, and Sheng-chi Liu. 1953. Tibet and the Tibetans. Stanford: Stanford University Press. [Also in the HRAF, 1955.]

Sherman, P. W. 1976. Natural Selection Among Some Group-living Organisms. Ph.D. dissertation, University of Michigan.

———— 1977. Nepotism and the Evolution of Alarm Calls. Science 197:1246–1253.

Shortridge, G. C. 1934. The Mammals of South West Africa. Vol. 2. Pp. 439–779. London: Wm. Heinemann, Ltd.

Siegler, S. L. 1944. Fertility in Women. Philadelphia: J. B. Lippincott Co.

Silvertsen, E. 1941. On the Biology of the Harp Seal, *Phoca groenlandica.* Hvalradet Skrifter 26:1–166.

Simonds, P. E. 1965. The Bonnet Macaque in South India. *In* Primate Behavior: Field Studies of Monkeys and Apes. I. DeVore, ed. pp. 175–196. New York: Holt, Rinehart and Winston.

Simpson, G. G. [1939–40.] Los indios Kamarakotos: tribu Caribe de la Guayana venezolana. Revista de Fomento (Caracas) 3(22/25):201–660.

———— 1953. The Major Features of Evolution. New York: Columbia University Press.

———— 1964. This View of Life, the World of an Evolutionist. New York: Harcourt, Brace, and World.

———— 1972. The Evolutionary Concept of Man. *In* Sexual Selection and the Descent of Man, 1871–1971. B. Campbell, ed. Pp. 17–39. Chicago: Aldine.

Siskind, J. 1973. Tropical Forest Hunters and the Economy of Sex. *In* Peoples and Cultures of Native South America. D. R. Gross, ed. Pp. 226–240. Garden City: Natural History Press.

Skinner, A. 1920. Notes on the Bribri of Costa Rica. Indian Notes and Monographs 6:37–106.

Skinner, E. 1964. The Mossi of the Upper Volta: The Political Development of a Sudanese People. Stanford: Stanford University Press.

Skoog, R. O. 1968. Ecology of the Caribou (*Rangifer tarandus granti*) in Alaska. Ph.D. dissertation, University of California at Berkeley.

Slaski, J. 1950. Peoples of the Lower Luapula Valley. *In* Bemba and Related Peoples of Northern Rhodesia. Wilfred Whiteley, ed. Pp. 77–100. London: International African Institute.

Slater, R. L. 1951. Paradox and Nirvana. Chicago: University of Chicago Press.

Smith, A. H. 1899. Village Life in China: A Study in Sociology. New York: F. H. Revell.

Smith, C. C. 1968. The Adaptive Nature of Social Organization in the Genus of Tree Squirrels *Tamiasciurus*. Ecological Monographs 38:31–63.

Smith, Carol A. 1976. Regional Analysis. Volume 1, Ecological Systems. Volume 2, Social Systems. New York: Academic Press.

Smith, E. W. 1949. Addendum to the "Ila Speaking Peoples of Northern Rhodesia." African Studies 8:1–9; 53–61.

Smith, E. W., and A. M. Dale. 1920. The Ila-speaking Peoples of Northern Rhodesia. London: Macmillan. [Also in the HRAF, 1961.]

Smith, M. G. 1954. Baba of Karo: A Woman of the Muslim Hausa. London: Faber and Faber. [Also in the HRAF, 1959.]

———— 1955. The Economy of Hausa Communities of Zaria. London: H. M. Stationery Office. [Also in the HRAF, 1958.]

Smithers, R. H. N. 1971. The Mammals of Botswana. National Museum of Rhodesia, Memoir 4: 1–340.

Smithson, C. L. 1959. The Havasupai Woman. University of Utah Anthropological Papers 38:1–70. [Also in the HRAF, 1960.]

Sociobiology Study Group of Science for the People. 1976. Sociobiology—Another Biological Determinism. Bioscience 26:3.

———— 1977. Sociobiology: A New Biological Determinism. *In* Biology as a Social Weapon. The Ann Arbor Science for the People Editorial Collective, ed. Minneapolis: Burgess Publishing Co.

Southwold, M. 1965. The Ganda of Uganda. *In* Peoples of Africa. J. L. Gibbs, ed. Pp. 81–118. New York: Holt, Rinehart and Winston.

Speck, Frank G. 1951. Utilization of Animals and Plants by the Micmac Indians of New Brunswick. Journal of the Washington Academy of Sciences 11.

Spencer, W. B., and F. J. Gillen. 1927. The Arunta: A Study of a Stone Age People. 2 vols. London: Macmillan and Co.

Spicer, R. B., and J. Chesky. 1949. The Desert People: A Study of the Papago Indians. Chicago: University of Chicago Press.

Spier, L. 1928. Havasupai Ethnography. American Museum of Natural History. Anthropological Papers 29(3):81–408.

——————— 1933. Yuman Tribes of the Gila River. Chicago: University of Chicago Press.

Spillius, J. 1957. Natural Disaster and Political Crisis in a Polynesian Society: An Exploration of Operational Research. Human Relations 10(1):3–27; 10(2):113–125.

Spoehr, A. 1949. Majuro: A Village in the Marshall Islands. Chicago: Chicago Museum of Natural History.

Spooner, Brian, ed. 1972. Population Growth: Anthropological Implications. Cambridge, Mass.: MIT Press.

Spuhler, J. N. and L. B. Jorde. 1975. Primate Phylogeny, Ecology, and Social Behavior. Journal of Anthropological Research 31:376–405.

Stair, J. 1897. Old Samoa or Flotsam and Jetsam from the Pacific Ocean. London: The Religious Tract Society.

Stander, H. J. 1936. William's Obstetrics. New York: Appleton-Century Crofts.

Staub, J. 1936. Beiträge zur Kenntris der materiellen Kultur der Mendi in der Sierra Leone. Solothurm: Buchdruckerei-Vogt-Schild. [Translated for the HRAF by C. Wood, 1958.]

Stebbins, G. L. 1977. In Defense of Evolution: Tautology or Theory? American Naturalist 111:386–390.

Stefansson, V. 1914. The Stefansson-Anderson Arctic Expedition of the American Museum: Preliminary Ethnological Report. New York: American Museum of Natural History.

Steggerda, Morris. 1941. Maya Indians of Yucatan. Carnegie Institution of Washington Publication no. 531.

Stein, Z., and M. Sausser. 1975. Fertility, Fecundity, Famine: Food Rations in the Dutch Famine 1944/5 Have a Causal Relation to Fertility and Probably Fecundity. Human Biology 47(1):131–154.

Steindorf, G. 1904. Durch die Libysche wüste zur Amonsoase. Leipzig: Velhagen und Klasing.

Stern, K. 1960. Principles of Human Genetics. 2nd Edition. San Francisco: W. H. Freeman.

Stevenson, M. C. 1902. The Zuni Indians: Their Mythology, Esoteric Fraternities, and Ceremonies. 23rd Annual Report of the Bureau of American Ethnology. [Also in the HRAF, 1961.]

Stewart, O. C. 1937. Northern Paiute Polyandry. American Anthropologist 39: 368–369.

————— 1941. Culture Element Distributions: XIV. Northern Paiute. Anthropological Records 4(3):361–445.

Stirling, I. 1969. Ecology of the Weddell Seal in McMurdo Sound, Antarctica. Ecology 50(4):573–586.

————— 1970. Observations on the Behaviour of the New Zealand Fur Seal (*Arctocephalus forsteri*). Journal of Mammalogy 51(4):766–778.

————— 1971a. Studies on the Behaviour of the South Australian Fur Seal, *Arctocephalus forsteri* (Lesson). I. Annual Cycle, Postures and Calls and Adult Males During the Breeding Season. Australian Journal of Zoology 19(3):243–266.

————— 1971b. Population Dynamics of the Weddell Seal (*Leptonychotes weddelli*) in McMurdo Sound, Antarctica, 1966–1968. *In* Antarctic Pinnipedia. W. H. Burt, ed. Pp. 141–162. Washington, D.C.: American Geophysical Union.

————— 1972. Observations on the Australian Sea Lion, *Neophoca cinerea* (Peron). Australian Journal of Zoology 20:271–279.

Stirling, I., and R. M. Warneke. 1971. Implications of a Comparison of the Airborne Vocalizations and Some Aspects of the Behaviour of the Two Australian Fur Seals, *Arctocephalus* spp., on the Evolution and Present Taxonomy of the Genus. Australian Journal of Zoology 19(3):227–241.

Stirling, M. 1938. Historical and Ethnological Material on the Jivaro Indians. Bureau of American Ethnology Bulletin no. 117.

Stone, D. Z. 1949. The Boruca of Costa Rica. Papers of the Peabody Museum of American Archaeology and Ethnology, vol. 26, no. 2. [Also in the HRAF, 1961.]

Stott, D. H. 1969. Cultural and Natural Checks on Population Growth. *In* Environment and Cultural Behavior. A. P. Vayda, ed. Pp. 90–120. Garden City: Doubleday.

Strehlow, T. G. H. 1947. Aranda Traditions. Melbourne: Melbourne University Press. [Also in the HRAF.]

Struhsaker, T. T., and J. S. Gartlan. 1970. Observations on the Behaviour and Ecology of the Patas Monkey (*Erythrocebus patas*) in the Waza Reserve, Cameroon. Journal of Zoology 161:49–63.

Stuard, S. M. 1976a. Women in Charter and Statute Law: Medieval Ragusa/ Dubrovnik. *In* Women in Medieval Society. S. M. Stuard, ed. Pp. 199–208. Philadelphia: University of Pennsylvania Press.

Stuard, S. M., ed. 1976b. Women in Medieval Society. Philadelphia: University of Pennsylvania Press.

Sturgis, S. H. and W. T. Pommerenke. 1960. The Clinical Signs of Ovulation— A Survey of Opinion. Fertility and Sterility 1:112–132.

Suggs, R. 1966. Marquesan Sexual Behavior. New York: Harcourt, Brace, and World. [Also in the HRAF.]

Sugiyama, Y. 1964. Group Composition, Population Density and Some Sociological Observations of Hanuman Langurs (*Presbytis entellus*). Primates 5:7–37.

———— 1967. Social Organization of Hanuman Langurs. *In* Social Communication Among Primates, S. A. Altmann, ed. Pp. 221–236. Chicago: University of Chicago Press.

Sugiyama, Y., K. Yoshiba, and M. D. Parthasarathy. 1965. Home Range, Mating Season, Male Group and Intertroop Relations in Hanuman Langurs (*Presbytis entellus*). Primates 6:73–106.

Sumner, William M. 1972. Cultural Development in the Kur River Basin, Iran. Ann Arbor: University Microfilms.

Sutherland, Ian. 1949. Stillbirths. London: Oxford University Press.

Sutherland, E. H., and R. Cressey. 1966. Principals of Criminology. 7th ed. New York: Lippincott.

Sutlive, V. H., Jr. 1973. From Longhouse to Pasar: Urbanization in Sarawak, East Malaysia. Ph.D. dissertation. University of Pittsburgh. Ann Arbor: University Microfilms.

Swan, J. G. 1870. The Indians of Cape Flattery, at the Entrance to the Strait of Fuca, Washington Territory. Washington, D.C.: Smithsonian Institution. [Also in the HRAF, 1960.]

Swane, H. G. C. 1900. Seventeen Trips Through Somaliland and a Visit to Abyssinia. London: Rowland Ward.

Swanton, J. R. 1928. Social Organization and Social Usages of the Indians of the Creek Confederacy. 42nd Annual Report of the Bureau of American Ethnology, pp. 23–472; 859–900.

Sykes, E. C. 1910. Persia and Its Peoples. New York: Macmillan.

Szulman, A. E. 1968. Significance of Chromosomal Abnormalities in Spontaneous Abortion. *In* Progress in Infertility. S. J. Behrman and R. W. Kistner, eds. pp. 847–866. Boston: Little, Brown & Co.

Taber, S., III., and J. Wendel. 1958. Concerning the Number of Times Queen Bees Mate. Journal of Economic Entomology 51:786–789.

Talayesva, D. C. 1942. Sun Chief: The Autobiography of a Hopi Indian. L. W. Simmons, ed. New Haven: Yale University Press.

Tanaka, J. 1965. Social Structure of Nilgiri Langurs. Primates 6:107–122.

Tanner, J. M. 1962. Growth at Adolescence. 2nd edn. Springfield, Ill.: Charles C. Thomas.

Tauber, I. 1958. The Population of Japan. Princeton: Princeton University Press.

Taussig, F. J. 1936. Abortion. St. Louis: C. V. Mosby Co.

Tauxier, L. 1912. The Black Population of the Sudan, Mossi, and Couroursi Country, Document and Analyses. Paris: Emile Larose.

————— 1917. The Black Population of Yatends Mossi, Nioniosse Samo, Yaise, Silmi, Mossi, Peul. Paris: Emile Larose.

Tax, Sol. 1955. Some Principles of Social Organization. In Social Anthropology of the North American Tribes. F. Eggan, ed. Pp. 3–32. Chicago: University of Chicago Press.

Taylor, C. R., K. Schmidt-Nielsen, and J. L. Raab. 1970. Scaling of the Energetic Cost of Running to Body Size in Mammals. American Journal of Physiology 219:1104–1107.

Taylor, C. R., R. Dmi'el, M. Fedak, and K. Schmidt-Nielsen. 1971. Energetic Cost of Running and Heat Balance in a Large Bird, the Rhea. American Journal of Physiology 221:597–601.

Taylor, C. R., and V. J. Rowntree. 1973. Running on Two or on Four Legs: Which Consumes More Energy? Science 179:186–187.

Taylor, Douglas Macrae. 1938. The Caribs of Dominica. Bureau of American Ethnology Bulletin no. 119.

Teitelbaum, Michael S. 1972. Factors Associated with the Sex Ratio in Human Populations. In The Structure of Human Populations. G. A. Harrison and A. J. Boyce, eds. Pp. 90–109. Oxford: Clarendon Press.

Temple, C., ed. 1922. Notes on the Tribes, Provinces, Emirates, and States of the Northern Provinces of Nigeria. 2nd ed. Lagos: CMS Bookshop.

Temple, Richard C. 1903. The Andaman and Nicobar Islands. Report on the Census of Calcutta: Office of the Superintendent of Government Printing, India.

Tenaza, R. R. 1975. Territory and Monogamy among Kloss' Gibbons (Hylobates klossii) in Siberut Island, Indonesia. Folia Primatologica 24:60–80.

Tenaza, R. R., and W. J. Hamilton, III. 1971. Preliminary Observations of the Mentawai Islands gibbon Hylobates klossii. Folia Primatologica 15: 201–211.

Tessman, G. 1913. The Fang Peoples: An Ethnographic Monograph on a West African Negro Group. Vol. 1. Pp. 51–344. Berlin. Wasmuth.

Theissen, D. D. 1972. A Move Toward Species Specific Analyses in Behavior Genetics. Behavior Genetics 2:115–123.

Thomas, Brooke. 1975. The Ecology of Work. In Physiological Anthropology. A. Damon, ed. Pp. 59–79. London: Oxford University Press.

Thompson, L. 1940a. Southern Lau, Fiji: An Ethnography. Honolulu: Bernice Bishop Museum Bulletin 162. [Also in the HRAF, 1959.]

————— 1940b. Fijian Frontier. San Francisco: American Council, Institute of Pacific Relations.

Thompson, Virginia. 1941. Thailand: The New Siam. New York: The Macmillan Co.

Thurn, E. F. 1883. Among the Indians of Guiana. London: Kegan, Paul, Trench, & Co.

Thurston, E. 1909. Toda. *In* Castes and Tribes of Southern India. Vol. 7:116–197. E. Thurston and K. Rangsehari, eds. Madras: Government Press.

Thurston, E., and K. Rangsehari. 1909. Nayar. *In* Castes and Tribes of Southern India. Vol. 5: 283–413. E. Thurston and K. Rangsehari, eds. Madras: Government Press.

Tietze, C. 1960. Probability of Pregnancy Resulting From a Single Unprotected Coitus. Fertility and Sterility 11:485–488.

Tiger, Lionel. 1969. Men in Groups. New York: Random House.

————— 1970. Biological Fabianism. Canadian Forum 50:112–117.

————— 1975. Somatic Factors and Social Behaviour. *In* Biosocial Anthropology. R. Fox, ed. Pp. 115–132. London: Malaby Press.

Tiger, Lionel, and Robin Fox. 1966. The Zoological Perspective in Social Science. Man 1:75–81.

————— 1971. The Imperial Animal. New York: Holt, Rinehart and Winston.

Tiger, Lionel, and Joseph Shepher. 1975. Women in the Kibbutz. New York: Harcourt Brace Jovanovich, Inc.

Tinbergen, N. 1951. The Study of Instinct. Oxford: Clarendon Press.

————— 1953. Social Behaviour in Animals, with Special Reference to Vertebrates. New York: Wiley.

————— 1965. Behavior and Natural Selection. *In:* Ideas in Modern Biology. Proceedings of the XVI International Zoological Congress, Washington, 1963. J. A. Moore, ed. Vol. 6:519–542. New York: Doubleday.

Tinley, K. L. 1969. Dikdik *Madoqua kirki* in South West Afrika: Notes on Distribution, Ecology, and Behavior. Madoqua 1:7–33.

Titiev, M. 1971. Old Oraibi: A Study of the Hopi Indians of Third Mesa. New York: Kraus Reprint. [Originally published in 1944.]

————— 1972. The Hopi Indians of Old Oraibi: Change and Continuity. Ann Arbor: University of Michigan Press.

Tobias, P. V. 1962. On the Increasing Stature of the Bushmen. Anthropos 57: 801–810.

Tod, J. 1829. Annals and Antiquities of Rajast'han. 2 vols. London: Routledge & Kegan Paul.

Topley, M. 1975. Marriage Resistance in Rural Kwangtung. *In* Women in Chinese Society. M. Wolf and R. Witke, eds. Pp. 67–88. Stanford: Stanford University Press.

Townsend, Charles H. 1912. The Northern Elephant Seal. Zoologica 1(8):159–73.

Tran-Nuong Hahn. 1882. Moeurs et coutumes annamites. Annales de l'Extrême-Orient 4:369–377.

Tran-van-Trai. 1942. La famille patriarcale annamite. Paris: Lapagesse. [Translated for the HRAF by C. A. Messner, 1950.]

Trexler, R. C. 1973a. Infanticide in Florence: New Sources and First Results. History of Childhood Quarterly 1(1):98–116.

———— 1973b. The Foundlings of Florence, 1395–1455. History of Childhood Quarterly 1(2):259–284.

Trivers, R. L. 1971. The Evolution of Reciprocal Altruism. Quarterly Review of Biology 46(1):35–57.

———— 1972. Parental Investment and Sexual Selection. In Sexual Selection and the Descent of Man, 1871–1971. B. H. Campbell, ed. Pp. 136–179. Chicago: Aldine.

———— 1974. Parent-Offspring Conflict. American Zoologist 14:249–264.

———— 1976a. Sexual Selection and Resource-accruing Abilities in Anolis garmani. Evolution 30(2):253–269.

———— 1976b. Foreword. In The Selfish Gene. R. Dawkins. Pp. v–viii. New York: Oxford University Press.

Trivers, R. L., and H. Hare. 1976. Haplodiploidy and the Evolution of the Social Insects. Science 191:249–263.

Trivers, R. L., and D. E. Willard. 1973. Natural Selection of Parental Ability to Vary the Sex Ratio of Offspring. Science 179:90–92.

Tseng, Chao-hun. 1945. [The Lolo District of Liang-Shan]. In [An Account of Investigation Trip to Liang-Shan]. Pp. 91–139. Chunking.

Tupper, C., and R. J. Weil. 1968. The Etiology of Habitual Abortion. In Progress in Infertility. S. J. Behrman and R. W. Kistner, eds. Boston: Little, Brown & Co.

Turnbull, C. M. 1965a. The Mbuti Pygmies: an Ethnographic Survey. Anthropological Papers of the American Museum of Natural History 50(3):39–283.

———— 1965b. Wayward Servants: The Two Worlds of the African Pygmies. Garden City: Natural History Press.

Turner, G. 1884. Samoa, a Hundred Years Ago and Long Before. London: Macmillan. [Also in the HRAF, 1965.]

Tylor, E. B. 1910. Anthropology. Encyclopaedia Brittanica, 11th ed. Vol. 2. Pp. 108–119.

———— 1958. The Origins of Culture. Pt. I. [Originally published as chapters I–X of Primitive Culture, 1871.] New York: Harper and Bros.

Tyndale-Biscoe, Cecil E. 1922. Kashmir in Light and Shade. London: Seeley.

Ullrich, J. 1976. Zur Biologie und Soziologie der Colobusaffen (Colobus quereza caudatus Thomas 1885). Zoologische Garten 25:305–368.

Ullyot, J.   1976. Women's Running. Mountain View, Cal.: World Publications.

Underhill, R. M.   1936. The Autobiography of a Papago Woman. Memoirs of the American Anthropological Association, no. 48. [Also in the HRAF, 1958.]

————   1939. Social Organization of the Papago Indians. New York: Columbia University Press. [Also in the HRAF, 1958.]

————   1946. Papago Indian Religion. New York: Columbia University Press. [Also in the HRAF, 1958.]

United Nations Educational, Scientific, and Cultural Organization.   1952. Education Mission to Afghanistan. Report. Paris: UNESCO.

Vaillant, G. C.   1941. Aztecs of Mexico: Origin, Rise, and Fall of the Aztec Nation. Garden City: Doubleday. [Also in the HRAF, 1958.]

Vallois, H. V.   1940. New Research on the Western Negrillas. American Journal of Physical Anthropology 26:449–471.

van den Berghe, P. L. and D. P. Barash.   1977. Inclusive Fitness and Family Structure. American Anthropologist 79:809–823.

Vanoverbergh, M.   1929. Dress and Adornment in the Mountain Province of Luzon, Philippine Islands. Catholic Anthropological Conference, Washington, D.C., 1929. Vol. 1:181–242.

Vassal, G. M.   1910. On and Off Duty in Annam. London: Heineman. [Also in the HRAF, 1951.]

Vavilov, N. I., and D. D. Bukinich.   1929. Agricultural Afghanistan. Applied Botany of Genetics and Plant-Breeding Supplement 33:535–618.

Vayda, Andrew P.   1969. Expansion and Warfare among Swidden Agriculturalists. *In* Environment and Cultural Behavior. A. P. Vayda, ed. Pp. 202–220. Garden City: Doubleday. *Also in* American Anthropologist 63:346–358.

Vayda, Andrew P., and Bonnie McCay.   1975. New Directions in Ecology and Ecological Anthropology. Annual Review of Anthropology 4:293–306. Palo Alto: Annual Reviews, Inc.

Vayda, Andrew P., and Roy A. Rappaport.   1968. Ecology, Cultural, and Non-Cultural. *In* Introduction to Cultural Anthropology. J. A. Clifton, ed. Pp. 477–497. Boston: Houghton Mifflin.

Veblen, T.   1899. The Theory of the Leisure Class. London: Allen and Unwin.

Venables, U. M., and L. S. V. Venables.   1959. Vernal Coition of the Seal, *Phoca vitulina* in Shetland. Proceedings of the Zoological Society of London 132(4): 665–669.

Veniaminov, I. E. P.   1840. [Notes on the Islands of the Unalaska District.] Vol. 3. St. Petersburg: Izdano Izhdiveniem Rossisko-Amefikanski.

Viedma, A.   1837. Description of the Southern Shores of the Region Commonly Called Patagonia. *In* P. DeAngelis, ed. Collection de Obras y Documentos Relativo a la Historia Antigua y Moderna de las

Provinces del Río de la Plata. Vol. 6: 63–81. [Also in the HRAF, 1958.]

Vigna, J. 1945. Bosquejo sobre los Indios Shuaras o Jibaros. America Indigena 5:35–49.

Villa Rojas, A. 1945. The Maya of East Central Quintana Roo. Washington, D.C.: Carnegie Institution of Washington.

Vincent, F., Jr. 1874. The Land of the White Elephant: Sights and Scenes in South Eastern Asia. New York: Harper Bros.

Viski, Karoly. 1932. Hungarian Peasant Customs. J. de Márffy-Mantuano, trans. Budapest: G. Vajna and Co.

Voegelin, C. F. 1935. Tubatulabal Texts. Berkeley: University of California Press.

Voegelin, E. W. 1938. Tubatulabal Ethnography. Berkeley: University of California Press.

Von Neumann, John, and Oskar Morgenstern. 1964. Theory of Games and Economic Behavior. New York: John Wiley and Sons, Inc. [Original edition, 1944.]

Voth, H. R. 1905. Oraibi Natal Customs and Ceremonies. Field Columbian Museum, Publication no. 97. Pp. 47–61.

———— 1912. Brief Miscellaneous Hopi Papers. Chicago: Field Museum of Natural History, Anthropological Series, Vol. 11:91–149.

Vyatkina, K. V. 1964. The Buryats. *In* The Peoples of Siberia. M. G. Levin and L. P. Potapov, eds. Pp. 203–242; 903–904. Chicago: University of Chicago Press.

Wafer, L. 1934. A New Voyage and Description of the Isthmus of America. Oxford: Hakluyt Society.

Wagley, Charles. 1945. Um Tapirapé atinge a maioridade. Revista del Museo National (Rio de Janeiro) 1:16. [Also in the HRAF.]

———— 1960. Champukwi of the Village of the Tapirs. *In* In the Company of Man. J. B. Casagrande, ed. Pp. 397–415. New York: Harper & Row (Torchbook edition).

Wagner, R. K., and A. Hughes. 1974. I. Current Views on Androgen Receptors and Mechanisms of Androgen Action. Handbuch der Experimentellen Pharmakologie 35(2):1–28.

Walker, S. S. 1976. Widow and Ward: the Feudal Law of Child Custody in Medieval England. *In* Women in Medieval Society. S. M. Stuard, ed. Pp. 159–172. Philadelphia: University of Pennsylvania Press.

Wallace, E., and E. A. Hoebel. 1952. The Comanches: Lords of the South Plains. Norman: University of Oklahoma Press.

Wallis, W. D., and R. S. Wallis. 1953. Culture Loss and Culture Change Among the Micmac of the Canadian Maritime Provinces. Kroeber Anthropological Society Papers 8/9:100–129.

———— 1955. The Micmac Indians of Eastern Canada. Minneapolis: University of Minnesota Press.

Wang, Hsing-shui. 1948. The Miao People of Hainan Island. Institute for Chinese Frontier Studies, Series B, No. 2. Canton, China: Chu-Hai University. [Translated for the HRAF by Te-Kong Tong, 1961.]

Warner, W. Lloyd. 1937. A Black Civilization: A Social Study of an Australian Tribe. New York: Harper Brothers. [Also in the HRAF, 1960.]

Washburn, S. L. 1942. Skeletal Proportions of Adult Langurs and Macaques. Human Biology 14:444–472.

———— 1959. Speculations on the Interrelations of Tools and Biological Evolution. In The Evolution of Man's Capacity for Culture. J. M. Spuhler, ed. Pp. 21–31. Detroit: Wayne State University Press.

———— 1960. Tools and Human Evolution. Scientific American 203:63–75.

Washburn, S. L., and I. DeVore. 1961a. The Social Life of Baboons. Scientific American 204:62–71.

———— 1961b. Social Behavior of Baboons and Early Man. In The Social Life of Early Man. S. L. Washburn, ed. Pp. 91–105. Chicago: Aldine.

Washburn, S. L., Phyllis C. Jay, and Jane B. Lancaster. 1965. Field Studies of Old World Monkeys and Apes. Science 150:1541–1547.

Washburn, S. L., and C. S. Lancaster. 1968. The Evolution of Hunting. In Man, the Hunter. R. B. Lee and I. DeVore, eds. Pp. 293–303. Chicago: Aldine.

Washington State University, Far Eastern and Russian Studies Institute. 1956. Mongolian People's Republic (Outer Mongolia). New Haven: Human Relations Area Files Press. 3 vols.

Watanabe, H. 1971. Running, Creeping and Climbing: A New Ecological and Evolutionary Perspective on Human Locomotion. Mankind 8(1): 1–13.

Waxenberg, S. E., M. G. Drellich, and A. M. Sutherland. 1959. The Role of Hormones in Human Behavior, I. Changes in Female Sexuality After Adrenalectomy. Journal of Clinical Endocrinology and Metabolism 19:193–203.

Waxenberg, S. E., J. A. Finkbeiner, M. G. Drellich, and A. M. Sutherland. 1960. The Role of Hormones in Human Behavior, II. Changes in Sexual Behavior in Relation to Vaginal Smears of Breast Cancer Patients after Oophorectomy and Adrenalectomy. Psychosomatic Medicine 22: 436–442.

Webster, D. 1975. Warfare and the Evolution of the State: A Reconsideration. American Antiquity 40: 464–470.

Wedel, W. R. 1936. An Introduction to Pawnee Archaeology. Bureau of American Ethnology Bulletin 112. [Also in the HRAF, 1961.]

Wedgwood, C. H. 1943. Notes on the Marshall Islands. Oceania 13:1–23.

Weinrich, J. D. 1977. Human Sociobiology: Pair-Bonding and Resource Predictability (Effects of Social Class and Race). Behavioral Ecology and Sociobiology 2(2):91–118.

Weisner, P. 1977. A Study of Reciprocity Among the Kalahari Bushmen. Ph.D. dissertation, Department of Anthropology, University of Michigan.

Weiss, K. M. 1975. The Application of Demographic Models to Anthropological Data. Human Ecology 3:87–103.

———— 1976. Demographic Theory and Anthropological Inference. Annual Review of Anthropology, Volume 5:351–381. Palo Alto: Annual Reviews Inc.

Weltfish, G. 1965. The Lost Universe: With a Closing Chapter on "The Universe Regained." New York: Basic Books.

West Eberhard, M. J. 1975. The Evolution of Social Behavior by Kin Selection. Quarterly Review of Biology 50(1):1–33.

Westerman, P. 1912. Shilluk People, Their Language and Folklore. Foreign Missions Board of the United Presbyterian Church of North America.

Weyer, E. M. 1932. The Eskimos: Their Environment and Folkways. New Haven: Yale University Press.

Whital, S. 1890. Pima Agency. In U.S. Department of the Interior, Census Office. Report on Indians Taxed and Indians Not Taxed in the United States (Except Alaska) at the Eleventh Census: 1890. Washington, D.C.: United States Government Printing Office.

White, L. A. 1949. The Science of Culture. New York: Farrar, Straus & Giroux.

Whitehead, A. N. 1930. Process and Reality. New York: The Macmillan Company.

———— 1938. Modes of Thought. Cambridge: Cambridge University Press.

Whiting, B. B. 1950. Paiute Sorcery. New York: Viking Fund.

Wilbert, J. 1958. Kinship and Social Organization of the Ye'cuana and Goajiro. Southwestern Journal of Anthropology 14:51–60.

Williams, B. J. 1974. A Model of Band Society. Memoirs of the Society for American Archaeology no. 29. Issued as American Antiquity, vol. 39, no. 4, pt. 2.

Williams, F. 1928. Orokaiva Magic. London: Oxford University Press.

———— 1930. Orokaiva Society. London: Oxford University Press.

Williams, G. C. 1957. Pleiotropy, Natural Selection, and the Evolution of Senescence. Evolution 11:398–411.

———— 1966. Adaptation and Natural Selection. Princeton: Princeton University Press.

Williams, G. C., ed. 1971. Group Selection. Chicago: Aldine Atherton.

———— 1975. Sex and Evolution. Princeton: Princeton University Press.

Wilson, Edward O. 1971. Competitive and Aggressive Behavior. In Man and Beast: Comparative Social Behavior. J. F. Eisenberg and W. S.

Dillon, eds. Pp. 181–217. Washington, D.C.: Smithsonian Institution Press.

———— 1973. On the Queerness of Social Evolution. Bulletin of the Entomological Society 19:20–22.

———— 1975. Sociobiology: The New Synthesis. Cambridge, Mass.: Harvard University Press.

———— 1976. Some Central Problems of Sociobiology. Social Sciences Information (Biology and Social Life) 14(6):5–18.

———— 1977. Biology and the Social Sciences. Daedalus 106:127–140.

———— 1978. On Human Nature. Cambridge: Harvard University Press.

Wilson, E. O., and W. H. Bossert. 1971. A Primer of Population Biology. Sunderland, Mass.: Sinauer.

Wilson, J. 1855. History of the Suppression of Infanticide in Western India Under the Government of Bombay. Bombay: Smith, Taylor.

Wilson, V. J., and G. Child. 1965. Notes on Klipspringer from Tsetse Fly Control Areas in Eastern Zambia. Arnoldia (Rhodesia) 35:1–9.

Wilson, V. J., and J. E. Clarke. 1962. Observations on the Common Duiker *Sylvicapra grimmia* Linn., Based on Material Collected from a Tsetse Control Game Elimination Scheme. Proceedings of the Zoological Society of London 138:487–497.

Wirtz, William O., II. 1968. Reproduction, Growth and Development and Juvenile Mortality in the Hawaiian Monk Seal (*Monachus schauinslandi*). Journal of Mammalogy 49(2):229–238.

Wiser, W. H., and Wiser, C. M. 1971. Behind Mud Walls: 1930–1960; With A Sequel: The Village in 1970. Berkeley: University of California Press.

Wolf, A. P. 1966. Childhood Association, Sexual Attraction, and the Incest Taboo: A Chinese Case. American Anthropologist 68:883–898.

———— 1968. Adopt a Daughter-in-Law, Marry a Sister: A Chinese Solution to the Problem of the Incest Taboo. American Anthropologist 70: 864–874.

———— 1970. Childhood Association and Sexual Attraction: A Further Test of the Westermarck Hypothesis. American Anthropologist 72:503–515.

Wolf, A. P., ed. 1974. Religion and Ritual in Chinese Society. Stanford: Stanford University Press.

———— 1975. The Women of Hai-Shan: A Demographic Portrait. *In* Women in Chinese Society. M. Wolf and R. Witke, eds. Pp. 89–110. Stanford: Stanford University Press.

Wolf, Eric. 1964. Anthropology. Englewood Cliffs, New Jersey: Prentice-Hall.

Wolf, M. 1975. Women and Suicide in China. *In* Women in Chinese Society. M. Wolf and R. Witke, eds. Pp. 111–141. Stanford: Stanford University Press.

Wolf, M., and R. Witke, eds. 1975. Women in Chinese Society. Stanford: Stanford University Press.

Wrangham, R. W. 1975: The Behavioural Ecology of Chimpanzees in the Gombe National Park, Tanzania. Ph.D. dissertation, University of Cambridge.

——— In press. *In* The Behaviour of Great Apes: Perspectives on Human Evolution. D. A. Hamburg and J. Goodall, eds. New York: Staples/ W. A. Benjamin.

Wright, P. L., and S. A. Dow, Jr. 1962. Minimum Breeding Age in Pronghorn Antelope. Journal of Wildlife Management 26:100–101.

Wright, S. 1922. Coefficients of Inbreeding and Relationship. American Naturalist 56:330–338.

Wrigley, E. A., ed. 1966. An Introduction to English Historical Demography: From the Sixteenth to the Nineteenth Century. London: Weidenfeld & Nicholson.

Wroughton, R. C. 1916. Bombay Natural History Society's Mammal Survey of India, Burma, and Ceylon. Journal of the Bombay Natural History Society 24:749–782.

Wylie, L., ed. 1966. Chanzeaux: A Village in Anjou. Cambridge: Harvard University Press.

Wynne-Edwards, V. C. 1962. Animal Dispersion in Relation to Social Behavior. New York: Hafner.

Yalman, N. 1971. Under the Bo Tree: Studies in Caste, Kinship and Marriage in the Interior of Ceylon. Berkeley: University of California Press.

Yang, Mou-ch'un. 1965. A Chinese Village: Taitou, Shantung Province. New York: Columbia University Press.

Yoshiba, K. 1968. Local and Intertroop Variability in Ecology and Social Behavior of Common Indian Langurs. *In* Primates, Studies in Adaptation and Variability. P. C. Jay, ed. Pp. 217–242. New York: Holt, Rinehart and Winston.

Young, J. Z. 1957. The Life of Mammals. Oxford: Clarendon Press.

Zimmerman, Carle C. 1937. The Stature and Weight of the Siamese. Genus 2: 295–323.

Index

Anthropology, 523–26; biology and, 31–39, 519–21; kinship and, 132–33
Apes, 459
Arbitrariness, cultural, 75–78
Archaeology, 63
Armadillos, 497
Ashanti, 160, 161, 162, 164, 169, 184
Asians, 417, 420, 421, 423, 435
Assam, 338
Attractivity, 458, 460, 461
Attributes, human, 437–41
Australia, 173–74, 456, 492; kinship classification in, 139
Avunculate ties, 84, 85, 145–57, 160–70, 175, 209–12, 213
"Ax Fight, The" (film), 85, 216
Ax fight, Yąnomamö, 213–37

Baba Nanuk, 333
Baboons, 412, 447, 449, 463, 464
"Baby farms," 350
Bachelors, 346, 357
Barkow, J. H., 508
Basle, Switzerland, 353
Bates, Daniel G., and Susan H. Lees, 81–82, 252–53, 254, 273–89
Bathurst Island, 162, 192
Bats, 495
Bedi Sikhs, 333
Bedouins, 471
Behavior: animal, 510, 513–14; anthropoid-hominid, 454–61; cultural restraints on, 34; culturally transmitted, 8–10, 33, 34; ecological restraints on, 34; facultative and obligate, 7; flexibility, 7–8; genealogical information on, 83; human, 39–59, 508, 509, 510, 522–26; learned

and genetic, 7–10, 65; maladaptive, 47–48; social, 35
Behavioral biology, anthropology and, 31–39
Behavioral evolution, anthropoid-hominid, 454–61
Belladonna, 465
Bemba, 162, 164
Benedict, Ruth, 32, 72
Bengal, 332, 338–39
Bernds, William P., and David P. Barash, 372, 487–506
Betrothal, child, 334, 336, 358, 364; prebirth, 192–93
Bhadauri Rajput, 332
Biases, learned, 45–46
Bighorn sheep, 407
Biochemistry, 519–20
Biological success, 257–72. See also Inclusive fitness; Reproductive success
Biology: and anthropology, 31–39, 519–21; vs. culture, 58; human, co-evolutionary, theory of, 39–59
Bipedal locomotion, sexual receptivity and, 454–61
Birds, warning calls and, 22–23
Birdsell, J. B., 294
Birth defects, 294, 304, 305, 306, 441
Birth, multiple, 294
Birth rate, 281
Bisaasi-teri, 379–82
Blood types, inheritance and, 5
Blunt, E. A. H., 340
Blurton-Jones, N. G., and R. Sibly, 508
Boas, Franz, 72
Bologna, Italy, 353
Bondservants, 345

Circumcision, as sexual fitness token, 465

"Circumstantial bias," 46

Clans, 139–40

Classification, kinship, 82–83, 87, 132–44

Clitoridectomy, 176

Cloak, F. T., Jr., 46, 72

Clogg, Clifford, 261, 271

Clutton-Brock, T. H., 403, 410

Coale, A. J., and P. Demeney, 261

Coalitions, flexibility in, 438

Coercion, 35, 189, 190

Coevolutionary theory, 39–59

Cohabitation, 104

Collective representations, independence of, 33

Colonial administration, 280

Communication, 75, 437. *See also* Language; Symbolism

Competition: intergroup, 439, 440, 447; for mates, 27–8, 62, 80, 81, 86, 87, 88, 99, 101, 102–9, 123, 163, 196, 197, 198, 199, 281, 284, 313, 363, 376, 377–78, 398, 403, 421, 434, 463

Conception, relationship between sexual intercourse and, 172–74

Concubinage, 344–45, 346, 358, 420

Conflict: in kin selection, Yąnomamö, 213–37; parent-offspring, 20–21, 167; sibling, 167, 170. *See also* Aggression; Competition

Consciousness (self-awareness), 158, 437; and concealed ovulation, 452–53

Conspicuous consumption, as sexual signal, 465

Conspicuousness, as sexual signal, 467

Continuity-discontinuity, 454–55

Convention, 173

Copper Eskimo, 409

Copulation, 83, 101, 104, 443; frontal, 438, 452

Co-residence, household, 85, 183; sister-sister, 193–95

Cosmetics, 469

Coulton, G. G., 355

Courtship, 28

Cousins: cross-, 96–99, 107, 155, 156, 397; first, 156; parallel, 107, 140, 155–56, 397

Cowgill, U. M., and G. E. Hutchinson, 421–22

Creation, divine, 59, 60–61

Creation Research Society, 60

Creationists, and humanity, 61

Cross-cousins: marriages, 96–99, 107, 200, 222, 342, 385, 397, 399; relatedness, 155, 156

Crow terminology, 139

Cuckoldry, 28–29, 101, 102, 148, 149, 161

Cultural evolution. *See* Evolution

Cultural materialism, 286

Cultural relativism, 33, 38, 511–19

Cultural selection, 1, 40–59; criteria for, 43, 48; between groups, 51–53; within groups, 44–51; social benefits and, 52

Cultural success, 257–72

Cultural traits: heritability of, 72, 73; retention of, 45–46

Culture: arbitrariness in, 75–78; behavior and, 8–10, 33, 34–35, 36; biological evolution and,

Kinship systems (*cont.*)
Tiwi, 192–97; Yąnomamö, 86–132, 197–200, 213–37; Yomut Turkmen, 200–203
Korea, 422
Kowalewski, Stephen, 277
Kroeber, A.L., and Robert H. Lowie, 136
Kshattriyas, 186–87
Kulin Brahmins (Bengal), 332
Kummer, H., 449
!Kung Bushmen, 240, 241
Kuri-Mar ("daughter-slayer"), 333
Kurland, Jeffrey A., 145–80, 241; and Steven J. C. Gaulin, 84
Kwangtung, 349

Labor: in lieu of bridewealth, 212; sexual division of, 38
Labrador Eskimo, 409
Lack, D., 503
Lactation, 20, 377, 495
Ladinos, 422
Lancaster, J. B., 451
Landlordism, 345
Land use, 280
Lang, O., 342
Langer, Suzanne, 455
Language, 7, 75, 135, 454, 455; kinship reckoning and, 86–87
Lapps, 409
Laws, system of, 439
Leach, E., 234
Leaders, appointed and elected, 439
Learning (nature vs. nurture), 8, 45–46; culture and, 8; vs. instinct, 58; genetic variation and, 65–67
LeBoeuf, B., 402, 407

LeVine, Robert, 45
Lévi-Strauss, Claude, 132, 133, 134, 139, 141, 144, 172, 249, 321, 365, 374–75, 523
Lewontin, R., 251
Life history, 32, 37
Lineage composition, 116–21
Lineage ranks, 314–16
Lineal classification, kinship systems, 137–41
Lineal descent, fertility and, 384–90
Lisbon, Portugal, 353
Livestock: breeding, 64; exchanging for women, 200, 201
Lizot, J., 385
Locomotion, upright, 438; bipedal, 454–61; and parental care, 452
Lorenz, Konrad, 507
Lotka, A. J., and Vito Volterra, 520
Low, Bobbi, 369, 372, 462–87

Macaques, 145, 146, 241, 442, 450, 458, 463
MacArthur, Robert H., 520
Madras, 338
Mahar, J. M., 336
Mainpuri (India), 333
Makeup, as sexual signal, 465
Maladaptive cultural practices, 47–48
Male chauvinism, 253
Male role in reproduction, theories of 27–29
Males, excess of, 338
Male supremacy, 281–82, 286, 287, 326
Malinowski, Bronislaw, 72, 76–77, 172, 173, 252, 278–79
Malnutrition, 11